Animal Welfare Law in Britain

Regulation and Responsibility

MIKE RADFORD

School of Law
University of Aberdeen

Foreword by

DONALD M BROOM

Colleen Macleod Professor of Animal Welfare
Department of Clinical Veterinary Medicine
University of Cambridge

OXFORD
UNIVERSITY PRESS

*This book has been printed digitally and produced in a standard specification
in order to ensure its continuing availability*

OXFORD
UNIVERSITY PRESS

Great Clarendon Street, Oxford OX2 6DP

Oxford University Press is a department of the University of Oxford.
It furthers the University's objective of excellence in research, scholarship,
and education by publishing worldwide in

Oxford New York

Auckland Cape Town Dar es Salaam Hong Kong Karachi
Kuala Lumpur Madrid Melbourne Mexico City Nairobi
New Delhi Shanghai Taipei Toronto
With offices in
Argentina Austria Brazil Chile Czech Republic France Greece
Guatemala Hungary Italy Japan South Korea Poland Portugal
Singapore Switzerland Thailand Turkey Ukraine Vietnam

Oxford is a registered trade mark of Oxford University Press
in the UK and in certain other countries

Published in the United States
by Inc., New York

ISBN 0-19-826245-0

Antony Rowe Ltd., Eastbourne

Foreword

What is the purpose of law? In my view, it is to promote co-operation among individuals and to discourage actions which harm individuals or society at large. The foundation of human society, like that of other social animals, is reciprocal altruism and the promotion of social cohesion by avoiding actions which could harm others despite the fact that it is easy to do so. An important consequence of this fundamental aspect of biology is that morality has evolved. Laws are mechanisms for promoting moral actions.

In their origins, laws in human society are often difficult to dissociate from the tenets of religion because religion is an important mechanism for promoting morality and hence stability in society. Laws should be promoting what is right and penalizing what is wrong. Inconsistencies are evident, however, between the actual laws which exist and my morality-based arguments. This is because, even if laws stemmed originally from moral codes, they often came to be designed and enforced by the strong rather than by the entirely altruistic. As a consequence, many laws were formulated to protect the possessions of the powerful and wealthy. These laws may still have furthered social stability in human society but have not necessarily always done so.

In the early stages of most legal systems, animals were referred to largely as possessions. In the same way, slaves, servants, and wives were often treated legally as possessions. Social attitudes did not universally correspond with such a view but the law lagged behind social development. The view of domestic and other animals as sentient beings who deserved respect became influential in the wake of a similar developing view that persons of other nations, creeds, or colours and women had such qualities. In each case there was a clear conflict between the possession-oriented and morally-oriented legal thinking.

Given the dramatic changes in knowledge of, and attitudes towards, animals in recent years, rapid legal developments were inevitable. The subject of animals in law is presented as an exciting and dynamically developing subject by Mike Radford. Many people will want to know what is happening and how it has come about. The structures of law are not easy to comprehend but Mike Radford is masterful in presenting a story which is dramatic and interesting, while informing in an expert and comprehensively reliable way. People from many backgrounds, and indeed many countries, will enjoy this book and find it very useful.

DONALD M BROOM

Cambridge
May 2001

Preface

A man may say 'I bought the beast with my money, it is my property; who shall hinder me from doing unto it according to my pleasure?' You bought him with your money, it is true, and he is your property; but, whether you are apprised of it or not, you bought him with a condition necessarily annexed to the bargain. You could not purchase the right to use him with cruelty and injustice. Of whom could you purchase such right? Who could make such a conveyance?

John Lawrence (1796)[1]

The completion of this book coincided with the outbreak of foot-and-mouth disease in Britain during the spring of 2001. It is always dangerous to attempt to draw long-term conclusions while in the midst of a crisis; the passage of time and a more considered approach can lead to a very different perspective after the event. Nevertheless, the nature of the State's response to the disease was revealing.

First and foremost, it highlighted the degree to which, even in an increasingly urbanized country, animals impact on human society, the central role they play in shaping both our landscape and our communities, and the extent to which our activities impose upon them. Secondly, it illustrated that, where there is a political will, a way can be found to address the issues raised by the keeping of animals. Massive resources were mobilized to deal with the perceived threat posed by the disease, in sharp contrast to the lack of urgency or importance which many statutory enforcement agencies charged with safeguarding animal welfare seem too often to display in carrying out their routine duties. Ironically, it may in time come to be shown that if those self-same agencies had been better resourced and more assiduous in their duties, the spread of the disease could have been, if not altogether prevented, at least rather more effectively contained. Thirdly, and most significantly, it demonstrated the extent to which animals continue to be regarded principally as economic units. Arising from the predicted financial consequences of Great Britain losing its disease-free status, no expense was spared to prevent such an outcome and no politician was placed above the fray: the Prime Minister took charge, the army was called upon to provide logistical support, and even elections went by the board. Indeed, other financial interests, most notably those of tourism, seemed to be sacrificed on the

[1] 'On the Rights of Beasts', in *A Philosophical Treatise on Horses, and on the Moral Duties of Man towards the Brute Creation*, 2nd edn, 1802 (1st edn, 1796), in Nicholson, EB, *The Rights of an Animal: A New Essay in Ethics* (1879) 93.

altar of preventing foot-and-mouth disease from becoming endemic in the national herd, notwithstanding that it poses no threat to humans, many animals recover from it, and its presence might lead to the development of at least some degree of resistance. Certainly, the immediate welfare of the animals involved took second place to the eradication of the disease: considerable suffering was inflicted as a direct result of movement restrictions; hundreds of thousands were killed in less than ideal conditions, perhaps needlessly (and possibly, time will show, unlawfully in some cases); and the alternative strategy of vaccination was rejected. The episode thus demonstrates a trait which has characterized our relationship with other species: an assumption that they exist merely for our use and their interests are therefore of little importance when compared with those of humans.

It was precisely this attitude which spurred reformers at the end of the eighteenth century to campaign for animals to be accorded legal protection. They were influenced by the intellectual fervour which characterized the period, and their concern captured a particular idea which is central to the eighteenth-century Enlightenment: namely, that individuals matter. Generally seen in terms of human beings, they extended the principle to encompass other species. The significance and profundity of this idea cannot be over-emphasized: not only did it have far-reaching implications for our relationship with other species, it also posed a fundamental challenge to traditional assumptions about our place in the world. It endowed other species with a moral status; it focused on the consequences of human treatment; it recognized that at least some species were sentient; and it underpinned the argument that humans had responsibilities towards them, which in turn formed the basis for the introduction of legal regulation.

Over the course of almost two centuries, the law in Britain has been developed to provide greater protection for individual animals because society at large and public policy makers have recognized that the way in which each is treated matters (although, as the reaction to foot-and-mouth disease demonstrates, it remains the case that the importance which is attached to an animal's interests varies according to the relationship which it happens to have with humans). The body of law which has built up over almost two centuries is, however, complicated and unwieldy; its form, substance, application, and effect can all be difficult to understand.

Accordingly, this book attempts to provide a broad overview of the law in Britain as it relates to the protection of animals. As such, it may be regarded as being akin to a progress report. It sets out to explain the factors which have influenced the law's development; the social and legal context within which it exists; and the nature of the protection which it affords. As tends to be the case with the law, the devil is often in the detail, but a conscious effort has been made to ensure that the text is accessible to those without a legal training, hence the inclusion of information which will already be familiar to lawyers. Informed consideration of the proper treatment of animals requires contributions from many different disciplines, and it is therefore essential that the literature should seek to encourage a readership which is as wide as possible. Most importantly, it is hoped that this volume will contribute to an understanding of why legal regulation is necessary and how far the law has progressed, while simultaneously drawing attention to its weaknesses.

Finally, the use of the term 'animals' throughout this book, in preference to the recently adopted term 'non-human animals', reflects both the traditional entrenched legal distinction between humans and other species, and the widespread failure by legislators to understand the significance of taxonomic terms. There is no intention to deny or ignore the fact that, scientifically speaking, humans are themselves animals. Indeed, the very opposite is the case. For our developing understanding of the profound implications inherent in the view that human beings have evolved by the same means as other species, and from shared progenitors, has been perhaps the most significant factor in developing our understanding of their capacities and needs. It has thereby contributed to a fundamental reassessment of our responsibilities towards them and hence provided much of the impetus for the development of legal regulation, initially to provide protection from cruelty, and latterly to promote higher standards of animal welfare and hence a better quality of life.

The law is stated as at 1 April 2001, although later developments have been noted wherever possible.

Acknowledgements

Many people have contributed to the writing of this book. I am grateful to them all. However, I would in particular wish to thank the following for their help, advice, and expertise: Roland Bonney; Donald Broom; Norman Burton; Samantha Callaghan; Jeremy Chipperfield; Francis Coleman; Walter Douglas; Janet Edward; Mike Flynn; David Fox; Roger Hancock; Anna Harrison; Stuart Harrop; Pat Hartley; Sue Haslam; Jo Keeley; Kate Kerr; Patrick Kitson; Hilary Koe; Ruth Layton; David Main; David Morton; Rachel Newman; Rosemary Pattenden; Paul Roger; Peter Stevenson; Pippa Swann; Gareth Thomas; Peter Thornton; Tim Wass; Stephen Wickens; Steven Wise; the staff of the RSPCA's Public Affairs Department; and, for their support and patience, at OUP, Becky Allen and Chris Rycroft.

In order to avoid any embarrassment or misunderstanding, I would like to make it clear that the views expressed in the following pages are my own. Although they may be generally sympathetic to my approach, it should not be assumed that any of the aforementioned unreservedly endorse all of my conclusions.

MIKE RADFORD

Aberdeen
May 2001

Contents—Summary

Contents

Part F   Effectiveness

Chapter 14   Enforcement   345

Table of Cases

Tables of Legislation

British Legislation

Other Jurisdictions

Abbreviations

AC	Law Reports, Appeal Cases
All ER	All England Law Reports
APC	Animal Procedures Committee
art	Article
B	Baron, as in Baron Smith
BSE	Bovine Spongiform Encephalopathy
BUAV	British Union for the Abolition of Vivisection
BVA	British Veterinary Association
C & P	Carrington and Payne's Reports
CA	Court of Appeal *or* Court of Appeal Reports
CB	Chief Baron, as in Chief Baron Smith
Ch	Law Reports, Chancery Division
CIWF	Compassion in World Farming
CJ	Chief Justice
CLY	Current Law Yearbook
CMLR	Common Market Law Reports
COD	Crown Office Digest
Coup	Couper's Justiciary Reports (Scotland)
Cox C C	Cox's Criminal Cases
CPS	Crown Prosecution Service
Cr App R	Criminal Appeal Reports
Crim LR	Criminal Law Review
DEFRA	Department for Environment, Food and Rural Affairs
DETR	Department of the Environment, Transport and the Regions
Dowl	Dowling's Practice Reports
DPP	Director of Public Prosecutions
EAT	Employment Appeal Tribunal
EC	European Community
ECJ	European Court of Justice
ECR	European Court Reports
EEC	European Economic Community
ER	English Reports
Ex	Exchequer
Ex D	Law Reports, Exchequer Division
FAWC	Farm Animal Welfare Council
FRAME	Fund for the Replacement of Animals in Medical Experiments
GATT	General Agreement on Tariffs and Trade
Hale PC	Hale's Pleas of the Crown
HC Debs	House of Common Debates (Hansard)
HL	House of Lords

HL Cas	Clarke's Reports, House of Lords
HL Debs	House of Lords Debates (Hansard)
IFAW	International Federation for Animal Welfare
ILR	Irish Law Reports
IR	Irish Reports
J	Justice, as in Mr Justice Smith (a judge of the High Court)
JC	Court of Justiciary Cases (Scotland)
JP	Justice of the Peace
KB	Law Reports, King's Bench Division
LACS	League Against Cruel Sports
LC	Lord Chancellor
LGA	Local Government Association
LGR	Local Government Law Reports
LJ	Lord Justice, as in Lord Justice Smith (a judge of the Court of Appeal)
LJKB	Law Journal, King's Bench
LT	Law Times Reports
MAFF	Ministry of Agriculture, Fisheries and Food
MEP	Member of the European Parliament
MP	Member of Parliament
MR	Master of the Rolls
MSP	Member of the Scottish Parliament
NACWO	Named Animal Care and Welfare Officer
NAVS	National Anti-Vivisection Society
NCDL	National Canine Defence League
NFU	National Farmers' Union
NVS	Named Veterinary Surgeon
OJL	Official Journal (Legislation)
PC	Privy Council
QB	Queen's Bench Reports (1841–1852) or (preceded by date) Law Reports, Queen's Bench Division
QBD	Queen's Bench Division or Law Reports, Queen's Bench Division
r	Rule
RCVS	Royal College of Veterinary Surgeons
RDS	Research Defence Society
reg	Regulation
RR	Revised Reports
RSPCA	Royal Society for the Prevention of Cruelty to Animals
s	Section
SC	Session Cases
SCCR	Scottish Criminal Case Reports
SCLR	Scottish Civil Law Reports
Sch	Schedule
Sh Ct	Sheriff Court
SI	Statutory Instrument
SLT	Scots Law Times
SR&O	Statutory Rules and Orders

SSI	Scottish Statutory Instrument
SSPCA	Scottish Society for the Prevention of Cruelty to Animals
TEC	Treaty of the European Community
TEU	Treaty on the European Union
TLR	Times Law Reports
V-C	Vice-Chancellor
WA	Written Answer
White	White's Justiciary Reports (Scotland)
WLR	Weekly Law Reports
WTO	World Trade Organization

Part A

Introduction

1

To Guard and Protect

Cruelty to animals pervaded eighteenth-century England; the majority of the population simply disregarded their suffering, but a significant proportion positively revelled in it. In 1798, for example, Thomas Young, a Fellow of Trinity College, Cambridge, observed that 'the English have more cruelty to animals in their sports in general, than any of their neighbours'.[1] The mistreatment of other species was deeply entrenched in the social fabric, and widely evidenced in daily life. 'Brutes are every day perishing under the hands of barbarity, without notice, without mercy,' complained the Reverend Richard Dean in 1768, 'famished as if hunger were no evil, mauled as if they had no sense of pain, and hurried about incessantly from day to day, as if excessive toil were no plague, or extreme weariness was no degree of suffering.'[2] Appalled by such callous and routine abuse, one John Lawrence, a gentleman farmer and sometime author, was prompted to put forward a novel and far-reaching proposal. Lawrence considered that the prevalence of cruelty could be largely attributed to there being no mechanism in place to regulate how animals were treated. To 'abandon them to the simple discretion of man in all cases without remedy', he wrote, was to 'deprive them in great measure even of compassion'. Accordingly, he concluded, the issue which needed to be addressed was society's failure to acknowledge that other species might have interests which it had a collective responsibility formally to safeguard. 'The grand source of the unmerited and superfluous misery of beasts exists, in my opinion, in a defect in the constitution of all communities', he declared. 'No human government, I believe, has ever recognized the *jus animalium*, which surely ought to form a part of the jurisprudence of every system founded on the principles of justice and humanity.' Writing in 1796, Lawrence was unusual in regarding animal suffering to be an issue of any significance. He was exceptional in arguing that it was properly to be regarded as a matter of public policy:

---

[1] 'An Essay on Humanity to Animals'; quoted in Ryder, RD, *Animal Revolution* (2nd edn, 2000) 59.
[2] 'An Essay on the Future Life of Brute Creatures'; quoted in Fairholme, EG and Pain, W, *A Century of Work for Animals. The History of the RSPCA, 1824–1924* (1924) 6.

I therefore propose that the Rights of Beasts be formally acknowledged by the state, and that a law be framed upon that principle, to guard and protect them from flagrant and wanton cruelty, whether committed by their owners or others.[3]

Today, such a suggestion is commonplace. The contention that 'it is the task of the Government to establish a framework in which animals are treated humanely'[4] represents the accepted view in Britain (although there may be dispute about what constitutes 'humanely'). It is difficult, therefore, at a distance of more than two centuries, fully to appreciate how radical Lawrence's proposal was. To the vast majority of his contemporaries, the notion of enacting legislation to protect animals would have seemed absurd. It is true that there was at the time a growing debate, at least among some intellectuals, about the moral status of animals and man's responsibilities towards them, but few would have agreed that government had any role in controlling how they should be treated. Yet Lawrence's foresight in appreciating the need for legal regulation 'to guard and protect' (to adopt his own phrase) animals from the consequences of man's cruelty, indifference, and ignorance has been shown to be entirely justified.

Exactly two hundred years after he identified the need for state intervention, it was officially estimated that the United Kingdom's legislation contained almost three and a half thousand provisions relating to animals,[5] and the number has subsequently continued to increase. This represents a significant body of law. It also reflects a potent social force, which, since Parliament first enacted such legislation in 1822 (due, in part, to Lawrence's influence), has succeeded in persuading public policy makers that it is both legitimate and necessary to regulate by law, in ever more detail, the way in which animals should be treated. It is a subject which has attracted the attention of writers drawn from a wide range of disciplines, many of whom are cited in the following pages, and yet, with a few notable exceptions, it has been largely overlooked by lawyers in the United Kingdom.[6] It is against this background that the present work seeks to trace the evolution of animal protection legislation in Britain; to place that legislation in its legal, political, and scientific context; to provide a detailed analysis of the substantive law and its application; to evaluate its effectiveness; and to suggest possible avenues for further reform. As

---

[3] From a chapter entitled 'On the Rights of Beasts', in *A Philosophical Treatise on Horses, and on the Moral Duties of Man towards the Brute Creation*, extracts of which were reproduced as an Appendix by Edward Byron Nicholson in *The Rights of an Animal: A New Essay in Ethics* (1879). Lawrence published the first edition of his *Treatise* as a single volume of more than 700 pages in 1796. A second edition in excess of a thousand pages followed in 1802, and it was this which was used by Nicholson. The above quotations are to be found at pp 82, 84, and 85 of Nicholson's book.

[4] Banner, M (Chairman), *Report of the Committee to Consider the Ethical Implications of Emerging Technologies in the Breeding of Farm Animals* (1995) 1.

[5] HC Debs, 12 March 1996, cols 574–575 (WA).

[6] For example, Sandys-Wynch, G, *Animal Law* (1984); Cooper, ME, *An Introduction to Animal Law* (1987); Sweeney, N, *Animals and Cruelty and Law* (1990); Brooman, S and Legge, D, *Law Relating to Animals* (1997); Harrop, SR, 'The Dynamics of Wild Animal Welfare Law' (1997) 9 Journal of Environmental Law 287.

such, it is intended to assist not only lawyers, but also those from other backgrounds whose work is concerned with the treatment of animals, as well as the general reader who has an interest in this topic.

Part B of this work focuses on the historical development of animal protection legislation in Britain. In Chapter 2 consideration is given, first, to the traditional view of our relationship with other species. This was grounded in religious teaching. Man was considered to have been given dominion over the rest of creation, which existed solely for his benefit. On this basis, humans were widely assumed to have a God-given licence to treat animals however they saw fit. Although there were isolated voices arguing from a different perspective, it was not until the latter half of the eighteenth century that one can perceive evidence of a significant reassessment of man's responsibilities towards animals, influenced by developments in natural and political science, religion, and moral philosophy. Although these contributed to a change in thinking among some of the well educated, it had little wider impact, not least because domestic and captive animals had the status of property (as, indeed, they still do), which entitled their owners to exercise complete discretion as to how they should be treated. In consequence, a small, but ultimately influential, number of people such as John Lawrence began to argue that it was necessary for Parliament to intervene by enacting legislation to prohibit the worst excesses of animal cruelty. Chapter 3 takes this story forward, and explains in detail how the first legislation came to be enacted, why it was not possible to rely on the State to enforce it, which thereby led to the establishment of an organization, one of whose objects was to bring private prosecutions for animal cruelty, wherein are to be found the origins of the Royal Society for the Prevention of Cruelty to Animals (RSPCA). An attempt is also made to view these developments in their social context. It is remarkable, for example, that having initially been greeted with derision, within less than forty years the campaign to secure greater legal protection for animals had succeeded in attracting the active support of the social establishment, including the express endorsement of members of the royal family. Similarly, although initially legal intervention had been vigorously opposed on the ground that it constituted an unacceptable intrusion by the State into private life and personal freedom, over the same period it came to be accepted as the legitimate exercise of public power. Chapter 4 demonstrates how, once established, the principle of protecting animals by means of legislation expanded to embrace vivisection, the regulation of the veterinary profession, measures to prevent disease, provisions to protect wildlife and wild animals kept in captivity, the first attempts to control the export of live animals, culminating in the Protection of Animals Act 1911, which remains the basis of animal protection law in England and Wales. Here again, an attempt is made to put these developments into a wider perspective by, for example, discussing the way in which the RSPCA developed a sophisticated strategy by which prosecutions and political lobbying were together used to advance the campaign for further legislative reforms. On the one hand, tracing the development of animal protection legislation provides a fascinating case study in legal and social history; on the other, it is essential for an understanding of the contemporary law, which continues to be shaped and influenced by the foundations which were laid down prior to the First World War. It explains, for example, the ad hoc nature of much of the legislation; the importance of political campaigning to secure change; the role of the RSPCA and the Scottish SPCA in supplementing enforcement by public authorities; and the origin of the fundamental concept of 'unnecessary suffering' in relation to animals.

In Part C, attention moves to the contemporary legal and political context. Much of the information here will be familiar to many readers, especially those who have some knowledge of the law. Nevertheless, it is useful to consider these matters with particular reference to animal welfare. Chapter 5 addresses the central issue of the continuing need for legal regulation. The origins and significance of the common law status of domestic and captive animals as property is explained, which itself continues to necessitate legislative intervention if animals are to be adequately protected under the law. The legal status of animals under European Community law is also examined, with particular reference to the Protocol annexed to the Treaty of the European Community which formally recognizes their sentiency. In addition, it is argued that neither the imposition of voluntary standards nor reliance on market forces is, in itself, sufficient to safeguard animal welfare. There is then a discussion of the nature of legal regulation, in which consideration is given to the distinction made by policy makers between activities deemed to be illegitimate, which are prohibited, and those which are accepted as legitimate, but generally regulated; the principles which may be said to underlie animal protection legislation; and its objects. Chapter 6 seeks to explain the legal framework, including the impact on animal welfare law of the World Trade Organization, the Council of Europe, and the European Community; the status of domestic legislation and associated statutory codes of practice and recommendations; and specific developments such as devolution in Scotland and Wales, the introduction of the Human Rights Act 1998, and the nature of judicial review. Chapter 7 complements this analysis by discussing the important relationship between law and politics, with particular reference to the means by which legislative change may be achieved.

Parts D and E concentrate on the substantive law. Cruelty and welfare are considered separately. This is, of course, something of an artificial distinction, since the welfare of an animal which is the victim of cruelty is in consequence adversely affected. However, despite the overlap, there are important differences. Cruelty, for example, is a well-established *legal* concept, whereas animal welfare is a much more recent *scientific* discipline. Cruelty legislation is generally *negative* in character, in that it specifies what may not be done; welfare legislation, on the other hand, tends (although it is not invariably so) to be *positive*, prescribing how an animal ought to be treated, housed, and cared for. Chapter 8 provides an extended analysis of the meaning and application of the offence of cruelty, which remains the cornerstone of animal protection legislation. Chapter 9 follows on by setting out those who may be held accountable for cruelty, and the sanctions which are available to the courts. There is no single objective which underpins animal protection legislation in Britain, but a thread which runs through it is the prevention of unnecessary suffering. It is central to the offence of cruelty, and the same phrase is also employed widely in welfare legislation. With reference to the relevant case law, Chapter 10 seeks to provide a detailed interpretation of the legal meaning of this ubiquitous term, knowledge of which is essential for an understanding of the basis of animal protection legislation. The following three chapters look at welfare. Chapter 11 contains nothing original. It represents an attempt by a non-scientist to synthesize the leading scientific writing on the subject and thereby to provide an overview of what those working in the field understand by the term 'welfare'. In the process, it also draws attention to some of the disputes which are inherent in this area of research. Although it is written by an amateur, this discussion is important, because the work which is referred to has had a very substantial impact on legislation both within Britain and the wider European Community. Familiarity with the scientific background is therefore necessary in order to appreciate the basis of the legislative provisions. It is also a prerequisite if one is to understand the concept of welfare, for it is in the scientific literature not the law that this is to be found: although the term is used extensively in legislation, nowhere is it defined. Chapters 12 and 13 then go on to consider the welfare requirements specified by law. Instead of providing separate chapters for each activity, such as farming, scientific procedures, transport, and so on, the analysis is presented in a way which enables direct comparison to be made with the nature and degree of legal regulation which applies in different contexts. So, for example, Chapter 12 considers the nature of public control, comparing, in particular, the demands of the various licensing and similar schemes which have been introduced to regulate activities involving animals, as well as the degree of competence required of those responsible for the care of animals in specific circumstances. Chapter 13 considers legal measures intended to promote quality of care, including requirements relating to: the treatment of animals; the accommodation in which they are kept; monitoring their condition; nurturing fitness; dealing with ill-health; preventing and controlling disease; and measures intended to ensure humane killing. Following this discussion of the relevant legal requirements, Chapter 14 focuses on the issue of enforcement, which is too often overlooked. Securing legislation is only half the story; to be effective, it must be adequately enforced, and the discussion here attempts to provide an insight into this important topic. Finally, Chapter 15 draws together some of the issues which have been discussed and suggests further possible reforms.

Having explained how the book is organized, it is appropriate to make four further comments by way of introduction. First, notwithstanding the volume of animal protection legislation currently in force, it applies in the main to a very small proportion of the animal kingdom. It has been estimated that there are more than 1.25 million species of miscellaneous invertebrates, arthropods, and insects, but these do not, in general, benefit from protection under the legislation discussed here. In the

main, this is reserved, in varying degrees, to the 40,000 species of chordates (including 17,000 species of bony fishes; 2,200 of amphibians; 6,000 of reptiles; 8,600 birds;
and 4,400 mammals[7]). By far the most extensive legislative requirements apply to
those species which live closest to man, especially companion animals, working animals, and farmed livestock. We should not be surprised by this. Many of these
species are among those which have the most demanding requirements if they are to
benefit from a high standard of welfare. More pertinently, individuals, and society
generally, clearly have a moral obligation to ensure the well-being of those animals
for which they have assumed responsibility. If a person chooses to have a companion
animal, their responsibility for it is greater than that of the population at large; if
society wishes to benefit from agricultural production and scientific procedures,
then it owes the animals involved a greater duty than animals living in the wild.
Moreover, although wildlife may have a precarious existence, such animals will usually enjoy a degree of autonomy, by which they can attempt to respond to their situation and thereby to improve their own welfare (although there will often be reasons
why this is not possible to achieve), whereas domestic and captive animals tend to be
entirely, or to a very significant extent, dependent on man.

Secondly, although one might wish that it were otherwise, we should not be surprised if the law reflects a confused attitude towards other species. This is indicative of the confusion which exists in society. For example, it is difficult to know
what to make of the statement by the British Veterinary Association, made in
response to the widespread slaughter of calves in the wake of the spread of Bovine
Spongiform Encephalopathy (BSE), that the 'pointless slaughter of healthy animals is abhorrent to the veterinary profession'.[8] There is a respectable moral argument that it is wrong to kill animals; conversely, one can see the logic in saying that
killing an animal is acceptable provided it is done without causing unnecessary
suffering; but what does it mean to speak out against a slaughter programme, carried out humanely, intended to prevent the spread of disease, when the profession
is actively involved in the routine killing of healthy livestock for human consumption? Similar inconsistency is apparent in many other areas, where the moral status
of animals appears to be dependent not on the application of principle, but on the
circumstances in which they find themselves.[9]

Thirdly, having mentioned the issue of the moral status of animals, it should be
stated that the important ongoing debate on this subject receives little attention in
these pages. In part, this is for reason of space; but it is also because there already
exists an enormous literature on this topic which the interested reader may consult.[10] This is not to deny the importance of the moral dimension. Indeed, legislators

---

[7] Storer, TI and Usinger, RL, *General Zoology* (4th edn, 1965) 270.

[8] (1997) 140 *Veterinary Record* 317.

[9] See further, Serpell, J, *In the Company of Animals. A Study of Human-Animal Relationships* (2nd edn, 1996).

[10] See, for example: Godlovitch, S, Godlovitch, R, and Harris, J (eds), *Animals, Men and Morals* (1971);
Clark, SRL, *The Moral Status of Animals* (1977); Frey, RG, *Interests and Rights* (1980); Frey, RG, *Rights,
Killing and Suffering* (1983); Midgley, M, *Animals and Why They Matter* (1983); Regan, T, *The Case for
Animal Rights* (1983); Sapontzis, S, *Morals, Reason and Animals* (1987); Rachels, J, *Created from Animals*

and policy makers *must* develop the regulatory regime by reference to a recognized ethical framework. In practice, the overriding concern has been to minimize animal suffering. It is not surprising, therefore, that much of the law is utilitarian in character. When so much significance has been attached to sentience, a moral theory which takes specific account of considerations such as pain and pleasure in determining the proper course of conduct would seem to be peculiarly suitable for deciding on the way in which animals ought to be treated. However, welfare legislation must have a wider ambit than simply to prevent unnecessary suffering. There are situations, for example, where an animal's welfare may be compromised without it actually suffering; or it may have needs which, if denied, will cause no obvious ill effect, but when fulfilled provide it with a significantly better quality of life. Moreover, new technologies present new dilemmas. These go beyond the traditional issue of suffering and confront fundamental questions about what it means to be a pig, a sheep, or a chicken. This is particularly true of the possibilities presented by advances in gene manipulation, a topic with which policy makers are currently grappling. It is important that boundaries be prescribed at an early stage defining what is, and what is not, acceptable in relation to the treatment of animals. For if the ultimate determinant of what may be done is whether it will cause them to suffer, genetic manipulation which either significantly reduces their capacity to suffer, or imposes fundamental changes to their very nature without inflicting suffering, would seem to be permissible. One therefore welcomes the view expressed by the Banner Committee that, even where there are no welfare implications, a proposed modification should still be regarded as morally objectionable if it amounts to 'treating the animals as raw materials upon which our ends and purposes can be imposed regardless of the ends and purposes which are natural to them'.[11]

Fourthly, this book focuses on human responsibilities, not animals' rights. Its underlying theme is that, for the foreseeable future, the protection of animals in Britain can best be promoted by a greater appreciation of their nature and capacities and the consequences for them of human activity, underpinned by increased and more effective legal regulation of their use and treatment, including the imposition of detailed and binding positive duties on those who assume responsibility for them. This incremental approach is decried in some quarters. The American academic lawyer, Gary Francione, for example, asserts that what he terms legal welfarism 'explicitly supports animal exploitation as morally justifiable, and rejects animal rights'.[12] In his view, 'welfarists seek the *regulation* of animal exploitation; the rightists seek its *abolition*', and he accuses the former of never having 'challenged the basic assumption . . . that humans are justified in

---

(1990); Rodd, R, *Biology, Ethics and Animals* (1990); Singer, P, *Animal Liberation* (2nd edn, 1990); Leahy, M, *Against Liberation* (1991); Carruthers, P, *The Animals Issue* (1992); Linzey, A, *Animal Theology* (1994); DeGrazia, D, *Taking animals seriously. Mental life and moral status* (1996); Scruton, R, *Animal Rights and Wrongs* (1996); Clark, SRL, *Animals and their Moral Standing* (1997).

[11] n 4 above, para 3.19.   [12] Francione, GL, *Animals, Property and the Law* (1995) 258.

exploiting animals'.[13] The notion of exploitation is widely used in this context in an entirely derogatory manner, but other species have long since been integral to our society, and exploitation is an inevitable consequence of social interdependence. It is the nature of the exploitation which is important. In 1965, Brigid Brophy published an influential article in which she complained that 'the relationship of *Homo sapiens* to the other animals is one of unremitting exploitation'.[14] It is the condemnatory adjective 'unremitting' which is significant. The interaction of animals with man need not be prejudiced inevitably in our favour; they, too, may benefit, and often do. At the same time, it is surely incontrovertible that humanity abuses the power which it is able to exercise over other species. However, to suggest that we should somehow isolate ourselves from them is not only fanciful, it is also a denial of the human condition. We are part of the animal kingdom, not separate from it, and, like all other forms of life, each of us has to exploit our environment in order to survive. 'No philosophy or legislation could completely prevent humans from imposing on other animals; imposition is a feature of the biosphere', observe Broom and Johnson. Notwithstanding this, as they point out, 'our use of animals need not be profligate and cruel'; rather, humans 'can afford, and have the knowledge, to reduce our impositions on the animals with which we share the world'.[15] Indeed; what distinguishes us is the capacity to understand the consequences of our actions and hence the effect of our conduct on other animals. Herein, surely, lies the basis of our responsibility towards them—and the more we know, the greater that responsibility becomes. The incremental approach of 'legal welfarism' may not satisfy the moral absolutists, but well drafted and effectively enforced animal protection legislation is an essential constituent in meeting man's responsibilities to other species, especially with regard to domestic animals and wild animals kept in captivity. To this end, it:

- defines the nature and extent of collective and individual responsibility towards animals;
- provides protection from cruelty and abuse;
- regulates the treatment of animals;
- prescribes minimum standards;
- promotes better welfare;
- encourages responsible ownership and husbandry;
- improves both animal and human health, together with public safety;
- educates the public as to the needs of animals;
- allows third-party intervention and thereby qualifies property rights;
- concentrates the minds of policy makers;
- influences judicial attitudes;

---

[13] Francione, GL, *Rain Without Thunder. The Ideology of the Animal Rights Movement* (1996) 1 and 11 (italics in the original).

[14] 'The Rights of Animals', *Sunday Times*, 10 October 1965.

[15] *Stress and Animal Welfare* (1993) 161.

- establishes the principle that the treatment of animals is a legitimate social concern; and
- provides the opportunity for further legislative development.

Marian Dawkins has observed that 'What we choose to do towards animals is up to us.'[16] The law is the means by which society expresses its collective choice. Any shortcomings are those of society itself. In the present state of public opinion, however, it is submitted that the most effective way of advancing the interests of animals is by the formal imposition of human responsibilities through legal regulation.

[16] *Animal Suffering. The Science of Animal Welfare* (1980) 127.

Part B

Historical Development

2

A Great Revolution

A. The Traditional Attitude Towards Animals

'I can entertain no doubt, after the most deliberate study and dispassionate judgment of which I am capable, that the view which most naturalists entertain, and which I formerly entertained—namely, that each species has been independently created—is erroneous', declared Charles Darwin in his Introduction to *The Origin of Species*, published in 1859. 'I am fully convinced', he continued, 'that species are not immutable; but that those belonging to what are called the same genera are lineal descendants of some other and generally extinct species.'[1] As a result, he suggested in parenthesis at the end of the book, 'Light will be thrown on the origin of man and his history.'[2] In response, Samuel Wilberforce, the Bishop of Oxford, denounced the theory of evolution by natural selection as being 'absolutely incompatible' not only with the Biblical account of creation, but also the 'whole representation of that moral and spiritual condition of man' inherent in Christian doctrine:

Man's derived supremacy over the earth; man's power of articulate speech; man's gift of reason; man's freewill and responsibility; man's fall and man's redemption; the incarnation of the Eternal Son; the indwelling of the Eternal Spirit—all are equally and utterly irreconcilable with the degrading notion of the brute origin of him who was created in the image of God, and redeemed by the Eternal Son assuming to himself of his nature.[3]

This quotation nicely encapsulates the traditional Western view of man's place in the world. Humanity considered itself to be pre-eminent because of its unique relationship with God. He had given us 'dominion over the fish of the sea, and over the fowl of the air, and over every living thing that moveth upon the earth',[4] all of which had been created specifically for our use. We were formed in God's own image; we had the power of speech and the capacity to reason; and we alone were

---

[1] 1996 edn, 7.   [2] ibid 394.
[3] Quoted in Clark, RW, *The Survival of Charles Darwin: A Biography of a Man and an Idea* (1984) 145.
[4] Genesis 1: 26–28.

possessed of an immortal soul. As the Psalmist put it, God had made man 'a little lower than the angels' and 'crowned him with glory and honour':

Thou madest him to have dominion over the works of thy hands; thou hast put all things under his feet:
All sheep and oxen, yea, and the beasts of the field;
The fowl of the air, and the fish of the sea, and whatsoever passeth through the paths of the seas.[5]

In view of the power exercised by the Church during the early modern period, it is to be expected that, historically, social attitudes to animals were defined almost exclusively by reference to religious doctrine. Of particular significance in this regard were the writings of St Thomas Aquinas (1225–1274), which represented a distillation of Aristotelian philosophy together with the theology of the Old and New Testaments. Aristotle, for example, regarded the natural world to be hierarchical, with humans at the apex, on the basis of which he concluded that 'if nature makes nothing incomplete, and nothing in vain, the inference must be that she has made all animals for the sake of man'.[6] This proposition was endorsed by Aquinas, but rationalized in the context of divine revelation: 'man, being made in the image of God, is above other animals', he wrote, and they are therefore 'rightly subjected to his government' and intended for his benefit.[7] Accordingly, 'it is not wrong for man to make use of them, either by killing or in any other way whatever'. There was only one exception to this general principle: 'If any passages of Holy Scripture seem to forbid us to be cruel to brute animals', he pronounced, 'this is either to remove man's thought from being cruel to other men, lest through being cruel to animals one become cruel to human beings; or because injury to an animal leads to the temporal hurt of man, either of the doer of the deed, or of another.'[8] On this basis, humans did not owe animals any *direct* duty to minimize their suffering, although there might be an *indirect* duty because of the detrimental social consequences which cruelty could engender. The Thomist tradition has had a profound influence on European attitudes towards animals, and is still reflected in the doctrine of the Roman Catholic Church which has recently reiterated its view that animals are 'by nature destined for the common good of past, present and future humanity', although it is now at least conceded that 'men owe them kindness'.[9]

It is therefore unsurprising that throughout the sixteenth and seventeenth centuries, theological and philosophical orthodoxy continued to be unremittingly anthropocentric. Margaret Cavendish, Duchess of Newcastle (1624–1674),

---

[5] Psalm 8: 5–8.
[6] *Politics*, Book 1, Ch 8; quoted in Regan, T and Singer, P (eds), *Animal Rights and Human Obligations* (1976) 109–10.
[7] *Summa Theologica*, Question 96; quoted in Clarke, PAB and Linzey, L (eds), *Political Theory and Animal Rights* (1990) 61.
[8] *Summa Contra Gentiles*, Third Book, Part II, Ch cxii; quoted in Clarke and Linzey, ibid 10.
[9] *Catechism of the Catholic Church* (1994) paras 2415–2417.

concluded a poem condemning hunting, entitled 'The Hunting of the Hare', by observing that man

> ... is so proud, he thinks only he shall live,
> That God a godlike nature did him give,
> And that all creatures for his sake alone
> Was made for him to tyrannize upon.

Francis Bacon (1561–1626) was reflecting accepted opinion in regarding humanity to be 'the centre of the world, insomuch that if man were taken away from the world, the rest would seem to be all astray, without aim or purpose'.[10] Animals were not considered to have an existence independent of human needs, a view which served both to emphasize man's special status, and to sanction the unrestricted exploitation of other species. Accordingly, animals fell outside the boundaries of moral concern, a conclusion which was endorsed by scientific opinion, most notably by the French philosopher and mathematician, René Descartes (1596–1650), who considered humans and other species to be essentially machines. The distinguishing feature of man, he argued, was the possession of a soul, in which resided human consciousness: 'I think, therefore I am.'[11] Animals, he argued, had no soul, and therefore lacked consciousness. No matter how sophisticated they might appear in their movements and reactions, they were merely automata, to be equated with clocks. They had no thoughts, no feelings, and therefore they could not suffer. They were simply things, and could be treated as such.[12]

Keith Thomas points out that the Cartesian view of animals was much more influential on the Continent than in Britain and was specifically rejected by English intellectuals such as Locke,[13] but it nevertheless served to underpin the prevailing religious and philosophical conventions. In 1796, for example, John Lawrence complained that 'It has ever been and still is the invariable custom of the bulk of mankind—not even excepting legislators, both religious and civil—to look upon brutes as mere machines; animated, yet without souls.' 'From these defects,' he observed, 'and from the idea, ill understood, of their being created merely for the use and purposes of man, have the feelings of beasts, their lawful, that is natural interests and welfare, been sacrificed to his convenience, his cruelty or his caprice.'[14] Whether or not social attitudes were directly influenced by Cartesian thinking, many of them were certainly redolent of it. For example, referring to rural Oxfordshire in the 1880s, Flora Thompson records that:

---

[10] Quoted in Thomas, K, *Man and the Natural World. Changing Attitudes in England 1500–1800* (1984) 18.

[11] *A Discourse on Method*—Discourse IV (1637).

[12] *A Discourse on Method*—Discourse V (1637); cited in Clarke and Linzey, n 7 above, 14–17.

[13] Thomas, n 10 above, 35.

[14] 'On the Rights of Beasts' in *A Philosophical Treatise on Horses, and on the Moral Duties of Man towards the Brute Creation* (1796), reproduced in Nicholson, EB, *The Rights of an Animal: A New Essay in Ethics* (1879) 82.

Ordinary country people at that time, though not actually cruel to animals, were indifferent to their sufferings. 'Where there's no sense there's no feeling,' they would say when they had hurt some creature by accident or through carelessness. By sense they meant wits or understanding, and these they imagined purely human attributes.[15]

Such an attitude helps to explain the widespread disregard for animal suffering. So, too, does the prevalence of animals in, and their fundamental importance to the functioning of, society; a case, perhaps, of familiarity breeding contempt. Eighteenth-century Britain was still overwhelmingly rural, but even in the growing towns, food animals were kept in houses and yards as a source not only of meat, but also milk, eggs, and essential by-products, such as tallow for candles. London was by far the most important centre of population. According to Linda Colley, 'at least one in every dozen Britons' lived there during this period.[16] In 1801, its population numbered 922,000; by comparison, the next largest conurbation was Manchester and Salford with 84,000.[17] Such a concentration of people created an insatiable demand for fresh food, and vast quantities of sheep and cattle were walked from the West Country, Wales, northern England, and Scotland. At the beginning of the nineteenth century, Thomas de Quincey described 'the vast droves of cattle upon the Great North Road all with their heads directed to London and expounding the size of the attracting body together with the force of its attracting power by the never-ending succession of these droves and the remoteness from the capital of the lines in which they were moving'.[18] Upon arrival, they were sold at Smithfield and killed in one of the many local underground slaughterhouses which served the market. Defoe, writing in the 1720s, was overawed by the scene: 'no description can be given of it, no calculation of the numbers of creatures sold there can be made'.[19] An attempt *was* made, however, and it has been estimated that in 1726 there were slaughtered in London 100,000 cattle, 100,000 calves, and 600,000 sheep.[20] Horses, ponies, and asses were ubiquitous, playing an essential role in agriculture, industry, transport, and the army. Many amusements centred on animals: hunting and horse racing for the aristocracy and their hangers-on, various forms of baiting and fighting for the lower orders. Bull-baiting involved tying a bull to a stake and setting one or more dogs upon it, the object being for the dogs to get hold of, and hang on to, the bull's nose. Other animals used for baiting included bears and badgers. Bull-running was a variation on this, during which a bull was chased through the town until it became exhausted, whereupon dogs were set upon it, or it was subjected to local variations, such as at Stamford in Lincolnshire, where the bull was traditionally thrown, or forced to jump, off the

[15] *Lark Rise to Candleford* (1945; 1973 edn) 152–153.

[16] *Britons. Forging the Nation 1707–1837* (1996) 68.

[17] Porter, R, *English Society in the Eighteenth Century* (1982) 381–384.

[18] *Autobiographical Sketches*, Vol XIV of *Works* (1863 edn) 179; quoted in Haldane, ARB, *The Drove Roads of Scotland* (1952; 1995 edn) 173.

[19] *A Tour Through the Whole Island of Great Britain* (1724–6; 1971 edn) 313.

[20] Thomas, n 10 above, 26.

town bridge into the river. Cocks and dogs were most commonly used for fighting. In addition, particular activities were traditionally associated with specific festivals; cock-throwing, for example, which involved tying a fowl to a post and throwing sticks and stones until the unfortunate bird died, was customarily associated with Shrove Tuesday.

The routine abuse of animals was therefore widespread and largely uncontested, being legitimated by theology, philosophy, science, and deep-seated social attitudes. As Lewis Gompertz observed in 1824, 'any one who takes a walk in our public streets . . . will, if possessed of any thought, be shocked at the wanton barbarity continually practised on dumb animals'.[21]

B. Challenging the Anthropocentric Tradition

Despite this widespread indifference to the plight of animals, there had long been isolated voices advancing a very different view of man's relationship with other species. In the 1590s, for example, Michel de Montaigne derided the vanity of man which 'makes him equal himself to God' and 'set himself apart from the mass of other creatures', notwithstanding that they are 'his fellows and his brothers'.[22] It would be more than two hundred and fifty years before such sentiments would gain anything approaching general acceptance, but a series of developments throughout the seventeenth and eighteenth centuries served to undermine the anthropocentric tradition. The period witnessed rapid development in a wide range of disciplines, culminating in the so-called 'Age of Enlightenment'. This intellectual fervour saw an outpouring of ideas—philosophical, scientific, economic, social, and political—which inevitably challenged the status quo.

(1) Impugning man's hubris

In particular, greater understanding across the scientific spectrum initiated a fundamental reassessment of man's status and his place in nature. Astronomers such as Brahe, Kepler, Hooke, and Newton established that the earth was not, after all, the centre of the universe, and the discovery of hitherto unknown species in newly explored parts of the world implied that the totality of creation did not exist simply for man's benefit. Indeed, the discovery by geologists of plants and animals which had lived and become extinct prior to man's existence further undermined the theory. Meanwhile, knowledge increased about the habits and behaviour of individual species and their interrelationship with one another. Gilbert White, whose *Natural History and Antiquities of Selborne* was published in 1788, is but the best remembered of a large number of amateur naturalists who, by recording their

---

[21] *Moral Inquiries on the Situation of Man and of Brutes* (1824) 6.
[22] Quoted in Regan and Singer, n 6 above, 82.

observations accurately and in meticulous detail, contributed significantly to our understanding of the natural world. Physiologists also made an important contribution. Ironically, while Cartesianism had been relied upon to justify the vivisection of conscious animals on the basis that they did not experience pain, the resulting observations, far from distancing man from other species, revealed the same organs, apparently performing the same functions. The degree of similarity led, at least in some quarters, to a realization that humans themselves might properly be regarded as animals. In 1753, for example, Carl Linnaeus published his *Systema Naturae*, in which he classified humans as part of the primate order, together with apes, monkeys, and lemurs. By the turn of the century, scientists such as Erasmus Darwin (grandfather of Charles) in Britain and Lamark in France were suggesting that species might have developed by evolutionary change. It was not, however, until the early years of the nineteenth century, when geologists established the earth to be millions of years old, that it could be demonstrated that life had existed long enough for mutability on the scale contemplated to have occurred.

'The explicit acceptance of the view that the world does not exist for man alone can be fairly regarded', suggests Keith Thomas, 'as one of the great revolutions in modern Western thought.'[23] It went to the heart of man's presumed status. It challenged established assumptions about our physical and spiritual condition, our authority, our purpose, our relationship with God. Little wonder, then, that Thomas considers it a development 'to which historians have scarcely done justice'.[24] It resulted, after all, in nothing less than a gradual, but ultimately fundamental, transformation of the way in which humans regarded their place in the world, one consequence of which was a reassessment of our responsibilities towards other species.

(2) The discovery of 'Nature'

It was not only scientists whose attitude to the natural world was changing; artists, poets, and writers discovered 'Nature' and began to present it as something to be admired and reflected upon, rather than subjugated: 'I love not man the less,' wrote Lord Byron, 'but nature more.'[25] This resulted in a novel reappraisal of man's relationship with other species. William Cowper, for example, took satisfaction that

> Well,—one at least is safe. One sheltered hare
> Has never heard the sanguinary yell
> Of cruel man exulting in her woes.

He went on to describe a close and affectionate bond with this 'Innocent partner of my peaceful home':

---

[23] Thomas, n 10 above, 166.   [24] ibid.
[25] *Childe Harold's Pilgrimage* (1812–1818), canto 4, st 178.

> For I have gained thy confidence, have pledged
> All that is human in me to protect
> Thine unsuspecting gratitude and love.
> If I survive thee I will dig thy grave;
> And, when I place thee in it, sighing say,
> I knew at least one hare that had a friend.[26]

On another occasion he opined,

> I would not enter on my list of friends
> (Tho' grac'd with polish'd manners and fine sense,
> Yet wanting sensibility) the man
> Who needlessly sets foot upon a worm.[27]

More philosophically, William Blake inquired of the fly,[28]

> Am not I
> A fly like thee
> Or art not thou
> A man like me?

Robert Burns, echoing the words of Genesis, apologized to the mouse:[29]

> I'm truly sorry man's dominion,
> Has broken nature's social union,
> An' justifies that ill opinion,
> Which makes thee startle
> At me, thy poor, earth-born companion,
> An' fellow-mortal!

While John Clare, addressing the robin, concluded:[30]

> In duty I'm bound to show mercy on thee,
> Since God don't deny it to sinners like me.

(3) Religious diversity

Running in parallel with these secular developments was a growing religious diversity, which allowed the prevailing theological orthodoxy respecting animals to be challenged. Despite the anthropocentric doctrine of the Roman Catholic and Anglican churches, the Bible itself appeared to be rather more ambivalent as to the relationship between humans and other species: 'A righteous man regardeth the life of his beast: but the tender mercies of the wicked are cruel.'[31] There was some basis for maintaining that animals might be included in God's covenant;[32] and, according to Christ, 'Are not five sparrows sold for two farthings, and not one of

---

[26] 'The Task' (1785).   [27] 'The Winter Walk at Noon' (1788).
[28] 'The Fly' (from *Songs of Experience*, 1789–1794).
[29] 'To A Mouse. On Turning Her up in Her Nest with the Plough, November 1785'.
[30] 'The Robin' (1809).   [31] Proverbs 12: 10.   [32] Hosea 2: 18.

them is forgotten before God' (albeit that the illustration was used to emphasize the importance of man: 'Fear not therefore: ye are of more value than any sparrows').[33] Ecclesiastes even ventured to suggest that humans 'might see that they themselves are beasts' and 'hath no pre-eminence above a beast; for all is vanity'.[34]

This alternative tradition had long been present in Christianity, although overwhelmed by the idea of domination over nature. St Basil (330–379), Bishop of Caesarea, for example, lamented that in relation to 'our brothers the animals',

> We remember with shame that
> In the past we have exercised the
> High dominion of man with ruthless
> Cruelty ...
> May we realize that they live not
> For us alone but for themselves and
> For Thee.[35]

Most notably, there was the example of St Francis of Assisi (1181–1226). 'The realization that everything comes from the same source', wrote St Bonaventure, 'filled Francis with greater affection than ever and he called even the most insignificant creatures his brothers and sisters, because he knew they had the same origin as himself.'[36] Those who knew him described Francis's 'affection and respect' for other creatures; of him speaking to animals 'with a great inner and exterior joy, as if they had been endowed by God with feeling, intelligence, and speech'; of how 'he caressed and contemplated them with delight'.[37] According to another contemporary account,

we who were with him often saw how much he loved them, and what pleasure he took in them. Indeed, his spirit was stirred by such love and compassion for them that he would not allow them to be treated without respect. He used to speak to them as though they were rational creatures with such inward and outward joy that at times he was rapt in ecstasy.[38]

Against this background, some were prepared to regard man's 'dominion' over creation as encompassing a duty to consider the suffering of other species. The seventeenth-century English lawyer Sir Matthew Hale, for example,

abhorred those sports that consist in torturing animals and, if any noxious creatures must be destroyed, it has been my practice to do this with the least torture or cruelty, ever remembering that, although God has given us dominion over His creatures, yet it is under a law of justice, prudence and moderation, otherwise we should become tyrants and not lords.[39]

---

[33] Luke 7: 7–8.   [34] Ecclesiastes 3: 18–19.

[35] Quoted in Wynne-Tyson, J (ed), *The Extended Circle. An Anthology of Humane Thought* (1990) 15.

[36] 'Lives of St Francis by St Bonaventure' in Habig, MA (ed), *St Francis of Assisi. Writings and Early Biographies. English Omnibus of the Sources for the Life of St Francis* (1983, 4th revised edition) 692.

[37] 'Legend of Perugia', ibid 1027 and 1029.   [38] 'Mirror of Perfection', ibid 1255.

[39] Quoted in Fairholme, EG and Pain, W, *A Century of Work for Animals. The History of the RSPCA, 1824–1924* (1924) 3.

During the eighteenth century a number of clerics began to concern themselves with the status of animals. To Humphry Primatt, writing in 1776, 'Every creature is to be considered as a wheel in the great machinery of nature; and if the whole machine is curious and beautiful, no wheel in it, however small, can be contemptible or useless.' In his view, 'there is no more demerit in a beast being a beast, than there is merit in a man being a man' and he expressed sorrow for religion's 'insensibility and indifference as to the happiness or misery of the inferior animals'.[40] At the same time, new denominations provided new insights. The Quakers were well known—as, indeed, they still are—for their concern with animal life, and the Methodists rejected the traditional gulf between humans and the rest of creation. Their founder, John Wesley, expressed strong opposition to cruelty and even went so far as to suggest the probability that animals had souls. 'The lion, the tiger or the shark, inflict pain on other animals', he wrote, 'from mere necessity, in order to prolong their own life; and puts them out of their pain at once.' In contrast, 'the human shark, without any such necessity, torments them of his free choice; and perhaps continues their lingering pain till, after months or years, death signs their release'.[41]

(4) New moral theories

Crucially, all these developments coincided with the emergence of the two most significant and influential moral theories of modern times: the claim for universal human rights, and utilitarianism.

The French Revolution, the framing of the American constitution, publication of Thomas Paine's *Rights of Man* and Mary Wollstonecraft's *A Vindication of the Rights of Woman*, and the debate over slavery, all served to put the question of rights on the political and intellectual agenda. Paine's invective was aimed principally at the hierarchical nature of society and the fact that the exercise of political power was restricted to a very small minority in the upper echelon. 'It is by distortedly exalting some men', he observed, 'that others are distortedly debased, till the whole is out of nature. A vast mass of mankind are degradedly thrown into the background of the human picture, to bring forward, with greater glare, the puppet-show of State and Aristocracy.' In contrast, Paine promoted the—literally—revolutionary idea of 'the unity of man', by which he meant that 'men are all of one degree, and consequently that all men are born equal, and with equal natural rights'.[42] Similarly, Wollstonecraft attacked convention by challenging 'the causes that, in the present corrupt state of society, contribute to enslave women', especially 'the prevailing opinion that woman was created for man'. 'Liberty is the mother of virtue', she asserted, and yet women, 'by their very constitution', were 'not

---

[40] *The Duty of Mercy and the Sin of Cruelty to Brute Animals* (1776; 1992 edn) 20, 22, and 27.

[41] 'Sermon LX: The general deliverance' in Jackson, T (ed), *The Works of John Wesley*, Vol 6 (3rd edn, 1829) 248; quoted by Kean, H, *Animal Rights. Political and Social Change in Britain since 1800* (1998) 19–20.

[42] *The Rights of Man* (1791–2; 1993 edn) 25 and 32.

allowed to breathe the sharp invigorating air of freedom'.[43] Such challenges to the status quo were, of course, intended to benefit the position of people, and were not in any way directly concerned with the lot of animals. However, the call for society to recognize that all human beings had the same moral and civil rights, on the basis of the innate nature of each individual, and regardless of their social status, caused at least some to consider applying a similar principle to other species. It is not suggested that such a notion was either common or widely accepted, but there are examples from this period of the language of rights being applied to animals. 'If we judge impartially, we shall acknowledge that there are the rights of a beast, as well as the rights of a man', wrote Hermann Daggett in 1791, in a pamphlet actually entitled *The Rights of Beasts: An Oration.* 'And I know of nothing in nature, in reason, or in revelation,' he continued, 'which obliges us to suppose, that the unalienated rights of a beast, are not as sacred, and inviolable, as those of a man: or that a person, who wantonly commits an outrage upon the life, happiness, or security of a bird, is not as really amenable, at the tribunal of eternal justice, as he, who wantonly destroys the rights and privileges, or injuriously takes away the life of one of his fellow creatures of the human race.'[44] In similar vein, John Lawrence, writing five years later, argued that 'life, intelligence, and feeling necessarily imply rights' and went on to suggest that 'the rights of animals . . . arise . . . spontaneously from the conscience or sense of moral obligation in man, who is indispensably bound to bestow upon animals, in return for the benefit he derives from their services, good and sufficient nourishment, comfortable shelter, and merciful treatment; to commit no wanton outrage upon their feelings, whilst alive, and to put them to the speediest and least painful death, when it shall be necessary to deprive them of life'.[45] A rather different instance of an analogy between human and animal rights was the publication in 1792 of *A Vindication of the Rights of Brutes,* by one Thomas Taylor. Intended as a satirical attack upon Paine and Wollstonecraft, the author attempted to demonstrate the absurdity of their advocacy of rights by taking the idea to what he considered to be its logical extreme and applying it to animals. Ironically, the proposition on which he based his parody—'the equality of all things, with respect to their intrinsic and real dignity and worth'[46]—would today attract a body of earnest support. Although a substantive theory of animal rights has been developed only relatively recently,[47] its theoretical origins can be traced back to the end of the eighteenth century.[48]

---

[43]   *A Vindication of the Rights of Woman* (1792; 1986 edn) 26, 30, and 41.
[44]   Quoted in Clarke and Linzey, n 7 above, 129–132.   [45]   Lawrence, n 14 above, 81 and 82.
[46]   1966 facsimile, 10.   [47]   See, for example, Regan, T, *The Case for Animal Rights* (1983).
[48]   See, for example, Salt, H, *Animals' Rights* (1892; reissued 1980). Salt, widely regarded as one of the founding fathers of the contemporary animal rights movement, not only cites eighteenth-century writers in developing his argument, but also assembled an important bibliography of English writing on the subject which he included as an appendix to the main work. This clearly demonstrates a continuity of thought throughout the nineteenth century.

(5) Bentham and Utilitarianism

It was, however, utilitarianism, a moral theory which is based on the premise that 'The greatest happiness of the greatest number is the foundation of morals and legislation',[49] which provided the immediate theoretical stimulus for reassessing man's responsibility towards other animals. Its best known proponent, Jeremy Bentham, dismissed the idea of natural rights as 'nonsense', and that of 'natural and imprescriptible rights' as 'rhetorical nonsense—nonsense on stilts'.[50] Instead, he considered that the answer to moral questions was to be found in the fact that 'Nature has placed mankind under the governance of two sovereign masters, *pain* and *pleasure*. It is for them alone to point out what we ought to do, as well as to determine what we shall do.' Accordingly, he suggested, 'Pleasures . . . and the avoidance of pains' should be 'the *ends* which the legislator has in view'.[51]

Bentham published his theory in 1789 and, from the outset, appreciated its far-reaching implications for the treatment of animals. He recognized that as 'sensitive beings' they, like humans, 'may be the objects of benevolence'.[52] If, as he suggested, ethical behaviour was to be defined as 'the art of directing men's actions to the production of the greatest possible quantity of happiness, on the part of those whose interest is in view',[53] then it followed that the interests of animals as well as humans were morally relevant. According to Bentham, animals 'at the same time that they are under the influence of man's direction, are susceptible of happiness', notwithstanding that 'on account of their interests having been neglected by the insensibility of the ancient jurists, [they] stand degraded into the class of *things*'.[54] Despite the unorthodoxy of this view, he observed that 'Under the Gentoo [Hindu] and Mahometan religions, the interests of the rest of the animal creation seem to have met with some attention', and he speculated that 'The day *may* come, when the rest of the animal creation may acquire those rights which never could have been withholden from them but by the hand of tyranny.'[55] After all, the French had 'already discovered that the blackness of the skin is no reason why a human being should be abandoned without redress to the caprice of a tormentor'.[56] Might it 'come one day to be recognized', he asked, that 'the number of the legs, the villosity of the skin, or the termination of the *os sacrum* [that is, whether the individual possesses a tail], are reasons equally insufficient for abandoning a sensitive being to the same fate'?[57]

---

[49] Bentham, J, *The Commonplace Book* in Bowring, J (ed), *The Works of Jeremy Bentham* (1843) Vol 10, 142.

[50] *Anarchical Fallacies*, in Bowring, J (ed), *The Works of Jeremy Bentham* (1843) Vol 2, 501.

[51] *An Introduction to the Principles of Morals and Legislation*, Ch 1, para 1, and Ch 4, para 1 (1789; 1970 edn) (italics in the original).

[52] ibid, Ch 5, para 10.   [53] ibid, Ch 17, part 1, para 2.

[54] ibid, para 4 (italics in the original).   [55] ibid, footnote to para 4 (italics in the original).

[56] ibid. The editors note that by the terms of Louis XIV's Code Noir, the treatment of slaves in the French West Indies had been regulated since 1685. The killing of slaves by their masters was prohibited, and the royal authorities were empowered to protect slaves from mistreatment.

[57] ibid.

Similarly, Bentham rejected the conventional basis for drawing a moral distinction between humans and animals, namely the faculties of reason and discourse, pointing out that 'a full-grown horse or dog, is beyond comparison a more rational, as well as a more conversible animal, than an infant of a day, or a week, or even a month, old'. Accordingly, he asserted, 'the question is not, Can they *reason*? nor, Can they *talk*? but, Can they *suffer*?'[58] Other eighteenth-century thinkers had come to a similar conclusion. Rousseau, for example, had suggested more than thirty years before that, 'by virtue of the sensitivity with which they are endowed', men were 'bound by a certain form of duty' towards animals: 'if I am obliged to refrain from doing any harm to my neighbour, it is less because he is a reasonable being than because he is a sentient one; and a quality which is common to beast and man ought to give the former the right not to be uselessly ill-treated by the latter'.[59]

(6) The growing denunciation of cruelty

The recognition that animals had the capacity to experience pleasure and pain led directly to the denunciation of cruelty. In 1750, William Hogarth published a series of prints entitled 'The Four Stages of Cruelty' which drew attention to the abuse of animals and suggested that such conduct led to the infliction of violence on people. They were produced 'with the hope of, in some degree, correcting the barbarous treatment of animals, the very sight of which renders the streets of our metropolis so distressing to every feeling mind', said Hogarth. 'If they have had this effect, and checked the progress of cruelty,' he remarked, 'I am more proud of having been the author than I should be of having painted Raffaele's [*sic*] cartoons.'[60] Similarly, Mary Wollstonecraft called for a more compassionate attitude towards animals, not simply for their own benefit but also because of the wider social consequences of their cruel treatment. 'Humanity to animals should be particularly inculcated as a part of national education', she argued, because

habitual cruelty is first caught at school, where it is one of the rare sports of the boys to torment the miserable brutes that fall in their way. The transition, as they grow up, from barbarity to brutes to domestic tyranny over wives, children, and servants is very easy. Justice, or even benevolence, will not be a powerful spring of action unless it extend to the whole creation; nay, I believe that it may be delivered as an axiom, that those who can see pain, unmoved, will soon learn to inflict it.[61]

During the second half of the eighteenth century 'scores of books and innumerable contributions to periodicals and newspapers' were published concerning man's responsibility towards animals and the extent of what was coming to be accepted

---

[58] ibid (italics in the original). This quotation is widely cited in the modern literature on the moral status of animals. See, in particular, Singer, P, *Animal Liberation* (2nd edn, 1990), the leading proponent of applying a utilitarian approach to determine how animals ought to be treated.

[59] *Discourse on the Origins and Foundations of Inequality among Men* (1755; 1984 edn) 71.

[60] Nichols, JB, *Anecdotes of William Hogarth* (1833) 64–65; quoted in George, MD, *London Life in the Eighteenth Century* (1925; 1966 edn) 30.

[61] Wollstonecraft, n 43 above, 190.

by many as their mistreatment.[62] 'Pain is pain,' wrote Primatt, 'whether it be inflicted on man or beast.' In his view, 'No creature is so insignificant, but whilst it has life, it has a right to happiness.' Accordingly, 'To deprive it of happiness is injustice; and to put it to unnecessary pain is cruelty', and 'cruelty to a brute is odious and abominable, whether it be to a beast, or a bird, or a fish or a worm'.[63] 'Justice, in which are included mercy or compassion, obviously refer to sense and feeling', asserted Lawrence, which led him to ask: 'Now is the essence of justice divisible? Can there be one kind of justice for men and another for brutes? Or is feeling in them a different thing to what it is in ourselves?'[64] Similarly, because 'Animals are endued with a capability of perceiving pleasure and pain', Thomas Young reasoned, 'we must conclude that the Creator wills the happiness of these his creatures, and consequently that humanity towards them is agreeable to him, and cruelty the contrary'. Young, a Fellow of Trinity College, Cambridge, thereby concluded, 'This, I take it, is the foundation of the rights of animals ... being the same sort of argument as that on which the moralists found the Rights of Mankind.'[65] William Blake reflected similar sentiments in verse:[66]

> A Horse misus'd upon the Road
> Calls to Heaven for Human blood.
> Each outcry of the hunted Hare
> A fibre from the Brain does tear.
> A skylark wounded in the wing,
> A Cherubim does cease to sing.
> The Game Cock clip'd and arm'd for fight
> Does the Rising Sun affright.

Referring to eighteenth-century London, Dorothy George writes that 'It is significant of the new spirit which runs through society that there is a growing feeling against cruelty to animals.'[67] The same could not, however, be said of the country at large. Despite the growing debate, the great majority remained completely unmoved by the plight of animals, as is reflected in the postscript the Reverend James Granger, vicar of Shiplake, Oxfordshire, added to his sermon entitled *An Apology for the Brute Creation or Abuse of Animals Censured*, published in 1772. 'This foregoing discourse gave almost universal disgust to two considerable congregations', he wrote, 'The mention of dogs and horses was censured as a prostitution of the dignity of the pulpit, and considered as a proof of the Author's growing insanity.'[68] Even among those who gave consideration to the matter, there was an ambivalence towards animal suffering when it conflicted with their own convenience or interests, an attitude which remains prevalent today. 'We may have uneasy sensations from seeing a creature in distress, without pity,' observed

---

[62] Thomas, n 10 above, 149.
[63] Primatt, n 40 above, 21 and 107.
[64] Lawrence, n 14 above, 82.
[65] 'An Essay on Humanity to Animals' (1798); quoted in Salt, n 48 above, 153.
[66] 'The Auguries of Innocence', c1803.
[67] n 60 above, 30.
[68] Cited in Turner, ES, *All Heaven in a Rage* (1964; 1992 edn) 72.

Johnson, 'for we have not pity unless we wish to relieve them. When I am on my way to a friend, and finding it late, have bid the coachman to make haste, if I happen to attend when he whips his horses, I may feel unpleasantly that the animals are put to pain, but I do not wish him to desist. No, Sir, I wish him to drive on . . .'[69]

Slowly but surely, however, attitudes *were* changing and the scope of morality was being extended to include other species. As Thomas Paine observed in 1794, 'everything of cruelty to animals, is a violation of moral duty'.[70]

C. The Need for Legislation

This process was gaining some momentum by the end of the eighteenth century, yet animals still lacked any formal protection against abuse. They were 'endowed with feelings', observed John Lawrence at the time, 'but utterly devoid of rights and placed without the pale of justice'.[71]

(1) Animals as property

The courts had long since regarded domestic animals simply as property. 'Whatever airy metaphysical notions may have been started by fanciful writers upon this subject', asserted the eighteenth-century jurist, William Blackstone, the dominion given to man by God had the effect that 'The earth, . . . and all things therein, are the general property of mankind . . . from the immediate gift of the creator.'[72] Initially, 'every one took from the public stock to his own use such things as his immediate necessities required', but gradually this 'communion of goods' was superseded as man began 'to gather together such animals as were of a more tame and sequacious nature; and to establish a permanent property in their flocks and herds . . . as absolute a property as in any inanimate beings'.[73] Accordingly, the owner had complete freedom to determine how his animals should be treated and disposed of, in the same way that he could do whatever he wished with his inanimate possessions. '[T]he injured brute hath neither speech to plead for him, nor law to protect him, nor hope of future recompense to support him', wrote Primatt in 1776.[74] 'As the law stands at present,' observed Lawrence, 'no man is punishable for an act of the most extreme cruelty to a brute animal but upon the principle of an injury done to the property of another', and 'the owner of a beast has the tacit allowance of the law to inflict upon it, if he shall so please, the most horrid barbarities'.[75] Addressing the House of Lords in 1809, Lord Erskine, a former Lord Chancellor, summarized the situation succinctly: 'Animals are considered as

---

[69] Hill, GB (ed), *Boswell's Life of Johnson* (1934) Vol 1, 437.
[70] *The Age of Reason*, Part One (1794); quoted in Foot, M and Kramnick, I (eds), *The Thomas Paine Reader* (1987) 540–541.
[71] Lawrence, n 14 above, 79.   [72] *Commentaries on the Laws of England* (1765–1769) Book II, 3.
[73] ibid 390.   [74] n 40 above, 32–33.   [75] n 14 above, 85.

property only: to destroy or abuse them, from malice to the proprietor, or with an intention injurious to his interest in them, is criminal; but the animals themselves are without protection; the law regards them not substantively; they have no rights!'[76]

In so far as the law was concerned with animals at all, its primary focus was on protecting the property interests of the owner. Between 1671 and 1831, for example, there were enacted more than fifty statutes concerned with game, deer stealing, and poaching. The most notorious of these was the so-called 'Black Act' of 1723 which, among its other provisions, made it an offence punishable by death unlawfully to hunt, wound, kill, destroy, or steal deer; to rob any warren or place where rabbits or hares were kept; to steal fish out of any river or pond; or unlawfully or maliciously to kill, maim, or wound any cattle.[77] Otherwise, the law would only intervene if a domestic animal was either treated in such a way as to cause a public nuisance, or harmed by a third party without the express or implied consent of the owner. If a domestic animal was killed or wounded, the owner might sue in trespass for compensation, but the perpetrator was only criminally liable if malicious intent could be proved, the courts having stated that 'In order to convict a man for barbarous treatment of a beast, it should appear that he had malice towards the prosecutor.'[78]

In none of these cases was the purpose to prevent suffering to the animal. The first was concerned with the maintenance of public order, and the others were intended to protect owners from damage being done to their property, although the public order provisions did have the potential to provide some, albeit very limited, protection. With the intention of suppressing the Shrovetide custom of cock-throwing, for example, the Norwich Court of Mayoralty, 'in just abhorrence of the cruel practice', in 1759 ordered the constables to patrol the streets 'to prevent such disorders as usually arise therefrom' and, in 1762, the Mayor and Justices of Northampton 'perambulated the Precincts' so as 'to prevent the scandalous and inhuman Practice' from taking place.[79] Some suggested that the authorities should do more: a letter to the *Gentleman's Magazine* urged magistrates and peace officers 'to exert themselves with the utmost vigour, in the suppression of the infamous and iniquitous custom';[80] Thomas Young pointed out that magistrates had the power to prevent shows with performing animals travelling about the country and 'by a proper exertion of it they would do much good, besides cutting off one source

---

[76] Parl Debs vol 14, col 554 (15 May 1809).

[77] See further, Thompson, EP, *Whigs and Hunters* (1990); McLynn, F, *Crime and Punishment in Eighteenth-Century England* (1991) Ch 11; Gilmour, I, *Riots, Risings and Revolution. Governance and Violence in Eighteenth-Century England* (1992) Ch 9.

[78] Heath J, *R v Parker* (July Sessions, 1794), cited in Nicholson, n 14 above, 9. 'The prosecutor' would have been the owner of the animal because the practice then was that such prosecutions were brought by the person against whom the crime had been committed rather than by the State.

[79] *Norwich Mercury*, 10 March 1753; *Northampton Mercury*, 1 March 1762; quoted in Malcolmson, RW, *Popular Recreations in English Society 1700–1850* (1973) 120–121.

[80] vol XXI (1751) 8.

of cruelty to animals';[81] and Lord Erskine was of the opinion that *public* cruelty to animals was, 'under many circumstances, an indictable offence'.[82]

Even if more rigorously enforced, however, such measures were in themselves insufficient to deal with the nature and scale of the problem. Much of the cruelty, such as that associated with the driving and slaughtering of cattle, and the beating of horses, was routine, widespread, largely uncontentious, and did not therefore pose a threat to public order. Similarly, the focus of the common law on protecting the value of property was ineffective in circumstances where the abuse was inflicted by the owner himself, or with his acquiescence. 'You cannot punish cruelty and aggression', declared Lawrence, 'without trespassing upon the right of property.'[83]

(2) The call for parliamentary intervention

Simply exhorting people to treat animals better, Lawrence argued, was insufficient: 'Experience plainly demonstrates the inefficacy of mere morality to prevent aggression, and the necessity of coercive laws for the security of rights.'[84] If, however, there were to be 'a law made for the protection of beasts', he asserted, 'its utility would consist in the recognition of the principle', and, as such, 'it would stand forth as an eminent precept and momento of humanity'.[85]

The argument that Parliament should provide protection for animals against ill-treatment was not entirely novel. In 1749, an anonymous contributor to the *Gentleman's Magazine*, in an article condemning cock-throwing, imagined the bird asking for kinder treatment and suggesting that 'Perhaps the legislature may not think it beneath them to take our said case into consideration.'[86] At the time, this was a lone voice, but by the end of the century there were calls for the introduction of legislation from a number of quarters. In addition to Lawrence, a correspondent to the *Gentleman's Magazine* opined, 'It is hard that there should be no law for brute animals, when they carry so large a proportion of representatives to every legislative assembly.' Another, bemoaning the 'innumerable and unwarrantable cruelties' committed upon 'the courageous cock', 'the majestic bull', 'the generous horse', and even 'some kinds of fish' (which are 'taken abroad, and made to endure a painful existence'), exclaimed: 'Surely the law should restrain the outrages committed against these, and other much injured animals!'[87] In 1789, Bentham had noted that the 'Interests of the inferior animals [had been] improperly neglected in legislation',[88] and he later asserted:

---

[81] 'An Essay on Humanity to Animals' (1798), quoted in Fairholme and Pain, n 39 above, 14–15.

[82] Parl Debs vol 14, col 554 (15 May 1809).

[83] n 14 above, 86.   [84] ibid 79.   [85] ibid 93.

[86] *Gentleman's Magazine*, April 1749, 147–148.

[87] 'Mr Humanus', *Gentleman's Magazine*, January 1789, 17; 'B' (anonymous author), *Gentleman's Magazine*, 1791, Vol 61, 334–336.

[88] *An Introduction to the Principles of Morals and Legislation*, n 51 above, Ch 17, Part 1, margin note to footnote to para 4.

The legislator ought to interdict everything which may serve to lead to cruelty . . . It is proper . . . to forbid every kind of cruelty towards animals, whether by way of amusement, or to gratify gluttony . . . Why should the law refuse its protection to any sensitive being? The time will come when humanity will extend its mantle over everything which breathes. We have begun by attending to the condition of slaves; we shall finish by softening that of all the animals which assist our labours or supply our wants.[89]

In 1797 George Nicholson, referring to a Manchester butcher who hung up live calves 'with the gambrel put through their sinews, and hook stuck through their nostrils, the dismal bleating of the miserable animals continuing till they had bled to death', complained that 'Attempts were made to prevent the hellish nuisances caused by this man, but in vain, for he did but torture his own property! Such are the glaring imperfections of the laws of a civilized, a humane, a Christian country!'[90] And Richard Sheridan, the politician and dramatist, told the House of Commons in 1802 that 'he must consider cruelty to brute animals as a crime, whether done for amusement, for sport or for gluttony; and therefore if there were not laws to prevent, if not to punish such cruelties, there certainly ought to be'.[91]

By the end of the eighteenth century, then, that great revolution in ideas which would fundamentally alter the way in which the British regarded animals was taking root; and among the (admittedly, relatively small number of) people who concerned themselves with such matters, attention was turning to Parliament with a view to securing legislation which would reflect the emerging moral status of other species.

[89] *The Principles of Modern Penal Law* (1811) in Bowring, J, *The Works of Jeremy Bentham* (1859) Vol 1, 562.
[90] Nicholson, G, *On the Conduct of Man to the Inferior Animals* (1797); quoted in Ryder, RD, *Animal Revolution* (2nd edn, 2000) 74.
[91] *Parliamentary History of England*, Vol 36, col 852 (24 May 1802).

3

The First Legislation

'[A]ll animals are endowed with sensation, or at least with irritability, which last has been considered as a distinctive character of animal life', wrote the Scottish writer William Smellie in 1790. 'Sensation', he suggested, 'implies a distinct perception of pleasure and pain',[1] the very characteristics which were central to the moral theory of utilitarianism. So, as Richard Ryder observes, by the end of the eighteenth century 'the basic principles of the modern animal welfare position were established'. Namely, a recognition that animals, like humans, can suffer pain, 'and that pain entitles them to legal as well as moral rights'.[2] While this would have a profound effect in the future, at the time it remained very much a minority view.

A. The 1800 and 1802 Bull-Baiting Bills

It is not surprising, then, that the first attempt at legislation was intimately bound up with wider social issues. On 3 April 1800, the Scottish MP, Sir William Pulteney, introduced a Bill into the House of Commons to prohibit bull-baiting. Formerly animal fighting and baiting had been considered respectable pastimes, being patronized by royalty and the aristocracy, but by the end of the eighteenth century they were associated with the lower orders of society, among whom such activities remained a popular form of entertainment. Indeed, the Bill's Preamble drew attention to the fact that bull-baiting 'hath of late much increased in Several Parts of the Kingdom'. Pulteney acknowledged that bull-baiting was 'cruel and inhuman' but gave greater emphasis to its social vices, complaining that 'it drew together idle and disorderly persons' and gave rise to 'many disorderly and mischievous proceedings'. In Staffordshire and Rutland, he claimed, 'the labouring poor often left their work to attend on this sport for days and even weeks together'.[3] William

---

[1] *The Philosophy of Natural History* (1790) Vol 1, Ch 1. Smellie is best remembered as the editor, printer, and co-producer of the first edition of the *Encyclopaedia Britannica*.

[2] Ryder, RD, *Animal Revolution* (2nd edn, 2000) 72.

[3] *Parliamentary History of England*, Vol 35, cols 202 and 209 (2 and 18 April 1800).

Wilberforce is reported to have been unhappy at the prominence Pulteney gave to the issue of public order at the expense of the treatment accorded to the bulls, and complained that, in presenting the Bill, he had 'argued it like a parish officer, and never once mentioned cruelty'.[4] Others, however, did; 'to tie the poor animal to a stake and set upon him a number of ferocious dogs, was cruel, disgraceful and beastly', charged Sheridan.[5]

In any event, regardless of the grounds on which it was promoted, the Bill received a hostile reception, especially from William Windham, MP for Norwich. 'This House ought only to legislate when an act of the legislature is gravely and generally called for; and not merely to gratify petty, personal, and local motives, such as are infinitely beneath the deliberate dignity of parliament', he told the House of Commons, and warned that 'This petty, meddling, legislative spirit, cannot be productive of good; it serves only to multiply the laws, which are already too numerous, and to furnish mankind with additional means of vexing and harassing one another.' Windham presented the proposal as an attack upon the freedom of the poor to pursue their traditional customs, asking 'Why should we set about to deprive them of the few enjoyments which are left to them?' It was, he thought, 'time to resist these unnecessary restraints' which, if they became law, would 'no doubt be followed by other regulations equally frivolous and vexatious'.[6] *The Times* agreed: 'It should be written in letters of gold that a Government cannot interfere too little with the people; that laws, even good ones, cannot be multiplied with impunity, and that whatever meddles with the private personal disposition of a man's time or property is tyranny.' According to the paper, the only justification for legal intervention was if someone got injured, and 'it is then to redress and not to restrain', otherwise 'we must eat and drink and play and sleep by Act of Parliament'.[7]

Windham raised a further objection, and one which was close to the hearts of MPs, pointing out that cruelty was also associated with the field sports enjoyed by gentlemen. 'The common people may ask with justice', he said, 'why abolish bull-baiting, and protect hunting and shooting?' 'What appearance must we make', he enquired of the Commons, 'if we ... become rigid censors of the sports of the poor, and abolish them on account of their cruelty, when they are not more cruel than our own?' This was to be a recurring objection to successive attempts at legislation. While Windham denied there was any real evil in bull-baiting, by implication he accepted it was cruel, but others denied even that. According to George Canning, 'The amusement was a most excellent one; it inspired courage, and produced a nobleness of sentiment and elevation of mind.' 'What could be more innocent', he asked, 'than bull-baiting, boxing, or dancing?'[8] The voting was close, but the Bill

---

[4] Wilberforce, RI and S, *The Life of William Wilberforce* (1838) ii, 366; quoted in Harrison, B, *Peaceable Kingdom* (1982) 83.

[5] *Parliamentary History of England*, Vol 35, col 213 (18 April 1800).

[6] ibid, cols 203, 204, and 206 (18 April 1800).   [7] 25 April 1800.

[8] *Parliamentary History of England*, Vol 35, cols 207, 208, and 211 (18 April 1800).

was lost by 43 votes to 41. A further, unsuccessful, attempt at prohibition was made in 1802. The opposition was again led by Windham, who reiterated his view that 'the discussion of such paltry local complaints was wholly unworthy of the legislature of a great nation', and accused the Jacobins and Methodists of attacking the amusements of the people for their own ends. Once more, he warned the Commons against applying double standards, enquiring why hunting, shooting, and fishing should not be judged by similar principles, and declaring that horse racing was 'infinitely more pernicious' than bull-baiting, attracting 'all the riff-raff from every part of the country' and encouraging gambling.[9]

B. Erskine's Cruelty to Animals Bill

It was seven years before the next attempt was made to introduce legislation, humane reformers being preoccupied with the campaign to prohibit slavery, which was successful in 1807. In 1809, Thomas Erskine presented a Bill to the House of Lords to prevent malicious and wanton cruelty to animals. Erskine had been born in Edinburgh in 1750 and had become both a King's Counsel and MP for Portsmouth in 1783. He was in sympathy with the French Revolution and during the 1790s became renowned for defending radicals facing prosecution, including Thomas Paine, Thomas Hardy, and John Horne Tooke. Despite this record, he served as Lord Chancellor between 1806 and 1807.[10]

The scope of his Bill, and the intellectual arguments he used to support it, were of a completely different order than those of 1800 and 1802. Although concern about public order and the manners of the lower orders was still present, Erskine's principal motivation was clearly to secure protection for animals against illtreatment. His purpose, he told the House of Lords, was to do something about 'the almost innumerable instances of cruelty to animals, which are daily occurring in this country, and which, unfortunately, only gather strength by any efforts of humanity in individuals to repress them, without the aid of the law'. This was in contrast to the previous attempts at legislation, whose 'One great object' was, he said, 'to put an end to sports which led away the servants and labourers of manufacture and husbandry from the service of their masters'.[11]

In a remarkable speech for the time, Erskine succeeded in marshalling the existing, but disparate, arguments in favour of statutory protection into a coherent and forceful thesis, based on a reinterpretation of the meaning to be attached to the biblical term, 'dominion'. Gone was any suggestion that animals were outside the ambit of moral concern; man owed them a direct duty: 'I am to ask your lordships,' Erskine told the House of Lords, 'in the name of that God who gave to man his dominion over the lower world, to acknowledge and recognize that dominion to be a moral trust.'[12] Gone, also, were distinctions based on language, reason, or the

---

[9] ibid, Vol 36, cols 831–833 and 837 (24 May 1802).
[10] See further, Campbell, JL, *Lives of the Lord Chancellors* (1857) Vols 8 and 9.
[11] Parl Debs vol 14, cols 553 and 559–560 (15 May 1809).   [12] ibid, col 554.

possession of a soul. It was the *similarity*, particularly as regards sentiency, between man and other creatures which was morally significant. Erskine conceded that 'if we found no organs in the animals for their own gratification and happiness; no sensibility to pain or pleasure; no grateful sense of kindness, nor suffering from neglect or injury; no senses analogous, though inferior to our own: if we discovered, in short, nothing but mere animated matter, obviously and exclusively subservient to human purposes,' then 'it would be difficult to maintain that the dominion over them was a trust'. The evidence, however, was self-evidently otherwise: 'it calls for no deep or extended skill in natural history', he said, 'to know that the very reverse of this is the case'.

'For every animal which comes in contact with man,' Erskine declared, 'nature has taken the same care to provide, and as carefully and bountifully as for man himself, organs and feelings for its own enjoyment and happiness.' So it was that, 'Almost every sense bestowed upon man is equally bestowed upon them; seeing, hearing, feeling, thinking; the sense of pain and pleasure; the passions of love and anger; sensibility to kindness, and pangs from unkindness and neglect, are inseparable characteristics of their natures as much as our own.' Was it possible 'to contemplate this wonderful arrangement', he asked the House of Lords, 'and to doubt for a single moment that our dominion of animals is a trust'? Other species might be exploited for human ends, but not unconditionally: 'They are created indeed for our use, but not for our abuse', he declared. In consequence, 'Their freedom and enjoyments, when they cease to be consistent with our just dominion and enjoyments, can be no part of their natures; but whilst they are consistent, I say their rights, subservient as they are, ought to be as sacred as our own.'[13]

On this basis, he condemned the way in which post-horses were treated ('I see no reason why . . . travellers should not endeavour to overcome the *ennui* of their lives without killing poor animals, more innocent and useful than themselves'), the use of old and diseased horses who were incapable of working, the conditions in which animals were kept awaiting slaughter, and the overloading of draught animals.[14] The situation would continue to get worse, he suggested, 'without the aid of the law'.[15] There was no new principle involved. Statutory protection for animals would, he argued, simply represent the extension of an established practice, for 'Every other branch of our duties, when subject to frequent violation, has been recognized and inculcated by our laws; and the breaches of them repressed by punishments.' Accordingly, 'why not in this', the treatment of animals, enquired Erskine, 'where our duties are so important, so universally extended, and the breaches of them so frequent and so abominable?' The effect of such legislation would be to establish and promote man's obligations towards animals which Erskine regarded as arising directly from his dominion over them: 'From the moral sense . . . created by the law, the next generation will feel, in the first dawn of their

---

[13] Parl Debs vol 14, cols 554–556.   [14] ibid, cols 561–564.   [15] ibid, col 553.

ideas, the august relation they stand in to the lower world, and the trust which their station in the universe imposes on them.'[16]

Unlike the bull-baiting Bills, Erskine's was not aimed at any specific activity, but, rather, sought to make it a misdemeanour for any person, including the owner, maliciously to wound or with wanton cruelty to beat or otherwise abuse any horse, mare, ass, ox, sheep, or swine (Erskine recognizing that 'For one act of cruelty in servants, there are an hundred in the owners of beasts of burthen' (*sic*)).[17] This was a clever tactic. Not only would such a provision apply in many different circumstances, it also sought to avoid either the charge that it was aimed at any particular section of the populace, or controversy in Parliament over whether a given practice was or was not cruel. That judgement would be left to the courts. 'The Bill says not a word about bull-baiting', explained Erskine, 'I only include a bull in my catalogue of protected animals. They, therefore, who support the practice, may still support it successfully, if they can convince a court and jury, and the other magistracies of their countrymen, that it does not fall within the description wilful and wanton cruelty.'[18] The strategy was, however, ultimately unsuccessful. The Bill passed through the Lords after it had been amended to apply only to beasts of burden, but was eventually lost in the Commons, by 37 votes to 27. Yet again, Windham was the principal antagonist and the focus of his criticism on this occasion was the generality of the proposals. It was an ingenious argument. At a time when most prosecutions were brought by private individuals rather than the State, he claimed that if the Bill became law, it would mean that 'All the fanatical views and feelings, all the little bustling spirit of regulation, all the private enmities and quarrels would be at work', and the accused would be subjected to 'the arbitrary and fluctuating standard, which the judge . . . happened to have in his breast'. Indeed, he suggested that the measure should have been entitled, 'A Bill for harassing and oppressing certain classes among the lower orders of the people'.[19] More fundamentally, however, he remained implacably opposed to the very concept of legislation to protect animals. In his view, such a subject was better left to manners and morals, to be promoted 'from the pulpit, from the press, by precept, by exhortation',[20] not by Parliament, not by means of law. And there was still the issue of field sports. According to Windham, if Parliament was to pass legislation which imposed a punishment for cruelty, while 'we continued to practise and to reserve in great measure to ourselves the sports of hunting, shooting and fishing, we must exhibit ourselves as the most hardened and unblushing hypocrites that ever shocked the feelings of mankind'.[21]

The following year, Erskine made a second attempt, but subsequently withdrew the measure because of the strength of opposition he now encountered. Notwithstanding that his Bill had been supported by the Lords the previous year, Windham's arguments appear to have had some impact. Lord Ellenborough, for

[16] ibid, cols 556 and 571.   [17] ibid, col 561.   [18] ibid, col 560.

[19] Parl Debs vol 14, col 1036 (13 June 1809).

[20] ibid, col 1027 (should be 1043, the column is wrongly numbered).

[21] ibid, col 1040.

example, predicted that 'it would cause more vexation to mankind than was now suffered by the brute creation', and suggested 'the moral sense of mankind was sufficient, as it hitherto had been, for the protection of animals'.[22] The Earl of Lauderdale, Lord Holland, and Lord Redesdale agreed, the latter suggesting that Erskine had 'so long contemplated this subject, that his mind had become so heated, as to prevent the exercise of his cool discretion'.[23]

Beyond Parliament, however, attitudes were becoming more receptive to the concept of legislation to protect animals. *The Times*, which had reacted with such hostility to the bull-baiting Bills, now thought it 'peculiarly worthy' of Erskine 'to lay the foundation for and establish a system of rights and privileges even for the mute and unconscious part of creation', and the *Gentleman's Magazine* for June 1809 suggested that 'few subjects in the whole compass of moral discussion can be greater than the unnecessary cruelty of man to animals'. Even so, the prevailing orthodoxy was yet to accept that animals should be protected in their own right. The *Edinburgh Review*, for example, considered that the only possible reason for such legislation could be that 'their protection be connected either directly or remotely with some advantage to man'.[24]

C. Martin's Act

It was to be more than ten years before the matter was again considered by Parliament, the instigator on this occasion being Richard Martin, MP for Galway. Born in Dublin in 1754, he was educated at Harrow and Cambridge, and trained as a barrister, although he did not practise. Among the causes he advocated were Catholic emancipation, abolition of capital punishment for forgery, and access to counsel at the State's expense for those charged with criminal offences who could not themselves afford legal representation. It is, however, his efforts on behalf of animals for which he is remembered. Martin, with the assistance of John Lawrence and Thomas Erskine, produced in 1821 a Bill 'to prevent the ill-treatment of horses and other animals' by third parties.[25] The familiar objections were rehearsed in the Commons: the Bill was 'altogether unnecessary', the subject was 'not a fit one for legislation', and 'when so many barbarities prevailed in fishing and hunting, and other species of amusement, it was idle to legislate without including all possible cases'.[26] However, there were now MPs on the other side of the debate, who did not think that it went far enough: one wished to protect all animals, another thought that cruelty by owners should be included.[27] Despite the opposition,

---

[22] Parl Debs vol 16, col 881 (8 May 1810).   [23] ibid, cols 882–884.
[24] Fairholme, EG and Pain, W, *A Century of Work for Animals* (1924) 23; Moss, AW, *Valiant Crusade* (1961) 15.
[25] Ryder, n 2 above, 82.
[26] Mr Monck, Mr Scarlett, and Mr Ricardo, Parl Debs (new series) vol 5, col 1099 (1 June 1821).
[27] Mr Alderman Wood and Lord Binning, ibid.

including that of the Attorney-General, who objected to the Bill because it introduced a new principle into the criminal law, it succeeded in the Commons by 48 votes to 16, but was lost in the Lords. Undeterred, Martin reintroduced the Bill on 24 May 1822 and, with assistance from Erskine in the Lords, it passed both Houses and received the Royal Assent on 21 June 1822. Formally titled 'An Act to prevent the cruel and improper Treatment of Cattle',[28] but generally referred to as 'Martin's Act', it was the first piece of legislation specifically intended to prevent cruelty to animals.[29] It became an offence for any person or persons (therefore including the owner) wantonly and cruelly to beat, abuse, or ill-treat any horse, mare, gelding, mule, ass, ox, cow, heifer, steer, sheep, or other cattle. A prosecution was to be initiated by making a complaint on oath to a magistrate and, upon conviction, the magistrates were required to impose a fine of at least ten shillings, up to a maximum of five pounds. In the event of a frivolous or vexatious complaint, the complainant could be ordered to pay the accused compensation of up to twenty shillings.

Martin's success encouraged him to press for further reform: in May 1823 he applied to bring in a Bill to prohibit bull-baiting and dog-fighting;[30] in February 1824 he tried to extend the 1822 Act to dogs, cats, monkeys, and other animals, and the same day he proposed a further Bill to prohibit bear-baiting and other cruel sports;[31] in the summer of 1824 his target was the treatment of horses awaiting slaughter;[32] in February 1825 he again sought to end bear-baiting, badger-baiting, and dog-fights and, the following month, he sought to make offences under the 1822 Act misdemeanours, which would have meant they were punishable with a fine and imprisonment;[33] and in April 1826 he introduced a Bill to protect dogs.[34] In a succession of speeches, Martin was able, by drawing on his considerable personal experience, to provide Parliament with an informed view of the way in which animals were being abused and to keep the issue in the public domain, but none of these measures passed into legislation. Martin was re-elected at the general election of 1826, but subsequently lost his seat as a result of alleged irregularities by his

---

[28] 3 Geo IV, c 71.

[29] Ryder cites an Irish law of 1635 which prohibited the pulling of wool off sheep and the attaching of ploughs to horses' tails which was enacted at least in part because of the cruelty caused by these practices. He also refers to the legal code of the Massachusetts Bay Colony which, in 1641, directed that 'No man shall exercise any Tirranny or Crueltie towards any bruite Creature which are usuallie kept for man's use': Ryder (n 2 above) 49–50. See also, Wise, SM, *Rattling the Cage* (2000) 43–44, who, in addition to the Massachusetts legislation, also refers to what he describes as the first anti-cruelty statute in the United States, enacted in Maine the year before Martin's Act was passed (Me Laws Ch iv, sec 7 (1821)).

[30] Bill to Prohibit Bull-Baiting and Dog-Fights, Parl Debs (new series) vol 9, cols 433–435 (21 May 1823).

[31] Cattle Ill-Treatment Bill, Parl Debs (new series) vol 10, cols 130–131 and 865–869 (11 February and 9 March 1824); Bear Baiting Bill, Parl Debs (new series) vol 10, cols 131–134, 368–369, and 486–496 (11, 24, 26 February 1824).

[32] Horse Slaughtering Bill, Parl Debs (new series) vol 11, cols 1095–1097 (4 June 1824).

[33] Bear-Baiting Prevention Bill; Cruelty to Animals Bill, Parl Debs (new series) vol 12, cols 657–661, 1002–1013, and 1160–1162 (24 February, 11 and 24 March 1825).

[34] Cruelty to Dogs Bill, Parl Debs (new series) vol 15, cols 530–532 (20 April 1826).

supporters during the election campaign. In spite of all his efforts, the 1822 Act was his single legislative achievement. The House of Commons was not, however, the only arena in which he worked on behalf of animals.

D. The Establishment of the SPCA

Legislation alone was not enough; it never is. To be effective, it must be enforced, and this clearly posed a problem. In the 1820s the State took little part in bringing prosecutions, most of which were initiated by private individuals. Indeed, there was a deep suspicion of suggestions that the State should take a more active role in enforcing the criminal law, and it was not until 1829 that the Metropolitan Police were established.[35] Without someone taking the initiative, there was a distinct danger that Martin's Act would be stillborn. It is therefore unsurprising that within a couple of weeks of its enactment, it was Martin himself who brought the first prosecution.[36] It was the first of many in which he became involved, but, on gaining a conviction, he often asked the court to impose the minimum fine of ten shillings, and it was not unknown for him to pay the penalty himself. The *Morning Chronicle* complained that he patrolled the streets looking for offences and then took up the time of the courts with charges which he invariably prefaced with a speech on the evils of cruelty to animals, and then frequently ended by pleading for leniency for the offender or paying the fine himself.[37] Such criticism was to misunderstand his motives; his purpose was not primarily to punish the individual defendant, but to gain publicity for his Act and to establish precedents before the courts.

Nevertheless, an individual, working alone, could only achieve so much; for greater effectiveness, a formal organization charged with protecting animals was required. This was not an entirely novel idea. The Society for the Suppression of Vice, established in 1802, ironically with the objective of suppressing radical literature and promoting adherence to established religion, had made the interests of animals one aspect of its work; in 1809 there had been established in Liverpool a Society for Preventing Wanton Cruelty to Brute Animals (although it is not clear how long it survived);[38] and in 1818 a correspondent in the *Monthly Magazine* had

---

[35]   10 Geo IV, c 44.

[36]   There is some confusion about the identity of the first person convicted under the Act. There is in existence a contemporary cartoon which purports to show Martin prosecuting a costermonger, one Bill Burns, and insisting on his ill-treated donkey being brought into court as evidence. It is often suggested that this was the first successful prosecution. It was certainly an early case (although there are doubts about whether the animal was actually present in the court). The better view is that the first convictions, reported in *The Times* of 12 August 1822, were by Martin of Samuel Clarke and David Hyde at the Guildhall, both men being fined twenty shillings for beating their respective horses. See further, Fairholme and Pain, n 24 above, 32; Moss, n 24 above, 66; Lynam, S, *Humanity Dick* (1975) 208; Ryder, n 2 above, 82–83.

[37]   Lynam, ibid 252.

[38]   Moss, n 24 above, 20–21. According to Linda Colley, the city founded the Society to commemorate the Jubilee of George III: *Britons* (1996) 237.

proposed the establishment of a society for the prevention of cruelty to animals.[39] In April 1821, the same publication contained a notice inserted by an individual calling himself 'Clericus', generally thought to be the Reverend Arthur Broome, lamenting 'the wanton cruelties which are so frequently exercised with impunity' upon animals, and proposing the formation of a society 'by whose united exertions some check may, if practicable, be applied' to this 'evil'.[40] Subsequently, the edition of *John Bull* dated 3 November 1822 reported that a 'meeting of Gentlemen, lately held at Old Slaughter's Coffee House, St Martin's Lane, the Rev Mr Broome in the Chair', had resolved to form a society 'for the purpose of preventing, as far as possible, the cruel treatment of brute animals'.[41]

Nothing more is known about the activities of this embryonic society but, on 16 June 1824, a further meeting at the same place agreed to establish a similar organization, to be known as the Society for the Prevention of Cruelty to Animals (SPCA). According to the minutes, twenty-one individuals were present and, significantly, they were men of some moment. Among them were four MPs—T Fowell Buxton (who took the chair), Richard Martin, Sir James Mackintosh, and William Wilberforce—all of whom were well-known humanitarians; three clergymen, including Arthur Broome, who was appointed secretary;[42] and William Mudford, the editor of the *Courier,* who reported upon the activities of the Society and provided it with editorial space. The parliamentary correspondent of *The Times* also attended, in an official capacity, and a full report of the meeting duly appeared in the following day's edition.

The Society's purpose, according to its prospectus, was to secure 'the mitigation of animal suffering, and the promotion and expansion of the practice of humanity towards the inferior classes of animated beings'. The means adopted to achieve these ends was to be a combination of education and enforcement. Accordingly, the inaugural meeting agreed to the establishment of two committees, one 'to superintend the Publication of Tracts, Sermons, and similar modes of influencing public opinion', the other to 'adopt measures for Inspecting the Markets and Streets of the Metropolis, the Slaughter Houses, the conduct of Coachmen, &c-&c'.[43] In respect of the latter, there was a debate about the proper role of the Society in relation to prosecutions. Martin appears to have reflected the mood of the meeting in stating that 'although prosecutions might be adopted in some cases, it would be ill-judged to stand forward as a prosecuting society'; better to 'appoint agents to watch the conduct of those who frequented markets; and those agents might prosecute upon their own responsibility, and at their own expense'. Based on his own experience, he conceded that 'nothing but punishment would have any

[39] Lynam, n 36 above, 195.   [40] Cited in Fairholme and Pain, n 24 above, 24–25.   [41] ibid 52.

[42] Arthur Broome is generally acknowledged to be the founder of the SPCA, despite suggestions that it was Richard Martin. It was reported in the *Courier* of 1 July 1825, that at the meeting to mark the first anniversary of the Society's establishment, Martin stated he had 'nothing at all to do with it', and that the SPCA was 'quite a child of Mr Broome's' who had 'acted the part of a good father to it'; quoted in Fairholme and Pain, n 24 above, 49.

[43] SPCA, First Minute Book.

effect', but he also cautioned that 'to form a confederacy of prosecutors would throw a great unpopularity upon the Society's proceedings'.[44] In fact, Martin had previously employed an agent to assist in enforcing his Act, and Broome had paid a man named Wheeler for the same purpose and to some effect: during the first half of 1824, Wheeler had secured sixty-three convictions, and he now became the Society's first inspector with the result that the SPCA successfully prosecuted 149 cases of cruelty during its first year, mostly arising from events at Smithfield.[45]

Unfortunately, however, the SPCA soon became a victim of its own success, failing to attract sufficient income to fund its activities. Indeed, within three years, Broome was imprisoned because of its debts and the committee came close to dissolving the Society. That outcome was narrowly avoided by receipt of a timely legacy and the efforts of the new secretary, Lewis Gompertz, a founder member and author of *Moral Inquiries on the Situation of Man and Brutes*. Nevertheless, its existence remained precarious. By the end of 1830, the Society was again in financial straits and its difficulties culminated in 1832 with the suspension of the inspectorate, a reduction in the number of prosecutions and the production of tracts—all to save money—and, following an internal dispute, the departure of Gompertz to found the Animals' Friend Society. Remarkably, however, the Society not only survived but, during the second part of the decade, positively prospered. With the benefit of hindsight, it is easy to overlook just how close it came to collapsing in its early years. That the SPCA did succeed was to have profound consequences for the legal protection of animals.

E. The SPCA's Early Accomplishments

Despite the 1822 Act, the plight of vast numbers of animals remained desperate. Among Martin's many complaints, for example, was the practice of using the same bear for baiting 'month after month', like the unfortunate creature he had seen which was employed for two years until, eventually, 'its eyes were out, its lip torn off, and the keepers said it was necessary to shoot it at last, as there was nothing left

---

[44] *The Times*, 17 June 1824. The term 'prosecuting society' had a particular meaning at this time. Before the establishment of an organized police force with responsibility for law enforcement, it was largely left to individuals to apprehend and prosecute offenders. The preparation and prosecution of an offence could be difficult, time-consuming, and expensive. Accordingly, there was a well-established practice of forming prosecuting societies from which, upon payment of an annual subscription, members would receive help and advice in bringing cases before the courts, including a contribution towards costs. Martin was not, therefore, arguing against the need to prosecute in appropriate circumstances, but was warning that the SPCA should not become merely a vehicle for providing practical and financial assistance for its members to pursue their own prosecutions.

[45] Fairholme and Pain, n 24 above, 40, 53, and 55. In February 1825, Fowell Buxton told the House of Commons that there had been 71 prosecutions under Martin's Act, 69 of which resulted in conviction. Although he did not say so, he was presumably referring to those cases the SPCA had been involved with since it was founded in June of the previous year; Parl Debs (new series) vol 12, col 660 (24 February 1825).

for the dogs to lay hold of '.[46] Another was the treatment of horses awaiting slaughter, such as those he had witnessed in Whitechapel, 'some with their eyes knocked out, others hopping on three legs, all miserably maimed, which had upon an average been kept there several days without food'.[47] Cats were commonly stolen and flayed alive, their skins being used as imitation fur; horses and ponies were driven until they dropped; baiting and fighting continued; and pigs were whipped to death. In 1829, Gompertz described how food animals were routinely treated: they were driven 'for hundreds of miles' to London, often without food, and many died from exhaustion during the journey; others had their eyes knocked out or their legs broken by the drovers. When they reached Smithfield, sheep were literally thrown into the underground slaughterhouses, to be killed 'according to the uncontrolled fancy of the operator', while cattle were subjected to 'repeated blows of hammers on their heads'. Calves were transported packed into carts with their legs tied together, and kept in the underground slaughterhouses for days, to be slowly bled so as to produce white flesh, during which time they were muzzled 'lest the public should be attracted by their moans'. Meanwhile, the streets reverberated with the 'unceasing sound of the lash'.[48] Much of the abuse was routine, mindless, and of long standing. Indeed, some magistrates were reluctant to convict drovers and slaughtermen who were following customary practices and could not be shown to have acted wantonly.[49] At the same time, new situations encouraged fresh examples of callousness towards animals. A speaker at the SPCA's annual meeting in 1837, for instance, complained that persons were being stationed on the Kent coast to shoot messenger pigeons from France to prevent financial information reaching London. 'Thus is afforded', he remarked, 'another instance of cruelty for the purpose of forwarding the rapacity of man.'[50]

Against this background, the Society did make progress in alleviating at least some of the suffering. It was instrumental in improving conditions at Smithfield: the market was enlarged, gas lamps replaced naked flames, only sticks approved by the City Corporation were to be used for driving cattle, and boards were installed to allow animals to walk down into the slaughterhouses. Robert Batson, a member of the Society's committee, devised a special cart for conveying calves to market; in 1835, William Youatt was appointed honorary veterinary surgeon and offered to treat animals of the poor referred to him by the SPCA; and, by the second half of the 1830s, enforcement activities had been recommenced with two inspectors—formally called 'constables'—in post and 270 successful prosecutions concluded in 1837. The Society had also started formally lobbying Parliament. Prior to Martin's attempt in 1825 to increase the penalties under his Act, for example, it contacted all sympathetic MPs asking them to support the measure at second reading.[51] Three particular occurrences, however, serve to demonstrate the growing influence of

---

[46] Parl Debs (new series) vol 10, col 488 (26 February 1824).
[47] ibid, vol 11, col 1096 (4 June 1824).
[48] Fairholme and Pain, n 24 above, 66–67.   [49] ibid 176–177.   [50] ibid 89.
[51] Lynam, n 36 above, 250.

the SPCA, and the importance of the 1830s as a watershed in the early development of animal protection legislation.

(1) Pease's Act

We have seen that, following the 1822 Act, Martin attempted to extend legislative protection to dogs, cats, monkeys, horses awaiting slaughter, and animals used for baiting and fighting. Bull-baiting had been a particularly contentious issue. The Attorney-General complained that, having failed to get the bull specifically included in his Act, Martin had been attempting to persuade magistrates that it should come within the category of 'other cattle', a contention that was ultimately rejected by the High Court.[52] In response, the SPCA petitioned the House of Commons, expressing their 'deepest concern' that, after the court's decision, bull-baiting had resumed 'to an unprecedented extent', and seeking legislative intervention to protect the animal.[53] A Bill to that effect was introduced in 1829, but was defeated by 73 votes to 28.[54] Despite the lack of progress, the Society continued to focus its attention on Parliament. William Alexander Mackinnon MP, a member of its committee, introduced a Bill to extend Martin's Act which, although unsuccessful, led to the establishment of a Select Committee which concluded that further legislation was required to prevent the cruel and improper treatment of animals. In the meantime, an Act concerned principally with the maintenance of public order in London was passed which, at the behest of Joseph Pease MP, included in its provisions a prohibition on animal baiting and fighting, including cockfighting, within the City.[55] Pease, another member of the SPCA's committee, then took up the cause for more extensive animal protection legislation, which succeeded in 1835.[56]

Pease's Act repealed and re-enacted Martin's Act and, in so doing, added 'torture' to the list of prohibited conduct, extended protection to bulls, dogs, and other domestic animals (a category which was not further defined) and, for the avoidance of doubt, calves and lambs. The fine upon conviction was reduced from a minimum of ten to five shillings, and the maximum from five to two pounds, but the possibility of imprisonment for up to fourteen days was introduced; the court could also make an order for compensation and costs. In addition, the Act increased protection in three distinct areas. First, the prohibition on animal fighting and baiting which was already applicable in London was extended to the country at large. Secondly, anyone responsible for impounding an animal was placed under a duty to provide it with sufficient food, the cost being recoverable from the owner and, in the event that the animal was confined for more than twenty-four hours without sufficient food, it was permitted for any person to enter the pound

---

[52] Parl Debs (new series) vol 10, cols 866–867 (9 March 1824); *Ex p Hill* (1827) 3 C & P 225.

[53] Moss, n 24 above, 18–19.   [54] Parl Debs (new series) vol 21, cols 1319–1320 (12 May 1829).

[55] 3 & 4 Will IV, c 19; An Act for the more effectual Administration of Justice in the Office of a Justice of the Peace in the several Police Offices established in the Metropolis (1833).

[56] 5 & 6 Will IV, c 59; An Act to consolidate and amend the several Laws relating to the cruel and improper Treatment of Animals, and the Mischiefs arising from the driving of Cattle.

to feed it. Thirdly, the duty to license knackers' yards (where the slaughtered animals are not used for human consumption), to display the name of the licensee outside the premises, and to keep adequate records, all of which had been mandatory since 1786,[57] was restated and the penalty for failure to comply was increased to £5. Furthermore, it was specified that all horses and cattle should be killed within three days of arriving at the knacker's and, in the meantime, had to be provided with sufficient daily food, and horses were not to be employed in any work. The Act also gave power of summary arrest and enacted that half of the fines imposed under its authority should be paid to those bringing the prosecution. In 1837, in order to remove any uncertainty, the provisions of Pease's Act were specifically extended to Ireland.[58]

To all intents and purposes, then, Pease's Act secured most of the reforms which Martin had attempted to introduce during the 1820s, but he did not live to see them enacted. Martin had died in January 1834. Although, in reporting his death, *The Times* referred to him merely as 'the late eccentric MP for Galway',[59] his contribution to animal protection was immense. Assisted by Erskine and Lawrence, he was instrumental in establishing the principle that Parliament should legislate to prevent cruelty; and he was a pioneer in enforcing the law, both personally and as one of the founder members of the SPCA. Martin's attitude towards animals was straightforward. 'Though they could not be said to possess rights in the same degree as man,' he explained, 'they were entitled, so far as was consistent with the use which was given to men over the brute creation, to be treated with kindness and humanity.' He thought, therefore, that 'unnecessary cruelty to animals . . . should be put down'.[60] In applying this philosophy, he recognized that it was only possible 'to prohibit those cruelties which public opinion would follow him in saying ought to be prohibited', and that progress would inevitably be gradual. 'The argument, that he had not by this bill done all that ought to be done,' Martin told the Commons, 'was no answer to his claim to do as much as was possible at this moment, any more than telling a man who attempted to save one hundred out of eight hundred persons on board a sinking ship, that he could not preserve all, would be a sufficient reason to induce him to abstain from attempting to rescue any of the 800 from a watery grave.'[61] Martin had to fight hard to counter the deep-felt hostility to which his views gave rise, but the combination of determination, persistence, expertise, and pragmatism which characterized his campaigning eventually overcame the opposition.

---

[57] 26 Geo III, c 71; An Act for regulating Houses, and other Places, kept for the Purpose of slaughtering Horses. The original purpose of this legislation was to regulate slaughterhouses in response to the growing practice of stealing horses and cattle and passing them on to disreputable dealers to be killed. It was not concerned with animal suffering and did not attempt to control conditions within slaughterhouses.

[58] 1 Vict, c 66.   [59] 10 January 1834.

[60] Parl Debs (new series) vol 10, col 487 (26 February 1824).

[61] ibid, vol 10, col 133 (11 February 1824); vol 12, col 1010 (11 March 1825).

(2) The Stamford bull-running

As with the 1822 legislation, Pease's Act posed the problem of enforcement, particularly in relation to the prohibition on animal baiting and fighting, activities which attracted large crowds and were deeply rooted in the community. Such a situation was very different from bringing an individual recalcitrant drover or costermonger before the courts; a determined effort to defy the law would require forces on a much greater scale than the SPCA could muster. Exactly this situation arose in Stamford, Lincolnshire, where bull-running had taken place since the beginning of the thirteenth century and was now held each November. Pease's Act came into force in September 1835 and, although the secretary of the SPCA wrote to the town authorities the following month, drawing their attention to the new legislation, the event still went ahead. The Society decided that it would be futile to bring a prosecution before the local magistrates, many of whom actively support- ed the event. Accordingly, it issued a further warning the following year and, when this too was ignored, the SPCA successfully prosecuted three of the promoters at the County Assizes in Lincoln. When the offenders appeared before the Court of Queen's Bench for sentence, the court confirmed that, regardless of local custom, the practice was now illegal.[62] In the meantime, the Home Secretary, Lord John Russell, had become involved, writing to the mayor and magistrates on 2 November 1837 indicating that he desired 'to impress upon you the necessity of active measures being taken to prevent a proceeding so disgraceful and contrary to law as Bull-running'. In response, nearly 221 special constables were sworn in, but even this was unsuccessful. However, two of those involved were convicted under Pease's Act by the local justices for wantonly and cruelly ill-treating a bull, and fined 20s and 10s respectively, and each was ordered to pay 7s 8d costs. In 1838, the Home Office ordered dragoons from Northampton and a detachment of officers from the Metropolitan Police to complement the local special constables, but again an attempt was made to stage the event. The following year, 20 London policemen together with 43 dragoons and 90 local constables partially succeeded in prevent- ing it taking place, in what was to be the last attempt at bull-running in Stamford. Ironically, it was not so much the show of strength by the authorities which put an end to the tradition, as its cost to the local ratepayers. In November 1840, 670 of them signed a memorial addressed to the mayor and magistrates of the town, com- plaining of the expense (which had risen from £49 8s in 1837 to £150 in 1838, and had nearly doubled the following year) and expressing 'deep regret that any neces- sity should exist for calling in foreign force, to do away with that which has been adjudged by the law to be illegal'. The signatories therefore gave an undertaking that they themselves would ensure there was no bull-running, so long as no outside force intervened: 'we feel that the time has arrived when we ought to manifest to

---

[62] The case is not reported in the law reports, but a summary of the hearing before the Queen's Bench is included as part of a detailed description of these events in Burton, G, *Chronology of Stamford* (1846) 49–69.

the Government that we are obedient to the law, and are able by our own exertions to support and vindicate the same'.[63] This strategy proved successful. The strength of Stamford's opposition lay in the fact that the town's residents did not consider that they were doing anything wrong; they were merely indulging in a well-established local tradition which had been enjoyed by many previous generations. The town clerk observed that those who participated in the bull-running were 'strongly impressed with the idea that their practise is a lawful ancient custom, warranted by an exercise of 600 years . . . and which they ought not to be deprived of except by express legislative enactment'.[64] The episode clearly demonstrates, however, that, by 1840, the SPCA was capable of mounting an effective and pro-tracted campaign outside London, and could call in aid the most senior politicians who, together with the courts, would use all their power and authority to override entrenched local customs to secure compliance with the law as determined by Parliament.

(3) Royal patronage

Although the early years of the SPCA had been precarious, from the outset its membership included men of influence. In six of its first ten years, for example, its chairman was a Member of Parliament. The real turning point in its fortunes came, however, when the Society and, by implication, the cause it stood for, received royal endorsement. Robert Batson reported to the committee in July 1835 that 'at the suggestion of several ladies he had presented a Report of the Society and a letter to their Royal Highnesses the Duchess of Kent and the Princess Victoria with a request that they would honor [sic] the Society by becoming Ladies Patronesses' and a reply had subsequently been received indicating that they 'very readily acceded' to the request.[65] Upon her succession to the throne in 1837, Victoria renewed her patronage of the Society and, in 1840, allowed it the use of the royal prefix, and so it became the RSPCA. In an age of deference, when both the aristocracy and the growing middle classes were keen to emulate the values espoused by the sovereign, the impact of Victoria's support cannot be overstated. It gave to the cause of animal protection both social standing and legitimacy.

The change in attitude to the treatment of animals had been remarkable. An issue which at the turn of the century had been regarded as, at best, eccentric and, at worst, subversive and anti-religious had become, within the space of a mere forty years, eminently respectable. When Martin's initial Bill was before the Commons in 1821 and it was suggested that protection should be extended to include asses, the mocking laughter from MPs was so loud that *The Times*' reporter could not hear the debate. Even after Martin's Act, MPs were still complaining that the protection of animals was 'a petty, trumpery, and . . . blundering kind of legislation', and 'too

[63] ibid 65.
[64] Quoted in Malcolmson, RW, *Popular Recreations in English Society 1700–1850* (1973) 134.
[65] RSPCA Minute Book No 1.

minute—too much the property of local custom and regulation—to be fit matters for legislation'.[66] Yet, as Pease's Act, the Stamford bull-running episode, and the involvement of Queen Victoria all demonstrate, by 1840 the principle of animal protection was not only established, but had been extended to render illegal sports and amusements which were part of the traditional fabric of society, and to restrict what an individual might do with his own property; it had been demonstrated that, if necessary, the regulatory forces of the State would be mobilized to enforce the new legislative framework; and all this had been achieved with the approval and support of the very highest echelons of society. It is undoubtedly the case that these developments 'owed a lot to utilitarian calculation and the associated rejection of traditional discriminations',[67] but they are not in themselves sufficient to explain *why* such a radical social and legal development took place in Britain at this time.

F. The Reasons for Change

The simplistic response is that the change in attitude merely reflected a sympathy for animals which is inherent in the psyche of the British, and is often contrasted, unfavourably, with their disposition towards children, not least because the RSPCA was founded in 1824, whereas the National Society for Prevention of Cruelty to Children (NSPCC) was not established until sixty years later (notwithstanding that the former was instrumental in setting up the latter). It is important to refute this fallacy. Hitherto, sensitivity towards animals had not been regarded as a national trait. Indeed, the very opposite was the case. The country's reputation was such that 'previously it had been the English themselves who had been notorious among travellers for their cruelty to brutes'.[68] Furthermore, legislation to protect animals developed in parallel with that to protect children. The first Factory Act was passed in 1802, and further legislation to regulate working hours and conditions relating to children was enacted in 1819, 1825, 1831, 1833, 1842, 1844, 1847, 1850, 1853, 1864, and 1874.[69] Of course, their provisions appear totally inadequate by contemporary standards but, as in the case of animals, reformers were at an early stage in the process of developing a detailed legal framework. The argument that the British cared more for animals than for children is simply not sustainable. Rather, animal protection can be seen as part of a general movement which gathered pace during the nineteenth century, often promoted by the same people, which was concerned to improve conditions across a range of areas, such as employment, slavery, schools, prisons, and the treatment of the poor.

[66]   Sir R Heron, Parl Debs (new series) vol 10, col 489; Robert Peel, col 493 (26 February 1824).

[67]   Clark, SLR, 'Utility, Rights and the Domestic Virtues' in Clark, SLR, *Animals and their Moral Standing* (1997) 99.

[68]   Thomas, K, *Man and the Natural World. Changing attitudes in England 1500–1800* (1984) 144.

[69]   42 Geo III, c 73; 59 Geo III, c 66; 6 Geo IV, c 63; 1 & 2 Will IV, c 39; 3 & 4 Will IV, c 103; 5 & 6 Vict, c 99; 7 & 8 Vict, c 15; 10 & 11 Vict, c 29; 13 & 14 Vict, c 54; 16 & 17 Vict, c 104; 27 & 28 Vict, c 48; 37 & 38 Vict, c 44.

(1) Animals and children

The reason that children did not benefit from greater statutory protection during the nineteenth century was due largely to deep-seated financial, legal, and political conventions. First, there were economic constraints. Many poor families relied on young children to bring in an income, and orphans and the destitute were expected to earn as soon as possible to offset the cost of their keep to local ratepayers. Secondly, most ill-treatment of children occurred in private, in either the workplace or the home, whereas that to animals—or those cases which led to prosecution—took place in public, thus allowing concerned individuals and the RSPCA (in the absence of any official agency specifically charged with the task) to initiate proceedings. As factories, mills, and the like were private property, access was impossible in the absence of the owner's consent, without statutory authority. A factory inspectorate was established in 1833, but it was grossly under-resourced and ill-equipped for its task. In respect of animals, a similar situation arose in relation to pit ponies: because the mines were private, RSPCA inspectors could not gain entry to establish how the ponies were being treated, and it was only in 1911 that an (again inadequate) inspectorate with statutory powers and duties was established for this purpose. Thirdly, children in the workplace were, unlike animals, party to a contract, and nineteenth-century judges were extremely reluctant to interfere with agreements which they regarded as having been freely entered into by both sides. In other words, employees, including children, were deemed to have consented to their conditions of employment,[70] notwithstanding that, as Mill observed, 'Freedom of contract, in the case of children, is but another word for freedom of coercion.'[71] Finally, what went on within the home was considered to be of no concern of the State. The man's status as head of the household was not merely titular, it represented a position of real power and authority underpinned by the law. Judicial divorce was not available until 1857,[72] and then only on very restricted grounds; prior to the Married Women's Property Act 1870,[73] a wife had no separate legal personality, she could not hold property in her own name and, upon marriage, that which was not already held in trust became her husband's; and it was not until the last decade of the century that the courts denied a husband the right to subject his wife to 'reasonable' chastisement for 'misbehaviour', including physical restraint.[74] Children fared no better. Blackstone, in claiming that a father had a duty to maintain, protect, and educate his children, conceded that it was a moral rather than a legal obligation;[75] he could discipline them as he chose, short of murder or very serious physical assault; and in civil matters the courts considered that the views of the father prevailed over all others. The

---

[70] *Ryder v Mills* (1850) 3 Ex 853.
[71] Mill, JS, *Principles of Political Economy* (3rd edn, 1852) Vol II, Bk V, Ch XI, section 9, 546.
[72] 20 & 21 Vict, c 85.   [73] 33 & 34 Vict, c 93.
[74] *R v Cochrane* (1840) 8 Dowl 630; overturned by *R v Jackson* (1891) QB 671.
[75] *Commentaries on the Laws of England* (1765–1769) Book I, 450.

Guardianship of Infants Act 1886[76] did lay down that in custody and access proceedings the court was to have regard to the welfare of the infant as well as the conduct and wishes of the parent, but it was not until its successor of 1925[77] that the welfare of the child was declared to be the first and paramount consideration. Mill had observed in the middle of the century that 'Parental power is as susceptible of abuse as any other power, and is, as a matter of fact, constantly abused', in consequence of which, he argued, 'Whatever it can be clearly seen that parents ought to do or forbear in the interest of children, the law is warranted, if it is able, in compelling to be done or forborne, and is generally bound to do so.'[78] Only towards the end of the century, and largely as a result of pressure from the NSPCC, did Parliament accept that it was legitimate for the State to intervene directly to protect children within the family. Under the Prevention of Cruelty to, and Better Protection of, Children Act 1889[79] it became an offence wilfully to ill-treat, neglect, abandon, or expose a child in a manner likely to cause it suffering or injury to health, and magistrates were given the power to remove children from their families and place them with a 'fit person'; two years later, the Custody of Children Act allowed the courts to refuse custody to a parent.

Although the relative delay in introducing legislative protection against domestic abuse was clearly detrimental to children, it should not be seen as reflecting an inherent lack of concern for their well-being, but as the expression of a patriarchal society's view of the proper boundary between the role of the State and individual autonomy. Indeed, it was even reflected in relation to animals: even after the principle of protecting agricultural and working animals had been accepted, there remained reservations about extending it to pets, which were part of the household. A vice-president of the RSPCA, for example, speaking at the annual meeting in 1835, expressed the view that dogs were 'beyond the reach of legislation': 'What law, I ask, could protect them, without the odious alternative of intrusion on private life. It is not because we wish to be less kind to dogs that we would exclude them from protection, but because we wish to avoid an inquisition into private life.'[80] Mill was an exception in taking the view that, on the contrary, 'the domestic life of domestic tyrants is one of the things which it is the most imperative on the law to interfere with'.[81]

(2) The political process

It can be appreciated, then, that the influences for social and legal change are complex. At the most basic level, the cause of animal protection legislation succeeded in the 1820s as a result of the prevailing legislative system and the personalities involved. Britain had comparative political stability during the early years of the nineteenth century and a relatively mature and established legislative process,

---

[76] 49 & 50 Vict, c 27.   [77] 15 & 16 Geo V, c 45.
[78] Mill, n 71 above, Vol II, Bk V, Ch XI, section 9, 546.   [79] 52 & 53 Vict, c 44.
[80] Fairholme and Pain, n 24 above, 73.   [81] n 71 above, Vol II, Bk V, Ch XI, section 9, 547.

which involved presenting grievances and claims for redress to the Commons by means of petitions or through the representations of individual MPs. To secure legislative change, the essential requirement was a forceful advocate in each House of Parliament, and the alliance in 1822 of Richard Martin in the Commons and Thomas Erskine in the Lords was therefore crucial. It was a close run thing: Erskine died in 1823. Incidentally, although the English take considerable pride that theirs was the first country to introduce legislation to protect animals, it will be noted that it was, in fact, achieved largely by the efforts of an Irishman and a Scot![82]

Although Martin experienced strong opposition in his subsequent efforts to legislate, once the 1822 Act was in operation, the benefits quickly began to be appreciated. Within three years of its enactment, MPs were acknowledging that it had: 'been productive of great diminution of cruelty to animals', 'affected a beneficial change in the manners of the people', 'done great good, and particularly in Smithfield market', and even convinced one member that 'There was no duty . . . more imperative upon the House than that of affording protection to animals.'[83] As the century progressed, a growing number of parliamentarians became genuinely appalled at the callous way in which animals were regarded. In 1809, Windham dismissed the reformers as 'those who allowed their sensibilities . . . to outrun their judgment',[84] but it was, in fact, precisely the exercise of judgement which led to the conclusion that legislative intervention was justified. Windham could declare in 1802 that a baited bull 'felt a satisfaction in the contest', but thirty years later it was inconceivable that a senior politician would propose such a view. Rather, the orthodoxy had swung behind Wilberforce's assessment in the same debate that the sport was 'cruel in its designs, cowardly in its execution', and subjected the bull 'to the most inhuman cruelties, till it sunk under the pressure of its complicated miseries'.[85]

(3) Popular support

The politicians could also point to a degree of popular support in the country: for example, petitions from eight towns (including, ironically, one from the mayor and aldermen of Stamford) were presented to the Commons in support of the 1802 Bill;[86] after presenting his Bill in 1809, Erskine received more than three trunk loads of letters in support, 'detailing the most horrid acts of cruelty';[87] George Nicholson, who had dedicated the first edition of his book, *On the Conduct of Man*

---

[82] Mention should also be made of John Lawrence's contribution. Ryder reports that there is a copy of Lawrence's *Philosophical Treatise* in the Bodleian Library, Oxford, into which EWB Nicholson claimed he transcribed annotations made by Lawrence during the 1830s. These include the note: 'Mr Martin MP for Galway, subsequently took up this cause on my recommendation, and got the animal protection bill with much difficulty thro' Parliament. Mr M and myself had many conferences on this subject': Ryder, n 2 above, 75.

[83] Sir J Mackintosh, Parl Debs (new series) vol 12, col 1006 (11 March 1825); Mr Lockhart, Mr Alderman Thompson, and Mr Maxwell, cols 1161–1162 (24 March 1825).

[84] Parl Debs vol 14, col 1025 (the column is incorrectly numbered, it should be 1041) (13 June 1809).

[85] *Parliamentary History of England*, Vol 36, cols 839 and 846–847 (24 May 1802).

[86] *Commons Journal*, 5, 7, and 24 May 1802.   [87] Parl Debs vol 16, col 881 (8 May 1810).

to the Inferior Animals, published in 1797, to the 'generous, enlightened and sympathising few', remarked in the fourth edition, published in 1819, that 'the few have increased to a numerous and decided body';[88] and Martin was always assiduous in demonstrating public backing. He claimed that there were 'millions of well-thinking people' in the country who considered that cruel sports ought to be prohibited. 'There was not a part of the kingdom that he was not in correspondence with, and he knew that to be the general opinion.'[89] He presented a petition from Manchester, signed by 700 'most respectable individuals', and forewarned of another coming from Liverpool. 'If they wanted petitions,' he told the Commons, 'petitions would flow in from every part of the united kingdom, supplicating them to put an end to the cruelty to animals... if any hon member would go and knock at the door of every man in London and Westminster, he would find a vast majority who would pray for the abolition of these cruelties.'[90] Later, he reminded the House that this support had indeed been forthcoming, stating that it had received petitions 'from all over the country'.[91]

Public opinion was changing, perhaps not on the scale suggested by Martin's hyperbole, but sufficient to have an impact. The major causes for this development have already been considered, the most important of which was the confluence of utilitarianism and a growing social abhorrence to pain. Time and again in the contemporary literature arguing for reform, one is struck by the utilitarian basis of the reasoning. Typical is the initial prospectus of the SPCA, which asserted: 'Morality consists in the desire, rationally directed, to promote general happiness, and secondly to diminish general pain, and it cannot be contended that the operation of a principle, so glorious to man, should not be made to embrace in its effects, the whole of animal life.'

(4) Concern for manners, mores, and social discipline

Improving the position of animals was, however, only one aspect of the impetus for reform. Of equal, possibly greater, concern was a desire to effect a change in the behaviour of the general population to reflect more closely that of the higher social orders, many of whom would have agreed with Johnson, who thought that 'Pity is not natural to men... Pity is acquired and improved by the cultivation of reason.'[92] For example, although the 1800 and 1802 bull-baiting Bills are generally presented as the first serious attempt to introduce legislative protection for animals, it is apparent from the parliamentary debates that the principal motivation was the maintenance of public order and an improvement in the conduct of the poor. This, remarked Lord Erskine, 'rather obscured the principle of protection to the animals'.[93] While the interests of animals became a greater priority in the later

---

[88] Quoted in Ryder, n 2 above, 74.   [89] Parl Debs (new series) vol 10, col 133 (11 February 1824).

[90] ibid, vol 10, cols 368–369 and 489 (24 and 26 February 1824).

[91] ibid, vol 12, col 1011 (11 March 1825).

[92] Hill, GB (ed), *Boswell's Life of Johnson* (1934) Vol 1, 437.

[93] Parl Debs vol 14, col 559 (15 May 1809).

debates, changing manners and mores remained the predominant theme. Martin, for example, argued that cruel sports ought to be suppressed 'as tending to corrupt morals, and endanger good order', and warned that they were attended by 'the lowest and most wretched description of people'. In his view, 'the places of amusements in London where these cruelties were exhibited, formed a nucleus for the great villains in the world'.[94] Indeed, he echoed the moral suggested by Hogarth seventy-five years before in 'The Four Stages of Cruelty', by reporting the magistracy's view, that 'nothing was more conducive to crime than such sports; that they led the lower orders to gambling; that they educated them for thieves; and that they gradually trained them up to bloodshed and murder'.[95] Others variously described those who frequented these events as 'the lowest', 'the most ignorant', and 'totally uneducated . . . as to any moral or religious knowledge'.[96]

Some idea of the potential threat to public order which they posed can be gleaned from the account of the Stamford bull-running alluded to above. In 1836, for example, 'a mob of people, chiefly of the town and neighbourhood, consisting of about 5000 or 6000' were involved. After running the bull through the streets, they congregated outside the house of an opponent of the practice, where 'the most deafening shouts, groans, and hisses were raised by the mob, and a few panes of a window were broken'. The prosecution arising from these events brought by the SPCA at Lincoln Assizes the following year was as much concerned with the breakdown in public order as the treatment of the bull. Thus, the defendants were charged with: (i) conspiring, combining, and confederating together to beat, bait, wound, and torment a bull, and thereby to disturb the peace of the town, and cause a riot and tumult; (ii) in pursuance of such conspiracy, riotously assembling with sticks, staves, and other weapons, and obstructing the free passage of the street; (iii) assault of an officer of the SPCA; and (iv) riotously breaking windows.[97]

At a time when, in the absence of an organized police force, the only means of restoring public order required the intervention of the militia, political radicalism was in the air and on the streets, and a monarchy had recently been overthrown by the mob across the Channel, any large gathering posed a potential threat to the authorities; one which encouraged gambling, drinking, and promiscuity was more dangerous still. It was not only to maintain public order that supporters wanted these activities banned, however; it was also for the personal improvement of those who participated. One MP, for example, noting the 'injurious effect such scenes had on the morals of society', made it clear that, in supporting the prohibition of animal fighting and baiting, 'he was not legislating on a principle of humanity towards brutes, but of men'.[98] Sir James Mackintosh, in the same debate, assured the Commons that 'The enactment of such measures would sink deeper and deeper into the minds of the people, and would, in the course of time, when aided

---

[94] Parl Debs (new series) vol 10, col 487 (26 February 1824); vol 12, col 1010 (11 March 1825).
[95] ibid, vol 12, col 657 (24 February 1825).   [96] ibid, vol 10, col 491 (26 February 1824).
[97] Burton, n 62 above, 54–56.
[98] Sir F Burdett, Parl Debs (new series) vol 12, col 1013 (11 March 1825).

by the diffusion of education and enlightened principles, be productive of the most beneficial effects upon that particular class of society whose habit of unnecessary cruelty the present bill was intended to repress.'[99]

Such views reflected the values of what has been called the 'sentimental revolution', which developed in the third quarter of the eighteenth century. Characterized by a mixture of benevolence and discipline, it was sustained by the expanding, urbanized middle class.[100] It represented a reaction against the brutal nature of society by emphasizing the importance of gentility, sensibility, and sympathy, together with an emphasis on character, godliness, manners, and 'proper' conduct. Its influence can be seen in art, literature, the beginnings of social reform, and the rise of the individual philanthropist. The provision of hospitals, schools, prison reform, the abolition of slavery, and changing attitudes towards the poor all reflected its values. At the same time, however, it contained a strict moral element, encouraged by a combination of religious evangelicalism and the need to secure obedience as labour moved from home working and small-scale workshops to the factory. According to Paul Langford, 'Much attention was bestowed on the need to discipline the poor, partly by eliminating all practices which seemed to threaten political order and religious conformity, partly by enforcing the kind of regimentation appropriate to the labour requirements of a rapidly industrializing society.'[101]

Thus, activities which did not engender moral and spiritual improvement, such as drinking, gambling, violence, sexual licence, idleness, and 'wasted' time, were all condemned, and clearly amusements such as animal baiting and fighting were included. In 1800, for example, Pulteney justified banning bull-baiting on the ground that it had 'much increased . . . particularly in Places where large Manufactories are carried on, to the great Encouragement of Idleness, Rioting and Drunkenness, and to the great Corruption of the Morals of the Common People'.[102] Against this background, it has been argued that legislation, such as that relating to animals, predominantly 'represented the efforts of the bourgeois to impose its classifications and definitions of "proper" human behaviour on all social groups', having 'appropriated to itself the virtues of kindness and compassion'.[103]

(5) The legitimacy of state intervention

This raised the fundamental question of whether it was either legitimate or desirable for the State to define and impose common standards of public morality. To understand the significance of this issue, it is essential to appreciate how deeply ingrained in the national consciousness was the notion of individual freedom, even if the reality for most was rather different from the rhetoric. Many among the

---

[99] Sir F Burdett, Parl Debs (new series) vol 12, col 1006 (11 March 1825).
[100] See further, Langford, P, *A Polite and Commercial People* (1989) Ch 10.
[101] ibid 499.   [102] *Parliamentary History of England*, Vol 35, col 202 (2 April 1800).
[103] Tester, K, *Animals and Society* (1991) 115.

political class saw it as their bounden duty to protect the liberties of 'the freeborn Englishman'. The importance attached to this issue can be demonstrated by the fact that in 1822 a parliamentary select committee, charged with considering the policing of London, agreed that it was 'difficult to reconcile an effective system of police, with that perfect freedom of action and exemption from interference, which are the great privileges and blessings of this country', and concluded that 'the forfeiture or curtailment of such advantages would be too great a sacrifice for improvements in police, or facilities in detection of crime, however desirable in themselves if abstractly considered'.[104]

Clearly, those such as Erskine and Martin who wished to see an improvement in the position of animals could counter such concerns by harnessing their campaign to the new morality. 'The violences and outrages committed by the lower orders of the people are offences more owing to want of thought and reflection, than to any malignant principle,' Erskine told the House of Lords, 'and whatever, therefore, sets them a thinking upon the duties of humanity . . . has an evident tendency to soften their natures, and to moderate their passions in their dealings with one another', for 'The effect of laws which promulgate a sound moral principle is incalculable.'[105] Accordingly, the preamble to the Bill Erskine presented to Parliament in 1809 sought to justify legislative intervention by associating arguments regarding man's duties towards animals with the social advantage of promoting a general improvement in social behaviour:

Whereas it has pleased Almighty God to subdue to the dominion, use, and comfort of man, the strength and faculties of many useful animals, and to provide others for his food; and whereas the abuse of that dominion by cruel and oppressive treatment of such animals, is not only highly unjust and immoral, but most pernicious in its example, having an evident tendency to harden the heart against the natural feelings of humanity.[106]

Similarly, it is unsurprising that at the inaugural meeting of the SPCA, Martin claimed his Act had produced 'a revolution in morals',[107] and the chairman, T Fowell Buxton MP, explained in his opening speech that the Society's purpose would be both to prevent cruelty to animals and 'to spread amongst the lower orders of the people . . . a degree of moral feeling which would compel them to think and act like those of a superior class'.[108] While the consequences were widely welcomed by those with influence, there was considerable unease at the use of legislation to achieve them. Those with traditional, libertarian, rural sympathies were appalled at such intrusion by the State into people's lives. Windham, for example, robustly criticized the magistracy for supporting the 1800 Bill, complaining that many of its members acted as though 'it is their duty at all times to control the common people in their amusements, like some to whom the care of children is committed, who think it right to deny them every thing which they seem eager to have

---

[104] Select Committee on the Police of the Metropolis, *Parliamentary Papers*, 1822 (440) iv, 107.
[105] Parl Debs vol 14, cols 556–557 (15 May 1809).   [106] ibid, col 557.
[107] *The Times*, 17 June 1824.   [108] Fairholme and Pain, n 24 above, 55.

or enjoy'. Such magistrates, he said, appeared 'to act on the opinion, that the common people have nothing to do with any amusement; but only to eat, to sleep, and to work'. Similarly, Canning in the same debate suggested that 'if the legislature were to interfere to put a stop to every practice which might possibly be productive of mischief to any individual, the House must sit unremittingly, making new laws, and many whimsical laws they would make'.[109] In Peel's view, it was preferable to 'let public opinion and the acts of individuals remedy the evils complained of', and, in the middle of the nineteenth century, there were those, such as Earl Grey, who continued to argue that 'cruelty amongst other vices, were not proper subjects of legislation'; instead, 'improvements were to be effected by the process of civilization, and the changes it produced on the tempers and character of individuals'.[110]

Furthermore, with the French Revolution still creating uncertainty and nervousness in Britain during the early years of the century, there was concern that antagonizing the lower orders by depriving them of their amusements might lead to something worse. 'The habits so long established among the people were the best fitted to resist the schemes of innovation', said Windham, emphasizing that 'it was among the labouring and illiterate part of the people that Jacobinical doctrines had made the smallest progress'. Echoing Edmund Burke, he urged caution against change, saying of bull-baiting that 'the antiquity of the thing was deserving of respect—for respect of antiquity was the best preservation of the church and state—it was by connecting the past with the future, that genuine patriotism was produced and preserved'.[111] Two decades later, Peel was still of the view that it was better 'the House should turn its eyes away, than select the sports of the people for penal enactment.... They would do well to take care, that in legislating for the abolition of cruelty, they did not introduce new vices among the people.'[112]

The magistracy was also divided in its response to the new legislative regime. Martin had the support of the magistrates in London and Middlesex for his 1822 Bill and claimed in 1824 that magistrates would vote 'ninety-nine to one' that cruelty should be put down, 'as tending to corrupt the morals of the people'. The following year he told the Commons that he had conversed 'with every alderman of the City of London, with almost every police magistrate in the metropolis, and with many magistrates in different parts of the country', and had collected from their conversation that 'It was their unanimous opinion, that these cruel practices ought to be put down.'[113] Individual magistrates certainly expressed their appreciation for the SPCA's role in enforcing the law. In the 1830s, for example, justices at Rochford spoke approvingly of the Society's efforts to prevent cruelty to donkeys and ponies on the beach at Southend, and a magistrate at Ramsgate described the

[109] *Parliamentary History of England*, Vol 35, cols 208 and 211 (18 April 1800).

[110] Parl Debs (new series) vol 15, col 530 (20 April 1826); (series 3) vol 54, col 929 (27 April 1849).

[111] *Parliamentary History of England*, Vol 36, cols 833–834 and 840 (24 May 1802).

[112] Parl Debs (new series) vol 10, cols 493–494 (26 February 1824).

[113] ibid, vol 7, col 759 (24 May 1822); vol 10, col 487 (26 February 1824); vol 12, col 657 (24 February 1825).

SPCA inspector appearing to give evidence as 'an officer acting under a Society, the existence of which is an honour to the nation', and asserted that he would 'receive every assistance and protection in the execution of his duty'.[114] Worthing magistrates 'expressed their approval of the Society's proceedings, and said that the inhabitants . . . were much indebted to the Society for its humane and praiseworthy interference'.[115] On the other hand, the Stamford magistrates were not alone in demonstrating reluctance to enforce the prohibition on animal baiting and fighting. In many parts of the country, the magistracy were aware that cockfights were continuing to take place in their area, but declined to suppress them, preferring to give precedence to local traditions rather than the new morality emanating from London. As late as 1850, a lawyer representing a defendant accused of cockfighting complained to the court in Newcastle that the prosecution had been brought by 'parties who did not reside on the spot' and had 'no interest in the welfare of the inhabitants of this town'. Presumably, regardless of the law, cockfighting was still regarded locally to be a legitimate activity as 'No attempt whatever had been made on the part of the authorities here to put it down, but they had to wait until a party came down from London to correct their morals and reform their manners.'[116] Further opposition was encountered from courts who took exception to what they regarded as 'paid informers' because of the financial reward due to prosecutors under Pease's Act. In response, the RSPCA adopted a policy at the beginning of the 1840s that no inspector should benefit personally as a result of bringing a case.

(6) Pursuits of the rich and poor distinguished

Concern about the effect on the general populace of a ban on animal baiting and fighting also raised the (still controversial) issue of the position of field sports. This was a matter close to the hearts of a political class made up almost exclusively of the aristocracy and the landed gentry; Brougham was in a very small minority of parliamentarians (of one?) when he objected to Martin's proposals to ban bull-baiting and dog-fights on the ground that the Bill 'did not go far enough'. He took exception that 'It aimed at the sports which formed the amusements of the lower orders, but did not interfere with those in which the most wealthy and powerful classes indulged', and he asked whether 'fishing, grouse-shooting, hare-hunting, horse-racing, foxhunting, and other diversions of the same kind were not every whit as cruel as those against which the bill was levelled'. In Brougham's view, the Bill 'tended to draw a distinction between the lower and higher classes of his majesty's subjects, with respect to amusements in which there was equal cruelty'.[117] However, his concern that the legislature might give the appearance of applying double standards was more widely shared, although others employed it as an argument to do nothing rather than to go further. 'What a pretty figure we must make

---

[114] Fairholme and Pain, n 24 above, 87 and 90.   [115] RSPCA, Annual Report 1842, 77.
[116] RSPCA, Annual Report 1850, 120; quoted in Ritvo, H, *The Animal Estate* (1987) 155.
[117] Parl Debs (new series) vol 9, col 433 (21 May 1823).

in the world,' Windham warned the Commons, 'a house of hunters and shooters ... affecting to take the brute creation under their protection.'[118] Peel was particularly insistent on the point, asserting that 'Every man who pursued field sports must know, that in the course of them a vast deal of unnecessary suffering was inflicted on animals', and asking 'Why were the monkey and bear to be protected, while the fox, and the stag, and the hare, were subject to the most unrelenting persecution?'[119] Here was a discrepancy which could be used by the press to cause trouble and encourage dissent. The *Edinburgh Review*, for example, attacked Erskine's Bill on the grounds that 'A man of ten thousand a year may worry a fox as much as he pleases ... and a poor labourer is carried before a magistrate for paying sixpence to see an exhibition of courage between a dog and a bear! Any cruelty may be practised to gorge the stomachs of the rich—none to enliven the holidays of the poor!'[120]

Little wonder, then, that many MPs were concerned to demonstrate that they were not abusing their position by protecting their own interests at the expense of the poor, but there is also evidence of the paternalism which the powerful traditionally showed to those for whom they had responsibility. 'There was no better principle for the legislature to proceed,' Canning told the Commons in 1800, 'than to make no distinction between the different orders of the state, and that if any should be made, the comfort and happiness of the lower orders should be preferably attended to.'[121] More typical, though, were those who drew a distinction between both the nature of field sports and the type of person who participated in them. Thus, while in bull-baiting 'a poor animal is tied to a stake, with no means of defence or escape, and tormented', hunting and shooting involved 'no such refinements of torture', the suffering that was caused by these activities was said to be 'incidental and unavoidable, and the rich man would be better pleased if he could prevent the occurrence', whereas the amusements of the poor were such that 'the degree of pleasure in the spectator was proportioned to the quantity of suffering which was inflicted on the animal'. Similarly, field sports were 'conducive to health and activity', while baiting and fighting were 'mere spectacles of unmixed barbarity'.[122] Unlike the latter, hunting and shooting were not considered to have a moral dimension; they were, according to Viscount Mahon, chairman of the SPCA's annual meeting in 1839, 'innocent amusements'.[123] Martin himself, who was often accused of discriminating against the poor by campaigning to ban their pastimes but not those of the rich, asserted that he was 'equally anxious to meddle with both, when he found them opposed to the dictates of humanity', but made the point that while baiting and animal fights were attended by 'the lowest and most wretched

---

[118] Parl Debs vol 14, cols 1040–1025 (the column is incorrectly numbered in the original, it should be 1041) (13 June 1809).

[119] Parl Debs (new series) vol 10, col 492 (26 February 1824); vol 12, col 1004 (11 March 1825).

[120] January 1809.   [121] *Parliamentary History of England*, Vol 35, col 210 (18 April 1800).

[122] Sir William Pulteney, ibid, Vol 35, col 209 (18 April 1800); Mr W Smith, Parl Debs (new series) vol 9, col 434 (21 May 1823); Sir F Burdett, vol 12, col 1013 (11 March 1825).   [123] Annual Report 1839, 24.

description of people . . . Those who sported on their own manors, or fished their own streams, were a very different sort of men', to such an extent that 'He had known men as humane as men could be who followed the sports of the field.'[124] Peel was alone among politicians in turning these arguments on their head, by suggesting that 'in uneducated persons, it might be said, an excuse can be found for these unphilosophical and barbarous sports; but educated men, who can derive amusement from literature or from other pursuits, were the very individuals who ought to be punished for resorting to cruel sports'.[125]

G. Conclusion

The impetus for the introduction of animal protection legislation during the first third of the nineteenth century was founded on much more than mere sentimentality. Greater understanding of animal physiology, a reassessment of man's place in the world, the development of a secular morality, the increasing influence of urban middle-class values, concern for social discipline and stability, a political and legislative system which was responsive, the individual campaigners to carry the cause forward, and the endorsement of the higher ranks of society were all factors in legislative protection becoming a reality. It represented a confrontation between the old, pre-industrial, paternal, rural community, dominated by local customs, identity, and administration, and the new, urbanized society governed from London. In spite of considerable opposition, local traditions had to give way to a standard, national morality, centrally defined, overriding established property rights, and enshrined in law. This was not only of importance for its impact on the treatment of animals; it was also of considerable social and constitutional significance.

[124] Parl Debs (new series) vol 12, col 657 (24 February 1825); vol 10, col 487 (26 February 1824).
[125] ibid, vol 10, col 492 (26 February 1824).

4

Extending Protection

A. Concerning Cruelty

By the 1840s, the principle of legislation to protect animals from cruelty had become firmly established. Referring in 1848 to 'those unfortunate slaves and victims of the most brutal part of mankind, the lower animals', John Stuart Mill observed, 'It is by the grossest misunderstanding of the principles of liberty, that the infliction of exemplary punishment on ruffianism practised towards these defenceless creatures, has been treated as a meddling by government with things beyond its province; an interference with domestic life', and he regretted that 'metaphysical scruples respecting the nature and source of the authority of government' had induced many supporters of legislative intervention 'to seek for a justification of such laws in . . . the interests of human beings, rather than in the intrinsic merits of the case itself'.[1] Not everyone, however, shared Mill's enthusiasm. In 1844, for example, TS Duncombe told the House of Commons that, in his view, the fact that the Bill under consideration had been proposed by the RSPCA was in itself 'a sufficient reason for opposing it, as no encouragement ought to be given to societies for meddling with everybody's business but their own'.[2] By this time, however, such sentiments were no longer representative of Parliament as a whole. Indeed, the measure itself, which sought to strengthen the regulation of premises where horses were slaughtered, went through the full legislative process and became law in just two months. Both the Society and the police were in possession of considerable evidence which demonstrated that worn-out horses were continuing to be treated with extreme callousness at knackers' yards, particularly by being denied food and water for long periods before they were killed, or simply left to die of dehydration and malnutrition. The Act put the licensing of knackers' premises onto an annual basis, and magistrates were empowered to cancel existing licences in the event of a breach of the present Act or those of 1786 or 1835. Powers

---

[1] *The Principles of Political Economy* (3rd edn, 1852) Vol ll, Book V, Ch XI, section 9, 546–547.
[2] Parl Debs (series 3) vol 76, col 1334 (24 July 1844).

to inspect premises were strengthened and new penalties were introduced for obstructing inspectors (as well as making inspectors themselves criminally liable in the event that they neglected to perform their statutory duties). In addition, it was made a specific offence wantonly or cruelly to beat, ill-treat, abuse, wound, or torture any horse or cattle on premises occupied or used by a licence holder.[3]

These were significant developments. Hitherto, prosecutions for cruelty were largely restricted to offences committed in public places, but now the State assumed the power to enter and enforce anti-cruelty legislation on private property. Furthermore, the Act sought to *prevent* cruelty (as distinct from punishing it after the event) by the imposition of a regulatory regime intended to secure minimum standards, contravention of which might lead to a fine, imprisonment, or even deprivation of a person's livelihood by denying him the necessary licence to operate as a knacker.

(1) The Prevention of Cruelty to Animals Act 1849

The next significant development was in 1849, when Pease's Act and the 1837 legislation extending its application to Ireland were both repealed, and their provisions re-enacted and extended.[4] It now became an offence cruelly to beat, ill-treat, over-drive, abuse, or torture any animal, or to cause or procure it to be so treated. This revised definition included two important changes. First, it was no longer necessary for the prosecution to establish that the defendant had acted both wantonly *and* cruelly. This was of practical significance since some courts had been reluctant to convict in cases where, even though they were satisfied that the defendant's behaviour was cruel, the prosecution had failed to demonstrate that he had acted wantonly. The magistrate at Bow Street Police Station, for example, is reported to have said that 'If there be no apparent wantonness, I think a man must be permitted to exercise his own judgement as to the chastisement he may inflict upon his horse.'[5] Secondly, liability was extended beyond those who actually committed the offence to include third parties, such as employers and owners, who were responsible for encouraging or condoning it. This was particularly significant; those who actually caused the suffering were very often acting at the express or implicit behest of those for whom they worked. So far as the penalty was concerned, the minimum threshold of five shillings was removed, but the maximum was increased, so that the court could impose a fine for any amount up to five pounds for each offence. The Act introduced the practice, still generally employed, of providing a specific definition of the term 'animal' for the purposes of the particular piece of legislation. In this case it encompassed 'any Horse, Mare, Gelding, Bull, Ox, Cow, Heifer, Steer, Calf, Mule, Ass, Sheep, Lamb, Hog, Pig, Sow, Goat, Dog, Cat, or any other domestic Animal'. Subsequent legislation

---

[3] 7 & 8 Vict, c 87; An Act to amend the Law for regulating Places kept for slaughtering Horses.
[4] 12 & 13 Vict, c 92; An Act for the more effectual Prevention of Cruelty to Animals.
[5] Quoted in Lynam, S, *Humanity Dick* (1975) 221.

provided that the term 'any other domestic Animal' was to be interpreted to include 'any other Kind or Species whatever, and whether a Quadruped or not', thereby confirming that birds came within the law's protection.[6] In addition, the prohibition on animal baiting and fighting, together with the duty to provide sufficient food and water for impounded animals, were both restated but, if the latter was not carried out, it was now permitted to enter the pound to feed and water the animals after twelve, instead of twenty-four, hours. Similarly, the conditions relating to the licensing of knackers' premises, the recording of animals received, the limit of three days within which they had to be killed, the requirement that they had to be fed and watered while awaiting slaughter, and the prohibition, once they were on the premises, of animals either leaving or being worked, were all re-enacted, and, by way of extra protection, a person licensed to slaughter horses was no longer permitted to carry on business as a horse dealer at the same time.

Finally, the Act made it an offence to convey or carry (or cause to be conveyed or carried) an animal in or upon any vehicle in such a manner or position that it was caused 'unnecessary Pain or Suffering'. This was not only the first time the law had been used to regulate animal transport, it also represented a significant development in the very concept of cruelty. Hitherto it had been restricted to a catalogue of specific actions—beating, ill-treatment, over-driving, abuse, and torture—all of which involved the infliction of a deliberate act of brutality. In contrast, the new test of unnecessary pain or suffering was concerned with the outcome rather than the cause. Not only was it wider, in that it could equally well apply to suffering caused as a result of carelessness or indifference, but it also, for the first time, defined cruelty by reference to the effect on the individual animal rather than the attitude or conduct of the perpetrator. The rationale was unequivocally animal protection, not social engineering aimed at improving the morals of the lower orders: to determine what constituted an offence, it was necessary to consider the position from the point of view of the animal, and therefore have some understanding of the animal's experience, perception, and needs. It is not suggested that the introduction of the unnecessary suffering test made an immediate impact, but it did mark a major change of principle, and its continuing significance lies in the fact that it remains the basis of the legal notion of cruelty.

(2) The first Scottish legislation

The Prevention of Cruelty to Animals Act 1849 was built on the foundation of its predecessors, but clearly went further in a number of important respects and thereby established a wide-ranging and reasonably sophisticated legislative framework, except in respect of Scotland, which was specifically excluded from its provisions. The reason why this and the previous legislation applied only to England,

[6] 17 & 18 Vict, c 60; An Act to amend an Act of the Twelfth and Thirteenth Years of Her Present Majesty for the more effectual Prevention of Cruelty to Animals (1854).

Wales, and Ireland is obscure; perhaps it can be explained by Scotland's separate legal traditions, particularly the practice of developing the criminal law through the common (judge-made) law rather than statute. Whatever the explanation, a meeting of interested individuals held in Edinburgh in December 1839 had resolved 'That as cruelty to the brute creation is contrary to Scripture and humanity, and as there is no legislative enactment in Scotland adequate to prevent this evil … it is expedient that in Scotland a Society be instituted, to be called "The Scottish Society for the Prevention of Cruelty to Animals".'[7] Like the RSPCA, the Scottish SPCA (SSPCA) appears to have experienced an uncertain start: the following July, the *Scotsman* carried a notice announcing that a number of supporters were 'uniting their exertions to resuscitate the Society for the Prevention of Cruelty, which seems to have been defunct for the last six months'. Their priority was to improve the condition of Edinburgh's horses and donkeys which, 'to the disgrace of this enlightened city, are shamefully used'. To this end, it was claimed—curiously, in the light of the resolution of the previous year—that 'As the laws are now sufficiently stringent as regards the protection of the dumb animals, those who witness cases of cruelty are greatly to blame if they do not report them to the police.'[8]

It is unclear why the SSPCA's perception of the law's effectiveness had altered. There had been no new legislation, the Society having prepared a Bill which made no immediate progress. Indeed, the position in Scotland at this time was much the same as it had been in England prior to Martin's Act: the law regarded domestic animals as property, and such protection as it afforded was only concerned to prevent damage by third parties. According to the Scottish jurist, David Hume, 'if anyone go and poison his neighbour's dogs, sheep or cattle, or mangle them by cutting out their tongies [sic], breaking their limbs, or the like, certainly this is a crime', by virtue of the common law offence of malicious mischief.[9] It was not until 1850 that Parliament went some way to rectifying this legislative lacuna by introducing statutory protection for animals in Scotland. The Act was in similar terms to that of 1849, except that the provisions relating to impounded animals and animal transport were for some reason omitted.[10] So began the practice of having separate enactments, and, more regrettably, different degrees of statutory protection, applying to animals in the constituent parts of the United Kingdom. There was a further significant distinction: although both the 1849 and 1850 Acts provided a 'constable' with statutory powers of enforcement, the Scottish legislation's inclusion of Sheriff Officers within the meaning of that term allowed a practice to develop, unique to Scotland, whereby SSPCA inspectors, having taken an oath before a Justice of the Peace, received a Warrant Card signed by the Clerk of the Peace

---

[7] Cited in 'A Short History of the Scottish Society for Prevention of Cruelty to Animals' (*sic*), in Scottish SPCA Annual Report 1939, 9.

[8] ibid 12.

[9] *Commentaries on the Law of Scotland, Respecting Crimes* (1844) Vol 1, 124. Hume defined 'malicious mischief', at 122, as 'great and wilful damage done to the property of another, and whether done from malice, or misapprehension of right'.

[10] 13 & 14 Vict, c 92; An Act for the more effectual Prevention of Cruelty to Animals in Scotland.

which, unlike his RSPCA counterpart, endowed him with the powers of a police constable for the purposes of the Prevention of Cruelty to Animals in Scotland Act.[11]

(3) The use of dogs for draught

Meanwhile, in the rest of the United Kingdom, notwithstanding the degree of legislative protection which had already been achieved, experience continued to expose particular weaknesses which, once identified, gave rise to campaigns for further legislation to meet the problem. One such example related to the recent but widespread practice of employing dogs to pull carts. Dogs had been protected against cruelty since 1835 by the provisions of Pease's Act and a number of successful prosecutions arose from their use as draught animals, but the scale of the problem was too great to be overcome by pursuing individual cases. Dog transport was an attractive option, especially for the poor; dogs were cheaper and easier to keep than horses, ponies, and donkeys, and they were exempt from road tolls, but their lack of value left them open to abuse. The RSPCA's annual report of 1837 complained of the degree of suffering inflicted on 'poor, overladen, cruelly beaten, and half-starved dogs', and the Society's President spoke of them 'seen dying under the lash'.[12]

The use of dog carts having been prohibited in 1839 within fifteen miles of Charing Cross,[13] due to the danger they posed to other road users rather than out of concern for the animals themselves, the RSPCA campaigned to extend the ban throughout the country. Largely at its behest, Bills were introduced into Parliament in 1840, 1841, and 1843, but all were unsuccessful. So, too, was an attempt to include provisions in the 1849 Act which would have established a registry of dog carts for each county, including details of the species of dogs licensed to draw them, as well as making it a specific offence to compel a dog to pull a load manifestly beyond its strength. Opposition to such restrictions focused on their implications for those who made a living by running dog carts and the 'many infirm and decrepit persons, who were in the habit of being drawn by that docile, well-behaved, and excellent animal'.[14] It is unsurprising then, that when the ban on the use of dogs as draught animals on the public highway was eventually extended throughout the United Kingdom in 1854, it was principally on the basis of 'the obstruction, danger, and, oftentimes, the loss of life to which they led'.[15] Two particular contributions from members of the House of Lords in connection with this

[11] SSPCA Annual Report 1939, 14–15.
[12] Fairholme, EG and Pain, W, *A Century of Work for Animals. The History of the RSPCA, 1824–1924* (1924) 111.
[13] 2 & 3 Vict, c 47; Metropolitan Police Act 1839.
[14] Lord Campbell, Parl Debs (series 3) vol 54, col 928 (27 April 1849).
[15] 17 & 18 Vict, c 60; An Act to amend an Act of the Twelfth and Thirteenth Years of Her Present Majesty for the more effectual Prevention of Cruelty to Animals; Lord St Leonards, Parl Debs (series 3) vol 84, col 1076 (4 July 1854).

measure provide examples respectively of old and new attitudes to the concept of legislation to protect animals. On the one hand, the Earl of Eglington harked back to a battle which was already lost, complaining that to prohibit the use of dog carts would amount to 'a case of over-legislation', and described the proposal as 'puerile and unnecessary'. In marked contrast, the Marquess of Westminster supported the measure, not on the basis of traditional arguments about maintaining public order, improving the conduct of the lower orders, or even the new concern over road safety, but on account of the animals' anatomy. 'Every one knew', the Marquess said, 'that the natural position of a dog was to stand on its toes, and that to put a collar on its neck, harness on its back, and weight upon its loins, was virtually forcing it from its natural position into one which it could only be educated to, and that with much suffering and pain.'[16]

(4) The first dogs' home

A further issue concerning dogs in London which prompted legislation on the grounds of public protection was that of strays, with the result that the State, in the form of the Metropolitan Police, assumed responsibility in 1867 for alleviating the problem by taking such animals into its possession.[17] In fact, responding to the number of unwanted and unkempt dogs on the streets, individual citizens had taken their own initiative six years previously by founding The Home for Lost and Starving Dogs, which was to become the Battersea Dogs' Home. The establishment of homes dedicated to taking in, looking after, and, wherever possible, rehoming unwanted animals, supported by volunteers and run on a charitable basis, was to become characteristic of the British animal welfare movement, but they were initially greeted with a combination of dismay and ridicule. *The Times*, for example, was prepared to accept it was 'perfectly right that the Legislature should have distinctly forbidden that dogs should be used as beasts of draught', but 'when we hear of a "Home for Dogs",' the paper commented disdainfully, 'we venture to doubt if the originators and supporters of such an institution have not taken leave of their sober senses'.[18]

B. Vivisection[19]

It was, however, vivisection which proved to be the single most contentious issue involving the use of animals during the latter part of the nineteenth century. The early campaigners had adopted a pragmatic approach to the subject. Richard Martin considered public demonstrations involving vivisection to be 'equally

---

[16] Parl Debs (series 3) vol 84, cols 1076 and 1077 (4 July 1854).
[17] 30 & 31 Vict, c 134; An Act to regulate the traffic and the metropolis and for other purposes.
[18] 18 October 1860.
[19] For a detailed account of these events, see further French, RD, *Antivivisection and Medical Science in Victorian Society* (1975) and Westacott, E, *A Century of Vivisection and Anti-Vivisection* (1949).

cruel' as animal baiting and fighting, and wanted the practice banned. He accepted, however, 'the necessity of making some experiments on living animals', so long as they were 'performed in such a manner as to cause as little suffering as possible'.[20] Similarly, the SPCA's original prospectus stated: 'However justifiable it may be to conduct certain experiments of a painful nature, under the control of a benevolent mind, with a view to determine some important question in science, not otherwise attainable, yet all must agree "that Providence cannot intend that the secrets of Nature should be discovered by means of cruelty".'

(1) Growing opposition

In fact, compared with the Continent, there was not a great deal of vivisection in Great Britain until the 1860s and calls for statutory intervention, such as the suggestion made at the RSPCA's annual meeting in 1847 to require the inspection of premises,[21] were uncommon. As Ritvo points out, it was not until 1862 that the RSPCA began to take a serious interest in the issue[22] and, perhaps not altogether incidentally, an international conference to discuss the subject was held at the Crystal Palace the following year. Largely in response to growing public awareness and concern about the way animals were being treated, the British Association for the Advancement of Science published in 1870 voluntary guidelines for those undertaking vivisection. These stated that experiments were not to be performed merely for improving skills; they were to be undertaken only by qualified experts properly equipped, and with the animal anaesthetized whenever possible; and no demonstrations to an audience were to involve the infliction of pain or suffering.[23] Despite these recommendations, an attempt by the French scientist Eugene Magnan to induce epilepsy in a dog as part of a public demonstration at the annual meeting of the British Medical Association held in Norwich in 1874 caused such an outcry that the event had to be abandoned. Magnan having returned to France and therefore outwith the jurisdiction of the English courts, the RSPCA attempted to prosecute the organizers under the 1849 Act, but was unable to demonstrate that they had been personally involved in the experiment. Nevertheless, the episode generated debate about the acceptability of using animals in such a way, as did the publication in the previous year of the *Handbook for the Physiological Laboratory*, 'intended for beginners in physiological work'.[24] Richard French considers that the impact of this book on those opposed to vivisection 'can be scarcely overestimated', indicating as it did the adoption in Britain of experimental practices already common on the Continent, together with the

---

[20] Parl Debs (new series) vol 12, cols 658 and 659 (24 February 1825). According to Fairholme and Pain, n 12 above, 192, Martin subsequently said that he had been misrepresented, and that he did not approve of cruelty to a living animal under any circumstances.

[21] Fairholme and Pain, n 12 above, 192. [22] Ritvo, H, *The Animal Estate* (1987) 159.

[23] *Report of the British Association for the Advancement of Science, 41st Meeting, Edinburgh 1871*, Appendix 1.

[24] Sanderson, JB (ed), *Handbook for the Physiological Laboratory* (1873) Vol 1, vii.

text's apparent indifference to pain, evidenced by its failure to specify the need to use anaesthetics.[25]

One consequence of these events was the presentation to the RSPCA of a memorial by Frances Power Cobbe expressing concern at the number and nature of experiments being undertaken, which had been endorsed by, among others, the Archbishops of York, Dublin, and Westminster; the Primate of Ireland; three dukes; five marquesses; sixteen earls; twenty-eight peers; ten bishops; three senior judges (the Lord Chief Baron, Sir Fitzroy Kelly; the Lord Chief Justice, Lord Coleridge; and the Rt Hon Sir William Erle); the Lord Mayor of London; the Lord Provost of Edinburgh; the deans of seven cathedrals; twenty-seven senior military officers; twenty-three MPs; Alfred Tennyson; Robert Browning; Thomas Carlyle; John Ruskin; and numerous clergymen, academics, and doctors. Not only was it clear that a significant swathe of the Victorian establishment was unhappy with the situation, so too was Victoria herself. While the memorial was being prepared, the RSPCA received a donation on behalf of the Queen which was accompanied by a letter expressing her concern at the treatment of animals by scientists. Cobbe's memorial called upon the RSPCA to establish a committee to consider practical steps to restrict vivisection and, in the meantime, to bring further test cases under the Prevention of Cruelty to Animals Acts. If this strategy was unsuccessful, then it was suggested that consideration should be given to promoting legislation to prohibit painful experiments except by registered persons in authorized laboratories, a strategy which coincided with the views of the RSPCA's secretary, John Colam, who proposed to the Sixth International Conference of Societies for the Prevention of Cruelty to Animals in 1874 that 'painful experiments on living animals, if not already illegal, should be forbidden by law except under licence'.[26] The Society responded by forming a subcommittee, but its deliberations lacked any sense of urgency; a reflection, perhaps, of the absence of a consensus among the wider membership as to the efficacy and morality, or otherwise, of animal experiments. Indeed, the Society itself conceded, 'The RSPCA is not so entirely unanimous as to desire the passing of any special legislative enactment on the subject.'[27]

Impatient at the delay, Cobbe and a number of her supporters prepared a Bill for Regulating the Practice of Vivisection. Introduced into the House of Lords on 4 May 1875, it provided that vivisection should only be carried out at premises subject to inspection and annual registration by the Home Secretary. Meanwhile, the scientific community, fearful that the legality of vivisection would fall to be determined by magistrates, as a result of their interpretation of the anti-cruelty legislation, were moving towards the view that legislation *specifically permitting* the practice might be required, even if this involved 'something in the way of regulation and supervision'.[28] Accordingly, eight days after Cobbe's Bill was presented to Parliament, an alternative measure was introduced into the House of

---

[25] French, n 19 above, 48.   [26] ibid 74.   [27] RSPCA, *Animal World*, vi (1875) 180.
[28] (1875) 1 *Lancet* 19–21; cited in French, n 19 above, 59.

Commons. This Bill would have made painless experiments, including those undertaken using anaesthesia, lawful, and therefore immune from prosecution, while scientists carrying out painful experiments would have been required to be licensed by the Home Secretary.

(2) The first Royal Commission

Confronted by these alternative proposals, the Government avoided coming down on one side or the other by the expedient of establishing a Royal Commission 'to inquire into the practice of subjecting live animals to experiment for scientific purposes'. The evidence presented to the Commission confirmed that there was a lack of control over those involved in vivisection and that there were problems in respect of repeated and pointless experiments. Cobbe did not appear before the Commission to give evidence. Colam, on behalf of the RSPCA, conceded that he was not aware of a single case of wanton cruelty by British experimenters, but he provided detailed examples of procedures and practices which the Society considered to be unacceptable, including information drawn from the *Handbook for the Physiological Laboratory*. Included in his submission was the text of a Bill which sought to prohibit painful experiments on living animals and all vivisection undertaken for the purposes of demonstration or improving technique, and to introduce regulation of those experiments which were carried out, involving the registration of premises, licensing of personnel, and associated inspections.[29] Although these proposals were to influence the eventual legislation, it was the evidence and attitude of some of the witnesses who supported vivisection, especially their apparent indifference to animal suffering, which had the greatest impact on the Commission. Of these, the most significant was Dr Emanuel Klein, a lecturer at St Bartholomew's Hospital and a contributor to the *Handbook for the Physiological Laboratory*, whose oral evidence included the following exchange:

KLEIN: Except for teaching purposes, for demonstration, I never use anaesthetics where it is not necessary for convenience . . .

CHAIRMAN: When you say that you only use them for convenience' sake, do you mean that you have no regard at all to the sufferings of the animals?

KLEIN: No regard at all.

CHAIRMAN: You are prepared to establish that as a principle which you approve?

KLEIN: I think that with regard to an experimenter, a man who conducts special research and performs an experiment, he has no time, so to speak, for thinking what will the animal feel or suffer. His only purpose is to perform the experiment, to learn as much from it as possible, and to do it as quickly as possible.

CHAIRMAN: Then for your own purposes you disregard entirely the question of the suffering of the animal in performing a painful experiment?

[29] Royal Commission on the Practice of Subjecting Live Animals to Experiments for Scientific Purposes, *Final Report* (1876), Questions 1515–1702; Appendix 3, section 5; Appendix 4.

KLEIN: I do.

CHAIRMAN: Why do you regard it then when it is for demonstration?

KLEIN: One must take regard of the feelings and opinions of those people before whom one does the experiment . . .'[30]

French concludes that 'without the testimony of Emanuel Klein, several members of the Commission would have been entirely unwilling to sign a report recommending legislation of any kind with regard to experiments on living animals'.[31] The Commission now accepted, however, that as it was 'manifest' that the practice was 'from its very nature liable to great abuse . . . [it] ought to be subjected to due regulation and control', observing:

Those who are least favourable to interference assume, as we have seen, that interference would be directed against the skilful, the humane, and the experienced. But it is not for them that law is made, but for persons of the opposite character. It is not to be doubted that inhumanity may be found in persons of very high position as physiologists.[32]

The Commission's final report was published in January 1876. It concluded that 'it is impossible altogether to prevent the practice of making experiments on living animals for the attainment of knowledge applicable to the mitigation of human suffering or the prolongation of human life'. Even if absolute prevention were possible, it 'would not be reasonable' since 'the greatest mitigations of human suffering have been in part derived from such experiments'. The Commission was also influenced by the fact that, in their view, prohibition would lead to 'evasion of the law or the flight of medical and physiological students from the United Kingdom to foreign schools and laboratories, and would, therefore, certainly result in no change favourable to the animals'. It was also relevant that the use of anaesthetics could greatly mitigate, if not altogether prevent, pain being inflicted on the animals used. The Commission did agree, however, that 'the infliction of severe and protracted agony' should be avoided and 'the abuse of the practice by inhuman or unskilful persons,—in short the infliction on animals of any unnecessary pain—is justly abhorrent to the moral sense of Your Majesty's subjects generally, not least so of the most distinguished physiologists and the most eminent surgeons and physicians' and, consequently, 'the support of these eminent persons, as well as of the general public, may be confidently expected for any reasonable measure intended to prevent abuse'.[33] Accordingly, it recommended that a system of licensing be introduced, similar to that proposed by Colam. A minority report argued that there should be a total ban on the use of dogs and cats, partly to deter the

---

[30] ibid, Questions 3538–3543. When he received a proof of his evidence, Klein attempted to alter it, no doubt aware of its potential impact. The Commission, however, considered the alterations were 'so much at variance with the letter and spirit of the answers that he had given us at his examination, that we felt unable to receive them as an authentic report of his evidence'. Klein then attempted to withdraw his evidence, but the Commission thought 'that this would not be right', and published the original record of evidence; Klein's version was reproduced as an appendix; vii and Appendix 2, section 2.

[31] n 19 above, 103.   [32] *Final Report*, n 29 above, xvii.   [33] ibid xvii–xviii.

unscrupulous from stealing domestic pets to sell to laboratories, and partly in recognition of the particular relationship humans had with them.

(3) The Cruelty to Animals Act 1876

By this time Cobbe had formed her own organization, the Victoria Street Society for the Protection of Animals from Vivisection (later to become the National Anti-Vivisection Society), which met with the Home Secretary in March 1876 and was invited to put forward proposals for legislation. A Bill based on the Commission's recommendations, which would have severely limited the circumstances in which experiments on animals could be carried out, was presented to Parliament, but again the scientists responded, with the medical establishment to the fore. They successfully lobbied the Home Secretary, Richard Assheton Cross, and persuaded him to bring forward a less stringent Bill, the object of which he described as being 'to place under necessary, but under no unnecessary, control or restriction those who should perform experiments'.[34]

The subsequent legislation, the Cruelty to Animals Act 1876, made it an offence to perform on a living animal any experiment calculated to give pain, unless it was carried out with a view to advancing physiological knowledge, saving or prolonging life, or alleviating suffering. In order to ensure that experiments met these criteria, a regulatory system was established, administered by the Home Secretary, involving the registration of premises where experiments were carried out and the licensing of personnel undertaking the work. Responsibility for enforcing this regime was placed in the hands of a newly-created Home Office inspectorate. In addition, the Act purported to impose a range of further restrictions. For example, an animal was required to be anaesthetized sufficiently to prevent it feeling pain; if it was seriously injured during the procedure or would continue to be in pain afterwards, the animal had to be killed before it recovered from the anaesthetic; no dog, cat, horse, ass, or mule was to be experimented upon without first being anaesthetized; and no procedure was to be carried out merely for the purpose of demonstration or the attainment of manual skills. In practice, however, there was provision for each of these stipulations to be waived, subject to the agreement of the President of the Royal Society, the Royal College of Surgeons, the Royal College of Physicians, the General Medical Council, the Royal College of Veterinary Surgeons, or the Royal Veterinary College. Furthermore, no prosecution under the Act could be brought against a licence holder without the written assent of the Home Secretary.

(4) The second Royal Commission

The issue of vivisection returned to the fore at the beginning of the twentieth century. Stephen Coleridge, secretary of the National Anti-Vivisection Society (Frances

---

[34] Parl Debs (series 3) vol 231, col 891 (9 August 1876).

Cobbe and a number of her supporters having broken with the organization they helped to found because of policy differences had, in 1898, formed the British Union for the Abolition of Vivisection), was successfully sued for defamation by a scientist he had criticized at a public meeting in 1903. He had quoted from *The Shambles of Science*, a recently published book by two anti-vivisectionists which detailed their experiences as medical students in London. Although Coleridge lost the case, the public were shocked by the evidence of animal suffering which was revealed at the trial, a consequence of which was the placing of a statue of a small brown dog in Battersea Park in 1906 by the International Anti-Vivisection Council, the inscription of which read:

In memory of the brown Terrier Dog done to death in the laboratories of University College in February 1903 after having endured vivisection extending over more than two months and having been handed over from one vivisector to another till death came to his release. Also in memory of the 232 dogs vivisected in the same place during the year 1902. Men and women of England: How long shall these things be?

This statue became the tangible symbol of the vivisection controversy and, over the following months, attracted a series of demonstrations and counter-demonstrations. Battersea Borough Council having refused to remove it, about 100 medical students attempted to do the deed themselves on 10 December 1907. Local residents gathered to defend the statue and, after several hours of confrontation, the gathering had to be dispersed by mounted police. There were many subsequent demonstrations, and hundreds of police were engaged in protecting the statue. It eventually disappeared in the spring of 1910.

In response to the renewed public concern about vivisection reflected in these events, the Government established a second Royal Commission in 1906. When it eventually produced its report, after six years of deliberation, the Commission concluded, like its predecessor, that 'experiments upon animals, adequately safeguarded by law, faithfully administered, are morally justifiable and should not be prohibited by legislation', and was satisfied that 'the present system . . . has been so worked as to secure a large degree of protection to animals subject to experiment and at the same time so as not to hamper or impede research'.[35] Accordingly, the Commission saw no necessity for any major revision of the statutory framework. Instead, it recommended a number of administrative changes, including an increase in the inspectorate; further limitations as regards the use of curare (a relaxant which blocks neuromuscular transmission); stricter provisions as to the definition and practice of pithing (slaughtering or immobilizing an animal by severing its spinal cord); additional restrictions regulating the painless destruction of animals which showed signs of suffering after an experiment; a change in the composition and the method of selecting those who advised the Home Secretary; and the keeping of special records by experimenters in certain cases. The 1876 Act was to remain in force for more than a century.

[35] Royal Commission on Vivisection, *Final Report* (1912) paras 97 and 112.

C. Animal Health and the Origins of the Veterinary Profession

(1) The development and early regulation of the veterinary profession

Fundamental to the welfare of humans and other animals is their health, and in parallel with legislation to regulate the way in which animals were treated there developed the foundations of the modern statutory and administrative regime to safeguard and improve animal health. The world's first veterinary school was established in France in 1762, but it was to be another thirty years before a similar development took place in Britain. Traditionally, the 'treatment' of animals continued to be regarded as an extension of farriery and, unsurprisingly, was characterized by ignorance and quackery, 'conducted without principle of science and greatly to the injury to the noblest and most useful of our animals'.[36] Improving the condition of animals, particularly the horse, was of both economic and military importance and, in 1791, the privately-operated Veterinary College was established in London to produce students 'qualified to practise the Veterinary Art'. However, the standard of training was, at best, rudimentary; it was not until the second quarter of the nineteenth century that veterinary practice began to establish professional status or a scientific basis. In the meantime, 'diagnosis' continued to be carried out predominantly by unqualified horse-surgeons, cow-leeches, cattle-doctors, farriers, castrators, spayers, gelders, charmers, spell-workers, and similarly exotic-sounding 'experts', who relied on customary, largely ineffectual, 'cures'. In the 1820s, the inadequacies of the London school were highlighted as a result of the opening of a rival institution in Edinburgh by William Dick, and the founding of two publications, the *Farrier and Naturalist* and the *Veterinarian*, which were the first journals to provide a forum for matters of veterinary interest. Progress, however, was slow. A retrospective article published at the end of the century in the *Veterinary Record* recalled that 'in 1837 every wretched animal that was submitted to veterinary treatment underwent a course of bleeding, physicing and blistering ... there was no veterinary pathology ... the most conscientious practitioner would never sew up the simplest ... wound until he had filled it with some filthy greasy compound ... men with the mere ability to read and write could enter the ranks ... [and] twelve months study was all that was demanded'.[37] Nevertheless, the importance of animal health to farming was becoming increasingly obvious. When, for example, the English Agricultural Society (subsequently the Royal Agricultural Society) was established in 1838, it included among its objectives the encouragement of veterinary education. This aspiration was given practical effect in 1842 when,

---

[36] From a motion to the Odiham Agriculture Society, 1785, which led, ultimately, to the establishment of the Veterinary College, London; quoted in Dunlop, RH and Williams, DJ, *Veterinary Medicine* (1996) 344.
[37] Quoted by Pattison, I, *The British Veterinary Profession 1791–1948* (1983) 116.

following a serious outbreak of foot-and-mouth disease, the Society agreed to subsidize a professorship in cattle pathology at the London school.

This period also saw the first concerted effort by veterinarians to win formal recognition for their vocation, which was achieved in 1844 with the granting of a Royal Charter, providing that the Veterinary Art was to be recognized as a profession and that all those who were qualified to practise were to form one body, to be known as the Royal College of Veterinary Surgeons (RCVS).[38] Henceforth, only members of the RCVS could call themselves veterinary surgeons, which necessitated the compilation of a register of eligible practitioners. These totalled around 1,500, but it was estimated that there were four times that number of unqualified people making a livelihood from treating animals.[39] In addition to providing an enhanced status, the Royal Charter also presented the opportunity to raise professional standards, particularly by removing responsibility for the examination of veterinary students from the private, commercially-run schools and placing it with the RCVS, effectively giving the Royal College control of entry into the profession. Progress, however, remained slow. Formal requirements for entry into the veterinary schools were not specified until 1870, and a practical element was included in the final examination only the following year. Previously, the competence of those qualifying as veterinarians varied enormously, with the worst being of a very low calibre. Indeed, it was 1893 before a formal four-year course, culminating in written as well as oral examinations, was introduced. Against this background, the maintenance of professional standards was a continual problem. A further Royal Charter, granted in 1876, provided some assistance by empowering the RCVS to remove names from its register, but the real weakness of the regulatory regime was its lack of legal status, making it virtually impossible to take effective action against interlopers. This situation was corrected in 1881 with the passing of the Veterinary Surgeons Act, endowing the Charters with statutory authority and making it an offence to obtain registration by false representation, or for an unregistered person to hold himself out to be, or to receive payment for acting in any way as, a veterinary surgeon or practitioner. The procedures and circumstances under which names could be removed from the register were formalized and the Privy Council was given responsibility for deciding whether an individual's name should be removed. In the meantime, additional veterinary schools had been established in Glasgow and Dublin, together with a second school in Edinburgh (which subsequently moved to Liverpool in 1904), and the *Veterinary Journal*, providing scientific, educational, practical, and political information, was first published in 1875, followed by both the *Veterinary Record* and the *Journal of Comparative Pathology and Therapeutics* in 1888.

---

[38] Hall, SA, 'The Struggle for the Charter of the Royal College of Veterinary Surgeons, 1844' (1994) 134 *Veterinary Record* 536; Porter, A, 'Veterinary Charters and Veterinary Statutes' (1994) 134 *Veterinary Record* 541.

[39] Pattison, n 37 above, 44.

(2) The first animal health legislation

At the same time as these institutional developments were taking place, so were advances in the treatment of animals. What had traditionally been labelled the veterinary 'art' increasingly took on the characteristics of a science. Diagnosis based simply on estimation and experience was gradually being replaced by close observation, measurement, and greater knowledge of animal physiology. In the long term, the single most important development in relation to both human and animal surgery was undoubtedly the introduction of general anaesthesia in the 1840s, but the availability of such down-to-earth aids as the humble thermometer (in 1865) greatly assisted in enabling a practitioner to make an informed assessment of an animal's condition.

Similarly, greater understanding about the nature of disease and the manner in which it spread led to novel possibilities in its diagnosis, treatment, and prevention, and a new role for the law. In September 1847, for example, there was a serious outbreak of what was then known as 'sheep-pox', which originated in imported sheep sold at Smithfield and eventually spread throughout the national flock. In response, Parliament was persuaded to enact legislation the following year to prevent the introduction and spread of contagious or infectious disorders among sheep, cattle, and other animals.[40] Although the basis for statutory intervention was essentially economic, the episode established the principle that the State had a legitimate role to play in promoting animal health. This was taken a stage further twenty years later when an outbreak of so-called 'cattle plague' killed an estimated 500,000 cattle. The situation was brought under control only when the Government accepted, albeit reluctantly, the advice of the veterinary profession to slaughter infected cattle and restrict the movements of those which remained unaffected.

The introduction of legislation to give effect to this policy, and its success, was a defining moment. 'In eighteen months cattle plague revolutionized the British veterinary profession', concludes Iain Pattison. 'Before June 1865 disease was treated on a single-animal basis, with the horse by far the most usual patient. There was minimal Government interest in animal welfare, except in the specialized military world, and veterinary surgeons were seen as men who treated lameness or colic. Suddenly all was changed. The profession had saved the country. It had a new status, a special place in the life of the Nation.'[41] Furthermore, if animal health, as distinct from the health of an individual animal, was recognized to be of public concern, and the Government was to become directly involved in promoting it, then a bureaucracy was required to carry out the necessary inspection, monitoring, and administration. As a result of the cattle plague epidemic, a veterinary department was therefore set up, first, as part of the Privy Council Office and then, in 1889, under the auspices of the Board of Agriculture. So began what was to become the State Veterinary Service.

---

[40] 11 & 12 Vict, c 105 and c 107.   [41] Pattison, n 37 above, 61.

The first legislation to control animal disease having been introduced in 1848, the law was re-enacted, extended, and made more detailed during the next two decades.[42] In 1869, these various measures were repealed and replaced by the Contagious Diseases (Animals) Act, which sought not only to promote animal health and control disease, but also to safeguard the welfare of cattle while in transit (hence the origin of the continuing practice that the regulation of animal transport is regarded in legislation principally as a matter of animal health[43]). Railway companies, for example, were now required to provide food and water at specified stations, and both the consignor and the person in charge of an animal were guilty of an offence if it was left for 30 consecutive hours without a supply of water, or other period (not being less than 12 hours) as prescribed by the Privy Council. Interestingly, statute specifically placed the burden of proof on the accused to establish the time within which the animal had had a supply of water, rather than on the prosecution to show that the offence had been committed.[44] Furthermore, the Privy Council was empowered to make Orders to ensure that cattle brought by sea to ports in Great Britain were given a proper supply of food and water during the passage and upon landing; to protect such animals from unnecessary suffering during the journey and at disembarkation; and to protect cattle from unnecessary suffering during inland transit.[45]

Parliament enacted further legislation on the subject in 1878, 1893, 1894, and 1910,[46] indicating its importance and, in the process, encouraging the development of an increasingly sophisticated statutory regime. 'These elaborate Acts,' observed de Montmorency in 1902, 'designed for the double purpose of protecting the health and property of man, play an important though indirect part in the entire idea of State protection of animals. Their strict enforcement has alleviated an immense amount of suffering amongst animals: the spread of disease was generally due to culpable negligence, and the measures taken to prevent such negligence are not the least important of the laws for the prevention of cruelty to animals.'[47]

In addition to promoting animal health, a series of miscellaneous provisions was also introduced to prevent it being adversely affected. The sale and use of poisoned grain and meat were both prohibited;[48] it was made an offence unlawfully to

---

[42] An Act to extend and continue an Act [11 & 12 Vict, c 107] to prevent the spreading of contagious and infectious Disorders among Sheep, Cattle, and other Animals (1853); Cattle Diseases Prevention Act 1866; An Act to amend 11 & 12 Vict, c 107 to prevent the spreading of contagious or infectious Disorders among Sheep, Cattle, and other Animals (1866); Cattle Diseases Prevention Amendment Act 1866; Contagious Diseases (Animals) Act 1867.

[43] See now, Animal Health Act 1981, ss 37–38.   [44] Contagious Diseases (Animals) Act 1869, s 64.

[45] ibid, s 75; these powers were subsequently transferred to the Board of Agriculture by virtue of the Diseases of Animals Act 1894, s 22.

[46] Contagious Diseases (Animals) Act 1878; Diseases of Animals Act 1893; Diseases of Animals Act 1894; Diseases of Animals Act 1910.

[47] de Montmorency, JEG, 'State Protection of Animals at Home and Abroad' (1902) 18 Law Quarterly Review 31, 37.

[48] Poisoned Grain Prohibition Act 1863; Poisoned Flesh Prohibition Act 1864.

administer a poisonous or injurious substance to horses, cattle, and domestic animals;[49] and authority was given to the police to order, on the advice of a veterinary surgeon, the slaughter of any horse, mule, or ass which was so severely injured that it could not without cruelty be led away, regardless of whether the owner consented.[50]

D. The Protection of Wildlife

The protection from cruelty provided by the 1849 Act (and that of 1850 in Scotland) related only to domestic animals; the treatment of wildlife remained unregulated. However, the second half of the nineteenth century saw the first attempt to use the law to promote conservation. Birds had traditionally been taken from the wild and used for numerous purposes, but this was now being undertaken on a commercial and unsustainable scale. In 1854 alone, for example, it was estimated that 400,000 larks were sent from the country to London, where they were sold either to be kept in cages or for human consumption.[51] Eating wild birds had become fashionable, and a number of species had the dubious distinction of being considered a delicacy, while song birds and those with colourful plumage were kept as companions or for decoration. Others were regarded as amusements for children; sparrows and starlings, for example, had string tied to their legs and were then 'flown' like kites. Furthermore, during the breeding season, nests, complete with a clutch of eggs, were collected in vast numbers and sold by street vendors. It was, however, the introduction of the breech-loader and the double-barrel shotgun which proved to be the impetus for legislative intervention, for they reduced the cost of firearms to such an extent that large numbers of working people could afford to take up shooting. These were, literally, loose cannons. Instead of participating in organized shoots, they went out at weekends to the country and, particularly, the coast, where there were large concentrations of birds, and indulged in what amounted to an unregulated massacre. Concern among the higher social orders was excited both by the effect on bird populations and the type of person who was now enjoying an activity which traditionally had been reserved for the upper classes. *The Times* referred to 'a great deal of murderous work against the birds', and complained that

high up in the hills and down in the valleys such a fusillade ensues on the day of rest as could hardly be justified by any event short of the landing of French invaders upon our shores. This is an unmitigated evil and no attempt is made to deny it. Should nine-tenths of the birds of England deserve capital punishment it is not such a set of ragamuffins that ought to be allowed to inflict it.[52]

In response to this situation, a number of groups such as the Seabirds Society, the Small Birds Society, and the RSPCA campaigned to introduce protection, and the

---

[49] Drugging of Animals Act 1876.   [50] Injured Animals Act 1894.
[51] Turner, ES, *All Heaven in a Rage* (1964, republished 1992) 196.   [52] 12 October 1869.

first success was secured in 1869 with the introduction of a statutory closed season between 1 April and 1 August for seabirds.[53] The extent of the decimation being inflicted is evident from the remarks of Christopher Sykes, MP for the East Riding, who told the Commons that the decline in the number of seabirds was having a serious effect on three classes of his constituents: farmers, who were used to seeing the birds picking up grubs in the wake of the ploughboy; merchant seamen, who relied on the sound of the birds to warn when they were close to shore (he claimed that as the number of birds had declined, the instances of ships running aground at Flamborough Head had increased); and deep-sea fishermen, who located shoals of fish by seeing birds hovering above them.[54] By Acts passed in 1872, 1876, and 1880, the category of birds protected during the breeding season was extended to designated species of wild birds, wild fowl, and then all wild birds between the beginning of March and the end of July. In 1894, a further Wild Birds Protection Act empowered the Home Secretary to prohibit the taking or destroying of wild birds' eggs, either generally, or in relation to particular species or within a specific area; two years later, powers were provided to confiscate the nets and decoy birds used by bird catchers; and in 1902 the courts were given the power to confiscate birds and their eggs if they had been illegally obtained. As welcome as these measures were, their enforcement was difficult and, in part, prompted the establishment in 1889 of a Society for the Protection of Birds (SPB), which subsequently became a national organization and received a Royal Charter in 1904. While birds attracted such statutory attention, mammals were ignored, with the exception of the hare, whose population had dramatically declined because of the numbers being taken for food. The Hares Preservation Act 1892 therefore prohibited their sale between March and July but, curiously, it remained lawful to kill them during that period. Finally, as de Montmorency points out, there had been 'from very early times important and continual legislation on the subject of fish',[55] a tradition which continued during the latter part of the century. The Salmon Fishery Act 1861, for example, repealed and replaced more than twenty predecessors on the same subject and between 1860 and the end of the century thirteen further Acts were passed dealing with fish.

It was a mark of the degree to which attitudes had changed that in 1902, little more than thirty years after the first law to conserve seabirds had been introduced, de Montmorency was suggesting, in one of the most staid and respectable legal journals, that 'the protection of rare and harmless butterflies, moths, beetles, and other insects seems as legitimate an object of legislation as the protection of rare and indigenous birds'.[56]

Acceptance that it was legitimate for the State to employ the law to protect wildlife was extremely significant in laying down the foundations for today's body of legislation concerned to conserve native fauna and its habitats. It was, however,

---

[53] Sea Birds Preservation Act 1869.   [54] Parl Debs (series 3) vol 194, cols 404–405.
[55] de Montmorency, n 47 above, 39.   [56] ibid.

primarily concerned to preserve species populations, not the treatment of individual animals. In particular, it failed to address the situation whereby domestic animals were protected from the cruelty inherent in many traditional pastimes, but no equivalent measures had been introduced in relation to those living in the wild. This was unsurprising, in view of the fact that it was the political class and their social circle which participated in field sports, but the inconsistency did not go unremarked. For example, Edward Freeman, Professor of History at Oxford, observed in 1869 that although animal baiting and fighting had been generally proscribed, there remained 'the anomaly that other sports precisely the same in principle, sports which, on any moral theory, must stand or fall together with those I have just mentioned, are tolerated and honoured'. Thus, 'To chase a calf or a donkey either till it is torn in pieces or till it sinks from weariness, would be scouted as a cruel act. Do the same to a deer and it is a noble and royal sport.' Likewise, it was 'a legal crime to worry a cat', but to treat a hare in the same way 'is a gallant diversion', and, referring back to the parliamentary debates earlier in the century, he pointed to the fact that 'men who share Windham's tastes without Windham's consistency, men who would lift up their hands in horror at the wanton torture of a bull or a bear, deem no praises too high for the heroic sport which consists in the wanton torture of a fox'.[57]

E. Influence and Impact

(1) Respectability

Queen Victoria remained an active supporter of the RSPCA throughout her reign, and her involvement gave the cause of animal protection a degree of status and influence out of all proportion to its relative novelty, especially in the early years. In congratulating the RSPCA on its golden jubilee in 1874, she confirmed 'her warm interest in the success of the efforts which are being made here and abroad for the purpose of diminishing the cruelties practised on dumb animals', and expressed her 'horror' at 'the sufferings which the brute creation often undergo through the thoughtlessness of the ignorant, and she fears also sometimes from experiments in the pursuit of science',[58] a statement of some constitutional significance as it coincided with the growing public controversy which would lead ultimately to the Cruelty to Animals Act 1876. Thirteen years later, the Queen repeated similar sentiments in acknowledging the Society's congratulations upon her own jubilee, writing of her 'real pleasure' at 'the growth of more humane feeling towards the lower animals' and commending the RSPCA for its work: 'The labours of your

---

[57] 'The Morality of Field Sports', *The Fortnightly Review*, No 34 (new series), 1 October 1869, 353 at 356; see Ch 3 F(6), above.

[58] Letter sent to the President of the RSPCA, 10 June 1874, by command of the Queen, quoted by Fairholme and Pain, n 12 above, 93.

Society have done much to promote this moral progress; and, for the sake alike of human nature and of the happiness of the animal creation by which we are all surrounded, I trust that you will steadily persevere in your noble aims, in which you will have my warm and entire sympathy.'[59]

Such statements represented more than the formal niceties exchanged between monarch and her subjects. Victoria did not simply approve from a distance. She became actively involved by, for example, encouraging the RSPCA to take steps to promote the protection of cats,[60] challenge the worst practices associated with vivisection, and increase the protection for wild birds. More than this, she was prepared to lobby among opinion formers and politicians in an attempt to secure their support, to the extent that she has been described as 'a persistent thorn in the side of ministers', particularly in respect of animal experiments.[61] Ryder points out that she wrote to Joseph Lister encouraging him to oppose vivisection and, following publication of the Royal Commission's report in 1876, she encouraged the Prime Minister, Disraeli, to legislate against the practice. To another incumbent, Gladstone, her secretary wrote that the Queen 'had seen with pleasure' that he 'takes an interest in that dreadful subject of vivisection, in which she has done all she could', and went on to express the hope that he would 'take an opportunity of speaking strongly against a practice which is a disgrace to humanity and Christianity'.[62] Little wonder, then, that the President of the RSPCA told the annual meeting in 1886 that the Society did not have a more active member. 'Many things that escape less observant eyes attract her attention,' he said, 'and prove her to be a vigilant apostle of humanity.'[63]

In an age of deference, the RSPCA's association with the monarchy attracted the support of the rich and powerful; from 1834 until the 1920s, the Society's president was invariably a member of the aristocracy, and by the 1880s its status was underpinned by the endorsement of a host of well-connected patrons and vice-presidents drawn from royalty, the House of Lords, and the higher echelons of the church, so that it could be accurately described, in the words of the Prince of Wales, as 'one of the great philanthropic societies of this country'.[64] Interestingly, the RSPCA was not unique among animal protection organizations in attracting support from the well-connected; during the 1830s, the Association for Promoting Rational Humanity towards the Animal Creation, a small, short-lived organization with just over 200 members, nevertheless counted among them a duchess,

---

[59] Letter sent to the President of the RSPCA, 10 June 1874, by command of the Queen, quoted by Fairholme and Pain, n 12 above, 93.

[60] Victoria seems to have had a particular regard for cats. On her initiative, the RSPCA introduced a medal—the Queen's Medal—for those who gave it distinguished service. When the proposed design was submitted to the Queen for approval, she directed that a cat should be placed in the foreground, and sketched one on the design, reputedly commenting that it was time that the royal family did something to change the general contempt shown towards cats.

[61] French, n 19 above, 123.   [62] *Animal Revolution* (2nd edn, 2000) 107.

[63] Fairholme and Pain, n 12 above, 94–96.

[64] Said at the Society's annual meeting in 1880; quoted in Fairholme and Pain, ibid 98.

an earl, sundry other titled members of the aristocracy, and three bishops; the original patrons of the SSPCA included members of the nobility, aristocracy, and the church, its first president was the Lord Provost of Edinburgh, and numbered among its ten vice-presidents were seven knights (including two MPs) and a cleric; within ten years of its establishment, the president of Cobbe's Victoria Street Society was the Earl of Shaftesbury and its supporters included more than twenty titled vice-presidents, nine bishops, MPs, Lord Coleridge (the Lord Chief Justice), Cardinal Manning, Browning, and Tennyson.

(2) A model of the contemporary pressure group

In itself, the social status of those with whom the RSPCA was associated would have made it a force to be reckoned with, but so too did the professional manner in which it pursued its objectives under the guidance of John Colam, who acted as the Society's secretary between 1860 and 1905. Harrison is correct in emphasizing how adept the Society had become by the 1880s in mobilizing public opinion, promoting legislation, and deploying its 'steadily accumulated knowledge on animal questions, particularly in their legal aspects', which was used to inform the public, police, politicians, and others who had an interest in the subject.[65] The Society's evidence to the first Royal Commission on Vivisection, for example, amounted to almost 800 pages, and, three years previously, it had conducted an inspection of all London's 1,500 slaughterhouses in order to prepare a report on conditions to present to the Government.

The RSPCA had become 'wealthy, prestigious, politically influential, adept in courts of law, publicity conscious, and, most important, vigilant',[66] and its impact was apparent across a wide range of issues affecting animals. Indeed, one of its defining characteristics was, and still is, that it never became a single-issue pressure group. The Society actively supported the development and increased status of the veterinary profession and assisted in the campaign which led to the Veterinary Surgeons Act 1881 (although there were also tensions, particularly over what constituted cruelty, to the extent that the Society was not averse to prosecuting veterinarians in circumstances where, for example, it was the veterinarian's view that a horse could work and its inspectors thought that it should not).[67] It sought practical solutions to practical problems, becoming actively involved, for example, in developing the long-handled humane killer, which was introduced in 1906 and represented the first effective commercial alternative to slaughtering animals by means of the pole-axe (which depended entirely on the strength and skill of the slaughterman). And its zeal for campaigning was, of course, endless. In 1869, Colam itemized its agenda for reform in the first edition of the Society's journal, *Animal World*. This included: the erection of public abattoirs; more humane methods of slaughter; prohibition on the slow bleeding of calves; a ban on the

[65] *Peaceable Kingdom* (1982) 108.   [66] French, n 19 above, 46.
[67] For example, *Benford v Sims* [1898] 2 QB 641.

shearing of sheep in cold weather; abolition of dog muzzles; improved horse shoes; an end to the use of 'barbarous instruments of torture' in game preservation; discontinuance of pigeon-shooting clubs; a ban on the offering of rewards for the destruction of small birds; improvement in the construction of roads; abolition of the bearing rein; appropriate harness for draught animals; suppression of experiments on animals for science when accompanied by torture; anaesthetics for animals; improved laws for the protection of animals; and better treatment for cattle in transit.

The Society's operations formed a virtuous circle: drawing on its experience, it lobbied politicians for reform, brought forward detailed proposals for statutory change, publicized the terms of new legislation, and was actively involved in enforcing the law, as a result of which it identified further problems which it considered demanded action, which led it to make further representations for change, and so on.

There was nothing intrinsically novel in bringing problems to Parliament's attention; receiving grievances and considering redress was one of its traditional functions. What was new was the ruthless way in which the RSPCA mounted its campaigns. 'Faced with a problem,' observes Harrison, 'its almost instinctive response was to approach the powerful',[68] and the powerful took notice. Public opinion was both influenced and brought to bear on decision makers through petitions, letter writing, and the like; the Society always succeeded in having MPs among its supporters, who were kept fully briefed and could be relied upon to raise issues on the floor of the House, bring forward proposals, and actively support measures as they proceeded through Parliament; many of its supporters had offices in the corridors of power, while others enjoyed ready access to them and took the opportunity to persuade, cajole, and inform. Here, then, is the Victorian model of the contemporary pressure group. But the RSPCA did not stop at campaigning for change; through education and enforcement, it was also intimately involved in giving effect to the measures it was instrumental in securing.

(3) . . . and a precursor of a modern test case strategy

After the passing of Pease's Act in 1835, for example, the Society issued 25,000 abstracts of the legislation; following the 1854 Act, it circulated all police forces to draw their attention to the prohibition on the use of dogs for draught; by 1873, it had produced 100,000 copies of the legislation relating to wild birds; and from the 1860s onwards, it published, and revised as necessary, *Cruelty to Animals*, which provided details of the relevant law and examples of successful prosecutions. By this means, the Society equipped its supporters to police their local areas, to the extent that in London, according to *The Times*, 'thousands of sharp eyes made it impossible for anyone to put a galled horse to work'.[69] This active involvement of its members and supporters became increasingly effective as the RSPCA developed

---

[68] n 65 above, 105.   [69] 18 October 1860. A gall is a painful swelling or a sore caused by chafing.

into a national organization. The original focus of its activities had been almost exclusively on London, with occasional sorties by its inspectors into the provinces, but during the second half of the century, a concerted effort was made to establish a permanent presence throughout England and Wales by the formation of local branches coupled with an expansion in the inspectorate. The increase was slow at first—from 2 inspectors in 1838, the number increased to 5 in 1842 and 8 in 1855; by 1878 there were 48, 80 by 1886, and 120 in 1897. These developments were reflected in the number of prosecutions brought by the Society, which practically doubled each decade between 1830 and 1900:[70]

1830–9	1,357
1840–9	2,177
1850–9	3,862
1860–9	8,846
1870–9	23,767
1880–9	46,657
1890–9	71,657

The decision to pursue prosecutions was always taken by the centre, and they constituted an integral part of the RSPCA's campaigning strategy. It used the courts to establish precedents, to highlight the law's weaknesses as well as its strengths, to identify and publicize conduct towards animals that was no longer lawful, and to enhance its image and status, thereby encouraging further public support and contributions. Little wonder, then, that RE Boughton, speaking at the Society's annual meeting in 1844, described it as 'the handmaid—the support—the carriers into effect of the acts of the legislature';[71] in more modern parlance, by the end of the nineteenth century, the RSPCA could be regarded as, adopting Ritvo's phrase, 'a quasi-governmental institution'.[72]

(4) The charge of class bias

While such a self-appointed role undoubtedly enhanced its authority and influence, there were also disadvantages. The Society was vulnerable to the accusation that it was happy to harry and correct the lower classes in respect of their 'improper' behaviour, while ignoring the questionable practices of the upper classes. Field

---

[70] RSPCA 77th Annual Report, 1901, 166. The Scottish SPCA demonstrated a similar rate of expansion. Its earliest existing annual report is that for 1867. In 1875 it employed an 'inspector' and 5 'constables' who investigated 292 cases that year, of which 180 were lodged for prosecution. All the Society's staff were resident in Edinburgh, although they did visit other parts of Scotland (a separate organization, Glasgow and West of Scotland SPCA, had been formed in 1856). The first officer to be stationed outside Edinburgh was appointed to Perth in 1890. By 1901 the Society had 22 officers, 7 based in Edinburgh and the remainder stationed in towns the length of the country. Between them, they were investigating more than 1,200 cases annually. See further, SSPCA Annual Report 1939.

[71] RSPCA 18th Annual Report, 37.   [72] Ritvo, n 22 above, 145.

sports were one example of this phenomenon,[73] but so too was vivisection: 'Scientists, in their view, automatically belonged to a different moral category from drovers and omnibus drivers.'[74] It was a characteristic of the RSPCA which served to alienate some who were otherwise sympathetic to the cause of animal protection, such as John Stuart Mill, who wrote to the secretary in July 1868 complaining that 'it is thought necessary or desirable to limit the Society's operations to the offences committed by the uninfluential classes of society', while other activities, such as pigeon-shooting, which took place 'under the patronage and in the presence of the supposed elite of the higher classes' were ignored. 'This respect of persons,' Mill remarked, 'though it may be prudent, is too foreign to my opinions and feelings.'[75] In addition, there was evidence of an unattractive authoritarian tendency among the Society. 'The doctrine of the sacredness of alleged rights of the citizen, the domicile, and of private property', complained the 1895 annual report, 'is a British fetish, and is responsible for the closure of private places against Officers of the Society. A sealed door bars mines, slaughter houses, and laboratories.'[76]

Without question, much animal abuse went on in such places because they were not adequately accountable for the way in which they conducted their businesses, but that does not necessarily justify providing a private organization with the power to ride roughshod over fundamental freedoms and liberties. One wonders what would have been the reaction of the Society's membership if, for example, a trade union had on similar terms demanded access to their domestic servants or, indeed, an animal protection society to their sporting estates. A further consequence of the RSPCA's status was that, unlike the early days when it actively attracted those who wished to challenge the status quo, by the end of the century it alienated sympathizers with radical views; John Stuart Mill had distanced himself from the Society in 1868, it had lost Frances Power Cobbe and her supporters in the 1870s, and those who had decided views on the proper treatment of animals which went much further than was contemplated by the RSPCA, such as George Bernard Shaw, John Galsworthy, and Henry Salt, remained aloof; as Ryder concludes, 'its preoccupation with established respectability caused it to lose touch with the more progressive and inspirational elements in the animal welfare movement'.[77] Where it had initially been prepared to challenge the way in which animals were used, in such matters as animal baiting and fighting, and the use of dogs for draught, it was now more concerned to control and regulate. It had lost its progressive edge, in stark contrast to the anti-vivisection organizations which had sprung up, largely as a result of disillusionment with the RSPCA's position. What it lost in intellectual

---

[73] The RSPCA was not alone in attempting to control how others behaved towards animals, while condoning the field sports enjoyed by its patrons. The RSPB's position was to be 'strictly neutral on the question of the killing of game birds and legitimate sport of that character'; quoted in Turner, n 51 above, 178.

[74] Ritvo, n 22 above, 158.

[75] Fletcher, R (ed), *John Stuart Mill: A Logical Critique of Sociology* (1971) 416.

[76] Cited in Ritvo, n 22 above, 145.   [77] n 62 above, 100.

vigour, however, was compensated for in terms of practical achievement which was unsurpassed and, it must be acknowledged, due in large measure to its close association with the governing elite.

F. Into the Twentieth Century

(1) The Wild Animals in Captivity Protection Act 1900 and other legislation

Whatever criticism is made of the RSPCA, the fact is that it got results, and the first years of the twentieth century witnessed a burst of activity which significantly extended the statutory protection afforded to animals. Hitherto only domestic animals were protected from cruelty, which left wild animals kept in captivity vulnerable to abuse, especially performing animals and those kept in zoos and the travelling menageries which were fashionable at the time. The English courts had held that cocks and captive linnets trained as decoy birds were 'domestic animals' and therefore entitled to protection under the Prevention of Cruelty to Animals Acts,[78] but declined to accord the same status to rabbits which had been caught and kept for five days before being used for coursing, performing lions, or a tame seagull which would go to its owner when called, feed from her hand, and was used by her in her business as a photographer.[79] These decisions turned on an apparently inconsistent distinction being made between animals which were 'tamed' or 'subservient' and served 'some useful purpose for mankind', and those which were 'really wild animals in confinement, neither more nor less'. According to the courts, 'It is impossible to say that a wild animal kept in a cage becomes by the mere fact a domestic animal' and 'It cannot be contended that . . . it is sufficient merely to prove that the animal in question, being an animal which is ordinarily wild, on the particular occasion which is brought to the notice of the Court remained tame.'[80] This problem was addressed in 1900 (but not until 1909 in Scotland), when it was made an offence wantonly or unreasonably to cause, or permit to be caused, any unnecessary suffering to a captive, maimed, pinioned, or imprisoned animal, or cruelly to abuse, infuriate, tease, or terrify such an animal, or permit it to be so treated (although at the insistence of the House of Lords, hunting and coursing were expressly excluded).[81] In addition to its subject matter, three particular aspects of the Act represent significant further advances in the scope of

---

[78] *Budge v Parsons* (1863) QB 367 (3 B & S 382); *Colam v Pagett* (1883) 12 QBD 66. In Scotland, the High Court of Justiciary held in 1892 that cockfighting (except in a place kept for the purpose) was not illegal under the 1850 Act on the ground that the statute applied only to four-footed domestic animals, and not to fowls or poultry. Following representations from the Scottish SPCA, the Lord Advocate introduced amending legislation to confirm that protection extended to any game or fighting cock, or other domestic fowl or bird: Cruelty to Animals (Scotland) Act 1895.

[79] *Aplin v Porritt* [1893] 2 QB 57; *Harper v Marcks* [1894] 2 QB 319; *Yates v Higgins* [1896] 1 QB 166.

[80] *Harper v Marcks*, ibid 322 (Cave J); *Yates v Higgins*, ibid 168 (Vaughan Williams J).

[81] Wild Animals in Captivity Protection Act 1900. The Act was eventually extended to Scotland by the Wild Animals in Captivity Protection (Scotland) Act 1909.

animal protection legislation. First, it specified that an offence could be founded on an omission as well as an act of commission. Secondly, its ambit extended to any non-domestic animal 'of whatsoever kind or species', specifically including fish and reptiles, the first time the legislature had expressly recognized a direct duty to avoid cruelty to animals beyond the traditional boundary of mammals and birds. Thirdly, the inclusion of 'tease' and 'terrify' in the catalogue of prohibited conduct extended the statutory definition of cruelty to include mental as well as physical suffering.

In 1906, the police nationally were given responsibility to seize stray dogs and to keep them for at least seven days; they were also prohibited from passing on for use in vivisection those which were not claimed.[82] The Injured Animals Act 1907 represented a further triumph of animal protection over property rights by extending the power of the police under the previous Act of 1894 to order the destruction of animals without the consent of the owner. In addition to equines, the provision now applied to cattle, sheep, goats, and pigs, and could be discharged not only when such an animal was severely injured, but also in circumstances where it was so diseased or in such a poor physical condition that, in the opinion of a veterinary surgeon, it could not be removed without cruelty. Further legislation relating to wild birds was passed in 1902, 1904, and 1908, including a ban on the use of the dreadful pole-trap; statutory power was given to the Minister of Agriculture to make Orders for protecting poultry from unnecessary suffering during transit or while exposed for sale;[83] and regulation of the use and keeping of pit ponies underground was introduced, together with provision for the establishment of an, albeit inadequate, inspectorate.[84]

(2) The export trade in live horses

However, the issue which aroused the most public concern during this period was the export trade of worn-out horses to the Continent. The number of horses in Britain reached a peak during the early years of the century. It is estimated that the number rose from around 2 million in 1871 to 3.5 million in 1902. Ironically, the primary reason for the increase was the expansion of the railway, which enabled freight to be routinely moved around the country, but relied upon the support of horse-drawn transport to convey it to and from the railheads.[85] When horses came to the end of their working life they were virtually worthless in Britain, unlike Belgium and Holland, where they were bought to be slaughtered for human consumption. Accordingly, money could be made by shipping these unfortunate beasts across the Channel. The trade had started in earnest during the 1890s, and

---

[82] Dogs Act 1906.

[83] Poultry Act 1911. The Act was passed as a result of representations in Parliament that the exclusion of Scotland from the provisions of the Protection of Animals Act 1911 would result in poultry transported by train between England and Scotland being subject to different statutory regimes en route (notwithstanding that such an anomaly had, in fact, existed since 1849); HC Debs, 30 June 1911, cols 756–758.

[84] Coal Mines Act 1911, Sch 3.   [85] Harrison, n 65 above, 83; Clarke, P, *Hope and Glory* (1996) 112.

the RSPCA and SSPCA had been campaigning against it since 1895, during which time special inspectors had been posted on the roads to the ports and hundreds of convictions were secured for transporting horses in an unfit state. This failed to stop the trade, however, as the fines imposed were insignificant compared with the profit. The Board of Agriculture did make it illegal to convey from British ports any horse which, because of its condition, could not be transported without cruelty during the intended passage and on landing, but it proved to be 'practically a dead letter', with the result that the RSPCA continued to prosecute 'in thousands of cases for travelling unfit horses to the docks'.[86] The problem with enforcing this Order was an absence of formal arrangements for inspecting the horses before they embarked, and the docks, as private property, were closed to the RSPCA's inspectors. Following three unsuccessful attempts to introduce legislation to provide for veterinary inspection at the ports, the Diseases of Animals Act 1910 required that every horse intended for export should be examined by a veterinary surgeon appointed by the Board of Agriculture immediately before shipment. The veterinary inspector was required to certify in writing that the horse was capable of being conveyed and disembarked without cruelty. If he found a horse to be in such poor physical condition that it would be cruel to keep it alive, he was permitted to destroy it without the owner's consent. The threshold for export was subsequently tightened, so that the veterinary inspector could only certify a horse fit for export if he was satisfied that it was capable of being worked without suffering.[87] That was in 1914, but it was not implemented until 1919. In the meantime, countless horses were, like their human counterparts, to cross the Channel to endure immense suffering.

(3) The Protection of Animals Act 1911

Finally, largely on the initiative of George Greenwood, MP for Peterborough, the existing anti-cruelty legislation applying to England, Wales, and Ireland was consolidated, clarified, and extended by the Protection of Animals Act 1911. Greenwood took a keen interest in animal protection matters; he had been at the forefront of the campaign in Parliament to end the horse trade to Belgium, argued for an extension of the Geneva Convention to include veterinary surgeons to enable them to treat horses injured in battle, served as a council member of the RSPCA, and was an early proponent of the now common practice of soliciting information from government on the treatment of animals by means of Parliamentary Questions.[88] The Act made it an offence cruelly to beat, kick, ill-treat, override, over-drive, overload, torture, infuriate, or terrify any domestic or captive animal, or wantonly or unreasonably to do or omit to do any act which caused such an animal unnecessary suffering. Those who caused or procured such treatment were also liable under the Act and, for these purposes, it was expressly

---

[86] Exportation of Horses Order 1898; Fairholme and Pain, n 12 above, 245.
[87] Exportation of Horses Act 1914.   [88] Ryder, n 62 above, 127.

provided that an owner should be deemed to have permitted cruelty if he had failed to exercise reasonable care and supervision to prevent it. The provisions relating to transport, fighting, and baiting, and the administration of poisonous or injurious drugs or substances, were restated, and it was made an offence to subject an animal to any operation performed without due care and attention. The regulation of knackers' premises, the duty to ensure the provision of food and water for impounded animals, the restrictions on the sale and use of poisoned grain and other edible matter, the prohibition on the use of dogs for draught on the public highway, and the power for a constable to order the destruction of an injured animal on the advice of a veterinary surgeon, were all re-enacted. Additionally, spring traps for catching hares and rabbits were to be inspected at least once a day. Lastly, while coursing or hunting a captive animal remained lawful, the use of an animal released in an injured, mutilated, or exhausted condition might now lead to prosecution.

Upon the conviction of the owner of an animal, the courts were provided with two important new powers to protect the victims from further suffering; if they were satisfied that it would be cruel to keep the animal alive, they could order its destruction. Alternatively, if there was evidence that it was likely to be exposed to further cruelty at the hands of its owner, they could confiscate the animal and dispose of it as they saw fit (which generally meant handing it over to an animal protection organization for rehoming). The maximum penalty for cruelty was also increased to a fine of twenty-five pounds and/or six months' imprisonment, but this allowed the accused the right to trial by jury. Unfortunately, because of the number of prosecutions arising from the horse trade, there were parts of the country where it was virtually impossible to empanel a jury which did not include members who had themselves been prosecuted for cruelty, or had personal knowledge of someone who had. Because of the obstacle this created to gaining convictions, the penalties were reduced the following year to a maximum fine of twenty-five pounds and/or three months' imprisonment, with the result that all cases returned to the exclusive jurisdiction of the magistrates' courts.[89] Similar provisions to those contained in the 1911 Act were introduced in Scotland the following year.[90]

The 1911 Act is something of a dichotomy. On the one hand, it represents continuity: the provisions which were consolidated into it reflect the development of animal protection legislation throughout the nineteenth century, dating back to Martin's original Act of 1822; and it continues to be the basis of the contemporary legislative framework in England and Wales. On the other, it can be seen as a break with what had gone before, in the sense that between 1822 and 1911 the degree and extent of protection provided by the law steadily increased in response to well-organized lobbying. After the First World War, however, the momentum for

---

[89] Protection of Animals Act (1911) Amendment Act 1912.
[90] Protection of Animals (Scotland) Act 1912.

reform was lost for the best part of fifty years. There were some positive innovations during the period, in response to particular problems: for example, mechanical stunning of cattle became mandatory; the courts were given additional
sanctions in cases of cruelty; and a series of licensing regimes was introduced in
respect of performing animals, pet shops, and riding and dog breeding establishments. But overall there was little evidence of direction and none of urgency. 'What
a strange era it was,' comments Ryder, 'moving from the sense of progress and confidence of the late Victorian and Edwardian periods through the First World War
to stagnation beyond the Second.' Attitudes towards animals, he suggests, changed
'from strong sentiment and idealism to excessive caution, practicality and a decline
of serious interest'.[91] It would not be until the second half of the 1960s that the
treatment of animals would re-emerge as a significant political and legal issue.

G. The Single Best Idea that Anyone Has Ever Had?

Before concluding this historical overview, it is essential to consider the most profound and far-reaching development during the course of the nineteenth century
concerning our understanding of the world and the position of humans within it.
Indeed, it has been described by one respected commentator as 'the single best idea
that anyone has ever had'.[92] Namely, the elaboration by Charles Darwin in *The
Origin of Species* of a theory of evolution by means of mutability, transmutation,
and natural selection.

The notion of natural selection was not in itself new. In Chapter 2, mention was
made that scientists such as Linnaeus, Erasmus Darwin, and Lamark had put forward
a similar idea in the eighteenth century, and others had continued to pursue this line
of thinking. Indeed, Darwin was induced to make his own theory public by the knowledge that the Welsh naturalist and collector, Alfred Russel Wallace, working in
south-east Asia, had independently come to a similar conclusion and was about to
publish. Darwin's singular achievement, however, was 'to weave an evolutionary
hypothesis into an explanatory fabric composed of literally thousands of hard-won
and often surprising facts about nature', and thereby to do 'such a monumental job of
clarifying the idea, and tying it down so it would never again float away'.[93]

The reason that Darwin's work has not been discussed earlier in this narrative is
that it had little immediate effect on public attitudes towards the treatment of animals. The ramifications of evolution are so radical, and pose such a threat to the
traditional view of the human condition, that society has still to come fully to
terms with its implications. It is little wonder, then, that our Victorian predecessors
failed to grasp all of its consequences. There were also other, practical, reasons why
its repercussions for the relationship between humans and other species were
overlooked.

---

[91] n 62 above, 145.   [92] Dennett, DC, *Darwin's Dangerous Idea* (1996) 21.   [93] ibid 33.

First, Darwin was deliberately circumspect in discussing human evolution in *Origins*. 'I think I shall avoid the whole subject, as so surrounded with prejudices,' he wrote while preparing the manuscript, 'though I fully admit that it is the highest & most interesting problem for the naturalist.'[94] Having said that, the implication was clear for those who thought about it. The 'truly wonderful fact' that 'all animals and all plants throughout all time and space should be related to each other', for example, raised the question of human origins, as did Darwin's assertion that 'the community of descent is the hidden bond which naturalists have been unconsciously seeking, and not some unknown plan of creation'.[95] The book therefore 'raised questions fundamental to the life of humankind without making humankind the centre of its enquiry'.[96] According to Darwin himself: 'During many years I collected notes on the origin or descent of man, without any intention of publishing on the subject, but rather with the determination not to publish, as I thought that I should thus only add to the prejudices against my views. It seemed to me sufficient to indicate in the first edition of my "Origin of Species", that by this work "light would be thrown on the origin of man and his history".'[97] It was not until 1871, by which time he was confident that 'The great principle of evolution stands up clear and firm',[98] that Darwin confronted the issue directly. In *The Descent of Man*, he stated unequivocally that 'man bears in his bodily structure clear traces of his descent from some lower form'.[99] Moreover, there was 'a crowd of analogous facts' which 'all point in the plainest manner to the conclusion that man is the co-descendant with other mammals of a common progenitor'.[100] With regard to 'man and all other vertebrate animals,' he asserted,

we ought frankly to admit their community of descent. . . . It is only our natural prejudice, and that arrogance which made our forefathers declare that they were descended from demi-gods, which leads us to demur this conclusion. But the time will before long come, when it will be thought wonderful that naturalists, who were well acquainted with the comparative structure and development of man and other mammals, should have believed that each was the work of a separate act of creation.[101]

Secondly, the single most important controversy concerning the use of animals during the second half of the nineteenth century concerned vivisection, and Darwin was deeply involved in 'master-minding a rear-guard action against the rising anti-vivisectionist movement'.[102] He was instrumental in producing the Bill in 1875 intended to counter that drawn up by Cobbe and her supporters. Indeed, Darwin's son-in-law, RB Litchfield, a lawyer, was largely responsible for its drafting. It was the presentation of this Bill which led directly to the establishment of the

---

[94] Quoted in Desmond, A and Moore, J, *Darwin* (1992) 462.
[95] Darwin, C, *The Origin of Species* (1859; 1996 edn) 105–106 and 340.   [96] ibid ix.
[97] Darwin, C, *The Descent of Man* (1871; 2nd edn 1874) 1. The statement quoted by Darwin is in the third from last paragraph of *Origins*, and in that context its meaning and implications are not nearly so explicit as the form of this later citation suggests.
[98] ibid 607.   [99] ibid 65.   [100] ibid 607.   [101] ibid 25.
[102] Desmond and Moore, n 94 above, 615.

Royal Commission, before which Darwin gave evidence in an attempt to counter the damaging testimony of Emanuel Klein: 'Ten minutes from him was worth two hours of risky vivisectionist apologias.'[103] Although he had never experimented on live animals himself, Darwin thought physiology was 'sure sooner, or more probably later, greatly to benefit mankind', but it could 'progress only by experiments on living animals'. He described the proposal to limit research by legislation as 'puerile' and warned that, if it succeeded, physiology in England 'will languish or quite cease'.[104] It is not surprising, therefore, that neither Darwin nor his work were regarded by contemporaries as being sympathetic to the way in which animals were to be treated. Cobbe remarked that he 'eventually became the centre of an adoring *clique* of vivisectors . . . .standing forth before all Europe as an advocate of vivisection'.[105] But the reality was more complicated. Darwin was deeply concerned about animal suffering. His son, Francis, recalled that 'The two subjects which moved my father perhaps more strongly than any others were cruelty to animals and slavery. His detestation of both was intense, and his indignation was overpowering in case of any levity or want of feeling on these matters.'[106] In *The Descent of Man*, Darwin himself described 'humanity to the lower animals' to be not only a 'virtue', but 'one of the noblest with which man is endowed', which 'seems to arise incidentally from our sympathies becoming more tender and more widely diffused, until they are extended to all sentient beings'. Hence, 'As soon as this virtue is honoured and practised by some few men', he observed, it 'spreads through instruction and example to the young, and eventually becomes incorporated in public opinion'.[107] In the final paragraph of the same work, Darwin specifically included among man's 'noble qualities' his 'benevolence which extends not only to other men but to the humblest living creature'.[108] His support for vivisection was intended to 'protect animals, and at the same time not injure physiology',[109] but it was not unqualified. 'You ask me about vivisection', he responded to one enquirer, 'I quite agree that it is justifiable for real investigations on physiology; but not for mere damnable and detestable curiosity. It is a subject which makes me sick with horror, so I will not say another word about it, else I shall not sleep tonight.'[110] In *Descent* he wrote, 'every one has heard of the dog suffering under vivisection, who licked the hand of the operator; this man, unless the operation was fully justified by an increase of our knowledge, or unless he had a heart of stone, must have felt remorse to the last hour of his life'.[111] On another occasion, he indicated that he would 'gladly punish severely any one who operated on an animal not rendered insensible, if the experiment made this possible'.[112] At a practical level, in 1874 he offered

[103] ibid 618.
[104] Darwin, F (ed), *The Life and Letters of Charles Darwin* (1888) iii, 202–203; quoted in Rachels, J, *Created From Animals* (1990) 216.
[105] Cobbe, FP, *Life of Francis Power Cobbe* (1894) ii, 449; quoted in Rachels, ibid 215.
[106] Quoted in Clark, RW, *The Survival of Charles Darwin* (1984) 76.
[107] Darwin, C, n 97 above, 123.   [108] ibid 619.
[109] Darwin, F (1888) iii, 204; quoted in Rachels, n 104 above, 214.   [110] ibid.
[111] Darwin, C, n 97 above, 70.   [112] Darwin, F (1888); quoted in Rachels, n 104 above, 216.

the RSPCA fifty pounds as a prize for anyone who could invent a humane device for controlling rabbits.[113]

Whatever the perception by Darwin's contemporaries of his attitude towards animals, the argument that all living things had evolved posed a fundamental challenge to the traditional relationship between humans and other species, something that both he and Wallace appreciated. First, it was incompatible with animals existing solely for human benefit and exploitation. Wallace, overcome by the beauty of the King Bird of Paradise (*Paradisea regia*) he had encountered on a remote island in Malay, wrote:

I thought of the long ages of the past, during which successive generations of this little creature had run their course—year by year being born, and living and dying amid these dark and gloomy woods, with no intelligent eye to gaze upon their loveliness—to all appearance such a wanton waste of beauty. . . . This consideration must surely tell us that all living things were *not* made for man. Many of them have no relation to him. The cycle of their existence has gone on independently of his, and is disturbed or broken by every advance in man's intellectual development; and their happiness and enjoyments, their loves and hates, their struggles for existence, their vigorous life and early death, would seem to be immediately related to their own well-being and perpetuation alone, limited only by the equal well-being and perpetuation of the numberless other organisms with which each is more or less intimately connected.[114]

Coupled with this fundamental change to the traditional orthodoxy was the loss of any sense of divine design. The assumption that animals had been 'custom-built by the Creator to carry out their specific purposes in life', including the service of man, was undermined; instead, 'All at once, humans, animals, plants and other organisms were flung together in the same boat, driven onwards by the inexorable pressure of natural selection.'[115]

Secondly, it was an inevitable consequence that, far from being separate and distinct from 'animals', humans were animals too: 'Man in his arrogance thinks himself a great work worthy the imposition of deity', Darwin observed as early as 1838, 'More humble and I think truer to consider him created from animals.'[116] Not only did this challenge the traditional status of man, it also followed that attributes which had been assumed exclusive to humans, such as intelligence, may well be shared by other species, albeit in a less developed form. 'To maintain, independently of any direct evidence, that no animal during the course of ages has progressed in intellect or other mental faculties', he pointed out, 'is to beg the question of the evolution of species.'[117] Darwin specifically turned his attention to these issues in *The Descent of Man*, arguing that:

---

[113] Moss, A W, *Valiant Crusade. The History of the RSPCA* (1961) 146–147.

[114] Wallace, AR, *The Malay Archipelago* (1869; 1986 edn) 448 and 449 (italics in the original).

[115] Serpell, J, *In the Company of Animals* (1996) 165.

[116] Barrett, PH et al (eds), *Charles Darwin's Notebooks, 1836–1844* (1987) 300; quoted in Rachels, n 104 above, 1.

[117] Darwin, C, n 97 above, 81.

there is no fundamental difference between man and the higher animals in their mental faculties. . . . [T]he lower animals, like man, manifestly feel pleasure and pain, happiness and misery. . . . The fact that the lower animals are excited by the same emotions as ourselves is so well established, that it will not be necessary to weary the reader by many details. . . . There can be no doubt that the difference between the mind of the lowest man and that of the highest animal is immense. . . . Nevertheless the difference in mind between man and the higher animals, great as it is, certainly is one of degree and not of kind. We have seen that the senses and intuitions, the various emotions and faculties, such as love, memory, attention, curiosity, imitation, reason, &c, of which man boasts, may be found in an incipient, or even sometimes in a well-developed condition, in the lower animals.

And he went on to suggest it seemed 'extremely doubtful' that 'certain high mental powers, such as the formation of general concepts, self-consciousness, &c, were absolutely peculiar to man'.[118]

Clearly, such a view of the nature and capacities of other species poses a fundamental challenge to the traditional view of their moral status and the nature of our duties towards them. It is an issue that scientists and policy makers have only recently begun to confront; gradually, hesitantly, the consequences are now beginning to be reflected in the law. Not before time. Darwin's dictum that 'Animals, whom we have made our slaves, we do not like to consider our equal'[119] is still too widely reflected in social and official attitudes towards the treatment of other species.

H. Conclusion

By the outbreak of the First World War, there had developed in Britain a complex and wide-ranging legislative regime, built up during the course of less than a century. Domestic and captive mammals, birds, reptiles, and fish were all protected from cruel treatment; the perpetrator, those responsible for his conduct, and, if different, the owner of the animal, were all subject to prosecution; the law now focused on the outcome of the alleged offence by reference to the effect it had on the animal, rather than being exclusively concerned with the behaviour and character of the accused; liability could arise from omissions as well as acts of commission; and the law was concerned with both mental and physical suffering. Animals in a wide range of circumstances—domestic, commercial, entertainment, transit, export, laboratories, in the wild—benefited from some degree of protection. The promotion of animal health and the control of disease had become a high priority, and the law had begun to regulate those whose work brought them into contact with animals, most notably the veterinary profession. Taken together, these developments constituted a revolution in the State's attitude to other species. When 'kindness towards animals . . . embodies itself in laws which fine and imprison a

---

[118] ibid 66, 69, 125, and 126. [119] Barrett et al, n 116 above, 328.

man for using what had been held time out of mind to be his rights over his own property,' observed Edward Nicholson in 1879, 'it is plain that we have already been silently recognizing that *some* animals at least have *some* rights. If these laws have not been founded on such a silent recognition, they are unwarrantable curbs on the rights of *men*.'[120]

The courts did not go this far; for the most part they continued to endorse legal intervention to prevent cruelty on the ground that it was a means of improving the human character: 'constant familiarity with unnecessary torture to and abuse of dumb animals cannot fail by degrees to brutalize and harden all who are concerned in or witness the miseries of the sufferers', observed Hawkins J, a consequence which was 'to be scrupulously avoided in the best interests of civilized society'. Similarly, Chitty J asserted, 'Cruelty is degrading to man; and a society for the suppression of cruelty to the lower animals . . . has for its object, not merely the protection of the animals themselves, but the advancement of morals and education among men.'[121] The protection of animals was no longer regarded as eccentric, but was seen in an entirely positive light, as tending 'to promote and encourage kindness towards them, to discourage cruelty, and to ameliorate the condition of the brute creation, and thus to stimulate humane and generous sentiments in man towards the lower animals, and by these means promote feelings of humanity and morality generally, repress brutality, and thus elevate the human race'.[122] There were, however, judges who acknowledged that legal protection amounted to something more; namely, a growing recognition that man owed to animals a direct moral duty to minimize their suffering. 'The lower animals', said Dowse B, 'are not to be entirely subordinated to man.' Accordingly, 'If men have their rights in respect of these animals they also have their duties . . . Most people—at least those not entirely given over to selfishness—are agreed that the lower animals should be taken due care of, treated with kindness, and guarded against the wanton or purposeless abuse of man.'[123]

The story of Britain's changing attitudes towards animals is, in itself, a fascinating case study in legal and social history, but an appreciation of the background is also essential for understanding the contemporary law. First, many aspects of the substantive law have their origins in the Victorian era. Secondly, the characteristics of the legal framework were established during that period: the ad hoc nature of much of the legislation, enacted in response to particular issues, often on the initiative of an individual Member of Parliament rather than the Government; the importance of lobbying to secure change; responsibility for enforcement of the criminal law shared between public authorities and charitable organizations; the practice of defining the statutory meaning of 'animal' differently depending upon the context; the enactment of separate legislation and varying degrees of protection in relation

---

[120] Nicholson, EB, *The Rights of an Animal* (1879) 16 (italics in the original).
[121] *Ford v Wiley* (1889) 23 QBD 203, 225; *Re Foveaux* [1895] 2 Ch 501, 507.
[122] *Re Wedgewood* [1915] 1 Ch 113, 122, CA (Swinfen Eady LJ).
[123] *Brady v McArdle* (1884) 15 Cox C C 516, 522–523.

to the constituent parts of the United Kingdom; responsibility for animal protection falling to a number of government departments; and administrative responsibilities assumed by the State such as licensing, inspection, regulation, and control. The form of animal protection legislation at the beginning of the twenty-first century remains rooted in that of the nineteenth. As with so many areas of the law, it is only possible to comprehend the present if one has some knowledge of the past.

Part C

The Legal and Political Context

5

The Continuing Need for Legal Regulation

A. The Legal Status of Animals

(1) At common law

From its inception in 1822, the protection of animals by the State developed steadily during the course of the nineteenth century, so that by 1914 there was in place in Britain an extensive and sophisticated regulatory regime. It is important to appreciate, however, that while this legislation imposed restrictions on how animals could be treated, none of it—nor, indeed, any enacted subsequently—changed the traditional legal status accorded to animals by the courts.

Parliament's enthusiasm for passing voluminous amounts of wide-ranging legislation, applicable throughout the country, did not develop to any appreciable extent until the end of the eighteenth century.[1] Previously, in the absence of relevant statutory provisions, it was left to the courts to decide upon the many important aspects of daily life which came before them by application of the common law.[2] Historically, trials concerning animals generally arose from disagreements over ownership, or the rights and liabilities which might ensue from ownership.[3] It is therefore not surprising that both English and Scottish common

---

[1] The only significant body of legislation relating to animals which pre-dated this period were the so-called Game Laws. In England, 53 principal statutes were passed between 1671 and 1831 concerned with game, deer stealing, and poaching. These largely reserved the right to take game to the landowning class. In addition, through the powers this legislation gave to their gamekeepers, it enabled that same class to disarm and control the movement of the local populace: Gilmour, I, *Riots, Risings and Revolution. Governance and Violence in Eighteenth-Century England* (1992) Ch 9.

[2] This term simply refers to those legal principles and rules which have been (and continue to be) created and developed by the senior judiciary, as distinct from law enacted by Parliament. Both the common law and legislation are equally binding on those who fall within their province but, if they conflict, the legislative provisions prevail.

[3] There was no equivalent in England, Scotland, or Wales of the curious practice prevalent up to the late sixteenth century in continental Europe, especially France, of holding animals criminally responsible for

law defined the legal status of animals by reference to their standing as property. Hence, the courts distinguished between, on the one hand, animals which were domesticated or tamed, and could therefore be said to belong to someone, and those which were wild, and were owned by no one.[4] 'In such as are tame and domestic, (as horses, kine [cows], sheep, poultry, and the like) a man may have as absolute a property as in any inanimate beings,' wrote the eighteenth-century jurist, William Blackstone, 'because these continue perpetually in his occupation, and will not stray from his house or person, unless by accident or fraudulent entitlement, in either of which case the owner does not lose his property.' It followed that stealing, or forcibly abducting, such property amounted to a felony, 'for these are things of intrinsic value, serving for the food of man, or else for the uses of husbandry'.[5] In contrast, a person could not own absolutely a wild animal, although he might have qualified (that is, temporary) property in it where, for example, the creature had been lawfully taken, tamed, or reclaimed, but his property rights would be lost if the animal was released, escaped, or reverted to the wild.[6] Similarly, young wild animals were regarded as belonging to the person on whose land they were born, but only until such time as they were old enough to leave of their own accord; and a landowner had the right to hunt, take, or kill wild animals while they remained on his land.[7]

their actions. This could involve a full-scale trial, at which the case against the accused animal, which would be legally represented, was heard and adjudicated upon. If found to be guilty, it would be formally sentenced, up to and including an order that it be executed. Such a view of the culpability of other species strikes one as bizarre in any circumstances, but it seems especially so when considered in the context of the traditional attitude of the Roman Catholic Church to the moral status of animals. See further, Evans, EP, *The Criminal Prosecution and Capital Punishment of Animals* (1906).

[4] According to the seventeenth-century political philosopher, John Locke, animals in their original state 'belong to Mankind in common, as they are produced by the spontaneous hand of Nature; and no body has originally a private Dominion, exclusive of the rest of Mankind, in any of them'. However, if, as he believed, animals had been 'given for the use of Men', Locke recognized that 'there must of necessity be a means *to appropriate* them some way or other before they can be of any use, or at all beneficial, to any particular Man'. This was accomplished, he suggested, when a person removed an animal 'out of the State that Nature hath provided and left it in'. By so doing, 'he hath mixed his *Labour* with, and joyned [*sic*] to it something that is his own, and thereby makes it his *Property*'. By his efforts, man could assume charge of animals and, in consequence, alter their legal status: ''tis allowed to be his goods who hath bestowed his labour upon it': *Two Treatises on Government* (1690; 1964 edn) Book II, paras 26, 27, and 30 (italics in the original).

[5] *Commentaries on the Laws of England* (1765–1769; 1979 edn) Book II, Ch 25, 390.

[6] *Case of Swans* (1592) 77 ER 435; *Blades v Higgs* (1865) 11 HL Cas 621. According to Blackstone, 'once they escape from [a person's] custody, or he voluntarily abandons the use of them', wild animals 'return to the common stock, and any man has an equal right to seize and enjoy them afterwards'. A reclaimed wild animal is one which man has placed under some restriction. This may be total, such as when it is confined in a cage. Alternatively, it may be partial, where the animal is allowed a degree of freedom: 'my tame hawk that is pursuing his quarry in my presence, though he is at liberty to go where he pleases, is nevertheless my property', wrote Blackstone. 'So are my pigeons, that are flying at a distance from their home (especially of the carrier kind) and likewise the deer that is chased out of my forest, and is instantly pursued by the keeper or forester; all of which remain in my possession, and I still preserve my qualified property in them. But if they stray without my knowledge, and do not return in the usual manner, it is then lawful for any stranger to take them': ibid Book II, Ch 1, 14 and Ch 25, 392.

[7] *Sutton v Moody* (1697) 91 ER 1063.

The extent to which the legal status of animals was defined by reference to their monetary worth to the owner is illustrated by the fact that traditionally only those domesticated for draught or food were regarded as of sufficient value to be the subject of larceny (theft). In respect of other animals, such as those kept as pets, the owner might be able to recover compensation if they were wrongfully taken, but the courts would not hold the perpetrator criminally liable.[8] Animals 'only kept for pleasure, curiosity, or whim, as dogs, bears, cats, apes, parrots, and singing birds', were to be regarded differently, explained Blackstone, 'because their value is not intrinsic, but depending only on the caprice of the owner'.[9]

For its part, then, the common law was concerned with animals only in so far as they constituted property, and the very minimal protection against abuse which it provided originated entirely in the importance the courts attached to safeguarding the inviolability of a person's possessions; there was no regard for an animal's inherent needs. Accordingly, the owner of an animal might bring proceedings against a third party who had injured or abused it, on the basis that such conduct had reduced the animal's value, but the owner himself could treat it howsoever he pleased, and authorize his employees likewise, in exactly the same way that he could choose to do whatever he wished with his inanimate property. There were no constraints on the way horses were harnessed or saddled; no limit to the distance or speed they were expected to travel; no restrictions on the loads they were made to pull. Livestock were similarly unprotected in respect of the way they were kept, the manner in which they were driven to market, and their treatment at slaughter. On the same principle, wild animals, with no permanent property interest for the courts to protect, were even more vulnerable.

(2) Under statute

It was exactly this freedom to abuse, bestowed on animal owners by the common law, which the early campaigners sought to fetter. 'Divest property of the usurped and fictitious addition to its right', declared John Lawrence at the beginning of the nineteenth century, 'and you have the means of protecting animals and securing the dearest interests of morality.'[10] In the meantime, those who were concerned about their treatment were powerless to prevent cruelty: 'Nothing is more notorious than that it is not only useless, but dangerous, to poor suffering animals, to reprove their oppressors, or to threaten them with punishment', Lord Erskine told the House of Lords in 1809. 'The general answer, with the addition of bitter oaths and increased cruelty, is, What is that to you?—If the offender be a servant, he curses you, and asks if you are his master? and if he be the master himself, he tells you that the animal is his own.'[11] It was this 'defect in the law',[12] as he described it, which led Erskine, like Lawrence, to conclude that legislative

---

[8] *Anon* (undated) 1 Hale PC 512; *Anon* (1527) 145 ER 130.   [9] n 5 above, Book II, Ch 25, 393.
[10] 'On the Rights of Beasts' (1802) in Nicholson, EB, *The Rights of an Animal* (1879) 86.
[11] Parl Debs vol 14, col 554 (15 May 1809).   [12] ibid.

intervention was necessary in order to regulate the treatment of animals by their owners. This represented a major change in principle to that reflected in the common law, and the fact that he and Martin eventually succeeded in securing a degree of statutory protection in 1822 was a remarkable achievement. It is too easy from this distance, when the principle of such legislation is well established, to overlook the enormity of what they accomplished in persuading Parliament to make cruelty to animals a criminal offence. Criminal liability is, after all, 'the strongest formal condemnation that society can inflict'.[13]

The effect of the 1822 Act, together with the significant and sophisticated body of protective legislation developed subsequently, has been to qualify the common law freedom which allowed humans, especially owners and those acting under their authority, to treat other species in whatever way they saw fit. This explains why the nature of statutory protection has traditionally been negative in character, proscribing what may *not* be done to an animal, rather than imposing positive duties as to how it should be treated. These measures have not, however, had the effect of fundamentally altering the traditional legal status of animals.[14] Rather, protective legislation regulates their treatment against the backdrop of the common law's traditional principles; and wherever these are not superseded by legislation, they continue to apply. For example, because legislation does not in the main protect an animal's life, the owner retains complete discretion to decide for himself whether it should live or die. *Legal regulation of the way in which animals are treated therefore continues to be essential in order to offset the otherwise unconstrained property rights of the owner under common law.*

(3) Should the legal status of animals be changed?

It has been argued that animals can never gain adequate protection under the law without a fundamental reappraisal of this legal status. For example, according to the American lawyer, Gary Francione, because their 'interests are evaluated against this status as property, the outcome is almost certain: people win and animals lose'.[15] He takes the view that, although an animal's treatment by its owner 'may ostensibly be limited by anticruelty laws', property rights are 'paramount in

---

[13] Ashworth, A, *Principles of Criminal Law* (3rd edn, 1999) 1.

[14] Statute continues to reflect the law's traditional differentiation of animals based on ownership. The basis of legal protection in Britain, the Protection of Animals Act 1911 and the Protection of Animals (Scotland) Act 1912, apply only to domestic and captive animals. Section 4(4) of the Theft Act 1968 provides that a wild animal which has not been tamed or ordinarily kept in captivity cannot be stolen unless it has been or is being taken into the possession of another person, and under the Criminal Damage Act 1971 (which makes it an offence without lawful excuse to destroy or damage property of another) domestic animals are included in the definition of 'property' together with wild animals which have been tamed or are ordinarily kept in captivity, and other wild animals if, but only if, they have been reduced into possession which has not been lost or abandoned (ss 1 and 10(1)(a)).

[15] *Animals, Property and the Law* (1995) 11. See also, Tannenbaum, J, 'Animals and the Law: Property, Cruelty, Rights' (1995) 62 *Social Research* 539; Kelch, TG, 'Toward a Non-Property Status for Animals' [1998] New York University Environmental Law Journal 531; Favre, D, 'Equitable Self-Ownership for Animals' (2000) 50 Duke Law Journal 473.

determining the ambit of protection accorded to animals by law'.[16] 'If we say that an animal is property,' he declares, 'we mean that the animal is to be treated under the law primarily (if not exclusively) as a means to human ends, and not as an end in herself.'[17]

It is certainly the case that animals' status as property does have at least six detrimental consequences. First, in the absence of relevant protective legislation, it allows the owner of a domestic or captive animal complete autonomy to decide for himself how it is to be treated, including whether it should be killed. Secondly, a similar principle applies to wild animals, except that *anyone* may benefit from the same impunity. Thirdly, it can place a considerable onus on those who wish to secure greater legislative protection to justify further interference by the State with property rights. Fourthly, in the absence of a conviction for cruelty, it imposes a barrier to empowering a third party to remove and dispose of animals which are being kept in situations which compromise their welfare.[18] Fifthly, it undoubtedly colours attitudes towards animals. This is particularly so with regard to those kept for commercial purposes, which are too readily considered to be just another commodity, and threats to their welfare as the inevitable consequence of competitive pressures and business imperatives. Finally, as the European Convention on Human Rights provides particular protection for owners to enjoy their property, its incorporation into British law by virtue of the Human Rights Act 1998 has the potential detrimentally to affect the protection of animals in some circumstances. Those opposed to a proposed ban on fur farming and hunting with dogs have questioned, for example, whether such action is compatible with the Convention.[19]

Taken together, these are significant drawbacks. Whether they would necessarily be overcome by changing the status of animals is, however, open to question. While the position of those affected could, potentially, be significantly improved if there were to be, in Francione's words, 'a recognition that at least some animals may be said to possess rights that are not subject to abrogation merely because humans will benefit from that abrogation', it is important to recognize that rights are seldom absolute. Where the application of one right is incompatible with that of another, something has to give. Francione defines a right as 'a type of protection that does not evaporate in the face of consequential considerations',[20] but disputes arising from conflicting rights are as often as not determined by recourse to consequences, even though the outcome may be presented as the application of principle. Leaving aside the difficult question of which animals would be accorded what rights, it follows that it is by no means clear that the concept of rights is the panacea for animals that is often suggested.

Furthermore, although in theory it may be technically accurate to say that, as long as animals have the status of property, their interests 'may *always* be sacrificed',[21] this has not prevented the imposition of important and far-reaching legal

---

[16] ibid 24. [17] ibid 46. [18] See Ch 14, s G(2) and Ch 14, s G(3) below.
[19] See further, Ch 6, s J(5) below. [20] n 15 above, 114. [21] ibid 106 (italics in original).

constraints to protect at least some of their interests. Similarly, it is surely an over-statement to assert that, because the law requires animals' interests to be balanced against human interests, 'in the light of the status of animals as property, this is a balance performed on a rigged scale: virtually every human use of animals is regarded as "significant" (i.e. more significant than the animals' interest in not being so used) because the desires of human property owners always trump the interests of the animal'.[22] It is certainly the case that few uses are prohibited out-right, but the law intervenes to provide a significant degree of legal regulation as to *how* practices which are lawful may be carried on. In consequence, although their traditional legal status has remained unaltered, it is no longer generally appropri-ate in Britain to regard animals to be 'property' in the sense of what Blackstone described as 'that sole and despotic dominion which one man claims and exercis-es over the external things of the world, in total exclusion of the right of any other individual in the universe'.[23]

More recently, the American legal academic and practitioner, Steven Wise, has advocated seeking to transform the legal status of at least some animals (initially chimpanzees and bonobos) from things to persons by developing the common law.[24] In practice, this means persuading the courts that they should take the ini-tiative in laying down new principles as to how such animals are to be regarded. This strategy may be appropriate for the United States, but it is doubtful whether it could ever be successfully adopted in Britain, because the relationship between the courts and the state and federal legislatures in the US is fundamentally different from that between Parliament and the British courts. In Britain, even if the senior judiciary could be prevailed upon to accept that the capacities of a particular species were such as to justify a change in their legal status, it is highly improbable that the judges would consider it appropriate for they themselves to introduce such a novel principle into the law. The courts' subordinate status in relation to Parliament militates against a radical development of this nature: because there already exists a significant body of animal protection legislation, the judges would most likely conclude that the territory has been occupied by Parliament and it would therefore be proper to leave it to that institution to take the initiative in deciding whether it should be further extended.

Hence, the underlying theme of the present work: for the foreseeable future, the protection of animals in Britain can best be promoted by a greater appreciation of their nature and capacities and the consequences for them of human activity, coupled with increased and more effective legal regulation of their use and treat-ment, including the imposition of detailed and binding positive duties on those who assume responsibility for them.

---

[22] Francione, GL, *Rain Without Thunder* (1996) 10.   [23] Blackstone, n 5 above, Book II, Ch 1, 2.
[24] *Rattling the Cage. Toward Legal Rights for Animals* (2000); see also, Wise, SM, 'Animal Thing to Animal Person—Thoughts on Time, Place, and Theories' (1999) 5 *Animal Law* 61.

(4) The legal status of animals under European Community law

So far as European Community (EC) law is concerned with animals, their legal status is defined by the Treaty of the European Community (the TEC, formerly the Treaty of Rome), as amended. Two of the original objectives of the Community were the establishment of a common market, and the adoption of a common agricultural policy. Implicit in both was the need for Member States to abide by the same rules and standards, including those relating to farm animals. In this sense the Commission was correct to observe, as it did in 1993, that the protection of animals 'has always been taken into account in Community legislation, particularly in the Common Agricultural policy'.[25] Taking it into account is, however, rather different from giving the matter the attention it merits. Moreover, the impetus for the introduction of animal protection measures in agriculture and other areas has hitherto been primarily to facilitate the working of the internal market, rather than for the benefit of the animals themselves. Progress has been slow, and even when legislation is in place there remains serious concern about the rigour with which it is transposed into national law and enforced by Member States. In the face of determined opposition from some quarters, and apathy on the part of others, campaigners, expert advisers, politicians, and officials arguing to raise standards have been confronted by considerable obstacles. It is a testimony to their efforts that they have succeeded in establishing animal welfare on the EC's legal agenda, and have achieved some success in persuading a sufficient number of the relevant decision makers that this is a subject which merits action.

The scale of the challenge has been largely a consequence of different cultural attitudes to animals among the Member States, together with the priority given to commercial considerations. It can also be attributed to the fact that, as originally conceived, the Treaty of Rome categorized live animals as nothing more than 'agricultural products'.[26] There was no recognition that their nature was any different from that of inanimate commodities, and hence no special provisions which acknowledged their particular needs. Indeed, welfare measures were originally introduced merely because they were coincidental to furthering the economically important objective 'to increase agricultural productivity by promoting technical progress and by ensuring the rational development of agricultural production'.[27]

In response to this situation, persistent efforts were made from the early 1980s by pressure groups, MEPs, and some national governments, including that of the UK, to amend the Treaty to recognize the sentiency of animals.[28] Some headway was made as part of the negotiations leading up to the Treaty on European Union (1991), with the result that a Declaration was appended to the Treaty which called

[25] Commission of the European Communities, 'Background Report: Animal Welfare', 11 October 1993.
[26] TEC, art 32 (formerly 38) and Annex II. Many of the existing articles of the Treaty were renumbered as a result of the provisions of the Treaty of Amsterdam, which came into effect on 1 May 1999.
[27] TEC, art 33 (formerly 39).
[28] See further, Wilkins, D (ed), *Animal Welfare in Europe* (1997) 131–133.

upon the European Parliament, the Council, and the Commission, as well as Member States, when drafting and implementing Community legislation on the common agricultural policy, transport, the internal market, and research, 'to pay full regard to the welfare requirement of animals'.[29] The Declaration represented the most that it was politically feasible to achieve at the time. Although welcome both as recognition of the issue and a statement of intent, it was not formally incorporated into the TEC, did not have the status of law, and was not therefore legally enforceable. Although the Declaration was subsequently relied upon as one of the grounds for the introduction of measures relating to the protection of, respectively, animals at the time of slaughter or killing, calves, and farm animals generally,[30] it was aspirational rather than mandatory, and thereby failed to meet the original objectives of the campaign, which continued—and to some effect.

In consequence, a 'Protocol on protection and welfare of animals' has been annexed to the TEC, by virtue of the Treaty of Amsterdam, which came into force on 1 May 1999. This states:

THE HIGH CONTRACTING PARTIES [ie the Member States]
DESIRING to ensure improved protection and respect for the welfare of animals as sentient beings
HAVE AGREED upon the following provision which shall be annexed to the Treaty establishing the European Community: In formulating and implementing the Community's agriculture, transport, internal market and research policies, the Community and Member States shall pay full regard to the welfare requirements of animals, while respecting the legislative or administrative provisions and customs of the Member States relating in particular to religious rites, cultural traditions and regional heritage.

A protocol forms an integral part of the TEC.[31] As such, its terms have the same legal standing as the text of the Treaty itself. It is therefore now the case that the sentiency of animals is formally acknowledged in EC law. Ironically, this is something which has never been expressly recognized in British legislation, although arguably it is implicit in the nature of the protection afforded. In addition, the Protocol imposes an explicit duty upon Community institutions and Member States to pay full regard to animals' welfare. This represents a very significant achievement. To have succeeded in having the founding Treaty amended in this way highlights the influence of the animal welfare lobby and the political importance now attached to the issue. At a practical level, the Protocol has the potential to make a real difference by changing attitudes and affecting the substantive law. It will clearly need to be taken into account when formulating future EC legislation and in transposing directives into national law. The Protocol will also become a factor in the deliberations of the European Court of Justice (ECJ), not only when

---

[29] TEU, Declaration on the Protection of Animals.
[30] See the respective recitals (preambles) to Directives 93/119, 97/2, and 98/58.
[31] TEC, art 311 (formerly 239). See further, Camm, T and Bowles, D, 'Animal Welfare and the Treaty of Rome—A legal analysis of the protocol on animal welfare and welfare standards in the European Union' (2000) 12 Journal of Environmental Law 197.

applying new legislation, but also in relation to *existing* legislation. This is because it is the TEC itself which has been amended, and all secondary legislation, such as regulations and directives, is required to be interpreted in accordance with its terms. Furthermore, in relation to matters with an EC law dimension, the Protocol will be enforceable in the domestic courts of Member States as well as the ECJ.

However, while the potential implications may be far-reaching, how the Protocol is applied in practice, and therefore the actual degree of protection which it affords, will be determined ultimately by the courts. Clearly, how liberal an interpretation they apply to the caveat relating to practices in individual Member States will be an important factor. Moreover, a duty 'to pay full regard to the welfare requirements of animals' does not amount to an overriding duty to give effect to them. They must be considered, but that does not necessarily prevent them being qualified or overridden by competing considerations, such as other objectives contained in the TEC, or international obligations, for example, the rules of the World Trade Organization. Although these undoubtedly have the potential to defeat the claims of animal welfare where they threaten commercial interests, it is nevertheless symbolically important, and possibly legally significant, that the Protocol contains no express authority to take account of economic factors. It is inevitable that in time animal welfare campaigners will challenge the way in which the Commission and Member States interpret it; no great leap of imagination is required to envisage a situation where the wording of a directive, or its transposition into national law, does not go as far as campaigners would wish and they turn to the courts, alleging that the Protocol has been contravened. Only then will its real impact become apparent.[31a]

B. The Case for Legal Regulation

It is therefore evident that at least some degree of legal regulation of the way in which animals are treated is necessary in both domestic and EC law. Without it, they would be vulnerable due to the want of protection inherent in the common law of both England and Scotland; and there is a need for uniform rules and minimum standards to prevail throughout the Community in order to enable the single market to function. As the late Lord Houghton correctly asserted, 'animal welfare, in the general and in the particular, is largely a matter for the law. . . . There is no complete substitution for the law.'[32] There are those, however, who continue to argue against state interference. 'The road from private intolerance to the collective dictatorship of the statute book is easy to tread', opines one leading newspaper columnist in the course of an argument against a ban on fox hunting: 'It is

---

[31a] See *Jippes and Others v Minister van Landbouw, Natuurbeheer en Visserij*, Case 189/01 (ECJ, 12 July 2001), discussed below at Ch 15, n 33.

[32] Houghton, Lord, 'Animals and the Law. Moral and Political Issues' in Blackman et al, *Animal Welfare and the Law* (1979) 209.

the road from a healthy democracy to one that settles every argument by calling in the state.'[33] Others suggest that legal regulation can have the effect of compromising the interests of animals. Roger Scruton, for example, warns against 'hasty legislation, introduced under pressure from lobbyists on one side of a many-sided debate', which may 'worsen the situation of other sentient species and increase the resentment of those on whom their welfare ultimately depends',[34] and the United Kingdom Egg Producers Association is unequivocal in its opposition: 'There is no need for welfare legislation. It simply gets in the way of scientific development of better conditions of livestock.'[35] Similarly, in relation to the UK's pig industry, the House of Commons Agriculture Committee has said that 'Politicians should simply resolve to meddle less.'[36] However, as Tony Blair acknowledged in 1993, when he was shadow Home Secretary, while 'there are always going to be vested interests to try to put pressure on you to relent from protecting animals', it was the case that 'on the whole most public pressure is towards greater rather than lesser protection for animals'.[37]

This is so despite arguments that the treatment of animals can be best determined by the market. Leaving aside for the moment the fact that a large number of animals, most notably those kept as companions, fall outside the commercial arena, it is important to acknowledge that society is more than a group of individual consumers making independent decisions about how to spend their money. One of the defining characteristics of a society is a sense of collective morality. The community's moral position may change over time, and there will often be a significant proportion of the population who reject the prevailing view but, in respect of most matters of public policy, it is possible to identify some degree of consensus. It is this which the law, including that concerned with the protection of animals, generally seeks to reflect. But then it may be asked, if a common concern for animal welfare really exists in Britain, why can this not be adequately expressed in the voluntary decisions of consumers? Surely, if they feel strongly enough about the matter, they will act on their own initiative. In reality, probably not; even assuming they were to be sufficiently informed about the relevant issues and the nature of the products, which the vast majority are not, it is simply unrealistic to expect the average shopper, preoccupied with more immediate concerns, to consider and weigh all the relevant moral questions connected with each purchase before making a choice and selecting a specific item. They are much more likely to be swayed by a spontaneous response to the price, appearance, advertising, or simply the force of habit. On the basis of his own considerable experience, the international market speculator, George Soros, has expressed the view that 'economic values, on their own cannot be sufficient to sustain

---

[33] Jenkins, S, 'Persuade, don't outlaw', *The Times*, 23 October 1993.

[34] Scruton, R, *Animal Rights and Wrongs* (1996) 9.

[35] House of Commons Agriculture Committee, *The UK Poultry Industry* (1994) para 74.

[36] House of Commons Agriculture Committee, *The UK Pig Industry* (1999) para 66.

[37] RSPCA, *Animal Life*, Issue 13, Autumn 1993, 19.

society' because they 'express only what an individual market participant is willing to pay another in free exchange for something else'. In such a situation, 'anonymous market participants are largely exempt from moral choices'. According to Soros, because 'social values do not find expression in the market behavior of individual participants' there is a need for them 'to find some other form of expression'. A market economy, he asserts, 'does not function as a community and a global economy even less so'.[38]

The imposition of common minimum standards through legal regulation overcomes this problem: by reflecting society's perceived collective values, it removes from the individual the responsibility of making a moral decision in respect of every purchase. If the market has a morality at all, it is not necessarily that of the community, and across a broad spectrum of issues it is considered both legitimate and appropriate to use legislation to offset the extremes of market forces, especially to protect the vulnerable.

Of course, it is open to producers and retailers to respond voluntarily to social concerns, and the widespread use of quality assurance schemes is an example of this in relation to animal welfare. Undoubtedly, these have the potential to promote high standards of animal husbandry, and are therefore to be welcomed, but this does not mean that they are an adequate substitute for law. Legislation provides uniformity of standards, and its terms are publicly available and all-embracing. Many of the voluntary schemes now in existence differ from one another in the standards they specify; in some instances, it is virtually impossible to establish what these are because they are considered to be commercially sensitive; and a significant number of producers remain outside such schemes. Because of variation between different schemes, accurate and informative labelling is essential, but the Director of the Meat and Livestock Commission has admitted that 'a substantial problem in raising the specification of existing retail labelling was that 90 per cent of British consumers did not want to be reminded that animals were slaughtered to provide meat for human consumption'.[39] Moreover, even though labelling can enable consumers to make an informed choice in their purchasing, it also has considerable potential to confuse and mislead. For example, the so-called 'Special Marketing Terms' applied to eggs—'free range', 'semi-intensive', 'deep-litter', 'perchery' ('barn'), and 'caged'—indicate the conditions in which laying hens are kept,[40] yet one suspects that few shoppers have an accurate idea of the respective systems of husbandry represented by these terms. Similarly, a survey commissioned by the RSPCA found that 40 per cent of those asked thought the slogan 'Farm Fresh' eggs meant that they had come from free range hens; 46 per cent

---

[38] Soros, G, *The Crisis in Global Capitalism. Open Society Endangered* (1998) 46, 197, and 199.

[39] House of Commons Agriculture Committee, n 36 above, para 46.

[40] Regulation 1274/91, as amended by Regulation 2401/95. The Agriculture Council agreed in December 2000 new rules governing the labelling of eggs in the EU, which include a requirement to inform consumers of the husbandry system under which eggs were produced: HC Debs, 8 January 2001, col 453.

thought 'Naturally Fresh' indicated free range hens; and 27 per cent considered 'Fresh' was to be equated with free range, whereas all these terms are essentially meaningless.[41] Furthermore, although the Government is seeking to address the issue in European and international discussions, there are currently legal restrictions under both EC law and the WTO on the State requiring labelling of imported products indicating that they have been produced under conditions which would be illegal in Britain.[42] It is also significant in this context that the managers of companies are answerable first and foremost to their shareholders, whereas the politicians and officials responsible for legal regulation are accountable to Parliament, the courts, the media, and, ultimately, the public in respect of the nature of the rules (including what prevails in the face of conflicting or uncertain scientific evidence), how they are determined, applied, and enforced, and whether they should be changed. Finally, voluntary schemes will continue for so long as business considers they are commercially advantageous. But the consumer is capricious, and particularly susceptible to the media's ever-changing agenda: factors which influence today's purchases may soon be overtaken by other considerations. Perhaps consumers' perceived concern for the way in which animals are reared will continue to have an influence on purchasing managers in the long term, but there is no guarantee of this. Even where quality assurance schemes are currently in place, they only apply in most cases to a limited range of products and MPs have expressed concern that retailers and manufacturers are failing to support animal welfare by continuing to direct their purchases to cheaper producers outside the UK without insisting that they meet the same standards as those required of home producers.[43] In contrast, legal regulation remains in place until the legislature expressly decides otherwise, and applies equally to all relevant products.

In situations where market forces do not apply, it may be suggested that self-regulation is an adequate alternative to legislative intervention. Although it may have a part to play, it is seldom a satisfactory substitute. The Burns Committee which recently reported on hunting with dogs observed, for example, that 'a great deal of hunting takes place which is not regulated in any way by the rules of the various hunting and coursing associations', and, even where it does fall within their jurisdiction, the Committee 'became aware of some lack of confidence in the procedures for dealing with complaints'.[44] A rather different illustration of the same problem is provided by the docking of dogs' tails. Since July 1993 it has been illegal for anyone other than a veterinary surgeon to carry out this procedure,[45] although the law imposes no formal restriction on the freedom of the profession to continue the practice. However, in deciding whether it would be

---

[41] RSPCA, *Home to Roost—the future for laying hens* (1999) Appendix.

[42] HC Debs, 21 December 1999, col 566.

[43] House of Commons Agriculture Committee, n 36 above, paras 40–44. The Farm Animal Welfare Council commenced a study in 1999 into the impact of farm assurance schemes.

[44] Burns, Lord (Chairman), *Report of the Committee of Inquiry into Hunting with Dogs in England and Wales* (2000) paras 9.40 and 9.44.

[45] Veterinary Surgeons Act 1966 (Schedule 3 Amendment) Order 1991, SI 1991/1412.

appropriate to dock the tail of a particular puppy, a veterinary surgeon is required to have regard to the relevant guidance issued by the RCVS. This states that the procedure is 'unethical unless done for therapeutic or truly prophylactic reasons'. In the view of the Royal College, 'Arguments for docking puppies on the grounds of tradition, or prevention of faecal soiling, or damage in "working" breeds unlikely ever to work, are considered scientifically and morally flawed by the majority of veterinary surgeons.'[46] If this guidance had been strictly adhered to, one might have expected the number of puppies whose tails are docked to be relatively few. It seems, however, to have had only a limited impact; an attempt by the RCVS to bring disciplinary proceedings against a veterinary surgeon for tail docking was unsuccessful, and the practice still appears to be widespread.[47]

C. Legitimate and Illegitimate Activities

In regulating how animals should be treated, legislators make a distinction between legitimate activities and those which society considers to be illegitimate. Practices which fall into the latter category, and are in consequence prohibited, include: the use of domestic animals for baiting or fighting;[48] the staging of certain public contests, performances, and exhibitions involving equines or cattle;[49] the docking and nicking of horses' tails;[50] the public exhibition of any film which involved animal cruelty in its making, or the supply of an unclassified video recording which to any significant extent depicts mutilation or torture of an animal or any other act of gross violence towards it;[51] the public display of a scientific procedure;[52] the selling of pet animals in markets, the street, and other public places;[53] the keeping of calves in restrictive crates;[54] confining sows in stalls and

---

[46] RCVS, *Guide to Professional Conduct* (2000) Annex 12. See also the statement on the subject issued by the RCVS in 1997: (1997) 141 *Veterinary Record* 506.

[47] (1995) 137 *Veterinary Record* 278. In passing, it is worth citing the opinion of Hawkins J in *Ford v Wiley* ((1889) 23 QBD 203, 219–220) on the subject of tail docking in the context of the offence of cruelty. In view of the date of the case, he was presumably referring to the tail docking of horses (a practice since expressly prohibited by the Docking and Nicking of Horses Act 1949). Nevertheless, the judge's comments would appear equally relevant to the docking of dogs' tails: 'Docking is another painful operation, which, no doubt, may occasionally be justified; but I hold a very strong opinion against allowing fashion, or the whim of an individual, or any number of individuals, to afford a justification for such painful mutilation and disfigurement.'

[48] Protection of Animals Act 1911, s 1(1)(c); Protection of Animals (Scotland) Act 1912, s 1(1)(c).

[49] Protection of Animals Act 1934, s 1.   [50] Docking and Nicking of Horses Act 1949, s 1.

[51] Cinematograph Films (Animals) Act 1937, s 1; Video Recordings Act 1984, ss 2(2)(b) and 9(1).

[52] Animals (Scientific Procedures) Act 1986, s 16.

[53] Pet Animals Act 1951, s 2, as amended by the Pet Animals Act 1951 (Amendment) Act 1983.

[54] Welfare of Calves Regulations 1987, SI 1987/2021, now superseded by the Welfare of Farmed Animals (England) Regulations 2000, SI 2000/1870, Sch 4, para 1; Welfare of Farmed Animals (Scotland) Regulations 2000, SSI 2000/442, Sch 4, para 1; Welfare of Farmed Animals (Wales) Regulations 2001, Sch 4, para 1. The Regulations relating to Wales came into force on 31 July 2001, but at the time this book went to press they had not been allocated an SI number. Henceforth, the three sets of regulations will be referred to collectively as the 'Welfare of Farmed Animals Regulations'.

tethers;[55] and the gift or sale of unclaimed stray dogs for the purposes of vivisection.[56]

The practical significance of an activity being regarded as legitimate or illegitimate is clearly demonstrated by considering the very different ways in which the law at present treats, respectively, badgers and foxes. Parliament has reflected society's view that badger-baiting is unacceptably cruel. Hence, it is an offence, except as specifically permitted: wilfully to kill, injure, or take a badger; to attempt to do so; to possess or have under one's control a dead badger, or any part of, or anything derived from, a dead badger; cruelly to ill-treat a badger; to use badger tongs; to dig for a badger; to interfere with a badger sett; or obstruct access to, cause a dog to enter, or disturb a badger when it is occupying, a sett.[57] Compare this level of protection with the attitude displayed towards 'legitimate' field sports, in respect of which it has been the practice to include in legislation measures specifically intended to enable them to continue unhindered. For example, in respect of hunting with hounds, provisions for the purpose of protecting game which relate to trespassers and persons found on land do not extend 'to any person hunting or coursing upon any lands with hounds or greyhounds, and being in fresh pursuit of any deer, hare, or fox already started upon any other land';[58] offences of cruelty do not apply to wild animals, or to the coursing or hunting of a captive animal, unless it is liberated in an injured, mutilated, or exhausted condition, or into an enclosed space from which it has no reasonable chance of escape;[59] the offence of being in charge of a dog at large (that is, not on a lead or otherwise under close control) in a field or enclosure in which there are sheep, intended to penalize the worrying of livestock, does not apply to a pack of hounds;[60] even provisions relating to the protection of badger setts are qualified for the purpose of hunting foxes with hounds;[61] and an act which would otherwise be an offence under recent legislation introduced with the specific intention of protecting wild mammals from unnecessary suffering does not apply if done by a dog lawfully used for the purpose of killing or taking any wild mammal.[62]

In considering the question of legitimacy, it is important to appreciate that, in Britain, the degree of autonomy enjoyed by the individual has originated not so much by the endowment of positive legal rights, but rather from a tradition of freedoms and liberties which endure unless qualified by law. Thus, the courts have asserted England is 'not a country where everything is forbidden except what is

---

[55] Welfare of Pigs Regulations 1991, SI 1991/1477, now superseded by the Welfare of Farmed Animals Regulations, ibid, Sch 6, paras 4 and 6 (paras 4 and 8 in the Scottish Regulations).

[56] Dogs Act 1906, s 3(5); Environmental Protection Act 1990, s 149(6).

[57] Protection of Badgers Act 1992, ss 1(1), (3), 2(1)(a), (b), (c), 3.   [58] Game Act 1831, s 35.

[59] Protection of Animals Act 1911, s 1(3)(b) and Protection of Animals (Scotland) Act 1912, s 1(3)(b), as amended by the Protection of Animals Act (1911) Amendment Act 1921, s 1.

[60] Dogs (Protection of Livestock) Act 1953, s 1(1)(2)(2A), as amended by the Wildlife and Countryside Act 1981, s 12, Sch 7, para 3.

[61] Protection of Badgers Act 1992, s 8(4)–(9).

[62] Wild Mammals (Protection) Act 1996, s 2(b), (d).

expressly permitted', but 'a country where everything is permitted except what is expressly forbidden'.[63] The same principle applies in respect of both Scotland and Wales. It is not therefore necessary for individuals or companies to be able to point to express legal authority for treating or using animals in a particular way; so long as it has not been prohibited by either Parliament or the courts, a practice will generally be considered lawful, and hence, by implication, legitimate.

This situation clearly benefits the status quo. First, regardless of the extent of public support for change, it places a very heavy burden on those seeking to challenge the way in which animals are treated. They need to secure sufficient support within both the House of Commons and the House of Lords (including, whenever possible, that of the Government),[64] gain the necessary parliamentary time, and avoid the many procedural hurdles which are available to frustrate the progress of a Bill. Secondly, any threat to the continuation of a hitherto lawful practice may be countered by ideologically powerful claims based on its assumed 'legitimacy' and the 'right' of adherents to pursue it, coupled with claims that it would be wrong 'to criminalize otherwise law-abiding citizens' (a claim often employed by those opposed to a legal ban on hunting with hounds). By allowing a practice to continue, the law lends a moral legitimacy to it. It is a common defence to criticism to say that 'I'm doing nothing wrong; I'm acting within the law', or 'I'm merely doing what I have a legal right to do'. Thirdly, where a dispute arises between those engaged in such a legal activity and those who oppose it, the police and the courts will regard it to be their duty to uphold the rule of law by ensuring, so far as they are able, that the activity can be carried on; that those concerned can continue to go about their lawful business unhindered, regardless of the amount of opposition it might engender. It may be that the law recognizes 'the right to meet together, to go in procession, to demonstrate, and to protest on matters of public concern', but only so long as 'all is done peaceably and in good order, without threats or incitement to violence or obstruction to traffic'.[65] Traditionally, applying the term 'right' to what is permissible has been something of an overstatement: 'English law does not recognize any special right of public meeting for political or other purposes. The right of assembly . . . is nothing more than a view taken by the Court of the individual liberty of the subject.'[66] However, this situation may be altered by virtue of the Human Rights Act 1998, which incorporates

---

[63] *Malone v Metropolitan Police Commissioner* [1979] Ch 344, 357 (Sir Robert Megarry V-C).

[64] In contrast, the Scottish Parliament has only a single chamber, a characteristic which may prove to be of some significance in securing legislation on devolved matters affecting animals. For example, it is assumed that any proposal to ban hunting with dogs in England and Wales would encounter stiff opposition in the House of Lords.

[65] *Hubbard v Pitt* [1976] QB 142, 176, CA (Lord Denning MR). The House of Lords has recently confirmed that there exists at common law a qualified right of peaceful assembly on the highway: *DPP v Jones* [1999] 2 WLR 625.

[66] *Duncan v Jones* [1936] 1 KB 218, 222 (Lord Hewart CJ).

into domestic law article 11 of the European Convention on Human Rights, relating to freedom of assembly and association.[67]

Unsurprisingly, the courts are deeply committed to the principle that 'The rule of law must prevail.'[68] In their view, 'Any suggestion that a section of the community strongly holding one set of views is justified in banding together to disrupt the lawful activities of a section that does not hold the same views so strongly or which holds different views cannot be tolerated and must unhesitatingly be rejected by the courts.'[69] Accordingly, when, during the winter of 1994–1995, the activities of protesters against live exports to the Continent threatened to disrupt the trade by the sheer weight of numbers who were present, they found themselves confronted at ports and airports by hundreds of police, many fully equipped with riot equipment, who had been drafted in to ensure that a lawful trade could continue. As the High Court asserted:

The export of live animals for slaughter is lawful. But many think it immoral. They object in particular to the shipment of live calves for rearing in veal crates, a practice banned in this country since 1990. The result is that for some months past the trade has attracted widespread concern and a great deal of highly publicised protest. Some of that protest is lawful; some alas is not. The precise point at which the right of public demonstration ends and the criminal offence of public nuisance begins may be difficult to detect. But not only is all violent conduct unlawful; so too is any activity which substantially inconveniences the public at large and disrupts the rights of others to go about their lawful business.[70]

A similar situation exists in relation to hunting with hounds. Leaving aside the respective arguments for and against the practice, because it is not prohibited it is, by definition, lawful, and, while it remains so, the overriding responsibility of the police will be to ensure, so far as is possible in the light of the particular circumstances and the resources available to the chief constable, that the activity can be carried on.[71] For those who oppose hunting, the only way in which this situation can be changed is to secure the parliamentary time and support necessary to enact appropriate legislation.

Where protests are perceived seriously to interfere with the pursuit of a lawful activity, Parliament may respond by introducing measures specifically intended to outlaw further disruption. In 1994, for example, the Home Secretary justified a new offence of 'aggravated trespass', by saying that 'In recent months, we have seen many examples of disruptive and threatening behaviour—at the Grand National, during country sports and even fishing.' He acknowledged that those who were

---

[67] Article 11 provides that everyone has the right to freedom of peaceful assembly and to freedom of association with others. This may be qualified, however, by such restrictions as are 'necessary in a democratic society in the interests of national security or public safety, for the prevention of disorder or crime, for the protection of health or morals or for the protection of the rights and freedoms of others'. See, for example, the remarks of Lord Irvine of Lairg LC in *DPP v Jones* (n 65 above), at 634–635.

[68] *R v Metropolitan Police Commissioner, ex p Blackburn* [1968] 2 QB 118, 138, CA (Lord Denning).

[69] *R v Caird* (1970) 54 Cr App R 499, 506, CA (Sachs LJ).

[70] *R v Coventry City Council, ex parte Phoenix Aviation* [1995] 3 All ER 37, 40–41 (Simon Brown LJ).

[71] *R v Chief Constable of Sussex, ex parte International Traders' Ferry Ltd* [1998] 3 WLR 1260, HL.

opposed to such activities 'have a perfect right to campaign to change the law, . . . but they do not have the right to trespass, threaten or intimidate'.[72] More recently, the definition of terrorism has been widened to include, in the words of a different Home Secretary, 'people who claim to be in favour of so-called animal liberation who have engaged in actions that not only caused risk but resulted in the most serious violence to individuals, and have put people under threat of their lives'.[73] In the same way, responding to the activities of those opposed to the use of animals in scientific procedures, which were targeted in particular at the management, employees, and financial backers of Huntingdon Life Sciences, the Government in January 2001 placed before Parliament measures intended to restrict the freedom to demonstrate outside a person's home; to tighten the law relating to the sending of malicious communications; in specified circumstances, to allow company directors to keep their residential addresses secure; and to widen the existing offence of harassment.[74]

Self-evidently, that which is regarded to be legitimate in relation to the treatment of animals varies between cultures, and may change over time within a particular society. An example is the rearing of veal calves individually in crates. Having previously been permitted in the United Kingdom, the practice was prohibited in 1990, largely in response to public opinion, and legislation has recently been agreed to phase out this method of livestock husbandry from the European Union by the end of 2006.[75] Likewise, legislation has recently been passed which will prohibit the farming of animals for fur in England and Wales after the beginning of 2003.[76] Similarly, evidence suggests that we are witnessing a transition in popular attitudes towards hunting with hounds: what was until recently considered to be an intrinsic part of the country's rural heritage and

---

[72] HC Debs, 11 January 1994, col 29 (Michael Howard MP). See now, the Criminal Justice and Public Order Act 1994, s 68.

[73] HC Debs, 1 December 1999, col 155 (Jack Straw MP). The official number of incidents and arrests involving animal liberation groups between 1995 and 1999 are as follows:

	1995	1996	1997	1998	1999
Incidents	907	727	800	935	1,200
Arrests	820	780	848	925	1,020

Most of these involved public order offences and/or minor criminal damage, but a small number were more serious:

	1995	1996	1997	1998	1999
Use of incendiary devices	36	15	12	10	6
Arson (without device)	14	2	0	5	8

Source: HL Debs, 6 May 2000, col 122 (WA).

The Terrorism Act 2000, s 1 defines terrorism to include the use or threat of action designed to influence the Government or to intimidate the public or a section of the public, and is made for the purpose of advancing a political, religious, or ideological cause.

[74] Criminal Justice and Police Act 2001, ss 42–45. See also, Home Office, 'Animal Rights Extremism: Government Strategy. A Consultation Document' (2001).

[75] See n 54 above; Directive 97/2.

[76] Fur Farming (Prohibition) Act 2000.

spectacle is now, apparently, seen by a growing majority of the population as an anachronistic, brutal, and unnecessary means of killing wild animals (although its supporters are mounting an extremely determined defence of the activity). If and when hunting with dogs is banned remains a matter of conjecture. The status quo, however, appears untenable. The Burns Committee which inquired into the issue in relation to England and Wales, having expressed surprise at the lack of existing regulation, concluded that 'it might be productive, in the absence of a ban, to explore the possibility of introducing some form of licensing system'.[77]

Questions of legitimacy are also coloured by deeply-held, but often overwhelmingly subjective, personal convictions. Despite suggestions to the contrary, there is no self-evident truth which defines how we should treat animals. Individuals may be certain in their own minds, but the law has to reflect a moral consensus, for if it does not attract a wide degree of acceptance, it will become impossible to enforce. It is then, literally, worse than useless; a law that is impotent because it lacks public support brings the values which it represents into disrepute. This does not mean that law cannot lead public opinion. There is no necessity to wait until the majority of the population is positively in support of a measure, and on occasions a law which is ahead of its time has had the effect of educating the public eventually to endorse the policy it represents. An example of such a process is the impact of the legislation prohibiting gender and racial discrimination introduced into Britain during the late 1960s and '70s; the same might be said of the original animal protection legislation enacted in 1822. Hart describes the impetus for reform precisely when he writes that the development of the law is 'profoundly influenced both by conventional morality and ideals of particular social groups, and also by forms of enlightened moral criticism urged by individuals, whose moral horizon has transcended the morality currently accepted'.[78] It is, however, fatal for the law to be too far in advance of public opinion. Such an analysis will offend the moral absolutists, but they delude themselves if they think it is either possible or desirable to use the law as an instrument to impose the views of a minority onto an unsympathetic majority. The onus is on those who are opposed to the status quo to persuade others of the merits of their case: liberal democracy is dependent upon law that is essentially consensual. Conversely, however, if minorities are not to be subject to Mill's 'tyranny of the majority',[79] popular support cannot *in itself* justify

---

[77] Burns, n 44 above, paras 9.48–49. The Hunting Bill, introduced into Parliament by the Government in December 2000, offered MPs the opportunity to decide on a free vote whether hunting with hounds should be permitted to continue, subject to either self-regulation or a statutory licensing scheme, or, alternatively, whether the practice should be prohibited. On 17 January 2001, the House of Commons rejected both the status quo of self-regulation, by 399 votes to 155, and the proposal to introduce a statutory licensing scheme, by 382 to 182. The option of introducing an outright ban was carried by 387 votes to 174. The House of Lords subsequently voted decisively against both a total ban (by 317 votes to 68) and statutory licensing, and endorsed the continuation of self-regulation by 249 votes to 108. The Bill fell when Parliament was dissolved in May 2001. At the opening of the new Parliament following the general election, the Government undertook to provide a further opportunity for a free vote on hunting, but failed to indicate whether it intended to bring forward its own bill on the issue.

[78] Hart, HLA, *The Concept of Law* (2nd edn, 1994) 185.   [79] Mill, JS, *On Liberty* (1859; 1982 edn) 62.

legislation. For example, even if an overwhelming majority of the population were vehemently opposed to the Jewish and Muslim methods of killing animals, by which their throat is cut without pre-stunning, would it be acceptable for a liberal democratic society, in which a high value is placed on freedom of conscience and religion, to prohibit such practices? Both the European Convention and EC law provide for religious slaughter to be exempt from the general requirement for pre-stunning.[80] In Britain, a similar dispensation pre-dates these international measures and the multicultural nature of contemporary British society, and continues to apply.[81] Moreover, freedom of religion is recognized by article 9 of the European Convention on Human Rights, and is now formally incorporated in British law by virtue of the Human Rights Act 1998. Accordingly, any attempt to enact legislation to prohibit the practice could potentially be challenged on the ground that it was incompatible with the Convention. This is so, despite concern over the effects of religious slaughter on the animal. When the Farm Animal Welfare Council investigated the subject it concluded that the 'up-to-date scientific evidence available and our own observations leave no doubt in our minds that religious methods of slaughter, even when carried out under ideal conditions, must result in a degree of pain, suffering and distress which does not occur in the properly stunned animal'.[82] On this basis, it recommended that the law be changed to prohibit the practice. For its part, the RSPCA, while recognizing that 'in any democratic country it is a fundamental right of religious groups to practice [sic] their beliefs without hindrance', has expressed the view that

where these beliefs are directly responsible for animal suffering, that right has to be challenged. Surely it is not unreasonable to suggest that, in the light of new scientific knowledge and society's more caring attitudes to animals, religious traditions might be changed to secure an animal's welfare before and during slaughter.[83]

To date, the Government has attempted a degree of compromise by doing nothing to challenge the continuation of the practice, but has introduced a requirement that it is carried out only at a slaughterhouse, where a veterinary surgeon and stunning equipment are both available, should the need arise.[84]

Such an issue clearly gives rise to difficult, but important, questions about the circumstances in which it is acceptable for the State to intervene to restrict the autonomy of the individual. Perhaps few are quite so sensitive, but there are many similar examples of conflicting interests which arise in the course of the debate about the degree to which the law should protect animals. The late Lord Devlin described the dilemma: 'There must be toleration of the maximum individual freedom that is consistent with the integrity of society', and yet, 'Not everything is

[80] European Convention for the Protection of Animals for Slaughter, art 17; Directive 74/577, art 2.
[81] Slaughter of Animals (Scotland) Act 1928; Slaughter of Animals Act 1933; see now, Welfare of Animals (Slaughter or Killing) Regulations 1995, SI 1995/731, regs 21 and 22, and Sch 12.
[82] *Report on the Welfare of Livestock when Slaughtered by Religious Methods* (1985) para 92.
[83] *Farm Animal Welfare* (1995) 27.
[84] Welfare of Animals (Slaughter or Killing) (Amendment) Regulations 1999, SI 1999/400.

to be tolerated.'[85] To Devlin, intoleration, indignation, and disgust are the crucial considerations. On the one hand, they are 'the forces behind the moral law'; on the other, without them, 'the feelings of society cannot be weighty enough to deprive the individual of freedom of choice'. He illustrates this by reference to changing attitudes towards animals:

> I suppose that there is hardly anyone nowadays [the mid-1960s] who would not be disgusted by the thought of deliberate cruelty to animals. No one proposes to relegate that or any other form of sadism to the realm of private morality or to allow it to be practised in public or in private. It would be possible no doubt to point out that until a comparatively short time ago nobody thought very much of cruelty to animals and also that pity and kindliness and the unwillingness to inflict pain are virtues more generally esteemed now than they have ever been in the past.[86]

More controversially, however, Devlin asserts that 'matters of this sort are not determined by rational argument'. Instead, in his view, 'Every moral judgement, unless it claims a divine source, is simply a feeling that no right-minded man could behave in any other way without admitting that he was doing wrong. It is the power of common sense and not the power of reason that is behind the judgements of society.'[87] This is a dangerous proposition. The feelings of the 'right-minded man'—or woman—can be highly subjective, and reliance on common sense at the expense of reason provides too great an opportunity for the prejudiced, the bigoted, and the ill-informed to hold sway. Reason must surely be *combined* with common sense in order to reach an informed and rational judgement. Hence the importance of being able to demonstrate an ethical and scientific basis for legislative intervention for the better protection of animals: *if law is the means, science and ethics together provide the justification.* As Marian Dawkins has observed, 'if people feel that it is important to try to change the laws about the treatment of animals, they must have more to go on than just their intuition', because to do otherwise will result in legislation which 'is almost bound to be arbitrary and might even fail to improve the lot of the animals much, if at all'.[88]

D. The Nature of Legal Regulation

(1) The principles underlying animal protection legislation

In general terms, it may be said that animal protection legislation in Britain is based on the broad principle that, in the words of the Banner Committee, it is acceptable to exploit animals, 'provided the use is humane'. This principle 'represents the culmination of a long tradition of moral reflection, as well as expressing the views of

---

[85] Devlin, P, 'Morals and the Criminal Law' in *The Enforcement of Morals* (1965) 16 and 17.
[86] Devlin, P, 'Morals and the Criminal Law' in *The Enforcement of Morals* (1965) 17.   [87] ibid.
[88] Dawkins, MS, *Animal Suffering. The Science of Animal Welfare* (1980) 2.

most members of society, that the use of animals is, morally speaking, neither absolutely impermissible, nor a matter about which one should be indifferent'.[89] Against this backdrop, the Committee suggested that the law reflects three more detailed principles centred on 'harm', which extends beyond physical mistreatment to include, for example, treatment which is degrading. Thus:

(a) Harms of a certain degree and kind ought under no circumstances to be inflicted on an animal. In other words, there are situations in which cost/benefit analysis or utilitarian calculation should not be regarded as the sole test of acceptability; they 'must be augmented by a consideration of whether the action which is proposed, either in itself or in virtue of its particular consequences, ought not to be done'.

(b) Any harm to an animal, even if not absolutely impermissible, nonetheless requires justification and must be outweighed by the good which is realistically sought in so treating it.

(c) Any harm which is justified by the second principle ought, however, to be minimized as far as is reasonably possible.[90]

It has been recommended to the Government by both the Banner Committee and FAWC that these general principles provide an appropriate framework within which the present and future uses of animals should be assessed.[91] In addition, the latter has suggested that a procedure may be considered intrinsically objectionable within (a) above for any one of the following reasons:

(i) if it inflicts very severe or lasting pain on the animals concerned;

(ii) if it involves an unacceptable violation of the integrity of a living being;

(iii) if it is associated with the mixing of kinds of animals to an extent which is unacceptable;

(iv) if it generates living beings whose sentience has been reduced to the extent that they may be considered to be mere instruments or artefacts.[92]

FAWC has also endorsed the view that animals are 'certainly deserving of respect as individuals as well as types and that they should not just be the means to humankind's ends'.[93]

(2) The prevalence of legal regulation

It is now generally the case that those activities involving animals which British society regards to be legitimate are subject to some degree of legal regulation. The whole question of the desirability or otherwise of legal regulation is, of course, a matter of continuing political and economic debate which spreads far wider than

---

[89] *Report of the Committee to Consider the Ethical Implications of Emerging Technologies in the Breeding of Farm Animals* (1995) para 2.3.

[90] ibid paras 2.4, 2.8, and 2.10.

[91] ibid para 2.18; FAWC, *Report on the Implications of Cloning for the Welfare of Farmed Livestock* (1998) para 17.

[92] FAWC, ibid, para 13.   [93] ibid para 14.

the treatment of animals. Even if the principle of legal regulation is accepted, the appropriate degree remains controversial. Suffice it to say, where legal regulation on the use and treatment of animals is imposed through legislation, as distinct from an outright ban, the objective will usually be to ensure that the rules do not stifle the activity by making it economically or practically impossible to pursue (although very onerous legal regulation can be used as an alternative to explicit prohibition by so restricting the conditions under which an activity may be carried on that it becomes impracticable to continue).

In considering the nature, extent, and effectiveness of domestic legal regulation it is important to appreciate that it exists in the context of a global economy. Treaties, international law, diplomatic relations, and economic considerations all have an influence. Moreover, markets are increasingly dominated by multinational companies which trade internationally and have the ability to move their activities around the globe. In such a situation, animal products can be brought into the home market from anywhere in the world. And herein lies a very real dilemma: assuming that proponents of improved animal welfare agree with Tannenbaum that 'it is not always morally correct to require that animals adapt to human preferences',[94] should they, in order to be ethically consistent, always seek the highest possible domestic standards of protection even though to do so may encourage manufacturers and producers to move their activities to other countries, with the result that animal suffering is simply exported to jurisdictions where the standards may be significantly less, or even non-existent? Or is it better to impose standards with which commercial undertakings can live, albeit that this means compromising the interests of animals in Britain? This is an extremely difficult conundrum. As long ago as 1876, the Royal Commission on The Practice of Subjecting Live Animals to Experiments for Scientific Purposes warned that one of the consequences of prohibiting such activities would be 'the flight of medical and physiological students from the United Kingdom to foreign schools and laboratories, and would, therefore, certainly result in no change favourable to the animals'.[95] A similar concern has recently been reiterated by senior scientists. In an open letter to the Minister for Science, 110 signatories (including 5 Nobel Laureates and 38 Fellows of the Royal Society) warned that

the UK may not be able to maintain its position as one of the world's leading scientific nations in many areas of biotechnology and biomedical science because of the way that bureaucracy and delays are impeding the use of animals in research. . . . If this situation persists or gets worse . . . it appears inevitable that a substantial part of the UK's research effort, in many vital areas, will either become uncompetitive or be forced abroad.[96]

---

[94] Tannenbaum, J, 'Ethics and animal welfare: The inextricable connection' (1991) 198(8) *Journal of the American Veterinary Medical Association* 1360, 1373.

[95] *Final Report* (1876) xvii.

[96] *The Times*, 13 June 2000; *RDS News*, July 2000. Acknowledging concern about the level of regulation, the responsible Minister indicated that he was 'keen to look at ways of reducing this, but only when it will not compromise animal welfare. The regulation is in place to create the right balance between protecting

Similarly, the National Farmers' Union has expressed 'the real concern that unilateral measures simply transfer a welfare issue elsewhere while British producers may be forced out of business'.[97] Ministers are particularly sensitive to this argument. Thus the policy of the Home Office is to 'pursue initiatives across Europe rather than risk exporting animal experiments to countries with less rigorous controls', and while ministers have confirmed that they have 'no intention' of 'allowing the proper welfare of animals to be undermined', neither will they permit 'unnecessary bureaucracy or red tape' to prevent 'proper scientific research'.[98] Likewise, the Minister of Agriculture has cautioned against making both British and EU agriculture uncompetitive: a situation which he has described as 'a defeat for animal welfare as well as for farmers'. So, although there is 'a view among EU Ministers that animal welfare issues are important, . . . we must protect the EU from exporting its industries'.[99]

By way of contrast, a more robust approach is represented by the Banner Committee, which was established to consider the ethical implications of emerging technologies in the breeding of farm animals. The Committee expressly rejected the suggestion that Britain should never act on its own initiative. 'Doubtless abolition of child labour in nineteenth century Britain could have been opposed on the grounds that it would have disadvantaged British manufacturers and simply resulted in the export of our child welfare problems,' observed the Committee, 'but neither contention should have been found persuasive.' While recognizing that moral conduct can be costly, it rejoined that

it can hardly be argued that we should delay behaving properly until we can guarantee that so behaving will cost us nothing. . . . Nor does the point about 'exporting our welfare problems' carry much weight. The fact that someone else is prepared to do something which we judge to be wrong and which we subsequently decline to do, is certainly regrettable—but it does not usually persuade us to behave wrongly in the first place.[100]

In the long term the objective must be to raise standards internationally, but there is a danger that, far from improving, they will in fact deteriorate. Free trade and protective legal regulation do not sit well together, and it remains to be seen whether it is possible to protect home producers who are complying with domestic regulations against competition from cheaper imports produced in countries where animal welfare standards are lower.

animals and ensuring that the United Kingdom science and biotechnology industry is able to move forward.' At the same time, he indicated that the local review processes, introduced in April 1999, had been identified as 'a significant source of delay in many instances in the processing of applications for project licences'. As a result, the Animals (Scientific Procedures) Inspectorate was undertaking a review of the ethical review processes, which was due to report by the middle of 2001: HC Debs, 20 December 2000, col 219 (WA) (Mike O'Brien).

[97] *Caring for Livestock. Report of the Animal Welfare Working Group*, June 1995, para 17.

[98] HC Debs, 30 July 1997, col 259 (WA) and 26 June 2000, col 696. The *Guardian* of 3 November 2000 reported that the Government was seeking to accelerate the decision-making procedure.

[99] HC Debs, 13 January 2000, col 413 (Nick Brown MP).

[100] n 89 above, para 2.15.

(3) The objects of legal regulation

Since the middle of the nineteenth century, as legislation relating to animals has increased in volume and sophistication, the law has been relied upon to further a number of different aims, not all of which are necessarily compatible. These include:

- preventing cruelty and reducing animal suffering;
- improving animal and human health;
- protecting or conserving some wildlife;
- promoting animal welfare;
- securing public safety;
- safeguarding commercial interests;
- encouraging responsible animal ownership; and
- reflecting a moral consensus.

Most of the relevant legislation is intended to protect the interests of animals to some extent, although the nature and degree of protection may vary greatly, depending upon the context. However, there are situations in which the interests of the animal are overridden in order to further some other purpose. For example, on the ground of public safety, it is mandatory for a pit bull terrier to be muzzled whenever it is in a public place; and the High Court has held that this means it is no defence to argue that the circumstances were such that the muzzle had to be removed 'for the good of the dog, and that to do otherwise would have been cruel to the dog'.[101]

Accordingly, legislation concerning animals has no uniform objective and therefore no abiding principle. The most consistent theme is the prevention of 'unnecessary suffering', but this is by no means universal and, when it does apply, suffering that might be considered unnecessary in one context may be tolerated in another. This is particularly so where the animal is being kept as part of a business. Thus, it is for the time being expressly permitted to keep laying hens under battery conditions in a commercial undertaking,[102] but to confine hens under similar conditions in one's back garden may amount to an offence: if it could be established that they had suffered, a court might be persuaded that it was unnecessary in a domestic context.

(4) The degree of legal regulation

That an animal benefits from varying degrees of protection depending upon the situation in which it finds itself is due not only to the use of relative criteria such as the term 'unnecessary'. It reflects both Parliament's intention in the light of the

---

[101] Dangerous Dogs Act 1991, s 1(2)(d); *Cichon v DPP* [1994] Crim LR 918 (Schiemann J).

[102] Welfare of Farmed Animals Regulations, n 54 above, reg 4 and Sch 2. Battery cages will eventually be banned in the EU in accordance with the terms of Directive 99/74.

different purposes for which animals are kept, and the ad hoc and piecemeal way in which the statutory regime has evolved. Consider, for example, the position of a rabbit, which is subject to different legislative provisions depending upon whether it is: kept as a pet; on sale in a pet shop; used for a scientific procedure; reared for its meat on agricultural land; transported by a commercial undertaking; on sale in a livestock market; killed at a slaughterhouse; on display in a zoo; used as part of a performance (do conjurors still pull rabbits out of hats?); or living in the wild. Yet, as the American legal academic, David Favre, has pointed out: 'If we are willing to admit that a rabbit is a rabbit regardless of who owns it or where it is being held, then it is apparent that only one set of standards is necessary to protect rabbits around the world.'[103] In practice, however, very different standards may be applied, depending on the circumstances. So, for the time being at least, it remains lawful to keep laying hens in a battery system where the space provided for each bird is less than that of an A4-sized piece of paper,[104] notwithstanding that it is an offence to keep other types of bird (specifically excepting poultry) in a cage which is not of sufficient size to allow it to stretch its wings freely,[105] a situation which led Ruth Harrison to exclaim that such a law 'brings derision on itself and on its enactors alike for its manifest casuistry'.[106]

It is tempting to conclude from this situation that the law is anthropocentrically pragmatic in the face of competing interests: the greater the importance humans attach to an activity, the less protection will be afforded to animals. This is true in the sense that it may be lawful, for example, to do things to a rabbit under the authority of the Animals (Scientific Procedures) Act 1986 which would, if carried out in any other circumstances, amount to an offence of cruelty. On the other hand, legislation specifies detailed and stringent requirements about how the laboratory rabbit should be kept and treated,[107] whereas the law does little more for the pet than to make it an offence to cause the animal unnecessary suffering. Similarly, those who keep rabbits on agricultural land are expected to comply with a detailed code of welfare recommendations produced by the Ministry of Agriculture[108] which, similarly, does not apply to pet rabbits. It is possible to argue, therefore, that a rabbit kept in a laboratory or on a farm is subject to significantly greater legal regulation, and therefore more stringent protection, under the law— *provided it is effectively enforced*—than its counterpart kept as a companion animal. Put in these terms, the notion of protection is more complicated than it might initially appear.

---

[103] Favre, DS, 'Movement toward an international convention for the protection of animals—the further adventures of four rabbits' in Blackman et al, n 32 above, 248.

[104] Welfare of Farmed Animals Regulations, n 54 above, Sch 2, para 1.

[105] Wildlife and Countryside Act 1981, s 8(1)(2). [106] *Animal Machines* (1964) 153.

[107] Home Office, *Code of Practice for the Housing and Care of Animals used in Scientific Procedures* (1989).

[108] MAFF, *Code of recommendations for the welfare of livestock: Rabbits* (1987).

(5) The meaning of the term 'animal'

One particular way in which the legislature may extend or restrict the scope of legal regulation is by applying different meanings to the same word. For example, the term 'animal' is used generally in law to refer to any non-human creature (in contrast to the scientific definition, which includes humans).[109] However, in animal protection legislation it is often given a narrower, more particular definition, depending upon the context. The meaning of 'animal' may therefore vary considerably, and it is always essential to confirm the precise scope and application of the word in relation to each specific legislative provision. For example, it may refer to only a dog or a cat,[110] or be so widely drawn as to encompass 'animals of the classes Mammalia, Aves, Reptilia, Amphibia, Pisces and Insecta and any other multi cellular organism that is not a plant or a fungus'.[111] It may be restricted to those which are domestic or captive;[112] exclude birds, fish, and reptiles,[113] or, conversely, specifically include birds and reptiles (but not fish in this particular context);[114] it may be confined to vertebrates.[115] Another strategy is for the word to encompass all types of animal, except those specifically excluded. Section 7 of the Animals (Scotland) Act 1987, for example, provides that for the purposes of the statute, 'animal does not include viruses, bacteria, algae, fungi or protozoa'. In other situations, 'animals' is given a specific definition in the statute, but there is provision for this to be widened subsequently by means of secondary legislation. Thus, while the meaning of 'protected animals' under the Animals (Scientific Procedures) Act 1986 is 'any living vertebrate other than man',[116] it is expressly provided that this may be extended to include invertebrates of any description, and the species *Octopus vulgaris* has thereby been brought within the scope of the Act.[117] Similarly, the meaning to be applied to 'animals' under the Animal Health Act 1981, 'unless the context otherwise requires', includes cattle, sheep, goats, and all other ruminating animals and swine, but this list may be extended to include any kind of mammal except man, and any kind of four-footed beast which is not a mammal. However, in respect of certain parts of the Act, it may also include fish, reptiles, crustaceans, or any other cold-blooded creatures.[118] Moreover, 'animal' can extend, where specified, to undeveloped forms, including 'an egg, larva, pupa, or other immature stage',[119] or, in respect of a mammal, bird, or reptile, when half its gestation or incubation period has elapsed or, in the case of any other vertebrate, when it becomes capable of independent feeding.[120]

---

[109] *Halsbury's Laws of England* (4th edn, reissue, 1991) Vol 2, para 201.
[110] Animal Boarding Establishments Act 1963, s 5(2).   [111] Zoo Licensing Act 1981, s 21(1).
[112] Protection of Animals Act 1911, s 15(a); Protection of Animals (Scotland) Act 1912, s 13(a).
[113] Protection of Animals (Anaesthetics) Act 1954, s 1(4).   [114] Veterinary Surgeons Act 1966, s 27.
[115] Performing Animals (Regulation) Act 1925, s 5(1); Pet Animals Act 1951, s 7(3).
[116] Section 1(1).
[117] Section 1(3); Animals (Scientific Procedures) Act (Amendment) Order 1993, SI 1993/2103.
[118] Section 87(1), (2), (3).   [119] Wildlife and Countryside Act 1981, s 27(3).
[120] Animals (Scientific Procedures) Act 1986, s 1(2).

'Livestock' is another term which carries different meanings depending upon its statutory context. It can include 'any creature kept for the production of food, wool, skin or fur or for use in the farming of land or for such purpose as the Minister may by order specify';[121] or be restricted to 'cattle, horses, asses, mules, hinnies, sheep, pigs, goats and poultry, and also deer not in the wild state', and, in respect of certain parts of the statute, pheasants, partridges, and grouse while in captivity.[122] Although including many of the same animals, 'horses' are variously defined as any mare, gelding, pony, foal, colt, filly, or stallion;[123] or the foregoing, together with any ass, mule, or jennet;[124] or any mule, donkey, or other equine animal.[125] Only the Animal Health Act 1981 specifically defines what is to be regarded as a pony.[126] 'Cattle' is used to mean bulls, cows, steers, heifers, and calves;[127] but it can also encompass horses, mules, asses, sheep, goats, and swine, in addition to bovines.[128] Even more bizarrely, the gender-specific term 'bull' may extend to any cow, bullock, heifer, calf, steer, or ox.[129] Similarly, in one context the term 'poultry' encompasses domestic fowls, turkeys, geese, ducks, guinea fowls, pigeons, peacocks, and quails.[130] In another, it includes the foregoing, with the exception of peacocks and quails, but with the addition of pheasants and partridges, and with the further complication that the meaning may be either extended by secondary legislation to comprise any other species of bird, or, alternatively, restricted to exclude pheasants and partridges.[131] Just for good measure, elsewhere the word 'fowl' is used to mean any cock, hen, chicken, capon, turkey, goose, gander, duck, drake, guinea fowl, peacock, peahen, swan, or pigeon.[132]

Similarly, under one provision the adjective 'wild' means an animal not normally domesticated in Great Britain,[133] whereas under another it refers to one which is not a domestic or captive animal within the meaning of the Protection of Animals Act 1911 or the Protection of Animals (Scotland) Act 1912.[134] Under the Wildlife and Countryside Act 1981, it carries a different meaning depending upon the context. Thus, the term 'wild animal' means any animal which is living in the wild; but 'wild bird' is a bird of any kind which is ordinarily resident in, or is a visitor to, Great Britain in a wild state.[135] A 'domestic animal' under the 1911 and 1912 Acts includes a horse, ass, mule, bull, sheep, pig, goat, dog, cat, or fowl, 'or any other animal of whatsoever kind or species, and whether a quadruped or not which is tame or which has been or is being sufficiently tamed to serve some

---

[121] Agriculture (Miscellaneous Provisions) Act 1968, s 8(1).
[122] Animals Act 1971, s 11.
[123] Protection of Animals Act 1911, s 15(d); Protection of Animals (Scotland) Act 1912, s 13(d).
[124] Riding Establishments Act 1964, s 6(4).   [125] Farriers (Registration) Act 1975, s 18.
[126] Any horse not more than 147 centimetres in height, except a foal travelling with its dam if the dam is over 147 centimetres: s 89.
[127] ibid.   [128] Dogs Act 1906, s 7.
[129] Protection of Animals Act 1911, s 15(d); Protection of Animals (Scotland) Act 1912, s 13(d).
[130] Animals Act 1971, s 11.   [131] Animal Health Act 1981, s 87(4), (5).
[132] Protection of Animals Act 1911, s 15(d); Protection of Animals (Scotland) Act 1912, s 13(d).
[133] Zoo Licensing Act 1981, s 21(1).   [134] Wild Mammals (Protection) Act 1996, s 3.
[135] Section 27(1).

purpose for the use of man'.[136] A 'captive' animal for the purposes of the same legislation is defined as 'any animal (not being a domestic animal) of whatsoever kind or species, and whether a quadruped or not, including any bird, fish or reptile, which is in captivity, or confinement, or which is maimed, pinioned, or subjected to any appliance or contrivance for the purpose of hindering or preventing its escape'.[137] In other circumstances, a bird is not to be regarded as having been bred in captivity unless its parents were lawfully in captivity when the egg was laid.[138]

This practice of applying different definitions to the same word, which may be both scientifically and literally inaccurate, might appear to reflect imprecise drafting, but it does have a purpose: the advantage of using a single collective noun to refer to a range of different types of animal reduces the complexity of legislative provisions, and therefore makes them easier to follow.

It should also be noted that terms which may be used generally in everyday speech may be given a very specific meaning in legislation. Under the Welfare of Farmed Animals Regulations, for example, a 'calf' is a bovine animal aged six months or less. If it is aged six months and one day it no longer qualifies, for these purposes, as a calf. Similarly, 'sow' refers to a female pig after the first farrowing, and 'weaner' means a pig from weaning to the age of ten weeks.[139]

Finally, the same word may be given different meanings in respect of particular sections within the same legislation. Thus under the 1911 and 1912 Acts the expression 'animal' generally means any domestic or captive animal (as defined above), but, in relation to provisions relating specifically to injured animals, it is restricted to any horse, mule, ass, bull, sheep, goat, or pig (as those terms are defined elsewhere in the Acts).[140]

The moral is clear. In considering the application of any legislative provision, it is essential to establish to which animals it applies by reference to the statute itself and any relevant secondary legislation made under its authority. Equally significant, this analysis, although somewhat technical, serves to demonstrate how Parliament is able to control the scope of a legislative provision by specifying discrete and particular definitions for everyday terms.

E. Complementing Legal Regulation

In arguing the case for continued legal regulation, it is not suggested that the law is a panacea. Law can be technical, obscure, and difficult to understand; enforcement through the courts is expensive, cumbersome, time-consuming, and uncertain;

---

[136] Protection of Animals Act 1911, s 15(b); Protection of Animals (Scotland) Act 1912, s 13(b); the terms horse, bull, sheep, pig, goat, dog, cat, and fowl are further defined in s 15(c) and s 13(c) respectively.

[137] Protection of Animals Act 1911, s 15(c); Protection of Animals (Scotland) Act 1912, s 13(c).

[138] Wildlife and Countryside Act 1981, s 27(2).

[139] Welfare of Farmed Animals Regulations, n 54 above, reg 2(1) and Sch 6, para 1.

[140] 1911 Act, ss 11(4) and 15(d); 1912 Act, ss 10(4) and 13(d).

and reform is a protracted process, influenced more by political expediency than principle. It was, for example, formally recommended in 1968 that the use of sow stalls and tethers should be discontinued, but it took more than thirty years before they were finally banned.[141] Similarly, the Home Secretary established a departmental committee in 1963 to investigate the use of animals in science. This reported in 1965, putting forward eighty-three recommendations as to how the regulatory regime might be improved,[142] yet it took a further twenty-one years before new legislation was finally enacted, with the passing of the Animals (Scientific Procedures) Act 1986. Little wonder, then, that Ruth Harrison observed in her seminal book, *Animal Machines*, 'Legislation alone will not provide the animals with an adequate charter.'[143]

Campaigners have therefore always looked to other methods to advance their objective: education, campaigning, and research all have a vital part to play in raising consciousness, developing understanding, and changing attitudes to the way in which animals are treated. By attempting to influence the behaviour of consumers it is hoped to bring pressure on retailers and producers. The campaign against the use of fur for fashion clothing spearheaded by the pressure group, Lynx, resulted in a significant decline in the market during the 1980s; the success of companies such as The Body Shop caused competitors to introduce lines of 'cruelty-free' products, which had not been tested on animals (although this did not always mean that none of the ingredients had been); and the sale of free-range eggs has risen dramatically in recent years. Latterly, health fears arising from salmonella, *E-coli*, and BSE have made many consumers more aware and concerned to know how food derived from animals has been reared. This has coincided with the development of quality assurance schemes, which indicate to the consumer that endorsed products have come from animals treated in accordance with the standards prescribed by the respective schemes. These can, of course, be higher than those required by law, and their effect can be wide-ranging. For example, the RSPCA claimed that in 1999 its own scheme, 'Freedom Food', had more than 4,000 members and covered 19 million animals.[144] Furthermore, consumer choice can have an impact where legislators are loath to intervene or in situations where effective legislation is difficult to draw up and implement. For example, in the United Kingdom the crisis over animal transport came to a head during 1994 as a

---

[141] Brambell, FWR (Chairman), *Report of the Technical Committee to Enquire into the Welfare of Animals Kept Under Intensive Livestock Husbandry Systems* (1965) para 125; see n 55 above. 'The keeping of sows and gilts in stalls with or without tethers raises serious welfare problems', MAFF conceded in its Code of recommendations for the welfare of pigs, published in 1983. 'It inevitably places severe restrictions on the animals' freedom of movement, denies them normal exercise, can give rise to patterns of abnormal behaviour and very commonly cause injuries and leg weaknesses.' The Ministry accordingly 'strongly recommended' alternative systems in which 'animals' behavioural and exercise needs can be more fully met' (para 48).

[142] Littlewood, S (Chairman), *Report of the Departmental Committee on Experimentation on Animals* (1965).

[143] Harrison, n 106 above, 178.

[144] RSPCA, *Annual Review* 1999 (2000) 17. See also, Main, DCJ and Green, LE, 'Descriptive analysis of the operation of the Farm Assured British Pigs Scheme' (2000) 147 *Veterinary Record* 162.

result of the major British ferry operators introducing a voluntary ban on exporting livestock to the European mainland for slaughter and further fattening. One assumes they considered that on balance the opposition to such trade from passengers outweighed the income which it generated.[145]

Another possible tactic is to link welfare standards with subsidies. In 1994, for example, MAFF warned claimants under the Hill Livestock Compensatory Allowance Scheme that they were required to maintain and manage their flock in accordance with sound husbandry practice, and a failure to feed ewes adequately could result in disqualification from the scheme.[146] The same year, FAWC recommended that payment of the Annual Ewe Premium should be conditional upon the maintenance of good husbandry and welfare standards based upon the principles of the Ministry's Sheep Welfare Code.[147] An extension of this principle is strongly advocated by, among others, the RSPCA and John Webster,[148] and it is of potential significance that the Minister of Agriculture recently announced that he was considering the possibility of payments to compensate for the extra costs of high animal welfare standards.[149]

However, although these developments are to be welcomed, and have an important part to play, they act to complement legal regulation; they are not a substitute for it because of the reasons considered earlier in this chapter. Against this background, Garner is correct to express doubts 'about whether the consumer strategy has *any* long-term worth without a parallel campaign for legislative change'.[150]

F. Conclusion

The foregoing discussion has drawn attention to the fact that legislative intervention by Parliament acts to counter the lack of protection accorded to animals as a result of their status at common law, but the legal status itself remains unaltered. There are those, such as Francione, for whom this situation is fatal to the imposition of adequate standards of treatment for animals. As was pointed out at the beginning of this chapter, there is no consistent principle underlying the law, and the degree and nature of the protection accorded to an animal depends very much

---

[145] See Ch 7, s F(3) below.   [146] MAFF, *Condition Scoring in Sheep* (1994).

[147] FAWC, *Report on the Welfare of Sheep* (1994) para 24. More recently, FAWC has suggested that the Government should consider whether there is any permissible means of linking receipt of livestock support payments to compliance with the welfare codes, including the possibility of withdrawing payments from those convicted of animal welfare offences. The Council indicated that it proposed to look again at this issue and will provide further advice in due course: *Advice to Ministers on the Enforcement of Animal Welfare Legislation* (1999) para B(ii).

[148] RSPCA, *Agenda 2000. The future for farm animal welfare in the European Union?* (1998) 26; Webster, J, *Animal Welfare* (1995) 262.

[149] MAFF News Release 76/00.

[150] Garner, R, *Animals, politics and morality* (1993) 188 (italics in the original).

on the situation in which it finds itself, rather than on its inherent needs as an individual. This regulatory relativism *is* a matter which requires further attention from policy makers, but, while Francione confronts an important question, it is submitted that he overstates the importance of altering animals' legal status. His contention, that 'the law has not developed any doctrines that require that animal property be treated differently because an animal is different from inanimate property',[151] would seem to be demonstrably inaccurate, at least in relation to Britain. Similarly, to say that as long as animals remain property, 'there is no baseline below which their treatment cannot fall'[152] is not borne out by experience. The theme underlying this chapter is that the question of legal status is something of a distraction, at least so far as Britain is concerned (the situation may well be different in the US); it is far more important to secure a level of legal regulation which recognizes the needs and capacities of animals, imposes a clear and explicit duty on those who assume responsibility for them to ensure that prescribed standards are met, and—crucially—to ensure that this strategy is *supported by adequate means of enforcement.*

---

[151] Francione, n 15 above, 35.   [152] Francione, n 22 above, 146.

6

The Contemporary Legal Framework

A. Introduction

During the nineteenth century, protection for animals was secured, almost exclusively, by means of primary legislation; that is, Acts of Parliament. Bills were introduced, the majority on the initiative of individual MPs, into a sovereign parliament whose legislative authority went unchallenged. In the years following the First World War, however, the treatment of animals ceased to feature as a significant political issue. A society which had to come to terms successively with the profound consequences of that conflict, followed by the economic turmoil of the twenties and thirties, and then the upheaval of the Second World War, simply had other priorities. As a result, the momentum for reform disappeared. When, in the 1960s and '70s, after half a century of inertia, the issue began to reassert itself on the public consciousness, it was in a very different political, legal, and administrative environment. Acts of Parliament continued to be enacted in considerable numbers, but there was much greater reliance on secondary legislation—regulations and orders—to introduce detailed and technical provisions; legislative and non-legislative codes of practice and recommendations were being used to lay down standards; and circulars and other forms of guidance were routinely issued by central government departments to provide advice for administrative bodies. The political parties had come to dominate MPs by means of patronage and the imposition of strict party discipline; and the government of the day now had considerable control over the domestic political agenda and the parliamentary timetable. In response, those who sought to influence policy were joining together into formal pressure groups which could more effectively lobby government for reform. At the same time, the traditional autonomy of government and Parliament was being challenged by international developments. In short, power was slipping away from Westminster to Whitehall, and soon it would begin to move from there to supranational organizations, most notably to what was then known as the European Economic Community.

Accordingly, in order to understand modern animal protection law, it is necessary to appreciate the background to, as well as the nature and significance of, this contemporary legal framework. In particular, if law is to be regarded as the principal means of regulating the treatment of animals, it is essential to recognize where in the polity legislative power is located.

B. Parliament's Legislative Supremacy

The United Kingdom is an exception among liberal democracies in not having its system of government prescribed by the terms of a formal written constitution. In the absence of such a document, ultimate power must lie elsewhere within the body politic and, in the case of the United Kingdom, it resides with the national Parliament. This power has manifested itself in the doctrine of parliamentary legislative supremacy. In short, Parliament has 'the right to make or unmake any law whatever', and, further, 'no person or body is recognized by the law of England [or, indeed, Scotland] as having a right to override or set aside the legislation of Parliament'.[1] In other words, Parliament's supremacy means that its legislative powers are legally unconstrained: if it is persuaded of the merits of a particular course of action, then it has the inherent power and authority to legislate accordingly, and consideration of the validity of an Act's provisions is not part of the judicial function.

By virtue of this doctrine, Parliament has—in theory, at least—complete autonomy to decide for itself what measures to introduce in respect of animals. However, domestic law exists against the backdrop of international obligations assumed by the Government as a consequence of agreeing to the terms of treaties and conventions, most importantly in this context, the World Trade Organization (WTO), conventions of the Council of Europe, and the Treaty of the European Community (TEC).

C. The World Trade Organization

(1) The nature of the WTO

The WTO, based in Geneva, was established on 1 January 1995. Simultaneously succeeding and incorporating the General Agreement on Tariffs and Trade (GATT), it became the legal and institutional foundation of an international, multilateral trading system in respect of goods, services, and intellectual property.

---

[1] Dicey, AV, *An Introduction to the Study of the Law of the Constitution* (10th edn, 1959) 40.

It is 'dedicated to open, fair and undistorted competition', reflecting the prevailing commercial orthodoxy that 'liberal trade policies which allow the unrestricted flow of goods, services and productive inputs multiply the rewards that come with producing the best products, with the best design, at the best price'.[2] In order to advance these objectives, WTO rules are binding on all the individual states which comprise its membership.[3] Indeed, its 'primary output' has been described as 'rule writing and enforcement of an explicit global regime'.[4] In the event of a dispute between members which cannot be settled by conciliation, a panel is established by the WTO's Dispute Settlement Body to examine the matter. Its conclusions and recommendations are normally binding, subject to any appeal to the standing Appellate Body. Failure to implement the panel's recommendations may result in the recalcitrant member having to pay compensation, or being subjected to retaliatory trade sanctions authorized by the Dispute Settlement Body.

(2) The implications for animal protection legislation

The WTO therefore has the power and authority to prevent independent nation states from determining their own trading policies, and to punish them should they contravene WTO rules. This may be considered desirable in securing one of the Organization's principal objectives, namely, preventing 'a self-defeating and destructive drift into protectionism'.[5] However, the effect can be to preclude a country from obstructing the importation of a product which has been produced in a manner it regards as ethically unacceptable: in relation to, for example, the terms and conditions of the workforce, the environmental impact, or, of course, the standards of animal welfare.

In particular, WTO rules do not allow any trade restriction based upon what are described as 'process and production methods' (PPMs), unless they change the character of a product in a discernible way. The significance of this constraint is that varying standards of animal welfare are not considered to result in meat, milk, eggs, and other animal products which are materially distinctive. For example, eggs produced by battery and free range methods are regarded as indistinguishable (at least by international trade lawyers). While it is not immediately obvious why a

---

[2] World Trade Organization, *Trading into the Future* (1995) 6 and 7.

[3] The United Kingdom is a party to the WTO in its own right, but so too is the European Community (Decision 94/800). In consequence, the institutions of the EC have assumed responsibility for WTO matters both within the Community itself and in its external relations. The Commission therefore oversees trade between Member States to ensure that it complies with the requirements of the WTO, and represents the Community collectively in international negotiations, including those arising from trade disputes, which undoubtedly gives EC Member States a much greater international presence than would be the case if each country acted alone. This has been particularly apparent in relations with the United States. At the same time, it results in EC Member States being bound by the collective decisions of the Community on matters of international trade and, in the event of the EC trade policy contravening WTO rules, each may have sanctions imposed against it.

[4] Vines, D, 'The WTO in Relation to the Fund and the Bank: Competencies, Agendas, and Linkages', in Krueger, AE (ed), *The WTO as an International Organization* (1998) 70.

[5] World Trade Organization, n 2 above, 7.

condition which is already applicable to home-produced goods should be considered a restriction on trade if it is similarly applied to imports, in practice this situation presents a fundamental obstacle to a WTO member, such as the EC or the UK, which might wish either to prohibit the importation of products from animals which have been reared in systems with lower welfare standards than those required by their own legislation, or to insist that the animals have been kept in conditions which meet those standards.

This is so, notwithstanding that article 20 of the GATT provides that 'nothing' in the Agreement shall be construed to prevent the adoption or enforcement by any contracting party of measures which are necessary to protect public morals; human, animal, or plant life or health; or which relate to the conservation of exhaustible natural resources; provided such measures are not applied in a manner which would constitute a means of arbitrary or unjustifiable discrimination, or as a disguised restriction on international trade.[6] Such restrictions are therefore required to be based on science, imposed only to the extent necessary, and to apply international standards where they exist, although more stringent conditions may be permissible if there is scientific justification or they are based on the findings of an appropriate risk assessment. In the same way, although WTO members ostensibly have the right to take what are described as 'sanitary and phytosanitary measures' for the protection of human, animal, or plant life or health, these too are similarly circumscribed. They may only be exercised 'to the extent necessary to provide such protection'; may be maintained only if there is sufficient scientific evidence to justify such action; and must not constitute a disguised restriction on international trade. In order to meet these criteria, it is incumbent on the WTO member concerned to demonstrate that the measures are both 'necessary' (that is, the protection itself is necessary and there is no alternative means—less restrictive to trade—of achieving such protection), and 'based on scientific principles', not on 'arbitrary or unjustified distinctions'.[7] It is therefore extremely difficult to justify taking action under article 20, and it is not surprising that its impact has been minimal, even though representatives of the European Commission, including the trade commissioner, Sir Leon Brittan, have stated that trade-related animal welfare measures could theoretically be afforded protection under article 20.[8]

In practice, however, the Commission has chosen not to test this view, preferring to retreat in the face of uncertainty, even if this involves unilaterally overriding

[6] General Agreement on Tariffs and Trade, Geneva, 1986, art 20(a), (b), (g).

[7] Agreement on the Application of Sanitary and Phytosanitary Measures, arts 2 and 3. The meaning of a sanitary or phytosanitary measure is widely drawn to include: all relevant laws, decrees, regulations, requirements, and procedures including end product criteria; processes and production methods; testing, inspection, certification, and approval procedures; quarantine treatments including relevant requirements associated with the transport of animals or plants, or with the materials necessary for their survival during transport; provisions on relevant statistical methods, sampling procedures, and methods of risk assessment; and packaging and labelling requirements directly related to food safety: Annex A, para 1. The full text of the Agreement is attached to Decision 94/800.

[8] Eurogroup for Animal Welfare, *Report of the 139th Session of the European Parliamentary Intergroup on the Welfare and Conservation of Animals* (1997).

existing EC law. For example, the EC agreed in 1991 to a Regulation which, from the beginning of 1995, prohibited use of the leghold trap in all Member States and banned the import of certain furs from countries where this type of trap continued to be used.[9] While the Community was undoubtedly entitled to suppress the leghold trap within its own borders, import restrictions based on the manner in which wild animals were caught brought it into dispute with those countries which would be affected, especially Canada and the United States. Neither claimed that the purpose of the ban was to secure a trade advantage for EC Member States, but they nevertheless indicated their intention to mount a challenge under the terms of the WTO. As a result, the European Commission first postponed implementation of the import ban for a year (as it was entitled to do under the Regulation), and then, in December 1995, conceded defeat. It informed Member States that the ban was 'for the time being unfeasible', indicated it would take steps to have the Regulation amended, and advised that, in the meantime, 'the Commission considers that your custom authorities should therefore refrain from taking any action at frontiers from the beginning of next year'.[10] The British Government subsequently announced that, because of uncertainty as to whether Member States would be in breach of international law, it had 'reluctantly concluded that it would not be appropriate to implement the ban'.[11]

This episode clearly demonstrates the impact of the WTO on attempts to improve animal welfare. It apparently enables the Commission, acting administratively, to set aside a binding legal provision which has been subject to the full legislative process involving Commission, Council of Ministers, and European Parliament, notwithstanding that the Regulation should have come into force automatically on 1 January 1996, the only postponement provided for in the legislation (of twelve months) having been exhausted. Furthermore, despite the fact that a regulation has direct effect in all Member States, thus automatically becoming part of their domestic law, governments can apparently ignore their legally-binding obligations in such a situation: in refusing IFAW and the RSPCA leave to challenge the UK Government's decision not to implement the import ban, the High Court's limp response was that such inaction was justified because 'it is evident that there is going to be a change in the law'.[12] It is the usual practice in

[9] Regulation 3254/91. See further, Nollkaemper, A, 'The Legality of Moral Crusades Disguised in Trade Laws: An analysis of the EC "ban" on furs from animals taken by leghold traps' (1996) 8 Journal of Environmental Law 237; Charnovitz, S, 'The Moral Exception in Trade Policy' (1998) 38 Virginia Journal of International Law 689; Harrop, SR and Bowles, D, 'Wildlife Management, the Multilateral Trade Regime, Morals and the Welfare of Animals' (1998) 1 Journal of Wildlife Law and Policy 64; Harrop, SR, 'The trapping of wild mammals and attempts to legislate for animal suffering in international standards' (2000) 12 Journal of Environmental Law 333.

[10] Communication to Member States from the Director General of External Relations, Commercial Policy and Relations with North America, the Far East, Australia and New Zealand, 8 December 1995; quoted by Macpherson J in R v Commissioners of Customs and Excise, ex parte IFAW and RSPCA (QBD, 27 March 1996).

[11] HC Debs, 29 March 1996, col 796 (WA).

[12] R v Commissioners of Customs and Excise, ex parte IFAW and RSPCA, n 10 above. A 'Framework Agreement' was subsequently made in 1997 between the EU, Canada, and Russia under which some forms of leghold trap would be phased out within four years. In separate negotiations between the EU and the US, the latter agreed to phase out non-padded leghold traps within six years.

Britain for the courts to apply the law as it is, not how they speculate it might become at some indeterminate point in the future. Yet, the force of the WTO is such that they are seemingly prepared to allow the Government unilaterally to disregard its incontrovertible existing legal duties.

This is not the only example of the harmful influence of the WTO on animal protection. The EC decided to postpone implementation of the directive which would have prevented the marketing of cosmetics tested on animals, where non-animal tested alternatives were available, because of fears that it was incompatible with the WTO (a cosmetic which has not been tested on animals being no different in character compared to one that has).[13] Again, the basis of the measure was specifically intended to prevent animal suffering, and had nothing to do with restricting imports so as to protect European producers from outside competition. The EC's ability to prevent the importation of beef from cattle treated with growth-promoting hormones (a policy opposed by the British Government) has been another area of contention with the United States. The disputes panel initially sided with the USA, but on appeal the WTO's Appellate Body was more circumspect, holding that a member may require higher health standards than the international norm if it can demonstrate appropriate evidence.[14] It is instructive to compare the WTO's approach in such a situation, which requires positive scientific evidence that growth promoters pose a threat, with the precautionary principle reflected in the European Convention on the Protection of Animals kept for Farming Purposes: 'No other substance with the exception of those given for the therapeutic or prophylactic purposes shall be administered to an animal unless it has been demonstrated by scientific studies of animal welfare or established experience that the effect of the substance is not detrimental to the health or welfare of the animal.'[15]

The underlying problem is that the WTO does not recognize the treatment of animals as a legitimate basis on which to impose restrictions. In consequence, it becomes difficult, if not impossible, to prevent live animals being exported to, or animal products being imported from, countries where the standards of animal welfare are lower than those prevailing in the EU generally, or the UK in particular. Opposition to the policy of banning battery cages within the European Union, for example, has raised the spectre of an uncontrollable influx of cheap eggs from other countries which continue to keep laying hens in such conditions. This situation not only raises important issues of principle concerning the respective weight to be attached to unrestricted trade on the one hand, and questions of public

---

[13] Directive 97/18. In May 2000, Member States agreed a further postponement until the end of June 2002. The European Parliament voted on 3 April 2001 to ban within five years the sale of all products tested on animals throughout the EU, but this decision requires to be endorsed by the Council of Ministers before it can be implemented.

[14] In the face of conflicting scientific evidence as to whether the use of such hormones poses a risk to consumers, the Commission's policy as at June 2000 was to maintain the current ban on a provisional basis while it seeks further scientific opinion.

[15] Article 6, as amended by the Protocol to the Convention.

morality on the other; it also has implications for the stringency of domestic regulation: measures to protect animal welfare may increase the cost of a product, and additional domestic regulation can therefore have a detrimental effect on the competitiveness of home-produced goods. The House of Commons Environment Committee has described animal welfare as 'something of a special case', and has recommended that it 'should be given separate consideration by the WTO'.[16] Similarly, the RSPCA and Eurogroup for Animal Welfare have warned: 'If the policy of trade liberalization is allowed to supersede policies to protect people, animals and the environment, public support for the multilateral trading system may be lost.' In order to benefit both animal welfare and trade liberalization, they have called for 'a complementary relationship' to be established 'in which policies to promote animal welfare, social justice and environmental protection are facilitated rather than obstructed by free and fair trade'. In the meantime, they are right to call on the WTO 'to distinguish between measures to secure trade advantage (its primary purpose) and trade-related measures taken to secure valid non-trade objectives'.[17] Both the British Government and the EU are sympathetic to these arguments; the Minister of Agriculture told the House of Commons in June 2000 that the 'European Union has made a commitment to taking forward the issue of farm animal welfare in the World Trade Organization negotiations. The UK has been a strong supporter of that commitment.'[18] Nevertheless, securing international agreement on this matter is fraught with difficulty.

It has been said that, by wishing to introduce restrictions on imports which have not been produced to the same welfare standards as those required of home producers, countries are attempting to impose their own moral view on other nation states, who may have a very different attitude towards animals. Not only is it equally possible to argue the same point the other way (unconstrained trade liberalization leads to those with low or non-existent standards imposing *their* view of the moral status of animals on the importing country), it is also to miss the point. The intention is not to institute a form of moral imperialism by forcing other countries to adopt a view of the world based on a British, or EU, perspective, but rather to allow Britain or the EU, as the case may be, to make their own moral choices, by enabling them to prohibit within their own territory the marketing of products (whether domestically produced or imported) derived from practices which they find unacceptable.[19]

---

[16] House of Commons Environment Committee, *World Trade and the Environment* (1996) para 205. See also, House of Commons Agriculture Committee, *The Implications for UK Agriculture and EU Agricultural Policy of Trade Liberalization and the WTO Round* (2000) paras 43–47.

[17] RSPCA/Eurogroup for Animal Welfare, *Conflict or concord? Animal welfare and the World Trade Organisation* (1998) 5 and 13. See also, RSPCA/Eurogroup for Animal Welfare, *Food for Thought. Farm Animal Welfare and the WTO* (1999); RSPCA, *Profit with principle: animal welfare and UK pig farming* (2000).

[18] HC Debs, 29 June 2000, col 1028.

[19] I am indebted to Peter Stevenson of Compassion in World Farming for drawing this argument to my attention.

D. The Council of Europe

(1) Council of Europe Conventions

The Council of Europe, not to be confused with the institutions of the European Community, was established after the Second World War with the intention of promoting greater European unity, upholding the principle of parliamentary democracy and human rights, improving living conditions, and promoting what were described as 'human values'. Its membership now extends to forty European states, compared to the fifteen which make up the European Community. The Council is an intergovernmental body which, unlike the EC, has no power to make legislation, but seeks to advance the values it represents by drawing up conventions, of which by far the most important and influential is the European Convention on Human Rights and Fundamental Freedoms. Conventions have also been produced on a wide variety of other topics, including the treatment of animals on the farm, during international transport, at slaughter, used for experimental and other scientific purposes, and kept as pets.[20] In involving itself with issues of animal welfare, the Council of Europe has been 'motivated by its concept of the dignity of man, which it views as in dissociable [sic] from the respect which man owes to his environment and to the animals which live therein'.[21]

None of these Conventions is automatically binding; each member country may decide for itself which, if any, to ratify and implement. Nevertheless, despite their voluntary nature and relative obscurity, they are of some significance. First, they can make a difference in those countries which implement them. Secondly, as 'international ethical standards for the use of animals by man',[22] they affirm that the treatment of animals is a legitimate concern for public policy makers throughout Europe. Thirdly, they provide a benchmark which individual countries can aspire to and against which their own standards may be judged. Finally, although formally separate and distinct from EC law, the Conventions have been used as a term of reference when drawing up Community legislation.

---

[20] European Convention for the Protection of Animals Kept for Farming Purposes (1976; Additional Protocol, 1992), supplemented by specific Recommendations drawn up by the Standing Committee of the Convention, concerning respectively, poultry, pigs, cattle, goats, sheep, calves, ratites (farmed ostriches, emus, and rheas), domestic geese and ducks, and fur animals; European Convention for the Protection of Animals during International Transport (1968; Additional Protocol, 1979); European Convention for the Protection of Animals for Slaughter (1979); European Convention for the Protection of Vertebrate Animals used for Experimental and other Scientific Purposes (1986; Additional Protocol, 1998); and the European Convention for the Protection of Pet Animals (1987).

[21] Wilkins, DB (ed), *Animal Welfare in Europe* (1997) 126, referring to a speech by the Deputy Secretary General of the Council to the Plenary Session of the Eurogroup for Animal Welfare, 23 November 1990.

[22] ibid.

(2) The relationship between Council of Europe Conventions and the European Community

The Commission has recommended that the EC should become a contracting party to all these Conventions;[23] to date, it has formally approved those relating to farm animals, slaughter, and experimental and other scientific purposes.[24] In consequence, EC legislation has been amended to comply with the provisions of these Conventions.[25] However, while the European Court of Justice (ECJ) has confirmed that their terms thereby become 'an integral part of the Community legal order', the more detailed Recommendations which underpin the farm animals Convention are not legally binding.[26] In any event, the Conventions are of a very general nature and therefore need to be supplemented before they can be implemented; ratification alone is insufficient to make them operative. For example, in a case challenging the Minister of Agriculture's refusal to ban the export of calves destined to be reared in veal crates, the Advocate General pointed out that 'Although the imperative form is used in the provisions of the Convention [for the Protection of Animals kept for Farming Purposes], the word "shall" being systematically used to lay down the principles contained in Chapter 1, those provisions are for the most part characterized by imprecision.' The Court agreed, and thereby concluded that it was 'clear from the very wording of those provisions that they were indicative only'.[27] Accordingly, where the Community has decided to give effect to a Convention, it has been thought preferable, instead of simply adopting it, to integrate its terms into EC legislation, together with whatever other provisions may be necessary to make them effectual.[28] Indeed, it is by this process of incorporation that they have proved to be particularly influential. For example, the definition of a 'procedure' in the European Convention for the protection of vertebrate animals used for experimental and other scientific purposes[29] is reproduced in essentially identical terms in the equivalent EC directive (except here the term 'experiment' is preferred to 'procedure'),[30] and is thereby carried over into British legislation.[31] Indeed, the Conventions are the source of many of the welfare provisions which have found their way into domestic law. Thus, the requirement that

---

[23] COM (93) 384.

[24] Decision 78/923, Decision 88/306, and Decision 99/575. In addition, the fact that all Member States independently ratified the Convention on the Protection of Animals during International Transport has enabled the Community as such to accede to it.

[25] See, for example, the recital to Directive 93/119 on the protection of animals at the time of slaughter or killing, which declares that a reason for the new legislation is that 'the scope of the Convention is wider than existing Community rules on the matter'; and one of the grounds for the introduction of Directive 98/58 concerning the protection of animals on farms was, according to its recital, the necessity for the Community to make further provision for the uniform application of the Convention and its Recommendations.

[26] *R v Minister of Agriculture, Fisheries and Food, ex parte Compassion in World Farming*, Case 1/96 [1998] 2 CMLR 661, ECJ, paras [31] and [36].

[27] ibid, Opinion of the Advocate General, para 129; Judgment of the Court, para [34].

[28] Commission of the European Communities, 'Background Report: Animal Welfare', 11 October 1993.

[29] Article 2(c).   [30] Directive 86/609, art 2(d).

[31] Animals (Scientific Procedures) Act 1986, s 2.

farm animals should be kept in a way which has regard 'to their physiological and ethological needs in accordance with established experience and scientific knowledge' was transposed from the relevant directive, which in turn was taken from the Convention.[32] Similarly, the condition contained in the Protocol to the farm animal Convention that 'no animal shall be kept for farming purposes unless it can be reasonably expected, on the basis of its phenotype or genotype, that it can be kept without detrimental effects on its health or welfare'[33] has been reproduced in identical terms in the on-farm directive and the corresponding national regulations.[34]

(3) The relationship between Council of Europe Conventions and domestic law

The United Kingdom has ratified the European Conventions relating to the protection of animals during international transport, kept for farming purposes, and used for experimental and scientific purposes. Under British law, however, accession by the Government to a treaty or convention is an executive, not a legislative, act. The Government itself may thereby assume obligations under international law, but the terms of the treaty do not as a result automatically become part of domestic law. A treaty is not, in the words of Lord Oliver, 'self executing', and is not enforceable in the United Kingdom 'unless and until it has been incorporated into the law by legislation'.[35] In the absence of formal incorporation into domestic law, a treaty will not normally give rise to any rights or obligations which can be enforced in the British courts, even though the United Kingdom, in the form of the Government, may have agreed to its terms: 'the most that can be said about the weight to be attributed' to such a convention, observed the High Court in 1985, is that 'it can be used in interpreting the domestic law of this country', where the meaning of this is ambiguous.[36] The courts adopt the view that in such a situation it is always open to the Government to legislate to ' "domesticate" or "patriate" ' the Convention, and, if this has not been done, it is their duty to apply domestic law 'as it is, and not as it would be if full effect were given to this country's obligations under the Treaty'.[37] This may be by means of legislation enacted entirely on Parliament's own initiative, or as a result of the terms of a treaty being transposed

---

[32] Welfare of Farmed Animals (England) Regulations 2000, SI 2000/1870, reg 3(3); Welfare of Farmed Animals (Scotland) Regulations 2000, SI 2000/442, reg 3(3); Welfare of Farmed Animals (Wales) Regulations 2001, reg 3(3). Welfare of Farmed Animals (Wales) Regulations 2001, Sch 4, para 1. The Regulations relating to Wales came into force on 31 July 2001, but at the time this book went to press they had not been allocated an SI number. Henceforth, the three sets of regulations will be referred to collectively as the 'Welfare of Farmed Animals Regulations'.

[33] Article 3, as amended by the Protocol of amendment to the European Convention for the protection of animals kept for farming purposes, art 2.

[34] Directive 98/58, art 21; Welfare of Farmed Animals Regulations, n 32 above, Sch 1, para 29.

[35] *Maclaine Watson & Co Ltd v Department of Trade and Industry* [1990] 2 AC 418, 500, HL.

[36] *Roberts v Ruggiero* (QBD, 3 April 1985) (Stephen Brown LJ).

[37] *R v Secretary of State for the Home Department, ex parte Brind* [1991] 1 AC 696, 718, CA (Lord Donaldson MR).

into European Community law, which then becomes binding on Member States. So, for example, the obligations contained in the European Convention for the Protection of Animals kept for Farming Purposes, as amended by the Protocol of 6 February 1992, are reflected in the EC Directives concerning farmed animals,[38] and are given effect in English, Scottish, and Welsh law by each jurisdiction's respective Welfare of Farmed Animals Regulations.[39]

A convention may also be influential in the development of administrative policy and standards. It is expressly acknowledged, for example, that the *Code of Practice for the Housing and Care of Animals Used in Scientific Procedures*, produced by the Home Office under the authority of the Animals (Scientific Procedures) Act 1986, is based on the principles contained in the European Convention for Vertebrate Animals used for Experimental and other Scientific Purposes.[40]

E. The European Union

(1) The nature of the enterprise

The European Economic Community (EEC) was established in 1957 by the Treaty of Rome, article 2 of which stated:

The Community shall have as its task, by establishing a common market and progressively approximating the economic policies of Member States, to promote throughout the Community a harmonious development of economic activities, a continued and balanced expansion, an increase in stability, an accelerated raising of the standard of living and closer relations between the States belonging to it.

Article 3 specified those activities which the Community was empowered to undertake in order to further its purposes. These included:

- the elimination, as between Member States, of customs duties and other quantitative restrictions on the import and export of goods, and of all other measures having equivalent effect;
- the abolition, as between Member States, of obstacles to freedom of movement for persons, services, and capital;
- the adoption of a common policy in the sphere of agriculture; and
- the institution of a system ensuring that competition in the common market is not distorted.

The original objectives were therefore economic, with particular emphasis on the promotion of free trade between Member States. If these aspirations were to become reality, it was necessary to establish appropriate mechanisms and institutions to initiate and develop policy; and, in order to ensure that such policy was

---

[38] Directive 88/166; Directive 91/629, as amended by Directive 97/2; Directive 91/630; Directive 98/58; Directive 99/74.

[39] See n 32 above.   [40] (1989) paras 2.3 and 2.4.

implemented and applied uniformly across the Community, means of enforcing and interpreting it were also required. Accordingly, the Treaty established Community institutions charged to exercise executive, legislative, and judicial functions. Furthermore, in order to ensure that Member States fulfilled their obligations, article 3 of the Treaty empowered these Community institutions to secure 'the approximation of the laws of Member States to the extent required for the proper functioning of the common market'. Article 10 (formerly 5)[41] places a corresponding duty on Member States to 'take all appropriate measures, whether general or particular, to ensure the fulfilment of the obligations arising out of this Treaty or resulting from action taken by the institutions of the Community', to which end they 'shall abstain from any measure which could jeopardize the attainment of the objectives of this Treaty'.

The comparison is not entirely accurate, but the Treaty of Rome (now the Treaty establishing the European Community, the 'TEC') is somewhat analogous to a written constitution, although it operates at a supranational level: it established the EEC (now the European Community); specified the extent of its competence (that is, the purposes for which it exists and the parameters within which it is authorized to act); provided for the creation of rules to further its objectives which were to be *common to*, and *binding upon*, Member States; established the institutions to carry out these functions, including defining the extent of their respective powers and their relationship with each other and the Member States; and *affirmed that the rules of the Community are to have a higher status than the domestic law of Member States.*

The term 'progressively approximating' in article 2 indicates that, from the outset, it was accepted that the Community would not remain static; it was created with an inherent dynamism. Its principal aims could be set down in the founding Treaties, but the implementation of those aims, and the harmonization of national laws in accordance with them, could only be achieved over a period of time. The project entailed, therefore, a momentum which would carry it forward towards its ultimate goal. Consequently, the founding Treaty has itself been amended as a result of the Single European Act (1986), the Treaty on European Union ('the Maastricht Treaty', 1991), and the Treaty of Amsterdam (1997). Together, these have established the European Union, widened the competence of the European Community, created the single market, provided for a single currency, introduced new institutions, and altered the powers and procedures of those already in existence.

---

[41] Many of the existing articles of the Treaty were renumbered as a result of the provisions of the Treaty of Amsterdam, which came into effect on 1 May 1999.

F. European Community Law[42]

Primary Community legislation consists of the TEC, as amended by the Single European Act, the Treaty on European Union, and the Treaty of Amsterdam. It is created directly by agreement between the Member States. Secondary legislation—regulations and directives—is created by Community institutions acting under the authority of the TEC. The EC can legislate only on matters, and to further purposes, for which there is specific authority in the treaties; that is, those which are within its competence. Because regulations prevail over national law and are directly applicable, meaning that they automatically become part of the law of each Member State without the need for further national legislation, they are used for measures which require uniform application throughout the European Union, such as the standards which lorries must meet if they are used to transport livestock on journeys of more than eight hours, and the criteria applicable to the staging points at which the animals are fed, watered, and rested en route.[43]

However, most of the measures relating to the treatment of animals are contained in directives, the terms of which are binding on Member States in so far as they prescribe the objective to be attained, but it is left to national governments to decide for themselves how this is to be achieved. It may be that this can be accomplished administratively. For example, the provision in the zoos directive requiring such institutions to engage in specified conservation activities has been implemented in Britain by incorporating appropriate conditions in the licensing regime.[44] Directives may be transposed into domestic law by means of primary legislation, as is the case with the Animals (Scientific Procedures) Act 1986, which implements the provisions of the 1986 Directive on the approximation of law, regulations and administrative provisions of the Member States regarding the protection of animals used for experimental and other scientific purposes;[45] more usually in respect of animal welfare, transposition is achieved by means of secondary legislation which is introduced under the authority of enabling provisions contained in an Act of Parliament. Thus, the Welfare of Animals (Slaughter or Killing) Regulations 1995[46] were made under the European Communities Act 1972 to give effect to the directive on the protection of animals at the time of slaughter or killing.[47] Similarly, the Welfare of Animals (Transport) Order 1997,[48]

---

[42] The organization was originally known as the European Economic Community and subsequently changed its name to the European Community. More recently, the European Union has been established under the authority of the Treaty on European Union. It has become common to treat the words 'Community' and 'Union' as being interchangeable. Technically this is incorrect; they are not synonymous. The European Community continues to exist as a discrete legal entity under the umbrella of the European Union. Accordingly, the description 'European Community law' is to be preferred, and it is the term which will be adopted henceforth, but 'European Union' will be used to describe the geographical area which incorporates the 15 Member States.

[43] Regulation 411/98; Regulation 1255/97.

[44] DETR, *Secretary of State's Standards of Modern Zoo Practice* (revised version, 2000).

[45] Directive 86/609.   [46] SI 1995/731.   [47] Directive 93/119.   [48] SI 1997/1480.

which implements the transport directives,[49] was introduced under powers contained in the Animal Health Act 1981. Where a directive lays down minimum (as opposed to common) requirements, it is incumbent on all Member States to meet these, but it does not prevent an individual government from adopting a higher standard. So, although it is not expressly required under EC law, since 1999 it has been illegal in Britain to keep sows tethered.[50] However, where a country chooses to adopt such a policy, it is prevented both by WTO rules and EC law from prohibiting the import of products from animals raised in systems which fail to meet the same standards.

A Member State which does not comply with its obligations under Community law may be liable to pay damages to an injured party.[51] As with the WTO, the threat of potentially costly sanctions may make the governments of Member States extremely cautious to take legislative or administrative measures in circumstances of uncertainty.

Ultimate legal power lies with the ECJ. Its decisions are binding in all Member States; there is no appeal. The role of the Court is to ensure that the terms of the TEC, as amended, are observed by Community institutions and Member States, and to provide in cases of dispute a conclusive interpretation as to the meaning of the Treaty and any secondary legislation made under it. These tend to be written in very broad terms, which has provided the ECJ with the opportunity to influence the direction and speed of the Community's progress. In part, such judicial activism is the result of the Court having regard to the dynamic nature of the Community's objectives, but it also flows from the fact that the Court's jurisprudence is founded on the continental system of civil law which, crudely, regards the judge's role as being first and foremost to identify and apply the principle underlying the legislation, unlike British courts, which have traditionally tended towards a forensic consideration of the meaning to be attributed to specific words and phrases, with particular regard to precedent. 'The European Court, in contrast to English courts, applies teleological rather than historical methods to the interpretation of the Treaties and other Community legislation', observed Lord Diplock,

It seeks to give effect to what it conceives to be the spirit rather than the letter of the Treaties; sometimes, indeed, to an English judge, it may seem to the exclusion of the letter. It views the Communities as living and expanding organisms and the interpretation of the provisions of the Treaties as changing to match their growth.[52]

The ECJ is therefore very much more than simply an arbiter of disputes; it has seen its role as contributing to the impetus driving the Community forward and promoting its primary objects, such as unrestricted trade.

---

[49] Directive 91/628, as amended by Directive 95/29.

[50] Directive 91/630; Directive 98/58; Welfare of Farmed Animals Regulations, n 32 above, Sch 6, para 4. These provisions were previously contained in the Welfare of Livestock Regulations 1994, SI 1994/2126.

[51] *Francovich v Italian Republic*, Cases 6 & 9/90 [1993] 2 CMLR 66, ECJ; *Brasserie du Pecheur SA v Federal Republic of Germany* and *R v Secretary of State for Transport, ex parte Factortame Ltd (No 4)*, Cases 48/93 and 46/93 [1996] 1 CMLR 889, ECJ.   [52] *R v Henn* [1981] AC 850, 905, HL.

G. The Legal Basis for Animal Protection Measures in European Community Law

'The welfare of animals, both domestic and wild,' declared the Commission in 1991, 'occupies an important part in the European Community's programme of work.'[53] However, the EC may legislate only on those matters which fall within its competence and serve to further the objectives set out in the TEC. In other words, it must be able to point to legal authority for all the provisions it introduces, which is set out in the recital (preamble) at the beginning of each regulation and directive. EC legislation relating to the protection of animals has been intended principally to minimize differences in the conditions prevailing in the Member States, which might otherwise distort competition within the single market, especially in the sphere of agriculture. Thus, legislation concerned with the protection of animals on the farm,[54] during transport,[55] and at the time of slaughter or killing,[56] are based on article 37 (formerly 43) of the TEC, which sanctions measures to establish a common organization for the market in agricultural products; that regulating the use of animals for scientific purposes[57] was introduced under articles 94 and 95 (formerly 100 and 100A), which permit the approximation of the laws of Member States in order for the internal market to function; and the zoos directive[58] was made under the authority of article 175 (formerly 130s), in furtherance of the Community's policy on the environment. While this represents the main body of EC legislation intended to protect domestic and captive animals, there is also a large number of other measures which impinge upon animal welfare, such as those relating to animal health, the licensing and availability of veterinary medicines, regulation of the veterinary profession, the standards laid down for organic production, and the provisions which establish EC bodies with advisory, administrative, and enforcement responsibilities in this area.

As originally conceived, concern for animal welfare was entirely incidental to promoting the objectives set out in the TEC. Of the original six members of the Community, only Germany and The Netherlands had a tradition of animal protection legislation, and the subject was not a priority in the early days of developing the common agricultural policy. By the early 1970s, when Denmark, Ireland, and the UK joined, public awareness of the treatment of animals was growing. In particular, public concern was being expressed in Germany and the UK about

---

[53] Commission of the European Communities, 'Background Report: Animal Welfare', 23 October 1991.

[54] Directive 88/166 (which ceases to have effect after the end of 2002); Directive 91/629, as amended by Directive 97/2 and Decision 97/182; and Directive 91/630; Directive 98/58; Directive 99/74. The Council of Ministers agreed in June 2001 to amend Directive 91/630 on the protection of pigs, including the introduction of a ban on individual sow stalls (which are already prohibited in the UK) after the end of 2012. However, at the same time the Council rejected a number of other measures intended to improve the welfare of pigs which had been proposed by the European Parliament: Eurogroup for Animal Welfare, Press Release, 19 June 2001.

[55] Directive 91/628, as amended by Directive 95/29; Regulation 1255/97; Regulation 411/98.

[56] Directive 93/119.   [57] Directive 86/609.   [58] Directive 99/22.

methods of slaughter, which led in 1974 to the first Community legislation for the protection of domestic animals, laying down requirements for pre-stunning.[59] According to its recital, in addition to commercial considerations, the motivation for this measure was an acceptance that the Community should take action to avoid in general all forms of cruelty to animals, an object which had no basis in the Treaty. In 1977, the first Directive on the protection of animals during international transport was adopted,[60] which was a verbatim transposition of the Council of Europe Convention on the same subject. The following year, the Council of Ministers approved, on behalf of the Community, the Council of Europe Convention for the Protection of Animals kept for Farming Purposes,[61] but, on this occasion, the instrument which gave effect to the decision specifically stated that the protection of animals was *not* in itself one of the objectives of the Community, a change of attitude which reflected increasing scepticism in Community political circles, fuelled by opposition from the powerful agricultural lobby, about the need or desirability for the EC to involve itself in issues of farm animal welfare. Although further protective measures were subsequently introduced, principally on economic grounds, there remained no formal authority for the Community to concern itself with welfare until first the Declaration, and then the Protocol annexed to the TEC on the protection and welfare of animals, expressly placed a responsibility on EC institutions and the Member States to pay full regard to the welfare requirements of animals in formulating and implementing the Community's agriculture, transport, internal market, and research policies.[62] It should be noted, however, that the Protocol only applies to those areas specifically mentioned; it does not give the EC a general competence to promote animal welfare. Consequently, it has no power to introduce legislation in respect of those matters which continue to fall outside its jurisdiction, such as most aspects of companion animal welfare. Notwithstanding this caveat, regulating the treatment of animals has established itself as a legitimate concern for EC policy makers and legislators. The Protocol gives cause for guarded optimism,[62a] as does the easing of the potential threat posed by subsidiarity. This principle is intended to prevent over-centralization and requires that the Community may only take action if it can be justified on the grounds that the proposed objective could not be sufficiently achieved by the Member States acting on their own initiative.[63] When it was originally introduced in 1992, the Council decided not to pursue a number of proposals for legislation which it had been contemplating, including the proposed zoos directive, but it was subsequently persuaded that this measure could be

---

[59] Directive 74/577, now superseded by Directive 93/119.   [60] Directive 77/489.

[61] Decision 78/923.

[62] See Ch 5, s A(4) above. The recitals to Directives 93/119, 97/2, and 98/58 each cite the Declaration as one of the grounds on which they were introduced. More recently, the recital to Directive 99/74 expressly states that 'The protection of laying hens is a matter of Community competence.'

[62a] However, see now *Jippes and Others v Minister van Landbouw, Natuurbeheer en Visserij*, Case 189/01 (ECJ, 12 July 2001), discussed below at Ch 15, n 33.

[63] TEC, Protocol on the application of the principles of subsidiarity and proportionality.

supported. The Council also suggested that accession by all the Member States to the European Convention on the Protection of Animals kept for Farming Purposes meant that there was no need to retain the existing directives for the protection of laying hens, calves, and pigs. This threat was subsequently countered by the Commission, which carried out a detailed study of EC legislation on the protection of animals, and concluded that the existing directives should remain in force and proposals on the welfare of animals on farms and at the time of slaughter, which were then before the Council, were necessary and warranted early adoption.[64]

H. The Relationship between Community Law and Domestic Law

'By contrast with ordinary international treaties', observed the ECJ in 1964, the Treaty establishing the Community had created its own legal system which became 'an integral part of the legal systems of the Member States and which their courts are bound to apply'. According to the Court, the terms of the Treaty represented 'a transfer of powers from the states to the Community', to the extent that Member States 'have limited their sovereign rights, albeit within limited fields, and have thus created a new body of law which binds both their nationals and themselves'. On the basis of this analysis, the Court declared that 'the law stemming from the Treaty'—that is, the terms of the Treaty itself and any secondary legislation made under its authority, such as regulations and directives—'could not . . . be over-ridden by domestic legal provisions, however framed, . . . without the legal basis of the Community itself being called into question'. In consequence, acceding to the Treaty involves 'a permanent limitation' of each Member State's sovereign rights, 'against which a subsequent unilateral act incompatible with the concept of the Community cannot prevail'.[65]

The supremacy of Community law over the domestic law of Member States was recognized by the UK Parliament in the European Communities Act 1972. Section 2(1) provides that all rights, powers, liabilities, obligations, and restrictions created or arising by or under the Treaties, together with all remedies and procedures, 'shall be recognized and available in law, and be enforced, allowed or followed accordingly'. Furthermore, section 3(2) lays down that the domestic courts, confronted by any question as to the meaning or effect of Community law, shall have regard to the Treaties, the Community's *Official Journal*, and any decision or expression of opinion of the ECJ. The effect is to incorporate EC law into the law of the UK, so that, first, it is binding on those to whom it is applicable; secondly, it is enforceable in the British courts; and, thirdly, in respect of issues with a Community law dimension, the courts are required to take account of, and give

---

[64] COM(93)384.   [65] *Costa v ENEL*, Case 6/64 [1964] ECR 585, ECJ.

effect to, the objects of the Treaties, secondary Community legislation, and the jurisprudence of the ECJ.[66]

The supremacy of Community law is a principle of particular legal and political potency. On the one hand, it means that a Community measure has an impact on the law of fifteen nation states, a factor which makes lobbying for change at a Community level especially attractive to pressure groups. On the other, the principle poses a fundamental challenge to the functioning of representative democracy within the Member States. The requirement laid down by the ECJ that 'every national court must, in a case within its jurisdiction, apply Community law in its entirety and protect rights which the latter confers on individuals and must accordingly set aside any provision of national law which may conflict with it, whether prior or subsequent to the Community rule'[67] has the effect not only of restricting the autonomy of legislatures and governments, but may also serve to frustrate the popular will of the people. In the case of the UK, the precedence of Community law over national law also goes to the heart of traditional constitutional arrangements, namely the legislative supremacy of Parliament. Whereas the traditional role of the courts has been to identify and enforce the will of the legislature, they may now be in a position where they are required to ignore the provisions of an Act of Parliament, or prevent its implementation.[68] Accordingly, notwithstanding that a policy may have widespread public support, the Government has been mandated by the electorate to implement it, and Parliament seeks to give effect to it by passing legislation, the policy may be overridden by the national courts if it is incompatible with EC law.

I. The Elimination of Quantitative Restrictions on Imports and Exports and All Measures Having Equivalent Effect

(1) Articles 28 and 29 (formerly 30 and 34)

As with the WTO, it is the paramountcy accorded to securing trade liberalization which poses the greatest threat to national self-determination in matters of animal welfare. Together, articles 28 and 29 (formerly 30 and 34) of the TEC prohibit quantitative restrictions on both imports and exports,[69] together with all measures

---

[66] See, for example, the reasoning of the High Court in *Ken Lane Transport Ltd v North Yorkshire County Council* [1995] 1 WLR 1416 (note that the point at issue, the definition of a journey under the Welfare of Animals during Transport Order 1992, SI 1992/3304, has been subsequently clarified by art 3(1) of the 1997 Transport Order, SI 1997/1480).

[67] *Amministrazione delle Finanze dello Stato v Simmenthal SpA*, Case 92/78 [1978] ECR 629.

[68] *R v Secretary of State for Transport, ex parte Factortame Ltd (No 2)* [1991] 1 AC 603, ECJ & HL; *R v Secretary of State for Employment, ex parte Equal Opportunities Commission* [1995] 1 AC 1, HL.

[69] It has been held that article 28 is not restricted to *commercial* imports; it is equally applicable where an owner wishes to enter the country accompanied by a dog or cat: *R v Minister for Agriculture, Fisheries and Food, ex parte Geiden* (QBD, 30 September 1999).

having an equivalent effect. The prohibition applies to the activities and decisions—legislative, executive, or judicial—of any public body or official. Moreover, according to the ECJ, these measures require Member States 'not merely themselves to abstain from adopting measures or engaging in conduct liable to constitute an obstacle to trade', but, when read with article 10 (formerly 5) of the TEC, place a positive duty on them 'to take all necessary and appropriate measures to ensure that that fundamental freedom is respected on their territory'.[70]

A quantitative restriction is any measure which amounts to a total or partial restraint on imports, exports, or goods in transit.[71] The ambit of measures having equivalent effect has been widely drawn by the ECJ, to include 'All trading rules enacted by Member States which are capable of hindering, directly or indirectly, actually or potentially, intra-Community trade'.[72] It is not therefore necessary to establish that a measure has actually hindered trade to fall foul of these provisions; it is enough to show that it is capable of having such a consequence. Moreover, it is the effect which is crucial, not the intention behind it. Accordingly, notwithstanding that a measure may have been introduced for some legitimate purpose, if the result is that intra-Community trade is hindered, it may amount to a contravention of these provisions. As the ECJ has observed, 'any provisions or national practices which might alter the pattern of imports or exports by preventing producers from buying or selling freely within the State in which they are established, or in any other Member State, . . . are incompatible with the principles of a common organization of the market'.[73] On this basis, any steps taken by the UK Government, or any other emanation of the State, to restrict the export of animals to, or the import of animals from, any other Member State on the basis of their treatment in that country, is prima facie a breach of Community law.

(2) Article 30 (formerly 36)

Despite the prescriptive tone, articles 28 and 29 (formerly 30 and 34) are subject to the terms of article 30 (formerly 36), which provides that they shall not preclude prohibitions or restrictions on imports, exports, or goods in transit justified on grounds which include public morality, public policy, or the protection of health and life of humans, animals, or plants, so long as they do not 'constitute a means of arbitrary discrimination or a disguised restriction on trade between member States'. Although this might seem at first sight to offer considerable scope for allowing a Member State to derogate from its overriding duty to secure the free movement of goods within the Community, this has not been the case in practice. The ECJ is

---

[70] *Commission of the European Communities v French Republic*, Case 265/95 [1997] ECR I–6959 para [32]. Article 10 (formerly 5) requires Member States to take 'all appropriate measures, whether general or particular, to ensure fulfilment of the obligations of this Treaty or resulting from action taken by the institutions of the Community'.

[71] *Riseria Luigi Geddo v Ente Nazionale Risi*, Case 2/73 [1974] 1 CMLR 13.

[72] *Procureur du Roi v Dassonville*, Case 8/74 [1974] 2 CMLR 436, para [5].

[73] *Pigs Marketing Board v Redmond*, Case 83/78 [1979] 1 CMLR 177, para [58].

clearly fearful of opening the floodgates and thereby undermining the fundamental objective of trade liberalization. It has therefore consistently construed the article extremely narrowly, and it is inaccurate to regard it merely as involving 'a balancing of, on the one hand, the legitimate interests of the Member State falling within the categories specified in Article 36 and, on the other hand, the Community interest in free movement of goods'.[74] Rather, it is the case that free movement will always prevail unless the Member State can meet the demanding and tightly-drawn requirements which will, exceptionally, justify ousting it. Most importantly, article 30 'is not designed to reserve certain matters to the exclusive jurisdiction of Member States but only permits national laws to derogate from the principle of the free movement of goods to the extent to which such derogation is and continues to be justified for the attainment of the objectives referred to in that Article'.[75] According to the ECJ, 'as an exception to a fundamental principle of the Treaty', article 30 'must be interpreted in such a way that its scope is not extended any further than is necessary for the protection of the interests which it is intended to secure', and measures adopted on its authority will be justified 'only if they are such as to serve the interest which that Article protects and if they do not restrict intra-Community trade more than is absolutely necessary'.[76] In order to demonstrate that a prohibition or restriction does not amount to arbitrary discrimination, the onus is on the Member State to establish that it is objectively justified. Furthermore, such justification is subject to the principle of proportionality: it must be shown to be necessary, no more than is necessary, and to continue only so long as is necessary.[77]

Applying these principles, the UK's (former) policy of imposing a six-month quarantine period on mammals entering the country from other Member States was held to be lawful in the light of the danger to public health from the introduction of rabies.[78] In contrast, arguments that article 30 could be relied upon to restrict the movement of animals on the basis of their welfare have been repeatedly unsuccessful before the ECJ, notwithstanding that it has conceded that protection of the health and life of animals 'constitutes a fundamental requirement recognized by Community law'.[79]

For example, the Court has held that recourse to article 30 is no longer possible where a directive provides for the harmonization among Member States of the measures necessary to achieve the specific objective which would be furthered by reliance upon this provision. So, where the UK alleged that the way in which sheep

---

[74] *R v Chief Constable of Sussex, ex parte International Traders' Ferry Ltd* [1998] 3 WLR 1260, HL, at 1285 (Lord Hoffman).

[75] *Denkavit v Minister fur Ernährung, Landwirtschaft und Forsten des Landes Nordrhein-Westfalen*, Case 251/78 [1980] 3 CMLR 513, para [14], ECJ.

[76] *Ministre des Finances v Richardt*, Case 367/89 [1992] 1 CMLR 61, para [20], ECJ.

[77] *Commission v Germany (Re Health Control on Imported Meat)*, Case 153/78 [1980] 1 CMLR 198.

[78] Rabies (Importation of Dogs, Cats and other Mammals) Order 1974, SI 1974/2211; *R v Minister for Agriculture, Fisheries and Food, ex parte Geiden* (QBD, 20 September 1999). See now, Pet Travel Scheme (Pilot Arrangements) (England) Order 1999, SI 1999/3443.

[79] *R v Ministry of Agriculture, Fisheries and Food, ex parte Hedley Lomas (Ireland) Limited*, Case 5/94 [1996] 2 CMLR 391, para [18], ECJ.

were treated in Spanish slaughterhouses was contrary to Directive 74/577 on stunning animals before slaughter, the Court held that because of the existence of Community legislation, the Government was not entitled to rely on article 30 to restrict the export of live sheep from Britain to Spain. This was the case, even though the particular directive failed to prescribe any Community procedure for monitoring compliance or any penalties in the event of breach of its provisions. In such a situation, the Court declared that 'Member States must rely on trust in each other to carry out inspections on their respective territories.' Accordingly, a Member State 'may not unilaterally adopt, on its own authority, corrective or protective measures designed to obviate any breach by another Member State of rules of Community Law'.[80] Similarly, where the UK had taken advantage of the opportunity provided for in a directive to adopt higher standards than those it laid down, and thereby to ban the rearing of calves in veal crates, it could not rely on article 30 to prevent calves being exported to other Member States to be reared by that method. In the view of the Court, although Member States retained considerable discretion under the directive to determine for themselves the conditions in which calves could be kept, and different standards could therefore be applied across the EU, the legislation nevertheless amounted to a harmonization measure. Considerations of public morality, public policy, and the protection of the health and life of animals, which are, theoretically, relevant considerations under article 30, were consequently overridden once again by the free trade juggernaut.[81]

The only example of article 30 being relied upon successfully in relation to animal exports arose from the refusal by a Chief Constable, at the height of the demonstrations in the winter of 1994–1995, to commit the manpower necessary to allow the livestock hauliers free access to a port within his area whenever they wished. Instead, he provided police protection to assist the lorries through the demonstrators on a limited number of days during any week or fortnight. The House of Lords held that this action was legitimate under article 30, on the ground of public policy.[82] The effect was not, however, to prevent exports, or to lessen to any appreciable extent the number of animals being sent abroad; the hauliers simply turned their attention to ports in other police areas.

J. Domestic Sources of Regulation

(1) Primary legislation

While the TEC may be described as 'the supreme law of the country, taking precedence over Acts of Parliament',[83] and the WTO also places significant constraints

---

[80] ibid, paras [18]–[20].

[81] *R v Minister of Agriculture, Fisheries and Food, ex parte Compassion in World Farming Limited*, Case 1/96 [1998] 2 CMLR 661, ECJ.

[82] *R v Chief Constable of Sussex, ex parte International Traders' Ferry Ltd* [1998] 3 WLR 1260, HL.

[83] *Stoke-on-Trent City Council v B & Q plc* [1991] 1 Ch 48, 56 (Hoffman J).

on governmental action in respect of international trade, it is important to appreciate that, except for those (albeit very significant) matters which fall within their respective competencies, neither EC law nor the WTO has any effect on Parliament's traditional legislative supremacy. Subject to these, admittedly important, provisos, however, an Act of Parliament remains supreme: it can change the existing law—whether laid down in a previous Act or by the courts; it may legislate on matters about which there is no existing legislation; and it can authorize the making of secondary legislation, within the terms it prescribes.

Even before Scottish and Welsh devolution (discussed further below), it was the case that some statutes applied to the whole of Great Britain; some to England and Wales only; and some to Scotland only. The best known example of such a situation in the field of animal welfare legislation is the Protection of Animals Act 1911, which applies to England and Wales, and the almost identical Protection of Animals (Scotland) Act 1912. Some sections in the same Act may apply to different jurisdictions. So, the Wild Mammals (Protection) Act 1996 applies to the whole of Great Britain, with the exception of section 6, which does not apply to Scotland. Similarly, sections 8 and 9 of the Pests Act 1954 are specific to England and Wales, while sections 10 and 11 apply exclusively to Scotland.

A statute may come into effect immediately upon completing its parliamentary passage and receiving Royal Assent; others on a specific date,[84] or after a specific period following Royal Assent;[85] while some Acts do not come into effect automatically, and require a minister to trigger them by means of a Commencement Order.[86] Furthermore, different parts of an Act may be brought into force at different times.[87] Care must always be taken, then, to ensure that a statutory provision is actually in force. This is particularly so with recently enacted legislation, but even old statutes may contain measures which are effectively dormant. Sections 2, 3, 4, and 6 of the Guard Dogs Act 1975, for example, have never been implemented.

---

[84] The Pet Animals Act 1951, s 8(3) specifies, for example, that the Act shall come into operation on 1 April 1952, while the Riding Establishments Act 1964 (s 9(3)) and the Breeding of Dogs Act 1973 (s 7(3)) came into force on 1 April 1965 and 1974 respectively.

[85] The Agriculture (Miscellaneous Provisions) Act 1968, s 54(2) provides that Part 1 of the Act shall come into operation on the expiration of two months beginning with the date on which it was passed, while the Dangerous Wild Animals Act 1976 (s 10(2)) came into force three months after it was passed.

[86] Section 23(2) of the Zoo Licensing Act 1981, for example, states that the Act shall come into operation on such day as the Secretary of State may by order made by statutory instrument appoint. It was subsequently brought into force on 30 April 1984 by virtue of the Zoo Licensing Act 1981 (Commencement) Order 1984, SI 1984/423. The Fur Farming (Prohibition) Act 2000 is to come into force on such day as the Minister of Agriculture may decide, but this may not be before the beginning of 2003: s 7(2).

[87] Section 30(3) of the Animals (Scientific Procedures) Act 1986 provides that the Act shall come into force on such date as the Secretary of State may by order appoint; and different days may be appointed for different provisions or different purposes. Sections 1–6, 8, 9, 10(1), (2), (4)–(7), 11–28, 30 and Schs 1, 3, and 4 were brought into force on 1 January 1987 by the Animals (Scientific Procedures) Act (Commencement) Order 1986, SI 1986/2088; and s 7 and Sch 2 were brought into force on 1 January 1990 by the Animals (Scientific Procedures) Act (Commencement) Order 1989, SI 1989/2306.

(2) Secondary legislation

Many statutes empower ministers to bring forward further provisions or amendments by means of secondary legislation, the ambit and nature of such powers being set out in the relevant Act. Indeed, in terms of volume, significantly more legislation is enacted by this method than by statute because of its inherent advantages. Although proposals for secondary legislation generally have to be presented to Parliament, they are not subject to the same degree of detailed and time-consuming scrutiny as primary legislation. It is therefore particularly useful as a means of: specifying detailed and technical requirements in furtherance of the general objectives laid down in the Act; introducing additional measures in the light of changed circumstances, new knowledge and understanding, or urgent need; and allowing those with an interest or expertise in the subject matter to be formally consulted in drawing up regulations. Section 2 of the Agriculture (Miscellaneous Provisions) Act 1968, for example, authorizes ministers to introduce, after consultation with such persons as appear to them to represent any interests concerned, regulations in respect of the welfare of livestock, including provisions relating to accommodation, diet, mutilation, marking, restraining, or interfering with the capacity of livestock to smell, see, hear, emit sound, or exercise any other faculty. By this means detailed requirements as to how such animals should be kept may be imposed.[88] Arguably, one of the most important weaknesses of the Protection of Animals Act 1911, and its Scottish equivalent, is the absence of a similar enabling power which would allow the introduction of more effective provisions without the need to secure further primary legislation.

The powers bestowed on ministers to introduce secondary legislation can be very broad indeed, such as section 1(a) of the Animal Health Act 1981, which permits ministers to make such orders as they think fit generally for the better execution of the Act, or for the purpose of preventing the spreading of disease. In other circumstances, it may enable the application of the primary legislation to be extended. Section 87 of the same Act, for example, provides specific definitions of the terms 'animals' and 'poultry', but provides that these may be widened by means of secondary legislation. Similarly, application of the Dangerous Wild Animals Act 1976 may be extended or restricted as the Secretary of State thinks fit,[89] and while section 1 of the Dangerous Dogs Act 1991, which relates to dogs bred for fighting, applied initially to any dog of the types known as the pit bull terrier or the Japanese tosa, the Secretary of State has the power to extend it to any other type of dog which appears to him to be bred for fighting or to have the characteristics of a type bred for that purpose.[90] Occasionally, the statute will impose a duty on ministers to

---

[88] Welfare of Farmed Animals Regulations, n 32 above.

[89] Dangerous Wild Animals Act 1976, s 8(1).

[90] Dangerous Dogs Act 1991, s 1(1)(c). This power has been used to include two types of mastiff, the Dogo Argentini and the Fila Braziliero, within the terms of s 1: The Dangerous Dogs (Designated Types) Order 1991, SI 1991/1743.

introduce secondary legislation. The wording of section 43 of the Animal Health Act 1981, for example, specifies that ministers shall by order make such provision as they think necessary or expedient in relation to the regulation of the export of ponies. More usually, however, it lies entirely within the discretion of ministers to decide whether secondary legislation should be introduced. So, although Parliament has agreed in principle to the introduction of a statutory dog registration scheme, no such scheme is in force because it lies with the Secretary of State to establish it by way of secondary legislation and, to date, no minister has chosen to do so.[91]

Probably the most important general power to introduce secondary legislation is contained in section 2(2) of the European Communities Act 1972, which provides that it may be used for the purpose of implementing the UK's obligations arising from EC law. Directives are therefore commonly transposed into British law by means of secondary legislation, under the authority of this provision. It should be noted, however, that the 1972 Act may only be relied upon by ministers to bring UK law into compliance with EC law; if the proposed regulations include provisions which go further than those required by a directive, then other statutory authority must be relied upon. So, although the Welfare of Livestock Regulations 1994 were primarily intended to give effect to the UK's obligations under EC law, they imposed more stringent requirements in respect of, for example, the keeping of calves reared for veal. Accordingly, the Regulations were introduced under the authority of both section 2 of the Agriculture (Miscellaneous Provisions) Act 1968 and section 2 of the European Communities Act 1972 (their successors in England and Scotland were introduced solely under the authority of the 1968 Act[92]). If secondary legislation introduces a measure which goes beyond that which is authorized in the relevant enabling statute, or any procedural requirements laid down in the statute have not been complied with, the validity of the secondary legislation may be challenged in the courts.

A particularly unfortunate practice which has developed recently is to incorporate technical or ambiguous provisions originating in EC legislation into domestic law by means of a bare statement to that effect in the relevant regulations. So, for example, the Marketing Authorisations for Veterinary Medicinal Products Regulations 1994 abounds with illuminating provisions such as:

The Ministers shall consider an application for, and where appropriate grant, a marketing authorisation for a veterinary medicinal product—

(a) in accordance with articles 4.2, 5b, 8 to 11, 15, 36.3, 40, 41, 42.1 and 43 of Council Directive 81/851/EEC, and, as appropriate, in accordance with article 12 of that directive and Title I, Part 4, Chapter II.1, sixth paragraph of the Annex to Council Directive 81/852/EEC, or

---

[91] Local Government Act 1988, s 37. The Government established a Dog Identification Working Group, which delivered its report in November 2000. At the time of writing, the Minister is consulting with interested bodies: HC Debs, 1 November 2000, col 447 (WA).

[92] Welfare of Farmed Animals Regulations, n 32 above.

(b) in the case of a product already authorised in another Member State, in accordance with article 4.1, second paragraph, or articles 4.2, 8, 8a, 40 and 41 and Chapter IV of Council Directive 81/851/EEC,

and in both cases, where appropriate, in accordance with article 4 of Council Directive 90/677/EEC.[93]

While this tactic ensures there is no possibility that the Government has failed to transpose the relevant EC provisions adequately, it singularly fails to indicate what legal obligations and responsibilities arise from them. These can only be ascertained by cross-referencing the domestic regulations with the relevant EC legislation, and then taking account of any applicable decisions of the ECJ. It is legislative drafting entirely for the benefit of the Government, regardless of the needs of those to whom it applies, their advisers, those required to enforce it, and the courts. It is a practice to be eschewed.

Although the duties, obligations, and prohibitions imposed by both primary and secondary legislation are equally enforceable before the courts, there are significant differences between the two types of legislation. First, subject to the constraints of EC law, the UK Parliament may enact any provisions it wishes in statute, whereas secondary legislation may only be used to further the objects of the relevant primary legislation and in the terms prescribed by the Act. Secondly, it must be introduced by the minister authorized to do so under the enabling Act. Hence, there is no role for backbench Members of Parliament to introduce such measures. Thirdly, secondary legislation is not subject to the detailed parliamentary scrutiny accorded to primary legislation. Indeed, although Parliament's endorsement is generally required, it is almost always perfunctory in nature. It is subject to one of two different procedures: either the legislation will become law automatically unless Parliament votes to reject it; alternatively, a positive vote to endorse it is required. The procedure to be followed will be prescribed in the enabling Act, so orders made under the Dangerous Wild Animals Act 1976 and the Animals (Scientific Procedures) Act 1986, for example, come into force automatically unless annulled by either House of Parliament;[94] whereas regulations with respect to the welfare of livestock require to be approved by a resolution of each House of Parliament.[95] On occasions, the two procedures appear in the same legislation: in the Dangerous Dogs Act 1991, orders under section 1 in connection with dogs bred for fighting come into force automatically, unless Parliament chooses to subject them to a vote, while orders made under section 2 relating to other specially dangerous dogs always require each House positively to endorse them. The fact is, however, that a very significant volume of secondary legislation becomes law without Parliament having debated or voted upon its provisions. When it does occur, parliamentary debate on secondary legislation is truncated,

---

[93] SI 1994/3142, reg 5.
[94] Dangerous Wild Animals Act 1976, s 8(2); Animals (Scientific Procedures) Act 1986, s 28.
[95] Agriculture (Miscellaneous Provisions) Act 1968, s 2(3).

and those votes which take place are generally held towards the end of the day's sitting, when attendance is sparse. Most significantly, it is not open to Parliament to amend secondary legislation: its power is limited to accepting or rejecting the Government's proposals in their entirety. Given Parliament's very limited role in respect of secondary legislation, it is essential that interested parties become aware of intended measures, and make their views known to the relevant department while the legislation is being drawn up. By the time secondary legislation reaches Parliament it is generally much too late to affect the outcome.

(3) Statutory codes of practice and recommendations

In addition to primary and secondary legislation, the Agriculture (Miscellaneous Provisions) Act 1968,[96] the Zoo Licensing Act 1981,[97] the Animals (Scientific Procedures) Act 1986,[98] and the Welfare of Animals (Slaughter or Killing) Regulations 1995[99] provide for the preparation and promulgation of statutory guidance, codes of practice, or recommendations.

Codes of recommendations for the welfare of livestock issued under the authority of the 1968 Act are intended to provide guidance for persons concerned with livestock.[100] As such, contravention of these codes does not in itself amount to an offence, but may be relied upon by the prosecution as tending to establish the guilt of the accused in the event that proceedings are brought alleging that livestock have been caused unnecessary pain or distress.[101] In other words, 'If a failure to comply with a recommendation is established, the court still has to consider whether a criminal offence is proved.'[102] However, any person who employs or engages others to attend to livestock is required to ensure that they are acquainted with the provisions of the relevant welfare codes; has access to them while attending the livestock; and has received instruction and guidance on them.[103] This results in the somewhat anomalous situation whereby it amounts to an offence not to bring the relevant codes to the attention of another person, but does not in itself amount to an offence if that person fails to follow their recommendations. Similarly, it is an offence for any person who keeps livestock to attend them unless he has access to

---

[96] Section 3.   [97] Section 9.   [98] Section 21(1), (2).   [99] SI 1995/731, reg 7.

[100] Agriculture (Miscellaneous Provisions) Act 1968, s 3(1)(a). Separate codes have been produced in relation to cattle (1983), pigs (1983), domestic fowls (1987), turkeys (1987), sheep (revised 2000), ducks (1987), rabbits (1987), farmed deer (1989), and goats (1987). At the time of writing, a code for broilers is in preparation. Before coming into force, each code is required to be approved by both Houses of Parliament: s 3(2).

[101] ibid, s 3(4). In the same way, a failure to follow guidance contained in a code issued under the authority of the legislation regulating the slaughter and killing of animals does not render a person liable to proceedings of any kind. However, where a person is accused of an associated offence, their non-compliance with the terms of such a code may be relied upon by the prosecution as tending to establish guilt: SI 1995/731, n 99 above, reg 7(6), (7).

[102] *Roberts v Ruggiero* (QBD, 3 April 1985) (Stephen Brown LJ).

[103] Welfare of Farmed Animals Regulations, n 32 above, reg 10(1). In the Welsh regulations, the verb 'care' is used in preference to 'attend'.

the appropriate welfare codes and is acquainted with their provisions,[104] but in the event that these are not complied with no offence is committed unless it can be demonstrated that the animals were caused unnecessary pain or distress.

According to the Ministry, codes rather than mandatory controls were originally adopted because the recommendations of the Brambell Committee,[105] on which they were based, 'could not be backed by scientific findings', and 'might soon require revision as knowledge of the subject improved'. Accordingly, 'the Government did not believe it was justified in making producers undertake large capital expenditure in order to meet standards which might require revision'.[106] Whether, more than thirty years later, this argument remains pertinent is open to question. In any event, many of the most important recommendations contained in the codes relate to husbandry procedures, and do not entail capital expenditure. Nevertheless, MPs appear to be persuaded of their merit. The House of Commons Agriculture Committee has recognized 'the flexibility and adaptability to new developments which is given by codes, and the difficulties of definition which confronts any one who tries to draft regulations clear and precise enough to be readily understood and enforced'.[107] The same Committee has latterly expressed the view that 'technical implementation of welfare requirements is more appropriately dealt with under Codes of Practice, once the basic framework has been provided by legislation'.[108]

While providing guidance for the welfare of livestock is discretionary, it is mandatory in respect of scientific procedures. The 1986 Act requires the Secretary of State to publish information to serve as guidance with respect to the manner in which he proposes to exercise his power to grant licences and certificates under the Act, including the conditions which he proposes to include in such licences and certificates; and to issue codes of practice as to the care of protected animals and their use for regulated procedures; he may also approve such codes issued by other bodies.[109] Again, a failure on the part of any person to comply with any provision of a code does not of itself render that person liable to criminal or civil proceedings, but may be taken into account in the event of a prosecution,[110] or may lead to administrative action, such as the revocation of a licence. The Secretary of State is

---

[104] ibid, reg 10(2).

[105] *Report of the Technical Committee to Enquire into the Welfare of Animals kept under Intensive Livestock Husbandry Systems* (1965).

[106] House of Commons Agriculture Committee, *Animal Welfare in Poultry, Pig and Veal Calf Production* (1981) Appendix 1, para 7.

[107] ibid, para 39.

[108] House of Commons Agriculture Committee, *The UK Poultry Industry* (1994) para 78.

[109] Animals (Scientific Procedures) Act 1986, s 21(1), (2). See further, Home Office, *Guidance on the Operation of the Animals (Scientific Procedures) Act 1986* (2000); Home Office, n 40 above; Home Office, *Code of Practice for the Housing and Care of Animals used in Scientific Procedures* (1989); Home Office, *Code of Practice for the Housing and Care of Animals in Designated Breeding and Supplying Establishments* (1995); Home Office, *The Humane Killing of Animals under Schedule 1 to the Animals (Scientific Procedures) Act 1986. Code of Practice* (1997).

[110] ibid, s 21(4).

required to lay before Parliament copies of any new or revised information or code, and it is open to either House, within forty days, to call for it to be withdrawn.[111]

The *Secretary of State's Standards of Modern Zoo Practice*, produced under the authority of section 9 of the Zoo Licensing Act 1981, provide guidance on the management of zoos and the animals in them.[112] Failure to meet these standards does not in itself amount to an offence, but local authorities are required to have regard to them in deciding the conditions subject to which a licence should be granted, and a zoo operator may be guilty of an offence if he fails without reasonable excuse to comply with a condition attached to the establishment's licence.[113]

On occasions, ministers may adopt or enforce the recommendations of other specialist organizations. So the Welfare of Animals (Transport) Order 1997 requires compliance with the standards set by the International Air Transport Association (IATA) and guidelines issued under the Convention on International Trade in Endangered Species (CITES);[114] the Home Office has previously acknowledged that its Guidance on the operation of the Animals (Scientific Procedures) Act 1986 has been greatly influenced by guidelines drawn up respectively by the Universities Federation for Animal Welfare (UFAW) and the Laboratory Animals Breeders' Association;[115] and the Code of Practice for the Housing and Care of Animals used in Scientific Procedures largely incorporates guidelines previously drawn up by the Royal Society and UFAW.[116]

Government departments may also issue administrative advice to those affected by legislation or responsible for its enforcement, setting out how they consider it should be applied and often providing a valuable insight into how ministers intend to exercise their discretionary legal powers, or the way in which they consider other agencies might carry out their duties. The Ministry of Agriculture has, for example, issued a wide range of such documents in relation to the welfare of animals on the farm, during transit, in livestock markets, and at slaughter.[117] Except in relation to scientific procedures, the Home Office tends to distribute advice by means of departmental circulars, such as the series of circulars addressed to Chief Constables, courts, the Crown Prosecution Service, and local authorities, as a result of the confusion caused by the provisions of the Dangerous Dogs Act 1991;[118] and, in response to media concern about conditions on puppy farms, it issued advice in the spring of 1997 reminding local authorities of their powers and responsibilities regarding dog breeding establishments in England and Wales.[119]

---

[111] Animals (Scientific Procedures) Act 1986, s 21(5), (6). [112] DETR, n 44 above.

[113] Zoo Licensing Act 1981, ss 5(4), 19(2). [114] SI 1997/1480, art 11.

[115] Home Office (1990) paras 1.24 and 1.25. [116] n 40 above, paras 1.7–1.11.

[117] For example: MAFF, *Code of Practice for the Welfare of Animals in Livestock Markets* (1990); *Code of Practice for the Welfare of Horses, Ponies and Donkeys at Markets, Sales and Fairs* (1990); *Guidance on the Transport of Casualty Farm Animals* (1993); *An Explanatory Guide to the Welfare of Animals (Slaughter or Killing) Regulations 1995* (1996); *Pig Space Requirements. Guidelines on Schedule 3 of the Welfare of Livestock Regulations 1994* (1997); *Guidance on the Welfare of Animals (Transport) Order 1997* (1998); *Assessment of Practical Experience in the Handling, Transport and Care of Animals* (1998).

[118] Home Office Circulars 67/1991, 80/1992, 9/1994, and 22/1995. [119] Circular 9/1997.

In addition to such official guidelines, there are in existence a large number of voluntary codes which represent the accepted standards within an industry. Where these prove ineffective because they are not widely adhered to, the Government may take powers to put them on a more formal footing. For example, in response to the failure by some operators of quarantine kennels to comply with a voluntary welfare code which had been drawn up in relation to such premises,[120] legislation has been introduced to enable ministers to make regulations to set welfare standards.[121]

(4) Devolution

The consequence of Scottish and Welsh devolution will be to reduce the UK Parliament's ability to legislate for those parts of Britain, and to relieve the Government of an extensive agglomeration of administrative powers.

Scotland

The Scotland Act 1998 provides for the devolution of all matters relating to Scotland, except for those which are specifically 'reserved'.[122] In relation to all devolved matters, law-making powers have passed to the newly-established Scottish Parliament, including the ability to amend or repeal existing Acts of the UK Parliament. Executive and administrative functions have become the responsibility of the Scottish Executive, which is accountable to the Scottish Parliament in a relationship modelled on that between the Government and UK Parliament.

Areas of animal welfare which are expressly reserved include scientific procedures on live animals, prohibition and regulation of the import and export of endangered species, regulation of the veterinary profession, xenotransplantation, and medicines, medical supplies, and poisons.[123] By implication, the treatment of animals in all other situations has been devolved, as was signalled in the Government's proposals for devolution. These specifically alluded to the Scottish Parliament being given the power to legislate for the protection of animals, including protection against cruelty to domestic, captive, and wild animals, zoo licensing, controlling dangerous wild animals and game, together with issues of animal health and welfare 'subject to suitable co-ordination arrangements to ensure consistency within the UK where required under European law or to protect the public, animal or plant health or animal welfare'.[124] The Scottish Parliament therefore has the potential to have a significant impact on animal welfare law north of the border.

---

[120] MAFF, *The Welfare of Dogs and Cats in Quarantine Premises. Voluntary Code of Practice* (1995).

[121] Animal Health Act 1981, Sch 2, para 4A; inserted by the Animal Health (Amendment) Act 1998. In December 2000, the Government published for consultation proposals to modernize the requirements for the care of animals which still enter quarantine: MAFF Press Release 453/2000.

[122] Scotland Act 1998, s 30(1) and Sch 5.   [123] ibid, Sch 5, paras B7, C5, G2, J2, and J4.

[124] Scottish Office, *Scotland's Parliament* (1997) para 2.4.

Relations with the EU continue to be the responsibility of the UK Government, but the Scottish Parliament is able to scrutinize EU legislative proposals. The Scottish Executive is required to implement EU legislation on devolved matters, and the UK Parliament retains the power to legislate to give effect to EU obligations in Scotland.

Wales

The arrangements for Wales are considerably less far-reaching. Most significantly, primary legislation relating to Wales continues to be the responsibility of the national Parliament at Westminster. The National Assembly for Wales does, however, have the power to pass secondary legislation under the authority of statute,[125] including measures to implement obligations arising under EC law.[126] The Assembly has also assumed responsibility for the functions previously exercised by the Secretary of State for Wales,[127] is entitled to be consulted on the Government's legislative programme, and may consider and make representations about any matter affecting Wales.[128] Although the ability of the Welsh Assembly to influence animal welfare legislation is substantially less than that of the Scottish Parliament, it still has the capacity to make a difference to the way in which animals are treated within its jurisdiction.

(5) The Human Rights Act 1998

Like the European Communities Act 1972, the Human Rights Act 1998 is destined to become an Act of singular status and influence, in the sense that its provisions will predominate and permeate all other legislation, judicial decisions, and state action. However, unlike the 1972 Act, it does not automatically prevail over legislative provisions with which it is incompatible. In short, the Human Rights Act provides that courts and tribunals must, so far as is possible, interpret primary and subordinate legislation in a way which is compatible with the European Convention on Human Rights and Fundamental Freedoms, and the jurisprudence of the European Court of Human Rights.[129] If it is not possible to do so, the higher courts may make a declaration of incompatibility, and it then falls to ministers to decide whether the Government will introduce appropriate amending legislation.[130] In addition, it is now incumbent on a minister in charge of a Bill (although, curiously, not a backbench MP introducing a Private Member's Bill) to make a statement before its Second Reading indicating whether, in his view, the provisions of the Bill are compatible with Convention rights.[131] If the minister indicates that

---

[125] Government of Wales Act 1998, s 44.   [126] ibid, s 29.   [127] ibid, s 22 and Sch 2.
[128] ibid, ss 31 and 33.   [129] Human Rights Act 1998, ss 2(1) and 3(1).   [130] ibid, ss 4 and 10.
[131] ibid, s 19. Time will tell how legally robust such statements of compatibility are required to be. For example, when pressed, Nick Brown, the Minister of Agriculture, justified his contention that a Bill which provided for the prohibition of fur farming in England and Wales was compatible with the Convention on the ground that the Government was of the view that 'fur farming is not consistent with a proper value and respect for animal life', which, he asserted, 'should not be destroyed in the absence of sufficient justification in terms of public benefit'. The Government believed that 'the rearing of animals solely or primarily for slaughter for their furs fails this test'. According to the Minister, fur farming is, for these purposes, 'quite distinct' from circumstances where the 'primary purpose' of keeping an animal is for food, which, apparently,

he is unable to make a statement of compatibility, it is then up to Parliament to decide whether it wishes to enact the legislation. If it does so, the courts will give effect to Parliament's intention, notwithstanding that it is incompatible with the UK's obligations under the Convention. Hence, the Act preserves the principle of the Westminster Parliament's legislative supremacy. In contrast, both the Scottish Parliament and the Welsh Assembly are expressly prohibited from passing legislation which is incompatible with the rights specified in the European Convention.[132]

The Act applies to the exercise of administrative as well as legislative power. It therefore becomes unlawful for a public authority to act in a way which is incompatible with a Convention right, unless it can be shown that the authority had no alternative because of the terms of the legislation under which it was acting.[133]

So far as animal welfare is concerned, the Human Rights Act may have an impact in two ways. First, it may place an additional hurdle in the path of those seeking to prohibit particular activities or undertakings concerning animals. One can foresee, for example, circumstances in which those adversely affected might seek to rely on the right to respect for private and family life, or freedom of thought, conscience, and religion, or freedom of assembly and association.[134] Potentially most problematical, however, is the protection of property which is contained in the First Protocol. This lays down that:

Every natural or legal person is entitled to the peaceful enjoyment of his possessions. No one shall be deprived of his possessions except in the public interest and subject to the conditions provided for by law and by the general principles of international law.

None of the Convention rights is absolute and, as we have seen, Parliament may override them in any event. However, they may make the Government cautious in seeking to ban (as distinct from regulating) a practice involving animals, or provide it with an apparently principled excuse for inaction in circumstances where its support for change is less than enthusiastic. At the very least, arguments based on Convention rights can give rise to uncertainty. For example, in evidence to the Burns Inquiry, counsel for the pro-hunting Countryside Alliance was of the opinion that there is 'a serious argument that the proposed ban on hunting with dogs will violate [both] Article 1 of Protocol 1 and Article 8', whereas legal advice obtained by the anti-hunting consortium, Deadline 2000, concluded that 'a ban on hunting wild animals with dogs would be compatible with the Convention'.[135] The

---

'provides a sufficient public benefit to justify breeding the animals for slaughter', even though 'the production of fur or hide is a secondary purpose of keeping the animal' (HC Debs, 22 June 2000, col 300 (WA); see also, HC Debs, 10 January 2000, col 102 (WA)). While many may agree with this as a moral position, and it may be appropriate as a *political* argument, it may be argued that it fails to provide a sufficient *legal* justification for introducing a measure which has the effect of removing a person's livelihood and is prima facie in contravention of the Convention.

[132] Scotland Act 1998, s 29(2)(d); Government of Wales Act 1998, s 107(1).
[133] Human Rights Act 1998, s 6(1)(2).
[134] European Convention on Human Rights, arts 8, 9, and 11.
[135] Burns, Lord (Chairman), *The Report of the Committee of Inquiry into Hunting with Dogs in England and Wales* (2000) para 10.6; see generally paras 10.5–17 for further discussion of this issue.

Government is of the view that a ban on hunting could be introduced in such a way that it did not contravene the Convention, as the Hunting Bill which it introduced into Parliament in December 2000, and which includes the possibility of such a ban, was endorsed with a ministerial statement of compatibility. One suspects that it will ultimately fall to the courts to decide the point.

Secondly, experts in the area have raised doubts as to whether important aspects of the criminal justice system comply with the Convention. If this is so, any changes introduced generally to the way in which offences are investigated and prosecuted may have an impact on cases arising from infringements of animal protection legislation.

(6) Judicial precedents

In England and Wales, prosecutions arising from contraventions of animal protection legislation are tried summarily in the magistrates' courts (with the exception of certain offences under the Animals (Scientific Procedures) Act, which may be tried in the Crown Court[136]), and in Scotland by the Sheriff Court. The outcomes of such cases are not binding on other courts, unlike the decisions of the higher courts, which are important in providing guidance on the meaning and application of legislation, particularly where the wording is ambiguous or the lower courts have misinterpreted it. Most particularly, every piece of legislation operates against the background of general legal principles, procedures, and rules which may not be specifically referred to in the text: the rules of evidence or the test of a defendant's mental state in the context of the criminal law, for example; or the principles which have been developed by the courts in relation to the granting, renewal, and revocation of licences. Without taking account of the relevant case law, simply referring to the legislative text may not in itself provide a complete or accurate view of what the relevant provisions mean in practice.

(7) Administrative powers

Animal protection legislation does not consist simply of a collection of rules; it also provides public bodies and individuals—ministers, their officials, local authorities, veterinarians and other inspectors, the police, and the Royal College of Veterinary Surgeons, to name but a few—with a range of powers in order that they may administer the various regulatory schemes. Most of these powers are discretionary, in that those who exercise them enjoy a degree of freedom to decide how they should be applied. The way in which they are employed may have a profound impact on the effect of a legislative provision; indeed, they may be used to introduce an important change of policy without the need for legislative change. For example, a ban on the use of wild-caught, non-human primates in scientific procedures was imposed administratively in 1995, and, following completion of a report by the Animals (Scientific Procedures) Inspectorate on

---

[136] Section 22(1). In addition, offences under CITES, which may contain a welfare element, can be tried in England and Wales by either the Magistrates' or the Crown Court: Control on Trade in Endangered Species (Enforcement) Regulations 1997, SI 1997/1372.

commercial dog facilities, the minister asked the Inspectorate to ensure that all its recommendations were implemented as far as was practicable in all establishments certified under the Animals (Scientific Procedures) Act 1986.[137] In 1999, the Home Secretary similarly used his administrative powers under the Act to stop authorization of the so-called LD50 test (a test employed to identify the dose of a chemical which produces a 50 per cent mortality among the animals used in the study) if a suitable alternative was available, and to require the establishment of a local ethical review process at every designated establishment.

(8) Judicial review

Judicial review of administrative action is a specialized procedure whereby the court *reviews* the way in which public power is employed to ensure that it is exercised lawfully. It is appropriately described as a 'supervisory jurisdiction'. That is to say, it provides a means by which the courts supervise or oversee the exercise of public power by central and local government and other organizations and officials whose powers are derived from statute. Private bodies may be reviewed, if the court considers their powers are of a public nature;[138] or, in a challenge arising under the Human Rights Act, they fall within the category of 'any person certain of whose functions are functions of a public nature'.[139] The essence of judicial review is accurately reflected in this exposition by Laws J, which arose from a challenge to a decision by Somerset County Council to prohibit deer hunting on its land:

[I]n most cases, the judicial review court is not concerned with the merits of the decision under review. The court does not ask itself, 'Is this decision right or wrong?' Far less does the judge ask himself whether he would himself have arrived at the decision in question. It is, however, of great importance that this should be understood, especially where the subject matter of the case excites fierce controversy, the clash of wholly irreconcilable but deeply held views, and acrimonious, but principled, debate. In such a case, it is essential that those who espouse either side of the argument should understand beyond any possibility of doubt that the task of the court, and the judgment at which it arrives, have nothing to do with the question, 'Which view is the better one?' Otherwise, justice would not be seen to be done: those who support the losing party might believe that the judge has decided the case as he has because he agrees with their opponents. That would be very damaging to the imperative of public confidence in an impartial court. The only question for the judge is whether the decision taken by the body under review was one which it was legally permitted to take in the way that it did.[140]

---

[137] HC Debs, 26 November 1998, col 15 (WA).

[138] *R v Panel on Take-overs and Mergers, ex parte Datafin plc* [1987] QB 815, CA.

[139] Human Rights Act 1998, s 6(3)(b).

[140] *R v Somerset County Council, ex parte Fewings* [1995] 1 All ER 513, 515, QBD. The decision had been reached because the majority of the councillors voting considered deer hunting to be morally repulsive. While it was not in dispute that statute gave the authority the power to determine the purposes for which its land was used, the court held that it was not wide enough to permit the council to take a decision prohibiting activities on its land which was based on free-standing moral perceptions, as distinct from an objective judgement about what would be conducive to the better management of the estate.

In reviewing the way in which a public power has been exercised, the court will have regard to whether the appropriate body or individual has acted reasonably and within the boundaries of their legal powers, in furtherance of the purpose for which they have been given the power, and in compliance with all appropriate procedures. Judicial review is therefore concerned with significantly more than simply establishing that a public body possesses the necessary legal authority for its decision. Increasingly, the courts are concerned to review *how* public power is being exercised, to the extent that it is claimed that there has evolved

a new relationship between the courts and those who derive their authority from the public law, one of partnership based on a common aim, namely the maintenance of the highest standards of public administration.[141]

Acting entirely on their own initiative, the courts have developed common law standards which, in the absence of statutory provisions to the contrary, they will require of public officials. By extending the grounds for judicial review to include 'irrationality' and 'procedural impropriety',[142] the courts have sought to structure the manner in which discretionary power is used and to shape the way in which public administration is conducted; as a former Lord Chancellor observed, 'The purpose of judicial review is to ensure that the individual receives fair treatment.'[143]

Recent examples of the use of judicial review in matters concerning animals include issues arising from: the prohibition on the non-therapeutic administration of hormone growth promoters;[144] the export of live animals;[145] decisions by public bodies and quasi-public bodies to ban the hunting of deer on their land;[146] the decision of HM Customs and Excise not to give effect to the prohibition on importing furs and fur products from third countries contained in Regulation 3254/91;[147] a determination by the body which regulates the advertising industry;[148] an attempt by a local authority to use its licensing powers to prevent a performance involving

---

[141] *R v Lancashire County Council, ex parte Huddleston* [1986] 2 All ER 941, 945, CA (Lord Donaldson MR).

[142] Adopting Lord Diplock's formulation in *Council of Civil Service Unions v Minister for the Civil Service* [1985] AC 374, 410, HL.

[143] *Chief Constable of North Wales v Evans* [1982] 1 WLR 1155, 1161, HL (Lord Hailsham LC).

[144] *R v Minister of Agriculture, Fisheries and Food, ex parte Federation Europeanne de la Sant & Animale* (QBD, 20 September 1988).

[145] *R v Minister of Agriculture, Fisheries and Food, ex parte Roberts* [1991] 1 CMLR 555; *R v Coventry City Council, ex parte Phoenix Aviation, R v Dover Harbour Board, ex parte Peter Gilder & Sons, R v Associated British Ports, ex parte Plymouth City Council* [1995] 3 All ER 37; *R v Ministry of Agriculture, Fisheries and Food, ex parte Live Sheep Traders Ltd* (QBD, 12 April 1995); *R v Ministry of Agriculture, Fisheries and Food, ex parte Hedley Lomas (Ireland) Ltd*, Case 5/94 [1996] 2 CMLR 391, ECJ; *R v Chief Constable of Sussex, ex parte International Traders' Ferry Ltd* [1998] 3 WLR 1260, HL; *R v Minister of Agriculture, Fisheries and Food, ex parte Compassion in World Farming*, Case 1/96 [1998] 2 CMLR 661, ECJ.

[146] *R v Somerset County Council, ex parte Fewings* [1995] 1 WLR 1037, CA; although not strictly a case of judicial review, see also, *Scott v National Trust* [1998] 2 All ER 705, Ch.

[147] *R v Commissioners of Customs and Excise, ex parte International Fund for Animal Welfare and RSPCA* (QBD, 27 March 1996).

[148] *R v Advertising Standards Authority, ex parte International Fund for Animal Welfare* (QBD, 11 November 1997).

animals in its district;[149] and a challenge to quarantine requirements on the ground that they contravened the right to the free movement of goods protected under EC law.[150] On occasions, the fact that a court has given its permission for judicial review is enough to persuade a decision maker to reconsider their decision without the need for a full hearing. For example, in the face of judicial review brought by the British Union for the Abolition of Vivisection, the Home Office agreed to stop licensing the oral LD50 test for chemical safety testing because a less severe alternative existed, and under both European and national legislation it was this method which was required to be used.[151]

K. Conclusion

At a practical level, it is clearly important to have some knowledge of the nature, source, and status of different types of law, and the relationship between them, in order to understand the operation of animal protection legislation in Britain. This chapter has attempted to provide such an insight. In addition, however, it has highlighted two important issues presently confronting those who are concerned to regulate the way in which animals are treated.

First, it has been pointed out that although the UK Parliament has traditionally relied on its inherent legislative supremacy to enact whatever legislation it considered appropriate, this autonomy has been severely curtailed. On the one hand, by means of the European Communities Act 1972, it has ceded legal authority to the institutions of the European Community in respect of those matters which fall within the Community's competence. On the other, it has chosen to devolve both legislative power and executive accountability to Wales and, more particularly, Scotland. While the UK Parliament may retain the inherent power to repeal the 1972 Act, the Government of Wales Act 1998, and the Scotland Act 1998, and can therefore be said to remain legislatively supreme, while those statutes remain in force, there are significant areas for which it either cannot legislate, or may legislate only in accordance with policies determined by external institutions. In consequence, it is no longer sufficient simply to look to Westminster to secure reform of animal protection legislation.

Secondly, the consequences of the predominance of trade liberalization as reflected in the ideology of both the WTO and the European Community, and the resulting impotence of national governments to secure competing policy considerations, have been discussed. The importance of this development to the protection of animals which are used in commercial undertakings cannot be overemphasized: it clearly threatens to impede further progress in farm animal welfare for example, and runs the risk of bringing about a reduction in the hard-won standards which

---

[149] *Gerry Cottle's Circus Ltd v City of Edinburgh District Council* 1990 SLT 235.
[150] *R v Ministry of Agriculture, Fisheries and Food, ex parte Geiden* (QBD, 30 September 1999).
[151] Home Office Press Release 330/99, 21 October 1999.

have been achieved: 'The unscrupulous come out on top', observes the international financier, George Soros, 'This is one of the most disturbing aspects of the global capitalist system.'[152] The questions to which such a situation gives rise go well beyond animal protection. To what extent should the citizens of a democratic nation state be allowed to determine for themselves the laws to which they are subject? Why should the interests of commerce be permitted to prevail over other values? In a global economy, the contention that the legal system of a modern state 'is characterized by a certain kind of *supremacy* within its territory and *independence* of other systems'[153] would seem to have been superseded, with profound consequences for representative democracy. Indeed, the issues discussed in this conclusion have important political implications, and it is therefore appropriate to move on to consider the question of animal protection law in its political context.

---

[152]   Soros, G, *The Crisis in Global Capitalism. Open Society Endangered* (1998) 199.
[153]   Hart, HLA, *The Concept of Law* (2nd edn, 1994) 24 (emphasis in the original).

7

Law and Politics

A. The Political Nature of Animal Protection Legislation

Determining those factors which have a bearing on an animal's welfare, together with their relative importance, is essentially a question of science. However, deciding upon the appropriate degree of protection afforded to animals by the law requires more than the mere mechanical translation of scientific opinion into legislation. Although scientific advice is generally an essential consideration, and will often be paramount, it is not necessarily decisive. Even on those rare occasions when there is a consensus among the relevant experts, ethical, economic, political, and health issues may also require to be taken into account. For example, in deciding how best to control sheep scab, prevent the introduction into Britain of rabies, or investigate the prevalence of TB in badgers and cattle, a balance has to be struck between conflicting interests. Developing public policies towards animals, therefore, requires the exercise of judgement—a responsibility which falls ultimately to politicians.

It is trite to observe—but, nevertheless, too readily overlooked—that legislation is the product of the political process. As such, both its subject matter and its form are determined as much by circumstance as by principle. The priorities of government, the interests of individual parliamentarians, the legislative timetable, the influence of pressure groups, the advice of relevant experts, the views of those who may be affected, the conflict of competing interests, the diversity of scientific interpretation, the attitude of the media, the state of public opinion, and existing legal constraints, are among the factors which may play a part in shaping the law, and will often be of greater significance than the intrinsic merits of the case for change.

Whatever its objectives, then, the law is rarely, if ever, neutral or entirely objective, and never finally settled. Through the priorities it reflects, the policies it advances, the conduct it permits or prohibits, and the obligations, duties, and rights it prescribes, the law is always an expression of power. John Griffith, formerly Professor of Public Law at the London School of Economics, has written:

I do not believe that the concept of law is a moral concept. Of course I will, as cheerfully and as seriously as the next person, engage in discussions about the value of individual laws and pass moral judgements about them. But laws are merely statements of a power relationship and nothing more. A law remains a political act about which it is indeed possible to hold opinions. But it can be called good only in the limited sense that a number of people hold that opinion of it.[1]

Whether or not hunting with hounds is banned, the degree of regulation under which farmers operate, the scientific purposes for which animals may be used, are all reflections of the relative influence of opposing viewpoints, and an expression of the balance between the autonomy of the individual on the one hand, and the authority endowed upon the State to intervene on the other. As Andrew Ashworth has observed, 'The boundaries of the criminal law are explicable largely as the result of exercises of political power at particular points in history.'[2]

B. Animals and Politics

(1) Changing attitudes

Debate about the nature of man's responsibility towards other species and concern arising from the way in which animals are routinely treated have together resulted in the issue of animal welfare steadily rising up the political agenda since the 1960s. 'We discuss the fall of this party or the rise of that leader', one of the UK's most astute political commentators has recently observed, 'but, taking the long view, the change in our attitudes to animals and nature will be seen by historians as one of the most important political changes of our times.'[3] There are several reasons for this: the ideas of philosophers such as Peter Singer[4] and Tom Regan[5] have fuelled a debate about the moral status of animals which has spread far beyond the confines of academe; the scientific community has greatly increased its understanding of animal behaviour, which has in turn been very effectively communicated to a huge audience through the quality and quantity of television programmes dedicated to natural history; and there has been a reaction against the business ethic which appears to regard animals as nothing more than commodities to be relentlessly exploited so as to produce the maximum possible profit. All this has taken place against a backdrop of relative social stability and increasing affluence. Such factors, together with a wider general concern about the state of the environment, have focused attention on man's place in the world and led to a recognition that although humans may be predominant, they are not necessarily pre-eminent.

  As we saw in Chapters 3 and 4, a tradition of vigorous campaigning in support of legal protection of animals developed in Britain from the beginning of the

---

[1] Griffith, JAG, 'The Political Constitution' (1979) 42 Modern Law Review 1, 19.
[2] Ashworth, A, *Principles of Criminal Law* (3rd edn, 1999) 2.   [3] Marr, A, the *Observer*, 19 July 1998.
[4] *Animal Liberation* (2nd edn, 1990).   [5] *The Case for Animal Rights* (1993).

nineteenth century up to the outbreak of the First World War. For the next fifty years, however, this trend went into abeyance: there was little pressure for reform, less major legislation, and the animal welfare organizations became predominantly concerned with looking after unwanted dogs and cats. In 1964, however, the issue was politically resuscitated with the publication of Ruth Harrison's book, *Animal Machines*, the first informed critique of the growing practice of intensively rearing livestock, the 'greatest condemnation' of which she identified as being 'that *the animals do not live before they die, they only exist*'.[6] At the time, control over the way in which farm animals were treated relied almost exclusively on the Protection of Animals Act 1911 and the Protection of Animals (Scotland) Act 1912. Harrison argued that these were insufficient to meet the new situation, and that further legislation was required.[7] In response, the Government established a committee to enquire into the situation, under the chairmanship of a zoologist, Frederick Brambell. It reported in 1965,[8] and led to the passing of the Agriculture (Miscellaneous Provisions) Act 1968, the first legislation intended specifically to regulate the way in which livestock on farms were to be kept. In the year following the appearance of Harrison's book, Brigid Brophy published a highly influential article on animal rights in the *Sunday Times*.[9] By the beginning of the 1970s, the debate about the moral status of animals had been taken up by a group based in Oxford, which included Stephen Clark, Roslind and Stanley Godlovitch, Andrew Linzey, Richard Ryder, and Peter Singer.[10] The first edition of Singer's seminal work, *Animal Liberation*, was to follow in 1975,[11] the same year that Ryder published *Victims of Science*, an attack on the use of animals for experiments in which he also developed his concept of 'speciesism', a term which has entered the language to mean, according to the *Oxford English Dictionary*, 'an assumption of human superiority leading to the exploitation of animals'.

This period represented a watershed in shaping attitudes to animals; the issue began to impact on the media, within political circles, and on the public's perception. Most significantly, however, it was instrumental in a revitalization of pressure group activity. Indeed, as Garner rightly acknowledges, pressure groups have made a 'crucial contribution' in this area, to the extent that 'without the concerted efforts of those who have perceived a need for greater legislative protection for, and a change in society's attitude towards, animals, there would not be a set of political issues here requiring resolution'.[12]

---

[6] *Animal Machines* (1964) 151 (italics in the original). [7] ibid Ch 9.
[8] *Report of the Technical Committee to Enquire into the Welfare of Animals Kept Under Intensive Husbandry Systems*.
[9] 'The Rights of Animals', *Sunday Times*, 10 October 1965.
[10] See further, Godlovitch, S, Godlovitch, R, and Harris, J (eds), *Animals, Men and Morals* (1971).
[11] n 4 above. [12] Garner, R, *Animals, politics and morality* (1993) 181.

(2) Pressure groups

The RSPCA, for example, while continuing its traditional function of providing practical protection for animals through the work of its inspectorate, the provision of animal shelters and veterinary clinics, and the initiation of prosecutions, has adopted an increasingly forthright approach towards lobbying and publicity. Ryder, who was himself involved with reinvigorating the activities of the Society, found an organization at the beginning of the 1970s with no formal policies and a 'powerful inclination toward inertia and blandness'. By the end of the decade, new priorities had been established and, in spite of considerable opposition from within the Society itself, a strategy had been adopted to campaign for legislative reform.[13] Similarly, a number of other long-established organizations, such as the British Union for the Abolition of Vivisection (BUAV), the National Anti-Vivisection Society (NAVS), and the League Against Cruel Sports (LACS), were reinvigorated during this period. At the same time, new groups were formed, such as Animal Aid, Compassion in World Farming (CIWF), and the International Fund for Animal Welfare (IFAW), with the specific intention of challenging the status quo and actively campaigning to change the way animals were regarded and treated.

Not only is the nature of all these organizations' campaigning activities far removed from the somewhat staid and genteel image traditionally associated with concern for animals, but the methods and resources at their disposal have become increasingly sophisticated. Without doubt, the most significant of these has been the development and utilization of the video camera. This has made it possible, often by filming covertly, to bring a whole range of controversial practices, which were hitherto carried on largely unseen and unknown, to the attention of both the general public and decision makers in a way, and with a directness, which was not previously possible. At the same time, such organizations have benefited from a growing disillusionment with the political establishment. As a result, many who might formerly have been persuaded to join a political party, campaigning across a range of policies, have instead become activists or supporters of single-issue pressure groups concerned with, for example, animal welfare, conservation, or the environment. Together, these developments provide both the motivation and the means to take the initiative in seeking to improve the condition of animals through the political process.

By the end of the 1970s, the rising profile and increasing influence of animal welfare pressure groups were clearly in evidence. In 1978, for example, as part of a campaign against the killing of common and grey seals, IFAW placed whole-page advertisements in the national press, exhorting readers to write to the Prime Minister. As a result, some 17,000 letters opposing the seal hunt were sent in a single week, claimed by Ryder to be more than a British Prime Minister had ever previously received on a single issue.[14]

---

[13] Ryder, RD, *Animal Revolution* (2nd edn, 2000) 174–183.   [14] ibid 181.

(3) 'Putting animals into politics'[15]

A further manifestation of the growing impact of pressure groups was the success of what the late Lord Houghton characterized as the campaign to 'put animals into politics', as a result of which all the major political parties for the first time included policies on animal welfare in their manifestos for the 1979 General Election.

This practice has not only continued, but the policies developed by the parties have become increasingly detailed, a sure sign that their own polling of the electorate is registering animal welfare as a widespread concern. In 1994, for example, the Prime Minister, John Major, recognized that 'The welfare of animals is no longer a fringe issue.'[16] While in opposition, the Labour Party formally appointed an official spokesman on animal welfare, Elliot Morley, who subsequently became the minister responsible for animal welfare within MAFF when the party entered into government in 1997. The significance it attached to this issue was also reflected in the decision to publish a document in advance of the 1997 General Election devoted exclusively to its policies intended to promote animal welfare. These included: better treatment of animals reared for food; protection for species threatened with extinction; protection against cruelty for wild mammals; a free vote on banning hunting with hounds; an end to fur farming; the highest possible welfare in the laboratory; cruelty-free testing of cosmetics; maximum journey times for animals and better conditions during transit; safeguarding the countryside; dog registration; improved standards of care in circuses and zoos; ocean sanctuaries for whales and no more commercial whaling; and a Europe-wide embargo on trapping exotic birds. In addition, it was indicated that the party wanted 'to see policies to improve animal welfare co-ordinated in government', and it indicated an intention to 'meet annually with relevant interest groups to review progress'.[17]

For their parts, the Conservative and Liberal Democratic manifestos echoed each other, declaring respectively, 'A civilized society respects its animals' and 'The way a society treats its animals is a measure of its civilization.'[18] The Conservatives did not formally put forward any specific policies on animal welfare issues, except a proposal to produce a consultation paper on rabies protection, and an undertaking not to introduce legislation which would interfere with the rights of people to participate in what were described as 'traditional country pursuits, including fishing'. In contrast, the Liberal Democrats proposed the introduction of a dog registration scheme; the establishment of an Animal Welfare Commission to enforce and improve animal welfare standards; bans on the use of snares, and animal

---

[15] See further, Hollands, C, *Compassion is the Bugler* (1980); Ryder, n 13 above; Garner, n 12 above; Garner, R, *Political Animals* (1998); Ryder, RD, 'Putting Animals into Politics' in Garner, R (ed), *Animal Rights. The Changing Debate* (1996).

[16] Conservative Political Centre, *Animal Welfare* (1994).

[17] Labour Party, *new life for animals* (sic) (1996). See also, *Who Cares?* (1992).

[18] Conservative Party, General Election Manifesto, 1997; Liberal Democratic Party, General Election Manifesto, 1997. See also, Conservative Political Centre, n 16 above; and Liberal Democrats, *A Matter of Conscience* (1992).

testing for cosmetics, weapons, and tobacco; and a free vote in the House of Commons on hunting with hounds and coursing.[19] The Welsh Nationalists undertook to support indigenous industries for the slaughter and processing of animal products, 'thereby reducing the transportation of live animals over long distances'; to legislate against neglect and cruelty; and to prohibit the use of live animals for testing cosmetic and domestic products.[20] Indeed, of the major parties, only the manifesto of the Scottish National Party failed specifically to mention animal welfare. The impact that the campaign to put animals into politics, and retain them there, has had on both policy makers and public perceptions is a tribute to the efforts of pressure groups. Animal welfare 'has become a key factor in British politics', observes John Gray, Professor of European Thought at the London School of Economics. 'How the parties stand on the treatment of animals and the larger issues surrounding our relationship to the natural environment', he suggests, has become 'a test of their sensitivity to public opinion'.[21]

Despite these achievements, it would be wrong to suggest that this is a story of uninterrupted or unopposed progress. As Garner points out, 'those who are generally hostile to the introduction of further restrictions on their ability to exploit animals have developed formidable lobbying and general public relations structures paid for by some of the wealthiest interests in their respective countries'.[22] As a result of such activities, political perceptions can change. In 1981, for example, the Agriculture Committee of the House of Commons recommended that EC Member States should make 'a clear statement of intention that after, say, 5 years from now egg production will be limited to approved methods which will not include battery cages in their present form'. Thirteen years later, however, the same committee, differently constituted, concluded that 'we do not feel that in the present circumstances it would be realistic to propose a ban'.[23]

(4) Political activity and charitable status

However, campaigning in the political arena runs the very real risk that a pressure group thereby becomes ineligible for charitable status. This has important implications; registration as a charity not only results in considerable financial benefits, it also bestows upon an organization a certain prestige in the eyes of the public.

Dating from the reign of Elizabeth I, in order to be considered charitable in law, an organization's primary object must fall into one of four arbitrary and anachronistic categories: relief of the poor, advancement of either religion or education, or any other purpose which the courts are prepared to recognize as beneficial to the community.[24]

---

[19] Liberal Democratic Party, General Election Manifesto, 1997.

[20] Plaid Cymru, General Election Manifesto, 1997.   [21] The *Guardian*, 31 July 1999.

[22] Garner, n 15 above, 67.

[23] House of Commons Agriculture Committee, *Animal Welfare in Poultry, Pig and Veal Calf Production* (1981) para 150; House of Commons Agriculture Committee, *The UK Poultry Industry* (1994) para 78. See now, Directive 99/74, laying down minimum standards for the protection of laying hens.

[24] *Commissioners for Special Purposes of Income Tax v Pemsel* [1891] AC 531, 583, HL (Lord Macnaghten).

Surprisingly, perhaps, in view of the Victorian judiciary's inherent conservatism, by the end of the nineteenth century, societies for the suppression of animal cruelty, including those established specifically to oppose vivisection, had achieved the conspicuous feat of persuading the courts that they might be regarded as existing to further a charitable object. 'The purpose of these societies,' declared Chitty J in 1895, 'whether they are right or wrong in the opinions they hold, is charitable in the legal sense of the term. The intention is to benefit the community.'[25] Half a century later, however, in the important case of the *National Anti-Vivisection Society v Inland Revenue Commissioners*,[26] this view was qualified by the House of Lords in two important respects.

First, the assertion that an organization which was committed to the abolition of vivisection could be regarded as charitable was overruled on the basis that any assumed public benefit in the advancement of morals would be far outweighed by the detriment to medical science and research, and therefore to public health. According to Lord Wright, 'it is impossible to apply the word cruelty to efforts of the high-minded scientists who have devoted themselves to vivisection experiments for the purpose of alleviating human suffering', and are thereby 'fulfilling a moral duty to mankind which is higher in degree than the moralist or sentimentalist who thinks only of animals'. In contrast, anti-vivisection societies were, in the view of the judge, seeking 'to destroy a source of enormous blessings to mankind', which he regarded to be 'a positive and calamitous detriment of appalling magnitude'.[27]

Secondly, and more far-reaching, the court applied to groups concerned to protect animals a pre-existing legal principle to the effect that an organization was to be regarded as political in nature, and could not therefore qualify as charitable, if it sought as one of its main objects to secure legislative change. The rationale for this position is based on judicial concern that 'the court has no means of judging whether a proposed change in the law will or will not be for the public benefit'.[28] This exclusion was not to be restricted only to those organizations whose *principal* purpose was political, but extended to situations where 'it is a main object, if not the main object, of the society, to obtain an alteration in the law, . . . even if its purposes might otherwise be regarded as charitable'.[29] The courts have subsequently held that an object will be regarded as political for these purposes if its direct and principal purpose is: to further the interests of a particular political party; to procure changes in either domestic law or that of a foreign country; to procure a reversal of government policy or of particular decisions of governmental authorities in this country or abroad; or to oppose a particular change in the law or a change in a

---

[25] *Re Foveaux* [1895] 2 Ch 501, 507. See also, the remarks of FitzGibbon and Holmes LJJ in the Irish case of *Re Cranston* [1898] 1 IR 431, 446, and 457.

[26] [1948] AC 31, HL.   [27] ibid 47, 48, and 49.

[28] *Bowman v Secular Society Ltd* [1917] AC 406, 442, HL (Lord Parker).

[29] *National Anti-Vivisection Society v Inland Revenue Commissioners* [1948] AC 31, 62, HL (Lord Simonds).

particular law.[30] The paradox of this situation is readily apparent, and was alluded to in the *NAVS* case itself by Lord Porter, who considered its effect in the context of earlier campaigns to secure social reform. He expressly rejected the contention that 'the anti-slavery campaign or the enactment of the Factory Acts or the abolition of the use of boy labour by chimney-sweeps, would be charitable so long as the supporters of these objects had not in mind or at any rate did not advocate a change in the laws, but became political and therefore non-charitable if they did so'. To take such a view, he suggested, would be 'to neglect substance for form', for although it might be possible to achieve such objects voluntarily, 'the only effective method' was 'to alter the law'.[31]

Groups which exist to end the use of animals in experiments, such as BUAV, NAVS, and Advocates for Animals, are on that basis alone ineligible for charitable status (although this does not extend to those which promote alternatives to the use of animals, such as the Fund for the Replacement of Animals in Medical Experiments (FRAME) and the Dr Hadwen Trust). Most, if not all, organizations which campaign to improve the treatment of animals would seem to fall foul of the second restriction, and several other high-profile organizations concerned with the treatment of animals in other situations, such as CIWF, LACS, and Animal Aid, are not classified as charities (although this does not prevent them setting up a separate fund which does have charitable objectives, unsullied by a political aim). At the same time, however, it is self-evident that others, although 'prominent in their espousal of political means to attain their ends',[32] nevertheless continue to enjoy charitable status. The explanation for this is that the courts make a distinction between a political *purpose*, which cannot be charitable, and the employment of political *means* to further a non-political purpose, which may be permissible.[33] In other words, a charity may employ political means to advance a non-political object.

According to the Charity Commission, such political activities 'must be in furtherance of, and ancillary to,' a charity's stated objects, and it must be able to show that there is 'a reasonable expectation' that they will further the purposes of the charity 'to an extent justified by the resources devoted to those activities'. So long as these requirements are met, charities may enter into dialogue with government; publish the advice or views they express to ministers; and seek to inform and educate the public on relevant issues, including 'the solutions they advocate'. They are warned, however, that 'they must do so on the basis of a reasoned case and their views must be expressed with a proper sense of proportion'.[34] The Commission recognizes that charities are well placed 'to make an important contribution to the development of

---

[30] *McGovern v A-G* [1982] Ch 321, 340 (Slade J); *Re Koeppler's Will Trusts* [1984] Ch 243, 260 (Peter Gibson J).

[31] *National Anti-Vivisection Society v Inland Revenue Commissioners* [1948] AC 31, 55.

[32] *R v Radio Authority, ex parte Bull* [1998] QB 294, 316, CA (Brooke LJ).

[33] *McGovern v A-G* [1982] Ch 321, 340 (Slade J).

[34] Charity Commissioners for England and Wales, *Political Activity and Campaigning by Charities* (1995) paras 8, 9, and 10.

public policy', and it is therefore open to them to engage in campaigning activities.[35] Where a charity's policy coincides with that of a particular political party, it may continue to promote it, but must ensure that the independence of its view is explained and understood; the information provided to the public in support of the campaign as a whole is accurate and sufficiently full to support its position; and, while it may have an emotional content, it is unacceptable for a charity to seek to persuade government or the public on the basis of material which is merely emotive.[36]

The Charity Commission's guidance is helpful in setting out its view of what charities may do while remaining within the parameters set down by the courts, but difficult situations may still arise. Clearly, a charity will always wish to adopt the tactics which it considers to be most effective in influencing the public and politicians, and this may lead it to push at the limits of what it may lawfully do. The nature and extent of political campaigning that an organization may undertake while still retaining its charitable status has posed a particular difficulty for the RSPCA, causing tension internally and providing a basis for attack by those who are opposed to the Society's policies. The Chief Charity Commissioner has expressed the view that 'While it would be proper for a charity to seek to promote the raising of standards of care and subsequent slaughter of farm animals by promoting more humane farming methods, it would clearly be unacceptable to seek to frustrate essential medical research involving experimentation on animals if no acceptable alternative could be found.'[37] Similarly, he has said that, in relation to hunting, 'it is open to the RSPCA to argue that hunting involves unnecessary suffering on the basis that, where it is necessary to control numbers, other more humane methods exist', but this must be based on 'reasoned argument and evidence, not on the personal viewpoint or emotions of members'.[38] While these statements may accurately reflect the law, it is little wonder that such legal niceties dismay many of the Society's members, who are primarily concerned to campaign against what they regard as the unacceptable treatment of animals, regardless of the circumstances in which it arises.

C. Promoting Reform

The factors which lead to change in the regulatory regime governing the treatment of animals in Britain include research findings; society's evolving attitude towards other species; the development of new practices, uses, and techniques involving animals; a response to a particular incident or controversy; and the necessity to introduce legislation in order to meet the UK's obligations under EC law. The impetus for reform may come from many different sources: the Government itself; parliamentarians, either individually or in recommendations from select committees[39] or at

---

[35] ibid para 16.   [36] ibid paras 18–20.   [37] Letter published in the *Guardian*, 28 March 1996.
[38] Letter published in *The Times*, 17 July 1996.
[39] For example, House of Commons Agriculture Committee, *Animal Welfare in Poultry, Pig and Veal Calf Production*, n 23 above; House of Commons Agriculture Committee, *The UK Poultry Industry*, n 23 above;

the behest of the Associate Parliamentary Group for Animal Welfare[40] or other parliamentary committees;[41] political parties; pressure groups;[42] standing committees established specifically to advise ministers, such as the (statutory) Animal Procedures Committee (APC),[43] the (non-statutory) Farm Animal Welfare Council (FAWC),[44] and the (non-statutory) Zoos Forum;[45] or the non-government appointed Companion Animal Welfare Council (CAWC); ad hoc groups charged to consider a particular issue in detail and make recommend-

House of Commons Agriculture Committee, *Animals in Transit* (1991); House of Commons Environment Committee, *London Zoo* (1991); House of Commons Agriculture Committee, *Health Controls on the Importation of Live Animals* (1994); House of Commons Home Affairs Committee, *The Operation of the Dangerous Dogs Act 1991* (1996); House of Commons Agriculture Committee, *The UK Pig Industry* (1999); House of Commons Agriculture Committee, *The Government's Proposals for Organophosphate Sheep Dips* (2000); House of Commons Agriculture Committee, *Badgers and Bovine Tuberculosis,* (2001); House of Commons Agriculture Committee, *Organic Farming* (2001); House of Lords Select Committee on Science and Technology, *Resistance to Antibiotics and Other Antimicrobial Agents* (1998); House of Lords Select Committee on Science and Technology, *Resistance to Antibiotics* (2001).

[40] For example, RSPCA et al, *The commercial breeding and sale of dogs and puppies* (1996), and *Welfare of circus animals* (1998).

[41] The House of Lords recently indicated its intention to establish an ad hoc committee on animal experimentation: HL Debs, 17 July 2000, col 158.

[42] There has been a recent trend for individual organizations to form loose coalitions to pursue specific campaigns. These may be on an informal basis, for example in relation to the export of live animals (RSPCA, CIWF, IFAW), or under the auspices of a specially formed umbrella organization. For example, the Dangerous Dogs Act 1991 Reform Group consisted of 17 animal welfare organizations, including the BVA, NCDL, and the RSPCA (now reconstituted as the Dog Legislation Advisory Group); the Quarantine Reform Campaign (members included the RSPCA, Passports for Pets, and Vets in Support of Change); the Campaign for the Protection of Hunted Animals, subsequently Deadline 2000 (RSPCA, IFAW, LACS); Scottish Campaign Against Hunting with Dogs (IFAW, LACS, Advocates for Animals).

[43] Established under the Animals (Scientific Procedures) Act 1986, ss 19 and 20, the APC's function is to advise the Home Secretary on such matters concerned with the Act and his functions under it as the Committee may determine or as he may refer to it. In its consideration of any matter, the Committee is charged to have regard both to 'the legitimate requirements of science and industry and to the protection of animals against avoidable suffering and unnecessary use in scientific procedures'. The statute specifies that its membership is to be dominated by medical practitioners, veterinary surgeons, or others who possess 'qualifications or experience in a biological subject approved by the Secretary of State as relevant to the work of the Committee', but, in making appointments, the Home Secretary is required 'to have regard to the desirability of ensuring that the interests of animal welfare are adequately represented'.

[44] Established by the Government in 1979, FAWC is a non-statutory independent advisory body which is charged to keep under review the welfare of farm animals on agricultural land, at market, in transit, and at places of slaughter, and to advise ministers of any legislative or other changes that may be necessary. The Council has the freedom to consider any topic falling within this remit. Ministers may request the Council to report on a specific issue or it may decide to do so on its own initiative. Members are appointed by the Government. They serve in a personal capacity and typically include farmers, veterinarians, animal welfarists, consumers, and researchers. The Committee's work is typically carried out by small working groups of members who undertake the detailed analysis of a particular issue and prepare recommendations for approval by the whole Council. Most such reviews culminate in the publication of a report, a full list of which is included in the bibliography at the end of this volume. At the time of writing, FAWC is conducting studies into the welfare of animals at market and at slaughter, and the impact on animal welfare of farm assurance schemes.

[45] The Zoos Forum was established in 1998 to encourage the role of zoos in conservation, education, and scientific research; to keep under review the operation and implementation of the zoo licensing system; and to advise or make recommendations to ministers on any legislative or other changes that may be necessary.

ations;[46] professional bodies and industry groups; the media; and public opinion. Where they are responsible for the appointment of members to a committee, ministers will seek to ensure that a range of views is represented. However, the identity of those they invite may influence the way in which the committee approaches its work. For example, the appointment of a philosopher as chairman of the APC has had a discernible effect on the manner in which it approaches its work; a development which coincided with a conscious decision by the Government to increase the number of members of the APC who have an expertise in animal welfare.[47] Conversely, there was some disquiet among MPs about the selection of members to serve on the Burns Inquiry into hunting.[48]

D. Westminster and Whitehall

(1) Lobbying

Traditionally in Britain, the attention of those seeking to improve animal protection has centred on Westminster and Whitehall. The primary target is generally the relevant minister. It may be that he or she already possesses legal powers which are sufficiently wide to enable a policy to be changed administratively. If not, the minister may be able to rely on existing enabling powers in primary legislation to amend the law by means of secondary legislation. If neither of these options is available, primary legislation will be required. In the case of controversial proposals, the attitude of the minister personally responsible for a Bill is often crucial. It is widely acknowledged, for example, that David Mellor's personal commitment as Under-Secretary of State at the Home Office was crucial in successfully steering the Animals (Scientific Procedures) Act 1986 through Parliament.[49] Even when a measure is introduced by a backbench MP in the form of a Private Member's Bill, it will generally require government support to succeed. As a result of the Government's majority in the House of Commons, party discipline, and its control over the legislative timetable, a Bill that does not have the executive's backing is almost certainly doomed to failure. Accordingly, a decision by the Government neither to support nor oppose such a measure is not the expression of neutrality it might seem. Parliamentary procedure so disadvantages initiatives by backbench MPs that, in practice, a Government's detachment is greatly to the advantage of those who wish to preserve the status quo. This can be seen in relation to the

---

[46] For example, Scott Henderson, J (Chairman), *Report on Cruelty to Wild Animals* (1951); Littlewood, S (Chairman), *Report of the Departmental Committee on Experimentation on Animals* (1965); Polkinghorne, JC (Chairman), *Report of the Committee on the Ethics of Genetic Modification and Food Use* (1993); Kennedy, I (Chairman), Report of the Advisory Group of Quarantine: *Quarantine and Rabies: A Reappraisal* (1998); Krebs, J (Chairman), *Bovine Tuberculosis in Cattle and Badgers. Report of the Independent Scientific Review Group* (1997); Burns, Lord (Chairman), *Report of the Committee of Inquiry into Hunting with Dogs in England and Wales* (2000).

[47] HC Debs, 27 November 1997, col 611 (WA).

[48] HC Debs, 1 and 3 February 2000, cols 504–506 and 707 (WA).   [49] Garner, n 15 above, 182–187.

repeated attempts to ban hunting with hounds by means of a Private Member's Bill; sixteen such Bills were introduced in the period 1980–2000 (in 1995, the House of Commons voted 253 to 0 in favour of a ban, and in 1998 by a majority of 411 to 151). In consequence, the Government has decided that the Private Member's Bill procedure is not adequate to bring such a hotly contentious issue to a conclusion and has therefore decided, while remaining neutral on the outcome, to settle the matter by bringing forward its own Bill, offering a range of different options, which MPs will decide on by a free vote.[50] A summary of animal protection and welfare Bills introduced into Parliament between 1985/1986 and 1999/2001 is provided in Appendix 1.

Once pressure groups have identified a need for legislation, they will attempt to lobby the relevant minister personally, at the same time seeking to mobilize public opinion. This is something at which they are adept. During the first ten months of 1993, for example, the Government received over 100,000 pieces of correspondence and 81 petitions, representing 27,000 signatures, concerning the welfare of animals during transport;[51] over 20,000 representations were received from members of the public in response to the European Commission's failure to implement the regulation banning the leghold trap;[52] and in 1998, when a Private Member's Bill to abolish hunting with dogs was before Parliament, the Home Office received 70,000 representations.[53] Importance is also attached to obtaining access to the minister's officials. Their attitude and the advice they provide are influential in developing ministerial policy, and they are always involved in drawing up proposed legislation. By seeking to persuade ministers and officials of the merits of their arguments, lobby groups hope to influence not only domestic policies but also the UK's negotiating position in EC negotiations within the Council of Ministers.

The ethos of a Department is extremely important. In 1981, for example, the House of Commons Agriculture Committee complained that within the Agriculture Departments 'the whole weight and thrust of policy has, until recently at least, been directed towards ever-greater productivity', and animal welfare had 'played at best a minor part in Ministerial and official thinking'. The Committee acknowledged that by the time it reported, 'whether owing to more enlightened ideas or in response to public pressure', the issue was receiving greater attention. Even so, it expressed concern that animal welfare was 'still regarded as a tiresome complication engendered by vocal sentimentalists who need to be placated at minimum cost to producers' profits', and to the extent that this was true, it was, said the Committee, 'high time for a change in attitude'.[54] Subsequently, a Division was established within MAFF specifically to advise ministers on animal welfare

---

[50] HC Debs, 7 July 2000, col 524; its Hunting Bill was introduced into Parliament in December 2000. See Ch 5, s C, n 77, above.

[51] HC Debs, 26 October 1993, col 562 (WA).

[52] HC Debs, 24 June 1997, col 483 (WA); see Ch 6, s C(2) above.

[53] HC Debs, 30 March 1998, col 395 (WA).

[54] House of Commons Agriculture Committee, *Animal Welfare in Poultry, Pig and Veal Calf Production*, n 23 above, para 62.

issues and to implement their policies. By contrast, those matters involving animals which fell within the jurisdiction of the Home Office were dealt with by a Unit which, in addition to overseeing the operation of the Animals (Scientific Procedures) Act 1986, the protection of domestic and wild animals against cruelty, dangerous dogs, field sports, and game law, was also responsible, somewhat bizarrely it might be thought, for the Home Secretary's functions in relation to by-laws, private Bills, coroners, the removal of human remains, and cremation and burial matters! In an attempt to ensure a degree of coordination within government, an Interdepartmental Ministerial Group on Animal Welfare has been established, involving ministers with animal welfare responsibilities including those from the Department of the Environment, the Home Office, the Ministry of Agriculture, and representatives of the devolved administrations in Scotland and Wales, which it is intended should meet at least twice a year.[55] This process may be assisted by the recent concentration of animal welfare issues within the newly established Department for Environment, Food and Rural Affairs (DEFRA). Formed immediately after the 2001 General Election as part of a wider reorganization of central government by the Prime Minister, DEFRA assumed all the responsibilities formerly undertaken by MAFF, which was abolished (although the formal position of Minister of Agriculture, Fisheries and Food was expressly preserved in the person of the Secretary of State for the Environment, Food and Rural Affairs). In addition, a number of activities formerly administered by other departments were moved to DEFRA. These included animal welfare matters, excepting regulation of scientific procedures, which had formerly been under the auspices of the Home Office, together with responsibility for CITES, action against wildlife crime, and regulation of zoos and the keeping of dangerous wild animals, previously overseen by the DETR. It will obviously take some time before the ethos and priorities of the new Department emerge, and it will therefore be a while before one can assess whether these arrangements will prove to be of benefit to the interests of animal welfare.

According to Garner, on the basis of his own research, despite 'the huge array of subjects preoccupying MPs', there exists among them 'a healthy concern for animal protection issues'.[56] It is therefore not surprising that considerable effort is also made to lobby backbench MPs, especially those known to be sympathetic to animal issues. They can make their own representations to ministers, either privately or on the floor of the House, they may agree to introduce their own Private Member's Bill which, although the chances of success are remote, may nevertheless draw media and public attention to the issue, and they can also publicize their concerns through parliamentary questions, adjournment debates, and early day motions.

Parliament has conventionally been the focus for lobbyists because of its legislative supremacy: if it could be persuaded of the merits of the argument, it had the

---

[55] HC Debs, 21 July 2000, col 373, and 21 December 2000, col 330 (WA).
[56] Garner, n 15 above, 18.

inherent power to give effect to it. In asserting that animal welfare, 'in the general and in the particular, is largely a matter for the law', for example, Lord Houghton concluded: 'This means that to Parliament we must go. Sooner or later that is where we will *have* to go. That is where laws are made and where the penalties for disobedience and the measures for enforcement are laid down.'[57] Today, however, such an exhortation is inadequate; for all practical purposes, Parliament's former supremacy has gone. The effect of the WTO, membership of the European Community, and devolution, has been to dissipate significant areas of legislative power to other institutions. Indeed, it is now difficult to identify *any* issue relating to the treatment of animals over which the Westminster Parliament continues to have the ultimate power to legislate as it sees fit for Britain as a whole. Accordingly, it is no longer only to Parliament that lobbyists have to go; their destinations must also include Cardiff, Edinburgh, Brussels, Strasbourg, and Geneva.

(2) Consultation

It is often the case that legislation requires ministers to consult with interested parties prior to introducing new measures. Specific organizations may be mentioned, it may be left to the minister's discretion to approach those which he considers appropriate, or it may be a mixture of both. Section 19(5) of the Veterinary Surgeons Act 1966, for example, empowers ministers to amend the provisions of Schedule 3 (which details treatment and operations which may be given or carried out by unqualified persons), but only after consultation with the Council of the RCVS and any others appearing to ministers to represent interests which would be substantially affected by the proposed change.[58] Similarly, before introducing regulations or codes of recommendations for the welfare of livestock under sections 2 and 3 of the Agriculture (Miscellaneous Provisions) Act 1968, ministers are required to consult with such persons as appear to them to represent any interests concerned.[59] Even where there is no express requirement to consult, ministers often choose to do so voluntarily if they are contemplating a significant change of policy or the introduction of new legislation.[60] Ministers may also be required to consult with relevant bodies in carrying out their administrative responsibilities. Under the Zoo Licensing Act 1981, for example, the Secretary of State is required to consult with a local authority which is intending to carry out a zoo inspection, before nominating two persons with the appropriate expertise to participate in the inspection.[61] Similarly, before granting or issuing a certificate under the Animals

---

[57] Houghton, Lord, 'Animals and the Law: Moral and Political Issues' in Paterson, D and Ryder, RD (eds), *Animal Rights—A Symposium* (1979) 209 (italics in the original).

[58] Similar provisions apply in respect of amending Schedule 1 of the Protection of Animals (Anaesthetics) Act 1954; see further, s 1(3) of the 1954 Act and s 5 of the Agriculture (Miscellaneous Provisions) Act 1968.

[59] Agriculture (Miscellaneous Provisions) Act 1968, s 2(1).

[60] For example, the discussion document, MAFF, *Quarantine for Pets* (1997), and the consultation paper, DETR, *Review of the Operation of the Zoo Licensing Act 1981* (1997).

[61] Zoo Licensing Act 1981, ss 8(1), 10(4)(a)(ii).

(Scientific Procedures) Act 1986, the Secretary of State must consult one of the inspectors appointed under the Act and may also consult an independent assessor or the APC.[62] In a rather different context, the Secretary of State may, in respect of England and Wales, vary the close season for deer, but only after consulting any organization that appears to him to represent persons likely to be interested in or affected by the proposed change.[63]

Consultation by ministers prior to introducing new legislation or changing policy is always desirable. At one level, it helps to protect them from a legal challenge that they have failed to take relevant considerations into account, or have acted unfairly towards those who may be detrimentally affected by their decision. More practically, however, it serves to improve the quality and legitimacy of the eventual decision: those who have practical experience, expertise, or a particular interest in a subject can make an informed contribution to the decision-making process; unforeseen aspects of the issue can be identified; possible problems resolved in advance; and differing objectives and priorities aired. Where the minister has a discretion, it has become a common practice in recent years formally to approach those professional and commercial organizations, pressure groups, researchers, and other individuals with a known interest in a particular subject for their reaction. In addition, proposals are often placed in the public domain, accompanied by a general invitation for comments. These practices have significantly extended the circle of those who contribute to policy development, and introduced a greater range of perspectives. '[W]e are now just one of many organisations which give views on animal welfare', the Chairman of the RCVS External Affairs Committee has observed. 'The days when we were the only source of opinion have gone, and this can be seen from the lists of other organizations that are consulted. . . . Animal welfare is driven by factors other than pure veterinary science . . . the RCVS is influential, but not the final arbiter.'[64]

Regardless of whether consultation is mandatory or undertaken voluntarily, the courts are concerned to ensure that the exercise does not become a pretence; the decision maker is required to demonstrate that it involves 'a genuine invitation to give advice and a genuine consideration of that advice'.[65] In order to demonstrate that these two criteria have been met, the process must be initiated when the proposals are still at a formative stage and all those with a relevant interest should be consulted and provided with adequate information in respect of all relevant issues about what is proposed and why.[66] In short, those consulted are entitled to adequate information and time in order that they may respond with 'sufficiently informed and considered information or advice' about the substance of the proposals and their implications for those affected,[67] which 'must be conscientiously

---

[62] Animals (Scientific Procedures) Act 1986, s 9.
[63] Deer Act 1991, s 2(5).
[64] (1998) 142 *Veterinary Record* 46.
[65] *R v Secretary of State for Social Services, ex parte Association of Metropolitan Authorities* [1986] 1 WLR 1, 4.
[66] *R v Secretary of State for Health, ex parte United States Tobacco International Inc* [1992] QB 353, 371.
[67] *R v Secretary of State for Social Services, ex parte Association of Metropolitan Authorities* [1986] 1 WLR 1, 4.

taken into account' by the minister in arriving at a final decision.[68] However, there is no requirement to give any particular weight to the responses received, regardless of their force, and in most cases the decision maker will therefore retain considerable discretion in arriving at the final decision.

E. Edinburgh and Cardiff

At the time of writing, it is not possible to predict how responsive the Scottish Parliament and the Welsh Assembly, and their respective executives, will be to issues of animal welfare. It is self-evident, however, that attention will have to be directed towards them with regard to those matters which fall within their respective jurisdictions. Initially at least, this may present something of a novelty to those used to concentrating their efforts on Westminster and Whitehall. The situation presents both a challenge and an opportunity. On the one hand, in respect of most matters relating to animals, legislation secured at Westminster will no longer be applicable throughout Britain; campaigns and lobbying will have to be duplicated as necessary. On the other, once a principle is established by legislation passed at either Edinburgh or Westminster, the other legislature will then be encouraged to follow suit. This may become significant because, at least in theory, it would appear easier to secure legislation in the Scottish Parliament, especially in relation to Private Member's Bills, because, first, its membership is less (129 in comparison to 659 at Westminster) and it is therefore necessary to persuade many less MSPs in order to secure a parliamentary majority; secondly, the Scottish Parliament consists of only a single chamber, unlike Westminster, where an animal protection Bill must be approved by both the Commons and the Lords before it becomes law; and, thirdly, more modern and straightforward procedures mean that there is much less opportunity to frustrate the passage of a Bill. The consequences of these different legislative jurisdictions are already becoming apparent: legislation has been passed to prohibit fur farming in England and Wales after the end of 2002, but a similar provision has not yet been introduced into the Scottish Parliament, although the Scottish Executive has indicated that it intends to do so in due course;[69] at the time of writing, the Scottish Parliament is considering a Bill intended to prohibit hunting with hounds,[70] while the Westminster Parliament has before it a Bill which gives MPs the choice as to whether hunting with hounds in England and Wales should continue to regulate itself, be subject to a statutory licensing scheme, or banned;[71] the courts in England and Wales have been given additional powers to make provision for the care, disposal, or slaughter of animals kept for commercial purposes while proceedings against the owner under section

---

[68] *R v Devon County Council, ex parte Baker* [1995] 1 All ER 73, 91.
[69] Fur Farming (Prohibition) Act 2000; HC Debs, 28 February 2000, col 15 (WA).
[70] Protection of Wild Mammals.   [71] Hunting Bill; see Ch 5, s C, n 77 above.

1 of the Protection of Animals Act 1911 are continuing;[72] a new edition of the welfare code for sheep has been produced by MAFF, but applies only to England; and each jurisdiction has introduced its own secondary legislation to implement the EC farm animal Directive, coming into force on different dates, and slightly different in content.[73]

F. Brussels and Strasbourg

(1) The significance of pressure groups

Pressure groups concerned with animal welfare have long since recognized the shift of power away from national legislatures to the institutions of the European Community, and have responded accordingly, targeting both the Commission and the Parliament. But neither of these is the ultimate decision maker. This remains the Council, which is made up of representatives from the government of each Member State. Pressure groups therefore need to continue to lobby ministers of national governments in the hope of influencing the stand which they take within the Council.

Clearly, their principal objective is to secure the highest possible standards of animal welfare throughout the Union. This is a long-term goal, and in practice progress has been slow and piecemeal. A secondary aim is to defend the relatively high standards which already exist in some Member States. In other words, in the move towards common standards, to ensure a levelling up, not a levelling down. If this is not politically possible, then their fall-back position is to seek to protect the status quo in those Member States where existing national standards are higher than those applicable across the Union, either through some form of opt-out[74] or by obtaining agreement that the Community standard represents a minimum, which individual Member States may improve upon if they so wish.[75] In addition, they attempt to keep the question of animal welfare to the fore, and thereby encourage decision makers to have regard to it on their own initiative. To date,

---

[72] Protection of Animals (Amendment) Act 2000; see further, Ch 14, s G(3).

[73] Welfare of Farmed Animals (England) Regulations 2000, SI 2000/1870, came into force on 14 August 2000; Farmed Animals (Scotland) Regulations 2000, SSI 2000/442, came into force on 15 December 2000; and the Welfare of Farmed Animals (Wales) Regulations 2001 came into force on 31 July 2001 (at the time this book went to press they had not been allocated an SI number). These three sets of regulations—henceforth referred to collectively as the 'Welfare of Farmed Animals Regulations'—replaced the Welfare of Livestock Regulations 1994, SI 1994/2126, as amended, which had applied uniformly throughout Britain. It may also be noted that the Directive to which they give effect specified that it should be transposed into national law by 31 December 1999.

[74] Thus, the condition that horses and ponies may only be exported from Britain if they are worth more than the minimum values laid down in legislation (see Animal Health Act 1981, ss 40–43), intended to prevent them being slaughtered for meat abroad, is contrary to the principle of free trade but continues to remain in force, at least for the time being, by virtue of art 3(3) of Directive 91/628, which permits Member States to apply relevant national rules for the transport of solipeds in order to safeguard their welfare.

[75] For example, Directive 91/629, Directive 97/2, and Directive 91/630 laying down minimum standards for the protection of calves and pigs; Directive 93/119 on the protection of animals at the time of slaughter or killing; Directive 86/609 regarding the protection of animals used for experimental and scientific purposes.

there have been some successes and many disappointments but, overall, it is incontrovertible that the position of animals within the Union is better as a result of the activities of pressure groups than would otherwise be the case.

Over and above the degree of success they achieve in respect of their particular objectives, however, pressure groups which seek to carry influence through public support, such as those concerned with animal welfare, perform an important democratic function within the Community which is all too easily overlooked. First, they help to *inform* the legislative process. The institutions of the Community do not have the same reservoir of expertise within their ranks which many national governments and legislatures can draw upon. While the objectivity of some pressure groups may be open to question, the most professional contribute an expertise and perspective which might not otherwise be available; they certainly provide a counterpoint to the agenda of the majority of lobbyists, who work on behalf of business and commercial interests. Secondly, they *publicize* what is happening at the Community level. The Community's administrative and legislative procedures are complex and obscure, and the deliberations of the Council lack transparency. Most citizens are not familiar with the extent of the Community's competence or the way in which it functions. Most do not know who the decision makers are, let alone what subjects the Community is grappling with at any particular time. Through their various campaigns, pressure groups bring to public attention what is being debated and decided at Community level, the issues that are involved, and their implications. Thirdly, they encourage *participation* in the legislative process. Because of the widespread ignorance of the Community's work, the chances of citizens individually taking the initiative to make representations to their MEP or the Commission are remote. However, even if it is only by signing petitions or forwarding pre-printed postcards, pressure groups' campaigns do provide an opportunity for citizens to attempt to influence directly the outcome of the decision-making process. Fourthly, by co-ordinating their campaigns and co-operating with each other, pressure groups based in different Member States provide a *transnational perspective* on issues, whereas the formal players in the legislative process, such as MEPs and ministers, tend to provide an intra-state view based, respectively, on the opinions of their constituents or the political imperatives of their particular domestic circumstances. Finally, they act as *agitators*, monitoring whether undertakings given by, and duties placed upon, Community institutions to bring forward proposals are acted upon. Together, this represents a formidable contribution to the workings of the Community.

Holding a pivotal position between animal welfare interests in individual Member States, the institutions of the Community, and the Council of Europe is the Eurogroup for Animal Welfare. Established in 1980 on the initiative of the RSPCA, its membership is made up of one animal welfare organization from each Member State, whose representatives meet in plenary session annually to determine its policies. At one level, then, Eurogroup is a lobbying organization, identifying areas of concern in the treatment of animals and pressing for the introduction and enforcement of Community legislation, but it also performs an additional significant function: in 1983, members of the European Parliament decided to form an all-party group on animal welfare—now known as the Intergroup on the Welfare and Conservation of Animals—and invited Eurogroup to act as their Secretariat.

The animal welfare lobby has consistently mounted sophisticated and effective campaigns to influence politicians. According to one MEP, 'Members of the European Parliament, if asked what was the single most important issue in the Community today, to judge by the relative size of their postbag on different issues, would have to reply, "Animal welfare" . . . [T]he Euro-voter continues to put pen to paper about perceived and real problems of animals more often than on any other subject.'[76] This concern has also been reflected in the number of EU citizens who have been prepared to sign petitions on the subject directed to the European Parliament: for example, 3.5 million to ban the import of baby seal products (1982); more than one million on the status of animals (1991); more than 2 million on animal transport (1991); and 2.5 million opposing the use of animals for testing cosmetics (1991).

(2) EC decision making

Detailed consideration of the EC's legislative procedure falls outside the scope of the present work. However, it is clearly advantageous for interested parties to lobby the Commission, its officials, MEPs, and the national governments of Member States. In doing so, it is important to appreciate that each is representing a different constituency. The Commission is exclusively concerned to further the objectives laid down in the Treaties. Depending on the issue, MEPs may be influenced by national or constituency considerations, but they organize themselves on the basis of political affiliation rather than the country they represent, and this is reflected in the way they vote. MEPs are uniquely accountable among the institutions of the EC, not only because they alone are directly elected, but the proceedings of the Parliament and its committees take place in public and are reported verbatim in the *Official Journal*. In contrast, members of the Council of Ministers, although ostensibly committed principally to furthering the objectives of the Community, are always deeply mindful of their respective national interests.

Indeed, as the only directly-elected EC institution, it is perhaps unsurprising that it is the European Parliament which has been particularly responsive to animal protection issues. In 1985, for example, it called on the Commission to create a special policy section to deal with animal welfare matters, a proposal which it reiterated two years later;[77] in 1991 it asked the Commission to set up a 'consultative committee on

---

[76] Simmonds, R, 'The Role of the European Community' in Ryder (ed), *Animal Welfare and the Environment* (1992) 189.

[77] EP's resolution of 12 July 1985 [1985] OJ C229/126; Report drawn up on behalf of the Committee on Agriculture, Fisheries and Food on animal welfare policy, Rapporteur: Mr Richard J Simmonds, 19 January 1987, A2–211/85.

animal rights', and to take the necessary steps to recognize animals as 'sentient beings' in EC law;[78] and in 1994 it urged the Commission to set up its own advisory committee on animal welfare, again urged that the Treaty be amended to give animals the status of sentient beings, and called on the Commission to ensure that the prospective Community veterinary inspectorate was 'explicitly assigned responsibility for guaranteeing respect for animal welfare requirements throughout the Community'.[79] Even here, however, tensions between opposing perceptions of human duties towards animals have been apparent. The Committee on the Environment, Public Health and Consumer Protection has expressed the view, for example, that 'The life of every individual animal has a value', and 'especially the ability to feel pain and pleasure, are sufficient to confer rights on those who possess them; more precisely, the right to proper consideration of their physiological and behavioural needs'.[80] In response, the Committee on Agriculture, Fisheries and Rural Development asserted that, while it supported proposals 'to combat the pointless suffering caused by the search for short-term profit', it could not 'associate itself with irrational campaigns aimed at restricting, in the name of vague, even unfounded, philosophical principles, legitimate activities which satisfy a genuine demand, and whose outcome can only be counterproductive to the Community'.[81]

However, although the Parliament's involvement in the legislative process has grown increasingly influential, it is the Council of Ministers which remains pivotal in the EC legislative process. It consists of one minister from each Member State having responsibility within his or her own government for the subject matter under discussion. The Council of Ministers is not, therefore, a single, identifiable body, but a collective term which relates to a number of separate and differently constituted groups, all of which have the same status and legal powers, but each having responsibility for a different area of the EC's competence. The Council of Ministers is assisted in reaching agreement by officials from the Member States who conduct negotiations between themselves on behalf of their respective governments.

Each Member State in turn holds the Presidency of the Union for six months during which time it chairs meetings of the Council of Ministers. While it holds the Presidency, a Member State is able to have some influence in determining the priority given to particular policies and can attempt to promote those to which it attaches the greatest importance. The United Kingdom, for example, has consistently given priority to animal welfare issues on each occasion it has held the Presidency.

In order for a decision to be endorsed by the Council, it requires to be accepted unanimously or, more usually, by a qualified majority. This attempts to give the vote of each Member State a weighting which (very approximately) reflects the size

---

[78] European Parliament: Report of the Committee on the Environment, Public Health and Consumer Protection on animal welfare and the status of animals in the Community, Rapporteur: Mr Gianfranco Amendola, 13 November 1991, A3–0321/91, pp 5–6.

[79] European Parliament: Report of the Committee on the Environment, Public Health and Consumer Protection on the welfare and status of animals in the Community, Rapporteur: Mr Gianfranco Amendola, 3 January 1994, A3–0003/94, pp 6–7.

[80] ibid 8.   [81] ibid 17.

of its population and, in order for a proposal to be adopted, it is therefore necessary to gain agreement among a number of Member States. The outcome can be as much the product of shifting alliances within the Council as the application of principle. Membership of the Community itself is also significant. It is generally accepted that the accession of Austria, Finland, and Sweden in 1995 was broadly favourable to animal welfare; proposed accession by eastern European states which have not traditionally been overtly concerned with the treatment of animals may have the opposite effect.

The way in which the Council operates cannot be equated with that of national governments and legislatures. Within Member States, the ability to propose and implement policy is a measure of the executive's strength and authority. In many national administrations, there is common agreement over the policies to be pursued, either arising from a shared political ideology or, where this is lacking, on the basis of self-preservation. If there is not a degree of collective consent about the direction in which the administration is going, then the consequential divisions will eventually cause its downfall. Furthermore, the elected government of a nation state has a limited existence before it has to submit itself for re-election. The situation within the Council of Ministers is completely different. There is no overriding cohesive force, and the pressure to disagree may well be stronger than that to agree, on the basis that a stand against change can be presented to the home electorate as a defence of national interests. Success in securing legislative change demonstrates an ability to find a compromise which (in most cases) can command at least a qualified majority; there is no need for the Council to underpin its continued existence by demonstrating its collective strength. Another significant characteristic is that, although the political make-up of the Council alters as the governments of Member States change, the Council does not have a specific term of office; as a body, it exists indefinitely. There is therefore no inherent need to bring difficult issues to a conclusion, which can result in a lack of urgency and lead to prevarication.

It is the Commission which prepares draft legislation. As it is relatively small and does not have within its own ranks a wide range of expertise, it normally consults widely with interested parties when drawing up a legislative proposal, including politicians and officials from Member States, producers and other commercial interests, consumers, lobby groups, others who have an interest in the matter, as well as committees of experts which have been established to provide advice. The most important in relation to animal welfare has traditionally been the Scientific Veterinary Committee, an advisory body made up of experts from Member States. This has recently been superseded by the Scientific Committee on Animal Health and Animal Welfare. These committees make an important contribution in providing independent scientific advice which is taken into account in drawing up legislation,[82]

---

[82] See, for example, Scientific Veterinary Committee's *Report on the Welfare of Calves* (1995), which led to the EC directive banning the keeping of calves in small veal crates; and its *Report on the Transport of Farm Animals* (1992), which influenced the 1995 transport directive. See also, Scientific Veterinary Committee, *Report on the Welfare of Intensively Kept Pigs* (1997); Scientific Committee on Animal Health and Animal

and are to be distinguished from the Standing Veterinary Committee, the membership of which comprises the Chief Veterinary Officer from each Member State, who generally vote according to the instructions of their respective governments. The latter is therefore an essentially political body.

(3) The sovereignty issue

The fact that EC legislation overrides that of the Member States has the consequence that national politicians may be unable to prevent practices which are widely regarded as cruel by their electorate. The Banner Committee reflected the traditional (and widely held) view by asserting that 'The task of the Government is to establish appropriate protection for farm animals in Britain whether or not that protection commends itself to our European partners',[83] but it has been overtaken by economic and legal reality. The power to exercise such self-determination is no longer available in relation to significant areas of policy. Such a situation raises an issue of fundamental constitutional importance. In 1981, for example, MPs urged the Minister of Agriculture in forthcoming negotiations on battery cages to take a strong initiative towards laying down a minimum standard for adult laying hens in battery cages of 750 sq cm per bird, and in any event, they said, he should 'refuse to agree to anything less than 550'.[84] At the time, the Government recommended a minimum of 600 sq cm per bird. Despite Parliament's insistence, however, the Government was ultimately forced to *reduce* the space allowance to 450 sq cm per bird.[85] Another example is provided by the controversy over the export of live animals which erupted in Britain during the winter of 1994–1995. One of the abiding impressions of that episode was the Government's powerlessness. The Minister of Agriculture, William Waldegrave, conceded that 'we really are, in Britain, more or less on the same side of this argument', and yet he was unable to act on his own initiative to resolve it, pleading instead that 'we really should be directing our anger and our national efforts towards getting things changed in Europe'.[86] Indeed, the most the Government could do was to trifle at the margins of the problem, introducing, for example, additional measures relating to hauliers' journey plans.[87]

Initially, MPs called on the Government to remain resolute in the face of threats to British standards of welfare. In 1991, for example, the House of Commons Agriculture Committee urged the minister to give an early indication that he

Welfare, *Report on the Welfare Aspects of the Production of Foie Gras* (1998); Scientific Committee on Animal Health and Animal Welfare, *The Welfare of Chickens Kept for Meat Production (Broilers)* (2000).

[83] Banner, M (Chairman), *Report of the Committee to Consider the Ethical Implications of Emerging Technologies in the Breeding of Farm Animals* (1995) para 2.16.

[84] House of Commons Agriculture Committee, *Animal Welfare in Poultry, Pig and Veal Calf Production*, n 23 above, para 163.

[85] See now, the Welfare of Farmed Animals Regulations, n 73 above, Sch 2, para 1, which implement Directive 86/113, readopted as 88/166.

[86] Quoted in the *Observer*, 5 February 1995.

[87] The Welfare of Animals During Transport Order 1994, SI 1994/3249, as amended by the Welfare of Animals During Transport (Amendment) Order 1995, SI 1995/131.

would block the export of live food animals from the UK to Member States which failed to meet the welfare standards demanded by EC legislation.[88] Latterly, however, they have shown a greater inclination to recognize the constraints imposed by EC law and, more recently, the WTO. Thus, in 1999, the House of Commons Agriculture Committee advised ministers against taking unilateral action, saying that it wanted to see 'any future changes in animal welfare legislation imposed and implemented on a uniform basis throughout the EU'. In its view, 'successive Governments have been too quick to impose costs and burdens on UK agriculture without adequate consideration of the impact on its competitiveness.'[89] While this may reflect the reality of the situation, it nevertheless has serious implications. If the law does not command widespread assent, its legitimacy is undermined, particularly when it appears in conflict with the moral consensus. If such a law cannot be changed, it is dangerous for both democracy and the rule of law. In these circumstances, it is not surprising that, if making their views known by constitutional means appears useless, people resort to direct action. In the context of protests against the live export trade, the High Court repeated the well-established position that any activity is unlawful which disrupts the rights of others to go about their lawful business.[90] But what if the body politic is impotent to redefine what constitutes lawful business? The bleakness of this situation was well summed up by the court itself:

It may, indeed, be doubted whether there remains any logic in protesting at the ports: the only body properly able to ban this lawful trade is Parliament itself—unless indeed the Secretary of State is rightly advised that even that would be unlawful under Community law, in which event the only solution lies across the Channel.[91]

The European Court of Justice subsequently confirmed that the minister had indeed been rightly advised.[92] There is a lesson here, with far-reaching repercussions for democracy: while the Government and Parliament were unable to respond to popular sentiment, commercial undertakings, which are not subject to the same legal constraints by the WTO and EC law, could, and did.

In June 1994, a campaign was launched in the UK by a lobby group, Respect for Animals, with the aim of boycotting ferry companies which carried animal transporters across the Channel.[93] Supporting the move, Alan Clark MP commented that 'the ferries are the choke-point at which pressure can be most easily applied; people who feel strongly about the cruelty and degradation of transporting live animals can switch their patronage.'[94] Throughout the summer, supporters distributed to passengers leaflets and pre-printed postcards to be sent to the ferry companies. Although the ferry operators initially insisted that they would

---

[88] House of Commons Agriculture Committee, *Animals in Transit*, n 39 above, para 20.

[89] House of Commons Agriculture Committee, *The UK Pig Industry*, n 39 above, paras 22 and 25.

[90] *R v Coventry City Council, ex parte Phoenix Aviation* [1995] 3 All ER 37, 41.   [91] ibid 64–65.

[92] *R v Minister of Agriculture, Fisheries and Food, ex parte Compassion in World Farming Ltd*, Case 1/96 [1998] 2 CMLR 661.

[93] Targeting the ferry companies was not new. In the spring of 1992, CIWF had encouraged its supporters to write to them, but the effort was now directed at getting *passengers* to make their views known.

[94] *The Times*, 24 June 1994.

continue to carry animals, at the end of August P&O broke ranks, announcing that it would stop carrying animals for slaughter unless European ministers could agree by October on improved welfare standards. A fortnight later, Brittany Ferries announced that it would, with effect from 20 September, refuse to carry live animals for slaughter, except those being sent for fattening in northern France. At the end of the month, Stena Sealink trumped them both by stopping all livestock transport immediately, with the exception of breeding animals. The President of the NFU complained that he did not see 'why ferry companies need to set themselves up as the moral conscience of the nation', but this was not the case; the same article quoted a director of Stena Sealink as saying, 'We have acted essentially for commercial reasons. Over the past few months we have received thousands of letters from our customers saying they do not want to travel on a ferry that carries livestock.'[95] Undoubtedly, competition from the Channel Tunnel, through which livestock are not permitted to travel for safety reasons, was a major factor in the decision. At a stroke the export trade from the UK had been undermined.[96]

As the rising power of the consumer coincides with the declining influence of politicians, pressure groups and their supporters will no doubt think less in terms of MP, MSP, or MEP, and rather more of PLC, in campaigning to further their objectives. One of the manifestations of this is that attention has turned increasingly to lobbying retailers, particularly the large supermarket companies. While this change of focus has had some effect, the marginalization of Parliament is unfortunate, to say the least. In 1981, the House of Commons Agriculture Committee declared as a matter of principle that

society has the duty to see that undue suffering is not caused to animals, and we cannot accept that that duty should be set aside in order that food may be produced more cheaply. Where unacceptable suffering can be eliminated only at extra cost, that cost should be borne or the product forgone.... [A] balance has to be struck, and this can only be done in the light of subjective judgement; but our emphatic view is that the welfare of animals must come first.[97]

A political system that has lost the power effectively to impose such a duty through public regulation raises profound questions about the present state of representative democracy in Britain. 'Market fundamentalism', warns the international financier, George Soros, 'undermines the democratic political process.'[98] Indeed.

G. The Impact of Science on Policy

The point was made at the beginning of this chapter that scientific opinion is central to developing animal welfare policy, but that it cannot in itself be the sole

---

[95] *The Times*, 5 September 1994.

[96] Of the other two major ferry companies, neither Sally Ferries nor Hoverspeed carried animals. The former was prohibited from doing so by local by-laws in Ramsgate, from which it operated, and the latter did not have the capacity to carry lorries.

[97] House of Commons Agriculture Committee, *Animal Welfare in Poultry, Pig and Veal Calf Production*, n 23 above, para 27.   [98] Soros, G, *The Crisis in Global Capitalism. Open Society Endangered* (1998) 199.

determinant of what that policy should be. This is so, notwithstanding that politicians have become increasingly dependent on scientific advice. In many circumstances, the subject matter dictates the need for the involvement of experts, but the adoption by ministers of such advice may also help to deflect political criticism of their decisions and make them less susceptible to legal challenge by way of judicial review. It is also significant that appropriate scientific evidence is one of the relatively few grounds on which interference with the principle of free trade under both EC law and WTO rules may legitimately be based. Nevertheless, it is important that policy makers should continue to exercise their own judgement when deciding what weight to give to the views of scientists. Not all would agree. Commenting on the way the BSE crisis had been handled, for example, the *Veterinary Record* complained that 'while individual decisions should be based on science, they inevitably form part of a wider picture in which science, politics, economics, public opinion and practical considerations all play a part', and went on to argue that proposals to deal with the situation 'should be viewed on their scientific merits, with every effort being made to keep the science and politics apart'.[99] Such exclusivity is neither desirable nor acceptable. The approach of FAWC is to be much preferred, having expressed the view that 'the many dimensions of animal welfare inevitably mean that an understanding of production conditions and scientific information alone cannot provide a sufficient guide for detailed recommendations'.[100] As a question of law, it is incumbent on a public official to take all relevant factors into account, and therefore mechanically to implement the advice they have received from scientists may be unlawful, either because by doing so they fetter their discretion or, alternatively, it effectively delegates the decision to those who have proffered the advice. More generally, it is wrong to presume that the view provided by science is entirely objective or represents the ultimate answer to any particular question. This is especially so in relation to issues concerned with animal welfare. First, scientific opinion should be considered in the light of an ethical framework; and, secondly, it will often be necessary and appropriate to develop policy on the basis of incomplete evidence. 'Science has become a supermarket for interested parties or pressure groups in search of specific arguments', Stafleu and colleagues suggest, a situation in which 'science becomes liable to opportunistic use by policy-makers'. For instance,

the diversity [of scientific argument] can be used to generate reasons for not having to make a moral decision and so postpone the development of what the animal welfare debate was all about: making decisions on how we ought to treat our animals. Part of what has been won in making vague common-sense concept concrete, has lost in diversity [*sic*]. What was started as a help for decision-making, ended in making it too complicated to make a decision at all.[101]

---

[99] Editorial, 'Separating science and politics' (1997) 140 *Veterinary Record* 613.

[100] *Report on the Welfare of Broiler Breeders* (1998) para 8. For a detailed investigation of the relationship between science and public administration, see Phillips, Lord (Chairman), *The BSE Inquiry: The Report*, Vols 1–15 (2000; the full report is also available at www.bseinquiry.gov.uk).

[101] Stafleu, FR, Grommers, FJ, and Vorstenbosch, J, 'Animal welfare: evolution and erosion of a moral concept' (1996) 5 *Animal Welfare* 225, 231.

To avoid such a situation, it is strongly urged that a precautionary principle in favour of animals should be applied. 'We consider that it is morally incumbent upon us to give the animal the benefit of the doubt and to protect it as far as is possible from conditions that may be reasonably supposed to cause it suffering,' the Brambell Committee asserted, 'though this cannot be proved.'[102] A similar view was put forward by the House of Commons Agriculture Committee in 1981, which criticized the Ministry of Agriculture on the basis that its 'touchstone of demanding "established experience or sound scientific evidence" before having recourse to regulation, put the onus of proof in the wrong place and can too easily be used to justify tolerating practices which are clearly undesirable even though this cannot be scientifically proved'. Rather, the Committee expressly sympathized with the view 'that some practices should be forbidden even though it cannot be proved that they inflict unnecessary pain or discomfort'.[103]

H. Conclusion

Seeking to change the law through legislation is a political act; achieving such an objective is an expression of power. This chapter has focused on the endeavour to put animals into politics. At the same time, the way in which significant areas of legislative power, previously exercised exclusively by the UK Parliament at Westminster, have been dispersed to other institutions has been considered. It has therefore become necessary for lobbyists to target these various centres of decision making. The constraints imposed on national politicians by such a situation have been highlighted, together with the implications for democracy. Although progress has been difficult, it has been demonstrated that public opinion has been successfully mobilized, and politicians and officials both within Britain and the EC recognize animal welfare to be a significant area of public policy.

Unsurprisingly, this heightened concern for animals has its detractors. It is often represented as being founded on irrational sentimentality on the part of an increasingly urbanized population. Carruthers may be in a minority in regarding 'the present popular concern with animal rights in our culture as a reflection of moral decadence', but he is by no means alone in expressing unease that 'many in the West agonize over the fate of seal pups and cormorants while human beings elsewhere starve or are enslaved'.[104] Leaving aside the wholly erroneous implication that concern for animals is somehow irreconcilable with a similar concern for humans, the fact is that there is a long-standing and honourable tradition of seeking improvements in the way animals are treated. Revitalized since the 1960s, its most enduring manifestation, an abhorrence of cruelty, goes back to the early years of the nineteenth century. It is to a detailed analysis of this offence, still the basis of animal protection legislation in Britain, that we now turn.

[102] *Report of the Technical Committee to Enquire into the Welfare of Animals Kept Under Intensive Livestock Husbandry Systems* (1965) para 30.

[103] *Animal Welfare in Poultry, Pig and Veal Calf Production*, n 23 above, para 39.

[104] Carruthers, P, *The Animal Issue* (1992) xi.

Part D

Cruelty

8

The Offence of Cruelty

A. Background

The basis of animal protection legislation in Great Britain is the Protection of Animals Acts, the most important of which is, in England and Wales, the Protection of Animals Act 1911 ('the 1911 Act') and, in Scotland, the Protection of Animals (Scotland) Act 1912 ('the 1912 Act'). It is in these statutes that the legal meaning of cruelty is set out. The 1911 and 1912 Acts are, in all essentials, identical; the reason for there being two separate pieces of legislation is historical. That of 1911 was principally a consolidation Act, by which means the existing law is, for the sake of convenience, brought together and restated in a single statute. At the time, the extent of the protection provided by Scottish law differed from the rest of Britain in a number of important respects and, by definition, it is inappropriate to introduce significant legislative change by means of a consolidation Act. Accordingly, in order to secure uniformity, it was necessary to introduce separate legislation in respect of Scotland.[1]

Having stated that the 1911 Act was principally a reiteration of the status quo so far as England and Wales were concerned,[2] it did include a number of modifications to the existing law. For example, the prohibition on causing mental suffering which already applied to captive wild animals[3] was extended to domestic animals; and, in the light of conflicting judicial decisions on the question,[4] it confirmed that cruelty could be caused to domestic animals by an omission as well as an act of

---

[1] 'This is not a new Bill, but a Consolidation Bill', the Lord Advocate, the principal law officer in Scotland, told the House of Commons. 'The object of it is to consolidate English Statutes. . . . The House may take it that our code of procedure is entirely different from the code of procedure in England, and it is quite impracticable to make this Bill applicable to Scotland': HC Debs, 30 June 1911, col 758.

[2] The Act repealed and re-enacted the provisions of the Cruelty to Animals Acts 1849 and 1854, the Poisoned Grain Prohibition Act 1863, the Poisoned Flesh Prohibition Act 1864, the Drugging of Animals Act 1876, the Wild Animals in Captivity Protection Act 1900, and the Injured Animals Act 1907.

[3] Wild Animals in Captivity Protection Act 1900.

[4] See, for example: *Everitt v Davies* (1878) 42 JP 248; *Powell v Knight* (1878) 38 LT 607; *Hooker v Gray* (1907) 71 JP 337; cf *Green v Cross* (1910) 74 JP 357.

commission. The Act also introduced new duties and powers. One such required operations on animals to be carried out with due care and humanity; another enabled courts to confiscate an animal whose treatment at the hands of its owner had been the subject of a successful prosecution. In the light of experience, these changes may be considered significant developments, but they were not so regarded in 1911. Despite its longevity, at the time of its enactment the Protection of Animals Act was neither seen as, nor intended to be, a major piece of reforming legislation. 'This is a consolidating Bill', its proposer, George Greenwood, told the House of Commons, 'We did not like to introduce into it any amendment which was not necessary.'[5] It is not surprising, then, that the legislation reflects the scope, concepts, and concerns of its Victorian and Edwardian predecessors, proscribing conduct which had come to be regarded as amounting to 'an offence of cruelty', and making miscellaneous provisions in respect of animal fights, impounded animals, use of poisons, use of dogs for draught, inspection of traps, and the regulation of knackers' yards, all of which had exercised reformers and legislators during the nineteenth century and the early years of the twentieth.

B.   The Offences of Cruelty

The legal definition of animal cruelty is widely drawn, for the most part in very general terms, and the resulting versatility is undoubtedly its most advantageous characteristic. It can be applied to a wide variety of different situations, and enables courts to interpret the offence in the light of developing scientific understanding about the nature of animals' suffering and changing social attitudes as to their proper treatment. The result is that, although the legislative wording has remained largely unchanged since prior to the First World War, the situations in which criminal liability may arise have widened considerably in the intervening years. The courts are able to take account of the fact that conduct and practices which were considered necessary and reasonable, and therefore acceptable, in the past may be regarded rather differently in the light of contemporary standards.

Many might agree with the colloquial assertion of Macpherson J that 'any human being who does not have the interests of animals at heart (at least where cruelty is involved) is a cruel person himself'.[6] It is, however, essential to appreciate that the term 'offence of cruelty' has a particular and specific meaning in the context of animal protection legislation. First, it is not to be confused with other offences relating to the mistreatment of animals, notwithstanding that the terminology used may be similar. For example, terms such as 'cruel', 'cruelly', and 'cruelty' are not applied exclusively to the offence of cruelty;[7] and the phrase

---

[5]   HC Debs, 30 June 1911, col 745.

[6]   *R v Minister of Agriculture, Fisheries and Food, ex parte Roberts* (QBD, 20 September 1990).

[7]   Protection of Animals Act 1911, ss 11 and 13(2); Protection of Animals (Scotland) Act 1912, ss 10 and 12(1); Performing Animals (Regulation) Act 1925, s 2(1); Cinematograph Films (Animals) Act 1937, s 1(1); Protection of Badgers Act 1992, s 2(1)(a).

'unnecessary suffering', which is central to the definition of the offence of cruelty, is employed in a number of other legislative contexts relating to animals. What distinguishes an offence of cruelty from all other offences involving treatment which may be loosely described as 'cruel' is the range and severity of the penalties available to the courts; in particular, confiscation and disqualification orders. Secondly, the concept of cruelty has a significantly more restrictive meaning in law than that applied to it in everyday use. This important point is well illustrated by the recent case in which the international fast-food company, McDonald's, brought proceedings against those responsible for distributing a leaflet which the company claimed was libellous.[8] The judge, Bell J, found that, among other things, 'the leaflet means that [McDonald's] are culpably responsible for cruel practices in the rearing and slaughter of some of the animals which are used to produce their food'. The judge having accepted that such an accusation was indeed defamatory, being 'clearly damaging to the trading reputation' of McDonald's, the onus passed to the defendants to satisfy the court, on the balance of probabilities, that their claims were justified. Although the court did not accept all their contentions, the defendants successfully defended a number of them. On the evidence before him, the judge found that the restriction of movement experienced by battery-kept laying hens throughout their lives, of broiler chickens in their last days, and of sows kept in dry sow stalls for virtually the whole of their lives, were all, in his words, 'cruel practices'. So too were the frequency with which chickens were still fully conscious when they had their throats cut; the incidence of calcium deficit resulting in osteopaenia (reduced bone density) in battery hens; the practice of restricting broiler breeders' feed with the result that they went hungry; leg problems in broilers bred for weight; rough handling of broilers taken for slaughter; and pre-stun electric shocks suffered by broilers on the way to slaughter. On this basis, the judge held that 'the sting of this part of the leaflet' to the effect that McDonald's were 'culpably responsible for cruel practices in the rearing and slaughter of some of the animals which are used to produce their food is justified, true in substance and in fact'. However, despite this finding, it was not suggested that McDonald's were criminally liable for causing or permitting cruelty. Indeed, a number of the practices the judge criticized, such as the stocking density of battery hens, were not only lawful, but were being carried out in accordance with the relevant regulations and official guidance. In reaching his decision, the judge said that he had applied his own judgment, helped by the evidence he had heard, 'to decide whether a practice is deliberate and whether it causes sufficiently intensive suffering for a sufficient duration of time to be justly described as cruel'. It should be noted that this does not represent the legal meaning of cruelty. Nevertheless, that he felt compelled, after detailed and dispassionate consideration of the information before him, to conclude that so many of the practices routinely *and legally* carried out in livestock production may be justifiably described as cruel inevitably casts doubt on the

---

[8] *McDonald's Corporation and McDonald's Restaurants Ltd v Steel and Morris* (QBD, 19 June 1997).

extent of the protection provided by legislation which purports to prevent cruelty to animals. It is also a powerful example of how the lawful treatment of animals varies according to the circumstances and the prevailing commercial imperatives. If pet animals were subjected to the same conditions as these agricultural animals, it may very well be that those responsible would have committed an offence.

C. The Statutory Definition of Cruelty

Cruelty is defined by reference to a number of separate and distinct courses of conduct, any one of which may form the basis for a prosecution. So, a person is guilty of an offence of cruelty if they:

(1) Cruelly beat, kick, ill-treat, override, over-drive, overload, torture, infuriate, or terrify any animal; or cause, procure, or, being the owner, permit any animal to be so used[9]

This catalogue of specific actions, which will be referred to here as 'the first limb' of section 1(1)(a) of the 1911 and 1912 Acts, is the direct descendant of the nineteenth-century anti-cruelty legislation. Cruelly beating or ill-treating an animal were both originally prohibited in 1822 and restated in subsequent legislation; torture was added in 1835; and over-driving in 1849.[10] The proscription on cruelly infuriating or terrifying had been introduced in 1900 in relation to wild animals kept in captivity[11] and was extended in 1911–1912 to include all captive and domestic animals, thereby indicating that Parliament intended cruelty to encompass the infliction of both psychological and physical suffering. Cruelly kicking, overriding, and overloading were expressly mentioned for the first time in 1911, but their inclusion confirmed the law rather than extended it, as such behaviour was already liable to prosecution under the general head of cruel ill-treatment. As has been judicially observed, these provisions have been 'borrowed extensively from the somewhat turgid and excessively detailed language of earlier statutes.'[12]

---

[9] 1911 Act, s 1(1)(a); 1912 Act, s 1(1)(a).

[10] 3 Geo IV, c 71; 5 & 6 Will IV, c 59; 12 & 13 Vict, c 92; in respect of Scotland, see 13 & 14 Vict, c 92.

[11] Wild Animals in Captivity Protection Act 1900; extended to Scotland by virtue of the Wild Animals in Captivity Protection (Scotland) Act 1909.

[12] *Patchett v Macdougall* 1984 SLT 152 (Note), 155 (Lord Hunter). The statutory definition of cruelty in relation to children takes a similar, but less cumbersome, form. Thus, it is an offence for any person, who has attained the age of sixteen years and has responsibility for any child or young person under that age, wilfully to assault, ill-treat, neglect, abandon, or expose him, or cause or procure him to be assaulted, ill-treated, neglected, abandoned, or exposed, in a manner likely to cause him unnecessary suffering or injury to health (including injury to or loss of sight, or hearing, or limb, or organ of the body, and any mental derangement). It is further provided that a parent or other person liable to maintain a child or young person, or the legal guardian of a child or young person, shall be deemed to have neglected him in a manner likely to cause injury to his health if he has failed to provide adequate food, clothing, medical aid, or lodging for him, or if, having been unable otherwise to provide such food, clothing, medical aid, or lodging, he has failed to take steps to procure it to be provided under the enactments applicable in that behalf: Children and Young Persons Act 1933, s 1(1), (2)(a), as amended.

The list clearly reflects the priorities for animal protection in a society which was still heavily dependent upon the horse. It also presents problems of interpretation: to torture cruelly appears tautologous, and it is difficult to define precisely what behaviour constitutes cruelly infuriating an animal.

The term 'cruelly' in the subsection relates to each of the words that follow and each constitutes a separate offence.[13] Under the nineteenth-century legislation 'cruelly' was taken to mean, in the words of Wightman J, 'the unnecessary abuse of any animal',[14] an interpretation which has been adopted in the context of the 1911 Act.[15]

(2) Wantonly or unreasonably do or omit to do any act causing unnecessary suffering to any animal; or cause, procure, or, being the owner, permit any such act[16]

This provision constitutes 'the second limb' of section 1(1)(a) of the 1911 and 1912 Acts. In terms of both defining the legal notion of cruelty and forming the basis for prosecutions, it is without question the most important single offence. The inclusion of omissions is of considerable practical importance, for it allows prosecutions on the basis of a failure to provide an animal with proper care and attention. If a person is unsure about what is required to meet this standard, they should seek professional advice, generally from a veterinary surgeon, not only in the interests of the animal but also to rebut an allegation of having caused unnecessary suffering in consequence of having failed to act.[17]

The meaning of the term 'unnecessary suffering' is discussed further in Chapter 10, but the idea that cruelty is to be defined by reference to necessity dates back to the early campaigners for animal protection legislation. Humphry Primatt wrote in 1776 that 'to put [a creature] to unnecessary pain is cruelty'; and the basis of Richard Martin's philosophy was that 'unnecessary cruelty to animals . . . should be put down'.[18] 'Cruelty', asserted the RSPCA in 1876, 'is the infliction of *unnecessary* pain.'[19] The term 'unnecessary suffering' was first enshrined in statute in the Cruelty to Animals Act 1849 in relation to the conveyance and carriage of animals, and reiterated in the same context twenty years later in the Contagious Diseases

---

[13] *Ford v Wiley* (1889) 23 QBD 203, 218 (Hawkins J); *Johnson v Needham* [1909] 1 KB 626.

[14] *Budge v Parsons* (1863) 129 RR 367, 368.

[15] *Barnard v Evans* [1925] 2 KB 794, in which the court equated 'cruelly' variously with 'not necessary', 'without justification', and 'not reasonably necessary'.

[16] 1911 Act, s 1(1)(a); 1912 Act, s 1(1)(a).

[17] In *May v Broxton* (QBD, 22 February 1983), for example, the High Court quashed the conviction of an owner for causing her horse unnecessary suffering because, having consulted a vet, she was merely 'following advice given to her by an expert who considered himself competent to make the appropriate diagnosis and prescribe the right treatment' (Ackner LJ).

[18] Primatt, H, *The Duty of Mercy and the Sin of Cruelty to Brute Animals* (1776; 1992 edn) 107; Parl Debs (new series) vol 10, col 487 (26 February 1824).

[19] RSPCA, *Vivisection. The Royal Society for the Prevention of Cruelty to Animals and the Royal Commission* (2nd edn, 1876) iii (italics in the original).

(Animals) Act 1869. Furthermore, as is described below, a similar concept was adopted by the judiciary in interpreting the meaning of the adverb 'cruelly' in both the 1849 Act and the Prevention of Cruelty to Animals in Scotland Act 1850. The precursor of the present provision was contained in the Wild Animals in Captivity Protection Act 1900, section 2 of which made it an offence wantonly or unreasonably to do or omit to do any act which caused unnecessary suffering to a captive or confined animal. Accordingly, adopting the term 'unnecessary suffering', arising either from a positive act or an omission, was not in itself novel in 1911. It represented the existing legal benchmark for the meaning of cruelty. The significance of the new provision lay in its general application (extending as it did to acts as well as omissions, and to captive wild animals in addition to domestic animals), with the result that cruelty was no longer restricted to a catalogue of specific actions. Henceforth, it was to be defined by reference to the detrimental effects upon the animal, regardless of how they were caused, or the circumstances in which they arose, provided a court was satisfied that the suffering was unnecessary and the defendant had acted either wantonly or unreasonably.

The relationship between the adverb 'cruelly' in the first limb and the term 'unnecessary suffering' in the second limb of section 1(1)(a) of the 1911 and 1912 Acts

As a consolidation statute, the 1911 Act repealed and replaced, among others, the Cruelty to Animals Act 1849 and the Wild Animals in Captivity Protection Act 1900. In consequence, section 1(1)(a) of the 1911 Act contains two apparently different offences of cruelty, both of which had previously appeared in separate legislation. The first limb prohibits specific treatment to an animal if carried out cruelly, and can be traced back through the 1849 and 1835 statutes to Martin's Act of 1822. The second, proscribing the more general conduct of causing unnecessary suffering, originated in its present form in the Wild Animals in Captivity Protection Act 1900. The two now lie uneasily together in section 1(1)(a) of both the 1911 and 1912 Acts. Not only is the subsection 'really rather unwieldy',[20] it also gives rise to the question of whether the adverb 'cruelly' is to be interpreted differently from 'unnecessary suffering'.

The contention here is that it should not. The Victorian courts consistently defined cruelty to mean something akin to unnecessary suffering. In 1889, for example, Lord Coleridge CJ observed that 'The mere infliction of pain, even if extreme pain, is manifestly not by itself sufficient' to amount to cruelty. 'If the suffering inflicted is necessary,' said the judge, 'it may be inflicted; if not, it is'—quoting a phrase previously adopted by Wightman J in *Budge v Parsons*[21]—'"unnecessary abuse of an animal" and we have neither the moral nor the legal right to inflict it, a conclusion not of sentimentalism but of good sense.'[22] Similarly, the Lord Justice-Clerk said of the

---

[20] *Bandeira and Brannigan v RSPCA* (2000) 164 JP 307 (Schiemann LJ).   [21] n 14 above.
[22] *Ford v Wiley* (1889) 23 QBD 203, 209 and 215.

equivalent Scottish Act of 1850: 'Cruelty in the statute means cruelty without reason, cruelty in making one of the lower animals suffer without any reasonable object, or to an unreasonable extent.'[23] By 1906, Lord Alverstone CJ was able to refer to 'A long series of decisions [which] have put upon the word "cruelty" the meaning not only of cruel in the sense of paining the animal, but cruel in the sense that it is unnecessary'.[24] The courts have continued to apply this established interpretation under the present legislation. In the leading case of *Barnard v Evans*, for example, Shearman J suggested that the word 'cruelly' could not be better defined than 'causing unnecessary suffering'.[25] Accordingly, the inclusion of the two terms in the respective limbs of section 1(1)(a) of the 1911 and 1912 Acts is essentially tautologous. This view has recently been endorsed by the English High Court. 'There is a good deal of overlap between the various terms used in s 1(1)(a)', observed Simon Brown LJ in *Hopson v DPP*, leading him to conclude 'that the selfsame conduct could generally be charged (depending always on the circumstances) in more than one way'.[26] Similarly, in the absence of any authority to the contrary, it is reasonable to assume that when the notion of cruelty is employed in other legislative contexts, its meaning is to be regarded as synonymous with unnecessary suffering, notwithstanding that (perversely it might be thought) they do not formally constitute offences of cruelty.[27]

(3) Convey or carry any animal in such a manner or position as to cause it any unnecessary suffering; or cause, procure, or, being the owner, permit any animal to be so conveyed or carried[28]

This is a restatement of the offence originally introduced in respect of England and Wales in 1849,[29] and extended to Scotland for the first time in 1912. It should be noted that this provision applies to all captive and domestic animals, regardless of the context, and would appear to include manual as well as vehicular conveyance. Hence, although much less detailed, it is significantly wider in its scope than the regulations laid down in the Welfare of Animals (Transport) Order 1997, which apply only to transport undertaken in the course of a trade or business.[30] In practice, however, it has fallen into disuse because conduct which would constitute an offence of cruelty under this provision would also be an offence under the more general terms of section 1(1)(a).

---

[23] *Cornelius v Grant* (1880) 4 Coup 327, 332.   [24] *Bowyer v Morgan* (1906) 70 JP 253, 255.
[25] [1925] 2 KB 794, 798.
[26] QBD, 11 March 1997. By 'depending on the circumstances', the judge is alluding to the fact that an offence can only be brought under the first limb of section 1(1)(a) if the unnecessary suffering has arisen as a result of one of the specified actions.
[27] See n 7 above.   [28] 1911 Act, s 1(1)(b); 1912 Act, s 1(1)(b).   [29] 12 & 13 Vict, c 92.
[30] SI 1997/1480, art 2(2), 3(1).

(4) Cause, procure, or assist at the fighting or baiting of any animal. Keep, use, manage, or act or assist in the management of, any premises or place for the purpose, or partly for the purpose of fighting or baiting any animal; or permit any premises or place to be so kept, managed, or used. Receive, or cause or procure any person to receive, money for the admission to such premises or place[31]

These provisions are the successors of the ban on animal baiting[32] and fighting originally introduced in 1835.[33]

Apparently, this offence is only committed when all the combatants are either domestic or captive animals; it has been held not to apply where one of them is a wild animal.[34] Leaving aside the question of principle as to whether wild animals should be protected in such circumstances, there seems no logic in the current situation that a domestic animal is protected if it is fighting another domestic animal, but not if it is pitted against a wild animal. However, the High Court has subsequently confirmed that it is open to magistrates to find a person guilty of cruel ill-treatment to a dog under section 1(1)(a), where it is injured as a result of a confrontation with a badger or fox in a confined space, such as a sett or an earth, in circumstances where it was unable to escape.[35]

Subsequent legislation has also made it illegal to possess any instrument or appliance, designed or adapted for use in connection with the fighting of any domestic fowl, for the purpose of using it or permitting it to be used in such a pursuit;[36] to be present without lawful excuse during an animal fight;[37] and knowingly to publish an advertisement for an animal fight.[38]

(5) Wilfully, without any reasonable cause or excuse, administer any poisonous or injurious drug or substance to any animal; or cause, procure, or, being the owner, permit such administration; or wilfully, without any reasonable cause or excuse, cause any such substance to be taken by any animal[39]

---

[31] 1911 Act, s 1(1)(c); 1912 Act, s 1(1)(c).

[32] Baiting has been interpreted to apply where 'an animal is tied to a stake or confined so that it cannot escape' and is then subjected 'to attack with violence'. It was suggested in the same case that only 'animals that by nature can defend themselves, can be baited', such as bulls, badgers, and rats: *Pitts v Millar* (1874) 9 QB 380.

[33] 5 & 6 Will IV, c 59; confirmed in respect of Ireland in 1837 (1 Vict, c 66) and extended to Scotland in 1850 (13 & 14 Vict, c 92).

[34] *DPP v Barry* [1989] Crim LR 645 (but note the accompanying editorial commentary in the law report, expressing the view that 'the arguments which prevailed are not necessarily convincing').

[35] *Bandeira and Brannigan v RSPCA* (2000) 164 JP 307.   [36] Cockfighting Act 1952, s 1.

[37] 1911 Act, s 5A, added by the Protection of Animals (Amendment) Act 1988, s 2(2); 1912 Act, s 1A, added by the Protection of Animals (Amendment) Act 1988, s 2(3). See also, the Metropolitan Police Act 1839, s 47, as amended by the Protection of Animals (Amendment) Act 1988, s 2(1), (4); and the Town Police Causes Act 1847, s 36, as amended by the Protection of Animals (Amendment) Act 1988, s 2(1), (4).

[38] 1911 Act, s 5B, added by the Protection of Animals (Amendment) Act 1988, s 2(2); 1912 Act, s 1B, added by the Protection of Animals (Amendment) Act 1988, s 2(3).

[39] 1911 Act, s 1(1)(d); 1912 Act, s 1(1)(d).

This provision replaced the Drugging of Animals Act 1876, which had made it an offence unlawfully to administer poisonous drugs to horses and other animals. The two separate limbs of the offence, involving respectively the administration of a prohibited substance or causing it to be taken by an animal, together have the effect that it can be committed either directly or indirectly. It should be noted that in order to secure a conviction under this head, it is necessary for the prosecution to establish that the accused acted both wilfully—that is, 'deliberately and intentionally, not by accident or inadventure'[40]—and without reasonable cause or excuse, but there is no apparent requirement to show that the animal actually suffered as a result. If, however, it has been caused unnecessary suffering, but it is not possible to prove that the person responsible acted intentionally, it may still be possible to prosecute under section 1(1)(a) of the 1911 or 1912 Acts.

(6) Subject any animal to any operation which is performed without due care and humanity; or cause, procure, or, being the owner, permit any animal to be subjected to such an operation[41]

Subsequent legislation has provided that in this context any operation *on a mammal* involving interference with its sensitive tissues or bone structure, regardless of whether instruments are used, which is carried out without the use of an anaesthetic shall, but for those procedures specifically excepted, be deemed to have been performed without due care and humanity.[42] The statutory requirement is the prevention of pain during the operation,[43] so either a local or general anaesthetic may be used, depending upon the circumstances. The use of an inappropriate anaesthetic, or an appropriate anaesthetic ineffectively administered, both constitute an offence if as a consequence the animal experiences pain while the operation is in progress.

The following procedures are expressly exempt from this general rule and may be performed without the use of an anaesthetic:[44]

(i) the making of injections or extractions by means of a hollow needle;
(ii) any procedure duly authorized under the Animals (Scientific Procedures) Act 1986;

---

[40] *R v Senior* [1899] 1 QB 283, 290–291 (Lord Russell of Killowen CJ).

[41] 1911 Act, s 1(1)(e); 1912 Act, s 1(1)(e).

[42] Protection of Animals (Anaesthetics) Act 1954, s 1(1), (2), (4).

[43] Protection of Animals (Anaesthetics) Act 1954, s 1(1).

[44] Protection of Animals (Anaesthetics) Act 1954, s 1(2)(a), (b), Sch 1 (as amended by the Protection of Animals (Anaesthetics) Act 1964, s 1; the Protection of Animals (Anaesthetics) Act 1954 (Amendment) Order 1982, SI 1982/1626; and the Welfare of Livestock Regulations 1994, SI 1994/2126, reg 8(2); see further n 46 below). Ewbank points out that the age component in these provisions is based on the assumption that such animals do not suffer a significant degree of pain, but recent research indicates that this may be a misconception. However, he indicates that to give an analgesic or anaesthetic to such young animals may cause them more pain and distress than the actual operation: 'Animal Welfare' in Ewbank, R et al (eds), *Management and Welfare of Farm Animals. The UFAW Farm Handbook* (4th edn, 1999) 8.

(iii) the rendering in emergency of first aid for the purpose of saving life or relieving pain;

(iv) the docking of a puppy's tail or the amputation of its dew claws before the animal's eyes are open (since 1 July 1993, only a veterinary surgeon may lawfully dock a puppy's tail[45]);

(v) the castration of a pig before it is four weeks old;[46] a bull or goat before it is two months old; or a sheep before it is three months old; but if a rubber ring or other device to constrict the flow of blood to the scrotum is used, it must be applied within the first week of life;

(vi) any minor operation performed by a veterinary surgeon or veterinary practitioner which, by reason of its quickness or painlessness, is customarily carried out without using an anaesthetic;

(vii) any minor operation which is not customarily performed by a veterinary surgeon or practitioner.

Whether a particular operation falls within (vi) or (vii) is a question of fact for the court to determine on the basis of the evidence before it. By definition, however, neither (vi) or (vii) can include an operation which has to be performed under an anaesthetic, for example stitching an albeit small wound, accidentally inflicted during the course of clipping a dog.[47] Notwithstanding that legislation provides authority for certain procedures to be performed without the use of anaesthetic, by reference to section 1(1)(a) of the 1911 and 1912 Acts, they must nevertheless be carried out without causing the animal any unnecessary suffering. Similarly, although the *automatic presumption* that an operation undertaken without anaesthetic has been performed without due care and humanity applies only to those carried out on mammals, this does not preclude an offence being committed under this head in respect of an operation on a fish, bird, or reptile, but the onus would be on the prosecution to establish beyond reasonable doubt that the defendant was guilty of the offence. It should also be noted that, regardless of the type of animal involved, the use of an effective anaesthetic is not in itself conclusive proof that an operation has been performed with due care and humanity; a prosecution may be founded on other aspects of the way in which the procedure was carried out.

[45] Veterinary Surgeons Act 1966 (Schedule 3 Amendment) Order 1991, SI 1991/1412.

[46] As originally enacted, a pig could be castrated without the use of anaesthetic up to two months of age. This was reduced to four weeks by virtue of the Welfare of Livestock Regulations 1994, SI 1994/2126, reg 8(2). However, in order to give effect to subsequent EC law, the 1994 regulations have been revoked: Welfare of Farmed Animals (England) Regulations 2000, SI 2000/1870, reg 14; Welfare of Farmed Animals (Scotland) Regulations 2000, SSI 2000/442, reg 14; Welfare of Farmed Animals (Wales) Regulations 2001, reg 14. It is understood that there was no intention to amend this particular provision, but it has been neither expressly preserved nor re-enacted in the 2000 regulations. It is submitted that, albeit inadvertently, it has therefore been revoked, and no longer has effect. In order to avoid confusion, it is strongly urged that the terms of reg 8(2) of the now defunct 1994 regulations should be re-enacted as soon as possible. The Regulations relating to Wales came into force on 31 July 2001, but at the time this book went to press they had not been allocated an SI number. Henceforth, the three sets of regulations will be referred to collectively as the 'Welfare of Farmed Animals Regulations'.

[47] *Braid v Brown* 1990 SLT 793.

For the avoidance of doubt, legislation expressly requires the use of an anaesthetic in carrying out the following procedures:[48]

- the castration of a male animal, except in the circumstances specified in (v) above;
- the dehorning of cattle;
- the disbudding of calves, except by means of chemical cauterization applied within the first week of life;
- the docking of lambs' tails by using a rubber ring or other device to constrict the flow of blood to the tail, unless the device is applied within the first week of life;
- the docking of the tails of pigs more than seven days old;[49]
- the removal of antlers in velvet;
- the collection or transfer of a bovine embryo *per vaginam.*

(7) Tether any horse, ass, or mule under such conditions or in such manner as to cause the animal unnecessary suffering[50]

Introduced in 1988, this offence applies only to England and Wales. It specifically relates to both the environment in which the animal is kept and the way in which it is tethered. The provision was originally introduced primarily to deal with travellers' horses left by the roadside or on waste ground, and horses and ponies bought by people, often at the behest of a child, who had failed to make appropriate arrangements to ensure adequate grazing. Depending upon the circumstances, it may also be possible to pursue cases of cruel tethering either under the offence of wantonly or unreasonably doing or omitting to do any act which causes unnecessary suffering or, alternatively, abandonment. However, as Parliament has seen fit to introduce a provision relating specifically to tethering, it would be desirable to extend it to Scotland (a decision which would now fall to the Scottish Parliament). Similarly, there is also a strong case for widening the scope of the offence to encompass any animal. Many species may be tethered in such a way as to cause unnecessary suffering, not least dogs, large numbers of which are left for long periods tied or chained in wholly inappropriate conditions. Furthermore, given that the

---

[48] Protection of Animals (Anaesthetics) Act 1964, s 1(4); Agriculture (Miscellaneous Provisions) Act 1968, s 5; Docking of Pigs (Use of Anaesthetics) Order 1974, SI 1974/798; Removal of Antlers in Velvet (Anaesthetics) Order 1980, SI 1980/685; Bovine Embryo (Collection, Production and Transfer) Regulations 1995, SI 1995/2478, reg 22.

[49] Under the Welfare of Livestock (Prohibited Operations) Regulations 1982, SI 1982/1884 (as amended by the Welfare of Livestock (Prohibited Operations) (Amendment) Order 1987, SI 1987/114) it is prohibited to dock the tail of a pig kept on agricultural land unless the operation is performed by the quick and complete severance of the part of the tail to be removed and either (a) the pig is less than 8 days old, or (b) the operation is performed by a veterinary surgeon who is of the opinion that the operation is necessary for reasons of health or to prevent injury from the vice of tail biting. Under the Welfare of Farmed Animals Regulations, n 46 above, tail docking of piglets may be carried out only when there is evidence, on the farm, that injuries to other pigs' tails have occurred as a result of not carrying out this procedure: Sch 6, para 27.

[50] 1911 Act, s 1(1)(f), inserted by the Protection Against Cruel Tethering Act 1988.

dangers of an animal suffering as a result of tethering may be apparent in advance (such as a collar or halter that is obviously becoming too tight; an animal which is insecurely tethered on the verge of a busy road; or situated in direct sunlight without access to shade or water), it is regrettable that the offence does not extend to situations in which the animal is *likely* to be caused unnecessary suffering. Both the RSPCA and the All Party Parliamentary Group for Animal Welfare have called for a review of this legislation;[51] action is long overdue.

(8) Being the owner or having charge of any animal, without reasonable cause or excuse, abandon it, whether permanently or not, in circumstances likely to cause the animal any unnecessary suffering; or cause, procure, or, being the owner, permit it to be so abandoned[52]

Introduced in 1960, the prospective nature of the wording is particularly significant. This is the only offence of cruelty which can be committed on the basis of either what has already occurred or, alternatively, what is *likely* to happen in the future.

Scope of the offence

The most common examples of abandonment include deserting unwanted animals by the roadside or at premises which have been vacated, or leaving pets unattended without making adequate arrangements for their care while the owners are temporarily absent, such as away on holiday. However, the provision applies equally to horses, agricultural animals, and animals which are released after having been kept in captivity. Accordingly, those who are responsible for horses, ponies, and other livestock which are left unsupervised at pasture may potentially be liable under this offence if they fail to check on them at appropriate intervals. Furthermore, it means there is a legal as well as a moral duty on those who return captive animals to the wild to ensure that they are released into an appropriate habitat and, if they have become dependent on man for food and protection, to prepare them adequately to fend for themselves.[53]

Potentially, then, the offence can be committed in a wide variety of circumstances, including abandonment which is not permanent. This 'unusual concept'[54] raises the difficult issue of when, exactly, a person's conduct becomes illegal. In *Hunt v Duckering*,[55] the English High Court emphasized that whether an animal

---

[51] (1995) 137 *Veterinary Record* 576.   [52] Abandonment of Animals Act 1960, s 1.
[53] See further: Robertson, CPJ and Harris, S, 'The condition and survival after release of captive-reared fox cubs' (1995) 4 *Animal Welfare* 281; Robertson, CPJ and Harris, S, 'The behaviour after release of captive-reared fox cubs' (1995) 4 *Animal Welfare* 295; Sainsbury, AW, Cunningham, AA, Morris, PA, Kirkwood, JK, and Macgregor, SK, 'Health and welfare of rehabilitated juvenile hedgehogs (*Erinaceus europaeus*) before and after release into the wild' (1996) 138 *Veterinary Record* 61; Morris, PA and Warwick, H, 'A study of rehabilitated juvenile hedgehogs after release into the wild' (1994) 3 *Animal Welfare* 163.
[54] *RSPCA v O'Sullivan* (QBD, 15 April 1986) (Schiemann J).
[55] [1993] Crim LR 678 (the 1911 Act is incorrectly referred to in the report as the Protection of Animals Act 1991). Quotations are taken from the unreported transcript of the full judgment.

has been abandoned is a question of fact to be determined in the light of the individual circumstances. The length of time that it has been left unattended is a relevant factor, but not conclusive. The court accepted there are circumstances in which one could say an animal had been abandoned immediately it was left. Conversely, the earlier case of RSPCA v O'Sullivan[56] demonstrates that a considerable period may elapse without any offence being committed, the defendant having left his dog alone for nearly seventy hours. Because he was due to return within the following two hours, and the animal had been left with the run of the house and an adequate supply of food, the High Court refused to interfere with the magistrates' decision to acquit, since there was no evidence that the dog was likely to be caused unnecessary suffering.

The decision in Hunt v Duckering considered

According to Evans LJ in the *Hunt* case, it is necessary to have regard to what he termed 'the character' of 'the act of abandonment'; specifically, whether 'there is sufficient evidence to prove that the defendant has disregarded his duty to care for the animal'. Stated in these terms, the test appears to be reasonably straightforward. Unfortunately, elsewhere in his judgment the judge added a gloss to this formula by suggesting a need for the prosecution to show that the owner had '*totally* disregarded his duty to care for the animal in question' or had '*relinquished*, or *wholly* disregarded, or *given up* his duty to care' (emphasis added). Not only do such phrases suggest a degree of finality which is incompatible with the concept of temporary abandonment, they also make the test unduly restrictive. Thus while the judge recognized that where the responsible person had made 'no arrangements at all' for an animal's welfare during his absence, it may be 'relatively easy to say that he has abandoned [it] in the sense of disregarding totally his duty of care', this is not so where 'some arrangements had been made but they were apparently insufficient to prevent the animal from suffering in some way'. In such a situation, observed the judge, 'it might be said that the duty to make arrangements for the [animal] had been neglected but it would be difficult, as I see it, to say that that duty had been totally disregarded'.

Accordingly, circumstances in which the defendant had 'either made or attempted to make arrangements for [the animal's] welfare during the time he was unable to attend to them himself' did not constitute abandonment. This emphasis on the defendant's intention as evidenced by his arrangements at the time of leaving the animal is to be deeply regretted.

First, as is argued further in the following chapter, the need to demonstrate the defendant's intention is inconsistent with the other offences of cruelty based on unnecessary suffering. Secondly, the apparent defence of having made some, albeit inadequate, arrangements undermines the purpose of the legislation, which is to protect animals left in circumstances where they suffer in fact or are likely to suffer.

---

[56] n 54 above.

Once it is established that an animal was left in such a situation, any defence should be based not on notions of intention or attempts to make provision for its welfare, but on the justification expressly provided for in the statute, namely by the defendant demonstrating 'a reasonable cause or excuse' for his conduct. Thirdly, the court's approach places too great an emphasis on the defendant's conduct at the time he left the animal, whereas the offence may be committed subsequently by simply failing to return. Finally, the present state of the law as represented by *Hunt v Duckering* gives rise to considerable practical problems for those investigating alleged cases of temporary abandonment. As the following table demonstrates, the effect of the decision was to cause a dramatic fall in the number of prosecutions for abandonment brought by the RSPCA, and in consequence the impact of this important offence has been significantly reduced.

Prosecutions brought by the RSPCA under the Abandonment of Animals Act 1960, 1989–1997

Year	Number of persons reported for alleged abandonment	Number of defendants convicted of abandonment
1989	237	143
1990	356	175
1991	366	156
1992	456	172
1993	Decision in *Hunt v Duckering*	
1994	243	32
1995	234	53
1996	266	41
1997	298	49

Source: *RSPCA*

Where an animal has *actually* suffered unnecessarily as a result of having been abandoned, the person responsible may be prosecuted under section 1(1)(a), regardless of the circumstances, and the difficulties thrown up by *Hunt v Duckering* may thereby be avoided.

Practical problems arising from Hunt v Duckering

Self-evidently, there are circumstances in which the intention of the accused will be decisive in establishing that an animal has been abandoned, but there are many situations where the evidence of a person's actions can point to him having (albeit temporarily) 'relinquished, wholly disregarded or given up his duty to care' for an animal, no matter what his intention may have been.

Consider, for example, an all too common scenario: a dog left in a car on a hot day. In many such cases, not only is there no intention to abandon the dog in a situation where it is likely to suffer, the owner specifically intends that it should *not* suffer. Regardless of the person's state of mind, however, the fact is that suffering may very well occur, possibly within minutes.[57] Does this amount to an offence? What if, at the time of leaving the car, the owner intends to return shortly, but his errand takes longer than he anticipated? Or he forgets about the dog? Or it becomes much hotter while he is away? Or the car, which was left in the shade, comes to be standing in the sun? Can these situations amount to an offence and, if so, when is it committed? If, as the court suggested in the *Hunt* case, the crucial test is the person's intention at the point of departure, then presumably there is no offence, even though the dangers of leaving a dog in a car on a hot day are well known, widely publicized, and the responsible dog owner can be assumed to be aware of them. And if the person leaves the windows of the car open, does that amount to an attempt to make arrangements for the animal's welfare and therefore excuse him from any suffering that might arise, notwithstanding that those arrangements may be totally inadequate? On the basis of the court's analysis, such situations would not seem to amount to an offence, yet they would appear to represent exactly the type of mischief which the legislation was intended to address. Furthermore, what if the person responsible fails to appreciate the risk of causing the animal unnecessary suffering? Suppose, for example, that the owner of a dog or cat leaves the animal with access to the exterior balcony of a flat while he goes to work, without considering the possibility that it might fall or jump. Does his oversight excuse him from prosecution for this offence?

A preferred test

The requirement imposed by the *Hunt* case to show intention unduly complicates the issue of abandonment and risks frustrating the clear purpose of the provision, which is to prevent animals suffering when they are left unattended. Furthermore, it appears inconsistent with the same court's own view that it is sufficient to demonstrate that the defendant had 'wholly disregarded' his duty to care for the animal; to disregard the consequences of an action is the antithesis of intending it. Accordingly, it is suggested that the term 'abandon' would be better interpreted simply as a question of fact: is there sufficient evidence that the defendant has disregarded his duty to care for an animal by leaving it unattended without any reasonable cause or excuse in circumstances where it is likely to be caused any unnecessary suffering? After all, such an approach not only promotes the purpose underlying the offence, it also—unlike the High Court's analysis—reflects the express wording of the legislation.

[57] Gregory, NG and Constantine, E, 'Hyperthermia in Dogs Left in Cars' (1996) 139 *Veterinary Record* 349.

D. Statutory Limitations to the Offence of Cruelty

(1) Applicable only to domestic and captive animals

Although the various offences of cruelty are widely drawn, there are important limitations to their scope. First, the provisions of the 1911 and 1912 Acts apply only to domestic or captive animals; they do not provide any protection for animals living in the wild.[58] A domestic animal is defined for this purpose to mean

any horse, ass, mule, bull, sheep, pig, goat, dog, cat or fowl, or any other animal of whatsoever kind or species, and whether a quadruped or not which is tame or which has been or is being sufficiently tamed to serve some purpose for the use of man.[59]

This is a clumsy phrase, imported from the Victorian case law,[60] when it was necessary to distinguish between domestic animals and wild animals kept in captivity because, prior to 1900, only the former benefited from statutory protection. Since the legislation now applies to both categories, the distinction is largely redundant, except in relation to hunting and coursing.[61]

As a matter of statutory construction, the phrase 'which is tame or which has been or is being sufficiently tamed to serve some purpose for the use of man' would seem to apply only to 'any other animal of whatsoever kind or species' not listed at the beginning of the sentence. If this is so, then all those individuals belonging to the species expressly mentioned come within the ambit of the Act, including those, such as cats, which may be living in a feral state (this would also, perversely, appear to extend protection to the so-called 'wild cat', *Felis sylvestris*).

If this interpretation is incorrect and protection relies on tameness, regardless of the type of animal, then the issue of feral cats needs to be considered. In a different context the courts have held that the question of whether an animal is to be regarded as domestic or wild is one of law, not fact.[62] This means the issue is to be determined by applying a legal rule rather than having regard to the facts of the particular case; and the appropriate rule, it is suggested, is to consider whether the type of animal under consideration is, as a class, generally considered to be wild or domestic. This has been the traditional approach of the common law. According to Blackstone, 'our law apprehends the most obvious distinction to be, between such animals as we *generally* see tame . . . and such creatures as are *usually* found at liberty'.[63] In *McQuaker v Goddard*, for example, which involved a claim for negligence, the Court of Appeal held that a camel was not a wild animal because it belonged to a class of animals which were domesticated.[64] A similar view has been

---

[58] 1911 Act, s 15(a); 1912 Act, s 13(a).   [59] 1911 Act, s 15(b); 1912 Act, s 13(b).

[60] *Harper v Marcks* [1894] 2 QB 319.   [61] See s D(4) below.

[62] *McQuaker v Goddard* [1940] 1 KB 687.

[63] *Commentaries on the Laws of England* (1765–1769), Book II, Ch 25, 392 (italics in the original).

[64] [1940] 1 KB 687. Scott LJ commented that a camel was 'in all countries, a domestic animal, an animal that has become trained to the uses of man, and *a fortiori* accustomed to association with man'.

adopted in respect of a statutory provision which made it an offence unlawfully or maliciously to kill any animal, except cattle, 'being ordinarily kept . . . for any domestic purpose'.[65] In *Nye v Niblett*,[66] Darling J held that this included any animal which 'belongs to a class of animals which, as a class, are kept ordinarily in a state of confinement or for domestic purposes', and, in relation to two farm cats which had been killed, it was not therefore necessary to prove that the particular animals were 'ordinarily kept in confinement'. Avory J agreed,

cats belong to a genus or class of animals that are ordinarily kept for domestic purposes. There is no doubt that is the usual description of cats. 'Domestic cats' is a well-known expression. That being so, it was not necessary to prove that the particular cats in question were at the time being kept for domestic purposes.

According to this approach, members of the species *Felis catus*, including those living an independent feral existence, would therefore be regarded as domestic animals, unlike the wild cat. Increasingly, however, *Felis sylvestris* is hybridizing with *Felis catus*; if necessary it would be for a court to decide which category such an animal falls within. Rabbits present an even more complicated problem, but it is suggested that, on the basis of the foregoing analysis, those species and varieties which as a class are normally kept in captivity should be regarded as domestic, whereas the standard form of *Oryctolagus cuniculus* is a wild animal. Those animals which are not classed as domestic may nevertheless benefit from the protection of the 1911 and 1912 Acts if they fall within the statutory meaning of a captive animal, but these distinctions highlight the somewhat arbitrary nature of the protection afforded by these statutes.

(2) The meaning of 'captive' animal

A captive animal means any non-domestic animal of whatsoever kind or species, specifically including any bird, fish, or reptile, which is in captivity, or confinement, or which is maimed, pinioned, or subjected to any appliance or contrivance for the purpose of hindering or preventing its escape.[67] It has been judicially observed that 'What the difference between captivity and confinement is no one has been able to say. Confinement, no doubt, contemplates some outside barrier confining the animal, while captivity may or may not mean much the same.'[68] In any event, the terms have been interpreted extremely narrowly. For example, a beached whale, stranded alive on the foreshore, which was attacked by a person with a knife, was not protected by the Act because the court considered that captivity or confinement 'means something more than temporary inability to get away from a particular spot'.[69] On the same basis, a wild stag which, while being hunted, jumped over a hedge into a road, slipped on the tarmac, and fell under a

---

[65] Malicious Damage Act 1861, s 41. [66] [1918] 1 KB 23.
[67] 1911 Act, s 15(c); 1912 Act, s 13(c). [68] *Rowley v Murphy* [1964] 2 QB 43, 49 (Lord Parker CJ).
[69] *Steele v Rogers* (1912) 76 JP 150, 151 (Pickford J).

stationary van from which it was dragged by a group of men into a nearby enclosure and killed with a knife, was not considered to be captive within the meaning of the legislation; nor a hedgehog which was repeatedly beaten with a stick and reacted, as hedgehogs do, by rolling itself into a ball rather than running away; nor a rabbit which was covered by a coat on the ground so as to prevent its escape and then kicked and hit with sticks until it was fatally wounded; nor a fox which, the court acknowledged, had been 'restrained in [a] land drain for a significant period of time'.[70]

According to the courts, what Lord Parker CJ described in the leading case of *Rowley v Murphy* as 'mere captivity' is not in itself sufficient to bring an animal within the protection of the 1911 Act. Rather, 'some period of time during which acts of dominion are exercised over the animal, is necessary before the animal can be said to be in a state of captivity'.[71] In consequence, it has been held that the statutory provision 'maimed . . . for the purpose of hindering or preventing its escape from captivity or confinement' does not apply in circumstances where the accused had injured a wild animal so seriously that it could not escape; the term only applies to animals which are *already* in captivity before the alleged offence is perpetrated. The same court rejected the contention that beating the animal amounted to exercising an act of dominion over it.[72] Similarly, where a hunted fox had gone to ground in a culvert, was unable to escape, and remained trapped while preparations were made to send down a terrier to flush the animal out, whereupon it would be shot, the court held that 'the continuing restraint in this case was incidental to the attempt at capture and the capture itself'. In the opinion of Pill LJ, 'the fox was temporarily restrained with a view to it being killed', with the result that 'it never passed into the state of captivity contemplated by the 1911 Act as construed in *Rowley v Murphy*'.[73]

(3) Critique of the court's approach in *Rowley v Murphy*

The rationale for the approach adopted in the *Rowley* case is based on a reading of the Wild Animals in Captivity Protection Act 1900, which was repealed and replaced by the 1911 Act. Section 2 of the former made it an offence to cause an animal unnecessary suffering while it is 'in captivity or close confinement, or is maimed, pinioned, or subjected to any appliance or contrivance for the purpose of hindering or preventing its escape from such captivity or confinement'. According to Lord Parker CJ:

It seems to me that certainly when one looks at the title of that Act . . . the natural meaning is that the Act applies to animals which are reduced to a state of captivity in the ordinary sense of the word or to a state where there is something more than mere capture.

---

[70] *Rowley v Murphy* [1964] 2 QB 43; *Hudnott v Campbell* The Times, 27 June 1986; *Woods v RSPCA* (QBD, 5 November 1993); *Barrington v Colbert* (QBD, 10 November 1997) (Pill LJ).

[71] *Rowley v Murphy* [1964] 2 QB 43, 51 (Lord Parker CJ).

[72] *Hudnott v Campbell* The Times, 27 June 1986.

[73] *Barrington v Colbert* (QBD, 10 November 1997).

It is to be observed that section 15 of the Act of 1911 follows exactly the words of section 2 of the Act of 1900 in regard to its definition of 'captive animal' save only that the words 'close confinement' in the Act of 1900 have become merely 'confinement'. . . . If, however, I am right in thinking that the Act of 1900 is clearly referring to something more than a merely captive animal, but to an animal reduced to a state of captivity in consequence of some further act or acts of domination, then it would seem that there is no reason to give the words in section 15 of the Act of 1911 any different meaning.[74]

Although the lacuna in statutory protection caused by this decision has, to some extent, been filled by the Wild Mammals (Protection) Act 1996,[75] it is submitted that the attitude of the courts is over-restrictive. Pauline Todd has argued that they are constrained by the technical rule in English law to the effect that, where the wording of a new Act simply reproduces the wording of a previous Act, a court should assume that Parliament does not intend to alter the meaning of those words. Consequently, she suggests, the courts have been 'obliged to interpret the word "captive" in the same way as it had been interpreted under the old legislation'.[76]

It is not apparent from the law report, however, that any authorities decided under the 1900 Act were cited in the above cases. If this is so, the courts did not have before them any indication of the way in which the earlier Act had been interpreted. Certainly, the remarks of Lord Parker CJ appear to be speculative rather than based on any established precedent. Indeed, his opinion was that 'there is really no case to which this court has been referred which is of any real assistance', and he based his decision on the well-established general principle that, if ambiguous, 'then this section being a penal one must be strictly construed in favour of the defendant'.[77] It is difficult, therefore, to see that the courts were bound by existing case law.

Furthermore, for the courts to draw pedantic judicial distinctions between, for example, '"in captivity" meaning a state of captivity' on the one hand, 'and the fact of being a captive, i.e., subject temporarily to restraint by human beings'[78] on the other, is not only overly legalistic, it also ignores the rationale of the statute, which would seem to be based on the principle that, where humans assume power over an animal, they have a duty not to abuse it. The judicial gloss applied to ordinary words, so that 'The mere fact that an animal has been captured does not by itself make that animal one which is in captivity',[79] is both unnecessary and undesirable. It needlessly complicates the law and serves to frustrate the purpose of the legislation which is, after all, to provide protection for animals. Wherever the everyday meaning of a word is in accordance with the intention underlying the legislation, that is the meaning it should be given. On this basis, the important consideration

---

[74] *Rowley v Murphy* [1964] 2 QB 43, 50–51.   [75] See s E below.

[76] Todd, P, 'The Protection of Animals Acts 1911–1964' in Blackman, DE et al, *Animal Welfare and the Law* (1989) 16.

[77] *Rowley v Murphy* [1964] 2 QB 43, 50 and 51.   [78] ibid 52 (Winn J).

[79] ibid 51 (Winn J).

is not the subtle nuances of 'captivity' and 'in captivity'; it is that the animal is either unable to escape, or is prevented from doing so of its own accord, as Fenton Atkinson J appreciated in suggesting that 'there was very much to be said for the view that, once a wild animal had been captured it was in captivity on the plain meaning of the word'.[80] The traditional, much more restrictive interpretation is, however, so well entrenched as a precedent that there is no reasonable prospect of persuading the courts to disregard it. In two recent cases, the English High Court has emphasized that it is bound by the decision in the *Rowley* case;[81] a broader meaning, as suggested by Fenton Atkinson J, can probably now be achieved only by means of legislation.

The situation in Britain is to be compared with that in Northern Ireland, where the corresponding legislation makes no distinction between domestic, captive, or wild animals. Indeed, it extends to all mammals, birds, fish, and reptiles, regardless of the circumstances in which they are living.[82] As a result, and notwithstanding the limited protection now provided under British law by the Wildlife and Countryside Act 1981, the Protection of Badgers Act 1992, and the Wild Mammals (Protection) Act 1996, wildlife in the Province continues to enjoy a significantly greater degree of protection than in Britain.[83]

(4) Three further limitations

Re-enacting three exemptions which were originally included in the Wild Animals in Captivity Protection Act 1900, it is further provided that conduct which would otherwise constitute an offence of cruelty is not illegal if it is carried out[84]

(i) lawfully under the Animals (Scientific Procedures) Act 1986;[85]

(ii) in the course of the destruction of any animal as food for mankind, unless accompanied by the infliction of unnecessary suffering (in practice, this provision has been superseded by the Welfare of Animals (Slaughter or Killing) Regulations 1995[86]);

(iii) during the coursing or hunting of any captive animal, unless it is liberated in an injured, mutilated, or exhausted condition, or into an enclosed space from which it has no reasonable chance of escape.

---

[80] *Rowley v Murphy* [1964] 2 QB 43, 51.

[81] *Hudnott v Campbell* The Times, 27 June 1986; *Barrington v Colbert* (QBD, 10 November 1997).

[82] Welfare of Animals (Northern Ireland) Act 1972, s 29(1).　　[83] See s E below.

[84] 1911 Act and 1912 Act, s 1(3), as amended by the Animals (Scientific Procedures) Act 1986 and the Protection of Animals Act (1911) Amendment Act 1921, s 1.

[85] Protection for those engaged in scientific procedures ceases to apply where the treatment of an animal at an establishment designated under the 1986 Act amounts to an offence of cruelty and is not authorized by the terms of the relevant project or personal licence. Thus, following the broadcast by Channel 4 of video material recorded in a dog toxicology unit by an undercover investigator which showed dogs being physically abused, two persons involved were subsequently convicted of offences under the 1911 Act: see further, Animal Procedures Committee, *Report of the Animal Procedures Committee for 1997* (1998) para 107.

[86] SI 1995/731.

Two issues arise from the third exemption. First, it applies only to captive animals; unnecessary suffering caused as a result of hunting or coursing a domestic animal is an offence. In respect of the 1911 and 1912 Acts, this is the one area where the distinction between the two classes remains legally relevant.[87]

Secondly, and somewhat perversely one might think, while a person may be prosecuted for being cruel to a captive animal *immediately before* it is liberated,[88] provided it is not injured, mutilated, or exhausted at the time of release, and it has a reasonable chance of escape, it loses the benefit of any protection under the 1911 or 1912 Acts once it is being pursued. As has been judicially observed, the legislative exemption applies to hunting per se, regardless of the circumstances: 'It does not say to sportsmanlike hunting; it does not say to hunting which is not cruel, or anything of that sort.'[89] The courts have expressed similar sentiments in relation to coursing.[90]

In Northern Ireland, the corresponding provision relating to the coursing and hunting of liberated animals relates to non-domestic, rather than captive, animals, and therefore avoids the problem of having to distinguish between a captive animal and one that is free-living. In addition, because wildlife falls within the scope of the Province's general anti-cruelty legislation, the equivalent field sports exemption provides that any act done during hunting, pursuit, coursing, capture, destruction, or attempted destruction of any wild animal is immune from prosecution, *unless unnecessary suffering is caused to the animal.*[91] Hunting with hounds, coursing, shooting, and angling are all thereby lawful activities, but those who participate in them are, unlike their counterparts in Britain, liable for prosecution if they cause their prey to suffer unnecessarily. These two small, but significant, differences both have much to commend them.

E. Additional Provisions to Prevent Suffering Especially to Wildlife

In addition to the offences discussed above, the 1911 and 1912 Acts contain a number of miscellaneous provisions relating to poisons and traps, which have

---

[87] In 1932, the High Court declined to interfere with the justices' decision that a tame deer, which was entirely dependent on her keepers for food and water and had been provided with a loose box for shelter, was a captive rather than a domestic animal, largely on the basis that the exemption must have been intended by Parliament to include the hunting of so-called 'carted' deer: *White v Fox and Dawes* (1932) 48 TLR 641. If similar facts came before the courts today, it is possible that, in the light of contemporary attitudes, the case would be decided differently. The practice of hunting carted deer dates back to at least the eighteenth century. It involves releasing and pursuing semi-tame animals. The intention was not to kill the deer but, once the chase was completed, to capture it alive for a similar use in the future.

[88] *Jenkins v Ash* (1929) 93 JP 229.

[89] *Rodgers v Pickersgill* (1910) 74 JP 324, 326 (Channell J); approved by Avory J in *White v Fox and Dawes* (1932) 48 TLR 641, 643.

[90] *Waters v Meakin* [1916] 2 KB 111, 117.   [91] Welfare of Animals (Northern Ireland) Act 1972, s 15.

their origins in the nineteenth-century legislation.[92] These are intended to prevent or minimize suffering not only to domestic animals, but also to wildlife. It is convenient to consider these, and associated, measures here, but it is important to appreciate that *none of the offences discussed in this section constitute an offence of cruelty*.

(1) Poisons

It is an offence: to sell, offer, expose for sale, or give away any grain or seed which has been rendered poisonous, except for bona fide use in agriculture; knowingly to put down any poison, or any fluid or edible matter (not being grown seed or grain) which has been rendered poisonous; or to cause or procure the foregoing, or knowingly to be a party to them.[93] Notwithstanding this general prohibition, it is lawful to use poison (not being sown seed or grain) to destroy insects and other invertebrates, rats, mice, other small ground vermin, grey squirrels, coypus, and, under licence, badgers, where it is necessary in the interests of public health, agriculture, or the preservation of other domestic or wild animals, or for the purpose of manuring the land, so long as all reasonable precautions are taken to prevent injury thereby (or to prevent access thereto in the case of Scotland) to dogs, cats, fowls, or other domestic animals and wild birds.[94] In Scotland, the proviso applies simply to 'vermin', regardless of their size, and has been held to include foxes.[95] In the same case, it was held that the duty to take *all* reasonable precautions against injury to domestic animals and wild birds meant that if a person took a number of reasonable precautions, but omitted one, he could be convicted. The court was also conscious that such precautions were required to protect not only animals over which man has an element of control, such as dogs, but also those like cats which can stray. On this authority, a very high threshold would have to be met before the proviso could be successfully relied upon. In addition, the Secretary of State may prohibit or restrict the use of a poison if he is satisfied that a particular poison cannot be used for destroying mammals without causing undue suffering

---

[92] For example, the Cruelty to Animals Acts 1849 and 1854; the Poisoned Grain Prohibition Act 1863; the Poisoned Flesh Prohibition Act 1864; the Injured Animals Act 1907.

[93] 1911 Act, s 8; 1912 Act, s 7. No offence is committed if the use of poison has been approved under the terms of the Food and Environmental Protection Act 1985 or the Plant Protection Products Regulations 1995, SI 1995/887, or licensed under either the Wildlife and Countryside Act 1981 or the Conservation (Natural Habitats, &c) Regulations 1994, SI 1994/2716.

[94] 1911 Act, s 8, as amended by the Protection of Animals (Amendment) Act 1927; 1912 Act, s 7; Agriculture (Miscellaneous Provisions) Act 1972, s 19(1), (2), (6); Protection of Badgers Act 1992, s 10(10). In addition, the Wildlife and Countryside Act 1981, s 5(1)(a), (b), and (4) makes it an offence to injure a wild bird by the use of poison unless it can be shown that the substance was being used lawfully to kill or take, in the interests of public health, agriculture, forestry, fisheries, or nature conservation, any wild animal and all reasonable precautions had been taken to prevent injury to wild birds. In England and Wales, it is also lawful to control rabbits by means of using a poisonous gas in a rabbit hole: Prevention of Damage by Rabbits Act 1939, s 4.

[95] *Walkingshaw v McClymont* 1996 SLT (Sh Ct) 107.

and an alternative method of killing them exists which is both suitable and adequate.[96]

(2) Use and inspection of traps and snares

It is an offence to use, knowingly permit to be used, sell, or possess a spring trap for the purpose of killing or taking animals which has not been approved by the Minister of Agriculture, or to use a legal trap in circumstances for which it has not been approved.[97] Under the Wildlife and Countryside Act 1981, it is also prohibited to use any springe (a noose or snare for catching small game), trap, gin, snare, hook, or line, or any electrical device for killing or taking wild birds; and any trap, snare, electrical device, or net in the case of named species.[98] It is a defence, however, to show that the article was used in the interests of public health, agriculture, forestry, fisheries, or nature conservation and all reasonable precautions were taken to prevent injury to wild birds or protected animals.[99] The same legislation makes it an offence to set or use a self-locking snare calculated to injure, or for the taking or killing of, any wild animal.[100] Any spring trap set for catching hares or rabbits must be inspected by a competent person at reasonable intervals, but at least once every day between sunrise and sunset. Similarly, a snare must be inspected at least once every day.[101] In England and Wales, a spring trap may only be set elsewhere than in a rabbit hole if it is used in accordance with regulations made by the Minister of Agriculture or the terms of a licence granted by him.[102] The Wildlife and Countryside Act also prohibits other forms of taking and killing wild birds and animals, such as by the use of any bow or crossbow, any explosive other than ammunition for a firearm, and any form of artificial lighting, mirror, or dazzling device.[103]

(3) Other relevant measures

It is an offence intentionally to kill, injure, or take most types of wild bird; to take, damage, or destroy their nest while it is under construction or in use, or to take or

---

[96] Animals (Cruel Poisons) Act 1962, ss 2, 3. By virtue of the Animals (Cruel Poisons) Regulations 1963, SI 1963/1278, elementary yellow phosphorus and red squill may not be used for destroying mammals of any description and strychnine may be used only for destroying moles. Warfarin is specifically permitted, under prescribed conditions, to control grey squirrels: Grey Squirrels (Warfarin) Order 1973, SI 1973/744.

[97] Pests Act 1954, s 8; see further, the Spring Traps Approval Order 1995, SI 1995/2427; Agriculture (Spring Traps) (Scotland) Act 1969; Spring Traps Approval (Scotland) Order 1975, SI 1975/1722, as amended by SI 1982/92, SI 1988/2213, and SI 1993/167.

[98] Sections 5(1)(a), (b) and 11(2)(a), (b); Sch 6.

[99] Sections 5(4) and 11(6); Sch 6. See also, Conservation (Natural Habitats, &c) Regulations 1994, SI 1994/2716.

[100] Section 11(1)(a), (b).

[101] 1911 Act, s 10; 1912 Act, s 9; Countryside and Wildlife Act 1981, s 11(3), as amended by the Wildlife and Countryside (Amendment) Act 1991, s 2.

[102] Pests Act 1954, s 9.   [103] Sections 5(c) and 11(1), (2).

destroy their eggs.[104] It is similarly prohibited intentionally to kill, injure, or take certain species of wild animal which are considered to be endangered and in need to be conserved. These include bats, whales, dolphins, otters, pine martens, red squirrels, together with certain species of reptile, fish, butterfly, amphibian, spider, and insect. It is also an offence to be in possession of any animal belonging to such a protected species, to destroy or damage any shelter used by these species, or to disturb the animals themselves.[105] The so-called Game Laws, which are principally intended to protect the landowner's interests, are occasionally employed for the benefit of the animals themselves, for example to prosecute those who engage in unlawful hare coursing (that is to say, without first obtaining permission to be on the land).[106] In addition, two species which have been the subject of particular persecution are protected. The Conservation of Seals Act 1970 restricts the way in which seals may be killed, and imposes a close season on killing grey or common seals, and a complete ban on killing, injuring, or taking these animals at any time in English territorial waters has been introduced subsequently.[107] Except as permitted by statute, it is an offence wilfully to kill, injure, or take a badger, or attempt to do so, or to interfere with a badger sett.[108] Cruelty to a badger is also expressly prohibited, which includes cruel ill-treatment, the use of badger tongs, or unlawfully to dig for it.[109] More generally, it is an offence for any person to mutilate, kick, beat, nail or otherwise impale, stab, burn, stone, crush, drown, drag, or asphyxiate any wild mammal with intent to inflict unnecessary suffering.[110] It must be emphasized, however, that although the language is similar, none of these offences amounts to an offence of cruelty under the Protection of Animals Acts.

F. Conclusion

The offences of cruelty are central to the statutory protection of animals in Britain; they therefore merit particular consideration. Although wide-ranging and largely effective, they are a somewhat odd collection to the contemporary observer, reflecting as they do the nineteenth-century origins of the 1911 and 1912 Acts.

---

[104] Wildlife and Countryside (Amendment) Act 1981, ss 1 and 2. It is, however, permissible for a person to take a wild bird if he shows that it had been disabled otherwise than by his unlawful act and it is done solely for the purpose of tending it and releasing it when it is no longer disabled. Similarly, it is lawful to kill it if it has been so seriously disabled that there is no reasonable chance of it recovering: s 4(2).

[105] ibid, s 9 and Sch 5; for exceptions, see s 10.

[106] See further, Game (Scotland) Act 1772; Night Poaching Act 1828, as amended; Game Act 1831, as amended; Game (Scotland) Act 1832; Night Poaching Act 1844; Hares Act 1848; Game Licences Act 1860; Poaching Prevention Act 1862; Game Law (Scotland) Amendment Act 1877; Ground Game Act 1880; Game Laws (Amendment) Act 1960; Deer Act 1991, ss 10, 11; Deer (Scotland) Act 1996.

[107] Conservation of Seals Act 1970; Conservation of Seals (England) Order 1999, SI 1999/3052.

[108] Protection of Badgers Act 1992, ss 1, 3, 6, and 7. A 'sett' does not include the ground rising to the top surface above the sett where the tunnel system itself has not been broken into: CPS v Green [2001] 1 WLR 505.

[109] ibid, s 2.   [110] Wild Mammals (Protection) Act 1996, s 1.

There are those who advocate a major overhaul of the legislation, but there are a number of relatively minor amendments which could have a significant effect, such as extending the prohibition on cruel tethering to animals other than equines, and clarifying the meaning of a captive animal (or, preferably, follow the lead of Northern Ireland, and do away altogether with the distinction between domestic, captive, and wild animals). Most importantly in terms of protecting animals from cruelty, the prospective element contained in the offence of abandonment should be extended to all offences of cruelty which are based on causing unnecessary suffering by the addition of the words 'or likely to'. Regrettably, the Government has recently expressly rejected such a proposal.[111]

[111] HC Debs, 8 February 1999, col 87 (WA).

9
Cruelty: Culpability and Consequences

Having considered conduct which can amount to an offence of cruelty, this chapter is concerned with the consequences: those who may be prosecuted; the nature of the offence; and the penalties available to the courts.

A. Liability for an Offence of Cruelty

As cruelty is a criminal offence, the prosecution is required to establish the defendant's guilt beyond reasonable doubt in order to secure a conviction. Those who may be prosecuted include:

- the person who is directly responsible for the cruelty;
- a person who causes or procures the cruelty;
- if not already within one of the foregoing categories, the owner of the animal, if he has permitted the cruelty to occur.

Criminal liability is therefore comprehensive, extending to all those who may be either directly or indirectly responsible.

(1) The owner's legal responsibility to care for an animal

It is expressly prescribed that an owner shall be deemed to have permitted cruelty if he has failed to exercise reasonable care and supervision so as to prevent the animal suffering unnecessarily.[1] His conduct is therefore to be judged not by his own standards, but by those of the reasonable person in the same situation. If it is alleged that the owner has failed in this regard, the onus passes to him to satisfy the court, on the balance of probabilities, that he has adequately fulfilled this

---

[1] 1911 Act, s 1(2); 1912 Act, s 1(2).

requirement.[2] Not only does this provision prevent an owner avoiding liability by claiming ignorance, it also establishes the principle that *the owner of an animal has ultimate responsibility for the way in which it is treated*. Ownership therefore incontrovertibly carries with it *a positive, continuing, non-delegable, legal duty to exercise reasonable care and supervision in order to prevent the animal suffering unnecessarily*. This will be obvious to the responsible owner, but too many who possess animals fall outside this category. It is a principle which should be given much greater emphasis. It should also be noted that, in consequence of this provision, those organizations and shelters which retain ownership of rehomed animals continue to have ultimate legal responsibility for the way in which they are treated.

B. The Issue of *Mens Rea*

(1) The principle underlying *mens rea*

In respect of a great many criminal offences it is not enough for the prosecution to prove that the defendant committed the proscribed act; it must also demonstrate that they were culpable by reference to their state of mind at the time of the offence. The technical term for this requirement is *mens rea* ('a guilty mind'); it is indicated in legislation by terms such as 'intentionally', 'recklessly', 'wilfully', 'knowingly', and 'unreasonably'. The principle reflects the importance attached to personal responsibility in establishing criminal liability: the onus is on the prosecution to demonstrate beyond reasonable doubt not only that the defendant perpetrated the offence, but also that he knew what he was doing and was aware, or should have been aware, of the likely outcome of his act or omission, so that he can 'fairly be said to have chosen the behaviour and its consequences'.[3] The practical significance of *mens rea* is twofold. First, it is crucial in defining the ambit and nature of the offence. Section 1(1) of the Protection of Badgers Act 1992, for example, makes it an offence if a person 'wilfully kills, injures or takes' a badger. If the word 'wilfully' were not present, killing or injuring a badger would amount to an offence, regardless of the circumstances. Its inclusion, however, means that where such a situation arises accidentally, as when a badger on the road is struck by a vehicle, no offence is committed. It can therefore be seen that the presence of a single word may have a profound effect in circumscribing the meaning of the offence. Secondly, the test of *mens rea* determines, at least in part, that which the prosecution must establish in order to secure a conviction.

If no such mental element is expressly alluded to in the legislation, the offence may be one of strict liability, meaning that the proscribed act alone constitutes the offence. However, the absence in the legislation of words relating to the defendant's

---

[2] *Whiting v Ivens* (1915) 85 LJKB 1878.
[3] Ashworth, A, *Principles of Criminal Law* (3rd edn, 1999) 160.

state of mind does not necessarily mean that it is irrelevant. On the contrary, the courts recognize that 'there has for centuries been a presumption that Parliament did not intend to make criminals of persons who were in no way blameworthy in what they did'. Accordingly, 'whenever a section is silent as to *mens rea* there is a presumption that, in order to give effect to the will of Parliament, we must read in words appropriate to require *mens rea*'. Such a presumption will be ousted only if, having examined 'all relevant circumstances', the court is satisfied that 'this must have been the intention of Parliament'.[4]

(2) The significance of *mens rea*

The practical importance of *mens rea* is that it defines the standard by which the defendant is to be judged.[5] Namely,

1. those offences where the defendant's mental state is considered subjectively;
2. those where it is viewed objectively; and
3. those where it is irrelevant.

In respect of offences where a *subjective* test is applied, the prosecution is required to demonstrate that the particular defendant before the court knew, or, on the basis of the evidence, must be assumed to have known, the consequences of his conduct. In contrast, the *objective* test involves comparing the defendant's behaviour against that which might be expected of the reasonable person in the same situation. Accordingly, it is enough for the prosecution to satisfy the court that the defendant *should* have been aware of the implications of his behaviour.

Self-evidently, where an offence of animal cruelty requires consideration of the defendant's mental state, the nature of the test to be applied is of great significance. If a subjective test is required, for example, three important consequences follow:

- an additional evidential burden is placed upon the prosecution;
- the degree of protection afforded to an animal will vary according to the extent of the particular defendant's knowledge of its needs and awareness of the possible consequences arising from his conduct (the less he understands the animal's requirements, the more difficult it will be to show that he was aware of the likely detrimental effect of his behaviour); and
- the defendant's own view (however misguided) of the appropriate manner in which to treat the animal becomes relevant.

The third group of offences are those of strict liability. This means that the defendant may be convicted solely on the basis of his conduct, regardless of his mental state. This is so whatever his intention may have been, and irrespective of how careful or reasonable his conduct.

---

[4] *Sweet v Parsley* [1970] AC 132, 148 (Lord Reid). See also the remarks of Lord Scarman in *Gammon (Hong Kong) Ltd v Attorney General of Hong Kong* [1995] AC 1, 14, PC; and *Wings Ltd v Ellis* [1985] AC 272, 295, HL.

[5] See further Ch 14, s B below.

C. *Mens Rea* and Offences of Cruelty

There is no single rule concerning *mens rea* in relation to offences of cruelty. Indeed, there are examples of such offences in each of the three groups: subjective *mens rea*, objective *mens rea*, and strict liability. Which category any particular offence falls into depends upon the context and the wording by which it is defined.

D. Offences to which a Subjective Test is to be Applied

The only offence of cruelty which clearly requires a subjective test is that of administering a poisonous or injurious drug or substance. This is connoted by the inclusion of the word 'wilfully' in the statutory definition. In addition, however, the courts have held that where the defendant was not personally responsible for inflicting the cruelty, in that he caused or procured someone else to do it, the prosecution must establish that he knew, or by inference must have known, the consequences of his conduct. In the absence of such evidence, the causation or procurement of the cruelty will not be established.[6] However, if it is the *owner* of the animal who is indirectly responsible, statute stipulates that he shall be deemed to have permitted the cruelty if he failed 'to exercise reasonable care and supervision' to prevent it.[7] The inclusion of the word 'reasonable' indicates that, in these circumstances, the defendant's conduct is to be judged by an objective standard.

E. *Mens Rea* and the Offence of Cruelly Beating, Kicking, Ill-Treating, Overriding, Over-Driving, Overloading, Torturing, Infuriating, or Terrifying an Animal

It was explained in the previous chapter that the 1911 statute was a consolidation Act. As such, the above offence (the first limb of section 1(1)(a)) was essentially a restatement of the 1849 and, in Scotland, 1850 Prevention of Cruelty to Animals Acts, and the way in which the courts interpreted this earlier legislation therefore remains relevant.

(1) The Victorian case law: Scotland

In the early cases, the Scottish courts were divided on what was required to secure a conviction. On the one hand it was said that the offence 'necessarily imports a

---

[6] *Sharp v Mitchell* (1872) 2 Coup 273; *Small v Warr* (1882) 47 JP 20; *Elliott v Osborn* (1891) 56 JP 38; *Greenwood v Backhouse* (1902) 66 JP 519.

[7] 1911 Act, s 1(2); 1912 Act, s 1(2).

certain state of mind on the part of the accused—an intention of purpose to inflict cruelty',[8] with the result that appeals against conviction were successful where there was no evidence of 'any intent to injure or inflict pain needlessly' or 'that cruel purpose which constitutes wanton cruelty in the sense of the statute'.[9] According to Lord Young, wanton cruelty to animals was limited to 'cruelty which proceeds from a wicked disposition, and where the acts practised are to gratify a cruel propensity'.[10]

Other Scottish judges, however, held that it was not necessary to prove that the cruelty had been inflicted either wantonly or intentionally, unless the accused was absent from the place where the alleged offence occurred. If he was 'not on the spot something must be relevantly set forth bringing home a knowledge of the offence to him,' said Lord Neaves, 'but when this is not the case I see no reason for requiring knowledge or intention to be libelled'.[11] In such circumstances, it was enough that 'a person neglect to do a thing which is his duty and within his power, and there-by ill-treat, abuse, or torture any animal',[12] or, alternatively, 'neglected that duty . . . when he must have known [the animal] was suffering, and took no means to protect it'.[13] A particular issue which arose, at a time when horses played an essential role in transport, agriculture, and other parts of the economy, was whether an employer could be held responsible for the cruel behaviour of his employees. The judiciary conceded that conduct by an employer which amounted to 'gross negligence in the management of his business' might be sufficient to entitle the court to convict him of cruelty for the act of his servant, but Lord Shand warned 'the carelessness must be of such a nature as would lead to the inference that the accused had reason to believe that the act complained of would occur, where it was not the act of the accused himself, and in every case also that suffering would be inflicted'.[14]

During the nineteenth century, then, the Scottish courts moved away from a requirement that the defendant be shown positively to have intended the cruelty to a position where it was sufficient that he was aware of it, either in fact or by inference: 'knowledge of the act complained of, and knowledge that it will produce pain or suffering, or obvious reason to believe that suffering will be caused, is essential to the charge'.[15]

---

[8] *Sharp v Mitchell* (1872) 2 Coup 273, 278 (the Lord Justice-General).
[9] *Cornelius v Grant* (1880) 4 Coup 327, 332 (the Lord Justice-Clerk); *Jack v Campbell* (1880) 4 Coup 351, 355 (Lord Adam).
[10] *Anderson v Wood* (1881) 4 Coup 543, 549 (dissenting).
[11] *Wilson v Johnstone* (1874) 3 Coup 8, 12.   [12] ibid.
[13] *Anderson v Wood* (1881) 4 Coup 543, 547 (the Lord Justice-Clerk). See also, *Carmichael v Welsh* (1887) 1 White 333.
[14] *Wright v Rowan* (1890) 2 White 426, 433 (the Lord Justice-Clerk).   [15] ibid 432 (Lord Shand).

(2) The Victorian case law: England

Similarly, there were English judges who considered that the defendant's intention was a necessary factor in establishing cruelty. The widely held view that the 1849 Act applied only to acts of commission led Cockburn CJ, for example, to suggest intention was necessary, on the basis that what he called 'passive cruelty' did not constitute an offence.[16] In general, however, the English courts considered it sufficient that the defendant knew the animal was caused to suffer.[17] 'Cruelty', it was said, 'must be something which cannot be justified, and the person who practises it knows cannot be justified',[18] although it was enough that the accused had been put on notice of the possibility that an animal might suffer and had not taken appropriate steps to prevent it.[19] Likewise, an employer was to be held responsible for the actions of his employees if he had knowledge of the cruelty or there was evidence that he had wilfully abstained from the knowledge of it.[20]

Unfortunately, not all courts were prepared to follow this approach. As late as the early years of the twentieth century, some were still requiring evidence of intention with, on occasions, perverse results in view of the purpose of the legislation. For example, the justices' decision that a man who shot and seriously injured a dog which was trespassing on his employer's land was not guilty of cruelty was upheld on appeal, on the basis that he intended only 'to sting the dog', not 'to injure it in the sense of cruelly ill-treating it'.[21] Conversely, where a person shot and seriously injured a cat but took no immediate steps to have it attended to, or its sufferings alleviated, the justices' decision that he was not guilty of cruelty was also upheld, because his intention was to kill, rather than to wound, the animal. 'He wounded it,' explained Darling J, 'but not because he desired merely to wound it . . . to say that this was cruelty within the statute would be to say what the statute does not say.'[22]

The need to show intention was, however, emphatically rejected in *Duncan v Pope*. The accused had savagely beaten a six-month-old puppy with various implements for about half an hour before eventually shooting it, treatment which had been induced because the animal had 'got into the habit of barking and running at children'. The magistrates dismissed the case on the ground that 'the defendant could have no intention to commit cruelty, because he was trying to destroy the animal'. On appeal, Lawrence J repudiated such reasoning:

In my opinion the justices have taken an erroneous view of the case. They seem to have thought that they had to consider whether there was any intention on the part of the respondent to commit cruelty, whereas their duty is to say whether there was cruelty in fact.

---

[16] *Powell v Knight* (1878) 38 LT 607, 608; see also, *Hooker v Gray* (1907) 71 JP 337; *Potter v Challans* (1910) 74 JP 114. Cf *Green v Cross* (1910) 74 JP 357.

[17] *Everitt v Davies* (1878) 42 JP 248.   [18] *Lewis v Fermor* (1887) 18 QBD 532, 534 (Day J).

[19] *Thielbar v Craigen* (1905) 69 JP 421.

[20] *Small v Warr* (1882) 47 JP 20; *Elliott v Osborn* (1891) 56 JP 38; *Greenwood v Backhouse* (1902) 66 JP 519.

[21] *Armstrong v Mitchell* (1903) 67 JP 329 (Lord Alverstone CJ).

[22] *Hooker v Gray* (1907) 71 JP 337, 338.

Having considered the evidence before the magistrates, the judge concluded, 'There is no doubt that is cruelty, and the intention of the respondent in doing this does not matter.'[23] Seven years later, Bray J agreed with this proposition, stating 'there may be cruelty without having a cruel intention'.[24]

(3) *Ford v Wiley*: the adoption of an objective test

Meanwhile, other judges were not only rejecting the notion of intention, they also appreciated the problem inherent in requiring a subjective test to establish cruelty. The need to show knowledge had been justified on the ground that the legislation was not to be interpreted so as 'to bring within the criminal law people who act honestly and without any evil mind or motive', even if their belief was erroneous, unless it was so widely known to be wrong that 'it would be impossible to establish the defence of a bona fide belief that it was reasonable'.[25] But in the leading case of *Ford v Wiley*, decided in 1889, Hawkins J, with whom Lord Coleridge CJ agreed, pointed out that if a defendant could excuse himself on the basis that he honestly believed the law justified his action, 'it is difficult to see the limits to which such a principle might not be pushed, and the creatures it is man's duty to protect from abuse, would oftentimes be suffering victims of gross ignorance and cupidity'.[26] Accordingly, the judge suggested it was appropriate to apply an objective test in determining whether an offence of cruelty had been committed. 'Where a desirable and legitimate object is sought to be attained,' he said, 'the pain caused . . . must not so far outbalance the importance of the end as *to make it clear to any reasonable person* that it is preferable the object should be abandoned rather than that the disproportionate suffering should be inflicted.'[27] On this basis, the crucial issue was no longer the accused's knowledge, but whether the court thought his conduct could be justified by reference to the standards of the reasonable person. Applying this principle to the facts of the case, which involved an operation to dehorn cattle, Hawkins J made an important distinction:

I am not prepared to deny that an honest belief based on reasonable grounds in the exercise of circumstances which if proved would justify a painful operation, would afford [the accused] a defence against a charge of cruelty, even though the circumstances relied on were not as he had believed them to be. I do dissent from any notion that a mistaken belief, however honest, that the law justified a painful operation, when in truth it did no such thing, could operate as any excuse at all, except, perhaps, in mitigation of punishment.[28]

(4) The contemporary position: an objective test

Clearly, if the prosecution establishes that the defendant intended or knew of the animal's suffering, *mens rea* will have been established. The reasoning in *Ford v Wiley*, however, clearly demonstrates that some members of the judiciary have

[23] (1899) 63 JP 217.
[25] ibid 535–536 (Wills J).
[27] ibid 220 (Hawkins J) (emphasis added).
[24] *Bowyer v Morgan* (1906) 70 JP 253, 255.
[26] (1889) 23 QBD 203, 225.
[28] ibid 224–225.

long since appreciated the inherent disadvantage of requiring a subjective test to establish cruelty; hence, the court's preference for an objective standard. The modern case law endorses this proposition. In *Easton v Anderson*, for example, the Scottish High Court held that the imposition of a subjective test would, in the words of Lord Justice-General Cooper, 'unwarrantably impede the administration of a beneficial statute by requiring the prosecution to assume a very difficult and often impossible onus and by perhaps penalizing the intelligent and sensitive, while allowing the callous, indifferent or ignorant to escape'. Accordingly, the appropriate test to be applied was 'whether the facts are such as to justify the inference either that the accused actually knew that he was inflicting unnecessary pain and suffering on a dumb animal, or at least that he ought to have known that, because the proved circumstances would have conveyed such knowledge to any normal and reasonable person'. Applying this formula to the facts before him, the judge upheld the conviction because there was sufficient evidence that the appellant had been 'so careless and indifferent' as to whether his horse suffered pain 'that he must be held guilty of a contravention of the Act'.[29] The other members of the court agreed. 'If we had come to the opposite conclusion', said Lord Mackay, it would have 'very much cramped the humanitarian intention of the Act of 1912'.[30]

Following this approach, it was said in the Scottish case of *Tudhope v Ross* that a defendant accused of cruelly beating a terminally ill dog (albeit in a vain and clumsy attempt to kill it and so put the animal out of its misery)

could not reasonably be described as being callous or indifferent to the wellbeing of the animal, but . . . to try to kill a dog, even a dog which is suffering pain and will have to be destroyed in due course, by hitting it on the head repeatedly with a piece of wood is to display, at least temporarily, a disregard for present-day sensibilities and intuitions. . . . [I]n adopting such a course . . . the accused . . . had the limited degree of *mens rea* to provide the foundation for a successful prosecution provided unnecessary suffering could be proved.[31]

Having regard to the standard of 'present-day sensibilities and intuitions' is simply another way of asking what the reasonable person would have done in the same situation; what is being applied here is an objective test.

The English High Court has recently adopted a similar approach. The case arose from the injury caused to a bird flying repeatedly into the side of its cage for at least six weeks. The magistrates accepted that the defendant did not deliberately or wilfully maltreat the bird, but convicted him on the basis that he was aware of the situation. In upholding the conviction, the High Court rejected the contention that the charge of cruel ill-treatment under the first limb of section 1(1)(a) of the 1911 Act requires 'more in the way of moral opprobrium, more in the way of *mens rea*, more in the way of deliberate cruelty' than an offence charged under the second limb, and found there was 'no need to establish that the appellant desired to bring about this bird's harm in order for him to be guilty of cruel ill-treatment'. According to the court, what '*objectively* constituted the offence . . . was to allow

---

[29] 1949 JC 1, 6.   [30] ibid 9.   [31] 1986 SCCR 467, 477 (Sheriff Kearney).

this bird, for six weeks, to traumatize itself by repeatedly flying into the netting and thus creating this open wound'.[32]

The application of this objective test in defining cruelty under the first limb of section 1(1)(a) of both the 1911 and 1912 Acts is to be welcomed for the reasons initially identified in *Ford v Wiley* and echoed in *Easton*. Namely, that to do otherwise risks undermining the effectiveness of the protection provided by the legislation. It should be noted that in *Barnard v Evans*, decided in 1925, Avory J said the expression 'cruelly ill-treat' applies where 'a person wilfully causes pain to an animal without justification for so doing'.[33] It is submitted, however, that if the judge meant that intention is an essential element of the offence, his interpretation was incorrect. It is not in accordance with the case law existing in 1911 (which does not appear to have been brought to the court's attention), there is no apparent reason to import such a requirement, and it is suggested that the approach of the other members of the court is to be preferred. Lord Hewart CJ referred simply to causing suffering that was 'not necessary', and Shearman J suggested that the test for cruelly beating or ill-treating an animal was whether the accused did 'something which it was not *reasonably* necessary to do'.[34] As we have seen, an objective test has been applied subsequently.

The significance of this test lies in the judicial acknowledgement that criminal liability for cruelty to animals can be founded on the defendant's negligence, measured by reference to the standards of the prudent and responsible person. Although the civil wrong of negligence gives rise to liability for damages, it is relatively rare for negligence to form the basis for criminal liability, because the objective test it represents is contrary to the subjective principle of focusing on the mental state of the individual defendant. It is not unknown, however, and it is contended that cruelty falls into this category. Accordingly, it is enough to prove that the defendant was indifferent to, or disregarded, the animal's plight.[35]

F. *Mens Rea* and the Offence of Causing Unnecessary Suffering by Wantonly or Unreasonably Doing or Omitting to Do Any Act

The assertion that criminal liability for cruelty can be founded upon negligence is further illustrated by reference to the way in which the courts have interpreted the second limb of section 1(1)(a) of the 1911 and 1912 Acts. This provision is unique in the context of cruelty by including the words 'wantonly or unreasonably'.

In terms of prosecutions, causing unnecessary suffering as a result of a wanton or unreasonable act or omission is by far the most important single offence of

---

[32] *Hopson v DPP* (QBD, 11 March 1997) (emphasis added).
[33] *Barnard v Evans* [1925] 2 KB 794, 797–798.
[34] ibid 796 and 798 respectively (emphasis added).
[35] *Ford v Wiley* (1889) 23 QBD 203; *Duncan v Pope* (1899) 63 JP 217.

cruelty. Its meaning has been considered recently by the English High Court in *Hall v RSPCA*,[36] a case involving alleged cruelty to pigs. The animals in question were suffering from septic arthritis in the joints, together with associated lesions. It was common ground that there was nothing in the origin of this condition which reflected badly on the defendants; the point at issue was their response to it. They failed to seek veterinary advice, treated the animals themselves with an antibiotic, and continued to fatten them for a further three weeks until they reached optimum slaughter weight. Holland J, with whom Mann LJ agreed 'unhesitatingly', held that the word 'unreasonably' connoted 'a purely objective test'. It refers, he said, 'not to a state of mind, but to a prevailing external standard so that a subjective input is essentially irrelevant'. Applying this principle to the facts of the particular case, the appropriate objective standard against which to compare the defendants' conduct was that of 'the reasonably competent, reasonably humane, modern pig farmer'. Similarly, the same court applied an objective test in *RSPCA v Isaacs*,[37] which arose from the failure of a dog owner to consult a veterinary surgeon. In these circumstances, the test applied by the court was whether a reasonably caring, reasonably competent owner would have made the same omission.

The decisions in the *Hall* and *Isaacs* cases are discussed further in the following chapter. However, the imposition of an objective test is greatly preferable to a subjective one based on the sensitivity and standards of the individual defendant, which may fall considerably below those of the reasonably caring and humane person. The significance of an objective test is well demonstrated by comparing *RSPCA v Isaacs* with the earlier case of *Turner v Kiely*,[38] which similarly arose from an owner failing to seek veterinary advice. Here, the court applied a subjective test in holding that the prosecution was required to demonstrate not merely that the defendant had caused unnecessary suffering, but also, in the words of Taylor J, that he had 'the necessary guilty knowledge' in being 'aware there was a need to call the veterinary surgeon, and in that state of knowledge failed to do what was necessary in the circumstances'. The *Hall/Isaacs* formula also has the advantage that it avoids the types of equivocal reasoning which arose in *Peterssen v RSPCA*.[39] Here, the High Court held that the prosecution is required to prove the accused had what it described as 'guilty knowledge' of the fact that unnecessary suffering would or might be caused, and expressly denied that either recklessness or negligence were relevant to an offence charged under section 1(1)(a). The defendant had failed adequately to confine his dogs, with the result that they escaped and attacked sheep in an adjacent field. Morland J found that 'the appellant had guilty knowledge in the sense that he knew of the consequences that would result if he did not securely house his dogs'. Although this appears to prescribe a subjective test, the author of the accompanying editorial commentary in the law report criticizes the basis of the reasoning and suggests otherwise:

[36] QBD, 11 November 1993.   [37] [1994] Crim LR 517.   [38] QBD, 9 December 1983.
[39] [1993] Crim LR 852.

The appellant is held to have guilty knowledge because he knew that, if he left the dogs un-secured, they could escape and cause unnecessary suffering to sheep. This is not *guilty knowledge*. It is the awareness of a prudent man. . . . His failure to take the usual precautions seems a clear case of an unreasonable omission. The offence is one of negligence. Talk of *mens rea* and 'guilty knowledge' is confusing and misleading.[40]

Quite so. The judgment is an example of the dangers inherent in the use of tortuous language and confused reasoning; perhaps it arises from an innate reluctance on the part of the courts overtly to acknowledge criminal liability arising from negligence.

G. Emergencies—Still an Objective Test under Section 1(1)(a)

Significantly, the courts have also applied an objective test in circumstances where a defendant, confronted by what he regards as an emergency, has attempted to kill a domestic animal instantaneously, but succeeds only in injuring it. In such circumstances, the court asks whether the defendant has acted reasonably, regardless of his own view of the exigencies of the situation. Thus, in the Scottish case of *Farrell v Marshall*,[41] the Sheriff Court was satisfied that in the specific circumstances the defendant was not guilty of causing unnecessary suffering where he shot and wounded a dog which had attacked his cattle. Conversely, where the defendant had attempted to kill a terminally ill dog which was in considerable distress (and after having unsuccessfully attempted to summon professional assistance) by repeatedly hitting it over the head with a piece of wood, such conduct was condemned by the Sheriff as not being in accordance with contemporary moral sensibilities, although the accused was not convicted because of a lack of evidence that he had caused the dog to suffer.[42] Similarly, the English High Court recently upheld the magistrates' decision that there was no reasonable necessity for the defendant to shoot a dog because he could have taken some other action. This was so despite the fact that the dog had previously been running loose upon the defendant's land, had chased his geese, and, on the day in question, was discovered in a pig pen about a metre away from a pig's face with its teeth bared and barking. The crucial factor was the magistrates' finding that on the evidence the defendant 'chose to take no steps to chase off the dog', but instead 'his first action was to fetch a shotgun and shoot and injure her'.[43]

H. The Focus of the Objective Test

It is emphasized that the issue the court is focusing upon in applying an objective standard in relation to the fault element is whether a reasonable person would have

---

[40] ibid (italics in the original).
[41] 1962 SLT (Sh Ct) 65.
[42] *Tudhope v Ross* 1986 SCCR 467, 476.
[43] *Isted v Crown Prosecution Service* [1998] Crim LR 194; the quotations are taken from the transcript of the full judgment.

thought that the suffering was unnecessary. This is a separate and distinct question from that of whether the suffering was *actually* unnecessary. In most circumstances, the answer will be the same, and the distinction will have no practical effect. However, this is not always the case. For example, a failure to seek veterinary attention for an animal may actually cause it unnecessary suffering, but if the court is satisfied that it would not have been apparent to the reasonable person that the animal required professional treatment, then no offence has been committed.

This may be demonstrated by reference to the decision of the English High Court in *May v Broxton*.[44] The appellant had been convicted of causing unnecessary suffering to her ponies on the basis of the magistrates' finding that she failed to communicate their condition to a veterinary surgeon and to require him to attend to the ponies. The ponies were very much underweight, the result of a long-standing condition, and it was factually correct that the ponies had not been inspected by a vet. The full facts were, however, more complicated. A horse belonging to the appellant's mother which was kept with the ponies had died some time previously. A vet who carried out a post-mortem advised the mother, who passed the information on to her daughter, that the horse had been suffering from worms and there was a real risk that other horses which had been kept in the same field might have the same condition. In response, the appellant contacted the vet, who prescribed a course of treatment which she proceeded to carry out. Unfortunately, although the treatment prescribed was appropriate for worms that had actually developed, it was ineffective against the larval stage. Indeed, the evidence before the High Court suggested that the treatment probably contributed to worsening the ponies' condition. So, notwithstanding that the animals' health was deteriorating, and in ignorance of the fact that she was administering the wrong treatment, which thereby caused unnecessary suffering, the appellant continued to follow the vet's advice. The High Court found that, in these circumstances, the appellant could not be said to have acted unreasonably: the vet had given advice which would have seemed perfectly correct and sensible to a layperson; as such, she would have no reason to differentiate between mature worms and worms that were only at a larval stage; and she would not know either that a different treatment was necessary or the treatment prescribed by the vet would have the very reverse effect of what was intended. In the light of this evidence, the court was satisfied that it could not be established that the appellant had acted unreasonably, and the conviction was quashed. The vet might be criticized for having prescribed a treatment without seeing the animals, 'but that does not mean that the layman [*sic*] was acting unreasonably', concluded Ackner LJ. 'She was following advice given to her by an expert who considered himself competent to make the appropriate diagnosis and prescribe the right treatment.'

---

[44] QBD, 22 February 1983.

I. *Mens Rea* in Relation to Causing Unnecessary Suffering by Conveying, Carrying, Abandoning, or Tethering an Animal

Having advanced the argument that the legislative terms 'cruelly' and 'wantonly or unreasonably' include liability arising from negligence, as a result of indifference, disregard, ignorance, neglect, or a failure to meet accepted standards of care and humanity, it is suggested that the same objective test should be applied to those offences of cruelty based on causing unnecessary suffering where there is no specific statutory indication as to the nature of the requisite *mens rea*. In most cases, the issue will not arise because it will be the animal's owner who is accused of cruelty towards it, and the legislation provides that an owner is deemed to have permitted cruelty if he has failed to exercise *reasonable* care and supervision so as to prevent the animal suffering unnecessarily.[45] There is, however, a dearth of judicial authority as to the appropriate test in other situations, but an objective standard is clearly desirable for the reasons identified in *Ford v Wiley* and *Easton v Anderson*.

Unfortunately, the single relevant recent case decided by the English High Court points the other way. In *Hunt v Duckering*,[46] the court imported the notion of intention into the offence of abandonment. For the reasons identified in the previous chapter, it is doubted whether the application of a subjective test in these circumstances is either practical or consistent with Parliament's intention. In his judgment, Evans LJ concluded that 'the question of intention must and does have some relevance' since, in his Lordship's view, 'the statute is not concerned only with cases where the animal has, in fact, been left unattended for a period however long'. Having made a distinction between abandonment and leaving an animal unattended, the judge was confronted with the need to differentiate between the two concepts. The period during which the animal had been left was, in itself, insufficient, because the legislation provides that the offence may be committed where abandonment is temporary.[47] Moreover, the court recognized that there may be circumstances where one could say, 'immediately after the animal was left', that it had been abandoned. Accordingly, the court took the view that the question of whether an animal has been abandoned 'must involve some consideration of what arrangements had been made for its welfare during the period when it will be left unattended'. Although this suggests it is only one of the factors to be taken into account, the court went on to make it decisive in defining the offence. 'If a person

---

[45] 1911 Act, s 1(2); 1912 Act, s 1(2).

[46] [1993] Crim LR 678 (the 1911 Act is incorrectly referred to in the report as the Protection of Animals Act 1991). Quotations are taken from the unreported transcript of the full judgment.

[47] Section 1 of the Abandonment of Animals Act 1960 makes it an offence for the owner or any other person having charge or control of a domestic or captive animal without reasonable cause or excuse to abandon it, whether permanently or not, in circumstances likely to cause the animal any unnecessary suffering.

has made no arrangements at all,' Evans LJ said, 'then it may be relatively easy' to say that he has abandoned the animal 'in the sense of disregarding totally his duty to care for it'. However, 'where some arrangements had been made but they were apparently insufficient to prevent the animal from suffering in some way', it might be said that the defendant's duty to make arrangements for the animal 'had been neglected, but it would be difficult, as I see it, to say that the duty had been disregarded'.

As was stated in the previous chapter, it is submitted that this decisive emphasis on the defendant's intention as evidenced by his arrangements at the time of leaving the animal is inappropriate. It stems from the court's concern that, 'on the face of it', abandonment appeared to be 'an absolute offence'. In its anxiety to avoid strict liability, it is understandable that it introduced a requirement of *mens rea*, but an objective test would have been preferable. Instead of focusing exclusively on intention, it would be more fitting to ask, first, whether the defendant had disregarded his duty to care for the animal by leaving it unattended in circumstances where it was likely to be caused unnecessary suffering. If so, the onus should then pass to the defendant to demonstrate, on the balance of probabilities, that he had a reasonable cause or excuse for his conduct. This approach is not only consistent with the objective standard applied to other offences of cruelty based on unnecessary suffering, thereby conforming with the dictum of Schiemann J who, in an earlier case of alleged abandonment, said that 'one has to construe this section in the context of the Cruelty to Animals legislation which preceded it';[48] it also appears more accurately to reflect the literal meaning of the legislation.

Until such time as it is superseded by an amendment to the legislation, or repudiated by the High Court, the decision in *Hunt v Duckering*, unfortunately, remains binding on magistrates in England and Wales, and of persuasive authority in Scotland. It is, however, strongly argued that the decision is wrong.

J. Strict Liability Offences of Cruelty

In respect of strict liability offences, the defendant's mental state is irrelevant in determining guilt, to the extent that he may be convicted even though it was his express intention not to act cruelly. On the basis of the relevant wording, it is suggested that offences of cruelty which carry strict liability are: subjecting an animal to an operation which is performed without due care or humanity;[49] assisting at the fighting or baiting of domestic or captive animals; keeping, using, managing, or acting or assisting in the management of, any premises or place for the purpose, or partly for the purpose, of fighting or baiting such an animal; and receiving money for admission to such premises or place.

---

[48] *RSPCA v O'Sullivan* (QBD, 15 April 1986).   [49] *Braid v Brown* 1990 SLT 793.

K. Penalties Available upon Conviction for an Offence of Cruelty

Compared with other offences arising from the mistreatment of animals, the distinguishing feature of an offence of cruelty is the nature of the penalties which are available to the court.

(1) Sentence

Upon conviction for an offence of cruelty, a court may[50]

- impose a fine not exceeding level 5 on the standard scale (currently £5,000); or
- a term of imprisonment not exceeding six months; or
- both; and
- make an order to pay costs incurred by the prosecution, including those arising from the care of, and treatment to, the animal which was the subject of the prosecution.[51]

Where the owner of an animal is convicted of permitting cruelty by reason only of his having failed to exercise reasonable care and supervision, he is not liable to imprisonment without the option of a fine.[52]

(2) Orders in relation to animals

In addition, a court may:

1) where the *owner* of an animal is convicted,
   a) order the animal to be destroyed if it is satisfied that to keep the animal alive would be cruel (such an order, against which there is no appeal in England and Wales,[53] may only be made with the consent of the owner or upon the evidence of a veterinary surgeon);[54]
   b) deprive the person of ownership of the animal, provided there is evidence (previous conviction, character of the owner, or otherwise) that not to do so is likely to expose it to further cruelty;[55]

---

[50] 1911 Act, s 1(1); 1912 Act, s 1(1); Protection of Animals (Penalties) Act 1987, s 1; Protection of Animals (Scotland) Act 1993, s 1. Where more than one animal is involved, they may all be included in a single summons, but in such circumstances, assuming the defendant is found guilty, it will only constitute a single conviction: *R v Cable, ex parte O'Shea* [1906] 1 KB 719; *R v Rawson* [1909] 2 KB 748. Where the prosecution seeks a conviction in respect of each animal, separate summonses must be issued.

[51] 1911 Act, s 12(2); Prosecution of Offences Act 1985, s 18(1). In Scotland, prosecutions are brought by the procurator fiscal. Consequently, the SSPCA, unlike the RSPCA in England and Wales, does not bear any of the costs involved in prosecutions. In respect of the costs involved in caring for an animal that is the subject of court proceedings, the SSPCA may claim for compensation from the owner under the Criminal Procedure (Scotland) Act 1995, s 249(1).

[52] 1911 Act, s 1(2); 1912 Act, s 1(2).   [53] 1911 Act, s 14(1).   [54] 1911 Act, s 2; 1912 Act, s 2.

[55] 1911 Act, s 3; 1912 Act, s 3.

2) regardless of whether it is the owner who is convicted, disqualify for such period as it thinks fit, the *defendant* from having custody of any animal at all, or one of a kind specified in the order.[56]

Also, where the owner of an animal kept for a commercial purpose is prosecuted under section 1 of the 1911 Act, the Protection of Animals (Amendment) Act 2000 now gives the courts in England and Wales the additional power to make an order relating to the care, disposal, or slaughter of the relevant animal(s) *before* the proceedings have been completed.[57]

These powers are significant in that they are intended to prevent further cruelty being inflicted upon the victim and, in the case of a disqualification order, other animals. It should be noted, however, that a confiscation order differs in two important respects from a disqualification order. First, a confiscation order can be made only in relation to an animal whose treatment has resulted in a conviction for cruelty and, secondly, there must be evidence before the court that further cruelty is likely. However, a disqualification order, while not being subject to these two restrictions, is solely concerned with custody; it does not prevent the person to whom it applies from owning animals or, indeed, having further contact with them.

From the point of view of the prosecution, the main advantage of a confiscation order is that the court directs the future fate of the animal and prevents ownership being transferred to another family member. In contrast, where a disqualification order is made against the owner of an animal, there is no control over who gains custody of it. Whenever a court makes a disqualification order against the owner, therefore, it should normally be accompanied by a confiscation order directing who is to assume responsibility for the animal. Perversely, although it is an offence for a person to have custody of an animal in contravention of a disqualification order,[58] there is no power to seize the animal and thereby to give practical effect to the order.

(3) The meaning of 'custody' in relation to disqualification orders

The English High Court has declined to provide a detailed and comprehensive definition of what constitutes 'having custody' in this context, regarding it as a question of fact to be determined in the light of the particular circumstances. Nevertheless, in *RSPCA v Miller*[59] it has asserted that the essence of custody is control, or the power to control, and a person with *sole physical control* of an animal, even for a short time, has custody of it. However, the court also recognized

---

[56] Protection of Animals (Amendment) Act 1954, s 1, as amended by the Protection of Animals (Amendment) Act 1988, s 1. The word 'cattle' in a disqualification order includes any horse, ass, mule, bull, sheep, goat, or pig: *Wastie v Phillips* [1972] 1 WLR 1293.

[57] See Ch 14, s G(3) below.

[58] Protection of Animals (Amendment) Act 1954, s 2, as amended by the Protection of Animals (Amendment) Act 1988, s 1.

[59] [1994] Crim LR 516.

that it is possible for physical control to be shared between two or more people, for example members of the same household, such that one person might have actual physical control over an animal while simultaneously remaining subject to the direction, supervision, or control of another. The court held that in these circumstances the supervision by the latter may be so close that the person with actual physical control could not be said to have custody. On the basis of this reasoning, a disqualification order does not necessarily impose a complete ban on a person having a degree of physical control over an animal, provided it is shared with another person, and subject to the effectiveness of the direction, supervision, and control which that person is able to exercise.

(4) The problem of the approach adopted in *RSPCA v Miller*

On the facts of the particular case, which involved a person who was disqualified from having custody of dogs holding and walking a dog in a carnival procession, at the owner's request and in her company, it might seem reasonable to conclude that the disqualification order had not been broken. The Divisional Court observed that it was hard to imagine Parliament intended to criminalize so innocuous an action, when the dog remained under the owner's full visual supervision throughout, and there was no real possibility of harm to the animal. However, the introduction of considerations such as shared control, and the degree of direction and supervision by another, makes the meaning and enforcement of disqualification orders unduly complicated, especially in domestic and agricultural situations which may be difficult to police.

It is submitted that 'custody' should be interpreted strictly to include a situation in which a person has *any* degree of physical control over an animal or *any* degree of responsibility, either temporarily or permanently, for its care, treatment, or well-being. It is, after all, relevant that disqualification orders exist to *protect* animals from being exposed to the risk of cruelty from a person who has *already been convicted* of such an offence. Furthermore, it is open to a person against whom a disqualification order has been made to apply to have it removed, once it has been in effect for twelve months. In the light of the applicant's character, his conduct since the order was made, the nature of the offence of which he was convicted, and any other relevant circumstances, the court may decide to remove the disqualification, vary it so as to apply only to animals of a specified kind, or refuse the application. Even if the applicant is unsuccessful, he may make repeated applications on an annual basis until either his request is granted or the order expires.[60] Against this background, it would seem entirely appropriate that the courts should err on the side of caution in their interpretation of custody, and give the term a wide meaning.

The only case involving the issue of custody which has come before the High Court since the decision in *Miller*—*Taylor v RSPCA*[61]—arose from a situation in

---

[60] Protection of Animals (Amendment) Act 1954, s 1(3).   [61] QBD, 7 February 2001.

which two women, having been disqualified from having custody of horses for a period of ten years, had transferred ownership of their animals by gift to their niece. However, the evidence before the court was that it was they who had made arrangements with a farmer regarding the field in which the horses were kept, and they had also been observed providing food and water for the animals, without any other person being present. Having quoted at length from the judgment in *Miller*, but without giving any detailed consideration to the problems thrown up by its reasoning, Brooke LJ concluded that the facts of the case 'could quite properly have been taken as evidence that the appellants had custody of the horses. The appellants were there; they were responsible for the care of the horses; and they were making arrangements to feed and water them. There was no sign of the owner and the field in which the horses were based was a field in relation to which it was the appellants, and not the owner of the horses, who had always had dealings with the field's owner'. According to the judge, the magistrates were entitled to conclude that such circumstances amounted to a breach of the custody order, 'given the emphasis that this court made in the case of *Miller* on the matter being fairly and squarely within the domain of the lower court'.

Given the importance which the court in *Taylor* attached to *Miller*—Brooke LJ observed that, 'It appears to me important that those who have the responsibility for prosecuting and defending in such cases and, more particularly, those who have the responsibility of adjudicating in cases of this kind where someone is brought to court for breach of a disqualification order, should have access to the full report of the judgment . . . or, at any rate, the parts . . . which I have read into the present judgment, and that they should not merely have to rely on the very brief summary in the Criminal Law Review'—it might appear that it unreservedly endorsed its reasoning. However, although the court in *Taylor* purported to apply the jurisprudence of *Miller*, it did little more than give rein to the wide discretion enjoyed by magistrates to determine what amounts to custody, which had been identified in the earlier case. A detailed analysis was perhaps unnecessary in the light of the facts of the present case, but it should be noted that the court did not base its decision on the concept of *control* as laid down in *Miller*, but rather on the fact that the appellants were 'responsible for the care of the horses'. The decision therefore does nothing to address the difficulties and uncertainty inherent in the reasoning of *Miller*.

(5) Other consequences of a conviction for an offence of cruelty

Conviction for an offence of cruelty may also result in refusal, revocation, or disqualification of registration to train or exhibit performing animals;[62] or a licence

---

[62] Performing Animals (Regulation) Act 1925, s 4(2).

to keep a pet shop, an animal boarding establishment, a riding establishment, or a dangerous wild animal.[63] In addition, a local authority may revoke a zoo licence if the holder (or, where the holder is a body corporate, the body itself or any of its senior officers) is convicted of an offence under the Protection of Animals Acts, or if any of the keepers it employs has been so convicted and the licence holder is aware of that fact.[64]

L. Conclusion

The present law defining cruelty to animals has been in force since before the First World War, and its antecedents go back to the original animal protection legislation enacted in 1822. Its longevity must owe something to its effectiveness. In most cases of cruelty which come before the courts, there is no necessity to consider the nuances and niceties of legislative interpretation. Once the animal's suffering has been established, there is seldom any excuse for it and, if not inflicted intentionally, it will generally be possible to prove that the defendant knew, or must have known, of the animal's condition. To that extent, the legislation works well, and many who have practical experience of its application consider it to be both efficacious and successful. John Webster, for example, has written, in his own inimitable style, that the 1911 Act 'is to welfare legislation rather as Plato is to philosophy, i.e. it says most of what needs to be said and in simple language'.[65] As we have seen, however, detailed legal analysis reveals a number of significant practical problems. In part, this is due to the merger in 1911 of the two existing statutory provisions relating to cruelty into a single legislative subsection. While this might have seemed logical at the time, its manner has led to confusion over whether the first and second limbs of section 1(1)(a) relate to similar or separate and distinct offences. The continuing reliance upon nineteenth-century language and concepts has also created difficulties. The Scottish courts have, for example, complained that the statutory provisions are written in 'somewhat turgid and excessively detailed language'.[66] Similarly, the English High Court has recently described the present state of the law as 'unnecessarily confusing'. Section 1(1) of the 1911 Act, observed Brooke LJ, 'is framed by reference to the antique law underlying words like wantonly or unreasonably which is bound to go on giving trouble to those concerned with the administration of the law', and he remarked that 'it is surely high time' that the policy underlying the legislation was expressed in 'clear, intelligible modern language'.[67]

---

[63] Pet Animals Act 1951, s 5(3); Animals Boarding Establishments Act 1963, s 3(3); Riding Establishments Act 1964, s 4(3); Dangerous Wild Animals Act 1976, s 6(2). The same principle formerly applied to a licence relating to a dog breeding establishment, but this is no longer the case: Breeding of Dogs Act 1973, s 3(3), as amended by the Breeding and Sale of Dogs (Welfare) Act 1999.

[64] Zoo Licensing Act 1981, ss 4(4), (5), 17(1)(c), (d).

[65] *Animal Welfare. A Cool Eye Towards Eden* (1995) 259.

[66] *Patchett v Macdougall* 1984 SLT 152 (Note), 155 (Lord Hunter).

[67] *Isted v Crown Prosecution Service* [1998] Crim LR 194; the quotations are taken from the transcript of the full judgment.

In the meantime, it has been argued in this chapter that, in relation to most offences of cruelty, the defendant's behaviour is to be judged by the standards of a reasonably humane counterpart confronted by the same situation. Such offences extend beyond the deliberate infliction of suffering to include that which arises as a result of negligence, neglect, or a disregard for an animal's needs and interests. This objective test carries with it two important consequences. First, while retaining a degree of judicial discretion, it should prevent the members of the court being guided solely by their personal values and attitudes towards animals. Secondly, and most importantly, it provides greater protection for animals by ousting the particular motives, standards, and circumstances of the defendant.

In consequence, factors such as a lack of appreciation of the animal's needs, the defendant's domestic or financial situation, or his health or mental state, may be relevant in deciding whether to prosecute or the severity of the punishment, but they should not be taken into account in determining guilt. Claims by defendants to the effect that they love animals and would never be cruel to them do not constitute a defence; the fact that the defendant was not in a position adequately to look after an animal does not make its suffering necessary; and the owner who, for example, over-indulges their pet out of affection, to the extent that it becomes grossly obese resulting in attendant conditions such as respiratory and heart problems, diabetes, and painful joints, is just as culpable of causing unnecessary suffering as the person who neglects their animal. Conceivably, breeders who disregard a high risk of congenital conditions developing in the offspring may have a case to answer. Similarly, a person who fails to have their dog vaccinated against the likes of distemper, hepatitis, or parvovirosis, or allows their dog to stray, potentially may be liable if their animal contracts one of these diseases or is injured in a road traffic accident. The suffering caused is unnecessary, and arises because the conduct of someone, generally the owner, has fallen below that of the reasonably conscientious person. It is not suggested that it would be desirable for such people to be hauled indiscriminately before the courts and criminalized, but these examples serve to demonstrate the potency of the statutory offences of cruelty. They may be used not only to punish deliberate and wanton abuse of animals, but also, *by reference to the objective standards of the reasonably caring, reasonably humane man or woman, to promote responsible attitudes towards the care and treatment of animals*—the 1911 and 1912 statutes are, after all, entitled the *Protection* of Animals Acts.

The concept of 'unnecessary suffering' has been alluded to throughout this and the previous chapter. It is now appropriate to consider in detail the meaning of this term in the context of animal protection legislation.

10

Unnecessary Suffering

A. The Importance of the Unnecessary Suffering Test

'Now it is important to settle in one's mind, so far as it can be settled, clearly what is cruelty', asserted Lord Coleridge CJ in the leading case of *Ford v Wiley*. 'The mere infliction of pain, even if extreme pain, is manifestly not by itself sufficient', he suggested, not least because pain may be caused 'for reasons of beneficence, as in surgery or medicine'. It was, said the judge, lawful to inflict pain if it was 'reasonably necessary', a proposition which he recognized demands 'consideration of what "necessary" and "necessity" mean in this regard'.[1]

It is this concept of 'unnecessary suffering' which has become central to the legal definition of cruelty. It is not, however, exclusive to this context. It has also been widely adopted in Council of Europe conventions and EC legislation intended to protect animals,[2] as well as being used in domestic welfare law to define the benchmark for the proper treatment of animals in relation to farming,[3] transport and trade,[4] markets,[5] religious methods of slaughter,[6] and

---

[1] *Ford v Wiley* (1889) 23 QBD 203, 209.

[2] European Convention for the Protection of Animals Kept for Farming Purposes, arts 4(1), 6, and 7(1), as amended by the Protocol; European Convention for the Protection of Animals during International Transport, arts 12 and 25; European Convention for the Protection of Pet Animals, arts 3(1) and 7; Directive 86/609, preamble and art 7(4); Directive 88/166, recital and Annex, para 2; Directive 91/628, arts 3(1)(b)(i), 3(c), 3(2), 5(1)(c); Directive 93/119, Annex A, paras 1(6), 2(2); Directive 98/58, art 3 and Annex, paras 7 and 14; Directive 99/74, para 7.

[3] Welfare of Farmed Animals (England) Regulations 2000, SI 2000/1870, reg 3(1)(b); Welfare of Farmed Animals (Scotland) Regulations 2000, SSI 2000/442, reg 3(1)(b); Welfare of Farmed Animals (Wales) Regulations 2001, reg 3(1)(b). The Regulations relating to Wales came into force on 31 July 2001, but at the time this book went to press they had not been allocated an SI number. Henceforth, the three sets of regulations will be referred to collectively as the 'Welfare of Farmed Animals Regulations'.

[4] Animal Health Act 1981, ss 37, 41, and 64; Export of Horses (Protection) Order 1969, SI 1969/1784, arts 7, 10, and 12; Importation of Animals Order 1977, SI 1977/944, arts 3, 17; Export of Animals (Protection) Order 1981, SI 1981/1051, arts 3, 5, 6, and 13; Fresh Meat (Hygiene and Inspection) Regulations 1995, SI 1995/539, Sch 18; Welfare of Animals (Transport) Order 1997, SI 1997/1480, arts 4–7, 10, 18; and Sch 1, parts 1 and 2; Sch 2, parts 1 and 2; Sch 3, parts 1 and 2; Sch 4, part 2; Sch 5, parts 1 and 2.

[5] Welfare of Horses at Markets (and Other Places of Sale) Order 1990, SI 1990/2627, arts 6, 11, and 15; Welfare of Animals at Markets Order 1990, SI 1990/2628, arts 6, 10, and 15.

[6] Welfare of Animals (Slaughter or Killing) Regulations 1995, SI 1995/731, Sch 12, part 1.

wildlife.[7] So although there is no single, common principle which underpins animal protection legislation in the United Kingdom, the prevention of unnecessary suffering is a recurring theme. The legislative prevalence and uncertain meaning of the term require consideration of the way in which it has been interpreted by the courts. For it is the judiciary who, by defining what 'unnecessary suffering' means in practice, largely determine the extent of the protection afforded to animals by the law.

B. The Legal Nature of the Unnecessary Suffering Test

'It cannot', said Ridley J in *Dee v Yorke*, 'be a question of law, whether unnecessary suffering has been caused.'[8] In other words, it is a practical test rather than the application of a legal principle. Accordingly, whether there has been unnecessary suffering is a question of fact: the members of the court are required to exercise their own judgement in the light of the evidence before them. Given the subjective nature of the exercise, it is inevitable that, except in the most flagrant cases, there may be circumstances in which individual magistrates and sheriffs differ in their view as to whether an animal has suffered unnecessarily. That courts may come to different conclusions upon similar facts is therefore an inherent characteristic of the process.

Furthermore, the higher courts are reluctant to overturn such decisions. In their view, it is the court of first instance which is charged with determining whether an offence has been committed and, having been presented with all the evidence, heard the cross-examination at first hand, and had the opportunity to assess the witnesses, is best placed to reach a decision on the facts. In order to succeed on appeal, it will generally be necessary to demonstrate that the court below misapplied the law, or there was insufficient evidence to support its finding. It is no part of a higher court's role to overturn a decision simply because its members would have decided the case differently. The point is illustrated by the remarks of Lord Alverstone CJ, arising from an appeal in 1906 against the acquittal of a farmer for causing cruelty by the way he branded his sheep. 'If I were judging this matter as a question of fact,' said the judge, 'I should certainly come to the conclusion that it was not necessary to brand the sheep on the nose, but, sitting here, it is important that we should follow the rule long laid down. I am unable to see that the magistrates have applied a wrong test at all, and it is impossible for me to say that there was no evidence on which they could come to that conclusion.'[9]

Magistrates and sheriffs therefore enjoy considerable discretion to decide for themselves whether unnecessary suffering has been caused, but it is not unfettered. By reference to the relevant case law, it is possible to piece together a body of guidance emanating from the higher courts as to the nature and application of the

---

[7] Animal Health Act 1981, s 21(4); Wild Mammals (Protection) Act 1996, s 1; Plant Protection Products Regulations 1995, SI 1995/887, reg 6.

[8] (1914) 78 JP 359, 360.   [9] *Bowyer v Morgan* (1906) 70 JP 253, 255.

unnecessary suffering test. It is this which will now be analysed, starting from the basic proposition, enunciated by Hawkins J in 1889, that 'two things must be proved—first, that pain or suffering has been inflicted in fact', and, secondly, 'that it was inflicted cruelly, that is, without necessity, or, in other words, without good reason'.[10]

C. Suffering

The nature of animal suffering is considered further in the following chapter. The prosecution must, however, establish that an animal has suffered, either on the testimony of an expert witness, most usually a veterinary surgeon, or by necessary implication in the light of the available evidence. It is in relation to this issue that developments in our understanding of animal behaviour, physiology, and ethology can make an important contribution to the legal process. Mason and Mendl point out that 'Science can never "prove" that an animal is or is not suffering', but that it can be used for 'the collection of evidence from which to make inferences'.[11]

Originally, the courts equated suffering exclusively with the experience of pain, but the modern meaning is wider. On the basis that infuriating and terrifying an animal are specifically mentioned in the legislation which defines offences of cruelty, both physical and mental suffering are clearly relevant. Similarly, it used to be said that the degree of suffering had to be substantial,[12] but this is no longer the case. Neither does it necessarily have to be prolonged. The fact that an act which inflicts pain is done quickly 'does not make any difference', observed Kelly CB in *Murphy v Manning*. 'Let any one try to hold his hand over a flame for two seconds,' the judge mused, 'and I think he would say that half a minute, not to say a minute, was a long time.'[13] According to Lord Hunter, in the Scottish case of *Patchett v Macdougall*, the meaning of unnecessary suffering 'imports the idea of the animal undergoing, for however brief a period, unnecessary pain, distress or tribulation';[14] but suffering there must be.

(1) Death is not itself sufficient

In *Patchett v Macdougall*, the appellant had shot and killed a dog and, although it is evident from their judgments that all three judges were appalled by his conduct, they were also unanimous that a lack of evidence as to suffering meant that his conviction could not be upheld. Lord Cameron, for example, considered, 'Where, as here, no skilled opinion or direct evidence is available to support a finding that

---

[10] *Ford v Wiley* (1889) 23 QBD 203, 218 (Hawkins J).
[11] Mason, G and Mendl, M, 'Why is there no simple way of measuring animal welfare?' (1993) 2 *Animal Welfare* 301.
[12] *Swan v Saunders* (1881) 14 Cox C C 566, 570 (Grove J); *Ford v Wiley* (1889) 23 QBD 203, 210 (Lord Coleridge CJ).
[13] (1877) 2 Ex D 307, 313.   [14] 1984 SLT 152 (Note), 154.

the occurrence of death was or was not instantaneous', the prosecution had failed to discharge the burden of proving that any suffering was caused to the animal which was killed. 'In these circumstances,' said the judge, 'an essential link in the chain of proof is lacking.' He added, 'I regret the result at which I feel compelled to arrive, as I regard the actions of the appellant as wholly reprehensible.'[15] Similarly, Lord Hunter concluded, 'the absence of a positive finding to the effect that the act of the appellant caused the animal suffering is fatal to the conviction'.[16]

The court specifically rejected the suggestion that the situation automatically came within the statute because the dog had suffered loss of life. 'Metaphysical considerations apart,' observed Lord Wheatley, 'I do not consider that the structure and purport of the Act opens the door to that view.'[17] A similar opinion has recently been expressed by the English High Court. In *Isted v CPS*,[18] the court held that a person could not be convicted under section 1(1) of the 1911 Act if an animal was killed outright. This view is consistent with the ambit of the legislation: its purpose is to protect domestic and captive animals from unnecessary suffering, which includes *the manner* in which they die, but does not extend to safeguarding their lives. The morality of killing animals may be the subject of continuing controversy, but at present the law is clear: it is permissible to kill an animal (excepting those particular species which benefit from statutory protection), provided it is not accompanied by unnecessary suffering.

If an animal has died in circumstances where it is not possible to establish beyond reasonable doubt that it suffered immediately prior to death, it will not, except in the particular situations discussed in the following section, be possible to secure a conviction for causing unnecessary suffering. The person responsible can then be held accountable for his actions before the courts only if his conduct is such as to amount to another, different offence. If, for example, the only evidence available to the prosecution is a whole or partial skeleton of a farm animal which has been found lying in a field, it will generally be impossible to show that the animal suffered before it succumbed, even though there may be a strong suspicion that its demise was the result of starvation or a lack of veterinary attention. However, it may be the case that an offence has been committed as a result of having failed properly to dispose of fallen livestock.[19] Alternatively, a successful prosecution may occasionally be forthcoming as a result of imaginative application of the criminal law. So, in 1992, for example, a defendant who imported videos showing dog fighting was convicted under obscenity laws; more recently, it was reported that a man who threw a cat belonging to another person to the ground, killing it instantaneously, was convicted of thereby causing criminal damage.[20]

---

[15] 1984 SLT 152 (Note), 154.

[16] ibid. Lord Hunter, at 155, pointed out that although no statutory offence had been committed, the defendant could have been charged under the Scottish common law crime of malicious mischief.

[17] ibid 152.　　　　　　　　　　　　　[18] [1998] Crim LR 194.

[19] Dogs Act 1906, s 6; Animal By-Products Order 1999, SI 1999/646.

[20] RSPCA, *Animal Life*, Spring 1992, 7; *The Times*, 18 August 2000.

(2) Situations in which it is not necessary to establish suffering

There are, however, two important exceptions to the general rule that suffering must be established beyond reasonable doubt. First, in relation to abandoned animals, markets, and commercial transport, it is sufficient to demonstrate that the circumstances were *likely* to cause the animal unnecessary suffering.[21] At a practical level, this avoids difficult decisions for the prosecution in assessing when an animal's situation has crossed the line from inadequate to unlawful, especially in cases of neglect where its condition and environment may deteriorate gradually over a period of time. More significantly, this prospective test meets the principle which underlies the legislation, namely the *protection* of animals. It is ironic that, in most circumstances where cruelty is alleged, the law is powerless to intervene until an animal is actually suffering. Prior to that point, prevention is entirely dependent upon persuasion and encouragement. It was ever thus: an account of 'A Tame Lion Bait with Dogs' at Wombell's Circus, dating from 1825, records that 'Mr Martin's agent came down the day before and applied to the local authorities to stop the exhibition, but the Mayor, and, afterwards, a magistrate, refused to interfere on the ground that under Mr Martin's present Act no steps could be taken before the act constituting "cruelty" had been committed.'[22]

It is entirely desirable that wording which includes both actual and potential suffering should become the norm in animal protection legislation. It is strongly urged that policy makers and politicians should be looking to introduce a similar provision wherever it is presently an offence to cause unnecessary suffering.

The second exception is under the Wild Mammals (Protection) Act 1996, which makes it an offence to subject a wild mammal to specified forms of abuse with intent to inflict unnecessary suffering. In order to secure a conviction, it is therefore necessary to establish the defendant's intention, but it is not a requirement that unnecessary suffering actually occurred.

D. Necessity

Once it has been demonstrated that the animal suffered (or, where appropriate, was likely to suffer), attention turns to the question of necessity. Causing *necessary* suffering does not constitute an offence. Whether suffering is deemed to be unnecessary depends upon a number of factors, including its nature, the circumstances in which it arises, and the perspective of the observer. 'What amounts to a necessity or

---

[21] Abandonment of Animals Act 1960, s 1; SI 1990/2627 and SI 1990/2628, n 5 above, art 6(2); SI 1997/1480, n 4 above, art 4(1). It is also an offence to hire out, or use for paid riding instruction, a horse which is in such a condition as would be likely to cause it suffering (there is no requirement in this context that the suffering should be unnecessary): Riding Establishments Act 1964, s 3(1)(a).

[22] Cited in Fairholme, EG and Pain, W, *A Century of Work for Animals. The History of the RSPCA, 1824–1924* (1924) 41.

good reason for inflicting suffering upon animals protected by the statute is hardly capable of satisfactory definition', said Hawkins J in the nineteenth-century case of *Ford v Wiley*. While he recognized that 'each case in which the question arises must depend upon a variety of circumstances', the judge asserted that 'the amount of pain caused, the intensity and duration of the suffering, and the object to be attained, must, however, always be essential elements for consideration'. What is envisaged, then, is a balancing exercise, in which different factors will be assigned varying degrees of importance, depending upon the circumstances. 'To attain one object,' the judge acknowledged, 'the infliction of more pain may be justified than would ever be tolerated to secure another.'[23]

To cause an animal to suffer in the absence of a legitimate object is prima facie evidence of unnecessary suffering. The situation is more complicated when suffering arises as a consequence of furthering a legitimate purpose. In these circumstances, the crucial issue is the respective weight the courts attach to the conflicting interests of man and animal, especially in commercial situations. This was the question which the High Court had to consider in *Ford v Wiley*. The case involved a farmer who had caused two-year-old cattle to have their horns sawn off as close to the head as could be done using a common flat saw, a procedure which all the expert evidence agreed would result in extreme and prolonged pain. The farmer sought to justify his conduct on the grounds that he would get a better price for dehorned cattle, they would take up less space, and they would be unable to gore one another. In determining whether these advantages to the farmer were enough to make the suffering he had caused to the cattle permissible, the court had before it two decisions of the Irish courts, both of which had arisen from a similar situation. However, each had been decided differently on the basis of the disparate reasoning which had been adopted by the respective courts which heard the appeals.

(1) *Brady*: a legitimate object does not of itself inevitably excuse suffering

In the first of these, *Brady v McArdle*,[24] the primacy of commercial advantage had been rejected because, in the words of Dowse B, 'there is a limitation to the power of owners of beasts, and that limitation is that the act done must not be unreasonable and unnecessary'. Accordingly, '*all the circumstances* of the case ought to be considered'.[25] Similarly, Andrews J thought dehorning done simply 'for the purpose of convenience and profit' was not in itself a sufficient defence; it still had to be shown 'to be necessary and reasonable under *all the circumstances*'.[26] Following this precept, the judge concluded, '*Even if there were no other means of effecting the same purposes*, regard must be had to the nature of the act complained of, the manner in which it was done, and the amount of suffering thereby inflicted on the animals.'[27] On this authority, undue suffering may be unlawful, notwithstanding that it arose in pursuit of a legitimate object, which led the court to conclude in *Brady*

---

[23] (1889) 23 QBD 203, 218.   [24] (1884) 15 Cox C C 516.   [25] ibid 524 (emphasis added).
[26] ibid (emphasis added).   [27] ibid (emphasis added).

that the defendant should have been convicted because 'the objects sought to be attained do not . . . justify the means which were used to accomplish them'.[28]

(2) *Callaghan*: a legitimate object overrides even extreme suffering

This approach is in stark contrast to that where the court focuses predominantly on the purpose of the suffering. Thus, in the second Irish case, *Callaghan v The Society for the Prevention of Cruelty to Animals*, which arose from almost identical facts, Morris CJ said that the suffering 'cannot . . . be considered unnecessary, for *the object is reasonable and adequate*'.[29] According to Harrison J, the practice of dehorning 'is a reasonable one, and necessary for the proper carrying on of this system of straw-yard winter feeding, which is largely and profitably practised in many parts of Ireland, and which is a reasonable and proper mode of cattle farming'. Having come to this view, the judge considered 'the fact that the operation is attended with pain is not sufficient to constitute it a cruel or criminal act'. On the basis of this analysis, the court took the view that a practice which is regarded as legitimate can only be considered unlawful if unnecessary pain is inflicted in the sense that it is not properly or skilfully performed.[30] Such reasoning disregards any relationship between means and ends, and fails to provide adequate protection, as the court's conclusion clearly demonstrates: 'The pain caused to the animals in this case cannot be said to be an unnecessary abuse of the animal . . . if the operation by which the pain is caused enables the owners to attain this object either more expeditiously or more cheaply.'[31]

(3) The significance of the approach adopted

These two cases provide a useful illustration of the way in which the courts, confronted by two very similar situations, can arrive at completely different conclusions, depending upon how they perceive the relevant issues. In consequence, *even though the judges in each case were applying exactly the same statutory provision, its application differed significantly*. Clearly, then, the wording of the legislation is not the ultimate determinant of the degree of protection afforded by the law; it is the courts' interpretation of the term 'unnecessary suffering' which is crucial.

(4) *Ford v Wiley*: the means must be proportionate to the object

Returning to the English case of *Ford v Wiley*, the court, confronted by these two conflicting Irish decisions arising from similar facts, emphatically rejected the functionalist approach endorsed in the *Callaghan* case. 'There is no necessity and it is not necessary to sell beasts for 40s more than could otherwise be obtained for them', asserted Lord Coleridge CJ, 'nor to pack away a few more beasts in a farm

---

[28] ibid.   [29] (1885) 16 Cox C C 101, 103 (emphasis added).   [30] ibid 104–105.
[31] ibid 105 (Murphy J). This conclusion was subsequently endorsed by the Irish courts in *R v McDonagh* (1891) 18 ILR 204.

yard, or a railway truck, than could otherwise be packed; nor to prevent a rare and occasional accident from one unruly or mischievous beast injuring others. These things may be convenient or profitable to the owners of cattle, but they cannot with any show of reason be called necessary.'[32] Similarly, Hawkins J expressly rejected the notion that the pursuit of profit could in itself legitimatize suffering. 'If the law were that any man or any body of men could in his or their own interests, or for his or their pecuniary benefit, cause torture and suffering to animals without legitimate reason,' he exclaimed, 'it is difficult to see the limits to which such a principle might not be pushed, and the creatures it is man's duty to protect from abuse, would oftentimes be suffering victims of gross ignorance and cupidity.'[33]

It does not follow from this that the interests of animals will always take priority over the convenience or commercial considerations of their owner, but neither can it be assumed that the interests of man automatically take precedence over those of an animal. Indeed, the court expressly dissented from previous judicial statements which appeared to suggest that no operation, however painful, amounted to cruelty if its purpose was to make an animal 'more serviceable for the use of man'.[34] As in *Brady v McArdle*, the court in *Ford v Wiley* balanced the purpose to be achieved against the consequences for the animal. According to Lord Coleridge CJ, even if the suffering arises from something which may 'fairly and properly' be done to the animal, it should nevertheless involve 'only such pain as is reasonably necessary to effect the result'. Accordingly, and in contrast to the conclusion reached in the *Callaghan* case, even though the *objective* is deemed to be necessary, and therefore lawful, the court must also have regard to the *means* by which it is achieved. This is so *even if there is no obvious alternative*. Echoing the judgments in the *Brady* case, the Lord Chief Justice said, 'Necessity to form an excuse under the statute does not mean ... simply that the effect of an operation cannot be otherwise secured.'[35]

On this basis, the judge suggested that determining necessity was a two-stage process. First, it must be shown that the animal's treatment was to effect an 'adequate and reasonable object'; secondly, 'There must be proportion between the object and the means.'[36] Applying these criteria to the facts, he concluded that 'to put thousands of cows and oxen to the hideous torments described in this evidence in order to put a few pounds into the pockets of their owners is an instance of such utter disproportion between means and object, as to render the practice as described here not only barbarous and inhuman, but I think clearly unlawful also'.[37] Hawkins J, with whom Lord Coleridge specifically agreed 'both in substance and in expression',[38] explained further that 'the beneficial or useful end sought to be attained must be reasonably proportionate to the extent of the suffering caused,

---

[32] *Ford v Wiley* (1889) 23 QBD 203, 209.   [33] ibid 225.
[34] *Murphy v Manning* (1877) 2 Ex D 307, 314 (Cleasby B).
[35] *Ford v Wiley* (1889) 23 QBD 203, 209 and 215.   [36] ibid 210 and 215.   [37] ibid 215.
[38] ibid 208.

and in no case can substantial suffering be inflicted, unless necessity for its infliction can reasonably be said to exist'.[39]

Following *Ford v Wiley* a quarter of a century later, Darling J, in *Waters v Braithwaite*, held that 'where unnecessary suffering is caused by some act of an owner it cannot be justified on the ground of old custom and of benefit to commercial persons'.[40] The prosecution had arisen from a tradition in Oxfordshire to expose cows for sale at market in an unmilked state in order to demonstrate their productivity. It was not denied that the practice caused considerable pain, and the court was categorical in its condemnation: 'The pain was unnecessary as far as the cow was concerned. . . . If the custom of doing this exists it is time that it should cease, and people must find some other means of judging whether a cow is a good milker or not.'[41] It is not accurate, therefore, to suggest, so far as English and Scottish law are concerned, that 'the only time an animal wins the balancing test is when the human has no recognized interest to balance against the animal's interests'.[42]

(5) Unnecessary suffering does not mean causing the least possible suffering

There is, however, an important caveat in respect of the *Ford v Wiley* formula of necessity. Namely, the courts will consider a practice which is expressly or by implication permitted by legislation (as opposed to originating in custom) to be legitimate, provided it is carried out in a reasonable manner. This is so, even though there may be an alternative means of achieving the same end which causes less suffering.

The term 'unnecessary suffering' does not therefore always require that animals be treated in the way which causes them the least possible suffering. The relevant test is that an animal is not caused to suffer unnecessarily by the standards of the legislatively sanctioned practice which has been adopted. This point is particularly important in relation to the commercial rearing of livestock. In *Roberts v Ruggiero*,[43] for example, the appellant argued that raising veal calves by keeping them continuously tethered individually in stalls, unable to turn round, with no bedding, and feeding them exclusively on liquids, was contrary to section 1(1)(a) of the Protection of Animals Act 1911. In upholding the magistrates' decision to dismiss the charges, the High Court specifically distinguished this situation from that in *Ford v Wiley*. According to Stephen Brown LJ, 'this case is very different indeed, because the magistrates did not find that suffering was caused to any of the calves in this instance beyond that which was general in animal husbandry', and he rejected the appellant's request that the court should take account of other methods of raising veal calves:

---

[39] ibid 219.   [40] (1914) 78 JP 124, 125.   [41] ibid; cf *Bowyer v Morgan* (1906) 70 JP 253.
[42] Francione, GL, *Animals, Property, and the Law* (1995) 160.   [43] QBD, 3 April 1985.

The alternative systems which were introduced into evidence . . . related to entirely different systems of husbandry. . . . The question indicates that the real purpose of the prosecutor in this case was to attack this system of intensive farming. This was a very much wider question than that which the magistrates had to consider. . . . They were not concerned with a general comparison of various forms of intensive farming which undoubtedly arouse considerable controversy.

Stocker J agreed, observing:

the specific allegations in the charges were supported by evidence not of any physically observable injury to or ill-health of the calves, but by the proposition that the method of husbandry practised must have been inappropriate to their physiological and ethological needs and, thus, the cruelty alleged is established. This proposition was supported by the contention that cruelty was 'self evident' (to quote [counsel for the appellant's] own phrase) and supported by the opinions of the experts and as alternative methods were available the proposition is established that the suffering was 'unnecessary'.

Such an approach seems to me to constitute a general criticism of the methods of husbandry . . . . but a Magistrate's Court is, in my view, not the appropriate forum in which, nor is a criminal prosecution the appropriate method by which, the legality of the system of husbandry should be established.

Clearly, there is an inherent danger that the law thereby sanctions what may be termed institutional cruelty. Ruth Harrison drew attention to the anomaly that 'if one person is unkind to an animal it is considered to be cruelty, but where a lot of people are unkind to a lot of animals, especially in the name of commerce, the cruelty is defended and, once large sums of money are at stake, will be defended to the last by otherwise intelligent people'.[44] Against this background, there is some force in Francione's contention that 'The question whether the conduct is "necessary" is decided not by reference to some moral ideal but by reference to norms of exploitation already deemed legitimate.'[45] It is, however, important to appreciate that unnecessary suffering is not the only test by which the treatment of animals is judged. It is always open to the legislature (subject to the constraints imposed by WTO rules and EC law) to introduce other regulatory standards, including those which expressly override traditional industry practices. Indeed, the system of raising veal calves which was at issue in the *Roberts* case has since been prohibited by legislation.[46]

(6) The meaning of necessity in the context of the second limb of section 1(1)(a) of the 1911 and 1912 Acts

We have seen that where a legitimate object is involved, determining whether suffering is necessary will normally involve a balancing exercise. However, a rather

---

[44] Harrison, R, *Animal Machines* (1964) 144–145.

[45] Francione, GL, *Rain Without Thunder. The Ideology of the Animal Rights Movement* (1996) 130.

[46] Welfare of Calves Regulations 1987, SI 1987/2021; now superseded by the Welfare of Farmed Animals Regulations, n 3 above, Sch 4. See also, Directive 97/2 and Decision 97/182, both of which amend Directive 91/629.

different meaning has been applied to necessity in the context of the second limb of section 1(1)(a) of the 1911 Act. This relates to wantonly or unreasonably doing or omitting to do any act which causes an animal unnecessary suffering. Because of its general nature, it is this provision which is most commonly relied upon in bringing prosecutions for cruelty; the way in which it is interpreted is therefore of particular practical significance. In two recent cases, *Hall v RSPCA*[47] and *RSPCA v Isaacs*,[48] the English High Court has held that 'unnecessary' in this context is to be interpreted to mean 'not inevitable' or 'could be avoided or terminated'. This suggests a much more restrictive test than that involving the balancing exercise, but in practice this is not so. The reason for the apparent discrepancy lies in the wording of the legislation. This is the only offence of cruelty which specifically includes the adverbs 'wantonly or unreasonably' in relation to causing unnecessary suffering. Uniquely, therefore, this particular offence of cruelty is made up of three separate components:

1. *unreasonable* conduct on the part of the defendant;
2. resulting in an animal *suffering*; and
3. that suffering being *unnecessary*.

In *Hall v RSPCA*, Holland J held that considerations such as the reason for the suffering, together with its nature, intensity, and duration—the balancing exercise referred to in *Ford v Wiley*—are to be taken into account in determining whether the defendant acted *unreasonably*. It would be inappropriate, he said, to repeat this exercise in deciding whether the suffering was *unnecessary*. It is this which allows the court to equate 'unnecessary' with terms such as 'avoidable', or 'not inevitable'. According to Holland J, 'unnecessary' is to be taken to mean that the statute 'implicitly postulates that for an animal there may be suffering which is inevitable despite proper husbandry so as to be "necessary"', and the word therefore 'seeks to distinguish as an element for a prosecution that suffering which is not inevitable; that suffering which could be avoided or terminated and is thus "unnecessary"'. Such a meaning cannot be applied to 'unnecessary' in relation to the other offences of cruelty defined by reference to unnecessary suffering, which are made up of only two components: *suffering*, which is *unnecessary*. To do so would oust the balancing exercise, thereby making *any* suffering which was not avoidable or inevitable potentially illegal, regardless of its purpose, nature, duration, or intensity. While this might be welcomed by some animal welfare campaigners, it is clearly not the intention underlying the legislation.

(7) The *Hall/Isaacs* test

It will be recalled from the previous chapter that the *Hall* case arose from the failure of the defendants to seek veterinary advice in respect of pigs which had septic arthritis and associated lesions. The Halls decided instead to treat the animals

---

[47] QBD, 11 November 1993.   [48] [1994] Crim LR 517.

themselves for three weeks until the pigs reached optimum slaughter weight. Combining the court's interpretation of 'unnecessary' under the second limb of section 1(1)(a) with its view that 'unreasonably' connoted an objective standard in relation to *mens rea*,[49] the court posed three questions:

1. Did the pigs suffer?
   - If yes,
2. was the suffering necessary 'in the sense of being inevitable'?
   - If no,
3. would a reasonably competent, reasonably humane modern pig farmer have tolerated such a state of suffering?
   - If the answer is again no, the defendant is guilty of the offence.

On the facts of the case, the court found that the pigs did suffer; such suffering was not inevitable because the animals could have been slaughtered sooner; and there was not sufficient evidence presented to establish that a reasonably competent, reasonably humane modern pig farmer would have allowed such suffering to continue for three weeks. In relation to the final point, it was not enough, the court said, for the defendant to demonstrate the presence of similarly afflicted pigs on well run farms; it appeared to place the onus on the defence to produce evidence that those running such farms would have considered it acceptable to prolong the animals' suffering in the same way as the Halls had done.

Incidentally, the case provides a useful insight into the role of the court under an adversarial system. Unlike an inquisitorial tribunal, it does not undertake its own enquiries, but reaches its decision entirely on the basis of the evidence presented by the parties. Similarly, the court may not surmise or conjecture what the situation might be in the absence of evidence to support its conclusion. Hence, the decision in *Hall v RSPCA* does not amount to authority for the proposition that anyone acting in the same way would automatically be guilty of cruelty. If a defendant was able to produce evidence that a significant body of competent and humane pig farmers would find the suffering acceptable, he might be acquitted. It is not for the court to establish this, the responsibility lies entirely with the defence. This is one reason why courts may come to different decisions on the basis of apparently similar facts. Quite simply, there may be significant differences in the evidence which is presented to the court or the manner in which it is argued. In the *Hall* case, the prosecution had made out its case that the animals had suffered unnecessarily, and the defendants failed to show that they had acted reasonably. Another defendant facing prosecution on the basis of similar facts might be able, by advancing a different argument in his defence, to persuade the court that his conduct was justified.

The day following their decision in *Hall v RSPCA*, the same two judges, in *RSPCA v Isaacs*, applied an identical formula to a case of omission, in which the

---

[49] Discussed at Ch 9, s F above.

defendant admitted that she had failed to seek veterinary treatment for her dog for ten years, fearing it might be put down because of its appalling condition.[50] In these circumstances, the questions posed were:

1. Did the dog suffer?
   - Yes.
2. Was the suffering inevitable, in that it could not be terminated or alleviated by some reasonably practicable measure?
   - No.
3. Would a reasonably caring, reasonably competent owner have made the same omission?
   - No.

This novel analysis of the meaning and application of the second limb of section 1(1)(a) of the 1911 Act laid down in the *Hall* and *Isaacs* cases is to be welcomed both for its clarity and effect. It is easy to understand, straightforward to apply, and the objective test it imposes is greatly preferable to a subjective one based on the sensitivity and standards of the individual defendant, which may fall considerably below those of the reasonably caring and humane person. There are, however, two important points to make about this test. First, the objective standard to be applied will vary according to the status of the defendant: a veterinary surgeon will be judged by the standards of that profession; a farmer by those common in the industry; and the owner of a companion animal would be expected to meet the standards of the responsible amateur. Thus, the conduct of a professional dog breeder should, for example, be assessed by reference to the assumed knowledge and experience of their peers, rather than that of the 'ordinary' pet owner. Secondly, in relation especially to the rearing of commercial livestock, the application of an objective test—the standards of the reasonably competent, reasonably humane pig farmer, for example—results in the defendant being judged by the prevailing standards within the industry. If these are themselves less than satisfactory, prosecutions will only be successful in the most extreme circumstances. Similarly, where there are different views within the industry as to what constitutes an acceptable degree of competence and humanity, the courts will not automatically require the *highest* of such standards to be met. Accordingly, the test of unnecessary suffering is not in itself an appropriate mechanism for ensuring best practice. Indeed, the court does not have to decide which of two accepted practices is the better; although not directly applicable to cases of cruelty, this situation is redolent of the well-known '*Bolam* test', applied by the courts in cases of medical negligence. This lays down that a doctor who acts in accordance with a practice accepted at the time as proper by a responsible body of medical opinion possessing the relevant skill or competence is not negligent merely because there is a body of

---

[50] n 48 above.

competent professional opinion which might adopt a different technique. This does not, however, permit a doctor 'obstinately and pig-headedly [to] carry on with some old technique if it has been proved to be contrary to what is really substantially the whole of informed medical opinion'.[51]

(8) The status of the decision in the *Hall* and *Isaacs* cases

As decisions of the High Court, the *Hall* and *Isaacs* cases are binding on magistrates in England and Wales. The wording of section 1(1)(a) of the 1912 Act is identical, and they are therefore of persuasive authority in Scotland. It must be appreciated, however, that because of the specific wording of this particular offence of cruelty, the *Hall/Isaacs* formula cannot be applied mechanically to other offences of cruelty. While the strength of the *Hall/Isaacs* test is its simplicity, its consequence is to complicate further the statutory meaning of unnecessary suffering. It is largely a result of the somewhat clumsy way in which the existing legislation was consolidated into a single statute in 1911. While never underestimating judicial capacity for creativity, it will probably require parliamentary intervention to overcome this anomaly.

E. *Mens Rea* in Relation to Unnecessary Suffering Otherwise than in the Context of an Offence of Cruelty

The meaning and significance of *mens rea* was discussed in the previous chapter. In was suggested that in relation to the offences of cruelty arising from unnecessary suffering, an objective standard should normally be applied unless the defendant was indirectly responsible, in which case a subjective test is required.

In relation to offences arising from unnecessary suffering other than those defined as offences of cruelty, prosecutions brought under the Wild Mammals (Protection) Act 1996 require a subjective test to be applied because the legislation stipulates that the defendant must be shown to have *intended* to inflict unnecessary suffering on the animal. In contrast, other offences are generally ones of strict liability, where the defendant's mental state is irrelevant in determining guilt. For example, the imperative nature of article 4(1) of the Welfare of Animals (Transport) Order 1997, which states that 'no person shall transport any animal in a way which causes or is likely to cause injury or unnecessary suffering to that animal', is characteristic of a strict liability offence. The wording takes the form of a mandatory prohibition, and there is nothing to indicate that the defendant's state of mind is a constituent of the offence. This is not so draconian as it may initially appear, as there is a statutory defence: notwithstanding that the animal was caused unnecessary suffering in transit, the defendant is not guilty of the offence if he can

---

[51] *Bolam v Friern Hospital Management Committee* [1957] 1 WLR 582, 586 (McNair J).

establish, on the balance of probabilities, that he had a lawful authority or excuse for his conduct.[52] Similarly, article 6(2) of the Welfare of Animals at Markets Order 1990 is a strict liability offence. This imposes a duty on any person in charge of an animal in a market to ensure that it is not, or is not likely to be, caused injury or unnecessary suffering by reason of exposure to bad weather, inadequate ventilation, as a result of being hit or prodded, or 'any other cause'. According to the High Court, the wording is such that 'there could be no controversy at all as to whether strict liability is imposed'.[53]

F. Unnecessary Pain and Unnecessary Distress, and Avoidable Excitement, Pain, or Suffering

Finally, consideration must be given to two other statutory offences arising from the treatment of animals where a slightly different formula has been employed. Namely, 'unnecessary pain and unnecessary distress' in relation to livestock on agricultural land,[54] and 'avoidable excitement, pain or suffering' while they are at an abattoir prior to slaughter.[55]

(1) Unnecessary pain and unnecessary distress

In the absence of judicial authority from the higher courts on the meaning in law of unnecessary pain or distress, the following is largely conjecture, but it is suggested that a similar formula should be applied to that developed for unnecessary suffering. Thus,

- Has the animal been caused pain or distress?
- Did the pain or distress arise in the pursuit of a legitimate object?
- If so, was the pain or distress proportionate to the objective to be achieved?

In addition, arising from the wording of the provision, three further questions must also be asked:

- Was the livestock on agricultural land at the time of the alleged offence?
- Did the accused cause the unnecessary pain or distress and were the animals under his control?
- Or, if not, did the accused permit the livestock to suffer unnecessary pain or unnecessary distress in the sense that he knew or may reasonably have been expected to know the state that the animals were in?

---

[52] Animal Health Act 1981, ss 72 and 73; Welfare of Animals (Transport) Order 1997, art 21.
[53] *Davidson v Strong* The Times, 20 March 1997. Article 6(2) of the Welfare of Horses at Markets (and Other Places of Sale) Order 1990 is similarly worded and may therefore also be regarded as a strict liability offence.
[54] Agriculture (Miscellaneous Provisions) Act 1968, s 1(1).   [55] SI 1995/731, n 6 above, reg 4(1).

This, of course, still leaves the important issue of what, if any, is the distinction between unnecessary *suffering* under the 1911 and 1912 Acts, and unnecessary *pain* and *distress* under the 1968 Act? At first sight, the two phrases would appear to be tautologous: self-evidently, an animal which has been caused unnecessary pain or distress could also be described as having suffered unnecessarily. Yet, it is reasonable to assume that there must be *some* difference, because the maximum penalty for each offence under the 1911 and 1912 Acts is a fine of £5,000, six months' imprisonment, or both; whereas under the 1968 Act it is either a fine of £2,500 or three months' imprisonment. Moreover, it is only the former which allow the courts to impose confiscation and disqualification orders.

The point has not come before the higher courts to be decided, but it is submitted that the distinction lies in the fault standard applicable to the respective offences. Those of cruelty under the 1911 and 1912 Acts have a *mens rea* element, albeit an objective test, whereas the wording of the first limb of section 1(1) of the 1968 Act ('any person who causes unnecessary pain or unnecessary distress to any livestock') suggests that it is intended to be a *strict liability* offence. In contrast, the second limb, relating to a person who *permits* the unnecessary pain or distress (as distinct from causing it), requires at least an objective standard of *mens rea* ('of which he knows or may reasonably be expected to know'), which is itself unusual; where the defendant is accused of permitting an offence, a subjective test is generally applied.

If this interpretation is correct, then it explains the difference in penalties. There is less culpability involved in the strict liability offence, hence a lower maximum sanction. It also has important practical implications: if the offence of causing unnecessary pain or unnecessary suffering *is* one of strict liability, then not only does the intention or knowledge of the accused become irrelevant, so too does the reasonable person test. Unlike offences of cruelty, criminal liability would then turn exclusively on whether the animal experienced unnecessary pain or distress.

(2) Avoidable excitement, pain, or suffering

Again, there is no judicial authority on the meaning of 'avoidable' in the context of the Welfare of Animals (Slaughter or Killing) Regulations 1995. The phrase 'avoidable excitement, pain or suffering' originates in the European Convention for the Protection of Animals for Slaughter,[56] from where it was adopted into EC legislation,[57] and thence into the domestic regulations. On the basis of the everyday meaning of the word, it is submitted that it ousts the proportionality test which is central to determining necessity. In other words, the degree, intensity, and duration of the excitement, pain, or suffering, together with the reason for causing it, all cease to be relevant considerations. The question focuses exclusively on whether it could have been avoided. This distinction between 'unnecessary suffering' and 'unavoidable suffering' is supported by the fact that the former phrase also appears

---

[56] Article 2(3).   [57] Directive 93/199, arts 3 and 4.

in both the directive[58] and the regulations.[59] That they are used in association with one another in the same legislation is a strong indication that the respective terms are intended to convey different meanings.

G. Conclusion

Because the 1911 Act was a consolidation statute, *Ford v Wiley* remains good law, despite having been decided in 1889. It is authority for the proposition that necessity amounts to having a good reason to cause an animal to suffer. To establish this involves a balancing exercise, in which account must be taken of *all* relevant considerations. The alternative approach, represented by *Callaghan v SPCA*, where undue emphasis is placed on the object to be achieved in isolation from other factors, especially the degree of suffering caused to the animal, is inapposite. Taken to its logical conclusion it leads to an absurd outcome, such as that in the nineteenth-century Scottish case of *Renton v Wilson*, where the local practice adopted in Fife, Forfar, and Kincardine of sawing off horns was held to be lawful, even though it was proved that the operation caused great pain, because the *purpose* (preventing the animals goring each other) was legitimate, notwithstanding that the pain itself was *unnecessary*, there being evidence before the court that, in other parts of Scotland, the same objective was achieved painlessly using an alternative method.[60]

In summary, determining whether suffering is unnecessary involves consideration of the following factors:

- It must be established that the relevant animal has suffered or, where appropriate in the light of the legislative wording, is likely to suffer.
- In order to amount to a legitimate purpose, the object must be, according to the court in *Ford v Wiley*, 'adequate and reasonable'.
- Demonstrating that the suffering arose to further a legitimate purpose is not in itself conclusive evidence that it is necessary (and therefore lawful). Considerations such as convenience, profitability, and lack of an alternative must be balanced against the degree of suffering involved. Accordingly, the presence of a legitimate purpose does not of itself inevitably sanction suffering. There must be, again adopting the language employed in *Ford v Wiley*, 'proportion between the object and means'.
- It is therefore important to have regard to all relevant factors. In particular, undue weight should not be accorded to the legitimate object in isolation from the effects upon the animal.

[58] ibid, Annex A, paras 1(6) and 2(2).   [59] SI 1995/731, n 6 above, Sch 12, para 2.

[60] (1888) 2 White 43; cf the English case of *Adcock v Murrell* (1890) 54 JP 776 where the court upheld the magistrates' decision to convict the appellant over the way in which he had slaughtered a pig, having rejected his defence that he had a legal right to kill the pig, and pain inflicted for a lawful purpose cannot amount to cruelty.

- The absence of a legitimate purpose, such as non-prophylactic cosmetic surgery, is prima facie evidence that suffering is unnecessary. In relation to tail docking, for example, Hawkins J, while acknowledging that it 'may occasionally be justified', nevertheless expressed as long ago as 1889 his 'very strong opinion against allowing fashion, or the whim of an individual, or any number of individuals, to afford a justification for such painful mutilation and disfigurement'.[61]
- In relation to the question of *mens rea*, offences arising from causing unnecessary suffering fall into each of the three categories: subjective, objective, and strict liability.

The concept of unnecessary suffering, which has been developed by the courts and widely adopted by the legislature, has two very considerable merits. First, it may be applied to a multitude of different situations. Secondly, it can be constantly reinterpreted by the courts in the light of greater understanding about animal suffering, and changing social attitudes regarding the proper treatment of animals. These valuable characteristics dispense with the need constantly to amend and update the legislation. The prohibition on causing unnecessary suffering has undoubtedly made a major contribution to improving the treatment of animals, but it is essentially negative in character; it focuses largely on what should *not* be done to an animal. The concept remains central to the legal protection of animals, but in recent years attention has focused increasingly on the welfare of animals, and with it the imposition of positive duties to further that end. As Webster correctly points out, 'The care of animals involves more than just the absence of cruelty.'[62] It is to this topic that we now turn.

---

[61] *Ford v Wiley* (1889) 23 QBD 203, 219–220.
[62] Webster, J, *Animal Welfare. A Cool Eye Towards Eden* (1994) 89.

Part E

Welfare

11

The Nature of Animal Welfare

A. Cruelty and Welfare Distinguished

To cause an animal to suffer unnecessarily, or to subject it to any other treatment which amounts to an offence of cruelty, is self-evidently detrimental to its welfare. To that extent, there is a degree of affinity between cruelty and welfare, but the two are far from being synonymous: prejudicing an animal's welfare does not of itself amount in law to cruelty. There are other important differences. An animal may or may not become the victim of cruelty during the course of its life, but *every* animal can be said to have a welfare, which persists for the duration of its existence. The state of this welfare will vary according to the circumstances which confront the animal, together with its physiological and behavioural response to them. In consequence, at any given time, the state of its welfare will be located on a point somewhere along a spectrum between very good at one end, indicating an excellent quality of life, and, at the other, so poor that it ultimately proves to be fatal. Welfare is therefore inherent to the individual, albeit influenced by external factors, whereas cruelty is something which is inflicted upon an animal as a result of the act (or omission) of, in law, a human being. Furthermore, cruelty is defined as much by reference to the attitude and behaviour of the perpetrator, and the object which he seeks to achieve, as it is by the effect upon the victim, while welfare is concerned exclusively with assessing the state of the individual animal. This involves taking account of influences which may be either positive or negative, while cruelty is concerned only with treatment that is deleterious. This distinction is reflected in the thrust of public policy. On the one hand, the intention is to *prevent* cruel treatment by proscribing particular forms of behaviour. On the other, the aim is to *promote* improved standards of welfare by identifying those matters which are important to animals, and translating these into rules, guidance, and advice, to which those responsible for their care are required to have due regard. Last, but by no means least, animal welfare is principally a *scientific* notion, which has emerged as a discrete area of study only comparatively recently;[1] cruelty, in contrast, is a long-established *legal* test.

B. The Brambell Committee

Indeed, notwithstanding that it has become a major factor influencing legislative, political, and administrative arrangements concerning the treatment of animals,[2] as well as defining the nature of a veterinarian's professional duty,[3] it is important to appreciate the relative novelty of welfare. Whereas the concept of cruelty to animals has been entrenched in the law since 1822, and a similar idea has existed in common parlance to refer to the abuse of animals for much longer, welfare did not emerge as an identifiable area of scientific study or a factor influencing public policy towards animals until the second half of the 1960s. The turning point came with the deliberations of the Brambell Committee and its subsequent report.[4] Established in the wake of the publication of *Animal Machines*, Ruth Harrison's critique of modern farming methods, the Committee was asked 'to examine the condition in which livestock are kept under systems of intensive husbandry and to advise whether standards ought to be set in the interest of their welfare and if so what they should be'. These terms of reference, the originality of which should not be overlooked, allowed the Committee to consider man's responsibilities towards agricultural animals in a new way, an opportunity which it exercised to the full.

'Welfare is a wide term that embraces both the physical and mental well-being of the animal', the Committee pronounced, and any attempt to evaluate it 'must take into account the scientific evidence available concerning the feelings of animals

---

[1] However, use of the term 'welfare' in relation to other species dates back to at least the eighteenth century. In 1796, for example, John Lawrence complained that man's view of animals as having been created merely for his use had resulted in their 'natural interests and welfare' having been 'sacrificed to his convenience, his cruelty or his caprice': 'On the Rights of Beasts' in Nicholson, ER, *The Rights of an Animal. A New Essay in Ethics* (1879) 72.

[2] See, for example, the European Convention for the Protection of Animals kept for Farming Purposes, art 2; European Convention for the Protection of Pet Animals; Treaty of the European Community, Protocol on protection and welfare of animals (see Ch 5, s A(4) above); Regulation 1255/97, preamble; Regulation 411/98, preamble; Directive 91/628, art 5A(1), as amended by Directive 95/29; Directive 97/2, preamble; Directive 98/58, art 3; Directive 99/22, art 3; Directive 99/74, preamble; Agriculture (Miscellaneous Provisions) Act 1968, ss 2 and 3; Animal Health Act 1981, s 39(1); Breeding and Sale of Dogs (Welfare) Act 1999; Welfare of Horses at Markets (and Other Places of Sale) Order 1990, SI 1990/2627; Welfare of Animals at Markets Order 1990, SI 1990/2628; Welfare of Animals (Slaughter or Killing) Regulations 1995, SI 1995/731; Welfare of Animals (Transport) Order 1997, SI 1997/1480; Welfare of Farmed Animals (England) Regulations 2000, SI 2000/1870; Welfare of Farmed Animals (Scotland) Regulations 2000, SI 2000/442; Welfare of Farmed Animals (Wales) Regulations 2001 (at the time this book went to press, the latter had not been allocated an SI number). Since 1992, an agriculture minister has been specifically assigned responsibility for animal welfare issues; he is supported by the Department's Animal Welfare Division.

[3] Upon admission to membership of the Royal College of Veterinary Surgeons, every veterinarian is required to make a declaration which includes a formal promise that 'my constant endeavour will be to ensure the welfare of animals committed to my care'.

[4] *Report of the Technical Committee to Enquire into the Welfare of Animals Kept Under Intensive Livestock Husbandry Systems* (1965).

that can be derived from their structure and functions and also from their behaviour'.[5] This involves paying 'special attention to the possible cumulative effect on the animal of the long continuance of conditions which might be tolerable or even acceptable in the short term', but which if they caused prolonged stress, discomfort, or deprivation may be of 'much more significance for the total welfare of the animal than more acute, but transitory, suffering'.[6] Most significantly, especially in relation to livestock production, the Committee rejected as 'oversimplified and incomplete' the view that an animal's productivity could be taken as 'decisive evidence' of the state of its welfare.[7]

On the contrary, it argued, there were many factors to be taken into account, and only by having regard to them all could an animal's welfare be measured and, ultimately, improved. Thus it attached importance to animal health; to threats posed by hazards such as fire risks, failure of environmental control and automatic feeding systems, slippery floors, the possibility of entanglement or strangulation to caged or tethered animals; and the need for adequate ventilation and lighting, and appropriate temperature controls.[8] On the basis that farm animals belong to species which have an organized social life, the Committee expressed the view that they needed companionship, and should not be kept in solitary confinement. The practice of providing a diet deficient in some essential component was repudiated, regardless of whether it led to an overt pathological condition, as was that of including in the diet components calculated to upset the normal functions of the animal, except in so far as these were necessary under veterinary prescription for the prevention or treatment of disease. Floors, it said, should be constructed in such a way that made an animal feel secure when standing, and not so as to produce undue strain on the legs or feet or to result in malformation of them; there should be appropriate balance between periods of illumination and darkness; and appropriate measures taken to prevent or minimize undesirable habits which can arise because of confinement, such as fighting, feather pecking, and tail and ear biting.[9] All mutilation of animals was condemned 'in principle', but mutilation which affected their normal behaviour and was carried out to counter a defect in the system of husbandry was singled out for particular criticism. According to the Committee, mutilation of an animal is only acceptable in circumstances 'where the overall advantage to the animal, its fellows, or the safety of man, is unmistakable'.[10]

Furthermore, the Committee emphasized the importance to an animal of being able to engage in its natural behaviour. While recognizing that confinement could be advantageous to an animal, in providing shelter and protection, the Committee cautioned that the advantages must be weighed against the inherent disadvantages. In determining whether particular situations were acceptable, it suggested that two factors should be taken into account. First, the degree to which the animal's behavioural urges were affected; and, secondly, the duration of the confinement: 'In principle

---

[5] ibid para 25.   [6] ibid para 29.   [7] ibid para 30.   [8] ibid paras 31, 33, and 40–43.
[9] ibid paras 38, 39, 40, 44, and 45.
[10] ibid para 34. This principle is equally applicable in other contexts, such as the tail docking of dogs.

we disapprove of a degree of confinement of an animal which unnecessarily frustrates most of the major activities which make up its natural behaviour and we do not consider such confinement or restraint permissible over a long period unless the other advantages thereby conferred *upon the animal* are likely to be very substantial.' At the very minimum, the Committee considered that the animal should have 'sufficient freedom of movement to be able, without difficulty, to turn round, groom itself, get up, lie down, and stretch its limbs'.[11]

C. The Five Freedoms

As a direct consequence of the Brambell Committee's report, the term 'welfare' was embodied for the first time into animal protection legislation in Britain,[12] and many of the factors which Brambell identified as being important to an animal's welfare have since been incorporated into legislation and official guidance. Unlike cruelty, however, the meaning of the term 'welfare' itself has not been explicitly defined in law.

The European Convention for the Protection of Animals Kept for Farming Purposes, agreed by the Council of Europe, lays down what are described as 'principles of animal welfare'. These include a requirement that livestock should be housed and provided with food, water, care, freedom of movement, and environmental conditions appropriate to their physiological and ethological needs in accordance with established experience and scientific knowledge. In addition, it is specified that no animal shall be provided with food or liquid in a manner, or containing any substance, which may cause unnecessary suffering or injury, together with requirements concerning inspection of the animals themselves and, in the case of intensive systems, the technical equipment which is in use.[13] These provisions are 'an integral part' of the EC's legal order by virtue of the fact that the Community is a contracting party to the Convention but, in the light of their very general wording, the ECJ has expressed the view that they are 'indicative only'.[14] Accordingly, merely to incorporate them verbatim into EC law would not of itself be sufficient. It has therefore proved necessary to stipulate in EC legislation requirements which seek to reflect the standards called for in the Convention, but are more precisely defined.[15]

In the absence of a legal definition, the nearest one comes to an 'official' statement of the nature of good welfare is that developed by the Farm Animal Welfare Council (FAWC). According to FAWC, 'good animal welfare implies both fitness

[11] *Report of the Technical Committee to Enquire into the Welfare of Animals Kept Under Intensive Livestock Husbandry Systems* (1965) paras 36 and 37 (emphasis added).

[12] Agriculture (Miscellaneous Provisions) Act 1968, ss 2, 3, and 4.

[13] Articles 2–7, as amended by the 1992 Protocol.

[14] *R v Minister of Agriculture, Fisheries and Food, ex parte Compassion in World Farming*, Case 1/96 [1998] 2 CMLR 661, ECJ, paras [31] and [34].

[15] See further, Ch 6, s D(2) above.

and a sense of well-being', and it suggests that these can be effectively promoted by reference to what are referred to as the 'Five Freedoms'. While these 'define ideal states rather than standards for acceptable welfare', FAWC suggests that they nevertheless 'form a logical and comprehensive framework for analysis of welfare'. They are:

1. *Freedom from thirst, hunger, and nutrition* by ready access to fresh water and a diet to maintain full health and vigour.
2. *Freedom from discomfort* by providing a suitable environment including shelter and a comfortable resting area.
3. *Freedom from pain, injury, and disease* by prevention or rapid diagnosis and treatment.
4. *Freedom to express normal behaviour* by providing sufficient space, proper facilities, and company of the animal's own kind.
5. *Freedom from fear and distress* by ensuring conditions and treatment which avoid mental suffering.[16]

'Freedom' in this context constitutes 'a possibility to have self determination by carrying out an action or avoiding a problem'.[17] It also means taking positive measures to ensure that these criteria are, as far as possible, achieved, not simply leaving the animal to fend for itself. Indeed, extensive husbandry can be just as demanding in terms of management and stockmanship as intensive methods. The House of Commons Agriculture Committee, for example, found that keeping it outside 'undoubtedly comes as close as practicable to giving the pig scope for its full natural behaviour', and recognized that 'in suitable conditions' such a system can work well, but went on to observe that 'the charms of a sunny May morning are less apparent on a wet January afternoon and, on heavy land in bad winter weather, conditions so far from being idyllic can be thoroughly unpleasant for both the stockman and the pigs'.[18] FAWC has made a similar point. Having concluded that outdoor pig production not only has welfare advantages for the animals, but can also achieve the objects of the Five Freedoms, it warned that it is nevertheless 'particularly susceptible to variations in management, stockmanship, climate and site suitability'.[19]

The Five Freedoms have no formal status in either English or Scottish law but they have been widely adopted as an appropriate benchmark for the development of animal welfare policy, not only in Britain but also further afield. Their influence is apparent in domestic legislation and official advice, such as the codes of recommendations for the welfare of livestock issued under the authority of the

---

[16] FAWC, *Report on Priorities for Animal Welfare Research and Development* (1993) paras 8 and 9. The concept of the Five Freedoms was originally proposed by John Webster, himself a founder member of FAWC: see, for example, Webster, AJF, *Calf Husbandry, Health and Welfare* (1984).

[17] Scientific Veterinary Committee, *Report on the Welfare of Intensively Kept Pigs* (1997) para 1.4.

[18] House of Commons Agriculture Committee, *Animal Welfare in Poultry, Pig and Veal Calf Production* (1981) para 79.

[19] *Report on the Welfare of Pigs Kept Outdoors* (1996) paras 14(g) and 25.

Agriculture (Miscellaneous Provisions) Act 1968, and has been explicitly acknow-ledged in relation to zoo standards;[20] they have formed the basis for a number of quality assurance schemes, most notably the RSPCA's Freedom Food; and the World Veterinary Association has endorsed the same criteria (albeit in a slightly different formulation).[21]

D. The Concept of Welfare

(1) A relative concept

As Webster concedes, the Five Freedoms are not 'a counsel of perfection', but 'an attempt to make the best of a complex and difficult situation'. He points out that they are, nevertheless, helpful in two respects: they offer 'a set of first principles for an approach to the understanding of welfare as perceived by the animal itself'; and, when used as 'the framework for an evaluation of the welfare of a particular group of animals in a particular environment', they serve to ensure 'there is a fair chance that nothing of importance will be forgotten'.[22] They are not, however, intended to constitute a formula which can be applied mechanically to each and every situation. Indeed, Webster suggests that absolute attainment of all Five Freedoms would be both unrealistic, because they are to some extent incompatible, and superfluous, since 'it is not, in fact, necessary to the welfare of an animal (or man) to have absolute freedom' from or to the factors enumerated in the formula.[23]

The Five Freedoms can therefore be regarded as aspirational rather than pre-scriptive. Moreover, while serving as indicators of good welfare, they do not in themselves provide an explication of the meaning to be attached to the term 'wel-fare'. This remains an issue of some controversy, and many writers have attempted to provide such a definition.[24] Broadly, these fall into two groups. On the one hand, the word is used in a way which reflects its dictionary definition—well-being, hap-piness, health, and prosperity. Hence, welfare is presented as an exclusively positive concept. Hughes, for example, describes it as 'a state of complete mental and phys-ical health where the animal is in harmony with its environment'.[25] Likewise,

[20]   DETR, *Secretary of State's Standards of Modern Zoo Practice* (2000) Introduction, para 4.

[21]   Freedom from hunger and thirst; from physical discomfort and pain; from injury and disease; from fear and distress; and to conform to essential behaviour patterns: World Veterinary Association policy state-ment on animal welfare, well-being and ethology (1991) 7(2) *World Veterinary Association Bulletin* 38.

[22]   Webster, J, *Animal Welfare. A Cool Eye Towards Eden* (1994) 13 and 251. Webster has written else-where: 'Philosophically, the Five Freedoms define a platonic ideal state, unachievable, but a worthy para-digm. More practically, they may be used as a comprehensive checklist by which to assess the welfare of animals whether in the farm, the home or the laboratory, in transit or at the place of slaughter'; Webster, AJF, 'What use is science to animal welfare?' (1998) 85 *Naturwissenschaften* 262, 263.

[23]   ibid.

[24]   See further: Mason, G and Mendl, M, 'Why is there no simple way of measuring animal welfare?' (1993) 2 *Animal Welfare* 301; Fraser, D et al, 'A scientific conception of animal welfare that reflects ethical concerns' (1997) 6 *Animal Welfare* 187.

[25]   Hughes, BO, 'Behaviour as an index of welfare', *Proceedings 5th European Poultry Conference, Malta* II: 1005–1012.

Tannenbaum suggests that it refers to 'a state that includes some measure of a successful life',[26] and the philosopher, Stephen Clark, has written that animal welfare 'must be that state of condition or habitual activity in which animals are "well-off"'.[27] In contrast, 'welfare' is also used as a relative, not an absolute, term. Thus, to Broom, 'The welfare of an individual is its state as regards its attempts to cope with its environment',[28] a definition which has regard 'to both how much has to be done in order to cope with the environment and the extent to which coping attempts are succeeding'.[29] It is this meaning which has been adopted by FAWC.[30] Similarly, in the sense that he also focuses on the animal's response to its circumstances, Webster offers as his 'best attempt at a single-sentence definition' the view that 'the welfare of an animal is determined by its capacity to avoid suffering and sustain fitness'.[31] There is an important distinction between these two approaches and it is the latter, represented here by Broom and Webster, which is to be preferred because it recognizes that the term encompasses a variety of different conditions. As Webster puts it:

The welfare of any animal is determined by the state of its mind and body; how it feels within a spectrum that ranges from suffering to pleasure and its ability to sustain physical and mental fitness. If an animal is to achieve a sense of mental wellbeing, its physical and social environment should allow it to act to avoid hunger, thirst, heat, cold, pain, sickness, fear, frustration, exhaustion, etc. before the intensity of these potential sources of suffering becomes too severe. If it is to sustain physical fitness, then imposed methods of breeding, feeding, housing and any artificial manipulations should not be allowed to compromise its ability to live its allotted, maybe brief, life span without suffering from physical problems such as chronic pain, hunger or exhaustion.[32]

(2) The significance of an animal's ability to cope

According to the European Commission's Scientific Committee on Animal Health and Welfare:

In the course of evolution every animal species has adapted to an environment in which it is able to regulate its internal state and to survive and reproduce. Regulatory systems in animals consist of the detection of changes in that environment and responses to these changes which allow the animal to keep internal and external conditions at an optimal level. In other words, the animal tries to control its environment by using various coping mechanisms. Feelings play an important role in these coping mechanisms, as do behavioural, physiological, biochemical and immunological responses.[33]

[26] Tannenbaum, J, 'Ethics and animal welfare: The inextricable connection' (1991) 198 *Journal of the American Veterinary Medical Association* 1360, 1362–1363.
[27] Clark, SRL, 'Ethical Problems in Animal Welfare' in Clark, SRL, *Animals and their Moral Standing* (1997) 114.
[28] Broom, DM, 'Indicators of poor welfare' (1986) 142 *British Veterinary Journal* 524.
[29] Broom, DM and Johnson, KG, *Stress and Animal Welfare* (1993) 75.
[30] For example, *Report on the Welfare of Dairy Cattle* (1997) para 6.   [31] n 22 above, 11.
[32] ibid 127.
[33] Scientific Committee on Animal Health and Animal Welfare, *Welfare Aspects of the Production of Foie Gras in Ducks and Geese* (1998) para 1.2.

In attempting to cope with its environment, then, an animal relies on the normal regulation of its body state such as the functioning of body repair systems, immunological defences, and a variety of behavioural responses. When these are inadequate, it falls back on emergency responses such as high adrenal activity and increased heart rate.[34] Fraser and Broom provide a useful explanation of the biology:

When conditions are difficult, individuals use various methods to try to counteract any adverse effects of those conditions on themselves. One set of methods involves the use of the adrenal gland whose products mobilize energy resources and minimize the use of energy for certain everyday bodily processes. Another way of trying to deal with difficult conditions is to modify behaviour so that the state of the animal is returned to the tolerable range. Behaviour can also be used to alter the motivational state and hence ameliorate the most extreme psychological disturbances. A coping system which has recently been discovered incorporates the use of naturally occurring opioid peptides in the brain which have an analgesic effect during pain or in other unpleasant conditions. The animal can reduce aversiveness by self-narcotization. Whatever the method used, the individual may try to cope and succeed, or it may try and fail. The extent of what is done to try to cope can be measured, as can the effects of lack of success. These measurements will show how poor the welfare is and other sorts of measures give some information about how good welfare is.[35]

It follows that, although the prevailing conditions are always going to have an extremely important bearing on an animal's welfare, it is the way in which it responds to them which is the ultimate determinant of the state of the individual: 'If an animal is affected by environmental conditions but its regulatory systems, with their behavioural and physiological components, allow it to cope, then *adaptation* is said to occur. This situation is fundamentally different from one in which the environmental effect has detrimental consequences.'[36] Three important implications arise from this analysis. First, a challenge—even a serious challenge—confronting an animal will not necessarily be inimical to the quality of its long-term welfare, so long as it is able to adapt effectually (hence, mild but prolonged suffering may be more detrimental to an animal's welfare than a short-term or transitory serious challenge). Secondly, there may be circumstances in which there is no moral obligation upon us to take steps to preclude *all* potential challenges to the welfare of animals for which we are responsible. Some such experiences may be beneficial as learning exercises; others may provide essential stimulation; none will pose an enduring threat so long as the animal concerned can cope. As Broom and Johnson point out, 'animals have evolved to cope with a degree of environmental disturbance', and animals 'cope better when they have previously faced occasional bouts of at least middle noxious stimulation'. Similarly, there are situations in which pain can be of value to animals, depending on the circumstances and the nature of their lifestyle, and it may be in their interests to allow

---

[34] n 29 above, 75.   [35] Fraser, AF and Broom, DM, *Farm Animal Behaviour and Welfare* (1990) 256.
[36] ibid 258 (emphasis in the original).

them to endure it, even though it is detrimental to them in the short term.[37] Thirdly, because they respond to it differently, the same challenge may prove detrimental to the welfare of one animal, but not to another. Hence it is not enough simply to provide conditions which are generally considered to be adequate for the species in question, or which are sufficient for the majority of a particular group of animals which are kept together. High standards of welfare require due regard to *each individual's* ability to cope satisfactorily with its environment.[38] 'It is, after all,' observes Marian Dawkins, 'individuals that have the subjective experiences and individuals that have the potential for suffering.'[39]

(3) The issue of sentiency

It follows from this contention that in order to assess the state of an animal's welfare one must attempt so far as is possible to establish how it feels. 'Let us not mince words', asserts Dawkins, 'Animal welfare involves the subjective feelings of animals.'[40] This assumes, of course, that at least some non-human species are sentient, in the sense that they not only respond to their environment, but also have the capacity to be *aware* of their condition. In other words, the circumstances in which such animals are kept, the way they are treated, and the extent to which they are successful in coping with their situation matters to them because they are to some extent conscious of the consequences.[41] If it were otherwise, the concept of good welfare would amount to little more than establishing that animals are functioning efficiently, as one might maintain and service a piece of machinery. This issue cannot be ignored. As recently as 1992, for example, the late JS Kennedy, one time Professor of Animal Behaviour at Imperial College, London, expressed the view that 'it seems likely that consciousness, feelings, thoughts, purposes, etc. are unique to our species and unlikely that animals are conscious'. This led him to regard what he described as 'the layman's approach to the problem of animal welfare' to be 'unhesitatingly anthropomorphic', and the public demand for legal protection of animals to be 'fuelled by this feeling more than logic'. Further, he considered the scientific community to be equally culpable, if not more so. Apparently, their 'overreadiness to believe that animal suffering has been as good as proved' shows that they also have 'an anthropomorphic bias, stemming from the

---

[37] n 29 above, 166.

[38] FAWC have, for example, expressed the view that 'welfare assessment concerns individual animals', albeit that 'where there are indications of poor welfare, we consider the problem to be more serious when more animals are affected': n 30 above, para 9.

[39] Dawkins, MS, *Animal Suffering. The Science of Animal Welfare* (1980) 33.

[40] Dawkins, MS, 'From an animal's point of view: Motivation, fitness, and animal welfare' (1990) 13 *Behavioural and Brain Sciences* 1.

[41] This is not the place to discuss the difficult and controversial concept of consciousness. Suffice it to say that there is considerable merit in Appleby's suggestion that consciousness should be considered 'not as all-or-nothing, but as something that animals may possess to a greater or lesser extent', and that different species experience different degrees and kinds of suffering with the result that 'it is not productive to attempt any categorization of animals into those that can suffer and those that cannot': Appleby, M, *What Should We Do About Animal Welfare* (1999) 48 and 50.

spontaneous fellow-feeling for higher animals which scientists have in common with other people'.[42]

In contrast, the development of animal welfare science has proceeded on an interpretation of the available evidence which comes to the diametrically opposite conclusion. Namely, that many species of animals are capable of experiencing physical pain and, of those, some may be said to have a degree of consciousness, and may therefore also suffer psychologically. The Brambell Committee, for example, both recognized that animals 'show unmistakable signs of suffering from pain, exhaustion, fright, frustration, and so forth', and accepted that they can also 'experience emotions such as rage, fear, apprehension, frustration and pleasure'.[43] Dawkins, more forthrightly, asserts that 'Scientific evidence as well as common sense now demand that we take the step of inferring consciousness in species other than our own.'[44] For Webster, meanwhile, the 'most simple and satisfactory way to interpret the motivation and conscious behaviour' of sentient animals is that they 'are aware of how they feel; *and it matters to them*', and he declares himself to be 'convinced by the evidence that mammals and birds have the capacity to experience both suffering and pleasure'.[45] Similarly, Broom and Johnson conclude that 'Our knowledge of the complexity of the organization of the brain and behaviour of other vertebrate animals is such that it now seems inconceivable that these animals do not also have subjective feelings', one consequence of which is that if an animal is suffering 'then the welfare will always be poor'.[46] Manning and Dawkins not only note that 'A substantial number of animal behaviour workers would now accept that, no matter how difficult they may be to study, it is no longer sensible to deny the possibility of true thought processes and even consciousness of some sort in some mammals and birds', they also point out that there is a powerful evolutionary argument to support this conclusion: 'It is hard to accept that the mind and consciousness in human beings have just arisen *de novo* without *any* precursors which were ancestral to us and probably very similar to the non-human primates which we observe now.'[47]

This modern debate over the sentiency of other species is reminiscent of the issues which the early reformers had to confront in the eighteenth and early nineteenth centuries. It might have been thought the Cartesian view of animals as automatons had long since been rejected. The body of legislation designed to protect them from cruelty and to promote their welfare is predicated in Britain on an acceptance, underpinned by scientific opinion, that animals are sentient, and, as we have seen, so much is formally acknowledged in EC law.[48] While it may not be possible to prove indisputably that other species are able to suffer, the (growing)

---

[42] Kennedy, JS, *The New Anthropomorphism* (1992) 24, 114, and 118.

[43] n 4 above, paras 26 and 28.

[44] n 39 above, 2. See also, Dawkins, MS, *Through Our Eyes Only? The search for animal consciousness* (1993) 178.

[45] n 22 above, 249 and 250 (emphasis in the original).   [46] n 29 above, 80 and 82.

[47] Manning, A and Dawkins, MS, *An Introduction to Animal Behaviour* (1998) 296 (italics in the original).

[48] See Ch 5, s A(4) above.

body of scientific evidence is such that, first, the precautionary principle requires that policy makers should proceed on the assumption that this is indeed so; and, secondly, the onus has passed to those who believe this not to be the case to demonstrate otherwise. As the geneticist, Richard Dawkins, warns,

there is a danger of elevating humanity to a moral status—a uniqueness—which is not justified. So, for example, in the infliction of pain, it is all too easy for people to assume that inflicting pain on humans is qualitatively of a different order than inflicting pain on, say, chimpanzees or cows. . . . I think that a great deal of evil is done in the world through erecting a wall around the species *homo sapiens* . . . and forgetting that we are animals; we are apes, we are African apes. There is no good reason to suppose that we are unique in the ability to suffer.[49]

E. Suffering

(1) The nature of suffering

While widespread acceptance that other species have the capacity to suffer is of enormous practical and symbolic importance, it raises a further question as to the nature of suffering itself. According to Marian Dawkins, 'Suffering occurs when unpleasant subjective feelings are acute or continue for a long time *because the animal is unable to carry out the actions that would normally reduce risks to life and reproduction in those circumstances*.'[50] She attaches importance to the words in italics because, away from the wild, she considers 'there is more likelihood that the animal will be prevented from taking the usual steps to remove itself from danger or correct other aversive conditions'.[51] So, for her, suffering is taken to mean 'a wide range of unpleasant emotional states', which may arise as a result of fear, pain, frustration, exhaustion, the loss of social companions, together with other states of suffering of which humans are not aware.[52] However, Broom and Johnson point out that the connection which Dawkins makes between suffering and the animal's inability to carry out actions that would normally reduce risks to life and reproduction is narrower than most people's understanding of the term suffering. This, they suggest, would also include 'all but the milder, briefer kinds of pain and many of the consequences of disease', not all of which necessarily pose a risk either to life or reproduction. Accordingly, they advocate that suffering would be better defined as 'an unpleasant subjective feeling which is prolonged or severe'.[53] To Webster,

Suffering occurs when the intensity or complexity of stresses exceeds or exhausts the capacity of the animal to cope, or when the animal is prevented from taking constructive action. Suffering may also occur when an animal is in a state of limbo, free from any sort of environmental stress but denied the opportunity to make any sort of constructive contribution to the quality of its own existence.[54]

---

[49] Interviewed for 'The Ascent of Man', broadcast on BBC Radio 3, 25 August 1999.
[50] n 40 above, 2 (emphasis in the original).   [51] ibid.   [52] ibid 25.   [53] n 29 above, 81–82.
[54] n 22 above, 38.

For their part, Kirkwood and colleagues draw attention to other interpretations of the term which have been proposed—for example, 'a severe emotional state that is extremely unpleasant, that results from physical pain and/or discomfort at a level not tolerated by the individual', and 'the unpleasant emotional response to more than minimal pain and distress'[55]—before they themselves endorse the broader definition which encompasses both pain and stress.[56]

Before going on to consider these two facets in more detail, it is necessary to comment upon a characteristic which is common to each of these scientific definitions of suffering, namely the proposition that the cause of the unpleasant emotional response, or the emotional response itself, must be either acute or prolonged before an animal can be said to suffer. It should be noted that such criteria do not apply to offences based on causing an animal unnecessary suffering, where *any* unpleasant emotional response may amount to suffering.[57] There are two reasons for this apparent discrepancy. First, in relation to the legal test of unnecessary suffering, factors such as severity and duration *are* taken into account, but in relation to the question of necessity rather than suffering. Secondly, the above definitions of suffering have been formulated in the context of *welfare*, where an animal's negative experiences are weighed against its ability to cope or adapt. In the normal course of events, minimal pain or stress will not constitute a serious welfare problem to an animal (indeed, the fact that it is negligible may itself be an indication that the animal is coping satisfactorily), whereas the fact that an animal's physiology may allow it to withstand cruel treatment is not a relevant consideration in determining whether a defendant is guilty of the offence. Accordingly, caution is needed in applying any of the above definitions literally to the legislative concept of unnecessary suffering in the context of the offence of cruelty.

(2) Pain

There is a widespread consensus among animal physiologists and behaviourists that mammals, birds, and possibly fish have the capacity not only to experience pain, but also to suffer from it.[58] Many, within the scientific community and beyond, would agree with Webster's contention that 'Whatever criteria one uses to rank problems of animal welfare—intensity, duration or numbers of animals affected—pain must rank as the most serious',[59] and public policy towards animals has been substantially influenced by a conviction that pain should be prevented or

---

[55] Spinelli, JS and Markowitz, H, 'Clinical recognition and anticipation of situations likely to induce suffering in animals' (1987) 191 *Journal of the American Veterinary Medical Association* 1216; Kitchen, H et al, 'Panel report on the colloquium on recognition and alleviation of animal pain and distress' (1987) 191 *Journal of the American Veterinary Medical Association* 1186.

[56] Kirkwood, JK et al, 'The welfare of free-living wild animals: methods of assessment' (1994) 3 *Animal Welfare* 257, 265.

[57] See Ch 10, s C above.

[58] Webster, n 22 above, 252; Broom and Johnson, n 29 above, 28; Gentle, MJ, 'Pain in Birds' (1992) 1 *Animal Welfare* 235.

[59] n 22 above, 252.

minimized so far as is practicable (although what *is* practicable may continue to excite controversy). In technical terms, pain may be described as 'an aversive sensory experience caused by actual or potential injury that elicits protective motor and vegetative reactions, results in learned avoidance, and may modify species specific behaviour, including social behaviour'.[60] In practice, the most obvious indications that an animal may be in pain can usually be gained from general observation of its behaviour and demeanour, although the relevant signs are harder to detect in some (especially prey) species because there has been selection against obvious display which might attract the attention of predators. Further evidence can be deduced from its heart rate, respiration, temperature, and hormonal response. The presence of acute pain will generally be readily apparent. However, while this will have implications for the immediate well-being of an animal, the fact that it is short term may indicate that the victim is coping satisfactorily with the problem. Of much greater significance in terms of welfare is chronic pain, which persists over a prolonged period. This is not merely a protracted version of acute pain; it typically results in a much more extensive and detrimental effect on the overall physiology and behaviour of the individual. The moral is clear: it is important to appreciate that conspicuous symptoms are not necessarily those which betray the most pressing welfare problems; it is always incumbent on the observer to look beyond the obvious.

(3) Stress

Ewbank points out that an animal relies on a variety of biological mechanisms constantly to adjust its bodily state to maintain internal homeostasis. Most of the time, the necessary response will be within the capacity of the animal. However, occasions may arise when a substantial response is necessary and the animal has to carry a biological cost in order to cope. Ewbank suggests that this adaptive response amounts to stress. On this basis, an animal can be said to be experiencing stress, even though it is ultimately able to cope with the challenge, although Ewbank recognizes that in the case of acute or prolonged stress there may be harmful side effects.[61] Similarly, Dawkins uses the term stress to refer to 'a series of physiological changes, such as the release of hormones, which go on within the body' when an animal is subjected to a challenge, and she draws attention to the

---

[60] Zimmermann, M, 'Behavioural investigations of pain in animals' in Duncan, IJH and Molony, V (eds), *Assessing Pain in Farm Animals* (1986) 30–35.

[61] Ewbank, R, 'Stress: a General Overview' in Phillips, C and Piggins, D (eds), *Farm Animals and the Environment* (1992) 255; Ewbank, R, 'Animal Welfare' in Ewbank, R et al (eds), *Management and Welfare of Farm Animals. The UFAW Farm Handbook* (4th edn, 1999) 3–4. Manning and Dawkins comment: '"Homeostasis" was the term coined by WB Cannon in his book, *The Wisdom of the Body* (1974) to describe the relative stability of the body despite the changes that go on in the outside world. . . . Homeostasis implies that the body has some means of correcting deviation, so that if temperature or fluid volume falls, steps are taken to restore the balance. . . . It would be quite wrong, however, to think of animals like simple thermostats, switching behaviour on and off whenever they are in particular states. Homeostasis is much more complicated than this in practice': n 47 above, 213–214.

argument that 'lesser stress symptoms may be a sign that an animal's body is coping with its environment'.[62] Broom and Johnson, however, use the word stress to refer to 'an environmental effect on an individual which overtaxes its control systems and reduces its fitness or appears likely to do so', in the sense that it is *unable* to cope, or it is likely that there will be such a failure. Such circumstances, they suggest, include substantial immunosuppression, injury, behaviour abnormality, and 'physiological overload' which increases the chances that food acquisition or the ability to avoid dangerous aggression will be reduced.[63] Today, the term stress is more generally used in this way, to describe an animal's state when it is 'challenged beyond its behavioural and physiological capacity to adapt to its environment'.[64] As Manning and Dawkins point out, the practical problem is in deciding when an animal's normal and adaptive response has crossed the line and 'become evidence for a pathological state that is likely to be indicative of suffering', to which end they suggest that it is most appropriate to pay particular attention to cases where stress is prolonged and severe; associated with situations that animals avoid if they possibly can; and 'where the body's normal motivational processes have been stretched beyond their normal adaptive range'.[65]

Distress can be said to occur when the animal demonstrates 'a severe stress response in which there is some indication that the animal is conscious of what is going on, and finds it unpleasant'. In other words, where there is some sign of suffering through behavioural signs of discomfort, pain, or emotional distress.[66]

(4) Poor welfare is not confined to suffering

Although poor welfare is generally associated with suffering, this is not invariably the case. For example, some deficiencies do not cause any subjective negative feelings, but rather *prevent* the animal from experiencing pleasures.[67] In other situations, welfare can be deficient for a period before the animal starts to suffer; where a group of animals are kept together, some but not all may be susceptible to suffering; and, although stereotypic behaviour ('the prolonged, obsessive performance of apparently purposeless activity',[68] such as repeatedly pacing out the same route, or rocking backwards and forwards) is widely regarded as amounting to evidence of an unacceptably barren environment, lacking adequate stimulation or social contact, we do not yet know whether this indicates that 'the animal is suffering from frustration, or attempting to cope with a problem of frustration before it reaches the point of suffering, or has simply discovered a pointless but satisfactory way of passing the time';[69] and poor welfare may result in consequences such as reduced life expectancy, impaired growth, impaired reproduction, body damage,

---

[62] n 39 above, 55 and 62.   [63] n 29 above, 72–73.

[64] Termouw, EMC et al, 'Physiology' in Appleby, MC and Hughes, BO (eds), *Animal Welfare* (1997) 143–144.

[65] n 47 above, 247–248.   [66] Ewbank (1992), n 61 above, 255; Ewbank (1999), n 61 above, 3–4.

[67] Fraser, D and Duncan, IJH, '"Pleasures", "Pains" and Animal Welfare: Toward a Natural History of Affect' (1998) 7 *Animal Welfare* 383.

[68] Webster, n 22 above, 35.   [69] ibid 255.

disease, immunosuppression, increased adrenal activity, behavioural anomalies, and self-narcotization, all of which can arise without the individual having any subjective experience of the problem.[70] In addition, Fraser and colleagues make the important point that animal welfare research cannot be limited to subjective experience, because science is unable to give empirical answers to many ethically relevant questions regarding the subjective experience of animals, for example whether keeping a bird in a cage reduces its welfare by depriving it of the pleasure of flying, or whether prolonging the life of a sick dog reduces its welfare because its suffering outweighs its enjoyment of living.[71]

(5) Death

An extremely important consequence of the emphasis which is placed on the presence of suffering is that, although it undoubtedly has an ethical dimension, death is not, in itself, considered to be a welfare issue (unless culling takes place as a result of inadequate management and care), although the manner in which an animal dies is clearly relevant.[72]

F. Assessing Welfare

In 1980, Dawkins proposed what she described as 'a tentative check-list' for helping to decide whether a particular treatment of animals might be causing suffering. Both the science and the philosophy of animal welfare have developed in the intervening period, but the questions she posed remain relevant as a starting point for assessing welfare, and they also reflect the factors which are represented in animal welfare legislation:

(1) What are the conditions under which the animals are kept?
(2) Are the animals physically healthy?
(3) Does the behaviour, physiology, and general appearance of the animals differ from that of genetically similar animals in less restricted conditions?
(4) Is there evidence of severe physiological disturbance?
(5) What is the cause of the behavioural differences established under (3)?
(6) What conditions do the animals themselves prefer?[73]

---

[70] Broom, DM, 'Animal Welfare: Concepts and Management' (1991) 69 *Journal of Animal Science* 4167, 4168–4169.
[71] n 24 above, 195–196.
[72] Broom, DM, 'Ethical Dilemmas in Animal Usage' in Paterson, D and Palmer M (eds), *The Status of Animals* (1989) 83; Fraser and Broom, n 35 above, 257; Webster, n 22 above, 15.
[73] n 39 above, 114–116.

(1) The role of the researcher

The ability to assess the state of an animal's welfare and the relative importance of those factors which impact upon it is essential not only for those directly involved with the animal's care, but also for legislators and policy makers if regulation is effectively to prevent conditions which are detrimental to welfare and promote those which contribute to a high standard. This is not easy. 'While the notions of coping and stress seem at first to provide a handle on welfare,' declare Barnard and Hurst, 'they amount to little more than conceptual labels. Attempts to define and measure them in particular cases are fraught with difficulty and disagreement.'[74] The welfare of animals is 'an intrinsically difficult subject to study scientifically', concedes Baxter, but it has, he suggests, nevertheless 'reached a stage of maturity at which firm conclusions can be drawn about whether or not an animal is suffering in particular circumstances'.[75]

In general terms it may be said that indicators of poor welfare include 'abnormal behaviour, abnormal physiology, injury, etc. and also measures of the aversion shown by animals to particular conditions or procedures'; and good welfare is indicated by the absence of these, together with 'the occurrence of normal functioning including normal behaviour and measures of positive preferences for conditions and resources'.[76] This still begs the question, however, of what constitutes abnormality and normality for these purposes?

Assessing an animal's welfare is an exercise in observation and measurement, but interpreting the relevant findings involves an attempt to understand what the animal itself is experiencing. The animal's viewpoint is an 'essential ingredient in all animal welfare studies', asserts Dawkins, 'because it provides the only plausible bridge between the observable events such as physiological and behavioural changes, which are the basic data at our disposal, and the subjective experiences of animals, which it is the ultimate goal of animal welfare studies to understand'.[77] Herein lies a very real problem. On the one hand, it may be reasonable to infer what an animal is experiencing, especially one that is physiologically similar to us, by reference to human sensations and behaviour: 'The evaluation of the feelings of an animal', the Brambell Committee concluded, 'must rest on analogy with our own and must be derived from observation of the cries, expression, reactions, behaviour, health and productivity of the animal.'[78] On the other, it is essential to remain objective, as Webster warns:

If we are to create real improvement in animal welfare we have, first, to acknowledge that an animal's perception of its own welfare may be very different from that of the general (human) public, especially when public perception is based largely on media images, rather

[74] Barnard, CJ and Hurst, JL, 'Welfare by design: the natural selection of welfare criteria' (1996) 5 *Animal Welfare* 405, 411.

[75] Baxter, MR, 'The welfare problems of laying hens in battery cages' (1994) 134 *Veterinary Record* 614.

[76] FAWC, n 16 above, para 17.

[77] n 40 above, 1.   [78] n 4 above, para 26.

than the realities of regular day-to-day contact with animals. We have then to do our best to understand how animals view the world and finally try to educate public opinion towards a perception of welfare that is as close as possible to that of the animals themselves.[79]

This assessment is essentially a scientific undertaking. Some contend that it is exclusively so. Broom, for example, has consistently maintained that 'Welfare can be measured in a scientific way that is independent of moral considerations.'[80] He has variously expressed the view that it is 'important' and 'essential' that the process of welfare assessment and the process of ethical judgement be separate.[81] Similarly, Garner considers that the question of how we ought to treat animals is distinct from the extent to which they suffer, and the House of Commons Agriculture Committee has suggested that it can be answered 'without relying on philosophical arguments about animal rights or the nature of animal suffering'.[82] Others, however, argue that this is neither possible nor desirable. According to Tannenbaum, 'animal welfare science is as much about ethics as it is about science', since 'the fundamental motivation for studying and promoting welfare is ethical', and 'the very concept of animal welfare forces one to make and rationally defend value judgments about what ways of treating animals is [sic] appropriate'.[83]

This is an issue of some significance. It reveals an important difference among researchers as to their role and the nature of their work. Thus Broom and Johnson argue that welfare measurements and their interpretation should be 'objective',[84] whereas Fraser, for example, suggests that quantifying greater or lesser degrees of animal welfare 'inherently imply [sic] something better or worse for the animal. Hence, to define or conceptualize animal welfare, we involve value notions.'[85] According to Tannenbaum, what he calls the 'pure science model of animal welfare' sees the researcher as providing 'a storehouse of objective factual information, which will be available when the public and government are ready to decide how much or what sort of animal welfare should be provided'.[86] In contrast, the approach represented by both Tannenbaum himself and Fraser sees the researcher as, at least in part, an advocate: 'scientists should not sit idly by, waiting for society to decide what animal welfare involves so that they will know what to study', Fraser argues. 'Instead, scientists should develop and use knowledge of animals to help society develop a more sound conceptualization of animal welfare and its ethical dimensions.'[87] Stafleu and colleagues warn that 'the moral aspect of welfare is lost

---

[79] Webster, n 22 above, 13.

[80] For example, Broom, n 70 above, 4168; Fraser and Broom, n 35 above, 256; Broom and Johnson, n 29 above, 75.

[81] Broom, n 70 above, 4168; Broom and Johnson, n 29 above, 158.

[82] Garner, R, *Animals, politics and morality* (1993) 5; House of Commons Agriculture Committee, n 18 above, para 19.

[83] n 26 above, 1361 and 1374.　　　　　[84] n 29 above, 75.

[85] Fraser, D, 'Science, values and animal welfare: exploring the "inextricable connection"' (1995) 4 *Animal Welfare* 103, 104.

[86] n 26 above, 1362.　　　　　[87] n 85 above, 112.

in the process of scientific definition';[88] other scientists may be concerned that if an ethical component becomes too great, research and the results which it produces then become too subjective, whereas work which is rigorously objective provides a much stronger basis for the introduction of welfare measures, especially in societies which do not have a cultural tradition of having regard to the interests of other species.[89] It is not suggested here that one approach is better than the other, although it is relevant to be mindful of the philosopher Bernard Williams' contention that 'morality is not just like science or factual knowledge, and it is essential that it should not be', because 'The point of morality is not to mirror the world, but to change it.'[90] What is incontrovertible, however, is that Tannenbaum is correct to regard the field of animal welfare as 'inherently interdisciplinary in nature'.[91] Manning and Dawkins forcefully emphasize the breadth of subject matter and disciplines which are relevant to the study of welfare:

At one end, neuroethology merges into cellular physiology and biochemistry. At the other, the study of animal groups moves into evolutionary theory and ecology. Psychologists, ethologists, physiologists, and behavioural ecologists all contribute to this diversity.[92]

Whichever approach one prefers, however, they are clearly different. As such, each may have a particular influence on the questions researchers ask, their attitude to the answers they obtain, and the role they see for themselves in the policy-making and legislative arena.

It is also important to recognize that, depending on their area of expertise, researchers may emphasize different aspects of an animal's welfare, whether it be physiology, health, or behaviour. This may cause them to be at variance as to the appropriate weight to be afforded to particular factors in reaching their overall assessment and, in consequence, 'different researchers may come up with the measurement of different parameters, which may indicate different levels of welfare'. This in turn poses difficulties for decision makers in determining which results are the most appropriate to take into account in the development of policy.[93]

Clearly, the way in which researchers define welfare will influence the types of measure they use when assessing it.[94] Also relevant in this context is Tannenbaum's

---

[88] Stafleu, FR et al, 'Animal welfare: evolution and erosion of a moral concept' (1996) 5 *Animal Welfare* 225, 232.

[89] I am grateful to Stephen Wickens for drawing this argument to my attention. For a useful discussion focusing on different approaches to the ethical issues raised by a particular issue, see Appleby, MC, 'Tower of Babel: Variation in Ethical Approaches, Concepts of Welfare and Attitudes to Genetic Manipulation' (1999) 8 *Animal Welfare* 381.

[90] Williams, B, *Morality. An Introduction to Ethics* (1976) 47; cf Marx, 'The philosophers have only *interpreted* the world in various ways; the point is to *change* it': 'Theses on Feuerbach', in *Karl Marx, Frederick Engels, Collected Works* (1975 onwards) Vol 5, 5 (emphasis in the original).

[91] n 26 above, 1373. A similar view is expressed by Sandøe, P and Simonsen, HB, 'Assessing animal welfare: where does science end and philosophy begin?' (1992) 1 *Animal Welfare* 257, 266.

[92] n 47 above, 33.   [93] Stafleu et al, n 88 above, 231; see also, Mason and Mendl, n 24 above, 302.

[94] Mason and Mendl, n 24 above, 302.

scepticism at the very notion of attempting to provide 'purportedly complete and exhaustive definitions of welfare', lest they serve to 'remove competing ethical and scientific viewpoints from one's universe of discourse' with the result that 'alternative ethical and factual enquiries become literally unthinkable because they do not fit a preconceived definition of welfare'.[95]

This debate about the very nature of animal welfare science arises in part because of its relatively recent development, but is also due in large measure to its particular characteristics. First, it is public concern about animal suffering which 'has provided the incentive for scientists to find empirical and quantitative ways of evaluating welfare'.[96] In consequence, 'the field of animal welfare science owes its existence not primarily to the curiosity of its scientific pioneers, but to the ethical concerns extant in society'.[97] Perhaps one way of reconciling the different approaches discussed above is to adopt the suggestion of Fraser and colleagues, that animal welfare should be viewed as a 'bridging concept' which links scientific research to the ethical concerns that the research is intended to address.[98] Secondly, as Sandøe and Simonsen put it, animal welfare science does not 'in all respects fit into the standard picture of what "real" science is': objective and capable of producing hypotheses which can be tested empirically.[99] Manning and Dawkins illustrate the point in relation to the problems of observation and measurement associated with studying animal behaviour:

In the physical science, and often elsewhere in biology, we have universally recognized units—molecules, milliamps, pH units, metres, etc.—for measuring and classifying our observations. When we watch animals we have no such framework. Behaviour is continuous for as long as life persists; anything and everything may count. Put this way, the task would seem to be impossible and in fact we cannot ever study behaviour unless we abstract and simplify. We have to make decisions about what it is important to record and what can safely be ignored.[100]

Such difficulties arise not because animal welfare is inherently unscientific, but as a result of the nature and complexity of the questions which it seeks to address. The evidence which researchers rely on is generally referred to as 'indicators' of an animal's welfare, and, 'because they are only indicators, there is often room for argument . . . about the extent to which a particular finding indicates poor welfare as opposed to, for example, exertion that can be regarded as falling within natural limits'.[101] Moreover, as Fraser points out, conventional scientific techniques can be employed to identify, solve, and prevent animal welfare problems, but they cannot provide an overall measure of an animal's welfare, nor any purely objective way of combining different measures, that eliminates value-related disagreements. When

[95] n 26 above, 1372.   [96] Baxter, n 75 above, 614.
[97] Fraser et al, n 24 above, 188. See also, Duncan, IJH and Fraser, D, 'Understanding Animal Welfare' in Appleby and Hughes, n 64 above, 20.
[98] n 24 above, 188.   [99] n 91 above, 258.   [100] n 47 above, 5.
[101] Burns, Lord (Chairman), *Report of the Committee of Inquiry into Hunting with Dogs in England and Wales* (2000) para 6.10.

systems of animal husbandry differ in a large number of features, science may be unable to show objectively whether welfare is better in one system than another. In such a situation, a judgement has to be made, and this, Fraser suggests, will be coloured by what the observer considers is better or worse, more important or less important, for the quality of life of the particular animals.[102] This leads Duncan and Fraser to conclude that scientific information may be of assistance in reaching a consensus about an animal's welfare, but an assessment of its quality of life 'can never be entirely objective because it involves a mixture of scientific knowledge and value judgements'.[103]

These issues are of more than academic significance; they have far-reaching implications. The different conceptions of animal welfare adopted by scientists determine the type of research they undertake. This not only has an impact on the information available to society for deciding questions of policy, it may also lead to conflicting conclusions about how animals ought to be treated.[104] However, although there may be a legitimate debate about the extent to which it is proper for ethical considerations to influence such research, it is nevertheless the case that animal welfare is essentially a scientific concept, concerned with assessing how an animal responds to its circumstances, and not a moral theory. It is inappropriate, therefore, to suggest that the term represents 'the view that it is morally acceptable, at least under some circumstances, to kill animals or subject them to suffering as long as precautions are taken to ensure that the animal is treated as "humanely" as possible' or that 'an animal welfare position generally holds that there is *no* animal interest that cannot be overridden if the consequences of the overriding are sufficiently "beneficial" to human beings'.[105]

(2) Indicators of the state of an animal's welfare

It is clear that it will seldom be appropriate to regard a single characteristic as conclusive evidence of the state of an animal's welfare. According to FAWC, 'Although one single measurement can indicate that welfare is poor, studies comparing welfare in different systems, or using different husbandry methods, should utilize a range of indicators.'[106] Conversely, a single factor which appears to suggest good welfare is not in itself conclusive that this is indeed the case. Thus the Brambell Committee, while accepting that growth rate and condition, 'as witnessed by a good coat or plumage, alertness, bright eyes and contentedness', when taken together are 'perhaps the best objective measure available', warned that they 'are not inconsistent with periods of acute, but transitory, physical or mental suffering'.[107] The House of Commons Agriculture Committee has made a similar point. 'We do not accept', it stated in 1981, 'that because five hens in a cage are eating and laying well, there is necessarily nothing wrong with their welfare. It is necessary to

---

[102] n 85 above, 103.   [103] n 97 above, 19.   [104] Fraser et al, n 24 above, 202.
[105] Francione, GL, *Animals, Property and the Law* (1995) 6 (italics in the original).
[106] n 30 above, para 6.   [107] n 4 above, para 30.

take account of all that is known about their physiological make-up heritage as well as their behavioural and ecological needs.[108] Not ev~, with this approach. The United Kingdom Egg Producers' Association, for e~~ ple, has claimed subsequently that hens 'will not lay eggs if they are under stress, and the livestock farmer who does not look after the welfare of his animals will soon go out of business'.[109] However, while it may be the case that, by keeping them in battery cages, the welfare of laying hens can be well catered for in respect of feeding, health, and protection from cannibalism, the birds are nevertheless prevented from dust bathing, foraging, nesting, or roosting, and the restriction of movement may result in frustration and prevent normal bone maintenance. This leads Baxter to conclude, despite the egg producers' contrary contention on the basis of egg production alone, that confinement in a battery cage causes suffering to laying hens in several different ways.[110] Similarly, Beattie and colleagues found that the overall production performance of piglets kept respectively in a barren and an enriched environment was similar, but an analysis of the behaviour of the two groups revealed the latter's welfare to be significantly better, a situation which, in the view of the researchers, 'illustrates the fallacy of the belief that meeting production requirements automatically ensures high standards of welfare'.[111]

Accordingly, the state of an animal's welfare is best considered as the outcome of a complex, interrelated amalgam of many different factors. It is therefore desirable to have regard to a number of measures in assessing welfare, each being considered in the context of, first, the relevant species; secondly, the circumstances in which the relevant animals are kept and the nature of their lifestyle; and, thirdly, the particular individual. These factors include: the animal's subjective experience, such as pain, fear, distress, excitement, pleasure; its biological functioning, as evidenced by health, condition, fertility, and injuries or other physical damage; and its behavioural needs.

The latter has given rise to particular difficulties. It used to be considered an indication of good welfare if an animal displayed the full range of behaviour that it would be expected to exhibit in the wild. However, it is now widely accepted that this approach is too simplistic. Studies of 'presumed wild ancestors have limited value', according to Dawkins. However, while they may be 'unconvincing as a standard for welfare on their own', she regards them to have 'an extremely important function' in telling us 'what the effects of captivity are and through this, to alert us to the possibility that suffering is being caused'.[112] Domestic animals may have a significantly different genetic make-up from their wild counterparts, or they may adjust satisfactorily to their confined environment, or it may be that the confined

---

[108] n 18 above, para 16.
[109] House of Commons Agriculture Committee, *The UK Poultry Industry* (1994) para 74.
[110] n 75 above, 614.
[111] Beattie, VE, Walker, N, and Sneddon, IA, 'Effects of environmental enrichment on behaviour and productivity of growing pigs' (1995) 4 *Animal Welfare* 207.
[112] n 39 above, 53–54.

environment provides sufficient, albeit significantly different, conditions for them. 'Confinement is not necessarily undesirable for the welfare of the animal', observed the Brambell Committee. 'It may well confer advantages, notably shelter from the weather and freedom from predators and bullying, three of the major hardships to which the wild animal is exposed.'[113] In assessing the use of battery cages, for example, FAWC pointed out that adopting such a system could result in:

- an environment which is easy to control throughout the year;
- aggression suppressed by space restriction;
- a small colony size;
- good disease control;
- low risk from endo and ectoparasites;
- no necessity to carry out beak trimming; and
- no predation problems.

In practice, of course, these must be weighed against its detrimental consequences:

- prevention or modification of certain normal behaviours;
- an inability to escape aggression from other birds if this occurs;
- feather damage by abrasion and foot problems caused by the (sloping) wire floor;
- weak bones and an increased risk of breakages;
- inspection difficulties, particularly the top and bottom tiers.[114]

Moreover, at least some of the behavioural traits which animals demonstrate in the wild represent an effort to survive in a hostile environment. Remove the threats, and the behaviour ceases to be important to the animal. Indeed, far from being evidence of good welfare, the presence of such behaviour suggests that the animal's welfare is under threat. Other types of 'natural' behaviour are a response to an external stimulus. If the animal is not exposed to the stimulus, it may have no need to express the associated behaviour.[115]

Undoubtedly, however, some behaviour patterns are deeply entrenched, and we may assume that an animal experiences frustration if it is unable to carry them out. As the House of Commons Agriculture Committee pithily observed in the context of intensive systems of livestock husbandry, 'it is not a convincing argument to say that because a man in the stocks is not seen to walk he needs no exercise'.[116] For example, calves demonstrate a strong urge to suckle which is not directly connected with the need to take in milk. Indeed, if presented with the opportunity, many domestic animals behave in a similar manner to their wild relatives.[117] Establishing through research the environment and behaviour which are important to the animal

---

[113] n 4 above, para 36.   [114] FAWC, *Report on the Welfare of Laying Hens* (1997) para 101.
[115] Dawkins, n 39 above, Ch 4; Veasey, JS et al, 'On comparing the behaviour of zoo housed animals with wild conspecifics as a welfare indicator' (1996) 5 *Animal Welfare* 13; Poole, T, 'Natural behaviour is simply a question of survival' (1996) 5 *Animal Welfare* 218.
[116] n 18 above, para 156.   [117] Appleby, n 41 above, 90–93.

is the key. Such work not only focuses on the animal's situation from its own point of view; it also makes it less likely to put a human gloss on what humans think a good environment is. It is the animal's sensibilities, not those of humans, that should dictate conditions. Poole identifies, for example, that it may appear preferable for gorillas to be kept in captivity in a grassy enclosure surrounded by a moat rather than in a cage, but they are forest animals and an open enclosure 'may be more impoverished than a well designed cage which can offer appropriate complexity in the form of a three dimensional habitat with facilities for climbing'.[118] Similarly, Webster points to hens, which have evolved from jungle fowl living in social groups of perhaps six hens with one cockerel. In a group of this size an individual knows her relationship with each of her companions, and is aware of what action to take in the event of an emergency. 'When 2000 birds are run together on a so-called free-range system they are not so much a social group as a dangerous mob', he observes. Hens are not socially adapted to crowding; the problem is not one of fear, but loss of control.[119]

Indeed, perhaps the major advantage enjoyed by wild animals is that, when problems arise, they are 'at liberty to make their own decisions as to how to deal with them'.[120] This autonomy is fundamental to their attempts to adapt to, and thereby to cope with, such challenges. It follows that a domestic animal or one kept in captivity should enjoy similar opportunities. Webster suggests that 'one of the most effective ways to cause suffering is to deny an animal the opportunity to make a constructive contribution to the quality of its own existence'.[121] Similarly, Broom and Johnson point out that 'many situations which result in poor welfare are those in which an animal lacks control over its interactions with the environment'.[122] This is particularly significant in the light of the growing body of evidence which suggests that animal behaviour and the mental abilities of at least some species are considerably more complex than was previously assumed.[123]

On the one hand, 'minimum mortality, low morbidity, little or no risk of injury, good body condition, the ability to express species-specific activities including social interactions, exploration and play, and the lack of abnormal behaviour and of physiological signs of stress, including alterations of immune responses, indicate that there are no major animal welfare problems'.[124] On the other, the most important indicators of poor welfare include:

- physiological changes, abnormalities of behaviour, or changes in the brain which show the extent to which the animal is having difficulty in coping or failing to cope;
- disease incidence, disease severity, and immunosuppression;

[118] Poole, TB, 'The nature and evolution of behavioural needs in mammals' (1992) 1 *Animal Welfare* 203, 207.

[119] n 22 above, 13.   [120] ibid 14.   [121] ibid 29.   [122] n 29 above, 138.

[123] Dawkins, n 44 above.

[124] Scientific Committee on Animal Health and Animal Welfare, *The Welfare of Chickens Kept for Meat Production (Broilers)* (2000) para 3.2.

- the extent of injury or of bodily malfunction;
- reduced ability to grow or breed and reduced potential life expectancy;
- the extent to which animals must contend with situations which they would avoid strongly;
- the extent to which animals are deprived of strongly preferred resources or of the opportunity to carry out behaviours which are important to them;
- the levels of any indicators of contentment or of a calm, untroubled life.[125]

It will be apparent that some indicators of the state of an animal's welfare lie principally within the domain of research scientists, who seek to increase our understanding of the behaviour, physiology, and biological needs of other species, in order that we can better appreciate what is important to them, the ways in which different conditions impact upon their lives, and the nature of their responses to such challenges. For example, an animal's preferences can be ascertained by providing it with a choice of options, or measuring how hard it is prepared to work to achieve a particular end.[126] Conversely, the strength of its aversion to a stimulus can be demonstrated by its efforts to avoid or escape it. Similarly, investigation of the pituitary-adrenocortical system, particularly the level of corticosteroids such as cortisol, together with other hormones such as prolactin, has also been used extensively to identify potential welfare problems.

In contrast, other characteristics which are indicative of an animal's state can be routinely observed and measured both by researchers and by those who own and look after animals. Indeed, FAWC has made the important point that 'evidence is required not only from scientific study but also from practical, objective observation within the industry and examples of best practice in animal husbandry'.[127] So, for example, the Association of Veterinary Teachers and Research Workers suggest that the severity of pain can be assessed on the basis of a wide range of parameters, including:

- History: signs and course of current problem; previous problems; stocking density, where appropriate; food and water intake; environment.
- Physiological signs (which are not necessarily the same for each species): dilation of the pupils; wide opening of the eyelids; transient increases or decreases in blood pressure; increased heart rate; increased rate and alteration of the character or breathing (gasping or panting); movements of whiskers; piloerection; increased body temperature; increased muscle tone; sweating; change in skin temperature; evacuation of rectum or para-anal sacs.
- Behaviour patterns: (a) mental status, such as dull, depressed, unresponsive, unaware, apprehensive, anxious, bright, alert, aware, excitable, hypersensitive, aggressive, or timid; the state of consciousness or awareness; (b) any abnormal activity.

---

[125] FAWC, n 30 above, para 8; when identifying welfare problems, it is necessary to consider both the extent of poor welfare and its duration.

[126] Dawkins, n 40 above, 5.   [127] FAWC, *Report on the Welfare of Broiler Breeders* (1998) para 7.

- Posture.
- Gait.
- Response to handling.
- Vocalization: growling, snarling, grunting, groaning, whimpering, whining, howling, yelping, screeching, crying.
- Appetite.
- Weight.
- Response to analgesics.
- Any species specific signs.

This list was originally drawn up in relation to animals used for scientific proce-dures, but it clearly has a wider application, to the extent that, although 'none of these signs singly or together gives definite evidence of pain . . . at our current level of understanding, it must be assumed that pain may be present and appropriate action taken to prevent or relieve it'.[128] Other relevant factors which fall within this group are: the presence of gastric ulcers; poor functioning of the immune system and the prevalence of disease; reduced fertility; other behavioural problems such as extreme apathy and stereotypy; and body damage or trauma.

In assessing the state of an animal's welfare, attention tends to focus primarily on the presence of factors indicating poor welfare, largely because these are easier to identify than those which are positive: poor welfare is associated with more obvious behavioural, physiological, and pathological signs.[129] However, the basis of responsible animal ownership should not be restricted to providing the mini-mum standards necessary to produce acceptable welfare; it extends to promoting the highest practicable standard. As Poole points out, psychological well-being, for example, is 'more than the absence of distress, it is a positive state of mental satis-faction resulting from the animal's psychological needs having been met'.[130]

(3) The complexity and interrelationship of factors affecting welfare

In order to achieve high standards of welfare it is necessary to have a thorough understanding of the physiology, behaviour, and ecology of the species concerned, together with the needs and response of individual animals. This knowledge is then given practical application through caring and responsible planning and management; skilled, informed, and conscientious care, appropriate environmen-tal design, and considerate and competent handling. The complexity and inter-relationship of the factors affecting an animal's welfare is well illustrated by

---

[128] Association of Veterinary Teachers and Research Workers, *Guidelines for the Recognition and Assessment of Pain in Animals* (1989) 23.

[129] Broom and Johnson, n 29 above, 87.

[130] n 118 above, 217. In Poole's view, these psychological needs appear to be 'unique to the mammalian mind', a contention specifically refuted by Dawkins, Bradshaw, and Bubier: 1 *Animal Welfare* 309 and 2 *Animal Welfare* 101.

FAWC's detailed consideration of the factors which are relevant in assessing the suitability of the cubicles in which dairy cattle are kept:

Cubicle design should take into consideration the size, shape and weight of the animals. Inappropriate cubicle housing can reduce a cow's lying time which can predispose to lameness and may contribute to teat damage. A well designed cubicle permits a cow to stand comfortably with all four feet on the cubicle bed. It should be wide enough for the animal to rest without undue pressure on the body, which may restrict rumination, or cause damage to the legs and udder. There should be sufficient head room to allow her to go down, lie and rise without difficulty. There should be a gentle slope from the front (head end) to the back which will encourage a cow to lie facing uphill, so reducing rumen pressure on the diaphragm. It is also essential for drainage from the cubicle base.

The Welfare of Livestock Regulations 1994 [now superseded by the Welfare of Farmed Animals Regulations] state that, when in a building, lactating cows or cows which are calving 'shall have access at all times to a well-drained and bedded lying area'. About 80% of a cow's weight when lying down is taken on her knees and hocks, so a dry bed which provides sufficient mechanical comfort to avoid leg problems is necessary to prevent lesions and pressure sores which may then become infected. FAWC believes that a bare, solid base is unacceptable and that each cow should be provided with a comfortable, bedded, dry lying area within the cubicle. All solid bases should be covered evenly with a suitable depth of bedding to provide cushioning. This bedding should be topped up and/or replaced at appropriate intervals for hygiene reasons. A thin layer of sawdust, chopped straw or other bedding material on a solid base can be displaced when the cow lies down. This does not therefore prevent the occurrence of contact abrasions and is not satisfactory.

Some farmers use rubber mats, carpets or mattresses, with or without a covering of straw or sawdust, which lie on top of the concrete base. Any mat or mattress should be provided with some form of bedding in order to keep teats, udders and flanks clean. Other farmers use beds of non-abrasive sand on lipped cubicle bases to a depth of 75–100 mm. Unless they are raked daily, with all foul material removed, and replenished as necessary, these beds are likely to become unhygienic, compacted and uncomfortable. Whatever cubicle bedding is used, the primary purpose should be to ensure that the cow is kept in as comfortable and clean condition as possible.

Badly designed cubicles lead to cows spending long periods standing in the slurry passages or, commonly, half-in the cubicle with the hind feet in the slurry channel. Kerb height is most important as very high kerbs impose strain on the hind legs of animals which stand in this way. However, the kerb should not be so low that the end of the cubicle becomes contaminated with slurry. Cows which spend much time standing in the slurry passage or half-in cubicles are likely to run an increased risk of lameness. Those which refuse to use cubicles and lie in slurry passages will become unacceptably dirty with an increased risk of mastitis, abrasions to the hocks and lameness.

It is most important that there is one cubicle per cow. Provision of extra cubicles means that subordinate animals do not find that the only spare cubicle is next to a dominant cow.[131]

---

[131] FAWC, n 30 above, 71–75.

This quotation also highlights that each species may have particular needs. There is not a generic body of factors which can deliver universal high standards of welfare. Evolution has produced a myriad of species, whose interests and capacities vary hugely. Such a situation not only justifies treating them differently; it makes it imperative to do so. The more complex the animal, the greater their needs.[132]

(4) Welfare and wild animals

Discussion of welfare thus far has focused on animals for which humans have direct responsibility. This reflects the primary concern of scientists, ethicists, and, indeed, legislators. However, attention is beginning to turn to the welfare considerations of wild animals. It is certainly the case that there has been a marked increase in recent years in the rescue, treatment, and rehabilitation of wildlife. Although our relationship with free-living animals is fundamentally different from those we have domesticated or keep in captivity, it is incontrovertible that human activity can have a profound effect on their quality of life. It is not surprising, then, that it is being argued by some that 'if it is accepted that high standards of welfare should be a guiding principle in the husbandry of production animals, then it is inconsistent not to apply this principle to man's interactions with wildlife'.[133]

G. Conclusion

This chapter has attempted to give a brief overview of the developing concept of animal welfare, and to identify some of the issues which are a matter of debate among those working in the field. During the course of thirty years or so, the issue of welfare has grown very significantly in importance so that, today, it is the principal factor influencing public policy relating to the treatment of animals, especially in respect of legislative reform, hence the relevance of the foregoing discussion.

Notwithstanding that there is clearly some overlap, a distinction has been made between cruelty and welfare. In particular, animal cruelty is a long-established *legal* term; welfare, on the other hand, is a developing, essentially *scientific*, concept whose origins are to be found in the Brambell Report and its contemporary meaning is summarized in the idea of the Five Freedoms. Although some scientists would argue otherwise, welfare is now widely regarded as a relative, not an absolute, notion, which focuses in particular on an animal's ability to cope with its

---

[132] Appleby, n 41 above, 53–55.

[133] Sainsbury, AW et al, 'The welfare of free-living wild animals in Europe: harm caused by human activities' (1995) 4 *Animal Welfare* 183. See also: Kirkwood et al, n 56 above, 257; Harrop, SR, 'The Dynamics of Wild Animal Welfare Law' (1997) 9 Journal of Environmental Law 287; Harrop, S and Bowles, D, 'Wildlife Management, the Multilateral Trade Regime, Morals and the Welfare of Animals' (1998) 1 Journal of International Wildlife Law and Policy 64.

situation. An assumption that at least some animals have the capacity to suffer results in there being a moral dimension to be taken into account in deciding how animals should be treated, but there is disagreement among scientists about the extent to which such ethical considerations should influence their research. Moreover, although concern to minimize suffering is the principal intent of those concerned with welfare, its absence is not in itself the definitive indication of good welfare. Indeed, perhaps the most important conclusion to emerge from this chapter is the complexity of, and the interrelationship between, the many factors which affect an animal's welfare. In extreme cases, one particular element may have an overriding impact, but much more usually there will be very many considerations which together have a bearing on an animal's state. This situation has consequences not only for those who are directly responsible for the treatment of animals, but also for public policy makers. Indeed, many measures whose principal focus is not animal welfare may nevertheless be relevant. For example, the fact that the State has the power to require a person occupying land to prevent certain weeds from spreading, including ragwort (*Senecio jacobaea*), is to the benefit of equines, to whom this particular plant is fatal.[134] By way of contrast, regulations introduced with the intention of improving hygiene have resulted in the number of slaughterhouses licensed to process red meat decreasing from 1,385 in 1975 to 350 in 1999,[135] with the consequence that a large number of animals have to be transported over far greater distances. The use of antibiotics to mask the effects of intensive farming systems,[136] the availability and use of sheep dips to prevent disease,[137] the relative interests of badgers and cattle in the context of the growing prevalence of TB in the national herd,[138] the availability of and ability to prescribe veterinary medicines,[139] and so on; all have implications for animal welfare, and one would not wish to ignore their relevance. However, the main core of animal welfare legislation consists of measures which seek to regulate activities involving animals by prescribing how they should be treated and cared for. It is this body of law which is considered in the following two chapters.

---

[134] Weeds Act 1959.   [135] HC Debs, 14 December 1999, col 182 (WA).

[136] House of Lords Select Committee on Science and Technology, *Report on the Resistance to Antibiotics and Other Microbial Agents* (1998); BVA, *Guidelines on the prudent use of antimicrobials* (2000).

[137] House of Commons Agriculture Committee, *The Government's Proposals for Organophosphate Sheep Dips* (2000).

[138] House of Commons Agriculture Committee, *Badgers and Bovine Tuberculosis* (1999).

[139] Medicines (Restrictions on the Administration of Veterinary Medicinal Products) Regulations 1994, SI 1994/2987.

12

Public Control

A. Towards Promoting Better Welfare

The offence of cruelty continues to be the cornerstone of animal protection legislation in Britain, notwithstanding that the principal English and Scottish statutes pre-date the First World War and, even when enacted, were not intended to be especially innovative. The durability of the offence is attributable to its generality, enabling it to be applied to a wide variety of situations, together with its scope: in relation to domestic and captive animals, only acts lawfully carried out under the authority of the Animals (Scientific Procedures) Act 1986 are completely beyond its reach. It is also unique in empowering the courts, upon conviction, to make confiscation and disqualification orders. However, while the offence continues to make a major contribution to animal protection, it merely defines the standard below which conduct towards animals becomes unlawful. It imposes no requirement to improve upon that basic benchmark. Importantly, it fails to direct how animals *ought* to be cared for. In consequence, the concept of cruelty is not in itself sufficient to protect animals from inappropriate treatment, since there are many ways in which their standard of care may be less than satisfactory without it amounting in law to an offence of cruelty. It is therefore significant that, while changes to the Protection of Animals Acts have been relatively infrequent, there has evolved, especially since the end of the 1960s, a separate, but complementary, body of legislation, the effect of which has been to extend the legal duty we owe to animals beyond simply ensuring that they are not treated cruelly. Increasingly, it now also embraces an obligation specifically to have regard for their welfare.

It is, of course, self-evident that the prevention of cruelty and the promotion of high standards of welfare are not discrete objectives. It is not surprising, therefore, that concern to prevent 'unnecessary suffering' is common to both strands of legislation; but while the legal definition of cruelty is defined almost exclusively by reference to this concept, welfare legislation also includes terms such as 'without suffering',[1] 'shall not be harmful',[2] and 'unfit'.[3] Such wording ousts the balancing exercise inherent in the 'unnecessary suffering' test, with the result that *any* suffering, harm, or injury may amount to an offence. Equally, an animal is either unfit or it is not; there is no requirement to consider the necessity of its condition. Furthermore, unlike the Protection of Animals Acts, welfare legislation may expressly require that those who care for animals positively 'prevent' or 'protect' them from suffering,[4] or take appropriate steps 'to avoid injury and unnecessary suffering and to ensure the safety of the animals'.[5]

Potentially the most significant feature of welfare legislation is, however, the introduction of criteria which are no longer defined exclusively by reference to suffering. For example, there are circumstances in which it is incumbent on those responsible to ensure the 'proper care and well-being' of animals,[6] 'their health and welfare',[7] or their 'physiological and ethological needs';[8] others where a duty is imposed 'to maintain them in good health, to satisfy their nutritional needs and to promote a positive state of well-being',[9] or 'to safeguard the welfare of the animals under their care'.[10] On the face of it, this is regulation of a significantly different order from that which has traditionally prevailed. Rather than being concerned with whether the treatment of an animal has fallen below the rudimentary threshold of unnecessary suffering, provisions of this nature would seem to focus instead on identifying and meeting the innate needs of the animal itself.

Supplementing these general injunctions, and in the absence of an express legal definition of 'animal welfare', the legislation also often contains provisions which regulate how particular types of animal should be treated in specific circumstances, with special reference to those factors which have a material bearing on their quality of life (and death). To this end, detailed specifications relating to the treatment of animals may be prescribed by Act of Parliament, but it is more usual for the statute to provide ministers with the necessary legal authority to introduce these by means of secondary legislation, codes of practice, recommendations, and formal guidance. The Agriculture (Miscellaneous Provisions) Act 1968, for example, contains nothing of substance in relation to the way in which animals should be treated but, crucially, it enables ministers to introduce by means of regulations and codes of recommendations such provisions relating to the welfare of livestock as they think fit and proper.[11] Likewise, ministers are empowered to make such

---

[1] Animal Health Act 1981, s 40(2)(b).

[2] Welfare of Farmed Animals (England) Regulations 2000, SI 2000/1870, Sch 1, para 11; Welfare of Farmed Animals (Scotland) Regulations 2000, SSI 2000/442, Sch 1, para 11; Welfare of Farmed Animals (Wales) Regulations 2001, Sch 1, para 11. Welfare of Farmed Animals (Wales) Regulations 2001, Sch 4, para 1. The Regulations relating to Wales came into force on 31 July 2001, but at the time this book went to press they had not been allocated an SI number. Henceforth, the three sets of regulations will be referred to collectively as the 'Welfare of Farmed Animals Regulations'.

[3] Welfare of Animals at Markets Order 1990, SI 1990/2628, art 5(1).   [4] ibid, arts 11(1) and 17(2).

[5] Welfare of Animals (Transport) Order 1997, SI 1997/1480, Sch 1, para 1.

[6] Zoo Licensing Act 1981, s 4(3).   [7] Animals (Scientific Procedures) Act 1986, ss 6(5)(b), 7(5)(b).

[8] Welfare of Farmed Animals Regulations, n 2 above, reg 3(3).   [9] ibid, Sch 1, para 22.

[10] SI 1997/1480, n 5 above, art 9(1).   [11] Sections 2(1) and 3(1).

orders as they consider appropriate for the purpose of protecting animals from unnecessary suffering while in transit or at markets;[12] to introduce, in the interests of animal welfare, orders regulating animal exports;[13] to publish standards of modern zoo practice;[14] and to issue guidance on the operation of the Animals (Scientific Procedures) Act 1986, together with codes of practice on the care of animals and their use.[15] Ministers may also rely on section 2(2) of the European Communities Act 1972 to introduce regulations intended to fulfil the United Kingdom's obligations under EC law. This is the basis, for example, of the legislation relating to the welfare of animals at slaughter.[16]

Some legislation, particularly that enacted before the 1980s, contains no such enabling powers, something which constitutes a very real weakness because it means that further measures intended to keep abreast of public opinion or scientific knowledge can be introduced only by securing additional primary legislation. This may be a realistic proposition if the government of the day considers the matter sufficiently important to include in its own legislative programme or, alternatively, a sympathetic backbench MP is successful in steering a Private Member's Bill through the legislative process, but given the competition for parliamentary time and the procedural problems involved, the instances of either are relatively few and far between.[17] Nevertheless, the combination of statute and secondary legislation, together with administrative provisions introduced under their authority, has resulted in an extensive system of regulation which supplements the Protection of Animals Acts, influenced to a very considerable degree by the developing science of animal welfare.

B. Licensing, Certification, and Registration

To require an activity to be licensed, certificated, or registered is not only of practical importance, it is also of great symbolic significance. The consequence is that there is no longer an unfettered freedom to engage in it. In effect, it may only be carried on lawfully with the consent of the State. In relation to animals, this not only represents a major qualification to the traditional common law right of an

---

[12] Animal Health Act 1981, s 37.   [13] Animal Health Act 1981, s 39.
[14] Zoo Licensing Act 1981, s 9.   [15] Animals (Scientific Procedures) Act 1986, s 21(1), (2).
[16] The Welfare of Animals (Slaughter or Killing) Regulations 1995, SI 1995/731.

[17] Examples include: the Riding Establishments Act 1970 and the Breeding and Sale of Dogs (Welfare) Act 1999 which amend, and make more effective, respectively the Riding Establishments Act 1964 and the Breeding of Dogs Act 1973; and the Animal Health (Amendment) Act 1998, which amended the Animal Health Act 1981 to enable ministers to make regulations laying down welfare standards for animals kept in quarantine. Similarly, the provisions of the Protection of Animals Act 1911 have been subsequently enhanced by the Protection of Animals Act (1911) Amendment Act 1921; Protection of Animals (Amendment) Act 1927; Protection of Animals Act 1934; Protection of Animals (Amendment) Act 1954; Protection of Animals (Anaesthetics) Act 1954; Abandonment of Animals Act 1960; Animals (Cruel Poisons) Act 1962; Protection of Animals (Anaesthetics) Act 1964; Protection of Animals (Penalties) Act 1987; Protection of Animals (Amendment) Act 1988; Protection Against Cruel Tethering Act 1988; Protection of Animals (Amendment) Act 2000.

owner to do as he wishes with his property, but it may also permit the regulating authority to impose specific conditions, monitor standards and performance, insist on necessary improvements, and, ultimately, to revoke the authorization or refuse an application for its renewal.

It is perhaps not widely appreciated that, in relation to commercial and professional activities involving animals, some form of licensing, certification, or registration is now the norm in Britain. Circuses,[18] markets,[19] and farms are the most notable exceptions, the latter being particularly significant because of the vast number of animals involved.[20] Shelters which take in stray and unwanted animals also remain unregulated.[21] In contrast, a licence is required: to run a pet shop;[22] an animal boarding establishment;[23] a riding establishment;[24] a dog breeding establishment;[25] to operate a zoo;[26] to carry out a scientific procedure involving a protected animal;[27] and to use premises as a slaughterhouse.[28] A licence is also necessary before one can keep a dangerous wild animal;[29] kill, take, or sell a badger, have such an animal in one's possession, or interfere with a badger sett;[30] kill, take, sell, or keep certain types of wild bird;[31] or carry out the duties of a slaughterman.[32] In addition, a person who either exhibits a performing animal at any entertainment to which the public are admitted, or trains such an animal, is required to

---

[18] The Government has recently indicated that it has no plans to introduce additional statutory measures for travelling circuses, but is assisting the Association of Circus Proprietors to prepare a voluntary Code of Practice: HC Debs, 28 July 2000, col 895 (WA). A circus is defined as any place where animals are kept or introduced wholly or mainly for the purpose of performing tricks or manoeuvres: Dangerous Wild Animals Act 1976, s 7(4); Zoo Licensing Act 1981, s 21(1). Where a local authority in Scotland refused a circus an entertainment licence because it considered the concept of performing animals to be morally unacceptable, the court held that, in the absence of an express statutory power, the authority was not empowered to prohibit acts of which it disapproved, being the very types of performance which Parliament required to be registered by it under the Performing Animals (Regulation) Act 1925: *Gerry Cottle's Circus Ltd v City of Edinburgh District Council* 1990 SLT 235. Under EC Regulation 338/97, which implements the Convention on International Trade in Endangered Species of Flora and Fauna (CITES), it is illegal to use or display for commercial purposes any of the species listed in Annex A of the Regulation—which includes a number of animals traditionally used in circuses—unless DEFRA (Formerly the DETR) has issued a certificate for that purpose: HC Debs, 1 June 1998, col 22 (WA).

[19] Lairs at markets were formerly required to be licensed by the local authority under the Markets, Sales and Lairs Order 1925, SR & O 1925/1349, r 2(1)(b), but this was revoked by virtue of the Markets, Sales and Lairs (Amendment) Order 1996, SI 1996/3265.

[20] FAWC recommended in 1990 that the Government should give consideration to the introduction of a licensing or registration scheme for all those having responsibility for livestock: *Report of the Enforcement Working Group* (1990) para 8.10. The suggestion was subsequently rejected by ministers.

[21] The Government presently has no intention to introduce licensing for sanctuaries as it does not consider there to be sufficient evidence of problems to warrant it: HC Debs, 9 November 1999, col 472 (WA). At the time of writing, the Companion Animal Welfare Council has a working party investigating this issue. The Association of British Dogs' Homes has recently introduced a voluntary *Code of Practice for Animal Rescue Organizations Caring for Cats and Dogs*.

[22] Pet Animals Act 1951, s 1(1). [23] Animal Boarding Establishments Act 1963, s 1(1).

[24] Riding Establishments Act 1964, s 1(1). [25] Breeding of Dogs Act 1973, s 1(1).

[26] Zoo Licensing Act 1981, s 1(1). [27] Animals (Scientific Procedures) Act 1986, s 3(a), (b).

[28] Fresh Meat (Hygiene and Inspection) Regulations 1995, SI 1995/539, reg 4(1).

[29] Dangerous Wild Animals Act 1976, ss 1(1) and 5. [30] Protection of Badgers Act 1992, s 10(1), (2).

[31] Wildlife and Countryside Act 1981, s 16. [32] SI 1995/731, n 16 above, reg 4(3) and Sch 1.

be registered with a relevant local authority;[33] a place where scientific procedures are carried out, together with the establishments which breed and supply the animals used in such procedures, must be certified by the Home Secretary;[34] and those who transport cattle, sheep, pigs, goats, or horses on journeys in excess of eight hours are required to obtain specific authorization from the Minister of Agriculture or other competent authority.[35] This is a wide-ranging list, and it reflects how well established this form of regulation has become in relation to animals. The effectiveness of each of these regulatory regimes is, however, always dependent on the legislative provisions which govern the particular scheme and the rigour with which they are enforced, and it is significant that there is considerable variation in their operation and the conditions they impose on those to whom they are directed. Such differences may be due to the character of the respective activities; what is considered appropriate in one situation may not be in another. A further factor is the primary purpose of the regulation. The requirement to obtain a licence to keep a dangerous wild animal was, for example, instituted principally out of concern to protect the public, and zoo licensing is as much to do with safety and the provision of appropriate amenities as it is with animal welfare. In the main, however, the nature of each scheme is largely a reflection of the attitudes which prevailed at the time when it was originally enacted. Some, such as those relating to performing animals and pet shops, pre-date the modern concept of welfare, and clearly require updating; more recent provisions, such as those which govern farm animals and transport, have been greatly influenced by contemporary perceptions of an animal's needs, particularly those factors represented by the Five Freedoms (although many would argue that these continue to be compromised to an unacceptable degree in the face of commercial pressures). In consequence, the degree of legal regulation varies considerably, depending upon when and why the particular legislation was originally introduced. Moreover, it is important to appreciate the extent to which domestic welfare provisions have been influenced by EC legislation.[36]

---

[33] Performing Animals (Regulation) Act 1925, s 1(1).

[34] Animals (Scientific Procedures) Act 1986, ss 3(c) and 7(1).

[35] SI 1997/1480, n 5 above, art 12(3) and Sch 9.

[36] The Welfare of Farmed Animals Regulations, n 2 above, implement Directive 88/166, Directive 91/629, as amended by Directive 97/2 and Decision 97/182, Directive 91/630, and Directive 98/58; the Animals (Scientific Procedures) Act 1986, as amended, implements Directive 86/609; SI 1997/1480, n 5 above, implements Directive 91/628 as amended by Directive 95/29 (Regulation 1255/97 and Regulation 411/98 have direct effect); SI 1995/731, n 16 above, implements Directive 93/119; and the revised edition of the *Secretary of State's Standards of Modern Zoo Practice*, published in 2000, takes account of Directive 99/22, but there will need to be some further legislative changes to give full effect to the Directive. Similar action will be required to implement Directive 99/74 on laying hens.

(1) Scientific procedures

The most detailed system of licensing and certification is that provided for by the Animals (Scientific Procedures) Act 1986, the immediate successor of the licensing scheme originally introduced in 1876.[37] The Act applies to 'regulated procedures' carried out on a 'protected animal', that is any living vertebrate other than man, together with the members of the (invertebrate) species, *Octopus vulgaris*.[38] Save for those situations excepted under the Act,[39] a regulated procedure means:

- Any experimental or other scientific procedure applied to a protected animal which may have the effect of causing it pain, suffering, distress, or lasting harm.[40] In practice, these terms are interpreted to 'encompass any material disturbance to normal health (defined as the physical, mental and social well-being of the animal)' including disease, injury, and physiological or psychological discomfort, whether immediately or in the longer term.[41]
- Anything done for the purpose of, or liable to result in, the birth or hatching of a protected animal if this may have the effect of causing it pain, suffering, distress, or lasting harm.[42]
- The administration of an anaesthetic or analgesic to a protected animal, or decerebration or any other such procedure, for the purposes of any experimental or other scientific procedure.[43]

The effects of the regulation imposed by the Act are twofold. These may be considered as being either complementary or contradictory in nature, depending upon one's attitude to the use of animals in scientific procedures. First, the Act provides a degree of protection for animals by placing constraints on what may be done to them and imposing conditions as to how they should be treated. Secondly, it protects those engaged in such work, since that which is done under the authority of the Act is legal, even though the same conduct might amount to an offence under the terms of other animal protection legislation.

---

[37] See Ch 4, s B above.

[38] Animals (Scientific Procedures) Act 1986, s 1(1), as amended by the Animals (Scientific Procedures) Act (Amendment) Order 1993, SI 1993/2103. A mammal, bird, or reptile becomes a protected animal when half the gestation or incubation period for the relevant species has elapsed; in any other case, it is when the animal becomes capable of independent feeding: s 1(2).

[39] The ringing, tagging, or marking of an animal, or the application of any other humane procedure for the sole purpose of enabling it to be identified, so long as it causes only momentary pain or distress and no lasting harm, does not constitute a regulated procedure. Neither does the administration of any substance or article to an animal by way of a medicinal test in accordance with the Medicines Act 1968, ss 32(4),(6) and 35(8)(b); nor any recognized veterinary, agricultural, or animal husbandry practice: ibid, s 2(5), (6), (8). Killing a protected animal is a regulated procedure only if it is killed for experimental or other scientific use, the place where it is killed is a designated establishment, and the method employed is not one appropriate to the animal under Schedule 1 to the Act: s 2(7).

[40] ibid, s 2(1).

[41] Home Office, *Guidance on the Operation of the Animals (Scientific Procedures) Act 1986* (2000) para 2.14.

[42] Animals (Scientific Procedures) Act 1986, s 2(3).   [43] ibid, s 2(4).

The statute requires that two separate licences must be granted by the Home Secretary before a protected animal may be lawfully subjected to a regulated procedure. Thus, the individual carrying out the procedure must hold a personal licence permitting him to do so;[44] and the procedure itself must be authorized as part of a programme of work specified in a project licence.[45] The place where the procedure is to be carried out is indicated in both the personal and the project licence,[46] and this will normally be at premises which have in turn been designated by the Home Secretary as a scientific procedure establishment.[47] An establishment which breeds or supplies mice, rats, guinea-pigs, hamsters, gerbils, ferrets, rabbits, quail, dogs, cats, primates, or genetically modified pigs or sheep, for use in regulated procedures is required to be similarly certified.[48] In exercising his regulatory powers, the Home Secretary is assisted by the Inspectorate established under the Act, whom he is required to consult before granting a licence or issuing a certificate. If he wishes, he may also consult an independent assessor or the statutory advisory body, the Animals Procedure Committee (APC).[49]

The Home Secretary may only grant a project licence if he is satisfied that the purpose of the work is to promote:

- human, animal, or plant health;
- understanding of physiological conditions in man, animals, or plants;
- the protection of the natural environment in the interests of the health or welfare of man or animals;
- the advancement of knowledge in biological or behavioural sciences;
- education or training otherwise than in schools;
- forensic enquiries; or
- the breeding of animals for experimental or other scientific use.[50]

Notwithstanding that the object of the proposed work falls within one of these categories, the Home Secretary must be further persuaded that:

- the purpose of the programme cannot be achieved satisfactorily by any other reasonably practicable method not entailing the use of protected animals; and
- the procedures to be used are those which

---

[44] ibid, ss 3(a), 4(1).   [45] ibid, ss 3(b), 5(1), (2).   [46] ibid, s 3(c).

[47] ibid, s 6(1). The Home Secretary may only permit regulated procedures to be carried out elsewhere if it appears to him that the nature of the work requires it: s 6(2).

[48] ibid, s 7 and Sch 2, as amended by SI 1993/2103, n 38 above, and the Animals (Scientific Procedures) Act (Amendment to Schedule 2) Order 1998, SI 1998/1674. 'Endangered species' in these latter provisions refers to those listed in Appendix 1 of CITES, or Annex C1 of Council Regulation 3626/82 (now superseded by Regulation 338/97).

[49] ibid, s 9(1). Applications involving tobacco and tobacco products on conscious animals, microsurgical training, the use of non-human primates in procedures of substantial severity, the use of wild-caught, non-human primates, and the testing of cosmetics, have been routinely considered by the APC: Home Office, n 41 above, Appendix G, para 33. The APC is keen to stress that the decision whether to grant a licence remains entirely with the Home Secretary; the role of the Committee is only to proffer advice: see APC, *Annual Report 1997* (1998) para 20.

[50] ibid, s 5(3).

(a) require the minimum number of animals,
(b) involve animals with the lowest degree of neurophysiological sensitivity,
(c) cause the least pain, suffering, distress, or lasting harm, and
(d) are most likely to produce satisfactory results.[51]

The policy underlying the operation of the licensing system is therefore promotion of the so-called '3Rs', which seek to *reduce* the number of animals used, to *refine* the procedures employed in order to minimize suffering, and to *replace* animals with alternatives wherever possible.[52] That is not to say, however, that, in order to use the least possible quantity of animals, a single individual may be subjected to a disproportionate number of procedures; indeed, there are strict limitations placed on the reuse of protected animals.[53] In the years since the 1986 Act came into effect the overall trend in the number of procedures has been downwards, although this has been recently halted, due in large measure to an increasing number of procedures involving animals which have been genetically modified.[54] The use of such animals was recorded as a separate category for the first time in 1990. By 1999, some 512,000 procedures, mainly involving mice, fell into this category, having more than doubled since 1995, and now representing 19 per cent of all scientific procedures.[55] The Government has cautioned, however, that the 'effectiveness of the Act

---

[51] Animals (Scientific Procedures) Act 1986, s 5(5), as amended by the Animals (Scientific Procedures) Act 1986 (Amendment) Regulations 1998, SI 1998/1974. See further, Home Office, n 41 above, paras 5.13–5.20.

[52] These criteria, first proposed by Russell, WMS and Burch, RL in their seminal work, *The Principles of Humane Experimental Technique* (1959), have had, and continue to have, a profound influence on public policy towards scientific procedures.

[53] Animals (Scientific Procedures) Act 1986, s 14, as amended by SI 1998/1974, n 51 above. According to the Government, 'The purpose of the 1986 Act is not to control the total number of procedures but to reduce suffering. . . . Often, if a procedure can be carried out either by using a large number of animals which would not experience much suffering or by using more severe testing on a smaller number of animals, the former option will be authorized': HC Debs, 11 May 1998, col 51 (WA).

[54] No of scientific procedures:

1987	: 3,631,400
1988	: 3,480,300
1989	: 3,315,100
1990	: 3,207,100
1991	: 3,242,400
1992	: 2,928,300
1993	: 2,827,700
1994	: 2,842,400
1995	: 2,709,600
1996	: 2,716,600
1997	: 2,636,000
1998	: 2,659,700
1999	: 2,656,800

Source: Home Office, *Statistics of Scientific Procedures on Living Animals. Great Britain* (published annually)

[55] Home Office, *Statistics of Scientific Procedures on Living Animals. Great Britain 1999* (2000) 16–17.

cannot be judged by the overall number of procedures', as its primary purpose is 'to reduce suffering'.[56]

Having assured himself that the foregoing criteria have been met, the Home Secretary is then required to weigh the adverse effects on the animals that will be used against the benefit likely to accrue as a result of the proposed programme.[57] The nature of the exercise therefore takes the form of a utilitarian cost-benefit assessment.[58] The potential benefit relates, first, to the extent to which man, animals, plants, or the environment may be advantaged if the project is wholly successful in meeting its declared objectives; and, secondly, to the value that may be placed on the specific outcomes of the programme of work (that is, the utility of the resulting data or product), rather than the importance of the general area of activity. Thus, although the long-term objective may be to find new medical treatments, the benefit for the purposes of the cost-benefit assessment relates to the progress likely to result directly from the programme outlined in the project licence application.[59] In addition, the Secretary of State must be satisfied that the programme is scientifically valid and likely to meet the stated objectives. The cost of the project is the adverse welfare effects (pain, suffering, distress, or lasting harm) likely to be experienced by the protected animals used during the course of the study.[60] In practice, the assessment requires more than establishing that the benefit is likely to exceed the costs to the animals. It must be demonstrated that the former will be maximized, and the latter, in terms of animal use and suffering, minimized. In any event, the outcome of the assessment is not binding on the Home Secretary; it remains open to him to refuse a licence, notwithstanding that the benefits are likely to outweigh the costs. Furthermore, although the Act formally requires only that the Home Secretary weighs the costs and benefits before granting a project licence, the Home Office takes the view that the cost-benefit analysis is not a single exercise which is conducted only at the beginning of the project, but continues throughout the life of the licence.[61] Indeed, it has been described as 'a process rather than an event'.[62] The emerging and actual costs and benefits are therefore expected to be evaluated and kept under review as the project progresses, in order to ensure that the original assumptions and assessments remain sound, and appropriate efforts are made to refine existing protocols.[63]

In considering the cost to the animals, each protocol which forms part of the proposed project is allocated one of four severity limits: unclassified (those performed entirely under general anaesthesia, from which the animal does not recover consciousness); mild (protocols which, at worst, give rise to slight or

---

[56] HC Debs, 26 October 2000, col 214 (WA).   [57] Animals (Scientific Procedures) Act 1986, s 5(4).
[58] See Home Office, n 41 above, Appendix I; also APC, *Annual Report 1997*, n 49 above, Appendix F: 'Review of the Operation of the Animals (Scientific Procedures) Act 1986', Ch 2. In a consultation letter issued in December 2000, the APC sought views concerning the application of the cost-benefit assessment.
[59] Home Office, n 41 above, para 5.11 and Appendix I, para 6.
[60] ibid, Appendix I, para 9.   [61] ibid, Appendix I, paras 1, 5, and 13.
[62] APC, n 58 above, Appendix F, Ch 2, Annex 1, para 1.2.
[63] Home Office, n 41 above, Appendix I, para 13.

transitory minor adverse effects); moderate (for example, toxicity tests which do not involve lethal end points, and many surgical procedures, provided that suffering is controlled and minimized by effective post-operative analgesia and care); and substantial (which encompasses protocols that may result in a major departure from the animal's state of health or well-being). The severity limit for each protocol is determined by the upper limit of the expected adverse effects that may be encountered by a protected animal. It represents the worst potential outcome for any animal subjected to the protocol, even if it may only be experienced by a small number of the animals used.[64] This exercise fulfils two purposes. First, if the project licence is granted, the band designated to each protocol becomes its 'severity limit', and it constitutes a breach of the licence to exceed this without promptly notifying the Home Office. Secondly, the cumulative effect of each protocol is taken into account to assess the overall severity of the proposed project. This is taken into account by the Home Secretary in weighing the likely adverse effects on the animals to be used against the benefits likely to accrue.[65] According to the Home Office:

The assessment of the severity band for the project as a whole reflects the number of animals used on each protocol and the actual suffering likely to be caused as a result. It is based on the overall level of cumulative suffering to be experienced by each animal, not just the single worst possible case. It takes into account the proportion of animals expected to reach the severity limit of the protocol and the duration of exposure to that severity limit, the nature and intensity of the adverse effects, and the actions to be taken to relieve suffering.[66]

At the end of 1999 there were 3,481 project licences in force. Of these, 1,406 were classified as mild; 1,861 as moderate; 66 as substantial; and 148 were unclassified.[67]

In deciding whether a project licence should be granted, the interests of cats, dogs, primates, and equidae are given more weight than other animals; their use may be permitted only if the Home Secretary is satisfied either that no other species is suitable, or that it is not practicable to obtain those which are.[68]

According to the Government, where an application cannot be granted in its present form, the reasons are made known to the applicant, who then generally either amends or withdraws the proposal. Accordingly, 'applications are only formally refused in rare cases'. The Home Office does not hold central records on why applications for a project licence are refused or withdrawn.[69] It is a widely held view among opponents to the use of animals in scientific procedures that, in practice, the decisions concerning project licences are weighted too much in favour of the applicants, to the detriment of the animals which will be used. Whether or not this is so, it must be recognized that the 1986 Act provides the only example of statutory regulation which requires the potential consequences for the animals involved to be formally assessed and taken into account in determining whether an activity should

---

[64] Home Office, n 41 above, Appendix I, paras 5.40–5.42.   [65] ibid, paras 5.43–5.47.
[66] ibid, para 5.48.   [67] Home Office, n 55 above, Appendix B, para 13.
[68] Animals (Scientific Procedures) Act 1986, s 5(6).   [69] HC Debs, 24 February 1999, col 178 (WA).

be permitted (subjected to 'critical scrutiny' in the words of the Chairman of the APC[70]), with the prospect that the interests of the animals may take precedence over those of humans. From the other side of the debate, concern has been expressed from within the scientific community at the length of time licence applications take to process which, it is claimed, puts those based in Britain at a competitive disadvantage. For example, an open letter addressed to the Minister of Science, signed by 110 leading scientists, was published in *The Times* of 13 June 2000, complaining that it can take 'six months or longer to obtain approval for a research project in the UK, whilst in other countries that permission can be obtained in weeks or even days'. In response, the minister said that historical data on this matter was not available but, during the early part of 2000, the average time to reach a decision on project licence applications was just under forty working days.[71] It should also be appreciated that not only may a decision on an application involve complex issues, but it is not a mechanical exercise. The length of time needed to process a project licence application varies according to 'the quality of the initial application; the complexity or originality of the proposed work; and whether it is necessary to consult a specialist inspector, an external assessor or the Animal Procedures Committee'.[72] Indeed, the Home Office advises applicants that the programme and individual protocols are subject to close scrutiny to determine if there is further scope for replacement, reduction, or refinement, and ministers have acknowledged that 'the vast majority of project licence applications are revised during negotiations' with the Animals (Scientific Procedures) Inspectorate.[73] For their part, the APC has expressed the view that the level of regulation is 'likely to be only one of a number of factors which may lead to work being carried out elsewhere than in the UK'.[74]

When granted, a project licence is required to include the following standard conditions:[75]

- unless the Home Secretary is satisfied that no animal suitable for the purpose of the programme can otherwise be obtained, all cats and dogs must have been bred at and obtained from a designated breeding establishment; and all mice, rats, guinea pigs, hamsters, gerbils, ferrets, rabbits, quail, primates, and genetically modified pigs and sheep must have been bred at a designated breeding establishment, or obtained from a designated supplying establishment;
- no vertebrate of an endangered species may be used unless the Home Secretary is persuaded that the work to be carried out under the project licence conforms

---

[70] APC, n 58 above, Appendix F, Chairman's (Professor Michael Banner) Introductory Letter addressed to the Secretary of State.

[71] HC Debs, 24 July 2000, col 468 (WA).   [72] HC Debs, 25 June 1998, col 588 (WA).

[73] Home Office, n 41 above, Appendix I, para 4; HC Debs, 20 June 2000, col 148 (WA).

[74] APC, n 58 above, Appendix F, Ch 9, para 8.

[75] Animals (Scientific Procedures) Act 1986, s 10(3), (3A), (3B), (3C), (3D), and Sch 2, as amended and inserted by the Animals (Scientific Procedures) Act (Amendment) Regulations 1993, SI 1993/2102; SI 1993/2103, n 38 above; SI 1998/1674, n 48 above; and SI 1998/1974, n 51 above. For the standard conditions attached to a project licence, see Home Office, n 41 above, Appendix D.

with Council Regulation 338/97 on the protection of species of wild fauna and flora by regulating trade (which replaced Regulation 3626/82), and it is to undertake research aimed at preservation of the species in question, or for essential biomedical purposes where the particular species exceptionally proves to be the only one suitable;

- no protected animal may be used which has been taken from the wild;
- where a project licence authorizes the setting free of a protected animal, it must contain a provision requiring that before the animal is released prior consent is obtained from the Home Secretary, who will need to be satisfied that the maximum possible care has been taken to safeguard the animal's well-being, its state of health allows it to be set free, and to do so would pose no danger to public health or the environment;
- at the conclusion of a series of regulated procedures, a veterinary surgeon or, if none is available, another suitably qualified person should determine whether a protected animal should be killed or kept alive (if it is likely to remain in lasting pain or distress, it must be destroyed; if it is kept alive, it must normally continue to be kept at a designated establishment); in practice the animal's fate will generally be prescribed in the project licence.

In the same manner, all personal licences[76] must include:

- a condition that the licensee shall take precautions to prevent or reduce to the minimum consistent with the purposes of the authorized procedures any pain, distress, or discomfort;
- an 'inviolable termination condition', which specifies the circumstances and manner in which a protected animal must in every case be immediately killed;
- such conditions as the Home Secretary considers appropriate to ensure that

    (a) all experiments are carried out under general or local anaesthesia, unless to do so is judged to be more traumatic to the animal than the experiment itself, or anaesthesia is incompatible with the object of the experiment;

    (b) anaesthesia is used in the case of serious injuries which may cause severe pain;

    (c) if anaesthesia is not possible, analgesics or other appropriate methods are used in order to ensure as far as possible that pain, suffering, distress, or harm are limited and that in any event the animal is not subjected to severe pain, distress, or suffering;

    (d) provided such action is compatible with the object of the experiment, an animal which suffers what is described as 'considerable pain', once anaesthesia has worn off, will be treated in good time with pain relief or, if this is not possible, will be immediately killed by a humane method.[77]

---

[76] See s C(7) below.

[77] Animals (Scientific Procedures) Act 1986, s 10(1), (2), (2A), and Sch 2A, as amended by SI 1998/1974. See further, Home Office, n 41 above, Appendix E.

Conditions which must be attached to a certificate designating a scientific procedure establishment, a breeding, or supplying establishment include provisions relating to:

- the method by which an animal is to be killed;
- the employment of adequately trained staff in relation to scientific procedure establishments;
- the availability of a person who is competent to kill animals in the required manner;
- the keeping of records relating to the source and disposal of animals;
- the marking for identification purposes of dogs, cats, and primates;
- the general care and accommodation of the animals, with particular emphasis on the environment, housing, freedom of movement, food, water, and care provided for each animal being appropriate for its health and well-being; and
- the care and supervision of a protected animal which is kept alive after having been subjected to a series of regulated procedures.[78]

Over and above these statutory requirements, the Home Secretary has a wide discretion to decide for himself what conditions to attach to licences and certificates of designation granted under the Act.[79] However, he is required, in consultation with the APC, to publish for the guidance of applicants information indicating how he intends to exercise his powers, and the conditions which he proposes to include in licences and certificates.[80] In practice, the courts would normally expect the minister to exercise his discretionary power in accordance with his published policy, although there is nothing to prevent him changing that policy, provided he undertakes the necessary consultation and gives those affected sufficient notice. So far as conditions relating to the treatment of animals are concerned, the approach of the Home Office is predicated on the principle that those used for scientific procedures should be maintained in good health and physical condition, behave in a manner normal for the species and strain, with a reasonably full expression of their behavioural repertoire, and be amenable to handling.[81] In addition, the administrative discretion inherent in the statutory scheme can be used, if the Home Secretary so chooses, to change and develop policy in relation to scientific procedures without the need for further legislation. In November 1997, for example, the Home Office announced that it would end the use of animals in cosmetic testing by means of a voluntary agreement with the industry. No licences authorizing such procedures would be granted in the

---

[78] ibid, s 10(5), (5A), (6), (6A), (6B), (6D), as amended by SI 1998/1974. See further, Home Office, n 41 above, Appendix B (scientific procedure establishments) and Appendix C (breeding and supplying establishments).

[79] ibid, s 10(1).

[80] ibid, s 21(1), (3). See further, Home Office, n 41 above.

[81] Home Office, *Code of Practice for the Housing and Care of Animals Used in Scientific Procedures* (1989) para 3.2.

future, and companies which at the time were still undertaking this work agreed voluntarily to discontinue it.[82] Similarly, since April 1999, every scientific procedure, breeding, and supplying establishment has been required to establish an ethical review process,[83] and, in October 1999, the Home Office announced that licences to conduct the LD50 test (a test to find the dose of a chemical which is lethal to 50 per cent of the animals in a study) would no longer be granted if a suitable alternative was available.[84]

(2) Performing animals

In complete contrast to the sophisticated regime established by the 1986 Act, that relating to the exhibition and training of performing animals is rudimentary in the extreme. It requires only that a person involved in such activities is registered by the local authority in whose area they live.[85] If they do not have a permanent residence, they must register with one of a small number of authorities which are prescribed for the purpose.[86] The single qualification for entry on to the register is the payment of any fee that may be levied. So long as such money is forthcoming, the authority has no discretion in deciding whether the person should be registered; the statute fails to provide it with any power to refuse or revoke registration, or even impose conditions. To take any of these measures requires a court order, and this may only be granted if the person concerned is found to have been guilty of cruelty.[87] In submitting an application for registration, the information an applicant is required to provide consists of nothing more than particulars of the animals involved and the general nature of the performances for which they are to be trained.[88] The scheme has no provision allowing an authority to specify standards

---

[82] Home Office Press Notice 310/97, 6 November 1997. This agreement related to finished products. To complement it, the Government announced in November 1998 an end to the use of animals in the testing of cosmetics' ingredients, again as a result of voluntary agreement with the relevant companies.

[83] Home Office, *The Ethical Review Process* (1998); see now, Home Office, n 41 above, paras 4.13–4.17 and Appendix J. The minister announced at the end of 2000 that he had asked the Animals (Scientific Procedures) Inspectorate to carry out a review of the operation of the ethical review process, with a view to identifying improvements in the way in which it is carried out: HC Debs, 1 November 2000, col 517 (WA).

[84] Home Office Press Notice 330/99, 21 October 1999. In the five years, 1995–1999, 14 licences authorizing the LD50 test were granted; by April 2000, 12 of these had been varied to remove this authority, and the remaining 2 licensees had, after initial reluctance, agreed to submit their licences to be amended: HC Debs, 4 April 2000, col 72 (WA).

[85] Performing Animals (Regulation) Act 1925, s 1(1), (2). The Act applies to exhibition of an animal at any entertainment to which the public are admitted, regardless of whether they are charged for admission, and training for such an event, but excepting animals used for bona fide military, police, agricultural, or sporting purposes: ss 5(1) and 7.

[86] These include the City of London, Birmingham, Bristol, Cardiff, Kingston upon Hull, Leeds, Liverpool, Manchester, Newcastle upon Tyne, Aberdeen, Dundee, Edinburgh, and Glasgow: Performing Animals Rules 1925, SR & O 1925/1219, r 2.

[87] Performing Animals (Regulation) Act 1925, ss 2 and 4(2).

[88] ibid, s 1(3); SR & O 1925/1219, n 86 above, r 1 and Sch 1.

which must be met. Indeed, the degree of regulation under the Act is so inadequate that its contribution to animal protection is negligible.[89]

(3) Pet shops, animal boarding establishments, dog breeding establishments, riding establishments, and the keeping of dangerous wild animals

Licensing of pet shops,[90] animal boarding establishments,[91] and dangerous wild animals kept in captivity[92] also falls to local authorities. In relation to all of these, the authority does have a discretion whether or not to grant the licence. In reaching its decision, it must have regard to a number of specific factors, including the suitability of accommodation, the provision of food and drink, precautions

---

[89] In January 2000, local authorities were reminded by the Home Office of their duty under s 1(7) of the Act to provide it with information of registrations. In the first five months of the year, it received details of over 2,000 animals, of which 1,390 were used in promotional, film, and television work: Home Office Circular 1/2000; HC Debs, 23 May 2000, col 406 (WA).

[90] Pet Animals Act 1951, s 1. The Act applies to any premises where a business of selling vertebrate animals as pets is carried on, including a private dwelling and premises where animals are kept with the view to their being sold in the course of such a business. It does not apply, however, where a person sells pedigree animals bred by him, or the offspring of an animal kept by him as a pet: s 7, as amended by the Pet Animals Act 1951 (Amendment) Act 1983. The licensing requirement relates, not to the operating, but the keeping of, a pet shop. So where birds were on premises only for a limited period, prior to being exported to buyers overseas (having been brought from a dealer), they were there for business purposes, namely, the selling of pet birds; the premises were therefore kept as a pet shop, notwithstanding that the birds were not sold to members of the public coming to the premises; nor, save on certain occasions, were a stock of birds kept on the premises: *Chalmers v Diwell* (1975) 74 LGR 173.

[91] Animal Boarding Establishments Act 1963, s 1. A boarding establishment means any premises, including a private dwelling, where a business is carried on involving the provision of accommodation for dogs or cats belonging to other people: s 5.

[92] Dangerous Wild Animals Act 1976, s 1. The kinds of animal for which a licence is required are specified in the Schedule to the Act. The Secretary of State has the power to vary the Schedule if he considers it appropriate: ss 7(4), 8. 'No person is entitled in terms of the Act to commence keeping such animals before he has actually obtained a licence. The whole tenor of the Act makes clear that the local authority must be satisfied as to the safety and suitability of the premises and also of the suitability of the applicant, before granting a licence': *Halpern v Chief Constable of Strathclyde* 1988 SCLR 137, 144 (Sh Ct). The provisions of the Act do not apply to animals which would otherwise fall within its ambit that are kept in a zoo, a circus, a licensed pet shop, or a designated establishment under the Animals (Scientific Procedures) Act 1986: s 5. According to McNeill J, the meaning of a circus in relation to the exemption under the Dangerous Wild Animals Act 1976 is to be interpreted 'as that word is commonly understood, namely, the aggregation of vans and cages in which wild animals may be kept and a big top into which they may well be introduced for the purpose of performing' (*Hemming v Graham-Jones* The Times, 23 October 1980, QBD). This decision led the Department of the Environment to suggest that winter quarters did not fall within this definition (Department of the Environment, Global Wildlife Division Circular 11/96), although there was no evidence that local authorities acted on this advice to insist on licensing of dangerous wild animals while in winter quarters (see further, Circus Working Group, *A Report into the welfare of circus animals in England and Wales* (1998) 5). However, the Court of Appeal, reversing the decision of the High Court, has recently confirmed that the meaning of 'circus' in this context does include the winter quarters where the animals are kept when not touring for performances, and animals kept there do not in consequence require to be licensed: *South Kesteven District Council v Mackie* [2000] 1 WLR 1461. The Government has accepted that winter quarters should be subject to licensing controls, but have indicated that there is little prospect of finding time in its legislative programme to secure this change: HC Debs, 28 July 2000, col 895 (WA).

against the spread of diseases, and arrangements in the case of fire or other emergency. Where it grants a licence, the authority is required to specify such conditions as it considers necessary or expedient for securing these objects.[93] However, in none of these cases do authorities have the power to impose conditions which fall outside the objects expressly mentioned.

The legislation relating to riding establishments and dog breeding establishments is similar in form, but there are some significant differences as a result of subsequent amendments. In relation to the former, for example, it is specified that the licensing authority should have regard to the need for securing that *paramount* consideration will be given to the condition of the horses.[94] The Act also introduces the concept of statutory conditions, which have effect regardless of whether they are actually specified in the licence.[95] For the purposes of licensing, keeping a dog breeding establishment means the carrying on by a person at any premises, including a private dwelling, of a business of breeding dogs for sale. It was formerly the case that premises fell within this definition if at least three bitches were kept there by the person running the business for the purpose of breeding puppies for sale.[96] However, it proved too easy for unscrupulous commercial breeders to arrange their business (generally referred to as 'puppy farms') so that it did not fall within these criteria, and they were replaced with effect from 1 January 2000. A person is now regarded as carrying on a business of breeding dogs for sale if (i) he keeps a single bitch at *any* premises for a period of twelve months, (ii) she gives birth to a litter of puppies during that period, and (iii) four or more other relevant litters are born during that period. In assessing the number of litters born under the third head, account is taken of those born to the bitch initially mentioned in (i); any other bitches kept by the person at the same premises; any bitches kept there by a relative (as defined by the statute) of the person; any bitches kept by him at other premises; and any bitches kept anywhere by any person with whom he has made a breeding arrangement under which he is provided with puppies or any part of the proceeds from their sale.[97] For the same purpose, the licensing authority is now required additionally to have regard to the need for securing that: bitches are not mated if they are less than one year old; they do not give birth to more than six litters of puppies; each litter must be at

---

[93] See further, British Veterinary Association, *Guidance Model Conditions for Local Authorities and Their Authorized Officers and Veterinary Inspectors for the Licensing of Dog Breeding Establishments* (2000); LGA et al, *The Pet Animals Act 1951. Model Standards for Pet Shop Licence Conditions* (1998); SSPCA (with Exotic Animal Services, University of Edinburgh, and the Pet Care Trust), 'A Code of Practice for Livestock Trading' (nd).

[94] Riding Establishments Act 1964, s 1(4)(b)(i), as amended by the Riding Establishments Act 1970. The Act applies to a business which keeps horses for the purpose of either letting them out on hire for riding, or for instruction in riding in return for payment: s 6(1). It therefore includes, for example, beach donkeys, but does not extend to livery stables.

[95] ibid, s 1(4A), as amended by the Riding Establishments Act 1970.

[96] Breeding of Dogs Act 1973, s 5.

[97] ibid, s 4A, inserted by the Breeding and Sale of Dogs (Welfare) Act 1999, s 7.

least a year apart; and accurate records be kept in the prescribed form and available for inspection.[98]

Any person aggrieved by either the refusal of a local authority to grant any of these licences, or any condition attached to them, may appeal to a court of summary jurisdiction in the place in which the premises are situated.[99]

(4) Zoos

Local authorities are also responsible for the licensing of zoos.[100] In applying for a licence, an applicant is required to advise the authority of the kinds of animals to be kept and their approximate number, together with the arrangements for their accommodation, maintenance, and well-being, the approximate numbers and categories of staff employed or to be employed in the zoo, and details of the number of visitors, motor vehicles, and means of access to the premises.[101] The latter considerations demonstrate that the Act is as much concerned with public safety and the impact on the area in which the zoo is situated as it is with animal welfare. Thus, in considering the application, the authority is required to take into account any representations submitted by, among others, the police, the fire service, the governing body of any national institution concerned with the operation of zoos, any person alleging that the zoo would injuriously affect the health and safety of persons living locally, and any other person whose representations might, in the opinion of the local authority, be relevant to its decision whether to grant a licence.[102] Moreover, the authority is *required* to refuse a licence if it is satisfied that the zoo would injuriously affect the health or safety of persons living in the neighbourhood of the zoo, or seriously affect the preservation of law and order,[103] while it can *choose* for itself whether to grant a licence if it is not satisfied that the standards of accommodation, staffing, or management are adequate for either the proper care and well-being of the animals or for the proper conduct of the zoo.[104] This is highly unsatisfactory. No establishment should have an expectation of holding a licence in such circumstances.

In granting a licence, the authority is given a wide discretion to attach whatever conditions it thinks necessary or desirable for ensuring the proper conduct of the

---

[98] ibid, s 1 (4) (f)–(i), inserted by the Breeding and Sale of Dogs (Welfare) Act 1999, s 2; Breeding of Dogs (Licensing Records) Regulations 1999, SI 1999/3192; Breeding of Dogs (Licensing Records) (Scotland) Regulations 1999, SSI 1999/176.

[99] Pet Animals Act, s 1(4); Animal Boarding Establishments Act 1963, s 1(4); Riding Establishments Act 1964, s 1(5); Breeding of Dogs Act 1973, s 1(5); Dangerous Wild Animals Act 1976, s 2(1).

[100] Zoo Licensing Act 1981, s 1(1). A 'zoo' in this context means an establishment where animals not normally domesticated in Great Britain are kept for exhibition to the public on more than seven days in any twelve months, regardless of whether there is a charge for admission, but the Act does not apply to circuses or pet shops: ss 1(2), 21(1). In circumstances where the zoo is owned by the local authority, it remains responsible for undertaking the licensing procedures, but the process is overseen by the Secretary of State: s 13. If the relevant local authority informs the Secretary of State that in their opinion a zoo should be exempt because of its small size or the small number of kinds of animals kept there, he may direct that the Act shall not apply to that zoo: s 14(1)(a).

[101] ibid, s 2(2).   [102] ibid, s 3.   [103] ibid, s 4(2).   [104] ibid, s 4(3).

zoo,[105] although it is required to have regard to the standards relating to the management of zoos and the animals in them published by the Secretary of State under the authority of the Act.[106] The Secretary of State may also direct it to attach conditions of his own choosing.[107] Although not formally part of the licensing process, zoos, like scientific procedure establishments, are now encouraged to initiate 'some form of ethical review process', particularly where the use of animals may be in conflict with the best welfare interests of the animals, such as acquisition, management, or disposal for conservation, education, or research.[108] Furthermore, it is only zoos which are required publicly to exhibit their licence; the original, or a copy of it, including the conditions, must be displayed at each public entrance of the zoo.[109]

(5) Slaughterhouses

For their part, slaughterhouses are required to be licensed by the appropriate Minister of Agriculture.[110] This is intended principally to safeguard public health, but among the factors taken into account when deciding whether to grant a licence is whether animal protection provisions contained in other legislation relating to the construction, equipment, and maintenance of slaughterhouses specified are being complied with.[111]

(6) Certification

An alternative means of influencing the welfare of animals is by certification. This takes two forms. The first involves formal confirmation, generally by a veterinary surgeon, that an animal is in a suitable condition for its intended use or the situation in which it will be placed. For example, it is an offence to export a horse unless immediately before shipment it has been examined by a veterinary inspector appointed by the minister and is certified to be capable of being conveyed and disembarked without cruelty, and of being worked without suffering.[112] The second type of certification relates to undertakings involving animals. We have seen already that scientific procedure, breeding, and supplying establishments each require a certificate of designation from the Home Secretary. Similarly, a person who transports cattle, sheep, pigs, goats, or horses on journeys of more than eight hours in road vehicles, or on any journey by sea, rail, or air, is required to obtain a specific authorization from the appropriate competent authority. In the case of those based in Britain, this will be from the relevant minister; where the transporter is based in another country, it is sufficient to have an equivalent authorization from an EU

---

[105] Zoo Licensing Act 1981, s 5(3).
[106] ibid, ss 5(4), 9. DETR, *Secretary of State's Standards of Modern Zoo Practice* (2000).
[107] Zoo Licensing Act 1981, s 5(5).   [108] DETR, n 106 above, Appendix 2.
[109] ibid, para 12.1.   [110] SI 1995/539, n 28 above, reg 4(1).
[111] Regulation 4(2)(a)(i) alludes to Parts 1 and 11 of Sch 2 to SI 1995/731, n 16 above.
[112] Animal Health Act 1981, s 40(1), (2).

Member State. In deciding whether to grant a specific authorization, the minister must have regard to any relevant circumstances, in particular any evidence tending to show that the applicant, or any of the applicant's employees, agents, or associates, has committed an offence involving animal welfare or contravened any provision of the legislation relating to the transport of animals, including failing to provide relevant information or providing false information.[113]

C. Professional Proficiency

It is widely acknowledged that a key factor influencing the treatment of domestic and captive animals is the attitude of those who are responsible for them. 'It has been impressed on us over and over again that in any system the most important factor affecting the welfare of animals is the standard of knowledgeable, conscientious and sympathetic care for them which can be summed up as good stockmanship', observed the House of Commons Agriculture Committee in 1981. 'Given enough skilled care, many systems are satisfactory; treated carelessly or unfeelingly, however good their outward surroundings, animals will suffer.'[114] Similarly, FAWC has expressed the view that the 'most welfare-friendly system may fail if not accompanied by competent stockmanship and sound management practice. A good stockperson can anticipate and avoid many potential welfare problems, will have a compassionate and humane attitude, and an ability to identify any problems and respond to them.'[115] While these two quotations relate specifically to farm livestock, it is self-evident that, whatever the circumstances, the greater the knowledge, interest, and experience of those who care for animals, the better they will be looked after.[116] Although there are no standards laid down for those who keep animals in a private capacity, there is a welcome trend towards requiring those who deal with animals in a commercial environment to be able to demonstrate an appropriate level of proficiency in their work.

(1) The veterinary profession

This is not in itself a new idea. The veterinary profession, for example, has been the subject of statutory regulation since 1881.[117] It is presently governed by the Veterinary Surgeons Act 1966, which provides that a person may only practise, or hold himself out as practising, veterinary surgery if he is included in the register of veterinary surgeons required by the Act to be maintained by the Royal College of

[113] SI 1997/1480, n 5 above, art 12 and Sch 9, paras 1(2) and 2(2), (3).
[114] *Animal Welfare in Poultry, Pig and Veal Calf Production* (1981) para 21.
[115] FAWC, *Report on the Welfare of Broiler Breeders* (1998) para 17. See also the importance attached to high standards of stockmanship in the Codes of recommendations for the welfare of livestock produced by MAFF, a full list of which is to be found in the bibliography.
[116] See, for example, Home Office, n 81 above, paras 1.9 and 1.10.   [117] See Ch 4, s D(1) above.

Veterinary Surgeons (RCVS).[118] 'Veterinary surgery' is statutorily defined for these purposes to mean 'the art and science of veterinary surgery and medicine', including the diagnosis of diseases in, and injuries to, mammals, birds, and reptiles (but not fish); the giving of advice based upon such diagnosis; medical and surgical treatment of animals; and the performance of surgical operations on them.[119] The Royal College also has responsibility for ensuring that professional standards are maintained. To this end, it is, on the one hand, empowered to appoint persons to visit UK veterinary schools to report on the standards of facilities, training, and examinations,[120] and, on the other, it is required to investigate and determine disciplinary matters, specifically those which, if upheld, may either render the veterinarian unfit to practise or amount to disgraceful misconduct in any professional respect. It is also responsible in appropriate cases for establishing whether a person's name has been fraudulently entered in the register. Significantly, however, the RCVS has no specific power routinely to monitor the performance of practitioners.[121]

Upon being accepted into membership of the Royal College, a veterinary surgeon is required to take an oath which includes an undertaking that 'my constant

---

[118] Veterinary Surgeons Act 1966, s 19(1). The register contains the names, addresses, and qualifications of all persons who hold a recognized veterinary degree from a university in the United Kingdom: ss 2, 3. The name of a person who has ceased to practise may be removed from the register: s 13(2), (3). A person who is a national of a Member State of the European Union and holds a recognized European qualification in veterinary surgery is also entitled to be registered: s 5A, inserted by the Veterinary Surgeons Qualifications (EEC Recognition) Order 1980, SI 1980/1951, and the Medical, Nursing, Dental and Veterinary Qualifications (EEC Recognition) Order 1982, SI 1982/1076. These give effect to Directive 78/1026 (as amended by Directive 89/594). The effect of these measures is that vets who are EU nationals are 'to be regarded as a separate, favoured, privileged group enjoying greater rights and freedoms than other non-EU nationals': *Choux v RCVS* (EAT, 7 May 1996). All veterinary schools in the EU are required to comply with Directive 78/1027, which specifies a minimum five-year course and lists the subjects to be included. In the past, the RCVS has expressed 'serious reservations' about the effectiveness of the European Commission in carrying out its responsibility to monitor and enforce standards in veterinary schools: (1997) 140 *Veterinary Record* 187. Veterinarians from other countries may be admitted to the register at the discretion of the RCVS: Veterinary Surgeons Act 1966, s 6.

[119] ibid, s 27. Certain procedures which would otherwise fall within this definition are permitted to be performed by a non-veterinarian, for example, any treatment given by an animal's owner, his family or employees; anything, except an operation involving the opening of the abdomen, done to an animal used in agriculture by its owner or his employee; the rendering in an emergency of first aid; and certain specific operations. In addition, a registered veterinary nurse is permitted, under the direction of a veterinary surgeon, to carry out medical or minor surgical treatment on a companion animal not involving entry into a body cavity: Sch 3, Part 1, as amended by the Veterinary Surgeons Act 1966 (Schedule 3 Amendment) Order 1988, SI 1988/526, and the Veterinary Surgeons Act 1966 (Schedule 3 Amendment) Order 1991, SI 1991/1412. Other exemptions are contained in the Protection of Animals (Anaesthetics) Act 1954; the Animals (Scientific Procedures) Act 1986, s 19(3)(a); the Veterinary Surgeons (Exemption) Order 1962, SI 1962/2557, as amended by the Veterinary Surgeons (Exemptions) Order 1973, SI 1973/308, and the Veterinary Surgeons (Exemptions) (Amendment) Order 1982, SI 1982/1267; Veterinary Surgeons (Blood Sampling) Order 1983, SI 1983/6, as amended by the Veterinary Surgeons Blood Sampling (Amendment) Order 1988, SI 1988/1090, and the Veterinary Surgeons Blood Sampling (Amendment) Order 1990, SI 1990/2217; and the Veterinary Surgery (Epidural Anaesthesia) Order 1992, SI 1992/696. See further, Ch 8, s C(6) above.

[120] ibid, s 5.   [121] ibid, ss 15, 16.

endeavour will be to ensure the welfare of the animals committed to my care'. This emphasis on welfare is reinforced in the RCVS *Guide to Professional Conduct*, by giving precedence, in what are described as the profession's 'Ten Guiding Principles', to a client's entitlement to expect that a veterinary surgeon will make animal welfare their first consideration in seeking to provide the most appropriate attention for animals committed to their care. In addition, veterinarians are advised that first among their responsibilities towards their patients is to treat all of them, 'of whatever species, humanely, with respect, and with welfare as the primary consideration'.[122] These sentiments raise a fundamental issue about the role of veterinarians and the nature of their basic professional obligation. Are they intended to mean that vets should give welfare priority in the context of providing entirely objective and dispassionate guidance? Or, do they imply that vets should act positively as the champion of animals' interests? In other words, to act as their advocate? This is much more than a technical point. It goes to the heart of how vets approach their work. While it has some relevance in the clinical and surgical contexts, it has fundamental implications when vets provide advice on animal welfare, contribute to policy development, or participate in the enforcement of animal protection legislation.[123]

Unlike veterinary surgeons, there is no statutory regulation of veterinary nurses, except where they provide medical treatment or undertake minor surgery.[124]

(2) Farriers

Farriers operate under a similar legislative regime. Except in the case of a person rendering emergency first aid, it is an offence for anyone who is neither a registered farrier nor a veterinary surgeon (or training to become one or the other) to carry out any farriery.[125] The regulation of farriers is overseen by the Farriers Company under the authority of statute, whose responsibilities include maintaining a register and securing adequate standards of competence and conduct of farriers.[126]

(3) Slaughtermen

A rather different method of promoting proficiency is used in relation to those employed at slaughterhouses and knackers' yards. First, at all times when there are live animals on the premises, the occupier must ensure that there is available a person who is both competent and authorized to take whatever action may be necessary to safeguard the welfare of the animals.[127] Secondly, only those who have the

---

[122] RCVS, *Guide to Professional Conduct* (2000) Part 1B, para 1, and 1C, para 1.

[123] See further, Legood, G (ed), *Veterinary Ethics, An Introduction* (2000); Thornton, P et al, 'Veterinary ethics: filling the gap in undergraduate education' (2001) 148 *Veterinary Record* 214.

[124] Veterinary Surgeons Act 1966, Sch 3, para 6, as inserted by SI 1991/1412, n 119 above.

[125] Farriers (Registration) Act 1975, s 16.

[126] See generally, Farriers (Registration) Act 1975, as amended by the Farriers (Registration) (Amendment) Act 1977.

[127] SI 1995/731, n 16 above, reg 5.

knowledge and skill necessary to perform the task humanely and efficiently are permitted to participate in the movement, lairaging, restraint, stunning, slaughter, or killing of any animal.[128] Thirdly, any person involved in these activities is required to be acquainted with, and to have received instruction and guidance on the requirements of, the provisions of the relevant legislation and associated welfare codes, and to have access to the latter.[129] Finally, only a person holding an appropriate licence may undertake procedures associated with the restraint, stunning, slaughtering, killing, or pithing of any animal, the shackling or hoisting of a stunned animal, or the bleeding of any animal which is not dead.[130]

(4) Market drovers

There are, however, no equivalent statutory provisions requiring market drovers to have the knowledge and skill necessary to move, lairage, and restrain animals humanely and efficiently. However, the Ministry of Agriculture's recent *Strategy for the Protection of Animal Welfare at Livestock Markets* envisages the appointment of an animal welfare officer at each market who, it suggests, should hold sufficient standing in the market together with the competence and time to perform the necessary duties, one of which is to satisfy themselves of the competence of the staff for the jobs allocated to them and, if necessary, to arrange appropriate training.[131]

(5) Transporters

The most recent scheme to introduce specified standards of competency is that relating to the transport of animals. This lays down that a person may transport vertebrate animals on journeys over 50 km only if they have been authorized to do so, by the minister in the case of a transporter established in Great Britain.[132] For these purposes, the Government has made a General Authorization, which covers the generality of transporters unless and until they are individually disqualified from operating under it. In addition, with effect from October 1998, any transporter who conveys cattle, sheep, pigs, goats, and horses, except for those concerned only with journeys of less than eight hours in road vehicles, must be in receipt of a specific authorization, which may be granted only if the minister is satisfied that they are a fit person to transport animals.[133] They are then required to ensure that those to whom they entrust the animals include at least one person who has either specific training or equivalent practical experience, qualifying them

---

[128] SI 1995/731, n 16 above, reg 4(2).   [129] ibid, reg 6(1)(a)–(c).

[130] ibid, reg 4(3) and Sch 1. 'Pithing' means the destruction of the animal's brain tissue after stunning so that irreversible loss of consciousness is ensured: reg 2(1). As a result of Dec 2000/418, as of 1 April 2001, it is no longer permissible to pith an animal slaughtered for human or animal consumption: Restriction on Pithing (England) Regulations 2001, SI 2001/447; Restriction on Pithing (Scotland) Regulations 2001, SSI 2001/73; Restriction on Pithing (Wales) Regulations 2001, SI 2001/1303 (W80).

[131] MAFF (1998), para 11(a), (b).

[132] SI 1997/1480, n 5 above, art 12(1); by a competent authority of an appropriate Member State in the case of those established elsewhere.

[133] ibid, Sch 9, paras 1(2), 2(1).

to handle and transport vertebrate animals and to administer appropriate care. Such a person is specifically required to possess sufficient knowledge and competence to safeguard the welfare of the animals.[134] This includes knowledge of the relevant law and associated documentation, vehicle construction, appropriate methods of handling animals during loading and unloading, the causes of stress in animals and ways in which the symptoms may be reduced; an understanding of when to seek veterinary help, the importance of temperature on the welfare of different species, and the need to adjust ventilation; and an ability to plan a journey in accordance with the legislation, to load, operate, and control a vehicle so as to ensure the welfare of the animals, to recognize the signs of stress and ill health, and to care for animals which become unfit or are injured in transit.[135]

(6) Farmers

The .time during which a slaughterman, a market drover, or a transporter is responsible for animals can be significant, and in each case there is the potential for animals to be caused considerable suffering, but it is nevertheless relatively short in comparison with the period for which farmers and their employees have charge of livestock. However long or short it may be, the vast majority of such an agricultural animal's life will be spent on the farm. This being the case, the relative paucity of legal standards in relation to stock keepers is striking. Indeed, those who are responsible for the welfare of animals on farms do not have to demonstrate *any* specific level of competency. An employer must merely ensure that his employees are acquainted with the provisions of all the relevant welfare codes, have access to them, and have received instruction and guidance on them.[136] Similarly, a person who keeps livestock must have access to the relevant welfare codes while he is attending to them, and be acquainted with their provisions.[137] Formerly, the *only* legal requirement relating to competence was that laying hens kept in battery cages must be cared for by a sufficient number of personnel with adequate knowledge and experience of the production system used.[138] Belatedly, however, it is now a requirement that *all* farm animals shall be cared for by a sufficient number of staff who possess the appropriate ability, knowledge, and professional competence,[139] although there are no specific standards which lay down how these criteria may be met.

---

[134] ibid, art 9(1). In relation to a journey which involves the transport of cattle, sheep, pigs, goats, or horses, either by road vehicle for a journey lasting 8 hours or more, or by another means of transport irrespective of the length of journey, it is specified that the attendant must have *demonstrated* their competence, either by obtaining a qualification approved by the minister or through an assessment of equivalent practical experience: art 9(2), (3), (4). See further, MAFF, *Assessment of Practical Experience in the Handling, Transport and Care of Animals* (1998).

[135] ibid, Sch 8.

[136] Welfare of Farmed Animals Regulations, n 2 above, reg 10(1).

[137] ibid, reg 10(2). The regulations relating to Wales adopt the verb 'care' in preference to 'attend'.

[138] Welfare of Livestock Regulations 1994, SI 1994/2126, Sch 1, para 8; see now the Welfare of Farmed Animals Regulations, n 2 above, Sch 2, para 6.

[139] Welfare of Farmed Animals Regulations, n 2 above, Sch 1, para 1.

(7) Personal licensees and others responsible for the care of animals used in scientific procedures

Surprisingly, neither was there until recently any express statutory provision requiring that those responsible for animals used in scientific procedures involving animals either hold a relevant qualification, or have undergone appropriate training, relating to animal welfare. Originally, the 1986 Act stipulated only that each designated animal procedure, breeding, and supplying establishment specify a person to be responsible for the day-to-day care of the animals (without specifying any prerequisites such a person must possess), and a veterinary surgeon or other suitably qualified person to provide advice on their health and welfare.[140] At a designated establishment undertaking a high volume of regulated procedures it might be that the named veterinary surgeon is a full-time employee of the company or institution. At other facilities, they may be a relatively infrequent visitor. In addition, the Act also required that there must be available a person competent to kill animals in the manner specified by the conditions imposed in the relevant licences.[141] In relation to those who actually carried out regulated procedures, the legislation specified only that they should be at least eighteen years of age, and their application for a personal licence be endorsed by someone with knowledge of the applicant's qualifications, training, experience, and character.[142] This apparent lacuna in the 1986 Act concerning standards of competency was, to a certain extent, filled by administrative measures, using the licensing procedures. The Home Office's *Code of Practice for the Housing and Care of Animals Used in Scientific Procedures*, for example, stipulates that those responsible for laboratory animals should be thoroughly trained in their care and familiar with their basic requirements under both normal and experimental conditions, and emphasizes the need for them to be fully aware of the legal and moral responsibilities of using animals in scientific procedures. They are expected to appreciate the importance of, and be competent in, correct animal handling and restraint, and in the procedures which they will be carrying out.[143] 'Only competent staff', the Code declares, 'should be given responsibility for the care and husbandry of animals.'[144]

However, the Act itself has recently been amended so that, since October 1998, the Home Secretary has been required before granting a personal licence to satisfy himself, first, that the applicant has the appropriate education and training to apply the relevant regulated procedures; and, secondly, that they are competent to apply them in accordance with the conditions contained in the licence, and to

---

[140] Animals (Scientific Procedures) Act 1986, ss 6(5), 7(5). The same person may be named if the Secretary of State thinks fit. See further, 'RCVS Code of Practice for Named Veterinary Surgeons employed in Scientific Procedure Establishments and Breeding and Supplying Establishments under the Animal (Scientific Procedures) Act 1986' in RCVS, n 122 above, Annex 4.

[141] ibid, s 10(6)(a).   [142] ibid, s 4(3)(b), (4).   [143] Home Office, n 81 above, para 2.8.

[144] ibid, para 2.36. The Code also specifies that only personnel who have been suitably trained may be allowed to kill animals: para 4.4.

handle and take care of laboratory animals.[145] In addition, it is now also prescribed by statute that the Home Secretary shall in designating a scientific procedure establishment attach such conditions as he considers appropriate to ensure that there will be sufficient trained staff, and the persons who take care of the protected animals, as well as those who supervise them, have appropriate education and training.[146] Furthermore, the certificate designating a scientific procedure, breeding, or supplying establishment must include conditions to ensure that the well-being and state of health of the animals are monitored by a suitably qualified person in order to prevent pain or avoidable suffering, distress, or lasting harm.[147] To this end, it is now a standard condition that the certificate holder shall take steps to provide such education and training as is necessary 'for all licensees and others responsible for the welfare and care of protected animals' at a scientific procedure establishment, and 'to those entrusted with the care and welfare of protected animals' at breeding and supplying establishments.[148] To meet these requirements, all applicants for personal and project licences have to undergo mandatory training, which includes instruction in the relevant legislation, ethics, the design and management of programmes of work, the performance of regulated procedures, anaesthesia and surgery, and the handling and use of animals. Evidence that appropriate training has been successfully completed must be provided when licence applications are made.[149] The mandatory training is largely theoretical and does not itself ensure technical competence. Until this is attained, personal licensees are required to accept supervision and training arrangements put in place by the project licence holder.[150] The person named on the certificate as being responsible for the day-to-day care of the animals is now known as the Named Animal Care and Welfare Officer (NACWO). Although there are still no formal training requirements for NACWOs, the Home Office encourages certificate holders to make available to them relevant training courses, such as those provided by the Institute of Animal Technology,[151] and it specifies that NACWOs should have expert knowledge and suitable experience of relevant animal technology, typically as a senior animal technician or an experienced stockman, in either case having an appropriate qualification.[152] In addition, they are required to be familiar with the legislation; to have an up-to-date knowledge of animal technology; to be aware of the prevailing standards of care, accommodation, husbandry, and welfare set out in the relevant Codes of Practice; and to be knowledgeable about the appropriate methods of killing.[153] There is a specific Home Office training requirement when a person is initially appointed as a Named Veterinary Surgeon (NVS).[154] Both the RCVS and the Home Office expect every NVS to keep abreast of developments in

[145] Animals (Scientific Procedures) Act 1986, s 4(4A), inserted by SI 1998/1974, n 51 above.
[146] ibid, s 10(5A), inserted by SI 1998/1974.   [147] ibid, s 10(6B)(d), inserted by SI 1998/1974.
[148] Home Office, n 41 above, Appendix B, para 19; Appendix C, para 19.
[149] ibid, paras 2.73–2.76 and Appendix F; see also paras 6.3–6.5.   [150] ibid, paras 2.82–2.84 and 6.21.
[151] ibid, paras 2.78 and 4.55.   [152] ibid, para 4.56.   [153] ibid, para 4.58.
[154] ibid, para 2.77.

the use of laboratory animals, to be able to advise on methods of reducing adverse effects on animals by refinement of experimental techniques and husbandry methods, and to contribute to ensuring that consideration is given to the use of non-sentient alternatives.[155] They should also be familiar with the legislation and with relevant methods of humane killing, have a thorough knowledge of the husbandry and welfare requirements of the species kept at the establishment, and, at a scientific procedure establishment, advise licensees, applicants, and others on how to implement the principles of replacement, reduction, and refinement.[156] In addition, although it is not a formal requirement, the Home Office advises that applicants for certificates of designation also undertake a specified course of formal training.[157]

(8) Zoos

It is legitimate for a local authority to refuse to license a zoo if it is not satisfied that the standards of staffing or management are adequate for the proper care and well-being of the animals.[158] The *Secretary of State's Standards of Modern Zoo Practice* stipulate that the number of staff and their experience and training must be sufficient to ensure compliance with the standards at all times, and all animal staff must be competent for their individual responsibilities and be given the opportunity to undergo formal training to achieve appropriate qualifications. In addition, it is a requirement that continuous in-house training must be a regular aspect of the zoo, to include matters such as animal husbandry and welfare, emergency euthanasia, and basic sampling for health monitoring and diagnosis.[159]

(9) Riding establishments

In determining whether to grant a licence for the keeping of a riding establishment, a local authority must have regard to whether the applicant appears to be suitable and qualified to be the holder of such a licence, either by experience in the management of horses or by having obtained an approved certificate (or by employing such a person).[160]

(10) Pet shops, animal boarding establishments, dog breeding establishments, and the keeping of dangerous wild animals

An applicant for a licence to keep a dangerous wild animal must demonstrate that he is a suitable person.[161] However, there is no specific legislative provision requiring

---

[155] ibid, para 4.61.   [156] ibid, paras 4.62 and 4.63.   [157] ibid, para 2.79 and Annex to Appendix F.
[158] Zoo Licensing Act 1981, s 4(3).
[159] DETR, n 106 above, paras 10.1–10.6 and Appendix 9.
[160] Riding Establishments Act 1964, s 1(4)(a), as amended by the Riding Establishments Act 1970, s 2(1)(ii). 'Approved certificate' means (a) the British Horse Society's Assistant Instructor's Certificate, Instructor's Certificate, and Fellowship; (b) Fellowship of the Institute of the Horse; or (c) any other certificate prescribed by the Secretary of State: s 6(4), as amended by the 1970 Act.
[161] Dangerous Wild Animals Act 1976, s 1(3)(b).

authorities to take account of the competence of applicants in relation to licences for pet shops, boarding establishments, or dog breeding establishments, although the (voluntary) model standards for pet shop licence conditions produced under the auspices of the Local Government Association recommend that no animal should be stocked or sold unless at least one member of staff is familiar with its care and welfare, and has a recognized qualification or suitable experience. In respect of new pet shop applications, it is suggested that at least one member of staff should hold a City and Guilds Certificate in Pet Store Management or some other appropriate qualification or, alternatively, to be in the course of training for such a qualification, which must be obtained within two years of the licence being granted. These unofficial conditions also suggest that each licensee must formulate a written training policy for all permanent staff, and be required to demonstrate that systematic training is in fact carried out.[162]

D. Conclusion

This chapter has demonstrated the extent of public control over activities involving animals and those who are responsible for them. The difference in the degree of sophistication between these various schemes has also been made apparent. At one end of the spectrum, there is a highly detailed and complex system in place to regulate the use of animals in scientific procedures, which places significant restrictions on what may be done, how the work is carried out, and who may undertake it. At the other extreme, undertakings such as circuses, markets, and farming are not subject to any formal scheme of licensing or certification. This is particularly significant in respect of livestock production because of the huge numbers of animals which are involved. It also appears to be strangely inconsistent that the place where such animals spend the greater part of their lives is not subject to such regulation, when it has been thought appropriate for transporters and slaughterhouses. It is also apparent that many of the older licensing schemes, particularly those concerned with companion animals, are in urgent need of updating. Their provisions fail to reflect modern notions of welfare, and do not contain appropriate provisions to enable licensing authorities adequately to ensure the interests of the animals involved. The general nature of the criteria they specify gives no guidance on the detailed requirements which it is appropriate for local authorities to demand. Moreover, there is no provision in the legislation to introduce mandatory or advisory standards by means of regulations or codes of guidance. As a result, it is left to each individual authority to define the standards it considers to be appropriate, which may lead to considerable variation between different areas. In addition, there may be genuine uncertainty as to the extent of an

---

[162] LGA, n 93 above, para 16. Similarly, the voluntary code drawn up by the SSPCA contains a requirement that pet traders should ensure that staff receive appropriate training: n 93 above, para 20.

authority's power in specifying conditions. Notwithstanding that in relation to pet shops, animal boarding establishments, riding establishments, and dog breeding establishments, the licensing authority is *required* to specify such conditions in the licence as appear to it to be expedient for securing the stated objects, the respective legislation provides no explicit power to impose conditions which go beyond these.[163] This is in contrast to the Dangerous Wild Animals Act 1976, for example, which, in addition to requiring an authority to impose such conditions as in its opinion are necessary or desirable for securing the objects expressly identified in the legislation, also provides it with a wide discretionary power to specify such other conditions as it thinks fit.[164]

A similar situation exists in relation to professional proficiency. Veterinarians, for example, are regulated by the RCVS under the auspices of statute, but the legislation fails to reflect the developments that have lately taken place in the regulation of comparable professions. In particular, the RCVS does not possess the necessary powers routinely to monitor and to hold to account members of the profession. Equally, the assumption underlying the legislation that a generalist veterinary qualification in itself adequately equips each and every member of the profession to undertake all aspects of veterinary work similarly ignores the far-reaching developments which have taken place since 1966 in veterinary and welfare science, and the changing role of the veterinary profession over the same period. The time has come when veterinary nurses should also be the subject of regulation.[165] Furthermore, while welcome steps have been taken by means of legislation to improve the competency of those working in the field of scientific procedures, and administrative measures have been taken to improve the training of those working in zoos, perhaps the most significant development in this area has been in respect of transporters. The nature of the competence which they are required to demonstrate would seem to be an appropriate model for those activities involving animals where appropriate regulation is blatantly insufficient: farms, pet shops, boarding establishments, dog breeding establishments, and in relation to performing animals.

Overall, however, the practical and symbolic significance of licensing, certification, and registration in respect of both undertakings and personnel must not be underestimated. Together, they impose an extremely important qualification to the traditional right of the owner of an animal to do with it and to treat it howsoever he sees fit. As such, they have the potential to act as a substantial bulwark against the consequences of the continuing common law status of animals as property.

---

[163] Pet Animals Act 1951, s 1(3); Animal Boarding Establishments Act 1963, s 1(3); Riding Establishments Act 1964, s 1(4), as amended by the Riding Establishments Act 1970; Breeding of Dogs Act 1973, s 1(4), as amended by the Breeding and Sale of Dogs (Welfare) Act 1999.

[164] Dangerous Wild Animals Act 1976, s 1(6), (7).

[165] See, for example, Anon, 'Regulation—the way forward for veterinary nurses' (2000) 147 *Veterinary Record* 495.

13

Quality of Care

A. Treatment

Those who are knowledgeable, expert, and solicitous about the animals for which they are responsible may be expected to provide a high standard of care on their own initiative. Unfortunately, many who have charge of animals do not demonstrate these characteristics and, increasingly, legislation is being used to impose standards and specify how animals should be treated. Here again, the more recent the measure, the more detailed and demanding it tends to be, and the greater the influence of the Five Freedoms.

(1) Provision of food and water

At the most basic, under the Dogs Act 1906, a police officer or any other person who has assumed charge of a stray dog is required to ensure that it is properly fed and maintained.[1] Similarly, while at a market, animals must be provided with an adequate quantity of wholesome water as often as is necessary to prevent them suffering from thirst, and with food and drink if they are kept there overnight, for which purpose an adequate supply of water and facilities for dispensing it must be available.[2]

In relation to the licensing of pet shops, animal boarding establishments, dog breeding establishments, and dangerous wild animals, the local authority is obliged simply to have regard to the need for securing that the animals will be adequately supplied with suitable food and drink, and must specify such conditions in the

[1] Section 3(8).
[2] Welfare of Horses at Markets (and Other Places of Sale) Order 1990, SI 1990/2627, arts 12 and 15(b), (d); Welfare of Animals at Markets Order 1990, SI 1990/2628, arts 11 and 15(b), (d). In relation to equines, 'market' refers to a market place, sale yard, fairground, highway, or any other premises or place to which horses, ponies, asses, hinnies, or mules are brought from other places and exposed for sale. Otherwise, the word means a market place or sale yard or any other premises to which cattle, sheep, goats, and all other ruminating animals, pigs, rabbits, or poultry are brought from other places and exposed for sale. In both cases, it includes a lairage and any place used as a parking area by visitors, providing they adjoin the market: art 3(1). Similar provisions apply to animals placed in pounds in England and Wales: Protection of Animals Act 1911, s 7; see also, *Dargan v Davies* (1877) 2 QBD 118.

licence as appear to it necessary or expedient for securing this object.[3] The requirements in respect of riding establishments are slightly more particular, stipulating the
need for horses maintained at grass to have access to adequate pasture, water, and
supplementary feeds when required;[4] for their part, stabled horses have to be adequately supplied with suitable food and drink. Again, appropriate conditions must
be included in the licence to this effect.[5] Similarly, the conditions of a certificate designating an animal procedure, breeding, or supplying establishment require the
Home Secretary to include such conditions as he considers necessary to ensure that
the animals are fed and watered in a way which is appropriate for their health and
well-being,[6] and more detailed advice relating to the standards required is contained
in the appropriate code of practice.[7]

Owners and keepers of farmed animals are required to take all reasonable steps
to ensure that the animals are fed with what is described as a wholesome diet,
appropriate to their age and species, in sufficient quantity to maintain them in
good health, to satisfy their nutritional needs, and to promote a positive state of
well-being.[8] In addition, all such animals must have access to feed at intervals
appropriate to their physiological needs (and in any case, at least once a day),
except where a veterinary surgeon directs otherwise, and to a suitable water supply
freshly provided each day, or be able to satisfy their fluid intake by other means.[9]
Further, it is prohibited to provide food or liquid in a manner, or containing
any substance, which may cause them unnecessary suffering or injury, or to
administer any other substance (with the exception of those given for therapeutic
or prophylactic purposes, or for zootechnical treatment) unless it has been
demonstrated by scientific studies or established experience that the effect is not

---

[3] Pet Animals Act 1951, s 1(3)(b); Animal Boarding Establishments Act 1963, s 1(3)(b); Breeding of Dogs
Act 1973, s 1(4)(b); Dangerous Wild Animals Act 1976, s 1(3)(c)(ii) and (6)(d).

[4] Riding Establishments Act 1964, s 1(4)(b)(iv), as amended by the Riding Establishments Act 1970.

[5] ibid, s 1(4)(b)(v), as amended by the Riding Establishments Act 1970.

[6] Animals (Scientific Procedures) Act 1986, s 10(6B)(a), inserted by the Animals (Scientific Procedures)
Act 1986 (Amendment) Regulations 1998, SI 1998/1974.

[7] Home Office, Code of Practice for the Housing and Care of the Animals Used in Scientific Procedures
(1989), paras 3.20–3.27, 3.29–3.35, et seq.

[8] Welfare of Farmed Animals (England) Regulations 2000, SI 2000/1870, reg 3(2) and Sch 1, para 22;
Welfare of Farmed Animals (Scotland) Regulations 2000, SSI 2000/442, reg 3(2) and Sch 1, para 22; Welfare
of Farmed Animals (Wales) Regulations 2001, reg 3(2) and Sch 1, para 22. Welfare of Farmed Animals
(Wales) Regulations 2001, Sch 4, para 1. The Regulations relating to Wales came into force on 31 July 2001,
but at the time this book went to press they had not been allocated an SI number. Henceforth, the three sets
of regulations will be referred to collectively as the 'Welfare of Farmed Animals Regulations'. A 'farmed animal' means any animal (including a fish, a reptile, or an amphibian) bred or kept for farming purposes,
including the production of food, wool, skin, or fur: Welfare of Farmed Animals Regulations, reg 2(1).

[9] ibid, Sch 1, paras 24 and 25. It is expressly required that calves confined for rearing and fattening shall
be fed at least twice a day, and pigs once a day. In both cases, where the animals are housed in a group and
have neither continuous access to feed nor an automatic feeding system, they must all be fed at the same
time: Sch 4, para 14; Sch 6, para 13. They must also be provided with a sufficient quantity of drinking water
daily, except that calves are required to have a continuous supply in hot weather or when they are ill: Sch 4,
para 15; Sch 6, para 14. Likewise battery hens must have access to adequate, nutritious, and hygienic feed
each day so as to maintain them in good health and satisfy their nutritional needs, as well as having an adequate supply of fresh drinking water at all times: Sch 2, para 5.

detrimental to the health or welfare of the animals.[10] Where calves are confined for rearing and fattening, each animal must receive bovine colostrum as soon as possible within the first six hours of life, and thereafter its diet has to contain sufficient iron to ensure a blood haemoglobin level of at least 4.5 mmol/litre and, once it is over two weeks of age, a minimum daily ration of fibrous food.[11] The practice of producing white veal meat by feeding calves a liquid, iron-free diet is thereby prohibited. Food and drink provided for zoo animals must be presented in an appropriate manner and be of a nutritive value, quantity, quality, and variety suitable not only for the particular species, but also for the individual animals, having regard to their condition, size, health, and physiological and reproductive state. Furthermore, operators are told to give consideration to the natural behaviour of the animals, particularly social aspects, when offering food and drink.[12]

Before being transported, animals must be offered liquid and food and given any necessary care.[13] In the case of cattle, sheep, pigs, goats, and horses (except registered horses), it is the general rule that the journey time should not exceed eight hours.[14] However, if the vehicle is equipped with sufficient bedding, appropriate feed, direct access to the animals, adequate, adjustable ventilation, movable panels for creating separate compartments, a connection to enable water to be supplied during stops, and, when transporting pigs, sufficient liquid for the animals to drink during the journey, the following extended maximum journey times apply:

- *unweaned calves, lambs, kids, piglets, and foals which are still on a milk diet*
  18 hours' travelling, with a 1-hour rest period after the first 9 hours;
- *pigs*
  24 hours' continuous travelling, on condition they have access to liquid for the duration of the journey;
- *horses*
  a maximum period of 24 hours, during which time they must be given liquid and, if necessary, feed every 8 hours;
- *cattle, sheep, and goats*
  28 hours' travelling, with a 1-hour rest period after the first 14 hours.[15]

Each of these journey times may be prolonged for a further 2 hours if this enables the animals to reach their final destination.[16] At the end of the respective maximum

---

[10] ibid, Sch 1, paras 23 and 27.

[11] ibid, Sch 4, paras 11 and 12; the quantity of fibrous food should be raised in line with the growth of the animal from an initial minimum of 100g to no less than 250g at 20 weeks old.

[12] DETR, *Secretary of State's Standards of Modern Zoo Practice* (2000) paras 1.1 and 1.14. It is advised that the live feeding of vertebrate prey be avoided save in exceptional circumstances, and then only under veterinary advice. In such a situation, the welfare of the prey must be considered as well as any potential injury which might be caused to the predator: para 1.6.

[13] The Welfare of Animals (Transport) Order 1997, SI 1997/1480, art 8(1).   [14] ibid, Sch 7, para 1.

[15] ibid, Sch 7, paras 2 and 3. There are separate limits for poultry, domestic birds, domestic rabbits, cats, and dogs: art 8(3), (4).

[16] ibid, Sch 7, para 7.

specified journey time, the animals must be unloaded, fed and watered, and rested for at least 24 hours.[17]

Those who transport horses (other than registered horses), cattle, sheep, pigs, or goats to another EU state, or export them to a third country, on a journey which exceeds eight hours, are required to draw up a route plan. This must be submitted to the ministry in advance, providing details of: the transporter; the number and type of animals involved; the name of the person who will be in charge during the journey; the place where the animals will be first loaded; the planned date and time of departure; an itemized itinerary; the destination; and the estimated arrival. Having been approved by the ministry, both the transporter and the person in charge of the animals during the journey must take all reasonable steps to ensure that the route plan is complied with. The plan itself has to be endorsed with the details of the actual journey and returned to the ministry, either confirming that the original arrangements have been met, or providing details of any variation, and the reasons for it.[18] For most other less extensive journeys, the transporter is required to arrange for the animals to be accompanied by an animal transport certificate, which is required to include details such as the name and address of both the transporter and the owner of the animals; the place that the animals were loaded and their final destination; and the date and time of loading, departure, and rest periods.[19] As the length and complexity of journeys increase, the way in which they are structured can have a profound effect on the animals' welfare.[20]

(2) Handling

An animal's welfare is clearly at particular risk of being compromised when it is being moved; this is especially so in a commercial environment, where large numbers may be involved and speed is of the essence. Accordingly, any person transporting animals is under a duty to ensure that they reach their place of destination without delay,[21] but, at the same time, it is an offence to transport any vertebrate or cold-blooded animal by road, rail, sea, or air in a way which causes, or is likely to cause, injury or unnecessary suffering.[22] More specifically, in the context of a commercial journey, mammals and birds must not be severely jolted or shaken, or loaded and unloaded in such a way that they are caused injury or unnecessary suffering, either by the excessive use of anything used for driving them, or through contact with any obstruction.[23] In addition, there are a number of provisions

---

[17] The Welfare of Animals (Transport) Order 1997, SI 1997/1480, Sch 7, para 4. It has subsequently been made an offence to transport animals for more than 8 hours if the vehicle is not equipped in accordance with the legislation: art 21A, inserted by the Welfare of Animals (Transport) (Amendment) Order 1999, SI 1999/1622. For provisions relating to staging points, see further the Welfare of Animals (Staging Points) Order 1998, SI 1998/2537.

[18] ibid, art 13 and Sch 11.   [19] ibid, art 14.

[20] See, for example, Murray, KC et al, 'Taking Lambs to the Slaughter: Marketing Channels, Journey Structures and Possible Consequences for Welfare' (2000) 9 *Animal Welfare* 111.

[21] SI 1997/1480, n 13 above, art 10(1).   [22] ibid, arts 2(1),(2),(3), 3(1), 4(1).

[23] ibid, Sch 1, paras 22 and 23.

intended to prevent the animals slipping, falling, or being thrown about during transport,[24] including requirements as to how they should be tied and segregated.[25] Likewise, animals carried in a receptacle must not be caused injury or unnecessary suffering either while waiting to be loaded on to, or after they have been unloaded from, the means of transport.[26]

In the case of cattle, sheep, pigs, goats, and horses, suitable ramps, bridges, gangways, or mechanical lifting gear must be used, with appropriate protection on each side to prevent them from falling or escaping.[27] It is prohibited to suspend such animals by mechanical means, to lift or drag them by the head, horns, legs, tail, or fleece; or to use excessive force to control them.[28] Similar provisions apply to the handling of animals in markets. In addition, while in a market, no animal may be: driven or led over any surface which is likely to cause it to slip or fall; knowingly obstructed; or wantonly or unreasonably annoyed.[29] Calves, young lambs, and kid goats are required to be removed from the market expeditiously,[30] and a foal may only be brought to market and exposed for sale if it is accompanied by its dam.[31]

Zoo animals must be handled and managed by, or under the supervision of, appropriately qualified and experienced staff, and the procedure carried out with care so as to protect their well-being and avoid unnecessary discomfort, stress, or harm. Any direct physical contact with the public should be for restricted periods and under conditions which are consistent with the animals' welfare and not likely to lead to their discomfort.[32] Similarly, the relevant code of practice provides detailed guidance on the handling of animals used in scientific procedures.[33]

(3) Prohibited practices

In regulating the treatment of animals, the law is in general used as a means to impose standards rather than outright prohibition. There are, however, certain practices which the legislature has considered to be so detrimental to the welfare of animals that they cannot be justified and, in consequence, are forbidden. The most recent example is fur farming, defined as keeping animals solely or primarily for slaughter for the value of their fur, or for breeding progeny for such slaughter, which will become unlawful in England and Wales on a date to be determined by the Government after the beginning of 2003.[34] Other prohibited practices include:

[24] ibid, Sch 1, paras 4, 11, 12, 16, 21, 28, 29; Sch 2, paras 5, 6, 8, 10(3); Sch 4, para 5; Sch 5, paras 5, 6, 8(3).
[25] ibid, Sch 2, paras 11–14 and 17–21; Sch 3, paras 5–9.
[26] ibid, art 10(2). [27] ibid, Sch 2, para 10(2), (4). See also, para 11 and Sch 7, para 8(2), (4).
[28] ibid, Sch 2, para 15.
[29] SI 1990/2627, n 2 above, arts 6(2)(c), (d), 8, 9, and 10; SI 1990/2628, n 2 above, arts 6(2)(c), 7, 8, and 9.
[30] SI 1990/2628, n 2 above, arts 14(7) and 6A, inserted by the Welfare of Animals at Markets Order 1993, SI 1993/3085.
[31] SI 1990/2627, n 2 above, art 7. [32] DETR, n 12 above, paras 5.1 and 5.2.
[33] Home Office, n 7 above, paras 3.39 et seq. [34] Fur Farming (Prohibition) Act 2000.

muzzling calves;[35] keeping pigs or calves tethered;[36] keeping an animal for farming purposes unless it can reasonably be expected, on the basis of its genotype or phenotype, that this can be done without detrimental effect on its health and welfare;[37] routine tail docking and tooth clipping of piglets;[38] applying an electrical current to any farm animal to immobilize it;[39] keeping pigs in an environment of high temperatures and humidity (the 'sweat-box system');[40] keeping farm animals in permanent darkness, or without an appropriate period of rest from artificial lighting;[41] bringing young calves to market, or older calves more than once in twenty-eight days;[42] exporting low value equines;[43] using dogs as draught animals on the public highway;[44] or docking and nicking horses.[45] In addition, certain public performances which by their nature cause suffering to cattle or horses, such as using an appliance to make them buck while being ridden,[46] films and videos involving cruelty to animals,[47] and the public display of a scientific procedure,[48] are all banned.

B. Accommodation

The physical environment in which an animal spends its time will often have a decisive effect on the state of its well-being, and it takes on a particular significance where the animal remains in the same environment for a prolonged period, or is unable to exert any control over it. Here again, the imposition of detailed regulation is a relatively recent innovation.

---

[35] Welfare of Farmed Animals Regulations, n 8 above, Sch 4, para 13.

[36] Sch 4, para 6(1), and Sch 6, para 4 (para 8 in the Scottish Regulations).

[37] ibid, Sch 1, para 29.

[38] ibid, Sch 6, para 27. These procedures should be carried out only where there is evidence, on the farm, that injuries to sows' teats or to other piglets have occurred or are likely to occur as a result of not doing so; where tooth clipping appears necessary, it must be performed within seven days of birth: para 29.

[39] ibid, Sch 1, para 30.   [40] ibid, Sch 6, para 16.

[41] ibid, Sch 1, paras 14 and 16.   [42] SI 1990/2628, n 2 above, art 14(1), (2).

[43] Animal Health Act 1981, ss 40, 41; statutory minimum values are intended to prevent old and unwanted equines being sent to the Continent for slaughter. At present, these stand at: £715 for a horse; £495 for a vanner, mule, or jennet; £220 for an ass; £300 for a pony, except in the case of one which does not exceed 122 centimetres in height (£220) or a Shetland-type pony (£145). These amounts have remained unaltered for a considerable period; ministers have consistently indicated that they have no plans to increase them to take account of inflation: HC Debs, 5 March 1996, col 125 (WA); HC Debs, 10 November 1997, col 399 (WA).

[44] Protection of Animals Act 1911, s 9; Protection of Animals (Scotland) Act 1912, s 8.

[45] Docking and Nicking of Horses Act 1949. This does not apply where a veterinary surgeon has certified in writing that the operation is necessary for the health of the horse because of disease or injury to the tail. 'Docking' and 'nicking' mean, respectively, deliberately removing bone, or severing a tendon or muscle, in a horse's tail.

[46] Protection of Animals Act 1934.

[47] Cinematograph Films (Animals) Act 1937; Video Recordings Act 1984, ss 2(2)(b) and 9(1).

[48] Animals (Scientific Procedures) Act 1986, s 16.

(1) Space

The most obvious consideration in this regard is whether an animal is provided with sufficient space to meet its physiological and behavioural needs. Legal regulation clearly has the potential to ensure that this is so but, in practice, its impact is mixed. At worst, the law can be used to sanction systems which are intrinsically antagonistic to achieving a high standard of welfare. For example, the provisions which currently govern the keeping of hens in battery cages allow four or more hens to be kept in a single cage so long as the total floor area allows each bird 450 cm². To put this in perspective, the size of a piece of A4 paper is approximately 620 cm². In addition, it is specified that the height of the cage, for 65 per cent of its area, shall not be less than 40 cm, and for the remainder not less than 35 cm.[49] The paucity of these dimensions is self-evidently dictated by commercial considerations, in the face of which the welfare of the birds comes a very poor second, even though the Ministry of Agriculture conceded as long ago as 1987 that battery cages can place 'severe restrictions on the birds' freedom to turn round without difficulty, groom themselves, get up and sit down, rest undisturbed, stretch their legs and body and perform wing-flapping and dust-bathing behaviour as well as to fulfil other health and welfare needs'.[50] This situation is to be contrasted with the requirement under the Wildlife and Countryside Act 1981, which provides that where 'any bird whatever'—but with the express exception of poultry—is kept or confined in a cage or receptacle, the height, length, or breadth must be such as to permit it to stretch its wings freely.[51] More bizarrely, although a hen may be kept for the duration of its life in the cramped conditions of a battery cage, where a bird, this time including poultry, is offered or exposed for sale prior to being slaughtered, they must upon arrival at the premises be 'forthwith placed in accommodation in which they are able, without difficulty, to stand upright, turn round and stretch their wings'.[52] It may be argued, of course, that the existing regulations relating to battery hens do at least lay down a minimum amount of space and thereby prevent birds from being kept in even more cramped conditions. This is indeed so. Nevertheless, it is ironic that such modest and potentially harmful criteria are formalized in regulations which purport to enhance welfare. This example illustrates an important moral: while legislation has a significant role to play in positively improving the position of animals, its effect can also be to endorse and entrench standards which public policy makers may consider to be acceptable, but which are incompatible with the promotion of a high standard of welfare for the

---

[49] Welfare of Farmed Animals Regulations, n 8 above, Sch 2, para 1(1)(a), (f); these provisions will have to be amended in due course to give effect to Directive 99/74 which requires the phasing out of battery cages by January 2012 and introduces in the meantime a range of interim measures progressing to this position.
[50] MAFF, *Code of recommendations for the welfare of domestic fowls* (1987) para 13.
[51] Section 8(1), (2).
[52] Welfare of Animals (Slaughter or Killing) Regulations 1995, SI 1995/731, reg 20(a).

animals concerned. It thereby demonstrates the continuing need to campaign to improve the legal standards which apply to domestic and captive animals.

In contrast to battery hens, it is expressly provided that the freedom of movement of all other farm animals is not to be so restricted as to cause them unnecessary suffering or injury, having regard to their species and in accordance with established experience and scientific knowledge.[53] In the few circumstances where it is lawful to keep them tethered or confined, they must nevertheless be given space appropriate to their physiological and ethological needs in accordance with established experience and scientific knowledge.[54] It is further specified that pigs may be kept only in accommodation where they are free to turn round without difficulty at all times (except, in the case of a sow, between seven days before farrowing and the day on which the weaning of her piglets is complete), to stand up, lie down, and rest without difficulty in a place which is clean.[55] Similarly, calves may not be confined in an individual stall or pen after the age of eight weeks, except on the advice of a veterinary surgeon.[56] Where they are kept in such circumstances, the stall or pen has to be of a minimum size calculated on the basis of the height and length of the individual animal occupying it. In the same manner, there are minimum space requirements for animals kept in groups.[57] In any event, each calf must be able to stand up, turn around, rest, and groom itself without hindrance.[58] By this means, sow stalls and the so-called 'veal crate' are both prohibited. Rabbits must be kept in hutches or cages which are of a sufficient size to allow them to move around and to feed and drink without difficulty, large enough for all the animals kept in them to lie on their sides at the same time, and of a height which enables them to sit upright on all four feet without their ears touching the top.[59]

In the case of commercial transport, it is prohibited to convey any animal on a journey of over 50 km in a way which is likely to cause injury or unnecessary suffering because of the amount of space available.[60] The room each animal should be given is calculated by reference to its weight, size, and physical condition, the means of transport, the weather conditions, the likely journey time, and the relevant provisions of the appropriate EC Directive.[61] In addition, the size and height of the accommodation provided must be such that the animals (except for poultry, domestic birds, and rabbits) have adequate space to stand in their natural position,[62] and, unless it is inappropriate because of the species or the nature of the journey, mammals and birds must be provided with adequate space to lie down.[63] Similar considerations apply in relation to markets, where it is the duty of the market operator to ensure that no animal is kept in a pen, cage, or hutch which is

[53] Welfare of Farmed Animals Regulations, n 8 above, Sch 1, para 9.   [54] ibid, Sch 1, para 10.
[55] ibid, Sch 6, paras 6 and 7 (paras 4 and 5 in the Scottish regulations); see also, paras 17, 19, 23, 26 and 31.
[56] ibid, Sch 4, para 1(1). These requirements do not apply until 1 January 2004 in relation to accommodation in use before the beginning of 1998: para 2(1).
[57] ibid, Sch 1, para 1(2), (4).   [58] ibid, Sch 4, para 1(5).
[59] ibid, Sch 7, para 1.   [60] SI 1997/1480, n 13 above, art 5(1).
[61] ibid, art 5(2)(a), (b); Directive 91/628/EEC, Chapter VI.
[62] ibid, Sch 2, para 1; Sch 4, para 3; Sch 5, para 2.   [63] ibid, Sch 1, para 3.

unsuitable for its size or species.[64] More particularly, the pen into which calves or pigs are placed must be sufficiently large to enable all the animals to lie down at the same time, poultry should have enough room to stand in their natural position, and rabbits be able to sit upright on all four feet without their ears touching the top of the cage or hutch.[65] For their part, horses must be kept in separate pens from other animals; be distributed, having regard to differences in age and size, to avoid unnecessary suffering; and not be kept in pens which are overcrowded.[66]

Animals kept in zoos have to be provided with suitable accommodation which allows for their normal defence reactions and appropriate escape or 'flight' distances, and enables them to express most normal behaviour, as well as taking into account the animals' growth and satisfactorily providing for their needs at all stages of their development.[67] In relation to pet shops, animal boarding establishments, dog breeding establishments, horse riding establishments, and dangerous wild animals kept in captivity, the licensing authority is required to have regard to the need for securing that animals will at all times be kept in accommodation which is suitable in size.[68] Like so much of this tranche of legislation, this criterion is woefully inadequate; it gives no indication of what is expected, provides no standard against which any particular accommodation can be compared, and relies too much on the subjective judgement of those responsible for deciding upon individual applications. Animals used for scientific procedures, on the other hand, are governed by a code of practice which contains detailed provisions of both a general nature and relating to specific species.[69] Furthermore, the Home Secretary has recently been given additional powers to attach to certificates designating animal procedure, breeding, and supplying establishments such conditions relating to accommodation of protected animals as he considers appropriate, specifically including measures to ensure that the environment, housing, and freedom of movement are appropriate for the animal's health and well-being.[70] To this end, a standard condition is attached to certificates of designation requiring all protected animals to be provided at all times with adequate care and accommodation appropriate to their type or species, and any restrictions on the extent to which such an animal can satisfy its physiological and ethological needs shall be kept to the absolute minimum.[71]

---

[64] SI 1990/2627, n 2 above, art 11(1); SI 1990/2628, n 2 above, art 10(1).

[65] SI 1990/2628, n 2 above, art 10(2)(a), (b)(i).

[66] SI 1990/2627, n 2 above, art 11(2)(a)(i), (ii), (iv); for exceptions to these conditions, see art 11(3).

[67] DETR, n 12 above, paras 2.2 and 4.4.

[68] Pet Animals Act 1951, s 1(3)(a); Animal Boarding Establishments Act 1963, s 1(3)(a), (b); Breeding of Dogs Act 1973, s 1(4)(a), (b); Riding Establishments Act 1964, s 1(4)(b)(iii), as amended by the Riding Establishments Act 1970; Dangerous Wild Animals Act 1976, s 1(3)(c)(i), (ii).

[69] Home Office, n 7 above, Part 2.

[70] Animals (Scientific Procedures) Act 1986, s 10(6B)(a), inserted by SI 1998/1974, n 6 above.

[71] Home Office, *Guidance on the Operation of the Animals (Scientific Procedures) Act 1986* (2000) Appendix B, para 9; Appendix C, para 9.

(2) Bedding and litter

The welfare of many animals is enhanced by the availability of bedding or nesting material. Depending on the species, it can make an important contribution to minimizing pain, injury, fear, and distress, as well as allowing animals to engage in their natural behaviour. The provision of adequate bedding material is therefore a factor to be taken into account in relation to the licensing of animal boarding establishments, dog breeding establishments, horse riding establishments, and dangerous wild animals kept in captivity, but is not specifically mentioned in relation to the licensing of pet shops.[72] In general, agricultural livestock living inside have to be kept on, or have access at all times to, a lying area which has either well-maintained dry bedding or, alternatively, is well drained.[73] In relation to those kept outside, it is specified that reasonable steps must be taken to ensure that they shall have access, at all times, to a well-drained lying area.[74] However, where lactating dairy cows or cows which are calving are kept in roofed accommodation they must have access at all times to a well-drained *and* bedded lying area;[75] calves and pigs reared indoors must be kept on, or have access at all times to, a lying area which is clean, comfortable, and does not adversely affect them, and is well drained or well maintained with clean, dry, and appropriate bedding;[76] and gilts and sows between weaning their piglets and the perinatal period should also be given, if necessary, suitable nesting material.[77] Poultry kept indoors must be provided with well-maintained litter or a well-drained area for resting, except for battery hens, for which no such basic amenities have to be provided.[78] The latter's only entitlement is to a (bare) floor which is constructed so as to support adequately each of the forward facing claws of each foot, and the slope of which does not exceed, when made of wire mesh, 14 per cent or 8 degrees, or in the case of other materials, 21.3 per cent or 12 degrees.[79] While at market, calves, dairy cattle and goats which are pregnant or in milk, pigs, young goat kids, and young lambs unaccompanied by the ewe, must be provided with dry suitable bedding.[80]

Requirements for animals used in scientific procedures are contained in the relevant Code of Practice.[81] The *Secretary of State's Standards of Modern Zoo Practice* advise that accommodation should take account of the natural habitat of the species and seek to meet the physiological and psychological needs of the animal.

---

[72] Animal Boarding Establishments Act 1963, s 1(3)(a), (b); Breeding of Dogs Act 1973, s 1(4)(a), (b); Riding Establishments Act 1964, s 1(4)(b)(v), as amended by the Riding Establishments Act 1970; Dangerous Wild Animals Act 1976, s 1(3)(c)(i), (ii).

[73] Welfare of Farmed Animals Regulations, n 8 above, Sch 1, para 4.

[74] ibid, Sch 1, para 17.   [75] ibid, Sch 5, para 1.

[76] ibid, Sch 4, para 10; Sch 6, para 11.

[77] ibid, Sch 6, para 22; see also paras 17, 18, and 25.

[78] ibid, Sch 3.   [79] ibid, Sch 2, para 1(g), (h).

[80] SI 1990/2628, n 2 above, art 12, as amended by SI 1993/3085, n 30 above, art 2(4).

[81] Home Office, n 7 above, Section 3.

To this end, enclosures should be equipped according to the needs of the particular species, with bedding material, branchwork, burrows, nesting boxes, pools, substrates, vegetation, and other enrichment materials designed to aid and encourage normal behaviour patterns and minimize any abnormal behaviour.[82]

(3) Environmental conditions

Where the effects of the weather might be detrimental to an animal's welfare, it is important that it be provided with protection, especially in circumstances where it is confined and therefore not able to take measures on its own initiative to escape the worst effects of the elements. So, for example, animals are required to be protected from inclement weather while being transported,[83] and horses which are kept at riding establishments must be provided with adequate shelter when they are maintained at grass.[84] Farm animals kept outside must, where necessary and possible, be given protection from adverse weather conditions, predators, and risks to their health;[85] and rabbits kept on agricultural land are required to have accommodation which allows them access to shelter from the action of the weather (including direct sunlight).[86] There is a general duty on those in charge of an animal in a market to ensure that it is not, or is not likely to be, caused injury or unnecessary suffering by reason of being exposed to the weather,[87] and there is a positive requirement that where a horse has been clipped, with the result that it lacks sufficient protection against the elements by its natural coat, it is either kept in covered accommodation or provided with suitable protective clothing.[88] Calves, dairy cattle which are in milk or pregnant, pigs, goats, rabbits, and poultry must all be provided with covered accommodation while in a market. The same applies to unaccompanied lambs and goat kids under four weeks of age, but they must also be placed in pens which have solid sides and are draught free.[89] Similarly, zoo animals kept in outdoor enclosures are expected to be provided with sufficient shelter for their comfort and well-being.[90]

The welfare of animals which are confined in an enclosed space, be it a building, a lorry, or other receptacle, is even more susceptible to harm as a consequence of poor environmental conditions. Hence, the suitability of accommodation as respects temperature, lighting, and ventilation is a relevant consideration in relation to the licensing of pet shops, animal boarding establishments, dog breeding establishments, horse riding establishments, and dangerous wild animals kept in

---

[82] DETR, n 12 above, paras 4.3 and 4.4.
[83] SI 1997/1480, n 13 above, Sch 1, paras 2, 5, 14; Sch 2, paras 4, 9; Sch 4, para 4; Sch 5, para 4.
[84] Riding Establishments Act 1964, s 1(4)(b)(iv), as amended by the Riding Establishments Act 1970.
[85] Welfare of Farmed Animals Regulations, n 8 above, Sch 1, para 17.
[86] ibid, Sch 7, para 2.
[87] SI 1990/2627, n 2 above, art 6(2)(a); SI 1990/2628, n 2 above, art 6(2)(a).
[88] SI 1990/2627, n 2 above, art 14.
[89] SI 1990/2628, n 2 above, art 13, as amended by SI 1993/3085, n 30 above, art 2(5).
[90] DETR, n 12 above, para 2.2.

captivity.[91] The insulation, heating, and ventilation of buildings in which farm animals are kept must ensure that air circulation, dust levels, temperature, relative air humidity, and gas concentrations are kept within limits which are not harmful.[92] Such animals must not be kept in permanent darkness, and they are required to have an appropriate period of rest from artificial lighting. Where the natural light available in a building is insufficient to meet their physiological and ethological needs, appropriate artificial lighting should be provided.[93] Likewise, transporters are required to ensure that animals are adequately protected from excessive humidity, extremes of temperature, inadequate ventilation,[94] and to avoid other detrimental effects of travel, such as undue exposure to noise and vibration.[95] The temperature, ventilation, lighting, and noise levels in zoo enclosures are expected to be suitable for the comfort and well-being of the particular species at all times;[96] and there is detailed guidance on the appropriate environmental conditions which should be provided for animals used in scientific procedures.[97]

In addition, there are provisions relating to the construction and maintenance of buildings and equipment, which broadly fall into four categories, requiring: the surfaces on which animals stand, walk, sit, or lie to be designed, built, and utilized in such a way as to avoid causing injury or unnecessary suffering;[98] automatic or mechanical equipment to be inspected regularly, and any defects rectified immediately;[99] the risk of injury or distress caused by sharp edges or protrusions to be eliminated;[100] and the pens, cages, and receptacles into which animals are placed to be designed, constructed, and maintained so as to prevent any injury or unnecessary suffering.[101] In relation to zoos, the Secretary of State's standards prescribe that measures should be taken to prevent stress or harm to the animals from defective barriers, equipment, tools, rubbish in enclosures, dangerous branches on trees, and smoking by staff.[102]

---

[91] Pet Animals Act 1951, s 1(3)(a); Animal Boarding Establishments Act 1963, s 1(3)(a), (b); Breeding of Dogs Act 1973, s 1(4)(a), (b); Riding Establishments Act 1964, s 1(4)(b)(iii), as amended by the Riding Establishments Act 1970; Dangerous Wild Animals Act 1976, s 1(3)(c)(i), (ii).

[92] Welfare of Farmed Animals Regulations, n 8 above, Sch 1, para 13.

[93] ibid, Sch 1, paras 14–16. In respect of calves and pigs, see also Sch 4, para 7 and Sch 6, para 8 (para 6 in the Scottish regulations) respectively.

[94] SI 1997/1480, n 13 above, Sch 1, paras 5, 14, 19; Sch 2, para 2; Sch 3, para 1; Sch 4, para 1; Sch 5, para 1; Sch 6.

[95] ibid, Sch 1, para 9.　　　　　　　　　　[96] DETR, n 12 above, para 2.1.

[97] Home Office, n 7 above, Sections 2, 3, and 5.

[98] SI 1990/2627, n 2 above, art 15(c); SI 1990/2628, n 2 above, art 19; SI 1997/1480, n 13 above, Sch 1, paras 4, 11, 12; Sch 2, paras 5, 6; Sch 5, paras 5, 6; Welfare of Farmed Animals Regulations, n 8 above, Sch 4, para 9; Sch 6, para 12.

[99] ibid, Sch 1, paras 18–21; DETR, n 12 above, para 1.9.

[100] SI 1990/2627, n 2 above, art 15 (a)(ii); SI 1990/2628, n 2 above, art 15 (a)(ii); SI 1997/1480, n 13 above, Sch 1, para 6; Welfare of Farmed Animals Regulations, n 8 above, Sch 1, para 11.

[101] SI 1990/2627, n 2 above, art 15(a)(i); SI 1990/2628, n 2 above, art 15(a)(i); SI 1997/1480, n 13 above, Sch 1, paras 1, 2, 8; Welfare of Farmed Animals Regulations, n 8 above, Sch 1, paras 11, 26; Sch 2, paras 2, 3, 4.

[102] DETR, n 12 above, paras 2.3–2.6.

(4) Behavioural needs

It is recognized by government that the shape of a cage or enclosure, together with the facilities provided within it, may be as important to an animal as its overall size; and social relations are as relevant to its welfare as stocking densities.[103] In response, requirements are gradually being introduced into legislation and official guidance intended to meet the behavioural and psychological needs of animals. Farm livestock kept in buildings, for example, have to be provided with sufficient lighting to meet their physiological and ethological needs, and feeding and watering equipment must be such as to minimize the harmful effects of competition between animals.[104] Neither calves nor pigs may be kept in such a way that they are unable to see other animals, and provisions are in place which, with effect from the beginning of 2004, require that the walls of all calf stalls and pens be perforated to allow the animals direct visual and tactile contact with their neighbours.[105] Pigs must be placed in groups as soon as possible after weaning, which should then be kept stable with as little mixing as possible, and they must have access to straw or other material or objects to satisfy their behavioural needs.[106] If pigs are kept together, measures must be taken to prevent fighting which goes beyond normal behaviour, and pigs which show persistent aggression are to be kept isolated or separate from the group.[107] The *Secretary of State's Standards of Modern Zoo Practice* require that the behaviour of animals, particularly social aspects, should be considered when offering food; refuge areas must be provided for nervous animals to escape the permanent gaze of the public; and enclosures must be of a size and design, and the groups or herds so managed, to avoid animals within them being unduly dominated by individuals and the risk of persistent and unresolved conflict between their members, or between different species or age groups in mixed exhibits.[108] Accommodation should take account of the natural habitat of the species and their physiological and psychological needs. To this end, enclosures must be equipped with appropriate enrichment materials in order to aid and encourage normal behaviour patterns and minimize abnormal behaviour. Animals of social species should usually be maintained in compatible social groups, and kept isolated only for the benefit of the group, so long as this is not detrimental to the individual specimen.[109] In addition, animals which may interact in an excessively stressful way must not be maintained in close proximity; suitable accommodation provided for pregnant animals and animals with young should minimize unnecessary stress; and animals temporarily accommodated away from others should not be separated for so long that there would be difficulties in reintroducing them to the group.[110]

[103] Home Office, n 7 above, para 3.21.
[104] Welfare of Farmed Animals Regulations, n 8 above, Sch 1, paras 15, 16, and 26.
[105] ibid, Sch 4, paras 1(3), (6); Sch 6, paras 6(2)(c) (para 4 (2)(c) in the Scottish regulations) and 17.
[106] ibid, Sch 6, paras 15, 22, and 30.
[107] ibid, Sch 6, para 9 (para 7 in the Scottish regulations).
[108] n 12 above, paras 1.4, 2.2, 3.4(a), (b).   [109] ibid, paras 4.3, 4.4, 4.5.   [110] ibid, paras 5.4–5.6.

In relation to animals used in scientific procedures, the declared aim is to maintain them in good health and physical condition; behaving in a manner normal for the species and strain; and with a reasonably full expression of their behavioural repertoire.[111] To this end, the relevant Code specifies that accommodation should be designed, sited, and constructed to provide a suitable environment, including any special requirement for exercise or social contact for the particular species; and the size, shape, and fittings of pens and cages should be designed to meet the physiological and behavioural needs of the animals.[112] Furthermore, since September 1998, the Home Secretary has been empowered to impose such conditions as he considers appropriate to ensure that any restrictions on the extent to which a protected animal kept at an animal procedure, breeding, or supplying establishment can satisfy its physiological and ethological needs are kept to what are described as 'the absolute minimum'.[113]

C. Monitoring

Appropriate treatment and accommodation are not in themselves sufficient to protect captive and domestic animals from experiencing poor welfare. It is essential that they are regularly observed so that their condition can be effectively assessed, and any problems identified and acted upon at the earliest opportunity. Farm animals kept in husbandry systems in which their welfare depends on frequent human attention—expressly including calves kept outside, pigs, hens in battery cages, and all other livestock kept in intensive systems—must be thoroughly inspected at least once a day to check that they are in a state of well-being; other livestock must be inspected at intervals sufficient to avoid any suffering.[114] Housed calves and zoo animals must be inspected at least twice daily,[115] while it is once a day in respect of animals at a slaughterhouse, and those bred, kept, or used in scientific procedures.[116] With regard to the latter, the standard conditions stipulate that the environmental conditions are checked daily, and the animals' well-being and state of health are monitored by a suitably qualified person in order to prevent pain or avoidable suffering, distress, or lasting harm.[117] Those undergoing scientific procedures must be inspected at a frequency commensurate with the severity of the procedure.[118] In relation to pet shops, boarding establishments, dog breeding

---

[111] Home Office, n 7 above, para 3.2.   [112] ibid, paras 2.10 and 3.21; see generally section 3.

[113] Animals (Scientific Procedures) Act 1986, s 10(6B)(b), inserted by SI 1998/1974, n 6 above. When considering what conditions are appropriate, the Home Secretary is required to have regard to the guidance in Annex ll of Directive 86/609: s 10 (6C). See further, the standard conditions for scientific procedure, breeding, and supplying establishments: Home Office, n 71 above, Appendix B, para 9; Appendix C, para 9.

[114] Welfare of Farmed Animals Regulations, n 8 above, Sch 1, para 2(1), (2); Sch 2, para 7; Sch 4, para 4; Sch 6, para 2.

[115] ibid, Sch 4, para 3; DETR, n 12 above, para 3.1.

[116] SI 1995/731, n 52 above, Sch 3, para 3; Animals (Scientific Procedures) Act 1986, s (6B)(c), (d), inserted by SI 1998/1974, n 6 above.

[117] Home Office, n 71 above, Appendices B and C, para 9.   [118] Home Office, n 7 above, para 3.3.

establishments, and riding establishments, the term used is 'visited at suitable intervals' or 'suitable times'.[119]

All automated or mechanical equipment essential for the health and well-being of farm animals must be inspected at least once daily and any defects rectified immediately or, if this is impracticable, appropriate steps taken to safeguard the animals' health and welfare until the defect has been rectified.[120] Likewise, the Home Secretary is required to impose such conditions on animal procedure, supplying, and breeding establishments as he considers appropriate to ensure that the environmental conditions in which protected animals are kept are checked daily and that arrangements are in hand to make certain that any defect or suffering is eliminated as quickly as possible.[121]

D. Fitness and Ill Health

Where animals are placed in particularly challenging situations which threaten to jeopardize their welfare, provisions may be introduced which impose a duty on those responsible for them to ensure that they are fit for the purpose. Thus, it is an offence to let out on hire or riding instruction any horse which is in such a condition as would be likely to cause it suffering; is less than 3 years old; is about to foal or has recently done so; or use defective equipment which it is apparent is likely to cause suffering. It also constitutes an offence to fail to provide such curative care as may be suitable for a sick or injured horse which is kept for these purposes.[122] In addition, all horses kept at a riding establishment are required to be adequately exercised, groomed, and rested,[123] and if, during a formal statutory inspection, such a horse is found to be in need of veterinary attention, it is forbidden to return it to work until the licence holder submits a veterinary certificate to the local authority confirming that the horse is fit.[124]

Likewise, it is prohibited to transport any animal in the course of a trade or business unless it is fit for the intended journey, and suitable provision has been made for its care during the journey and on arrival at the place of destination.[125] This

---

[119] Pet Animals Act 1951, s 1(3)(b); Animal Boarding Establishments Act 1963, s 1(3)(b); Breeding of Dogs Act 1973, s 1(4)(b), as amended by the Breeding and Sale of Dogs (Welfare) Act 1999; Riding Establishments Act 1964, s 1(4)(b)(v), as amended by the Riding Establishments Act 1970.

[120] Welfare of Farmed Animals Regulations, n 8 above, Sch 1, paras 18-21.

[121] Animals (Scientific Procedures) Act 1986, s 10(6B)(c), (e), inserted by SI 1998/1974, n 6 above.

[122] Riding Establishments Act 1964, s 3(1)(a), (aa), (b), (c), as amended by the Riding Establishments Act 1970.

[123] ibid, s 1(4)(vi).   [124] ibid, s 1(4A)(a).

[125] SI 1997/1480, n 13 above, art 6(1). An unfit animal is one that is ill, injured, infirm, or fatigued: art 6(2). There are also restrictions on the transport of animals likely to give birth during transport or which have given birth during the preceding 48 hours; newborn animals whose navel has not completely healed; and infant mammals and birds which are not able to feed themselves, unless accompanied by their mother: art 6(3), (4). See further, MAFF, *Guidance on the Transport of Casualty Farm Animals* (1993; amended reprint 1998).

requirement applies to cattle, sheep, pigs, goats, or horses regardless of whether or not the transport is of a commercial nature, except where they are being taken to the nearest available place for either veterinary treatment or slaughter, so long as the animal is not likely to be subjected to unnecessary suffering in the process.[126] The only other circumstances in which an otherwise unfit animal may be transported are, first, if it is only 'slightly' unfit and the intended journey is not likely to cause it unnecessary suffering, and, secondly, the journey is authorized under the Animals (Scientific Procedures) Act 1986.[127] If an animal falls ill or is injured during transit, the person in charge of it must ensure that first aid treatment is provided as soon as possible, it is given appropriate veterinary treatment, and, if necessary, is slaughtered in a way which does not involve unnecessary suffering.[128] In the same way, it is an offence to permit an unfit animal or one that is likely to give birth while there to be exposed for sale in a market,[129] and no lamb or goat kid may be brought to market or exposed for sale if it has an unhealed navel.[130] If an animal does arrive in an unfit state, or becomes unfit while it is at the market, there are powers to have it removed from sale, isolated, detained, examined, treated, and managed in any other way that a veterinary inspector considers is necessary to protect it from suffering.[131]

Farm livestock which appear to be ill or injured must be cared for appropriately without delay; if they do not respond, veterinary advice must be obtained as soon as possible.[132] Where necessary, sick or injured animals are required to be isolated in suitable accommodation with, if appropriate, dry comfortable bedding.[133] Where battery hens do not appear to be in good health or show behavioural changes, steps must be taken to establish the cause and appropriate remedial action taken.[134]

Primary responsibility for the welfare of animals used in scientific procedures is entrusted to the personal licensee carrying out the work, who has a duty to ensure the animals are properly monitored and cared for, and must take effective precautions, including the appropriate use of sedatives, tranquillizers, analgesics, or anaesthetics, to prevent or reduce to the minimum level consistent with the aims

---

Veterinary inspectors are required to examine horses and ponies for export immediately prior to shipment to confirm that they can be conveyed and disembarked without cruelty or unnecessary suffering, for which purpose an inspector may enter any vessel or aircraft: Animal Health Act 1981, ss 40(1),(2) and 49(1).

[126] SI 1997/1480, n 13 above, arts 2(3), 6(6). Where an unfit animal is transported under the authority of this latter provision it may not be dragged or pushed by any means, or lifted by a mechanical device, unless this is done in the presence of and under the supervision of a veterinary surgeon who is arranging for it to be transported with all practicable speed for veterinary treatment. See also the Fresh Meat (Hygiene and Inspection) Regulations 1995, SI 1995/539, reg 17 on delivering diseased or injured animals to a slaughterhouse.

[127] ibid, art 6(2), (5).   [128] ibid, art 7(1).

[129] SI 1990/2627, n 2 above, art 5; SI 1990/2628, n 2 above, art 5. 'Unfit' in this context includes infirm, diseased, ill, injured, or fatigued: art 3(1); cf n 125 above.

[130] SI 1990/2628, n 2 above, art 5A, inserted by SI 1993/3085, n 30, art 2(2).

[131] SI 1990/2627, n 2 above, art 17; SI 1990/2628, n 2 above, art 17.

[132] Welfare of Farmed Animals Regulations, n 8 above, Sch 1, para 5.

[133] ibid, Sch 1, para 6; Sch 4, para 5; Sch 6, para 3.   [134] ibid, Sch 2, para 9.

of the procedure any pain, suffering, distress, or discomfort caused to the animals used.[135] It is expected that the Named Animal Care and Welfare Officer (NACWO) will ensure that the highest standards of husbandry and care are practised. If the health or welfare of a protected animal is giving rise to concern, the NACWO or Named Veterinary Surgeon (NVS) must notify the personal licensee; if this is not possible, they must take steps to ensure that the animal is cared for and, if necessary, destroyed.[136] The NVS should visit all parts of the establishment designated in the certificate at a frequency which will allow effective monitoring of the health and welfare of the protected animals under their care.[137] Similarly, personal licensees must obtain veterinary advice and treatment where necessary.[138] If, at the conclusion of a series of regulated procedures, a protected animal is suffering or is likely to suffer adverse effects as a result of what has been done, it must be immediately and humanely killed.[139] In other circumstances, a veterinary surgeon (or, exceptionally, another suitably qualified person) is required to determine whether the animal should be killed or kept alive.[140]

Any zoo animal which gives cause for concern must be thoroughly assessed as to whether it is unduly distressed, sick, or injured and, where necessary, be given immediate attention and treatment.[141] A comprehensive programme of care should be established and maintained under the supervision of a veterinary surgeon familiar with current practice in the care of zoo animals, and who should be responsible for, or actively involved in, routine inspections, directing and carrying out treatment of sick animals, preventative medicine, and health monitoring.[142] A daily record has to be kept by those in direct charge of the animals, indicating changes to the prescribed diet, health checks carried out, any unusual behaviour or activity or other problems, and remedial action taken.[143] In addition, there must be systems for regular review, by the relevant veterinary and curatorial staff, of clinical, behavioural, and pathological records and mortality. Husbandry and preventative medical practices should be reviewed where problems become apparent.[144]

E. The Prevention and Control of Disease

Self-evidently, an animal's welfare may be seriously compromised if it becomes ill. Hence, a failure to seek veterinary assistance can amount to an offence of cruelty, if the animal has suffered as a consequence. Prevention, however, is better than cure, and in order to protect public safety, the economic value of livestock, and animal welfare, there is an extensive body of legislation concerned with animal health.

---

[135] Home Office, n 71 above, Appendix E, para 12.
[136] ibid, paras 4.57 and 4.62; Appendices B and C, paras 10 and 11; Appendix C, paras 10 and 11.
[137] ibid, para 4.62.   [138] ibid, para 6.17; Appendix E, para 16.
[139] Animals (Scientific Procedures) Act 1986, s 15.
[140] ibid, s 10(3D)(a), inserted by SI 1998/1974, n 6 above.
[141] DETR, n 12 above, para 3.2.   [142] ibid, paras 3.7 and 3.9.   [143] ibid, para 3.3.
[144] ibid, para 3.12.

Ministers have a general enabling power to make such orders as they think fit for the purpose of preventing the spread of disease and are authorized to expend such sums as they consider appropriate for this purpose, including, with the Treasury's approval, the provision of veterinary services in order to promote good health.[145] In addition, ministers may make orders in relation to the cleansing and disinfection of places and transport used for animals,[146] together with prohibiting or regulating their movement and import for the purpose of preventing the introduction or spread of disease into or within Great Britain.[147] In order to protect human health, ministers may also take appropriate measures to control zoonoses (diseases which can be transmitted to humans from animals).[148] Ministers are empowered in the interests of animal or human health to introduce provisions regulating the export of livestock to other EU Member States, and it is mandatory that prior to export such animals undergo a veterinary check for the purpose of preventing the spread of disease.[149]

Complementing these measures, specific duties are imposed on those responsible for animals to take steps to minimize the risk of disease. Every time battery cages are emptied they must be thoroughly cleansed and disinfected before the next batch of laying hens is introduced. While the cages are occupied, the surfaces and all equipment have to be kept satisfactorily cleaned[150] (although, in view of the anecdotal evidence of the state of some units, this provision is either not adequately enforced or the acceptable standard is not particularly high). The housing, pens, equipment, and utensils used for calves or pigs must be properly cleansed and disinfected as is necessary to prevent cross-infection and the build-up of disease-carrying organisms; faeces, urine, and uneaten food must be removed with sufficient frequency to minimize smell and avoid attracting flies or rodents.[151] Likewise, feeding and watering equipment used for livestock is required to be designed, constructed, placed, and maintained so that contamination of feed and water is minimized.[152] In the same way, means of transport and receptacles must be constructed, maintained, and operated so as to allow appropriate cleaning and disinfection, and the animals should be loaded only after these procedures have been carried out. Floors on which animals are transported must be covered with sufficient litter to absorb urine and droppings (unless equally effective alternatives

---

[145] Animal Health Act 1981, ss 1(a), 3(1), 5.   [146] ibid, s 7.

[147] ibid, ss 8 and 10. Quarantine requirements intended to prevent the introduction of rabies into Britain have traditionally been authorized under s 10: Rabies (Importation of Dogs, Cats and Other Mammals) Order 1974, SI 1974/2211, as amended by SI 1977/361, SI 1984/1182, SI 1986/2062, SI 1990/2371.

[148] ibid, ss 29 and 30.

[149] Animal Health Act 1981, s 11; Animals and Animal Products (Import and Export) Regulations 1995, SI 1995/2428, implementing Directive 90/425.

[150] Welfare of Farmed Animals Regulations, n 8 above, Sch 2, para 10.

[151] ibid, Sch 4, para 8; Sch 6, para 10.   [152] ibid, Sch 1, para 26.

are in place) and removed as soon as possible after use.[153] Similar provisions exist in relation to markets.[154]

The various licensing regimes also require factors relating to health to be taken into account. In deciding whether to license a pet shop, an animal boarding establishment, a dog breeding establishment, or grant a licence to keep a dangerous wild animal, the local authority is required to have regard to: cleanliness and the need for securing that all reasonable precautions will be taken to prevent the spread among animals of infectious diseases; take appropriate steps in case of fire or other emergency; and to specify such conditions in the licence as appear to it necessary or expedient for securing these objects.[155] The same applies to riding establishments, but, in addition, before granting a licence a local authority must have regard to the need for securing that 'paramount consideration' will be given to the condition of the horses and that they will be maintained in good health and kept physically fit; that the feet of all the animals are properly trimmed and in good condition; that all reasonable steps will be taken to prevent and control the spread among horses of infectious and contagious disease; that veterinary first aid equipment and medicines shall be provided and maintained in the premises; that appropriate steps will be taken for the protection and extrication of horses in case of fire and relevant instructions with regard to such an event will be kept displayed in a prominent position on the outside of the premises.[156] Similarly, the *Secretary of State's Standards of Modern Zoo Practice* provide guidance on hygiene, sanitation, the control of disease, and veterinary care and facilities.[157]

Although the prevention and control of disease is important for animal welfare, the primary impetus for legislation in this area is the need to safeguard human health and to protect the value of livestock. The draconian nature of the legal powers the State is authorized to exercise to protect economic interests was well illustrated by its response to the outbreak of foot-and-mouth disease (which is harmless to humans) in the spring of 2001. Relying initially on the powers contained within the pre-existing Foot-and-Mouth Order 1993,[158] the whole of Great Britain was, within hours of the confirmation of the outbreak, declared to be a 'Controlled Area', which prohibited the movement of all sheep, cattle, pigs, and goats within the country; fairs and markets were closed; and hunting suspended. In addition, footpaths were closed by local authorities. Once a place was designated as being 'infected' it was subject to extensive restrictions, including the prohibition of any person entering or leaving except under the authority of a licence issued

---

[153] SI 1997/1480, n 13 above, Sch 1, paras 7, 26, and 27.

[154] Markets, Sales and Lairs Order 1925, SR & O 1925/1349, as amended by the Markets, Sales and Lairs (Amendment) Order 1926, SR & O 1926/546, Markets, Sales and Lairs (Amendment) Order 1927, SR & O 1927/982, and the Markets, Sales and Lairs (Amendment) Order 1996, SI 1996/3265. [155] Pet Animals Act 1951, s 1(3)(a), (d), (e); Animal Boarding Establishments Act 1963, s 1(3)(a), (c), (d); Breeding of Dogs Act 1973, s 1(4)(a), (c), (d); Dangerous Wild Animals Act 1976, s 1(3)(c)(i), (d), (e).

[156] Riding Establishments Act 1964, s 1(4)(b)(i), (ii), (iii), (vi), (vii), as amended by the Riding Establishments Act 1970.

[157] n 12 above, paras 22, 24–26, and 29–50.   [158] SI 1983/1950, as amended.

by a Ministry inspector. In addition to animals actually infected and suspected of infection, those kept on contiguous premises were also killed as a preventative measure, regardless of whether there was any indication that they had been infected. In many cases this was against the stated wishes of the owners, and included incidents where Ministry officials entered private dwelling houses to slaughter sheep kept as pets. At the time, doubts were expressed in some quarters as to whether the Ministry was invariably acting under proper legal authority.

F. Killing and Slaughter

Notwithstanding the extensive volume of legislation existing in Britain to regulate the treatment of animals while they are alive, in general the law does not impose any restriction on killing them. The only exceptions to this principle relate to members of a relatively small number of species which have gained special protection because their continued survival is precarious, their habitats are of environmental importance, or they are considered to be at particular risk of persecution. Moral claims to the effect that at least some non-human species may be considered to have a right to life[159] have, to date, made no impact whatsoever on either English or Scottish law. In consequence, it is in relation to this issue that the status of animals as property continues to have particular significance. In the absence of any overriding legislative provisions, the axioms of the common law apply, including the right of the owner to dispose of his property in whatever way he wishes. For these purposes an animal is no different from an inanimate object: the owner may give it away, sell it, or decide that it should die. The one thing they may not do is abandon it without reasonable cause or excuse in circumstances likely to cause the animal any unnecessary suffering.[160]

The only other limitation on the owner's autonomy to decide for himself what the fate of his animal should be relates to circumstances in which it *must* be destroyed. First, the owner will be guilty of an offence of cruelty if to keep the animal alive would cause it to suffer unnecessarily.[161] Secondly, where an animal is in such a situation and the owner refuses to give his permission to carry out euthanasia or he is not available to give his consent, there are circumstances in which the law provides authority for third parties to intervene to end the suffering.[162] Where an animal is fatally injured, diseased, or some other factor has meant that its quality of life has irrevocably deteriorated below that which is reasonably considered to

---

[159] See, for example, Regan, T, *The Case for Animal Rights* (1984).

[160] Abandonment of Animals Act 1964, s 1. See above, Ch 8, s C(7).

[161] Protection of Animals Act 1911, s 1(1)(a); Protection of Animals (Scotland) Act 1912, s 1(1)(a); see also, s 2 of each Act, which, when the owner has been convicted of cruelty, gives a court the power to order destruction of an animal, if it is satisfied on veterinary advice that it would be cruel to do otherwise.

[162] See, for example: Protection of Animals Act 1911, s 11(1), (4); Protection of Animals (Scotland) Act 1912, s 10(1), (4); Animal Health Act 1981, ss 44 and 46(1).

be acceptable, the law may therefore regard the animal's interest in having its suffering terminated as overriding the owner's property rights. Thirdly, an animal may be destroyed, regardless of the owner's wishes, on grounds of public policy, either because it poses a threat to animal or human health,[163] or it endangers public safety.[164]

However, while in most cases it will be up to the owner to decide *when* the life of his animal should be terminated, there are detailed requirements about *how* it should be killed. Such regulation is not only important in practice, the principle it represents is also significant. Namely, notwithstanding that the duration of the procedure may be relatively short and will not, by definition, have long-term implications for the welfare of the animal, its subjective experience immediately before and up to the point of death is considered to be of equal importance as that during the rest of its life. In short, what it feels *matters*, regardless of the circumstances, the duration, or the animal's prospects.

This moral obligation is widely reflected in the law through the imposition of a duty on those responsible to ensure that in dispatching the animal they avoid or at least minimize its suffering and distress, and treat it humanely and with dignity. While it remains alive, however briefly, it continues to be a sentient being; like us, it is only when it is dead that it can no longer be harmed.

For example, in relation to the movement, lairaging, restraint, stunning, slaughter, and killing of animals bred or kept for the production of meat, skin, fur, or other products, killing animals for the purpose of disease control, and the killing of surplus (predominantly male) chicks, it is required that no animal shall be caused or permitted to sustain any avoidable excitement, pain, or suffering.[165] Significantly, however, these restrictions specifically do not apply to any animal which is killed during a sporting event or to the killing of wild game.[166] There is absolutely no reason in principle why this should be: if such standards are considered to be important for the welfare of the animals in one context, they should apply in all others unless it can be demonstrated that it is in the interests of the animals involved to do otherwise.

Detailed standards are set down in relation to the construction, equipment, and maintenance of slaughterhouses and knackers' yards;[167] the manner in which animals are moved and lairaged;[168] restrained;[169] stunned or killed;[170] and bled or

---

[163] For example, Animal Health Act 1981, ss 31 and 32.   [164] For example, Dogs Act 1871, s 2.

[165] SI 1995/731, n 52 above, regs 3(1), 4(1). The term 'slaughter' means causing the death of an animal by bleeding; 'killing' means causing its death by any other process: reg 2(1). The exceptional use of 'avoidable' rather than the more usual term 'unnecessary suffering' originates in the European Convention for the Protection of Animals at Slaughter (art 2(3)), whence it was adopted into EC law (Directive 93/119, art 3) and thereby transposed into UK legislation: see Ch 10, s F(2) above.

[166] ibid, reg 3(3), (4).

[167] ibid, reg 8 and Sch 2. A slaughterhouse means premises used for the commercial slaughter or killing of mammals or birds for human consumption; a knacker's yard only handles animals not intended for human consumption: reg 2(1).

[168] ibid, regs 9(a) and 10(a) and Sch 3.   [169] ibid, regs 9(b), 10(b) and Sch 4.

[170] ibid, regs 9(c), 10(c), 11, and Sch 5, Parts l and ll, and 7. 'Stunning' means any process which causes immediate loss of consciousness which lasts until death: reg 2(1).

pithed in the case of slaughter.[171] Similar provisions apply to an animal killed or slaughtered elsewhere than in a knacker's yard or slaughterhouse,[172] except in circumstances where it has to be killed immediately for emergency reasons relating to its welfare,[173] or the animal is killed or slaughtered for private consumption (although this must be done without causing the animal any avoidable excitement, pain, or suffering, and, if slaughtered, the provisions relating to stunning must be complied with).[174] In addition, special provisions apply in relation to disease control,[175] the killing of any fox or mink farmed for its fur,[176] and the killing of surplus chicks and embryos in hatchery waste.[177]

The animals themselves must be unloaded as soon as possible after their arrival at a slaughterhouse or knacker's yard, protected from adverse weather conditions, and provided with adequate ventilation. Those which might injure each other have to be kept apart, as do any which are sick or disabled.[178] Any animal which has experienced pain or suffering during transport or following its arrival, and any which is too young to take solid feed, must be killed or slaughtered immediately.[179] If an animal is unable to walk, it must be slaughtered or killed without being moved or, if it is possible to do so without causing any unnecessary pain or suffering, transported on a trolley to a place of emergency slaughter or killing where it is then immediately dispatched.[180] Those engaged in the movement of animals are required to ensure that care is taken not to frighten, excite, or mistreat them,[181] no animal which has been stunned or killed is dragged over one that is conscious,[182] and they are handled and driven in compliance with the Regulations.[183] If animals are to be lairaged, requirements relating to their treatment are similar to those which apply while they remained on the farm, and include arrangements for regular inspection, provision of bedding if necessary, food and water, and adequate space to lie down, stand up, and turn round without difficulty.[184]

Animals are subjected to an ante-mortem inspection by a veterinary surgeon which, among other things, is concerned to determine whether they are diseased, injured, fatigued, or stressed.[185] Once brought into the slaughter hall, animals must be slaughtered without delay.[186] Every animal which is slaughtered must first

---

[171] ibid, reg 9(d) and Sch 6. 'Pithing' means the destruction of an animal's brain tissue after stunning to the extent that irreversible loss of consciousness is ensured: reg 2(1). As a result of Dec 2000/418, as of 1 April 2001, it is no longer permissible to pith an animal slaughtered for human or animal consumption: Restriction on Pithing (England) Regulations, SI 2001/447; Restriction on Pithing (Scotland) Regulations, SSI 2001/73; Restriction on Pithing (Wales) Regulations 2001, SI 2001/1303 (W80).

[172] ibid, regs 14, 15.   [173] ibid, reg 13(2).   [174] ibid, reg 16.
[175] ibid, reg 17 and Sch 9.   [176] ibid, reg 18 and Sch 10.
[177] ibid, reg 19 and Sch 11; see also, SI 1995/539, n 126 above, Sch 2, para 1 and Sch 5, Pt ll, para 1.
[178] ibid, Sch 3, para 2(a)–(f).   [179] ibid, Sch 3, para 4.   [180] ibid, Sch 3, para 5.
[181] ibid, Sch 3, para 6(a).   [182] ibid, Sch 3, para 2(f).
[183] ibid, Sch 3, paras 7–12; similar requirements apply to the handling of animals delivered in containers: para 14.
[184] ibid, Sch 3, para 13(a)–(f); see also paras 15(b) and 16. An animal may not be kept in a lairage for more than 72 hours without the consent of a veterinary surgeon: SI 1995/539, n 126 above, reg 16(1).
[185] SI 1995/539, n 126 above, Sch 8, paras 2 and 4.   [186] ibid, Sch 9, para 1(1)(a).

be stunned.[187] Prior to being stunned, slaughtered, or killed, every animal must be restrained in such a way as to spare it any avoidable pain, suffering, agitation, injury, or contusions,[188] and both the occupier of the premises and the relevant operatives are required to ensure that the procedure is carried out rapidly and effectively.[189]

Similarly, there are detailed provisions relating to when and how protected animals used in scientific procedures, and others kept at scientific procedure establishments, breeding, and supplying establishments, should be killed, including the method to be used for the particular species.[190] The Home Office expects that, wherever practicable, animals should be removed from the immediate presence of others and handled carefully to ensure that they are not frightened or antagonized. With methods that are not instantaneous, unconsciousness should be induced as quickly as possible with minimum stress and fully maintained until death, which must be confirmed by physical checks or ensured by exsanguination, severance of the major blood vessels or ventricles of the heart, before disposal of the body.[191]

G. Breeding and Supply

Under the Pet Animals Act 1951, it is prohibited to sell mammals as pets at too early an age; or to sell any pet in the street or a public place, or from a stall or barrow at a market; or to a child under twelve years of age.[192] Otherwise, the breeding and supply of animals has remained largely unregulated. The wholly irresponsible practice of offering animals as prizes, for example, remains legal. Recently, however, there has been a move to introduce some, albeit limited, measures in relation to these

---

[187] SI 1995/731, n 52 above, reg 9(c). Special provisions apply in relation to slaughter by a (Jewish or Muslim) religious method, during which the animal is not stunned, as provided for under Directive 74/577. This practice remains controversial. The Farm Animal Welfare Council has recommended that it should be prohibited (*Report on the Welfare of Livestock when Slaughtered by Religious Methods* (1985)), but ministers have adopted the view that the exemption from pre-stunning 'recognizes a fundamental matter of religious belief to communities that are an important part of our national life': HC Debs, 2 February 1997, col 659. However, because of the difficulties encountered in ensuring that such animals were killed humanely, it is now the case that religious slaughter may be carried out only at a slaughterhouse, where an official veterinary surgeon will be present and a stunner available to prevent unnecessary suffering should a problem arise: regs 21, 22, and Sch 12, as amended by the Welfare of Animals (Slaughter or Killing) (Amendment) Regulations 1999, SI 1999/400.

[188] ibid, Sch 4, para 2.

[189] ibid, Sch 5, para 2. Further detailed requirements to this end are contained in Schs 5, 6, 7, 8.

[190] Animals (Scientific Procedures) Act 1986, ss 10, 15 and Schs 1 and 2. See also, Home Office, *Code of Practice for the Humane Killing of Animals under Schedule 1 to the Animals (Scientific Procedures) Act 1986* (1997).

[191] Home Office, n 7 above, para 4.4.

[192] Sections 1(3)(c), 2, and 3. In the Scottish case of *White v Kilmarnock and Loudon District Council* 1991 SLT (Sh Ct) 69, the court held that a unit in an indoor market, which was a semi-permanent structure, separated from the neighbouring units by a plywood partition, constituted a market stall for these purposes. The court rejected the argument that 'a stall is not included unless it has some sort of impermanence as a barrow'.

matters. Breeding of animals for use in scientific procedures must normally take place only at a designated establishment, and designation is also required in respect of premises from which such animals are supplied. In consequence, they have to meet many of the same standards as are imposed on a scientific procedure establishment, including the appointment of a NAWCO and NVS, the duty to take appropriate steps if the health or welfare of any animal gives rise to concern, and they also fall within the jurisdiction of the Animals (Scientific Procedures) Inspectorate.[193] Furthermore, the Home Secretary is authorized to grant a designation subject to such conditions as he thinks fit.[194] These are in addition to those which are specified by statute, including a requirement that the certificate holder ensure that the environment, housing, freedom of movement, food, water, and care provided for each animal are appropriate for the animal's health and well-being, and any restrictions on the way it can satisfy its physiological and ethological needs are kept to an absolute minimum.[195] Certificate holders are also advised to minimize overbreeding so far as is reasonably possible.[196] Zoo operators are expected where appropriate to comply with the Animal Transaction Policy of the Federation of Zoological Gardens of Great Britain and Ireland.[197] When disposing of surplus stock operators are advised to ensure that they are passed only to persons with the appropriate facilities, resources, and expertise, and to take (unspecified) precautions that the recipients are likely to safeguard the animals' welfare in any subsequent transactions. Although culling of surplus stock may be justifiable where overcrowding of the animals compromises their welfare, it is advised that measures should be taken to control unwanted or unnecessary breeding in preference to destroying healthy stock.[198] Additional provisions have also recently been introduced in an effort to address the unscrupulous and indiscriminate breeding of dogs on so-called puppy farms. Conditions must now be attached to a dog breeding establishment licence requiring that bitches should not be mated if they are less than one year old, and should neither give birth to more than a total of six litters each nor to more than one litter in any period of twelve months.[199] Furthermore, a keeper of a licensed breeding establishment (and, in Scotland, a rearing establishment) is now guilty of an offence if they sell a dog anywhere other than at such an establishment or a licensed pet shop.[200] In relation to farm animals, it is prohibited to practise natural or artificial breeding or breeding procedures which cause, or are likely to cause, suffering or injury to any of the

---

[193] Animals (Scientific Procedures) Act 1986, ss 7, 9(1), 10(1), and Sch 2.   [194] ibid, s 10(1).

[195] ibid, s 10(6), (6A), (6B), (6C), and (6D), as inserted by SI 1998/1974, n 6 above. See further, the standard conditions applicable to designated breeding and supplying establishments: Home Office, n 71 above, Appendix C.

[196] Home Office, n 71 above, paras 8.25–8.28; see also Ch 8 generally, and the Annual Report of the Animal Procedures Committee for 1997, Annex F, Chapter 5.

[197] DETR, n 12 above, para 4.1.   [198] ibid, paras 4.9 and 4.10.

[199] Breeding of Dogs Act 1973, s 1(4)(f), (g), (h), inserted by the Breeding and Sale of Dogs (Welfare) Act 1999.

[200] Breeding and Sale of Dogs (Welfare) Act 1999, s 8(1), (2).

animals, although this does not preclude procedures which are likely to cause minimal or momentary suffering or injury or that might necessitate interventions which would not cause lasting harm.[201]

H. Conclusion

It is apparent from the foregoing that there is now in place in Britain a large volume of increasingly sophisticated legislation which lays down detailed standards for the care and treatment of animals. The detailed provisions owe much to scientific research which has led to a greater understanding of the needs of animals if they are to benefit from a high standard of welfare. As one would expect, the more recent the legislation, the higher the standards which are imposed. This means, however, that older legislation may lag behind contemporary standards of welfare. This is particularly so in relation to companion animals. Why this should be is not immediately obvious. Perhaps the attention of pressure groups has quite understandably focused principally on commercial activities because, in the absence of adequate regulation, animals in such an environment too easily become the victims of economic pressures and market forces. It may also be explained in part by the fact that in recent years the campaign for reform has largely concentrated on influencing changes to EC law, the jurisdiction of which does not extend to the keeping of companion animals. Whatever the reason, there is an increasingly urgent need to enhance the standards of care required of those who choose to keep pets. For too long, the Protection of Animals Acts have been relied on to ensure that companion animals are well treated; but this legislation is concerned with cruelty, not welfare.

It is also important to keep the progress which has been made in perspective. Notwithstanding the advances that have been achieved, it must be recognized that welfare legislation continues to sanction practices which many find offensive and unacceptable. It is certainly the case that it may allow the interests of other species to be compromised for the benefit of humans, especially where commercial considerations are involved. Nevertheless, it is the case that the introduction, and continuing development, of a body of welfare legislation represents a very significant extension to the protection afforded to animals.

[201] Welfare of Farmed Animals Regulations, n 8 above, Sch 1, para 28.

Part F

Effectiveness

14

Enforcement

As Richard Martin discovered immediately after the passing of his Act in 1822,[1] if legislation to protect animals is to be effective, it *must* be adequately enforced. This means more than merely bringing alleged offenders before the courts. Prosecution is an integral part of the process, but represents the option of last resort. The ambit of enforcement is far wider, and includes the need to ensure:

- the various regulatory schemes prescribed by the European Community, the national Parliament, and, where appropriate, the Scottish Parliament and the Welsh Assembly, are duly implemented;
- those to whom legislation applies are mindful of the nature and extent of their legal responsibilities;
- the treatment of animals meets the standards required by the relevant legislation;
- advice and guidance is made available as to how the care of animals might be improved to meet those standards; and
- in circumstances where this proves to be ineffectual, the appropriate authorities exercise the powers which are available to them in order to make certain that the welfare of the animals does not continue to be compromised.

Enforcement also has an important role to play in identifying problems or weaknesses in the law, and thereby to lay the foundation for further reform. This is particularly important in Britain, where legislation once enacted generally continues in force indefinitely. This is in contrast to EC legislation, which often includes provisions intended to initiate further reform in the future.[2] Conversely,

---

[1] See Ch 3, s D above.

[2] For example, the 1991 transport directive required the Commission to submit to the Council, by July 1992, a report drawn up on the basis of an opinion from the Scientific Veterinary Committee on such matters as maximum journey times, feeding and watering intervals, rest periods, and loading densities (Directive 91/628, art 13.2), which, in turn, formed the basis for the 1995 transport directive (Directive 95/29, recital). Similarly, the 1988 battery hens directive required the Commission to prepare by the beginning of 1993 a report on scientific developments regarding the welfare of hens kept under different systems, together with any appropriate proposals for reform (Directive 88/166, art 9), which led to its successor of

where it is found to be wanting, better enforcement of existing legislation may serve to forestall calls for yet more change.

A. The Importance of Good Drafting

It is self-evidently desirable that legislation is understood by those to whom it is addressed, and those who have the duty to enforce it. Every provision should be unambiguous in its wording, equitable and practicable in its application, and certain in its impact. Poorly drafted legislation has a tendency to result in confusion, inconsistency, and unforeseen consequences.

(1) The case of the Dangerous Dogs Act 1991

The dangers inherent in such a situation are well demonstrated by the Dangerous Dogs Act 1991. An extempore response by the Government to a series of well-publicized attacks on humans by dogs, especially pit bull terriers, it was rushed through Parliament, completing all its legislative stages in the House of Commons in a single day, having been published only four days previously.[3] Section 1 of the Act makes it an offence to have possession or custody of a dog bred for fighting, including specifically 'any dog of the type known as the pit bull terrier', unless a certificate of exemption has been granted in respect of the particular animal. In order to be eligible for exemption, the dog must be, among other things, neutered, permanently identified, insured, kept secure, and both muzzled and on a lead whenever it is in a public place.[4] Failure to comply with any of these requirements not only constitutes an offence, but, as originally enacted, also resulted in a mandatory destruction order, regardless of the circumstances.[5]

Unfortunately, the legislation failed to clarify what, precisely, was meant by the phrase 'any dog of the type known as the pit bull terrier'. Not only was the ambit of the term 'type' unclear, but, in Britain, the pit bull terrier is not recognized as a distinct breed. Hence, as the courts acknowledged, there was 'an absence of any precise criteria by which a pit bull terrier may be identified positively as a breed and by this means distinguished from all other dogs',[6] notwithstanding the stringency of the requirements which were applicable if an animal came within this definition,

---

1999 (Directive 1999/74, recitals (2) and (7)). The on-farm directive adopts a rather different tactic by requiring the Commission every five years to submit to the Council a report detailing the experience acquired since its implementation, together with any appropriate proposals (Directive 98/58, art 5.2).

[3] See further, Hansard Society for Parliamentary Government, *Making the Law. The Report of The Hansard Society Commission on the Legislative Process* (1992) Appendix 6.

[4] Dangerous Dogs Act 1991, s 1(1)(a), (3), (5), (7); the Dangerous Dogs Compensation and Exemption Schemes Order 1991, SI 1991/1744, as amended by SI 1991/2297, SI 1991/2636. The other types of dog covered by these provisions are the Japanese tosa, the Dogo Argentino, and the Fila Braziliero: s 1(1)(b); The Dangerous Dogs (Designated Types) Order 1991, SI 1991/1743.

[5] Dangerous Dogs Act 1991, ss 1(7), 4(1)(a).

[6] *Parker v Annan* 1993 SCCR 185, 190, High Ct (Lord Justice General Hope).

and the seriousness of the consequences for both dog and owner if they were ignored. The English High Court eventually held that in deciding whether a particular animal fell within the scope of the provision, it was relevant to take account of the basic physical and behavioural characteristics of the pit bull which had been established by the American Dog Breeders' Association,[7] but both the English and Scottish courts have stated that whether or not an animal is aggressive—the principal characteristic associated with pit bulls, and the basis on which the statutory provision had been introduced in the first place—is not decisive in determining if a particular animal is to be regarded as of the pit bull type.[8] It may be, as Lord Justice General Hope suggested, that the lack of precision in relation to what constitutes a pit bull terrier was 'no doubt deliberate, in view of the many variables produced by crossbreeding', but, as the judge conceded, in consequence, there was 'inevitably some risk that different judges will form different views on the same facts'.[9] In itself such a situation is clearly unsatisfactory, but it was made significantly worse as a result of a reversal in the normal burden of proof. This disregard for the fundamental constitutional principle, that a person should be considered innocent unless the prosecution can satisfy the court beyond reasonable doubt that they are guilty, arose because the Act provided that once the prosecution alleged that a dog was of a pit bull type, the court was to presume that this was indeed so, unless the accused could show otherwise.[10] It may be that the Act was 'ultimately aimed to exclude these dogs from the country *in toto*', and, in the meantime, was intended to keep 'the public as secure as is conceivably possible',[11] but legislation is to be judged not simply by whether it achieves its ultimate objective: it must also be comprehensible and fair. For an Act of Parliament to be described judicially as both 'Draconian'[12] and 'Delphic'[13] offends against the principle of fairness.

The confusion engendered by section 1 was further compounded by the way in which the courts interpreted the term 'public place'. Defined in the statute as 'any street, road or other place (whether or not enclosed) to which the public have or are permitted to have access',[14] it has been held that the garden path leading to the front door of a private dwelling does not for this purpose constitute a public place (notwithstanding that anyone could enter from the street and walk along it), but the inside of a car does, if the vehicle itself is situated in a public place (even though the car was secure, the dog could not escape, and the public could not gain access to it).[15]

---

[7] *R v Knightsbridge Crown Court, ex parte Dunne; Brock v DPP* [1994] 1 WLR 296.

[8] ibid; *Parker v Annan* 1994 SLT 675.   [9] *Annan v Troup* 1994 SLT 679, 681, High Ct.

[10] Dangerous Dogs Act 1991, s 5(5).   [11] *Bates v DPP* (1993) 157 JP 1004, 1007 (Waller J).

[12] A phrase employed by both Waller J and Rose LJ in *Bates v DPP* (1993) 157 JP 1004, 1007 and 1009.

[13] *Rafiq v Folkes* (1997) 161 JP 412, 413 (Popplewell J).   [14] Dangerous Dogs Act 1991, s 10(2).

[15] *Fellowes v DPP* (1993) 157 JP 936, [1993] Crim LR 523; *McGeachy v Normand* 1994 SLT 429; *Bates v DPP* (1993) 157 JP 1004.

The consequences of 'this ill-considered, unjust law', as it was described by the *Veterinary Record*,[16] were not only a series of arbitrary and inequitable decisions;[17] there were also welfare implications for the large number of dogs that were seized, many of which remained in kennels for a prolonged period as their increasingly desperate owners explored (generally unsuccessfully) the possibility of challenging mandatory destruction orders. At one point, the Metropolitan Police were holding 448 such animals,[18] and the cost to them of kennelling dogs under the 1991 Act from its introduction to the beginning of 1997 was more than £3,000,000.[19] More significantly, it was estimated that such a dog's average period of detention was two years and four months; in one case this extended to four years and five months.[20] After three abortive attempts, a Private Member's Bill was eventually passed in 1997 which went some way to addressing the problem by providing the courts with a limited discretion to decide for themselves whether it is necessary to order that the dog be destroyed, so long as they are satisfied that it would not constitute a danger to public safety.[21]

B. Legal Responsibility

The issue of enforcement, and thereby the very effectiveness of animal protection legislation, is intimately bound up with the nature of the responsibility which it imposes, and the scope of those whom the law holds to account for their conduct towards animals.

(1) The nature of legal responsibility

The nature of legal responsibility depends upon the circumstances: the *context* in which the relevant legislation applies; the *objective* it is intended to attain; the *scope* of those to whom it is addressed; its *character* (positive or negative, permissive or prohibitive, mandatory or discretionary, general or specific); and the *mental element* associated with any particular offence. Each of these may vary considerably, even among provisions contained within the same legislation, as can be demonstrated by reference to the following examples relating to markets:

---

[16] Editorial: 'A dog's dinner of a law' (1995) 137 *Veterinary Record* 573. In contrast, the House of Commons Home Affairs Committee, while conceding that the Act was 'not perfect' and contained 'some harsh measures', largely rejected the widespread criticism made of it, pointing to the fact that it had 'largely succeeded in eliminating the breeding and holding of a kind of dog for criminal or anti-social purposes—the pit bull terrier—which was causing increasing concern both to the public and the police': *The Operation of the Dangerous Dogs Act 1991* (1996) para 86. See also, Hood, C et al, 'Assessing the DDA: When does a Regulatory Law Fail?' [2000] Public Law 282.

[17] See, for example, *Normand v Freeman* 1992 SLT 598; *Bates v DPP* (1993) 157 JP 1004; *Cichon v DPP* [1994] Crim LR 918; *R v Secretary of State for the Home Department, ex parte James* [1994] COD 167.

[18] House of Commons Home Affairs Committee, n 16 above, para 81.

[19] HC Debs, 5 February 1997, col 605 (WA).   [20] HC Debs, 4 June 1996, col 328 (WA).

[21] Dangerous Dogs (Amendment) Act 1997.

- No person shall cause or permit any injury or unnecessary suffering to an animal in a market.
- No person shall use excessive force to control any animals in a market.
- No person shall drive or lead any animal over any ground or floor, the nature or condition of which is likely to cause the animal to slip or fall.[22]

The objective of each of these provisions is to prevent the specified events from occurring. They therefore apply generally, and are both negative and mandatory ('shall').

- It shall be the duty of a market operator to ensure that no animal is kept in a pen, cage, or hutch which is unsuitable for the size and species of that animal.[23]

Again, the aim is prevention, but here it is achieved by placing a specific person, the market operator, under a positive, mandatory duty to take appropriate steps to make certain that the eventuality does not happen.

- It shall be the duty of the person in charge of an animal to ensure that the animal is provided with an adequate quantity of wholesome water as often as is necessary to prevent it suffering from thirst.
- It shall be the duty of the owner (or his duly authorized agent) of an animal which is kept in a market from one day to the next to ensure that the animal is provided with an adequate supply of suitable food and with an adequate supply of wholesome water . . .[24]

Here, the intention is to promote a particular outcome, and it is given effect by imposing a positive, mandatory duty to that end, although the identity of those on whom the duty falls varies depending on the particular circumstances.

- Where a veterinary inspector is of the opinion that any animal in a market is unfit, he may treat it, or cause it to be treated, and take, or cause to be taken, any other steps that he considers necessary to protect it from suffering . . .[25]

In this context, the power provided is permissive ('may') and discretionary ('he considers necessary'). One does not want to labour the point, but these examples demonstrate three important issues: first, by means of precise wording, each provision can be fashioned in such a way that it fulfils a particular object; secondly, it must always be assumed that the specific language has been carefully and deliberately chosen in order to give effect to that purpose; and, thirdly, in order to determine the precise nature of the legal responsibility under each legislative provision, it is necessary to pay close attention to its particular construct.

Furthermore, in order to establish the extent of a person's *criminal* responsibility in any particular situation, it is essential to have regard to the *mental element* of the relevant offence. This issue of *mens rea* has already been extensively discussed

---

[22] The Welfare of Animals at Markets Order 1990, SI 1990/2628, arts 6(1), 8(1), 8(4).
[23] ibid, art 10(1).   [24] ibid, art 11(1), (2).   [25] ibid, art 17(2).

in relation to offences of cruelty and the concept of necessary suffering,[26] but it must be briefly alluded to once more because the duty any particular legislative provision imposes upon those who fall within its ambit is influenced by whether the state of mind of the accused is relevant (*mens rea*), or the offence is defined entirely by reference to their conduct (strict liability). Again, it is essential to have due regard to the specific wording of the particular provision; the subtlety of language and terminology can have a profound effect on its meaning. For example, the terms 'knowingly' and 'permit' both generally connote a subjective test. However, where they are used in association with a word such as 'reasonably', the test becomes objective, as where it is provided that 'a person permits any act or omission if he knows of, or might reasonably be expected to know of, that act or omission'.[27] Similarly, the provision which makes it an offence to cause unnecessary pain or distress to livestock, or to permit such suffering of which the accused knows or may reasonably be expected to know, offers, as the High Court has observed, three possible charges: 'The first is causing unnecessary pain or distress. . . . The second is permitting such pain or distress of which he knew, and the third is permitting such pain or distress of which he might reasonably be expected to know.' In consequence, even though the prosecution may not be able to establish that the defendant had actual knowledge of the animals' condition, he may still be guilty if the circumstances are such that—in the court's phrase—'constructive knowledge' may be inferred.[28]

By once more using the Markets Order as an example, it can be readily appreciated how language is used to specify the mental element of an offence, and thereby define the nature of the legal responsibility it imposes. Thus, the provisions which stipulate that

- . . . it shall be the duty of any person in charge of an animal in a market to ensure that the animal is not, or is not likely to be, caused injury or unnecessary suffering by reason of: the animal being exposed to the weather, inadequate ventilation being available to the animal, the animal being hit or prodded by any instrument or other thing, or any other cause;

and

- . . . no person shall handle an animal in a market by: lifting it off the ground; dragging it along the ground; or suspending it clear of the ground; by the head, ears, horns, legs, feet, tail, fleece, or wing;

both constitute strict liability offences.[29] On the other hand, the injunction that

---

[26] See Ch 9, s B and Ch 10, s E above.

[27] Welfare of Animals (Slaughter or Killing) Regulations 1995, SI 1995/731, reg 2(2).

[28] Agriculture (Miscellaneous Provisions) Act 1968, s 1(1); *Holliday v Armstrong* (QBD, 6 February 1995) (McCowan LJ).

[29] SI 1990/2628, n 22 above, arts 6(2), 7(1); see further, *Davidson v Strong* The Times, 20 March 1997.

- No person shall knowingly obstruct any animal which is being driven or led through any part of a market,

and

- No person shall wantonly or unreasonably annoy any animal in a market,

each have a mental element; a subjective test in the case of the former ('knowingly'), and either subjective or objective in respect of the latter ('wantonly', 'unreasonably').[30]

Furthermore, where detailed provisions are contained in a series of schedules, the *mens rea* for each is not always the same. So, the regulations relating to farmed animals in England require that owners and keepers 'shall take all *reasonable* steps' to meet the conditions under which such animals generally are required to be kept, as specified in Schedule 1,[31] but they *must* meet the standards laid down in Schedules 2 to 7, which relate to particular types of animals.[32] It should also be noted that devolution has begun to result in subtle variations respecting *mens rea*. Thus, the equivalent Scottish regulations specify that owners and keepers '*must*' ensure that the conditions laid down in Schedule 1 are complied with.[33]

Having identified that the wording of the legislation indicates that there is a mental element to an offence, there is a need to establish to what, precisely, the *mens rea* requirement applies. For example, confronted with the need to interpret the provision which directs that 'No person shall permit an unfit animal to be exposed for sale in a market',[34] the High Court expressed the unremarkable view that the inclusion of the word 'permit' required the prosecution to prove that the defendant *knowingly exposed an animal for sale in the market*, but the question before the court was whether it was necessary to demonstrate that the defendant's knowledge extended to the fact that the animal was indeed *unfit*. At first reading, the answer may appear to be in the affirmative, which would impose a significantly greater burden on the prosecution than the alternative. However, the court's conclusion, and its reasoning, is instructive. In particular, the court paid regard to the wider legislative context, and the purpose and policy it was intended to address. Having noted that the legislation provided elsewhere a defence of lawful excuse, proof of which lies on the defendant,[35] it held that the prosecution was required to prove, first, that an animal was unfit; and, secondly, that the defendant knowingly allowed that unfit animal to be exposed for sale. It was not necessary, the court concluded, to show that the defendant actually knew the animal to be

---

[30] ibid, art 9(1), (2); see further, *Davidson v Strong* The Times, 20 March 1997.
[31] Welfare of Farmed Animals (England) Regulations 2000, SI 2000/1870, reg 3(2); Welfare of Farmed Animals (Wales) Regulations 2001 (at the time this book went to press, these regulations had not been allocated an SI number) (emphasis added).
[32] ibid, regs 4–9.
[33] Welfare of Farmed Animals (Scotland) Regulations 2000, SSI 2000/442, reg 3(2) (emphasis added).
[34] SI 1990/2628, n 22 above, art 5(1).
[35] ibid, art 20, echoing s 73 of the parent Act, the Animal Health Act 1981.

unfit, although it would amount to a defence to establish on the balance of probabilities that the accused reasonably believed the animal to be fit. 'A construction
which required a prosecution to prove that the person exposing the animal for sale
knew that the animal was unfit or was wilfully blind to that fact, would allow a person to escape liability by mere careless disregard of the welfare of the animal which
he proposes to sell', observed Moses J (sitting with Lord Bingham CJ, who con-
curred with the judgment). 'On the other hand,' said the judge, 'a construction
which does not require proof of knowledge that the animal was unfit will put the
onus upon those exposing animals for sale, to see that the animal is fit for sale and
to take steps that there is a proper procedure in place to ensure that is done.' This
being the case, the court did not consider there to be 'anything unduly harsh in
exposing a farmer to liability and leaving it to him to show, on the balance of probabilities, that he had reasonable grounds for believing that the animal was fit'.[36]

The reference in this example to 'a defence of lawful excuse' illustrates a further
important factor in determining the extent of a person's legal responsibility in any
particular context. Namely, that legislation may be structured in such a way that it
imposes obligations, failure to comply with which would appear to amount to an
offence, but elsewhere within the text this may be qualified by a statutory defence.
The provisions relating to the treatment of animals in markets quoted above, for
example, allow that a person shall not be guilty of an offence if they can show that
they had lawful authority or excuse for their failure to comply.[37] Similarly, a person
who contravenes any provision of the regulations governing the slaughter and
killing of animals is not guilty of an offence if they can prove that by reason of accident, or other emergency contravention, it was necessary for preventing injury or
suffering to any person or animal.[38]

In order to ascertain the nature of legal responsibility, it is therefore essential to
have regard to the precise wording of each provision, the policy and purpose
underlying the legislation, and related provisions which might have a bearing on
that under consideration.

(2) The scope of those whom the law holds responsible for the treatment of animals

Clearly, where an offence has been committed, the principal perpetrator may be
prosecuted. It is often the case, however, that there are others standing behind the

---

[36] *Davidson v Strong* The Times, 20 March 1997. This decision is consistent with those in *Cheshire County
Council v Clegg* (1991) 89 LGR 600 and *R v Cheshire County Council Trading Standards Department, ex parte
Alan Helliwell & Sons (Bolton) Ltd* [1991] Crim LR 210, both of which concerned a similarly worded provision in the Transit of Animals (Road and Rail) Order 1975; see now, Welfare of Animals (Transport) Order
1997, SI 1997/1480, art 21.

[37] SI 1990/2628, n 22 above, art 20(c)(d)(e); see also, the Welfare of Horses at Markets (and Other Places
of Sale) Order 1990, SI 1990/2627, art 19(c)(d)(e). A similar defence is available in respect of contraventions
on the farm and during transport: Welfare of Farmed Animals Regulations, nn 31 and 33 above, reg 13(1);
SI 1997/1480, n 36 above, art 21.

[38] SI 1995/731, n 27 above, reg 27.

person directly responsible for the situation, typically those with some authority over them, who may also be culpable, and it is important that they too are answerable before the courts in situations where animals have been mistreated. So liability for offences of cruelty, for example, extends beyond the person immediately at fault for the relevant act or omission, to include any other person who may have caused or procured it (except, curiously, in the context of the cruel tethering of horses).[39] Likewise, the legislation relating to the welfare of animals on farms, during transport, and at markets specifies that not only those who contravene or fail to comply with its provisions commit an offence, but so too does a person who causes or permits such an event,[40] as does a project licence holder who procures or permits a person under his control to act beyond the authority of either the project licence or that individual's personal licence.[41] There is no similar general provision in relation to the regulations which apply to the slaughter or killing of animals, but a number of the individual measures have the same effect.[42] Furthermore, senior managers may be held personally responsible for the treatment of animals used by commercial undertakings. Thus, in relation to farms, zoos, transport, slaughter, and killing, it is specifically provided that where a body corporate is guilty of an offence, any director, manager, secretary, or similar officer shall also be guilty if the offence is proved to have been committed with their consent or connivance, or to be attributable to neglect on their part.[43] It is suggested that such a measure should be introduced in all other commercial contexts, most particularly in relation to pet shops and the carrying out of scientific procedures, as well as to any offence of cruelty inflicted on an animal for which a body corporate was responsible at the time. Where an activity involving animals is carried on under the authority of a licence, the licence holder will be guilty of an offence if its provisions are contravened or there is a failure to comply with the conditions attached to it, regardless of whoever is directly to blame for the transgression.[44]

In general terms, therefore, the scope of criminal liability is sufficiently wide to encompass those who may be indirectly responsible for a failure to meet the relevant legislative standards. Most importantly, if they are not themselves the immediate offender, these provisions will normally extend to the owner of the animal. *This is crucial.* For it is in respect of accountability for the treatment of animals that their legal status as property continues to be significant. By definition,

[39] Protection of Animals Act 1911, s 1(1), as amended by the Protection Against Cruel Tethering Act 1988; Protection of Animals (Scotland) Act 1912, s 1(1); Abandonment of Animals Act 1960, s 1.

[40] Agriculture (Miscellaneous Provisions) Act 1968, s 1(1); Welfare of Farmed Animals Regulations, nn 31 and 33 above, reg 13(1)(d).

[41] Animals (Scientific Procedures) Act 1986, s 22(2).

[42] See, for example, SI 1995/731, n 27 above, Schs 3, 4, and 5.

[43] Agriculture (Miscellaneous Provisions) Act 1968, s 50(4); Zoo Licensing Act 1981, s 19(5); SI 1997/1480, n 36 above, art 20(1); SI 1995/731, n 27 above, reg 25(1).

[44] Pet Animals Act 1951, s 1(7); Animal Boarding Establishments Act 1963, s 1(8); Riding Establishments Act 1964, s 1(9); Breeding of Dogs Act 1973, s 21(2); Dangerous Wild Animals Act 1976, s 2(6); Zoo Licensing Act 1981, s 19(2); Animals (Scientific Procedures) Act 1986, s 22(1); Fresh Meat (Hygiene and Inspection) Regulations 1995, SI 1995/539, reg 21(2).

property belongs to someone, and, in the case of an animal, that individual *must* be held ultimately answerable in law for its treatment. While the contention that at least some animals should be regarded as having legal personality in their own right[45] is not necessarily inconsistent with a particular individual having an ongoing duty to look after them (using a concept such as guardianship, for example), the nature of legal responsibility inherent in *ownership* of an animal should not be overlooked or readily abandoned, amounting as it does to a continuing and non-delegable duty to exercise reasonable care and supervision to protect it from suffering unnecessarily. Hence, failure to fulfil this obligation amounts to an offence of cruelty, even though the owner may be neither directly responsible nor, indeed, aware of the situation.[46] It is strongly urged that this important principle should be extended to include situations in which the animal is *likely* to be caused unnecessary suffering. It should also embrace welfare, so that the owner of any animal is placed under a positive legal duty to take all reasonable measures to promote its welfare, possibly by reference to the Five Freedoms. A significant move towards this position has recently been introduced in relation to the owners and keepers of farmed animals, who are now under an explicit duty to take all reasonable steps 'to ensure the welfare of the animals under their care'.[47]

There are, however, two circumstances in which the issue of ultimate responsibility may be less definite. The first is where animals belong to children. While it is an offence to sell an animal as a pet to a person whom the vendor has reasonable cause to believe to be under the age of twelve years,[48] legislation does not specify a minimum age which must be attained before a person assumes the legal obligations of ownership. The age of criminal responsibility is ten in England and Wales, and only seven in Scotland; neither is an appropriate age to be held accountable in law for the care and supervision of an animal. In relation to a dog which may cause damage or is dangerous, it is expressly provided that where it belongs to a person of less than sixteen years, the head of the household shall be regarded as its keeper or owner,[49] and, for the avoidance of doubt, there is merit in extending this principle to the generality of animals kept by children (although the notion of 'the head of the household' may no longer be appropriate; the Scottish alternative of the person who has 'actual care and control'[50] of the child would seem preferable).

The second situation is where it is difficult to identify the owner. There is, however, another concept in British law which is wider than ownership, and is used to hold individuals to account for animals, namely that of 'keeper'. Under the Dangerous Wild Animals Act 1976, for example, it includes any person who has an animal in their possession,[51] while the Animals Act 1971 defines the term as

---

[45] For example, Wise, S M, *Rattling the Cage. Toward Legal Rights for Animals* (2000).
[46] Protection of Animals Act 1911, s 1(2); Protection of Animals (Scotland) Act 1912, s 1(2).
[47] Welfare of Farmed Animals Regulations, nn 31 and 33 above, reg 3(1)(a).
[48] Pet Animals Act 1951, s 3.   [49] Animals Act 1971, s 6(3); Dangerous Dogs Act 1991, s 6.
[50] Dangerous Dogs Act 1991, s 6; see also n 52 below.   [51] Section 7.

encompassing the owner, any other person who has the animal in his possession, and the head of a household of which a member under the age of sixteen owns the animal or has it in his possession.[52] Both statutes specify that once a person falls within these respective definitions of a keeper, they shall continue to be regarded as such, unless and until some other person formally becomes its keeper (even though they may no longer actually possess the animal). More recently, the notion of 'keeper' has been introduced into welfare legislation, meaning, in this context, 'any person responsible for or in charge of animals whether on a permanent or temporary basis'.[53] Again, consideration should be given to applying this concept more widely in animal protection legislation. Alternatively, it may be time to revitalize and significantly widen the scope of 'deemed ownership', which is currently something of a historical anomaly, having applied to animals delivered to knackers since the nineteenth century.[54]

(3) Legal responsibility for dogs

Because of the threat posed to the health and safety of humans and other animals when they are inadequately supervised, particular legal responsibilities have traditionally been imposed in relation to dogs. The requirement for them to be licensed was abolished in 1988;[55] notwithstanding that the Secretary of State was at the same time empowered to establish a dog registration scheme, this has not, to date, been initiated.[56] There are, however, a range of provisions intended to address situations where dogs are not kept under proper control. The police and local authorities may seize, detain, return to their owner, or otherwise dispose of stray dogs found in a public place or on any other land or premises.[57] The Minister of Agriculture also has the power to introduce provisions relating to: the control of dogs; the seizure, detention, and disposal of strays; and the wearing of a collar which indicates the name and address of the animal's owner.[58] A constable or local authority dog warden may seize a dog to which section 1 of the Dangerous Dogs Act 1991 applies if it is in a public place and appears to be in contravention of the requirements of the Act, or *any* dog which is in a public place and appears to be

---

[52] Section 6(3); cf the Animals (Scotland) Act 1987, s 5(1), which defines a keeper to include a person who owns the animal, has possession of it, or has actual care or control of a child under the age of sixteen who owns the animal or has possession of it.

[53] Welfare of Farmed Animals Regulations, nn 31 and 33 above, reg 2(1).

[54] See now, Protection of Animals Act 1911, s 5(3); Protection of Animals (Scotland) Act 1912, s 5(4).

[55] Local Government Act 1988, s 38.

[56] Local Government Act 1988, s 37(1). The Government established a Dog Identification Group which reported to ministers in September 2000. The report, recommending a voluntary scheme for the permanent identification of dogs by either microchip or tattoo, was published in December 2000, and is currently out to consultation: HC Debs, 12 December 2000, col 5 (WA); see further, DETR, *Dog Identification Group Report* (2000). A decision to establish a similar inquiry was taken by the Scottish Parliament in March 2001.

[57] Dogs Act 1906, s 3, as amended by the Local Government Act 1988, s 39(1), (3); Environmental Protection Act 1990, s 149.

[58] Animal Health Act 1981, s 13; Control of Dogs Order 1992, SI 1992/901.

dangerously out of control.[59] It is an offence to be the owner, or in charge, of a dog which worries livestock on agricultural land,[60] and the keeper of a dog which kills or injures livestock is liable to pay compensation for the damage caused.[61] Where a complaint is made to a court that a dog is dangerous and not kept under proper control, the magistrates may, if they are satisfied it is justified, make an order directing that the dog be kept by the owner under proper control or, alternatively, destroyed.[62] This is an administrative measure, precautionary in nature, and is not dependent on any offence having been committed.[63]

The owner, and, if different, the person for the time being in charge of it, is guilty of an offence if a dog is either dangerously out of control in a public place, in the sense that there are grounds for 'reasonable apprehension' that it will cause someone injury, whether or not it actually does so,[64] or it is allowed to enter a private place where it is not permitted to be, and there are grounds for reasonable apprehension that it will injure a person.[65] In spite of the wording of the legislation, the English courts have held that this includes circumstances where a dog attacks and causes injury with no prior warning, although the basis of their reasoning has varied.[66]

C. Responsibility for Enforcement

(1) Statutory responsibility

Statutory responsibility for implementing and enforcing animal protection legislation falls to a number of different agencies, which vary considerably in the nature of their functions and mode of operation. The Animals (Scientific Procedures) Inspectorate and the State Veterinary Service, for example, are specialist bodies,

---

[59] Dangerous Dogs Act 1991, s 5(1).

[60] Dogs (Protection of Livestock) Act 1953, s 1, as amended by the Wildlife and Countryside Act 1981, s 12 and Sch 7, para 3.

[61] Animals Act 1971, s 3. See also, Animals (Scotland) Act 1987, ss 1 and 2.

[62] Dogs Act 1871, s 2; see also, Dogs Act 1906, s 1(4), as amended by the Dogs (Amendment) Act 1928; Dangerous Dogs Act 1991, s 3(5)(a), (b), (6). The court may direct that the dog be destroyed without first giving the owner the option of keeping it under proper control: *Pickering v Marsh* (1874) 38 JP 678. 'Dangerous' is to be given its ordinary everyday meaning: the test is whether the dog has a dangerous disposition, including presenting a danger to another dog: *Briscoe v Shattock* [1999] 1 WLR 432. Whether a dog is under control is a question of fact; in the absence of positive evidence to the contrary, if it is neither muzzled nor led this is sufficient proof that the dog was not under proper control: *Ex parte Hay* (1886) 3 TLR 24.

[63] *Haldane v Allan* 1956 SC(J) 41; *R v Nottingham Justices, ex parte Brown* [1960] 1 WLR 1316.

[64] Dangerous Dogs Act 1991, ss 3(1), (2), 10(3); the owner will only avoid liability if there is plain evidence that the dog has been placed in the charge of some other person: *R v Huddart* (24 November 1998). However, once that person has been given charge of the dog the responsibility rests with him until the owner takes charge of it again himself and resumes responsibility: *Swinlay v Crowe* 1995 SLT 34, High Ct.

[65] Dangerous Dogs Act 1991, s 3(3). 'Allow' extends to situations where the accused has acted negligently: *Greener v DPP* (1996) 160 JP 265.

[66] *R v Bezzina; R v Codling; R v Elvin* [1994] 1 WLR 1057, CA; *Rafiq v Folkes* (1997) JP 412. Cf *Tierney v Valentine* 1995 SLT 564, High Ct of Justiciary.

having a specific remit and staff with training and experience which is relevant to their particular duties. In contrast, for the police, animal law forms only a very small part of their general duty to enforce the criminal law and investigate the commission of offences. It is, however, local authorities which have the most extensive statutory responsibilities for enforcing animal protection legislation. Thus, it is they who are charged with registering those who train or exhibit animals; administering the licensing of pet shops, animal boarding establishments, riding establishments, dog breeding establishments, dangerous wild animals kept in captivity, and zoos; as well as being responsible for enforcing the legislation appertaining to markets and transport.[67] Yet no objective and informed assessment has been made of how effectively they carry out these duties. This raises an important issue. In the same way that those to whom animal protection legislation is addressed are required to meet the obligations imposed upon them, so too are the agencies charged with its enforcement. Not only does inadequate enforcement on the part of a public body undermine the purpose of the legislation, it also damages public confidence in the law's ability to ensure proper protection for animals in accordance with the will of Parliament. It is therefore essential that those whom statute charges with responsibility for enforcement are accountable for the way in which they carry out their duties and exercise their powers, and are seen to be independent of those whose activities they oversee.

(2) Accountability of statutory enforcement bodies

All the statutory enforcement agencies are indirectly accountable to the public in the sense that ministers will provide information (assuming it is available) about their activities to MPs in replying to parliamentary questions; local authorities are also answerable to their local electorates both collectively and through individual councillors. While this is to be welcomed, it is no substitute for the routine provision of material directly to the public, from which they can gain an accurate impression of these agencies' performance.

The Animals (Scientific Procedures) Inspectorate

To an extent, the Animals (Scientific Procedures) Inspectorate meets this criterion. Information about its activities is regularly published in consequence of the provisions in the Animals (Scientific Procedures) Act which require the Animal Procedures Committee (APC) to produce an annual report, and the Home Secretary to publish each year information about the use of protected animals for experimental or other scientific purposes (the latter duty originating in EC law).[68] However, while this may provide a valuable insight into some aspects of the Inspectorate's activities, together with the background to specific incidents or issues, little detailed information is made available about important aspects of its

---

[67] SI 1990/2627, n 37 above, art 20; SI 1990/2628, n 22 above, art 21; SI 1997/1480, n 36 above, art 17.
[68] Sections 20(5), 21(7); Dir 86/609, art 13(1).

work. For example, while statistics about the number of visits made to designated establishments are in the public domain, these fail to explain in any detail *how* inspectors carry out their duties on site. Moreover, not only is the policy advice which the Inspectorate provides to ministers shielded from public scrutiny, but the Act itself similarly protects all information which is provided to the Inspectorate in confidence.[69] This is wider than the requirement under EC law, which applies only to information which is shown to be commercially sensitive.[70]

This culture of secrecy means that it is virtually impossible to hold the Home Secretary to account for the way in which he applies his policy in relation to licensing, or to gain any insight into the way the conditions attached to the licences and certificates of designation are enforced. It also forestalls third parties from making representations on the desirability or otherwise of a licence application. In other words, the effectiveness of the regulatory scheme has to be taken largely on trust. It may be the case that it works in a way which it would be difficult to fault; alternatively, it may be administered in an entirely implicit and mechanistic manner. Ministers and the APC have been considering the extent of this restriction in the light of recently enacted freedom of information legislation;[71] at the time of writing, future policy is unclear. For its part, the APC has expressed the view that the 'overall presumption' should be that the information provided in the course of the licensing procedure should be 'disclosable on demand', with any exceptions being determined on a case by case basis. According to the Committee, 'increased openness about these matters might serve to dispel some of the suspicions which surround the issue of animal use'.[72] At present, however, it can be said that there is inadequate information available for the public to make a judgement as to the significance of the work carried out under the authority of project licences, its outcome, its effects on the animals involved, or the proficiency and sensitivity of the staff involved. Neither is one able to make an informed assessment of the way in which the cost-benefit analysis is implemented.

Unlike other statutory enforcement agencies, the Animals (Scientific Procedures) Inspectorate is intimately involved with administering the regulatory scheme it is charged with overseeing. Thus, its responsibilities include:

- advising the Secretary of State on applications for licences and certificates, requests for their variation or revocation, and, in relation to the former, their periodical review;
- visiting places where regulated procedures are carried out for the purpose of determining whether the requisite licences and certificates are being complied with; and

---

[69] Section 24(1). [70] Directive 86/609, art 13(2).

[71] Freedom of Information Act 2000 (the Act extends to Scotland in relation to reserved (undevolved) matters, which include regulation of scientific procedures). The APC has consulted on this issue, see n 87 below.

[72] APC, *Annual Report 1999* (2000) Appendix E.

- reporting to the Secretary of State any breach of the Act's provisions or failure to comply with the conditions attached to a licence or certificate, and to advise him on the action to be taken in any such case.[73]

The scope of the Inspectorate's responsibilities is therefore formidable. More so, if one considers that, at the end of 1999, just 21 inspectors, assisted by 15½ licensing staff (full-time equivalents), were in post to monitor the 2,931 project licence holders reporting procedures during the year, who were based in 296 designated establishments.[74] Such a situation has raised questions about the Inspectorate's ability to carry out its functions. David Taylor MP, for example, recently described the present level of inspection as 'inadequate'. Speaking in the House of Commons, he pointed out that:

They have to assess all new projects, many of which will be at the leading edge of research. They have to examine those projects and apply, wherever feasible, the principle of the 3Rs: reducing the number of animals used; refining experiments to cut down on suffering; and replacing them, where possible with non-animal methods.

Inspectors must ensure that all licence holders receive up-to-date training and education; and that all conditions of project licences are kept. In the light of its range of duties and the size of the industry, I contend that the size of the Inspectorate is patently too small.[75]

Such a sentiment sits uneasily beside the assertion by the Chairman of the APC, that public acceptance of the regulatory system is dependent upon 'a belief that the Act's provisions are rigorously and effectively applied in the regulation and conduct of animal experimentation'.[76] In March 2001, the Government announced that over the next three years it intended to appoint 12 additional inspectors, bringing the total to 33.[77] While this expansion is to be welcomed, the size of the Inspectorate remains extremely small when considered in the context of its extensive responsibilities.

In order that they have familiarity with, and an understanding of, the relevant *scientific* issues, each inspector is required to have either medical or veterinary qualifications (although it might be argued that there are those from other scientific disciplines who would be equally well equipped to carry out this function). However, while they are institutionally independent of licensees, the suspicion has been expressed that their training may make them unduly sympathetic to the use of animals in scientific procedures (although the establishment of local ethical review committees has the potential to introduce a non-scientific perspective into decision making and monitoring).

---

[73] Animals (Scientific Procedures) Act 1986, s 18(2).
[74] Home Office, *Statistics of Scientific Procedures on Living Animals in Great Britain 1999* (2000).
[75] HC Debs, 26 June 2000, cols 688–698. [76] APC, n 72 above, Chairman's Introduction, para 4.
[77] HC Debs, 22 March 2001, col 323 (WA).

The State Veterinary Service

The State Veterinary Service (SVS) is also a specialist agency, but, unlike the Animals (Scientific Procedures) Inspectorate, its duties are not specifically defined in legislation. Comprising of just over 300 veterinarians (full-time equivalents) under the direction of the Chief Veterinary Officer,[78] it exercises powers which are delegated to it by ministers under the authority of statute. As such, its role is

To assist MAFF and other Government Departments in achieving their aims in the field of animal health, public health, animal welfare and international trade by:
• providing timely, up-to-date and objective veterinary advice to Government on all relevant matters;
• implementing agreed policies efficiently, effectively and in conformity with the legislation;
• monitoring the implementation of policies and providing reliable and timely feedback on their effectiveness or otherwise;
• representing the Government effectively both in the UK and abroad and ensuring that the UK interests are robustly defended in negotiation;
• providing advice, guidance and training to the veterinary profession on matters relating to State veterinary medicine.[79]

The principal responsibility of the SVS remains, as has been the case since it was established,[80] the diagnosis and control of disease, and the promotion of animal health. These are in themselves important aspects of animals' welfare, but more recently there has been greater emphasis on monitoring wider aspects of welfare on farms, during transport, and at market, as a result of developments in both EC and national law. It is manifested in the SVS's routine contact with farmers, hauliers, and market operators, and through the development of special projects, such as the recent strategy for protecting welfare standards in markets.[81] Once again, however, apart from the most basic summary provided each year in the Chief Veterinary Officer's Annual Report, there is little detailed information about how the SVS routinely goes about its business. However, it is important that such data should be available, in order that the public may be assured that the SVS is acting in a way which is consistent and effective. If the public is to have confidence in the SVS's credibility it is incumbent on the organization to demonstrate its independence, objectivity, and determination to ensure high standards of welfare in relation to those activities which fall within its jurisdiction. There needs to be, for example, evidence that the SVS carries out a planned, comprehensive, and regular programme of farm inspections, as well as responding to ad hoc complaints from the public; the application of consistent standards throughout the country; and information about the action taken when the welfare of animals is found to be unsatisfactory. However,

---

[78] HC Debs, 31 July 1997, col 437 (WA).
[79] MAFF, *Animal Health 1998. The Report of the Chief Veterinary Officer* (1999).
[80] See Ch 4, s C(2) above.
[81] MAFF, *The 1998 Strategy for the Protection of Animal Welfare at Livestock Markets: Report on SVS Assessment of Compliance* (1999).

if the SVS is to fulfil its responsibilities, it must be adequately resourced. It is little short of scandalous that its present strength is less than half what it was twenty years ago. In 1979, it employed 597 vets; by 2001, this had been reduced to only 286, of whom just 220 were field officers.[81a]

Local authorities

Information about the way in which local authorities exercise their administrative and enforcement powers under the relevant legislation is sparse, sporadic, and unreliable. It is therefore impossible to provide an informed assessment of their performance. As the House of Commons Agricultural Committee observed in 1991,

the official responsible for animal welfare is located within a number of different departments depending on the individual local authority. We see no problem with this arrangement so long as the relevant post-holder is easily accessible and identifiable, but doubt whether this situation pertains at the moment. No guidance is issued by the Government as to how local authorities' animal welfare staff should be allocated, nor any central record held of their location. This is not altogether satisfactory. The Government should monitor the situation more closely and satisfy itself that there are adequate administrative arrangements at local level to handle any problems.[82]

Similarly, in relation to transport, the RSPCA has more recently pointed to 'a lack of adequate official policing and failure to enforce certain rules', and 'the need to strengthen the quantity and quality of monitoring systems';[83] and the Home Office has been compelled to remind authorities of their responsibilities under the Performing Animals (Regulation) Act 1925.[84] This is not to suggest that all authorities are failing in their duties; many are conscientious, and some

---

[81a] HC Debs, 4 April 2001, col 223 (WA).

[82] House of Commons Agriculture Committee, *Animals in Transit* (1991) para 54.

[83] RSPCA, *Live animal transport in the UK* (1998) 25.

[84] Home Office Circular 1/2000. Section 1(7) requires local authorities to provide the Secretary of State with a copy of each certificate of registration which they issue. Following the issue of the circular, during the first five months of 2000, the Home Office received details of over 2,000 animals which had been registered. This is to be compared with the number of animals listed in the registration documents held by the Home Office between 1988 and 1997:

1988	1,416
1989	1,355
1990	1,090
1991	613
1992	2,040
1993	2,857
1994	143
1995	611
1996	151
1997	545

Source: HC Debs, 21 January 1998, col 583 (WA) and 23 May 2000, col 406 (WA).
The Home Office has provided no explanation for the variation in these figures.

proactive. There is, however, a legitimate concern that not every authority possesses the appropriate expertise, allocates the necessary resources, or regards the matter sufficiently important to ensure effective enforcement. At the very least, there is a need to identify best practice and to ensure that it is extensively and uniformly implemented.

FAWC recommended in 1990 that each local authority should appoint an 'Animal Welfare Officer', who would assume overall responsibility for animal welfare, assisted by a nucleus of full-time staff dedicated to this area of work, and whose existence, the Council suggested, should be publicized, with a view to making them more readily identifiable and easily accessible to the general public. It emphasized the importance of local authorities giving what it described as 'proper priority' to animal welfare by devoting adequate resources to enforcement and training. The Council recommended that local authorities 'should ensure that their inspectors are fully trained and competent in animal welfare', and went on to suggest that shared training courses for all the statutory enforcement agencies should be introduced 'with a view to standardization of enforcement'.[85] More recently, the Council has called on the Government to provide detailed guidance to local authorities in order to clarify and emphasize their responsibility for enforcement. According to FAWC, such a document would 'serve as a reminder to authorities of their responsibilities, that they are a major component of the enforcement framework and that they should devote sufficient resources to animal welfare'.[86]

(3) The Animal Procedures Committee and the Farm Animal Welfare Council

Neither the APC nor FAWC has any direct responsibility for enforcement, but by examining and commenting upon the impact of legal regulation they both exercise an influence on the way in which the law is applied and developed.[87] Moreover, to their credit, each has made a conscious effort to account for its activities and make them more transparent, and has become increasingly proactive in this regard. In part this may be anticipating the impact of the Freedom of Information Act, but it also seems to be the result of a genuine belief among their respective members that this is an appropriate way forward. It is an approach which could usefully be adopted by the statutory enforcement agencies. Both have established useful websites. In addition, the APC has, for example, recently undertaken consultation exercises in relation to the effect of new and emerging biotechnologies on the use and welfare of laboratory animals and other animals which are used in scientific procedures, on the application of openness to the use of animals in scientific experiments or

---

[85] FAWC, *Report of the Enforcement Working Group* (1990) paras 8.4(d), (e), 8.5(ii), and 8.6.

[86] FAWC, *Advice to Ministers on the Enforcement of Animal Welfare Legislation* (1999) para A(i).

[87] See the bibliography for details of reports produced by FAWC. In 1997, the APC published a review of the 1986 Act, see n 72 above.

other procedures, and the application of the cost-benefit assessment.[88] For its part, FAWC has indicated that it wishes to operate as openly as possible, and has brought in new working practices in order to make information more widely available. On its own initiative, it has since 1998 published an annual review, and places the agenda and summary of its meetings on its website, together with the text of its reports, advice to ministers, and other relevant information.[89] It also held an inaugural open meeting in 1999 in order to allow interested parties the opportunity to hear about the Council's work and question its members. It is intended that this should become an annual event.

(4) The RSPCA and SSPCA inspectorates

It is not, however, the statutory agencies which figure foremost in the public mind when it comes to the enforcement of animal protection legislation; rather, it is the uniformed inspectors of the RSPCA and SSPCA. At the end of 1999, these numbered 328 and 63 respectively. The RSPCA also operates a Special Investigations and Operations Department, which pursues 'undercover' investigations, focusing on areas such as live animal transport and slaughter methods on the European mainland, cock- and dog-fighting, badger baiting, puppy farming, and the trade in exotic animals. The RSPCA describes its inspectorate as 'the largest non-governmental law enforcement agency in England and Wales';[90] the same may well be true of the SSPCA's inspectorate within its own jurisdiction. Together, their work includes the investigation of complaints about the treatment of animals, the provision of assistance and advice, the inspection of commercial establishments where animals are kept or used, and, where appropriate, the collection of evidence with a view to prosecution. All this is achieved without any public funding or the benefit of any special legal powers. In 1999, the cost to the RSPCA of operating its inspectorate, pursuing prosecutions, and the necessary operational support amounted to £27 million; the SSPCA's inspectorate required more than £2 million.[91]

It is something of a constitutional novelty for a significant body of law to be largely enforced through the efforts of a charitable organization, funded entirely by voluntary contributions. As Harrop remarks, animal welfare law is 'extensively enforced by the private sector without an official mandate or express accountability'.[92] Although there is a historical explanation for this situation,[93] it is generally

---

[88] Letters sent to interested parties by the APC asking for comments, dated 26 November 1999, 13 January 2000, and 6 December 2000.

[89] FAWC, *Annual Review 1999/2000* (2000) 6.   [90] RSPCA, *Annual Review 1998* (1999).

[91] ibid; SSPCA, *Annual Report 1999* (2000).

[92] Harrop, SR, 'The Dynamics of Wild Animal Welfare Law' (1997) 9 Journal of Environmental Law 287, 298. The Society is required to act within the terms of the Royal Society for the Prevention of Cruelty to Animals Act 1932 and its own rules, but the Society nevertheless enjoys considerable autonomy to develop its own policies and to determine who should be permitted to become a member, and thereby permitted to participate in its policy-making process: see further, *RSPCA v Attorney-General* The Times, 13 February 2001.

[93] See Ch 3, s D above.

the State, using public funds, which is regarded as having primary responsibility for enforcing the criminal law. There is, however, considerable advantage in having two specialized organizations, whose sole concern is the protection of animals, actively involved in enforcing the relevant legislation. Not only do they have a particular expertise, but it also means that the enforcement of animal protection legislation does not have to compete with the myriad of other law and order issues which confront the public investigatory and prosecuting authorities, such as the police, the Crown Prosecution Service, and, in Scotland, the procurator fiscals. Commenting on the contribution made by the RSPCA, Stuart Harrop, a former Director of the Society's legal services, observes, 'either the vast majority of animal cruelty transgressions would go unpunished or the public purse would be forced to bear the cost of processing thousands of specialist charges each year'.[94] Statute provides that the objects of the RSPCA are 'to promote kindness and to prevent or suppress cruelty to animals and to do all such lawful acts as the Society may consider to be conducive or incidental to the attainment of those objects'.[95] This represents legal authority for the inspectorate to undertake its work, but does not confer on individual inspectors any additional rights or privileges over and above those of the ordinary citizen. The courts have, for example, held that an RSPCA inspector has no statutory authority to take an alleged offender into custody.[96] This situation is in contrast to that of inspectors of the National Society for the Prevention of Cruelty to Children (NSPCC), who, since 1904, have had statutory authority to act in their own right to remove an endangered child to a place of safety. The NSPCC may also act as an agent for local authorities.

(5) Wildlife

Responsibility for the enforcement of wildlife law rests predominantly with the police, and all British police forces have appointed a specialist Wildlife Liaison Officer, but administrative oversight falls primarily to DEFRA (formerly the DETR).[97] In addition, Her Majesty's Customs and Excise take a leading role in pursuing illegal imports and exports.[98] However, a number of other bodies are also

---

[94] Harrop, S, 'Challenges and Dilemmas Faced by Conservation and Animal Welfare Charities Who Both Enforce the Law and Press for Charges', in Dunn, A (ed,) *The Voluntary Sector, The State and the Law* (2000) 211.

[95] Royal Society for the Prevention of Cruelty to Animals Act 1932, s 4.

[96] *Line v RSPCA and Marsh* (1902) 18 TLR 634. In Scotland, there is a long-standing practice that, where an SSPCA inspector has reasonable grounds for suspecting that an offence has been committed, a Sheriff may issue a warrant authorizing the inspector to enter land or premises for the purpose of obtaining evidence of the offence and, if necessary, to remove any animal for the purpose of it being examined by a veterinary surgeon in order to determine whether an offence has been committed. See above, Ch 4, s A(2), n 11.

[97] Department of the Environment, *Wildlife Crime: A Guide to Wildlife Law Enforcement in the UK* (1996).

[98] Endangered species are protected by the Convention on International Trade in Endangered Species (CITES), which bans trade in the rarest species, and strictly controls the trade in others. CITES was originally implemented in Britain by the Endangered Species (Import and Export) Act 1976, and subsequently into EC law by Regulation 3626/82; see now, the Control of Trade in Endangered Species (Enforcement) Regulations 1997, SI 1997/1372 ('COTES').

involved. DEFRA's Wildlife Inspectorate, for example, carries out inspections to gather and verify information relating to the licensing of trade in endangered species and the registration of certain wild birds kept in captivity, as well as providing specialist advice on species identification;[99] and organizations such as the RSPCA, SSPCA, and the Royal Society for the Protection of Birds also undertake their own investigations, as well as assisting the statutory enforcement agencies.

(6) The role of the veterinary profession in enforcement

Although not formally responsible for enforcement, the contribution of veterinarians is central to the effectiveness of animal protection legislation. This is self-evident in relation to the SVS and the Animals (Scientific Procedures) Inspectorate, but the profession in general has a crucial role to play in making legal regulation work, whether as expert witnesses in legal proceedings; through monitoring, inspecting, and enforcing legally defined standards and procedures; or by providing advice on the development and implementation of policy. It carries out these functions in a situation where, as the *Veterinary Record* has acknowledged, 'despite numerous attempts to define animal welfare objectively, it remains, essentially, a subjective topic, and views vary as widely as individual prejudices and beliefs'.[100] This gives rise to the important, and controversial, issue of whether a veterinary qualification is, in itself, sufficient to constitute expertise for the purposes of evaluating welfare in the context of enforcement. According to their *Code of Professional Conduct*, veterinarians are expected to be familiar with all relevant legislation;[101] but neither this, nor their basic training, it is suggested, equips them adequately for their enforcement role. Traditionally, veterinarians have relied on developing the necessary expertise through experience; but this is something of a hit-and-miss affair, and fails to guarantee either consistency or effectiveness. It is therefore to be welcomed that the profession itself has taken some initiative in this regard, the RCVS having recently introduced both a Certificate and a Diploma in Animal Welfare Science, Ethics and Law. In addition, two veterinary organizations have been established which have among their objectives the promotion of a better understanding of the relevant law and its application.[102] Consideration should be given to further specialization for those veterinarians whose work or inclination extends to implementation of animal welfare law. Ideally, animal protection legislation should specify requirements that veterinarians and other professionals involved with its enforcement should be required to meet.

---

[99] HC Debs, 11 April 2000, col 118 (WA). In February 2000, the Environment Minister announced the establishment of a National Wildlife Crime Unit to counter organized wildlife crime: DETR Press Release 111/2000.

[100] Comment (1996) 138 *Veterinary Record* 145.   [101] RCVS (2000), para G.1.

[102] The Animal Welfare Science, Ethics and Law Veterinary Association (AWSELVA) and the Veterinary Association for Arbitration and Jurisprudence (VAAJ).

(7) Expertise and independence

In some contexts, this important principle has already been established. The provisions for the appointment of zoo inspectors, for example, seek to ensure that they possess the appropriate expertise and independence. The Secretary of State is required, after consultation with the presidents of the British Veterinary Association, the National Federation of Zoological Gardens, and the National Zoological Association and with such other persons as he thinks fit, to compile a list consisting of two parts. The first part contains the names of veterinarians who have experience of the kinds of animals kept in zoos; the second, the names of people whom the Secretary of State considers competent to inspect animals in zoos, to advise on keeping them and on their welfare, and to advise on the management of zoos generally.[103] Not only does this list assist local authorities in identifying persons with the relevant skills for appointment as inspectors, it is also used by the Secretary of State in selecting his nominees to participate in a formal inspection (for which purpose he is required to nominate two inspectors, one drawn from each part of the list).[104] None of these individuals may be directly connected with the zoo. However, up to three representatives of the operator may accompany them during the inspection; in addition, the inspectors may require the attendance of any veterinary surgeon employed or retained by the zoo.[105]

It is not suggested that the same degree of complexity is necessary in relation to the other licensing schemes administered by local authorities, but the current arrangements fail to ensure that those carrying out inspections are properly equipped for the task. In relation to pet shops, boarding establishments, and dog breeding establishments, for example, the local authority may authorize any of its officers (generally those involved with environmental health) or any veterinary surgeon to carry out the inspection.[106] There is no specific requirement that those involved should have any particular expertise in animal welfare science or the relevant law. The same situation applies in relation to local authority officers who may be required to undertake the inspection of a riding establishment. However, in this case, a veterinarian carrying out an inspection of such premises on behalf of the authority must be one chosen by them from a list drawn up jointly by the Royal College of Veterinary Surgeons and the British Veterinary Association.[107] Inspections carried out in connection with the keeping of dangerous wild animals may be undertaken by any veterinary surgeon or such other person as the local authority may deem competent (although the nature of the competence is not specified).[108]

---

[103] Zoo Licensing Act 1981, s 8(1), (2), (3); a person's name may be contained in both the first and the second parts of the list: s 8(4).

[104] ibid, s 10(4)(a).   [105] ibid, s 10(4)(c).

[106] Pet Animals Act 1951, s 4(1); Animal Boarding Establishments Act 1963, s 2(1); Breeding of Dogs Act 1973, ss 1(2A) and 2(1), as amended by the Breeding and Sale of Dogs (Welfare) Act 1999.

[107] Riding Establishments Act 1964, s 2(1), (3).   [108] Dangerous Wild Animals Act 1976, s 3(1).

In the interests of both consistency and effectiveness, it is desirable that the law should require those enforcing its provisions to be able to demonstrate an up-to-date knowledge and understanding of the relevant legislation, the nature and extent of the legal powers they are exercising, and the developing science of animal welfare. Furthermore, there is no express requirement in any of these schemes that where a veterinarian conducts the inspection, they must be unconnected with the licensee. In order to avoid any conflict of interest, a local authority should be required to ensure that any such veterinarian is completely independent of the applicant or licence holder (although that would not necessarily prevent the licensee's vet being present when the inspection took place). The principle of independence is reflected in the practice adopted by the Home Office that, when a third party makes an allegation against an establishment or individual licensed under the Animals (Scientific Procedures) Act 1986, it is investigated by a superintending inspector from another region who has no connection with those complained of, and no management responsibility for the relevant inspector. In addition, the Government, having considered introducing greater independence, has recently announced the appointment of a small scrutiny team, drawn from the APC, and reporting directly to the Home Secretary, which is intended to provide assurance that investigations by the Inspectorate are carried out with the necessary objectivity and thoroughness.[109]

Furthermore, the Government has also recently acknowledged, in the context of establishing that animals for export are fit for the journey, the importance of those who carry out inspections being sufficiently expert and independent. Whereas exporters have previously been free to engage and pay any veterinarian to carry out this procedure, it has been proposed that in future they should pay MAFF in advance for the inspections, who would then reimburse veterinarians with a fixed hourly fee, based on the time taken for the work, with minimum times being laid down for the inspection. Moreover, instead of being nominated by the exporter, it was envisaged that in future the veterinarian would be nominated by the ministry from a panel of Local Veterinary Inspectors specifically authorized to undertake such work. To be eligible for inclusion on the panel, a veterinary surgeon would be required to undergo relevant training.[110] Some of these measures have been introduced administratively, others require legislation to implement. While the delay in giving full effect to them is regrettable, the principle of promoting specialization and independence is to be thoroughly welcomed, and should be widely adopted generally in relation to the enforcement of animal protection legislation.

In 1990, FAWC recommended that local authorities should ensure that their inspectors are fully trained and competent in animal welfare, and that shared training courses for all statutory enforcement agencies might be introduced to

---

[109] HC Debs, 23 May 2000, col 405 (WA), and 1 November 2000, col 517 (WA).

[110] MAFF, 'Proposed revised pre-export procedures for sheep/pigs destined for fattening/production or slaughter in other EC member states' (1998); MAFF, 'Revised pre-export procedures for sheep/pigs destined for fattening/production or slaughter in other member states' (1999).

promote standardization of the way in which they carry out their duties.[111] Unfortunately, consistency remains a problem. The Council has subsequently reiterated that there remains 'a serious lack of uniformity' in the application and enforcement of animal welfare legislation. In its view, if enforcement is to be effective,

> it is essential to have both good liaison between all enforcement agencies and also for all such agencies to be consistent in the manner and vigour with which they pursue their responsibilities. A uniform approach across all enforcement bodies to the training of inspectors is also crucial.[112]

Ideally, FAWC would like to see the establishment of a UK enforcement agency, responsible for all animal health and welfare matters, at least within its own purview of livestock farming; it argues that, 'logically some such body is essential if the government really does wish to give animal welfare issues a high priority'.[113] In the meantime, the Council stresses that successful enforcement is 'directly dependent on the commitment and skills of the personnel involved; their willingness to co-operate; the support framework they are given; and the political will of enforcement agencies to devote sufficient resources to the task'. To this end, it advocates that the role of animal welfare enforcement should have a specific professional status, with all relevant officers being suitably trained and qualified.[114]

D. Monitoring Standards and Enforcement Powers

In order to ensure the effectiveness of animal protection legislation, it is necessary to provide sufficient and appropriate powers to enable the treatment and care of animals to be effectively monitored so as to identify problems and seek improvements; to promote best practice and thereby raise welfare standards further; and, where the need arises, to obtain the evidence necessary to pursue formal action against those who fail to meet their legal responsibilities. 'Securing compliance with prescribed standards, whether by persuasion or compulsion,' the House of Commons Agriculture Committee observed in 1981, 'depends in the first instance on efficient inspection and detection.'[115]

(1) Inspections under statutory licensing schemes

One of the major advantages of a (well-drafted) statutory licensing scheme is that it provides for routine mandatory inspections by those with the relevant knowledge and expertise. In practice, however, the extent of these powers varies considerably, depending upon the context.

---

[111] n 85 above, para 86.   [112] n 86 above, para A(i).
[113] ibid, para A(ii).   [114] ibid, para A(iii).
[115] House of Commons Agriculture Committee, *Animal Welfare in Poultry, Pig and Veal Calf Production* (1981) para 41.

Thus, a local authority may require an inspection of any licensed pet shop, or animal boarding establishment situated in their area, for which purpose a person duly authorized by the authority may enter the premises (including a private dwelling) at all reasonable times and inspect them and any animals found there.[116] However, the frequency and manner of such inspections is left entirely within the discretion of each individual authority. Furthermore, while it is incumbent on the licensing authority to satisfy itself of a number of matters before initially granting a licence, which will normally necessitate an inspection, there is no express legal requirement to this effect. Neither is there any specific duty to carry out an inspection prior to the annual renewal of such a licence.[117] By way of contrast, in addition to similar general powers of inspection while a licence is in force,[118] a local authority is required to take account of a report of an inspection carried out on their behalf by a veterinary surgeon, *before* deciding on an application for a licence to keep either a riding establishment or a dangerous wild animal. In both cases, the report must contain appropriate information to enable the authority to determine whether the premises are suitable.[119] It is specified that a riding establishment must be inspected either following receipt of the licence application or, alternatively, at some time in the preceding twelve months.[120] As each such licence is subject to annual renewal,[121] the effect of this provision is to require the premises to be inspected prior to the first licence being granted, and at least once a year thereafter, whereas the provisions relating to dangerous wild animals specify only that the licensing authority must consider a veterinarian's report before reaching a decision.[122] In consequence, although the premises must be inspected prior to the initial grant of the licence, and notwithstanding that it too lasts only for a year,[123] the same report may theoretically be relied upon when it comes up for renewal, thus avoiding the need for annual inspection.

Ideally, legislation should impose a duty that the premises covered by each of these licensing schemes must be inspected prior to the grant of the initial licence, and at least once a year thereafter, not more than four and less than three months prior to the date on which the licence is due for renewal.

The requirements applying to dog breeding establishments were formerly the same as for pet shops and boarding establishments, but annual inspections are now mandatory. If a dog breeding establishment licence has not previously been granted to the applicant in respect of the premises, the inspection must be carried out by a vet *and* a local authority officer. In the case of subsequent applications for renewal of the licence, the inspection may be carried out by a vet *or* a local authority officer, or both. In either case, before reaching its decision, the authority must

---

116 Pet Animals Act 1951, ss 4(1), 7(1); Animal Boarding Establishments Act 1963, ss 2(1), 5(1).
117 Pet Animals Act 1951, s 1(5); Animal Boarding Establishments Act 1963, s 1(5).
118 Riding Establishments Act 1964, s 2(1), (2); Dangerous Wild Animals Act 1976, s 3(1).
119 Riding Establishments Act 1964, s 1(3); Dangerous Wild Animals Act 1976, s 1(5).
120 Riding Establishments Act 1964, s 1(3).   121 ibid, s 1(6).
122 Dangerous Wild Animals Act 1976, s 1(5).   123 ibid, s 2(2).

consider a report from the inspector(s) about the premises, the applicant, and any other relevant matter.[124]

A further weakness of the licensing schemes for pet shops and boarding establishments is that the relevant legislation fails to provide the necessary powers for an enforcement authority to enter unlicensed premises which it has reason to believe are being used for either purpose. The same situation previously applied in respect of an unlicensed dog breeding establishment. Now, however, except in the case of a private dwelling, a justice of the peace may, if satisfied that there are reasonable grounds for suspecting that unlicensed premises are, or have been, used for such a purpose, issue a warrant authorizing a local authority officer or their nominated veterinary surgeon, accompanied by anyone else specified in the warrant (members of the RSPCA inspectorate, for example), to enter those premises, by reasonable force if need be, and to inspect them and any animals found there.[125] It is unclear why it is considered necessary to obtain a warrant in these circumstances, when statute provides local authorities with the inherent power to inspect unlicensed premises which they have reason to believe are being kept as a riding establishment without first having to obtain the leave of the court.[126]

The arrangements for the inspection of zoos are significantly more detailed. Before granting a licence, the local authority must either consider inspectors' reports or, alternatively, consult experts nominated by the Secretary of State.[127] Thereafter, a zoo is required to be formally inspected at least twice during the lifetime of the licence: during the first year it is in force, and not later than six months before the end of the fourth year in the case of an original licence; during the third year and not later than six months before the end of the sixth year where the licence has been renewed.[128] Such inspections are carried out by up to three inspectors appointed by the licensing local authority, at least one of whom must be a veterinary surgeon, and two nominated by the Secretary of State following consultation with the local authority.[129] The inspection extends to all features of the zoo directly or indirectly relevant to the health, welfare, and safety of the public and the animals.[130] Upon completion, the inspectors submit a report to the local authority, which may include advice on the keeping of records, together with recommendations for any practicable improvements designed to bring any features of the zoo up to the normal standards of modern zoo practice specified by the Secretary of State.[131] Should the inspectors disagree over their recommendations relating to animal welfare, the issue

---

[124] Breeding of Dogs Act 1973, s 1 (2A), (2B), (7), inserted and amended by the Breeding and Sales of Dogs (Welfare) Act 1999.

[125] Breeding of Dogs Act 1991, s 1. A private dwelling does not include for these purposes adjoining buildings such as an outhouse or garage. The very limited evidence available suggests that this power is either not being used or, alternatively, is not proving to be effective. In 1996, for example, on the basis of two counties in Wales, there were 62 breeders registering with the Kennel Club more than 10 litters in the previous year, but only 27 could be confirmed as being licensed by the relevant local authority: Puppy Farming Working Group, *The commercial breeding and sale of dogs and puppies* (1996) 6.

[126] Riding Establishments Act 1964, s 2(1)(a).   [127] Zoo Licensing Act 1981, s 4(1).

[128] ibid, s 10(3); an original licence lasts for four years, thereafter for six years: s 5(1), (2).

[129] ibid, s 10(4)(a).   [130] ibid, s 10(4)(d).   [131] ibid, s 10(5).

may be referred to the Secretary of State.[132] Within one month of receiving the report, the local authority must send a copy to the zoo operator, who is entitled to comment upon its findings.[133] Further to these periodic inspections, the local authority may at any time carry out a special formal inspection if they consider it to be appropriate.[134] In addition, they are required to undertake an informal inspection during the course of any year during which no formal inspection is carried out.[135] Unlike other licensing regimes, a zoo operator is expressly entitled to be given prior notice of a formal inspection, together with the names of the proposed inspectors (in respect of any of whom he may lodge an objection).[136] Furthermore, in the case of a special inspection, the local authority is required to inform the zoo operator of its purpose and scope.[137]

Surprisingly, the legislation is silent on the frequency of visits to designated establishments by the Animals (Scientific Procedures) Inspectorate; this lies entirely within the discretion of the Inspectorate itself or the Home Secretary. Even more remarkable is the fact that there is no express statutory power which gives inspectors the right to enter premises. It is, however, a standard condition applied to certificates designating scientific procedure, breeding, and supplying establishments that inspectors shall be provided with access at all reasonable times to all parts of the establishment relating to the holding or care of protected animals.[138] In the absence of the occupier's permission, it may be necessary to seek the leave of the courts to authorize entry, but a justice of the peace or, in Scotland, a sheriff may only grant a warrant if they are satisfied that there are reasonable grounds for believing that an offence has been committed. This power is therefore inappropriate for routine monitoring. Moreover, the responsibility for executing such a warrant falls to the police rather than the Inspectorate, although it may authorize an inspector to be in attendance if the place in question is a designated establishment.[139] In practice, the Inspectorate carried out 2,730 visits during 1999, of which 2,174 were for the purpose of inspecting designated establishments and work in progress.[140] However, notwithstanding the activities of the Inspectorate, enforcement relies heavily on self-regulation. For example, when an undercover investigation revealed abuse of dogs at a licensed toxicology department operated by Huntingdon Life Sciences,[141] the APC responded by describing criticism of the Inspectorate for its failure to identify the problem as 'unfair'. 'Even if the Inspectorate was significantly enlarged, inspectors could not be present at an establishment all the time', it asserted. Against this background, the statement by a former Chairman of the Committee that 'Evidence of bad faith, insensitivity or any deliberate defiance of the Act is rarely to be seen'[142] cannot be regarded as the

---

[132] ibid, s 10(6). [133] ibid, s 10(7). [134] ibid, s 11.

[135] ibid, s 12. [136] ibid, s 10(2), (4)(a), (b). [137] ibid, s 11(4).

[138] Home Office, *Guidance on the Operation of the Animals (Scientific Procedures) Act 1986* (2000) Appendix B, para 18; Appendix C, para 17.

[139] Animals (Scientific Procedures) Act 1986, s 25. [140] Home Office, n 74 above.

[141] See further, n 211 below.

[142] *Annual Report 1996* (1997), Chairman's Introduction and Forward Look.

endorsement of the system which it was undoubtedly intended to be. In the opinion of the Committee, the successful operation of the 1986 Act 'depends upon self-regulation by the scientific community, assisted by the Home Office'.[143] If, however, it is the case that the Act's principles 'are not a matter of external constraint alone, but have to be internalized' because its effectiveness 'could not be ensured' by the Home Office,[144] then it underscores the need for greater openness and increased accountability on the part of project licence holders and those responsible for designated establishments, if the public are to be reassured that the requirements which exist to safeguard the interests of animals used in scientific procedures are consistently and effectively applied. While the APC may be satisfied that there is 'no evidence that such abuse is widespread',[145] one is tempted to ask: how can they be certain? It is a matter of concern that the most notorious examples of the Act's failure to protect animals which have become public knowledge—that involving Huntingdon Life Sciences referred to above, and the exposé of the practices employed by the late Professor William Feldberg[146]—both came to light as a result of undercover investigations carried out by those opposed to the use of animals in scientific procedures. That neither the much vaunted self-regulation within the respective institutions, nor the 'assistance' (to adopt the APC's language) of their inspector, managed either to prevent or bring to light such blatant infringements of the Act does not inspire confidence. The APC has acknowledged that 'Many establishments do take pride in operating within the letter and spirit of the Act; in improving animal welfare; and in reducing animal use and suffering.' However, it has also recognized that 'there is room for improvement in many establishments. Best practice is not always readily disseminated and implemented.'[147] It is high time that appropriate procedures were put in place to rectify this situation.

(2) Other powers of entry

In addition to the powers of entry provided for under the various licensing schemes, there are also other contexts in which statute permits various officials to enter premises. For example, a duly authorized officer of a local authority and a police officer may enter at all reasonable times and inspect any premises in which any performing animal is being trained or exhibited, or kept for training or exhibition, together with the animals found there, and may require to see the certificate confirming registration under the Performing Animals (Regulation) Act 1925.[148] This power is inadequate on two grounds. First, while a person may be prosecuted under the Protection of Animals Acts where there is evidence of cruelty, and the animals removed under the provisions of that legislation, if the condition of the premises, the animals, or their treatment is unsatisfactory, but falls short of an

---

[143] n 72 above, paras 109 and 114.
[144] ibid, Appendix F, Ch 1, para 11.   [145] ibid, para 113.
[146] MacDonald, M, *Caught in the Act. The Feldberg Investigation* (1994).
[147] n 72 above, Appendix F, Ch 6, paras 43 and 44.   [148] Section 3(1).

offence of cruelty, the legislation provides no power for the authorities to prosecute, impose conditions, or insist on improvements. Secondly, according to the
wording of the provision, the power of entry may be exercised only when animals
are actually present. Accordingly, there is no entitlement to enter premises from
which the animals have been removed or where there is reason to suppose they may
be, if this supposition turns out to be wrong. Like most aspects of this legislation,
these powers are in urgent need of reform.

In contrast, a person duly authorized by the minister may (accompanied by any
other person they consider to be necessary), at any time, enter a slaughterhouse,
knacker's yard, or any other land or premises (except where they are used wholly or
mainly as a dwelling) if they reasonably suspect that any activity governed by the
relevant regulations is, or has been, carried on, for the purpose of ascertaining
whether there is, or has been, any contravention of the regulations.[149] To this end,
such a person is empowered to carry out all checks and examinations necessary for
their enforcement and, where the inspector has reasonable suspicion that the regulations have been contravened, they may take samples; remove any carcase, or part
of it; inspect records and documents; and take copies or the originals.[150]

Similarly, under the Agriculture (Miscellaneous Provisions) Act 1968, a person
acting on the authority of the minister may at any reasonable time enter upon any
land (it is not restricted to agricultural land), other than premises used wholly or
mainly as a dwelling, for the purpose of ascertaining whether livestock have been
caused unnecessary pain or distress, or there has been any contravention of the regulations relating to welfare. Again, they may be accompanied by such other persons as
they consider necessary (for example, the police or members of the RSPCA or SSPCA
inspectorate).[151] Where the authorized person is a veterinarian, they are entitled to
examine any livestock which they find during the course of their inspection and apply
to, or take from, the animals such tests and samples as they consider appropriate.[152]

The number of inspections of farms carried out by the SVS specifically to assess
welfare standards are as follows:

1992	4,135
1993	4,090
1994	5,053
1995	4,711
1996	5,100
1997	4,344

It has to be said that these figures do not look impressive when one considers that
in 1997, for example, there were 70,742 holdings registered with the ministry

---

[149] SI 1995/731, n 27 above, reg 23(1), (4). The activities governed by the regulations include the movement, lairaging, restraint, stunning, slaughter, and killing of animals bred or kept for the production of
meat, skin, fur, or other products; killing animals for the purpose of disease control; and the killing of surplus chicks and embryos in hatchery waste: reg 3(1).

[150] ibid, reg 23(2), (3).   [151] Section 6(1), (3)(b).

[152] Agriculture (Miscellaneous Provisions) Act 1968, s 6(5).

where either sheep or goats were kept.[153] In 1998, the SVS carried out 6,592 inspections specifically to check welfare standards on farms, of which 1,961 were in response to complaints or allegations. Additional inspections were made when the SVS were visiting premises for other purposes.[154] In 1981, the House of Commons Agriculture Committee observed that inspection of farms 'directed to animal welfare is neither so frequent or so rigorous as to ensure that abuses do not go undetected', and recommended that 'all premises where indoor intensive production is carried on should receive at least once a year a formal inspection specifically directed to welfare' and that the SVS 'should be maintained at a strength which enables this to be done'.[155] FAWC has recommended that the number of unannounced SVS inspections should be increased, particularly at intensive pig and poultry farms, with a proportion being undertaken out of normal working hours.[156]

An inspector[157] acting under the authority of the Animal Health Act 1981, which relates to the welfare of animals during transit and at markets, as well as to the eradication and prevention of disease, is endowed with all the powers which a constable would have in the same situation.[158] They are expressly authorized to enter any land, shed, pen, vehicle, vessel, boat, or aircraft if they have reasonable grounds for supposing that there is or has been a contravention of the Act, or of an order or regulation made under its authority.[159] Furthermore, an inspector may at all reasonable hours enter any land, building, or other place, or any vessel, boat, aircraft, hovercraft, or vehicle of any other description, for the purpose of ascertaining whether the provisions of any order made under the 1981 Act intended to implement an EC obligation have been or are being complied with, and carry out such inspections (including inspection of documents) as may be necessary for that purpose.[160] Where a person is seen or found committing, or is reasonably suspected of being engaged in committing, an offence against the Act, a constable may, without warrant, stop and detain him, together with any animal, vehicle, boat, or thing to which the offence or suspected offence relates.[161] Where an inspector appointed by the minister is satisfied that there has been a failure to comply with the provisions of the statute or any secondary legislation made under its authority on board a vessel in port, he may detain it until the appropriate minister otherwise

---

[153] As required by the Sheep and Goats (Records, Identification and Movement) Order 1996, SI 1996/28, art 3; HC Debs, 2 February 1997, col 657 (WA).

[154] Statistics published in MAFF, *Animal Health. The Report of the Chief Veterinary Officer* (published annually). See further, MAFF, *State Veterinary Service: Service standards for the veterinary field and investigation services, including the code of practice on enforcement* (1994).

[155] House of Commons Agriculture Committee, n 115 above, para 45.   [156] n 86 above, para A(iv).

[157] This refers to a person appointed to be an inspector for the purposes of the Act by either the minister or a local authority, and, in relation to an officer of the ministry, includes a veterinary inspector: s 89(1); each local authority is required to appoint as many inspectors and other officers as it thinks necessary for the execution and enforcement of the Act: s 52(1).

[158] Animal Health Act 1981, s 63(1)(a).   [159] ibid, s 63(2)(c), (d), (3).

[160] ibid, s 64A, inserted by the Animal Health Act 1981 (Amendment) Regulations 1992, SI 1992/3293.

[161] ibid, s 60(2),(4)(a).

directs.[162] FAWC would like to see the introduction of a minimum number of checks on livestock hauliers and dealers.[163]

Finally, something of a historical anomaly, any constable has the right to enter a knacker's yard for the purpose of examining whether there is or has been any contravention or non-compliance with the provisions of the Protection of Animals Acts.[164]

(3) Inspections by the RSPCA and SSPCA

Although they have no statutory power entitling them access to premises (and the occupiers therefore have complete discretion to decide whether to co-operate and permit them onto their property), RSPCA and SSPCA inspectors carry out an extensive programme of visits to stables, boarding and breeding establishments, abattoirs, knackers' yards, pet shops, markets, and other places where activities involving animals are carried on. The number of establishment inspections carried out by these two organizations between 1995 and 1999 was as follows:[165]

	RSPCA	SSPCA
1995	20,294	4,835
1996	18,293	4,581
1997	21,531	4,517
1998	16,941	4,336
1999	15,708	4,600

These figures represent a significant contribution to the maintenance of acceptable standards. In addition, members of other specialist organizations may be invited to visit and advise on facilities and working practices. In 1998–1999, for example, the Humane Slaughter Association's staff made more than 50 visits to slaughter plants, giving advice and making recommendations.[166]

E. Improvement Notices

Ultimately, it may be necessary to have recourse to the courts in order to ensure that animals are properly treated. However, prosecution is only appropriate, or desirable, in the most serious of cases. Even then, the procedure is uncertain, cumbersome, costly, and slow. Most importantly, if prosecution is the only formal option, enforcement authorities too often have to bide their time while the condition of the animal(s) deteriorates, and an offence is eventually committed, before

---

[162] ibid, s 65(1).   [163] n 86 above, para A(iv).
[164] Protection of Animals Act 1911, s 5(2); Protection of Animals (Scotland) Act 1912, s 5(3).
[165] RSPCA, *Annual Review*; SSPCA, *Annual Report.*
[166] Humane Slaughter Association, *Annual Report 1998–99* (1999).

they can initiate formal proceedings. In the interim, all they can do is to attempt to achieve improvement through persuasion. Such a situation is clearly unsatisfactory. It undermines the effectiveness of the legislation and, crucially, results in needless suffering and continuing poor welfare. Wherever possible, therefore, it is desirable that enforcement agencies should be equipped with administrative powers which they can use to intervene at an early stage and thereby secure an early improvement in the situation. Some of the statutory licensing schemes—such as those which apply to the keeping of dangerous wild animals, zoos, scientific procedures, and slaughtermen—go some way to achieving this by giving the licensing authority the power administratively to vary and/or revoke a licence.[167]

However, a welcome development has been the introduction of statutory improvement notices. For example, where an inspector considers that animals are being transported, or are about to be transported, in a way which is likely to cause injury or unnecessary suffering, or in any other way which contravenes the transport legislation, they may serve a notice on the person appearing to be in charge of the animals, requiring them to take any necessary action to ensure compliance with the law. Such a notice may prohibit the animals being transported, either indefinitely or for a particular period; specify conditions under which the animals may be transported; or require that the journey be completed, the animals returned to their place of departure by the most direct route, held in suitable accommodation with appropriate care until the problem is solved, or slaughtered humanely. If a person fails to comply with the requirements of such a notice, the inspector is empowered to give effect to them, or cause them to be carried out, and the transporter is liable for the cost of such action.[168] According to MAFF, 1,168 such notices were served between 1 November 1997 and 19 November 1999, and 404 in the six months to 29 February 2000.[169] Similarly, where an authorized person considers that farmed animals are being kept in a way which is likely to cause unnecessary pain, suffering, or injury, or in any other way which contravenes the welfare regulations, they may serve a notice on the person appearing to be in charge of the animals requiring them, within the period stated in the notice, to take any action which is reasonably necessary to ensure compliance with the regulations. In the absence of a lawful authority or excuse, failure to comply with such a notice constitutes an offence.[170] This is an entirely positive development. Consideration should be given to extending the availability of such improvement notices generally in relation to all cruelty and welfare legislation.

---

[167] Dangerous Wild Animals Act 1976, s 1(9); Zoo Licensing Act 1981, ss 16 and 17; Animals (Scientific Procedures) Act 1986, s 11; SI 1995/731, n 27 above, Sch 1, para 9(1); see further, s H(1) below.
[168] SI 1997/1480, n 36 above, art 18(1), (2), (3).
[169] HC Debs, 30 November 1999, col 183 (WA) and 23 March 2000, col 589 (WA).
[170] Welfare of Farmed Animals Regulations, nn 31 and 33 above, regs 11 and 13(1)(b).

F. Seizure of Animals

In principle, it is desirable that, in the interests of the animals concerned, enforcement authorities should be able to remove them from situations which seriously compromise their welfare. In practice, however, it is a fundamental tenet of both the common law and the European Convention of Human Rights that a person should be left alone to enjoy their possessions with the minimum of interference from the State, consistent with the demands of public policy. Accordingly, a high threshold will generally have to be satisfied to justify seizing animals (here again, their status as property is relevant), such as the interests of public safety. Thus the Dangerous Wild Animals Act provides that a local authority may seize an animal where it is being kept in contravention of the statute, and thereafter retain, destroy, or otherwise dispose of it without compensation.[171] Similarly, the police and local authorities may seize stray or dangerous dogs.[172]

However, the only circumstance in which statute provides that an animal can be seized solely in the interests of animal protection is where a person having charge of it is arrested by a police constable for an offence of cruelty. In these circumstances the police (but only the police) may take charge of the animal(s) and deposit them in a place of safe custody until the termination of any legal proceedings or the courts order their return.[173] If the matter goes to trial, it takes several months for the case to be resolved, and there is always the possibility of further delay arising from procedural complications or a subsequent appeal. Unless the owner voluntarily relinquishes ownership in the meantime, the animal remains their property, and cannot therefore be rehomed. Furthermore, where significant numbers of large animals are involved, such as might be the case where the allegation of cruelty is against a farmer, looking after the animals in the interim can present very real logistical difficulties. In an attempt to address this problem, provisions have recently been introduced authorizing courts in England and Wales to make an order for the disposal of animals kept for a commercial purpose while proceedings for cruelty against the owner remain outstanding.[174]

Alternatively, there may be grounds for seizing an animal as evidence that an offence has been committed. For example, while the Protection of Animals Act 1911 does not itself authorize the police to enter premises, other than a knacker's

---

[171] Section 4(1).

[172] Dogs Act 1906, s 3, as amended by the Local Government Act 1988, s 39(1), (3); Environmental Protection Act 1990, s 149; Dangerous Dogs Act 1991, s 5(1).

[173] Protection of Animals Act 1911, s 12(2); Protection of Animals (Scotland) Act 1912, s 11(2). A police constable may apprehend without warrant any person whom he has reason to believe is guilty of an offence of cruelty, except where the owner is deemed to have permitted cruelty under s 1(2) by virtue of having failed to exercise reasonable care and supervision of his animal(s): ss 12(1) and 11(1), respectively. In relation to the seizure of animals by an inspector of the SSPCA under the authority of a sheriff's warrant, see n 96 above.

[174] Protection of Animals (Amendment) Act 2000; see further, s H(2) below.

yard,[175] it does provide the power of arrest where a police officer has reason to believe that a person is guilty of an offence of cruelty,[176] and, in England and Wales, the Police and Criminal Evidence Act 1984 (PACE) allows entry to premises where the police intend to make an arrest.[177] Having made an arrest, PACE provides the police with powers to search and seize evidence, which may of course include animals.[178] The exercise of these powers is dependent on an arrest having first been made. Where there has been no arrest, but an animal is believed to be in a poor condition due to abuse or negligence, it has been suggested that the police may enter premises under the authority of section 17(1)(e) of PACE, which permits police officers to enter and search any premises for the purpose of saving life or limb or preventing serious damage to property. It is an ingenious argument, and yet to be tested in the higher courts.

G. Prosecutions

It is simplistic to suggest, as is sometimes the case, that the effectiveness of animal protection legislation is to be assessed by the number of prosecutions which are brought before the courts. Indeed, prosecution is a reflection of failure in the sense that if regulation were working perfectly, there would be no need to prosecute. However, where there are serious or repeated contraventions, prosecution is clearly desirable, in part by way of punishment, but of equal if not more importance, as a means of safeguarding the animals concerned. Prosecution also serves as a public reinforcement that the legislation must be complied with. In relation to animal protection legislation, the House of Commons Agriculture Committee has accepted, for example, that, '*so long as it is seen to be effective*, persuasion is better than compulsion', but has also warned of the danger that if 'disregard of the law goes unpunished this may bring the law into disrepute', and has urged authorities to prosecute 'not only cases of wilful or persistent disregard of the law but also cases of neglect or carelessness in which exemplary consequences would have a useful deterrent effect'. It also suggested greater use of carefully chosen test cases in order 'to determine the adequacy of the terms used, to show that the legislation actually means something', and to assess the need for reform.[179] A prosecution must normally be instituted within six months of the alleged offence. FAWC has recommended that this time limit should be abolished. Alternatively, the Council considers that it should start to run from the day on which the offence came to the notice of the authorities, rather than from the date of its commission.[180]

---

[175] Section 5(2).   [176] Section 12(1).   [177] Section 17(1)(b).   [178] Sections 18 and 19.
[179] House of Commons Agriculture Committee, n 115 above, paras 37–39 (italics in the original).
[180] n 86 above, para B(vi).

(1) Prosecuting authorities

Where, having completed their investigations, the police in England and Wales are satisfied that there is sufficient evidence to prosecute, the case is submitted to the Crown Prosecution Service (CPS) for a decision as to whether the matter should be pursued. If so, the CPS then becomes responsible for undertaking the prosecution. A similar situation exists in Scotland, where potential prosecutions are referred to the procurator fiscal (it should be noted that in Scots law, in order to be admissible, all evidence must be independently corroborated). In some contexts, legislation provides express power for specific authorities to take a prosecution. For example, local authorities are provided with express powers to prosecute proceedings for any offence in relation to the licensing of pet shops, animal boarding establishments, and riding establishments.[181] In other situations, legislation places important restrictions on the power to prosecute. Thus, in England and Wales, it is *only* a local authority which may bring proceedings in respect of a contravention of or failure to comply with a condition attached to a riding establishment licence, and even then, only after receiving and considering a report by a veterinarian authorized by them to carry out inspections under the Act, which in the authority's opinion indicates that such an offence has been committed.[182] Similarly, no proceedings for either an offence under the Animals (Scientific Procedures) Act 1986 or an offence of cruelty under the Protection of Animals Act 1911 committed at an establishment designated under the 1986 Act may be brought in England or Wales without first having obtained the consent of the Director of Public Prosecutions.[183]

In deciding whether to bring proceedings, prosecuting authorities in England and Wales have regard to the criteria laid down by the CPS. First, an evidential test must be satisfied. This requires the prosecutor to be satisfied that there is enough evidence to provide a realistic prospect of conviction against each defendant on each charge. That is to say, taking account of the evidence, its admissibility, and reliability, together with consideration of what the defence case may be, it would seem that a court would be more likely than not to convict the defendant of the charge alleged. Where the evidence is less than overwhelming, this is a hard test to satisfy. Secondly, the prosecutor must be able to demonstrate that prosecution is in the public interest. There is no mechanical formula for determining this; various factors are taken into account in reaching a decision, including: conviction is likely to result in a significant sentence; there is evidence that the offence was premeditated; the defendant was in a position of authority or trust; the victim of the offence was vulnerable; or there are grounds for believing that the offence is likely to be continued or repeated. Conversely, prosecution is less likely to be needed where, for example: the court will

---

[181] Pet Animals Act 1951, s 6; Animal Boarding Establishments Act 1963, s 4; Riding Establishments Act 1964, s 5(1).
[182] Riding Establishments Act 1964, s 5(2).   [183] Animals (Scientific Procedures) Act 1986, s 26(1).

probably impose a very small or nominal penalty; the offence was committed as a result of a genuine mistake or misunderstanding; or the defendant is elderly or is, or was at the time of the offence, suffering from significant mental or physical ill health, unless the offence is serious or there is a real possibility that it may be repeated.[184]

Where there is sufficient evidence to pursue a prosecution, the offender has admitted the offence, and they consent to the procedure, it is open to the police or a prosecuting authority formally to caution them in accordance with Home Office guidelines.[185] Such a caution counts as if it was a conviction, and can be cited against the accused for up to three years, should there be a similar event which leads to prosecution. In less serious cases, it may be decided to deal with the matter with an informal caution, or 'warning letter'. These inform the recipient of the facts and of the offences which *may* have been committed, and they are advised to avoid a repetition of similar incidents in the future. In this case, there is no evidential test which must be satisfied, nor is the alleged offender required to acknowledge their liability. Such warning letters are not admissible in future proceedings.

(2) The role of the RSPCA and SSPCA

The RSPCA is not a prosecuting authority, and may therefore have regard to the CPS Code, but is not bound by it. In pursuing alleged offenders, it is acting entirely as a private prosecutor. The Protection of Animals Act 1911 imposes no restriction on those who may bring a prosecution, but other legislation may do so, which can limit the Society's ability to pursue cases. Nevertheless, the courts have on occasions recognized that the RSPCA holds a special position within its field of activity. It was decided, for example, that it could prosecute under the Transport of Animals Road and Rail Order 1975, notwithstanding that the legislation expressly stated that it 'shall, except where otherwise specified, be executed and enforced by the Local Authority'.[186] Furthermore, without actually deciding the point, the courts have proceeded on the assumption, as indeed has the Society, that RSPCA inspectors are investigating officers for the purposes of the Police and Criminal Evidence Act, and are therefore subject to the detailed Codes of Practice issued under that legislation, especially Code C, which concerns the detention, treatment, and questioning of suspects.[187]

It is sometimes suggested by those who do not sympathize with the activities of the RSPCA that it prosecutes primarily as a means of securing publicity and thereby encouraging donations from its supporters. This accusation not only fails to appreciate the reaction which would inevitably—and quite rightly—be forthcoming from the courts if they felt that the Society's prosecution strategy was either vexatious or oppressive, it also ignores the huge expense involved in undertaking investigations and pursuing prosecutions. The cost to the Society of prosecutions for the four years 1996–1999 was £1,461,046, £1,668,397, £2,017,343, and

---

[184] See further, Crown Prosecution Service, *The Code for Crown Prosecutors* (2000).
[185] Home Office Circular 18/94.
[186] *RSPCA v Woodhouse* [1984] CLY 693.   [187] *RSPCA v Eager* [1995] Crim LR 59.

£1,812,465 respectively. Notwithstanding that the courts may award costs against a defendant, including those arising from looking after and treating the animal which was the subject of the prosecution,[188] the amount is only ever a proportion of the expenditure actually incurred. First, an order for costs must not be beyond the means of the defendant, and, secondly, the amount of the costs awarded should be broadly in line with the size of any fine which is imposed.[189] In 1997, the Society was awarded total costs of £373,528; the following year, £438,695, and the chances are that it succeeded in recovering only a very small proportion of these amounts. Clearly, as a means of fund-raising, initiating litigation leaves much to be desired.

There is no tradition of private prosecution in Scotland, and the SSPCA does not itself bring prosecutions. The Society investigates complaints and, where it considers prosecution may be warranted, refers the matter to the public prosecutor, the procurator fiscal. This situation has the effect that the agency prosecuting the offence is independent of the body which has investigated it, a principle which was considered to be sufficiently important for the Crown Prosecution Service to be established in England and Wales in order to remove responsibility for prosecuting from the police. However, the RSPCA remains in the somewhat anomalous position of acting as both inspector and prosecutor.[190]

Confronted by evidence that an offence has been committed, the RSPCA and SSPCA, like the police, local authorities, and other prosecuting authorities, consider whether it would be appropriate to issue a caution rather than to initiate a prosecution. The number of cautions issued by these two organizations during the three years 1997–1999 is as follows (the distinction between an informal and formal caution is as described above):

	1997	1998	1999
RSPCA informal cautions	5,092	4,632	n/a
RSPCA formal written cautions	491	449	414
SSPCA informal cautions	976	862	715
SSPCA formal written cautions	12	15	16

(3) The number of prosecutions

Various statistics relating to prosecutions are produced and placed in the public domain, further details of which may be found in Appendix 2. The SVS, Animals (Scientific Procedures) Inspectorate, RSPCA, and SSPCA produce these annually; information about enforcement by local authorities is not held centrally, but a

---

[188] Protection of Animals Act 1911, s 12(2).

[189] *R v Newham Justices, ex parte Samuels* (QBD, 12 April 1991). But note the subsequent view of Collins J, who remarked that he could 'well envisage circumstances where a lack of proportionality would be wholly correct', and that the mere fact that the amount of costs might be considerably greater than the amount of the penalty could not of itself indicate that the former was not just and reasonable: *Cozens v Hobbs* (QBD, 29 October 1998).

[190] See further, Harrop, n 94 above, 215.

general overall picture may be gained by reference to ministerial answers to Parliamentary Questions. However, very great care needs to be taken in drawing conclusions based on any of these figures. They are useful in providing an impression of the volume of cases which come before the courts, together with their outcomes, but little else. They certainly do not provide a reliable insight into the prevalence of cruelty, the degree to which welfare legislation is ignored, the rigour with which it is enforced, or its effect. Much more information is required about the way in which enforcement bodies carry out their duties, how they deal with infringements, together with their strategies for pursuing prosecutions, before any meaningful assertion could be made about the significance of this raw data; only following further research and analysis could an informed view of the effectiveness of the legislation be advanced.

What is clear, however, is that the vast majority of prosecutions arising from the treatment of animals are brought for offences of cruelty under the Protection of Animals Acts. This is to be expected because of their general nature and wide application, together with a widespread acknowledgement that they represent the most appropriate means of pursuing those alleged to be responsible for serious mistreatment (culpability for cruelty being generally regarded as greater than that for causing poor welfare). Furthermore, because of the availability of confiscation and disqualification orders, the Protection of Animals Acts provide more effective sanctions than other legislation. However, there is a suspicion that this may encourage a view among enforcers that an infringement which does not amount to an offence of cruelty is therefore not sufficiently serious to merit prosecution. Again, this is an area which merits further research. In the meantime, it is appropriate to reiterate the views of the House of Commons Agriculture Committee which, although dating from 1991, remain relevant. 'There seems to be a disinclination to prosecute: the tendency has been to issue a caution or to offer advice',[191] the Committee observed in relation to infringements under the transport legislation then in force. It took the view that, while there was 'no objection to this low-key approach provided a record is kept and a follow-up procedure is instigated to ensure that matters are rectified', it was 'no use checking vehicles if the checks are not taken seriously', but 'how seriously they have been taken up to now', the Committee concluded, was questionable. According to the evidence presented to it by the Road Haulage Association, 'The risk of being apprehended whilst operating illegally is small and to many it is a risk worth taking.'[192] According to the Committee,

This casual approach is intolerable. . . . We therefore want these checks to be more stringent, so that hauliers and drivers become well aware that non-compliance with the law will be detected and penalized. The Council of Justice to Animals and Humane Slaughter Association and the Universities Federation for Animal Welfare suggested to us that: 'Wide publicity of prosecutions would also act as a reminder to other livestock hauliers of the need to obey the law'. This struck us as a valid point.[193]

---

[191] House of Commons Agriculture Committee, n 82 above, para 51.   [192] ibid, para 52.
[193] ibid, para 53.

Indeed. Work is also required to investigate the attitude of the magistrates' and sheriff courts when confronted with allegations of animal mistreatment. It is to be hoped that it was an unrepresentative JP who, after the journal of the Magistrates' Association published a feature on cruelty prosecutions with an accompanying cover photograph supplied by the RSPCA from one of its case files, depicting a dog which had been the victim of neglect, was moved to complain to the magazine. In his view, the illustration (which was typical of the material which would be presented to him in evidence during the course of such a prosecution) was 'clearly emotive and designed to both shock and cause offence', and he expressed the hope that 'in future we may look forward to covers that we are happy to have in our sitting rooms and which are more appropriate for the work which we are called upon to do'.[194]

H. Protective Sanctions

Penalties for infringements of the law are generally thought of in terms of fines and imprisonment. However, legislation also provides a number of sanctions designed to provide protection for animals against further mistreatment or threats to their welfare. From the animals' point of view, these may be of significantly greater importance than more conventional forms of punishment.

(1) Licences

Licences relating to pet shops, animal boarding establishments, riding establishments, dog breeding establishments, and for the keeping of dangerous wild animals, are each granted for a year, and must be renewed annually.[195] Only in the case of a riding establishment may a provisional licence (for three months, renewable for a further three months) be issued if the local authority considers that the circumstances warrant it.[196] In each case, the licence may be cancelled only by a court, and in circumstances where the licensee has been convicted of an offence against the relevant Act; or, with the exception of a licence for a dog breeding establishment, a conviction under one of the associated licensing schemes, or an offence of cruelty under the Protection of Animals Acts.[197] In other words, the licensing authority

---

[194] (1993) 49 *The Magistrate* 153. In fairness to the magistracy, a number of correspondents took issue with the view expressed: 49 *The Magistrate* 180 and 201.

[195] Pet Animals Act 1951, s 1(5), (6); Animal Boarding Establishments Act 1963, s 1(5), (6); Riding Establishments Act 1964, s 1 (6), (7); Breeding of Dogs Act 1973, s 1(6), (7), as amended by the Breeding and Sales of Dogs (Welfare) Act 1999; Dangerous Wild Animals Act 1976, s 2(2), (3).

[196] Riding Establishments Act 1970, s 1(1), (2).

[197] Pet Animals Act 1951, s 5(3); Animal Boarding Establishments Act 1963, s 3(3); Riding Establishments Act 1964, s 4(3); Breeding of Dogs Act 1973, s 3(3), as amended by the Breeding and Sale of Dogs (Welfare) Act 1999; Dangerous Wild Animals Act 1976, s 6(2). The Pet Animals Act only permits cancellation of a licence granted under its provisions; the Animal Boarding Establishments Act permits cancellation of both a boarding establishment and pet shop licence; the Riding Establishments Act permits cancellation of riding establishment licences, boarding establishment licences, and pet shop licences;

itself cannot revoke these licences. Furthermore, it is only in relation to the keeping of a dangerous wild animal that a local authority may vary or revoke the conditions attached to a licence while it is in force;[198] in all other cases, the original conditions remain unaltered until the licence expires, except if a court orders otherwise.

An original zoo licence is granted for a period of four years.[199] Where the application for the renewal of an existing licence is made, the local authority may either extend the period for which it remains valid, or direct the applicant to apply for a new licence. In either case, where the request is acceded to, the subsequent licence lasts for six years. Extending an existing licence is a straightforward administrative procedure. However, seeking a new licence requires the applicant to submit themselves to the same procedure as applies for an original licence.[200] There are two important differences between this licensing scheme and those discussed in the preceding paragraph. First, the local authority has an administrative power to alter a licence during the period it is in force by varying, cancelling, or attaching conditions, or by a combination of any of those methods, if in their opinion it is necessary or desirable to do so for ensuring the proper conduct of the zoo (the Secretary of State may also direct a local authority to alter the licence).[201] Secondly, the licensing authority may, having given the holder an opportunity to be heard, revoke the licence in four circumstances: if any reasonable requirements relating to the premises or conduct of the zoo identified during the course of an inspection are not complied with within a reasonable period; if the authority are satisfied that the zoo has been conducted in a disorderly manner or so as to cause a nuisance, or in breach of any conditions of the licence; if the holder (or, where the holder is a body corporate, a senior officer) is convicted of an offence under the Protection of Animals Acts or any of the licensing schemes already discussed; and, finally, if any person who, to the knowledge of the holder, has been so convicted is employed as a keeper in the zoo. However, no licence may be revoked on grounds involving the care or treatment of the animals unless the authority first consults an expert nominated by the Secretary of State for this purpose.[202]

Under the Animals (Scientific Procedures) Act 1986, a personal licence continues in force until revoked, but the Secretary of State is required to review each personal licence granted by him at intervals not exceeding five years.[203] Similarly, unless revoked, a project licence continues in force for such period as is specified in the licence and may be renewed for further periods but (without prejudice to the grant of a new licence in respect of the programme in question) no such licence

---

whereas a conviction under the Dangerous Wild Animals Act can lead to cancellation of any of the aforementioned licences and, additionally, a licence for a dog breeding establishment. There is clearly an anomaly here: a conviction under any of these schemes should allow cancellation of a licence granted under each of the others. However, this situation has recently been made more complicated. It used to be the case that the Breeding of Dogs Act provided for cancellation of pet shop and animal boarding establishment licences, but this is no longer the case by virtue of the Breeding and Sale of Dogs (Welfare) Act 1999, s 5.

[198] Dangerous Wild Animals Act 1976, s 1(9).   [199] Zoo Licensing Act 1981, s 5(1).
[200] ibid, ss 5(2) and 6.   [201] ibid, s 16.
[202] ibid, s 17.   [203] Animals (Scientific Procedures) Act 1986, s 4(5).

shall be in force for more than five years in all.[204] A certificate designating a scientific breeding establishment or a breeding and supplying establishment continues in force indefinitely.[205] The breach of a condition in a licence or certificate does not invalidate it, but is a ground for its variation or revocation.[206] Unless it is in response to the holder's request, they must be notified of the Secretary of State's intention to vary or revoke a licence or certificate, together with his reasons. If they object to what is proposed, the licence holder may make representations to a lawyer appointed by the Secretary of State (who may be assisted by a person with scientific or other appropriate qualifications).[207] If, however, it appears to the Secretary of State to be urgently necessary for the welfare of any protected animals, he may suspend a licence or certificate for up to three months.[208] According to the Government, at an early stage in the investigation of a suspected breach of the controls, the Inspectorate review whether a criminal offence has been committed and whether its gravity is likely to justify referral for prosecution. This depends on its origins, scale, and consequences. Thus, deliberate infringements will be viewed more seriously than those due to negligence, ignorance, confusion, or adherence to inappropriate instructions from those in authority over the alleged guilty party; repeated failures will generally be viewed more seriously than single incidents; and any unnecessary animal suffering will significantly increase the gravity of any infringement.[209]

It is not Home Office policy to provide detailed information about infringements relating to specific establishments or programmes of work.[210] Consequently, little information is available about the way in which the Inspectorate or the Home Secretary respond. Exceptionally, however, some light is thrown on to the process. For example, in response to an undercover television programme featuring video material recorded by an undercover investigator which revealed both cruelty to animals and contravention of the 1986 Act at Huntingdon Life Sciences, the largest commercial scientific procedures establishment in the UK,[211] the Home Secretary concluded that the establishment was inappropriately staffed and the animals did not always receive adequate care. It was announced on 24 July 1997 that he had decided to revoke its certificates of designation, but to do so from 30 November, 'because if the establishment closed earlier than that up to 62,000 animals may have to be unnecessarily destroyed'. Furthermore, because revocation would result in the closure of the company and the loss of 1,400 jobs, the Home Secretary indicated that he would be prepared to consider a replacement certificate if the company could demonstrate that it would meet sixteen specified conditions.[212] In the event, these were met, and a new certificate of designation was granted on 29 September.[213]

---

[204] ibid, s 5(7).   [205] ibid, ss 6(8), 7(8).
[206] ibid, ss 10(7), 11(a); see further, Home Office, n 138 above, Ch 7.
[207] ibid, s 12.   [208] ibid, s 13.   [209] HC Debs, 13 March 2000, col 85 (WA).
[210] HC Debs, 25 July 2000, col 512 (WA).
[211] 'It's a Dog's Life', broadcast by Channel Four, 26 March 1997; see n 141 above.
[212] HC Debs, 24 July 1997, col 680 (WA). The conditions are set out in APC, n 72 above, Appendix D.
[213] HC Debs, 13 November 1997, col 647.

Registration under the Performing Animals (Regulation) Act 1925 normally remains in force indefinitely. The only way in which conditions may be imposed on the training and exhibition of performing animals, or a person prevented from undertaking such activities, is by means of a court order, which is obtained by a constable or local authority officer applying to the court and satisfying it that the training or exhibition of a performing animal has been accompanied by cruelty.[214] Alternatively, a court which convicts a person of an offence against either the 1925 Act itself, or the Protection of Animals Act 1911, as amended, may order their name to be removed from the register permanently, or for such time as the court determines.[215]

(2) Orders for the care, disposal, or slaughter of animals

Even though animals may be confiscated by the court if their owner is successfully prosecuted for cruelty towards them, such an order can only be made once the person is convicted. Until then, the animals remain the property of the accused, even though they may have been seized by the police and placed in the hands of an animal welfare organization. Given the protracted nature of legal proceedings, animals can therefore be in a state of limbo for a considerable period, pending the outcome of the case. Such a situation is less than satisfactory in relation to companion animals; it poses considerable logistical and financial problems when a significant number of large animals are involved, such as might arise when cruelty occurs on a farm. This issue has recently been addressed in respect of England and Wales by the Protection of Animals (Amendment) Act 2000, which enables a person, who has brought a prosecution for an offence of cruelty under section 1 of the 1911 Act against the owner of animals which are kept, or have been kept, for a commercial purpose, to apply to the court for the animals to be disposed of, notwithstanding that the outcome of the case is yet to be decided.[216] If it appears to the court from evidence given by a veterinary surgeon that it is necessary in the interests of the welfare of the animals in question, the court may make an order authorizing the prosecutor to:

- take charge of the animals and make appropriate arrangements for their care on the premises at which they are kept, or elsewhere;
- sell them at a fair price;
- dispose of them by some other means;
- arrange for them to be slaughtered.

In determining which course of action to authorize, the court must have regard to all the circumstances, including the desirability of protecting the owner's interest in the

---

[214] Section 2(1). The court is required to send a copy of any such order to the local authority with whom the person is registered so that details of it are entered on the register, and to the Secretary of State: s 2(4).

[215] Section 4(2).

[216] The persons who may apply for such an order are restricted to the Director of Public Prosecutions, a Crown Prosecutor, a government department, a local authority, or a person who, at the request of MAFF or the National Assembly for Wales, has entered into a written agreement under which they may perform the functions conferred on a prosecutor by the Act: s 1(3).

value of the animals.[217] Where such an order is made, the prosecutor is entitled to be reimbursed for any reasonable expenses. Subject to this, the proceeds arising from the disposal or slaughter of the animals are to be returned to the owner.[218]

Regardless of the type of animal involved, or the purpose for which it is kept, courts throughout Britain retain the power to deprive a person of ownership when they have been convicted of treating it cruelly, and to make an order for its disposal.[219]

(3) Disqualification orders

It is essential that, where it is established that a person has failed to fulfil their responsibilities towards an animal, others should not be exposed to the possibility of similar mistreatment at their hands. The most important provision in this regard is that which enables the court, upon conviction for an offence of cruelty, to make an order against the defendant disqualifying them, for such period as it thinks fit, from having custody of any animal whatsoever, or any animal of a kind specified in the order. Indeed, the RSPCA has consistently stated that its primary intention in pursuing prosecutions for cruelty is to secure a disqualification order. It is important that the magistrates' and sheriff courts fully understand the nature of these; as has been acknowledged judicially, their object is 'the protection of animals from persons who have subjected an animal to cruel treatment'.[220] They are not to be regarded as part of the punishment for the offence, and it is therefore inappropriate for the court to assume that the severity of any other sanction it may impose can offset the need to make a disqualification order. They are also to be distinguished from similarly worded provisions intended to protect the public from the consequences of irresponsible dog ownership.[221] The RSPCA has repeatedly complained about the proportion of convictions for cruelty which do not result in a disqualification order. Perhaps because of their representations it has increased in recent years, but there remains a significant minority of cases where an order could be made, but is not. Thus, in 1992, nearly 50 per cent of eligible defendants involved in prosecutions brought by the RSPCA in England and Wales did not receive a disqualification order. More recently, the figures are as follows:[222]

	1995	1996	1997	1998	1999
Banning orders	650	681	795	819	723
Defendants who could have been banned but were not	225 25%	222 25%	261 25%	249 23%	170 19%

---

[217] ibid, s 2(1), (2), (3). [218] ibid, s 4(1).
[219] Protection of Animals Act 1911, s 3; Protection of Animals (Scotland) Act 1912, s 3.
[220] *RSPCA v Miller* [1994] Crim LR 516.
[221] Dangerous Dogs Act 1989, s 1(1)(b); Dangerous Dogs Act 1991, s 4(1)(b).
[222] RSPCA, *Annual Review*.

Only time will tell whether this demonstrates a permanent downward trend towards the expectation that a banning order will be made. It is a crude comparison, but the situation would appear to be worse in Scotland, where the courts seem to be even more reluctant to impose such an order:[223]

	1995	1996	1997	1998	1999
Cases dealt with by courts	100	100	75	60	60
Banning orders	19	14	12	15	8

These figures seem particularly low given that, because of delays in bringing cases to court, the SSPCA has adopted a policy of referring only the most serious allegations to the procurator fiscal.

At present the courts have complete discretion to decide whether to impose a banning order. This should now be limited by legislation. For its part, FAWC has recommended that the Protection of Animals Acts should be amended to prevent anyone from benefiting financially from the keeping of animals if they have been convicted of cruelty,[224] but it is essential that the courts retain a limited discretion in this matter. Mandatory orders inevitably lead to arbitrary decisions and injustice, as is illustrated by the consequences of the Dangerous Dogs Act 1991. As originally enacted, courts were *bound* to order that a dog be destroyed if, for example, a certificate of exemption had not been obtained in respect of an animal subsequently deemed to be a pit bull terrier type of dog, or such a dog was found in a public place without being muzzled and kept on a lead. The pitfalls inherent in such a situation are apparent from the case law. 'What then is the position in law when an owner has made every reasonable attempt to get a certificate of exemption and has been foiled by reason of the conduct of others, and in particular the police? My reaction, I confess, is to ask myself: is there really no remedy?' asked an exasperated McCowan J, before being forced to answer his rhetorical question in the negative.[225] In the same way, where it was claimed that the muzzle had been removed because the dog had kennel cough, there was no defence that to keep the muzzle in place while the dog was coughing would be cruel. The terms of the statute were such that it was not open to the person in control of the dog 'to make a value judgment as between what is good for the dog and what is good for the rest of mankind', observed Schiemann J. 'We have here an absolute prohibition,' he concluded, 'and a breach of that prohibition is to be followed by an order for the dog's destruction, however blameless the dog and its owner.'[226] A similar situation arose when a dog was seized by police, who came across it being walked in a public place by its owner's nephew without a muzzle, which had been removed to allow the dog to be sick. Commenting on the mandatory destruction order which

---

[223] SSPCA, *Annual Report.*   [224] n 86 above, para B(i).

[225] *R v Secretary of State for the Home Department, ex parte James* [1994] COD 167.

[226] *Cichon v DPP* [1994] Crim LR 918.

resulted from the ensuing prosecution, Rougier J felt moved to exclaim in unusually outspoken terms:

Whilst acknowledging the obvious need to prevent dogs which are, or have become, savage from injuring people, yet it seems to me that the Dangerous Dogs Act 1991 bears all the hallmarks of an ill-thought-out piece of legislation, no doubt in hasty response to yet another strident pressure group. Add to that the foolish nephew, an observant and zealous policeman and the result is that a perfectly inoffensive animal has to be sent to the gas chamber, or whatever method of execution is favoured, its only crime being to have a cough. It would take the pen of Voltaire to do justice to such a ludicrous situation.[227]

It is therefore submitted that the courts' ultimate discretion to make disqualification orders should be preserved, but it would be desirable for the legislation to be amended to introduce a presumption that such an order will be imposed, unless the court is satisfied that it is in the interests of the welfare of any animals which were at the time in the custody of the convicted person to decide otherwise. An associated amendment is required in relation to a breach of a disqualification order; at present, legislation provides only that a person may be fined or imprisoned (or both). Provision should also be made for the immediate and permanent seizure of any animal found to be in the custody of a person who is subject to a disqualification order.

In addition to offences of cruelty, it is also provided that where a person is convicted of an offence under the Protection of Animals Acts, the Performing Animals (Regulation) Act, or any of the licensing schemes relating to pet shops, animal boarding establishments, riding establishments, or the keeping of wild animals, the court may order that they are permanently, or for such time as may be specified in the order, disqualified from being registered to train or exhibit performing animals,[228] or from keeping a pet shop, a boarding establishment, a riding establishment, or a dangerous wild animal, for such period as the court thinks fit.[229] Where a person is convicted under the Breeding of Dogs Act 1973, in addition to being disqualified from keeping a dog breeding establishment, they may also be disqualified from having custody of any dog of a description specified in the order.[230] Furthermore, where a dog has been used in, or was present at, the commission of an offence under the Protection of Badgers Act 1992, the court, on convicting the offender, may make an order for the destruction or other disposal of the dog, and an order disqualifying the offender, for such period as it thinks fit, from having custody of a dog.[231]

---

[227] *R v Ealing Magistrates Court, ex parte Fanneran* (1996) 160 JP 409, 416.

[228] Performing Animals (Registration) Act 1925, s 4(2).

[229] Pet Animals Act 1951, s 5(3); Animal Boarding Establishments Act 1963, s 3(3); Riding Establishments Act 1964, s 4(3); Dangerous Wild Animals Act 1976, s 6(2).

[230] Section 1(3)(b), (c), as amended by the Breeding and Sale of Dogs (Welfare) Act 1999.

[231] Section 13(1).

I. Europe

Responsibility within Britain for implementing and enforcing EC legislation concerned with animal welfare rests with the UK Government. The question of how rigorous other Member States are in fulfilling their obligations has arisen in two contexts. First, if a Member State fails fully to meet its responsibilities the effect can undermine the fundamental principle of the single market. Put bluntly, if high standards of welfare have cost implications, a country which fails to meet the requisite conditions may enjoy a competitive advantage, at least so far as price is concerned. Secondly, it offends those who are concerned about animal welfare that animals which have been raised in Britain are exported to another Member State where standards may be significantly more lax.

The European Commission has a general responsibility to ensure compliance with EC law throughout the EU, but the resources it devotes to the task are wholly inadequate. In 1994, for example, the Commission confirmed that with just twenty-three inspectors, 'no checks have been made on compliance with Community rules on protection of animals during transport' because all of its meagre staff were otherwise engaged on other matters.[232] Similarly, in May 1997, Emma Bonino, the Commissioner for Consumer Affairs, admitted that the veterinary inspectorate was capable of satisfactorily performing only a quarter of its responsibilities, and that nearly 100 additional staff would be needed to carry out its obligations under EC legislation.[233] Moreover, in *R v MAFF, ex parte Hedley Lomas (Ireland) Ltd*, the ECJ has held that the government of one Member State may not, on the pretext that another Member State has failed to meet its obligations under EC law, initiate action against it which has the effect of interfering with free trade. The case arose from a decision by the Minister of Agriculture to adopt a policy of refusing to grant licences for the export of sheep from the UK to Spain, in response to allegations that the treatment of animals in at least some Spanish slaughterhouses was contrary to Directive 74/577 on the stunning of animals before slaughter. According to the Court, Member States 'must rely on trust in each other to carry out inspections on their respective territories'. A Member State, the Court ruled, 'may not unilaterally adopt, on its own authority, corrective or protective measures designed to obviate any breach by another Member State of the rules of Community law'. This was so, even though the Directive in question failed to specify any procedure for monitoring the application of its provisions, or any penalty in the event of their breach.[234]

Yet, it is quite clear that the standard of enforcement by Member States varies considerably throughout the EU. For example, the Commission has recently complained about the 'low level of priority given by the competent authorities of

---

[232] Reply to Caroline Jackson MEP, quoted in (1994) 134 *Veterinary Record* 340.
[233] (1997) 141 *Veterinary Record* 538.   [234] Case 5/94, [1996] 2 CMLR 391, paras [19]–[21].

Member States' to enforcement of the transport Directive, and has admitted that incomplete and inconsistent reporting to it by Member States has resulted in a situation where 'the Commission is not able to give a comprehensive view of the efforts at enforcement by the competent authorities of Member States'.[235] According to the Commission,

Member States must allocate in the near future adequate resources to informing, training and co-ordinating the actions of their field inspectors in order to apply the current legislation more efficiently. Animal welfare issues must be given high priority by professionals throughout the Community.[236]

Time will tell whether these worthy sentiments have any effect in practice. Unfortunately, one has one's doubts.

J. Conclusion

FAWC has recently reminded ministers that, in legislating to promote high standards of welfare, 'stronger law is only part of the equation as without effective enforcement any system of control will inevitably fail'.[237] Quite so. Securing legislative change is never to be regarded as an end in itself; if it is to fulfil its purpose, it must be implemented in a robust and consistent manner. Furthermore, the process of enforcement encompasses much more than simply hauling alleged offenders before the courts. First, legislation should be certain as to its object, application, and consequences. To this end, its provisions are required to be unambiguous, equitable, and practicable. Secondly, it is essential in the context of animal protection that the nature of the legal responsibility which every measure imposes is appropriate for its subject matter and its purpose. In particular, such responsibility should extend to *all* those whose conduct may have an impact on the welfare or treatment of the relevant animals. Thirdly, those charged with enforcement have to be provided with the necessary authority and powers to enable them to ensure that the law is complied with. It is also important that they should be able to demonstrate a relevant degree of training, knowledge, and independence. Fourthly, the legislation must provide sufficient and appropriate sanctions. These will include the imposition of a punishment, such as a fine or imprisonment, but it is crucial that measures are available which provide protection for the animals involved. Hence the importance of judicial powers, such as the availability of confiscation and disqualification orders. However, of equal significance are administrative measures, such as improvement notices, or licensing powers. Fifthly,

---

[235] Commission of the European Communities, *Report of the Commission to the Council and the European Parliament on the experience acquired by Member States since the implementation of Council Directive 95/29/EC amending Directive 91/628/EC concerning the protection of animals during transport* (2000) paras 2.1 and 2.2.

[236] ibid, para 3.2.   [237] n 86 above, Introduction.

statutory enforcement agencies should be adequately resourced to allow them properly to execute their responsibilities. It is acknowledged that recent enactments have the potential to make enforcement more effective, but, nevertheless, it is submitted that as presently constituted, and taken as a whole, the regulatory framework intended to protect animals fails satisfactorily to meet *any* of the foregoing criteria. Indeed, if it were not for the activities of the RSPCA and the SSPCA, enforcement would be wholly inadequate. The fact that these two organizations, operating without public funding or the advantage of any special legal power, make at their own volition such a major contribution to animal protection should not be allowed to provide the statutory agencies with an excuse for abdicating their responsibilities in this regard. Finally, such statutory enforcement agencies should be publicly accountable for the way in which they perform their functions. Enforcement should therefore be open and transparent. In dismissing a call from FAWC for 'the publication of statistics which give a clear picture of national and regional levels of enforcement', ministers of the time accepted that 'published annual statistics for all agencies concerned with welfare enforcement would be of academic interest to some', but concluded that 'the necessary commitment of resources to achieve this would not in the Government's view be justified'.[238] This is, however, to miss the point. Such statistics would undoubtedly be of academic interest, but much more importantly they would be an exercise in accountability: the information would provide the public with an insight into how the law intended to protect animals is working in practice, and how effectively it is being enforced. Only by gaining access to such information can the public judge whether statutory bodies responsible for enforcement are adequately carrying out their duties, and can they, together with politicians and policy makers, come to an informed view of whether further legislative reform is necessary.

---

[238] FAWC, n 85 above, para 8.3; Government's Response, para 35.

15
Enhancing Regulation and Responsibility

From the time that the first animal protection legislation was introduced in Britain in 1822, Parliament has accepted that it is both necessary and legitimate for the State to develop an extensive regulatory regime, intended to protect other species from cruel treatment; to prevent and to control the spread of disease; and, especially latterly, to promote high standards of welfare. Inherent in this body of law is a recognition that individual citizens and society collectively have a responsibility for the way in which other species are treated. The nature of that responsibility varies depending on the type of animal concerned, the situation in which it finds itself, and the relationship which a particular person has with it. At the very minimum, it encompasses a general duty to avoid causing unnecessary suffering.[1] However, those who accept responsibility for animals assume a significantly greater obligation towards them than the public at large. Legal regulation has played an essential role in defining and enforcing such responsibilities. Indeed, it is argued here that, for the foreseeable future, the protection of animals in Britain can best be achieved by increased and more effective legal regulation.

Initially, legislative intervention was necessary (as, indeed, it still is) to offset the otherwise unconstrained property rights enjoyed by owners under the common law to decide for themselves how their animals should be treated. More recently, the implications of our developing scientific understanding about the requirements which must be met if other species are to benefit from a high quality of life have also needed to be formalized through regulation. As Broom and Johnson point out, 'people's desire to keep animals often outstrips their knowledge of the animal's biology, and sometimes their appreciation of an animal's suffering'. Hence, the need to establish standards and 'codify what is commonly left to human judgement', not least because 'Humans have difficulties in setting benchmarks for

---

[1] Protection of Animals Act 1911; Protection of Animals (Scotland) Act 1912; Wild Mammals (Protection) Act 1996.

their own animal husbandry.'[2] Legal intervention thereby acts as both a regulatory mechanism and an educative tool.

It follows that the greater our insight into the nature of other species' physiology, behaviour, and sentiency, the more onerous the obligations towards them become. Our forefathers' (mis)treatment of animals can arguably be excused on the ground of ignorance, but, increasingly, such a defence is no longer available. Indeed, even though it may not be possible indisputably to establish the effect that specific treatment has on an animal, there will often be enough evidence to apply the precautionary principle. In the words of the Brambell Committee, 'it is morally incumbent on us to give the animal the benefit of the doubt and to protect it so far as is possible from conditions that may be reasonably supposed to cause it suffering, though this cannot be proved'.[3] In other words, science cannot provide all the answers; it will often be necessary to make a moral judgement in order to determine how an animal ought to be treated. So, if science provides the authority for imposing standards, and ethics the justification for doing so, then it is legal regulation which supplies the means. 'Attitudes to animal welfare cannot be set by law', Broom and Johnson observe, 'but procedures to prevent poor welfare can.'[4]

There are those, however, who argue that the very notion of animal welfare law is misguided. For example, according to the American legal academic, Gary Francione, 'laws and regulations that purport to protect animals are unable to achieve even a minimally acceptable level of protection as long as humans are the only rightholders and animals are regarded as "property"'. On the contrary, he argues, 'legal welfarism permits any animal exploitation that is not wholly gratuitous';[5] in Francione's view, it is 'structurally defective and conceptualizes the human/animal conflict in ways that animal interests never prevail'.[6]

This uncompromising dismissal of animal welfare law is unequivocally rejected by the present writer. While it is recognized that legislation may always endorse and entrench standards which public policy makers consider to be acceptable, but which are incompatible with the attainment of a high standard of welfare for the animals concerned (hence the need always to keep the law under review), the message of this book is that legislative intervention *has* made a positive difference, continues to do so, and reform has the potential to improve the situation further. This is not to suggest that the state of the law is ideal, and that all is well with the world. Quite clearly, significant shortcomings characterize the present situation. At one level, these are practical; animal protection law in Britain urgently requires to be consolidated, being at the moment much too diffuse; at another, there remains insufficient recognition of animals' inherent interests. Taken together, these weaknesses make it imperative to enhance regulation and responsibility by consolidating and

---

[2] Broom, DM and Johnson, KG, *Stress and Animal Welfare* (1993) 172.

[3] Brambell, FWR (Chairman), *Report of the Technical Committee to Enquire into the Welfare of Animals Kept Under Intensive Husbandry Systems* (1965) para 30.

[4] n 2 above, 170.   [5] *Animals, Property and the Law* (1995) 26.

[6] *Rain Without Thunder. The Ideology of the Animal Rights Movement* (1996) 4.

strengthening the law. New Zealand has shown the way forward, with its recently enacted Animal Welfare Act 1999, which came into force on 1 January 2000.[7]

The degree of compromise inherent in the law inevitably offends the moral absolutists, especially those who adopt the view that other species have an inalienable right to life and complete autonomy for its duration. From such a perspective, *any* interference or imposition by humans is morally abhorrent, and *any* measure which formalizes such a situation is thereby unacceptable. However, Francione makes a rather more serious charge. In his view, despite (or perhaps because of) legal intervention, 'things are worse for animals than they were one hundred years ago', which leads him to conclude that 'the present strategy is simply not working'.[8] This contention is more complicated to address than might seem initially to be the case. Take the view of a country vet, Dr Tim Swift, speaking at the end of the 1960s. Looking back twenty years, he recalled a time when the number of animals typically owned by a farmer 'was small and "knowable" as you might say—twenty cows, each with a name, each milked by hand, more often than not; five or six sows with their litters and their funny old ways'. There was, however, another side to this apparent bucolic ideal:

Animals often lived a long time, particularly horses, of course. I would be treating a horse with a discharging joint for months—maybe for years. Many of the horses were lame and had to wear surgical shoes. Nobody would put a horse down until it was absolutely useless. The sick animals were affectionately treated but they suffered a lot. I had almost no drugs, no antibiotics. The sick horses would be nursed and worked until another day's work couldn't be got out of them, then they were shot. If you could keep a horse going, you did. Ethics were different then. My job was to keep a horse on its feet.[9]

A very significant number of animals *are* treated vastly better than would have formerly been the case. Standards in many contexts *are* much higher than in previous times, and the law has played an important role in this improvement. This is not to deny that huge numbers of animals continue to be treated in a wholly unacceptable manner. One of the reasons for this has been the introduction of new practices, especially in relation to livestock: intensive methods of rearing; transit over long distances; greater and accelerated productivity. This highlights one of the shortcomings which has traditionally undermined the effectiveness of animal protection legislation in Britain. Namely, that it has too often been used after the event to counter the worst effects of practices which have already been introduced. Rather, the law should define fundamental principles of animal treatment in advance, with which every new practice would normally be expected to comply from the outset. It is therefore submitted that legislation be introduced which would have the effect of making *any* practice, procedure, or means of rearing or husbandry, unlawful unless either it met a prescribed standard of care, or there was express legislative authority permitting it. The continuing and non-delegable duty to exercise reasonable care and

---

[7] The full text of the Act is available on the New Zealand Government's website, http://www.govt.nz/.
[8] n 6 above, 5.   [9] Blythe, Ronald, *Akenfield. Portrait of an English Village* (1969) 260 and 261.

supervision to protect an animal from suffering unnecessarily, imposed on the owner by virtue of the Protection of Animals Acts, should be extended to welfare. A significant move towards this position has recently been introduced, whereby the owners or keepers of farmed animals are now under an explicit duty to take all reasonable steps to ensure the welfare of the animals under their care.[10]

A positive duty to ensure the care, supervision, and welfare of an animal?

- To this end, it should become a legal obligation that the keeper of any animal must exercise reasonable care and supervision of it, and take all reasonable steps to promote and ensure its welfare.
- A keeper for these purposes should be defined as the owner of the animal, and any other person who, whether on a permanent or temporary basis,

    (a) has possession of the animal,
    (b) is responsible for or is in charge of the animal, or
    (c) is responsible for or has actual care or control of a child under the age of sixteen years who owns the animal or has possession of it.

- In deciding whether the owner or keeper of an animal has exercised reasonable care or supervision, or taken all reasonable steps to ensure its welfare, regard should be had to:

    - the species concerned;
    - the degree of the animal's development, adaptation, and domestication; and
    - its physiological and ethological needs in accordance with established experience and developing scientific knowledge.

- A keeper should continue to be regarded as such unless and until some other person formally becomes the animal's keeper by meeting the criteria set out above (even though they may no longer actually possess the animal).
- In addition, an express duty should be imposed on a person proposing to become the keeper of an animal, whether permanently or temporarily, to take all reasonable steps to acquaint himself with the physical, physiological, and behavioural needs of the particular animal and to satisfy himself that he is able to meet these needs.
- For the avoidance of doubt, it should be specified that the keeper of an animal is under a continuing duty to take all reasonable steps to ensure that it is provided with

    - proper care and attention at all times;
    - a wholesome and suitable diet, in quantities and at intervals appropriate to the animal's species, breed, size, age, condition, lifestyle, and other relevant physiological needs;

---

[10] Welfare of Farmed Animals (England) Regulations 2000, SI 2000/1870, reg 3(1)(a); Welfare of Farmed Animals (Scotland) Regulations 2000, SSI 2000/442, reg 3(1)(a); Welfare of Farmed Animals (Wales) Regulations 2001, reg 3(1)(a) (at the time this book went to press, the regulations relating to Wales had not been allocated an SI number); cf Children (Scotland) Act 1995, s 1(1), which imposes on parents a positive responsibility to safeguard and promote their children's health, development, and welfare.

- unless the requirements of the species are recognized by reputable scientific opinion to be otherwise, a supply of fresh water, in quantities and at intervals appropriate to the animal's species, breed, size, age, condition, lifestyle, and other relevant physiological needs;
- a living environment which is constructed and maintained so as to avoid injury or unnecessary suffering to the animal;
- a living environment which is appropriate as regards the behavioural and physiological needs of the individual animal, including size, space, privacy, nesting and bedding, lighting, ventilation, temperature, protection from the elements, cleanliness and hygiene, health, adequate opportunity to exercise, contact with its own kind, security, and other facilities sufficient to meet its behavioural needs.

- In the same manner, the recently introduced provisions relating to the breeding of farm animals[11] should be extended, so as to have general application. Thus,

   (a) Natural or artificial breeding or breeding procedures which cause, or are likely to cause, suffering or injury to an animal shall not be practised. This shall not preclude the use of natural or artificial breeding procedures that are likely to cause minimal or momentary suffering or injury or that might necessitate interventions which would not cause serious or lasting injury.

   (b) It shall be the duty of any person who selects an animal for the purpose of breeding from it to have due regard to any anatomical, physiological, or behavioural characteristic apparent in the individual or the breeding line which is likely to put at risk the health or welfare of the offspring or the female parent.

   (c) No domestic or captive animal shall be kept by a person unless it can reasonably be expected, on the basis of their genotype or phenotype, that they can be kept without detrimental effect on their health or welfare.

- Furthermore, it is submitted that the previous requirements should also apply to methods of raising and keeping animals.
- Extending the principle already laid down in EC law, it should become the duty of every public authority or official in exercising their legal or administrative powers to pay full regard to the welfare requirements of animals which would be affected by their decisions.
- The principle that directors and senior managers of a body corporate may be held personally responsible for the treatment of animals used by commercial undertakings where it can be proved that the offence was committed with their consent or connivance, or is attributable to any neglect on their part, which is already contained in welfare legislation relating to farms, zoos, transport, and slaughter, should be extended to all other commercial situations, most particularly in

---

[11] Welfare of Farmed Animals Regulations, ibid, Sch 1, paras 28 and 29.

respect to pet shops and the carrying out of scientific procedures. A similar provision should also be introduced in relation to any offence of cruelty inflicted on an animal for which a body corporate was responsible at the time of the offence.

Amending the offence of cruelty

Section 1(1)(a) of both the 1911 and 1912 Acts needs clarifying. The Scottish courts have complained of the 'turgid and excessively detailed language',[12] while the English High Court has predicted that the wording is 'bound to go on giving trouble to those concerned with the administration of the law'.[13] It is, however, important that the generality of the definition of cruelty is maintained, so that, as now, it can be applied to a wide variety of different situations, and thereby enables the courts to interpret the offence in the light of developing scientific understanding about the nature of animals' suffering and changing social attitudes as to their proper treatment. The offence should also become prospective, thereby avoiding the need to establish that an animal has actually suffered. Thus,

- It shall be an offence of cruelty, without reasonable cause or excuse,
    - (a) to do or omit to do, or
    - (b) to cause, encourage, or procure, or
    - (c) being the keeper, to permit,

any act or omission which results in, or is likely to result in, any unnecessary suffering to any animal.
- In subparagraph (c) above, a keeper of an animal shall be deemed to have permitted an offence of cruelty if he has failed to exercise reasonable care or supervision of the relevant animal.
- The occupier of premises shall be guilty of an offence if he is shown to have unreasonably failed to prevent the commission or continuation of an offence of cruelty on those premises.

The meaning of 'keeper' would be the same as that proposed above in the context of welfare.

Clarifying the meaning of 'abandonment'

Furthermore, the effect of the decision in *Hunt v Duckering*[14] should be overturned by legislation to make it clear that the defendant's intention is irrelevant to the offence of cruelty arising from abandonment. This would return the law to the situation which seemed to be envisaged when the offence was originally introduced. Namely, that the defendant would be guilty, unless they could demonstrate that they had a reasonable cause or excuse for their behaviour.

---

[12] *Patchett v Macdougall* 1984 SLT 152 (Note), 153 (Lord Hunter).
[13] *Isted v Crown Prosecution Service* [1998] Crim LR 194 (Brooke LJ); the quotation is taken from the transcript of the full judgment.
[14] [1993] Crim LR 678.

Extending the offence of cruel tethering

The offence of cruelty arising from tethering[15] should be extended beyond equines to encompass all domestic and captive animals, and be amended to include circumstances in which a tethered animal is likely to suffer. The offence should also be introduced into Scotland.

Bringing wild animals within the ambit of the Protection of Animals Acts

Ideally, the offence of cruelty should not only apply to domestic and captive animals, but also to wild animals, as is already the case in Northern Ireland.[16] Otherwise, the meaning of a captive animal under the Protection of Animals Acts must be redefined to counter the effect of the decision in *Rowley v Murphy*[17] and associated case law. Notwithstanding the introduction of the Wild Mammals (Protection) Act 1996, it is both morally reprehensible and jurisprudentially illogical that an animal which is either unable to make good its escape because of its condition, natural behaviour, treatment, or the circumstances in which it is situated, or which is prevented from doing so as a result of human intervention, should not be protected from cruelty. As Fenton Atkinson J sensibly remarked in the *Rowley* case, 'there was very much to be said for the view that, once a wild animal had been captured, it was in captivity on the plain meaning of the word'.[18]

Addressing the problems surrounding 'custody'

To counter the confusion which has arisen from the English High Court's interpretation of 'custody' in *RSPCA v Miller*,[19] it needs to be made clear that the concept of 'custody' extends to situations where the person has *any* degree of physical control over an animal, whether temporarily or permanently, for its care, treatment, or well-being. The notion of shared custody advanced by the courts is not helpful. Ideally, the word 'custody' should be replaced with a less ambiguous term, such as 'responsibility'. The court would then be empowered to disqualify a person convicted of an offence of cruelty for such period as it thinks fit from assuming any degree of responsibility, either temporarily or permanently, shared or exclusive, for the control, care, treatment, or well-being of any animal at all, or one of a kind specified in the order.

The need for an enabling power

The Protection of Animals Acts should be amended to include an enabling power in order that further changes may be introduced by way of secondary legislation.

---

[15] Protection of Animals Act 1911, s 1(1)(f), inserted by the Protection Against Cruel Tethering Act 1988.
[16] Welfare of Animals (Northern Ireland) Act 1972, s 29(1).   [17] [1964] 2 QB 43.   [18] ibid 51.
[19] [1994] Crim LR 516.

Companion animals

Ministers have repeatedly rejected calls to introduce better legal safeguards for the benefit of companion animals on the ground that they are already adequately protected by virtue of the 1911 and 1912 Acts.[20] This is misleading. These statutes focus on *cruelty*; they do not expressly seek to promote high standards of welfare. As it has been thought appropriate to introduce complementary welfare legislation in relation to animals used in (most) commercial activities, so the same principle should be applied to companion animals. If the general duty to ensure the care, supervision, and welfare of an animal were introduced, as proposed above, this would go a long way to addressing the problem, although it would be desirable if provision were made to introduce welfare codes for companion animals, similar to (and with the same legal status as) those which are published for livestock.

There is also a need for the respective licensing regimes which apply to companion animals to be dragged into the twenty-first century, particularly to provide enforcement bodies with wider powers expressly to impose conditions to promote all aspects of welfare, and to place on them more stringent obligations to ensure compliance.

Many of the shortcomings relating to the welfare of companion animals would be addressed if the United Kingdom acceded to and implemented the provisions of the European Convention for the Protection of Pet Animals. Again, ministers have consistently refused to do so, arguing that it would not make any appreciable difference.[21] This is demonstrably not so. The Convention lays down requirements on keeping animals, breeding, acquisition, training, licensing, surgical operations, killing, and the provision of information and education, which go significantly beyond what is expressly prescribed in British law.

For example, the Convention specifies that any person who is keeping a pet animal or who is looking after it shall provide accommodation, care, and attention which take account of its ethological needs in accordance with its species and breed, in particular by giving it suitable and sufficient food and water; providing it with adequate opportunities for exercise; and taking all reasonable measures to prevent its escape.[22] The Convention states that an animal should not be kept as a pet in circumstances where either these requirements cannot be met or, notwithstanding that they are fulfilled, the animal cannot adapt itself to captivity.[23] Furthermore, the Convention provides that any person who selects a pet animal for breeding is placed under a responsibility to have regard to the anatomical, physiological, and behavioural characteristics which are likely to put at risk the health and welfare of either the offspring or the female parent;[24] provides for the

---

[20] See, for example, HC Debs, 8 June 1998, col 435 and 3 February 1999, col 706 (WA).

[21] See, for example, HC Debs, 27 February 1996, col 519 and 11 March 1999, col 43 (WA); HL Debs, 27 February 1996, col 94 (WA).

[22] European Convention for the Protection of Pet Animals, art 4(2).   [23] ibid, art 4(3).

[24] ibid, art 6.

licensing of animal sanctuaries, including requirements as to the competency of those who are responsible for such establishments;[25] and lays down specific requirements concerning the way in which pet animals should be killed as and when the need arises.[26]

Court orders

Except where it relates to a question of public safety, a court, when determining whether to make any order relating to an animal, should be placed under an express duty to give its welfare paramount consideration.[27] This would replace the existing requirement that the court may grant a confiscation order only if it has heard evidence of either a previous conviction or other evidence to suggest that if the animal is left with the owner it is likely to be exposed to further cruelty. Furthermore, a confiscation order should not be dependent on the *owner* of the animal being convicted of cruelty; it should also be available to the courts to make such an order against the keeper of an animal. Similarly, consideration should also be given to extending the scope of disqualification orders beyond custody and/or responsibility, to include the possibility of disqualifying a person from being the keeper of animals. There is also merit in providing the courts with the power to make a disqualification order against the occupier of the premises on which an offence of cruelty took place where they are convicted of an offence.

Enforcement

It should be a basic requirement that those charged by statute to enforce the legislation should be independent, and have relevant training, knowledge, and expertise in animal welfare science and the relevant law. Moreover, there needs to be much more detailed information available to the public about the activities of the statutory enforcement agencies. It is of the foremost importance that enforcement should be carried out consistently, diligently, and rigorously. However impressive legislative provisions may appear to be on paper, they will never fulfil the purposes for which they were introduced unless they are properly applied and enforced. There are serious concerns about the way in which the statutory enforcement agencies carry out their functions; it is incumbent on them to dedicate sufficient resources to the task and to demonstrate that they are giving this work the priority which Parliament has indicated it requires.

Licensing of farms?

FAWC recommended in 1990 that the Government should give consideration to the introduction of a licensing or registration scheme for all those having responsibility for livestock.[28] The Council has reconsidered this idea, but has not pursued

---

[25] ibid, art 8. [26] ibid, art 11.

[27] Such a requirement already exists in respect of children: Children Act 1989, s 1(1); Children (Scotland) Act 1995, s 16(1).

[28] FAWC, *Report of the Enforcement Working Group* (1990) para 8.10.

it, largely on the basis of the introduction of measures in the wake of BSE which require the keepers of cattle, pigs, sheep, and goats to notify the appropriate authorities and to maintain movement records. It has, however, proposed a registration scheme for poultry.[29] It is submitted here that the present arrangements are not adequate to secure the welfare of farm animals. In part, this is due to inadequate resources being devoted to the State Veterinary Service. It is, however, clearly anomalous that, whereas a person who breeds dogs on a very limited scale is required to be licensed by the local authority, it is open to a person to keep any number of livestock without first having to demonstrate that they possess the necessary knowledge and facilities to look after them properly. It might also be helpful to think about specifying a statutory definition of 'farmer', or perhaps 'livestock keeper' might be better. At the moment, it is an imprecise term which can be applied equally to multinational corporations, small family run businesses, hobby farmers, and those who would be more appropriately regarded as traders. One of the apparent shortcomings highlighted by the outbreak of foot-and-mouth disease in the spring of 2001 was that, despite the requirements as to movement and identification, the statutory enforcement agencies really did not have an accurate understanding of where animals were, or the extent to which they were being moved around the country. In short, despite claims to the contrary from within the industry, monitoring of, and accountability for, the keeping of livestock has been shown to be woefully inadequate.

The wider picture

Although there is a need for reform of the domestic law, the time has long gone when animal protection measures were determined exclusively by the UK Parliament: the Welsh Assembly, the Scottish Parliament, the institutions of the European Community, and the WTO together have a profound effect on the law, and thereby impose significant restrictions on both the legal power and the political feasibility of unilateral action by Westminster. It is both inevitable and necessary that attention continues to be focused on these other centres of power.

The crucial forum is the WTO. There are those who argue that it does not pose the threat to national standards which many fear. Robert Madelin, a senior official at the European Commission's trade directorate, has been quoted as saying that 'the question of whether we can impose requirements on importers based on principles of their production is extremely unclear', while Erik Wijkstrom, economics affairs officer at the WTO's agriculture and commodities division, considers 'the issue is open for argument. It is not clear cut.'[30] In contrast, the House of Commons Agriculture Committee is much more pessimistic. The problem, they argue, lies 'in persuading some other EU members and the EU's trading partners that animal welfare is a legitimate concern in WTO trade rules'. The Committee pointed to the Ministry of Agriculture's assessment that 'there is "very little

---

[29] FAWC, *Annual Review 1998* (1999).   [30] *Farmers Guardian*, 20 November 2000.

support for [the inclusion of animal welfare] outside the EU"'. By way of illustration, the Committee cited the attitude of the United States Department of Agriculture. '"Factors that are related to 'consumer preference', such as production methods, socio-economic factors, and ethical or religious preferences," it said in evidence, "must be addressed through the marketplace".' Against this background, the Committee concluded that issues such as animal welfare should not, 'when push comes to shove, be permitted to prevent agreement on a further round of "classic" trade liberalization', and warned that national governments 'which introduce unilateral animal welfare measures should consider their impact on trade at the time of their introduction, not seek to use the WTO to sustain these actions'.[31]

It is indisputable, however, that the nature of the WTO regime and the uncertainty it engenders has made the UK government and the institutions of the EC increasingly cautious when considering the introduction of further measures intended to promote higher standards of welfare in the commercial sector. As a result, debate about the extent to which EC law should regulate and prescribe how animals are to be treated seems set to continue, notwithstanding the recent introduction of the Protocol on the protection and welfare of animals.[32] Indeed, the ECJ has taken an early opportunity expressly to reject the proposition that the Protocol makes it a basic principle of EC law to safeguard animal welfare. According to the court, 'it is apparent from its very wording' that the Protocol 'does not lay down any well-defined general principle of Community law which is binding on the Community institutions'.[33]

The issue arose during the course of a challenge to a ban imposed by the Community on the use of routine preventative vaccination as a means of controlling foot-and-mouth disease, when it was argued before the court that 'there exists a general principle of Community law to the effect that, save in so far as may be necessary, animals are not to be exposed to pain or suffering and that their health and welfare are not to be impaired ("the principle of animal welfare")'. It was claimed that such a principle 'forms part of the collective legal consciousness and may be inferred from the intention expressed by the Member States and the Community in ratifying the [Council of Europe] Convention [for the Protection of Animals kept for Farming Purposes], from a 1987 resolution of the European Parliament, from various Community directives applying that principle and from the Protocol, which, according to Article 311 [T]EC, forms an integral part of Community law'. The effect of this purported principle of animal welfare, so it was said, was to require that all relevant EC legislation 'must be laid down and applied in such a way as to take account of the obligation to adopt adequate measures to

[31] House of Commons Agriculture Committee, *The Implications for UK Agriculture and EU Agricultural Policy of Trade Liberalization and the WTO Round* (2000) paras 46 and 47.
[32] See Ch 5, s A(4) above.
[33] *Jippes and Others v Minister van Landbouw, Natuurbeheer en Visserij,* Case 189/01 (ECJ, 12 July 2001).

avoid the exposure of animals to unnecessary pain or suffering and to prevent their health and welfare from being impaired'. While this would 'not preclude the adoption of measures which result in the exposure of animals to pain or the impairment of their welfare', such detrimental effects would have to be 'weighed against the objective pursued, bearing in mind the fundamental rule that animal health must not be impaired and that the aim pursued must not take precedence over animal welfare unless this can be justified'.[34]

The response of the ECJ was unequivocal. It rejected the contention that any such principle of animal welfare existed in EC law, either before the Protocol came into force, or since. The court emphasized that ensuring the welfare of animals did not form part of the objectives of either the TEC or the common agricultural policy; it was not possible to infer any principle of general application from the Council of Europe Convention; and, although there were various provisions in regulations, directives, and decisions referring to animal welfare, they did not contain any indication that the need to ensure animal welfare was to be regarded as a general principle of Community law. In the opinion of the court, the Protocol did not change this situation. Its effect was not to introduce any new principle into EC law, but rather (the court having 'held on several occasions that the interests of the Community include the health and protection of animals') 'to reinforce the [existing] obligation to take the health and protection of animals into consideration by providing that full regard must be had to the welfare requirements of animals' in the formulation and implementation of the Community's policies. Moreover, because it is expressly limited to four specific spheres of Community activity and it provides that the legislative and administrative provisions and customs of Member States must be respected as regards, in particular, religious rites, cultural traditions and regional heritage, this obligation is clearly not absolute. As the court observed, it recognizes 'that differences currently exist between the legislation of the respective Member States and the various sentiments harboured within those Member States'. As to the nature of the duty imposed by the Protocol to pay full regard to animal welfare, the court suggested the 'Fulfilment of that obligation can be verified, in particular, in the context of a review of the proportionality of the measure'.[35]

This general principle of EC law requires that 'measures adopted by Community institutions do not exceed the limits of what is appropriate and necessary in order to attain the objectives legitimately pursued by the legislation in question; when there is a choice between several appropriate measures recourse must be had to the least onerous, and the disadvantages caused must not be disproportionate to the aims pursued'. Thus, in reviewing the proportionality of a decision, 'the criterion to be applied is not whether the measure adopted . . . was the only one or the best one possible but whether it was manifestly inappropriate'.[36] Presumably, what constitutes action which is 'manifestly inappropriate' is to

---

[34] ibid, paras [48]-[51].   [35] ibid, paras [71]-[79].   [36] ibid, paras [81]-[83].

be assessed in this context by reference not only to the purpose of the particular measure, but also the differences mentioned above in the sentiments towards animal welfare which exist within the European Union. If this interpretation is correct, then the implication is that it remains relatively easy for those who are unsympathetic to higher standards of welfare to frustrate their implementation. Thus, the need to have regard to, and to campaign for the improvement of, the treatment and care of animals is as important today as it was when the likes of Richard Martin, Thomas Erskine, and John Lawrence took the initiative two centuries ago, but its focus now extends far beyond the traditional confines of Westminster.

Progress in securing adequate legal protection for animals may seem depressingly slow and frustratingly incomplete, but, however strongly held one's views may be, it requires evidence, time, and persuasion to take them forward. To seek to impose them where there is no consensus smacks of tyranny. 'There never yet was any truth or any principle so irresistibly obvious that all men believed it at once', wrote Thomas Paine. 'Time and reason co-operate with each other to the final establishment of any principle; and therefore those who may happen to be first convinced have not a right to persecute others, on whom conviction operates more slowly. The moral principle of revolutions is to instruct, not to destroy.'[37] There are long-standing issues to be addressed; long accepted practices will come to be challenged in the light of scientific development;[38] innovations such as organ transplantation and genetic engineering will pose new challenges; and, as human society continues inexorably to impinge on natural habitats, more attention will come to be focused on our responsibility for the welfare of wildlife, rather than, as at present, being derived 'unobtrusively, incidentally or accidentally from measures to conserve species'.[39] Much has been achieved since the pioneers of animal protection embarked on their unlikely and novel project. Much still remains to be done. 'Historically, the evolution of our society has been marked by increasing concern for the welfare of animals', the Brambell Committee reflected. 'It appears to us reasonable to anticipate a continuing development of concern for animal welfare and that conditions which appear to us tolerable today may come to be considered intolerable in the future.'[40]

[37] 'Dissertation on the First Principles of Government' (1975), reproduced in Foot, M and Kimnick, I (eds), *The Thomas Paine Reader* (1987) 469.

[38] Bateson, P and Bradshaw, E, 'Physiological effects of hunting red deer' (1997) 264 *Proceedings of the Royal Society* 1707.

[39] Harrop, SR, 'The Dynamics of Wild Animal Welfare Law' (1997) 9 Journal of Environmental Law 287.

[40] n 3 above, para 9.

Appendix 1: Animal Protection and Welfare Bills Introduced into Parliament, Sessions 1985/1986–2000/2001

Title of Bill	Government/Private Member's Bill	Progress
1985–1986		
Animal Welfare (Royal Commission)	Private Member's Bill	First Reading
Animals (Scientific Procedures)	**Government Bill**	**Completed**
Cruelty to Animals (Amendment)	Private Member's Bill	First Reading
Dog Fighting (Penalties)	Private Member's Bill	First Reading
Dog Fighting (Penalties) (No 2)	Private Member's Bill	First Reading
Dog Fighting (Penalties) (No 3)	Private Member's Bill	First Reading
Protection of Animals Act 1911 (Amendment)	Private Member's Bill	First Reading
Salmon	**Government Bill**	**Completed**
1986–1987		
Animals (Scotland)	**Private Member's Bill**	**Completed**
Deer	**Private Member's Bill**	**Completed**
Prevention of Cruelty to Animals	Private Member's Bill	First Reading
Protection of Animals (Penalties)	**Private Member's Bill**	**Completed**
Wildlife and Countryside Act (Protection of Birds) (Amendment)	Private Member's Bill	First Reading
1987–1988		
Horses, Ponies and Donkeys	Private Member's Bill	First Reading
Protection Against Cruel Tethering	**Private Member's Bill**	**Completed**
Protection of Animals (Amendment)	**Private Member's Bill**	**Completed**
Slaughter of Deer	Private Member's Bill	Second Reading
1988–1989		
Animal Protection	Private Member's Bill	First Reading
Ban of Useless Animal Experiments	Private Member's Bill	First Reading
Dangerous Dogs	**Private Member's Bill**	**Completed**
Hare Coursing	Private Member's Bill	First Reading
1989–1990		
Abolition of Deer Hunting	Private Member's Bill	First Reading
Abolition of Fox Hunting	Private Member's Bill	First Reading
Animals (Welfare in Transit)	Private Member's Bill	First Reading
Dogs	Private Member's Bill	First Reading
Hare Coursing (Abolition)	Private Member's Bill	First Reading
Performing Animals	Private Member's Bill	First Reading
Protection of Badger Setts	Private Member's Bill	Committee

1990–1991

Abolition of Deer Hunting	Private Member's Bill	First Reading
Badgers	**Private Member's Bill**	**Completed**
Badgers (Further Protection)	**Private Member's Bill**	**Completed**
Breeding of Dogs	**Private Member's Bill**	**Completed**
Dangerous Dogs	**Government Bill**	**Completed**
Dangerous Wild Animals Act 1976 (Amendment)	Private Member's Bill	First Reading
Deer	**Government Bill**	**Completed**
Hare Coursing	Private Member's Bill	Report
Pet Animals (Amendment)	Private Member's Bill	Second Reading
Pig Husbandry	Private Member's Bill	Report
Protection of Badgers	Private Member's Bill	First Reading
Trade Descriptions (Animal Testing)	Private Member's Bill	First Reading
Welfare of Animals at Slaughter	**Private Member's Bill**	**Completed**
Welfare of Calves (Export)	Private Member's Bill	First Reading
Wildlife and Countryside (Amendment)	**Private Member's Bill**	**Completed**
Zoo Animal Welfare	Private Member's Bill	First Reading

1991–1992

Animal Experimentation (Cosmetics)	Private Member's Bill	First Reading
Dog Control and Welfare	Private Member's Bill	Second Reading
Hare Coursing	Private Member's Bill	First Reading
Protection of Badgers	Government (Consolidation) Bill	Completed Lords; First Reading Commons
Wild Mammals (Protection)	Private Member's Bill	Second Reading

1992–1993

Animal Experimentation (Cosmetics)	Private Member's Bill	First Reading
Dog Control and Welfare	Private Member's Bill	Third Reading
Fox Hunting (Abolition)	Private Member's Bill	First Reading
Hare Coursing	Private Member's Bill	First Reading
Hare Coursing (No 2)	Private Member's Bill	First Reading
Protection of Animals (Scotland)	**Private Member's Bill**	**Completed**
Protection of Badgers	**Government (Consolidation) Bill**	**Completed**
Slaughterhouses	Private Member's Bill	First Reading
Welfare of Animals	Private Member's Bill	First Reading
Welfare of Animals at Markets	Private Member's Bill	First Reading

1993–1994

Dangerous Dogs (Amendment)	Private Member's Bill	Completed Lords; First Reading Commons
Dog Control and Welfare	Private Member's Bill	Second Reading
Hare Coursing	Private Member's Bill	First Reading

Protection of Dogs	Private Member's Bill	Second Reading
Stray Dogs	Private Member's Bill	First Reading

1994–1995

Animal Health (European Law)	Private Member's Bill	First Reading
Dangerous Dogs (Amendment)	Private Member's Bill	Third Reading
Eradication of Mink	Private Member's Bill	First Reading
Pet Animal Welfare	Private Member's Bill	First Reading
Protection of Animals	Private Member's Bill	First Reading
Protection of Animals (Amendment)	Private Member's Bill	First Reading
Protection of Calves (Export)	Private Member's Bill	First Reading
Transport of Animals for Slaughter	Private Member's Bill	Second Reading
Welfare of Calves (Export)	Private Member's Bill	First Reading
Wild Mammals (Protection)	Private Member's Bill	Completed Commons; Third Reading Lords

1995–1996

Dangerous Dogs (Amendment)	Private Member's Bill	Completed Lords; First Reading Commons
Deer (Amendment) (Scotland)	**Government Bill**	**Completed**
Deer (Scotland)	**Government (Consolidation) Bill**	**Completed**
Intensive Husbandry (Review)	Private Member's Bill	First Reading
Quarantine	Private Member's Bill	First Reading
Welfare of Broiler Chickens	Private Member's Bill	First Reading
Wildlife	Private Member's Bill	Completed Commons; First Reading Lords
Wild Mammals (Protection)	**Private Member's Bill**	**Completed**

1996–1997

Birds (Registration Charges)	**Government Bill**	**Completed**
Breeding and Sale of Dogs	Private Member's Bill	First Reading
Dangerous Dogs (Amendment)	**Private Member's Bill**	**Completed**
Dogs (Electric Shock Collars)	Private Member's Bill	First Reading
Great Apes (Prohibition of Experiments)	Private Member's Bill	First Reading
Welfare of Broiler Chickens	Private Member's Bill	Completed Lords; First Reading Commons

1997–1998

Animal Health (Amendment)	**Private Member's Bill**	**Completed**
Breeding and Sale of Dogs	Private Member's Bill	Committee
Farming of Animals for Fur (Prohibition)	Private Member's Bill	First Reading
Hare Coursing	Private Member's Bill	First Reading
Pet Ownership (Residential and Sheltered Accommodation)	Private Member's Bill	First Reading

Protection of Animals (Amendment)	Private Member's Bill	First Reading
Reform of Quarantine Regulations	Private Member's Bill	First Reading
Registration of Dogs	Private Member's Bill	First Reading
Welfare of Broiler Chickens	Private Member's Bill	First Reading
Welfare of Pigs	Private Member's Bill	First Reading
Welfare of Pigs (No 2)	Private Member's Bill	First Reading
Wild Mammals (Hunting with Dogs)	Private Member's Bill	Report
Wildlife	Private Member's Bill	First Reading

1998–1999

Animal Welfare (Prohibition of Imports)	Private Member's Bill	First Reading
Breeding and Sale of Dogs (Welfare)	**Private Member's Bill**	**Completed**
Fur Farming (Prohibition)	Private Member's Bill	Committee
Hare Coursing	Private Member's Bill	First Reading
Transport of Farm Animals	Private Member's Bill	First Reading
Use of Antibiotics in Farm Animals	Private Member's Bill	First Reading

1999–2000

Export of Farm Animals	Private Member's Bill	Second Reading
Fur Farming (Prohibition)	**Government Bill**	**Completed**
Hare Coursing	Private Member's Bill	First Reading
Marine Wildlife Protection	Private Member's Bill	First Reading
Pet Animals Act 1951 (Amendment)	Private Member's Bill	First Reading
Protection of Animals (Amendment)	**Private Member's Bill**	**Completed**
Welfare of Broiler Chickens	Private Member's Bill	First Reading
Welfare of Racing Greyhounds	Private Member's Bill	First Reading
Wild Animals (Hunting with Dogs)	Private Member's Bill	Second Reading
Zoo Licensing (Amendment)	Private Member's Bill	First Reading

2000–2001

Hunting	Government Bill	Completed Commons; Secondary Reading Lords
Transport of Farm Animals	Private Member's Bill	First Reading
Wild Mammals (Protection) (Amendment)	Private Member's Bill	Second Reading

---

Source: *House of Commons Sessional Information Digest* (London: HMSO/Stationery Office, published annually).

The third column indicates the stage in the legislative process reached by the Bill before it was lost, ran out of time, or was withdrawn. Bills in heavy type indicate those which successfully completed the legislative procedure and became Acts of Parliament

Appendix 2: Prosecutions

Table 1
The number of prosecutions for cruelty to livestock in England and Wales taken by MAFF and the Welsh Office between 1985 and 1993 under the Protection of Animals Acts 1911 to 1988 and the Agriculture (Miscellaneous Provisions) Act 1968

1985	2
1986	6
1987	8
1988	6
1989	4
1990	5
1991	0
1992	6
1993	2

Source: HC Debs, 5 July 1994, col 140 (WA)

Table 2
Number of prosecutions brought by the police for offences relating to animal welfare by result, England and Wales 1991, 1992, and 1994

	1991		1992		1994*	
	police pros.	conv.	police pros.	conv.	police pros.	conv.
Total offences of cruelty to animals	437	326	475	367	284	204
Animals (Scientific Procedures Act) 1986, ss 22(3), 23, & 25(3)	1	1	3	2	2	2
Protection of Animals Act 1911, as amended	337	254	359	283	217	160
Wildlife & Countryside Act 1981, s 8	0	0	4	4	0	0
Performing Animals (Regulation) Act 1925	0	0	0	0	0	0
Protection of Animals (Cruelty to Dogs) Act 1933	10	7	5	4		
Protection of Animals Act 1934	1	1	0	0	1	1

	1991		1992		1994*	
	police pros.	conv.	police pros.	conv.	police pros.	conv.
Docking and Nicking of Horses Act 1949						
Pet Animals Act 1951	2	0	2	0	2	1
Cockfighting Act 1952						
Protection of Animals (Amendment) Act 1954	10	5	10	9	11	9
Animal Health Act 1981, ss 40–42, 46, 49 and Orders under ss 8, 9, 37, 38, 39, and 43	24	19	24	19	5	1
Slaughterhouses Act 1974	0	0	0	0	0	0
Abandonment of Animals Act 1960, s 1	19	16	26	22	6	3
Animals (Cruel Poisons) Act 1962						
Animal Boarding Establishments Act 1963	4	3	1	1	0	0
Riding Establishments Acts 1964 and 1970	0	0	0	0	0	0
Slaughter of Poultry Act 1976						
Agriculture (Miscellaneous Provisions) Act 1968, ss 1, 2, and 6	1	1	2	2	2	1
Protection of Badgers Act 1973	19	12	32	16	32	22
Wildlife and Countryside Act 1981, s 9	2	0	3	3	4	2
Wildlife and Countryside Act 1981, s 11	4	4	1	1	2	2
Breeding of Dogs Acts 1973 and 1991					0	0
Diseases of Animals Act	47	31	27	15	10	9
Wild Birds Protection Acts	76	63	62	43	49	32
Other	3	3	3	1		

Source: HC Debs, 8 March 1994, col 177 (WA)
          HC Debs, 18 June 1996, col 386 (WA)

Table 3
RSPCA Prosecution Statistics

	1995	1996	1997	1998	1999
Complaints investigated	110,175	101,751	117,332	124,374	132,021
Prosecutions*	812	790	872	853	701
Convictions*	2,201	2,282	2,650	3,114	2,719

* One prosecution may include several convictions

Table 4
SSPCA cases reported to procurator fiscal with a view to prosecution

1990: 160	1991:167	1992:156	1993:106	1994:129
1995: n/a	1996:97	1997:95	1998:89	1999:79

Because of delays in the Scottish courts, the SSPCA has adopted a policy of only lodging the most serious cases with the procurator fiscal

Table 5
Cases dealt with by the courts following referral to the procurator fiscal by the SSPCA

1995	1996	1997	1998	1999
100	100	75	60	60

Apparent discrepancies between the figures in Table 4 are due to the fact that a case will not necessarily come before the courts in the same year that it was reported to the procurator fiscal

Table 6

Total number of prosecutions at the magistrates courts and convictions at all courts for offences relating to the welfare of animals, England and Wales, 1989–1999 (1999 data are provisional)

	1989	1990	1991	1992	1993	1994	1995	1996	1997	1998	1999
Pet Animals Act 1951											
Prosecutions	9	9	10	23	9	13	7	5	4	7	10
Convictions	6	6	6	18	8	12	6	5	4	6	9
Breeding of Dogs Act 1973											
Prosecutions	3	11	11	23	5	2	1	4	4	4	5
Convictions	2	10	9	18	3	2	1	4	3	4	4
Breeding of Dogs Act 1991											
Prosecutions	n/a————————————————————————n/a								1	1	0
Convictions	n/a————————————————————————n/a								1	0	0
Performing Animals (Regulation) Act 1925 and 1968											
Prosecutions	—	1	—	—	1	—	—	—	—	—	—
Convictions	—	1	—	—	—	—	—	—	—	—	—
Wild Mammals (Protection) Act 1996											
Prosecutions									7	8	—
Convictions									3	7	—
Protection of Animals Act 1911 (including Protection Against Cruel Tethering Act 1988)											
Prosecutions	1,050	1,167	1,202	1,154	1,084	908	927	967	1,051	1,107	1,051
Convictions	895	968	862	926	861	731	754	764	867	889	828
Protection of Animals (Amendment) Act 1954											
Prosecutions	17	21	39	29	39	33	18	18	34	23	23
Convictions	17	21	30	26	33	27	17	16	30	20	19
Abandonment of Animals Act 1960											
Prosecutions	51	52	47	62	53	21	18	25	26	36	17
Convictions	44	41	41	54	38	16	13	19	21	26	12
Protection of Badgers Act 1992											
Prosecutions									44	19	30
Convictions									25	4	10

HC Debs, 28 July 2000, col 1135 (WA)

Bibliography

Select Website Addresses

Increasingly, legislation, court decisions, and official documents are available on the World Wide Web. Relevant websites include:

Act of UK Parliament	www.hmso.gov.uk/act
British and Irish Legal Information Institute	www.bailii.org
Convention on International Trade in Endangered Species of Flora and Fauna	www.cites.org
Council of Europe	www.coe.int
Department for the Environment, Food and Rural Affairs:	www.defra.gov.uk
Department of the Environment, Transport and the Regions	see www.defra.gov.uk
Eurogroup for Animal Welfare	www.eurogroupanimalwelfare.org
European Commission	http://eu.int/comm/index_en.htm
European Community legislation	http://europa.eu.int/eur-lex/en/index
European Court of Justice	http://europa.eu.int/cj/en/index
European Union	http://europa.eu.int
Home Office	www.homeoffice.gov.uk
Ministry of Agriculture, Fisheries and Food	see www.defra.gov.uk
National Assembly of Wales	www.wales.gov.uk
Scottish Executive	www.scotland.gov.uk
Scottish legislation	www.scotland-legislation.hmso.gov.uk
Scottish Parliament	www.scottish.parliament.uk
Statutory Instruments	www.hmso.gov.uk/stat
UK Government	www.ukonline.gov.uk
UK Parliament	www.parliament.uk
World Trade Organization	www.wto.org

In the interests of uniformity, the citation of all journal articles is provided in the following form: Author(s); Title; Year of Publication; Volume (where appropriate); Journal; Page Number.

Animal Procedures Committee, *Annual Report* (London: HMSO/Stationery Office, published annually)

Anon, 'Regulation—the way forward for veterinary nurses' (2000) 147 *Veterinary Record* 495

Appleby, MC, 'Tower of Babel: Variation in Ethical Approaches, Concepts of Welfare and Attitudes to Genetic Manipulation' (1999) 8 *Animal Welfare* 381

—— *What Should We Do About Animal Welfare* (Oxford: Blackwell Science, 1999)

Ashworth, Andrew, *Principles of Criminal Law* (Oxford: Clarendon Press, 3rd edn, 1999)

Association of British Dogs' Homes, *Code of Practice for Animal Rescue Organizations Caring for Cats and Dogs* (London: Association of British Dogs' Homes, nd)

Association of Veterinary Teachers and Research Workers, *Guidelines for the Recognition and Assessment of Pain in Animals* (South Mimms: Universities Federation for Animal Welfare, 1989)

Banner, Michael (Chairman), *Report of the Committee to Consider the Ethical Implications of Emerging Technologies in the Breeding of Farm Animals* (London: HMSO, 1995)

Barnard, CJ, and Hurst, JL, 'Welfare by design: the natural selection of welfare criteria' (1996) 5 *Animal Welfare* 405

Barrett, Paul H et al (eds), *Charles Darwin's Notebooks, 1836–1844* (Ithaca: Cornell University Press, 1987)

Bateson, Patrick and Bradshaw, Elizabeth, 'Physiological effects of hunting red deer' (1997) 264 *Proceedings of the Royal Society* 1707

Baxter, MR, 'The welfare problems of laying hens in battery cages' (1994) 134 *Veterinary Record* 614

Beattie, VE, Walker, N, and Sneddon, IA, 'Effects of environmental enrichment on behaviour and productivity of growing pigs' (1995) 4 *Animal Welfare* 207

Bentham, Jeremy, *An Introduction to the Principles of Morals and Legislation* (1789), edited by Burns, JH and Hart, HLA (London: Athlone Press, 1970)

Blackstone, William, *Commentaries on the Laws of England. A Facsimile of the First Edition of 1765–1769* (Chicago: University of Chicago Press, 1979)

Blythe, Ronald, *Akenfield. Portrait of an English Village* (London: Allen Lane, 1969)

Bowring, John (ed), *The Works of Jeremy Bentham* (Edinburgh: William Tait, 1843) Vol 2

—— (ed), *The Works of Jeremy Bentham* (Edinburgh: William Tait, 1843) Vol 10

—— *The Works of Jeremy Bentham* (Edinburgh: William Tait, 1859 edn) Vol 1

Brambell, FWR (Chairman), *Report of the Technical Committee to Enquire into the Welfare of Animals Kept Under Intensive Husbandry Systems*, Cmnd 2836 (London: HMSO, 1965)

British Veterinary Association, *Guidance: Model Conditions for Local Authorities and Their Authorized Officers and Veterinary Inspectors for the Licensing of Dog Breeding Establishments* (London: BVA, 2000)

Broom, DM, 'Indicators of poor welfare' (1986) 142 *British Veterinary Journal* 524

—— 'Ethical Dilemmas in Animal Usage' in Paterson, D and Palmer, M (eds), *The Status of Animals* (Wallingford, UK: CAB International, 1989)

—— 'Animal Welfare: Concepts and Management' (1991) 69 *Journal of Animal Science* 4167

—— and Johnson, KG, *Stress and Animal Welfare* (London: Chapman and Hall, 1993)

Brooman, S and Legge, D, *Law Relating to Animals* (London: Cavendish Publishing, 1997)

Brophy, Brigid, 'The Rights of Animals', *Sunday Times*, 10 October 1965

Burns, Lord (Chairman), *Report of the Committee of Inquiry into Hunting with Dogs in England and Wales*, Cm 4763 (London: Stationery Office, 2000)

Burton, Geo, *Chronology of Stamford* (Stamford: Robert Bagley, 1846)

Camm, Tara and Bowles, David, 'Animal Welfare and the Treaty of Rome—A legal analysis of the protocol on animal welfare and welfare standards in the European Union' (2000) 12 *Journal of Environmental Law* 197

Campbell, John Lord, *Lives of the Lord Chancellors*, Vols VIII and IX (London: John Murray, 1857)

Cannon, WB, *The Wisdom of the Body* (London: Kegan Paul, 1974)

Carruthers, Peter, *The Animal Issue* (Cambridge: Cambridge University Press, 1992)

Catholic Church, *Catechism of the Catholic Church* (London: Geoffrey Chapman, 1994)

Charity Commissioners for England and Wales, *Political Activity and Campaigning by Charities* (London: Charity Commission, 1995)

Charnovitz, Steve, 'The Moral Exception in Trade Policy' (1998) 38 Virginia Journal of International Law 689

Circus Working Group, *A Report into the welfare of circus animals in England and Wales* (Horsham: RSPCA, 1998)

Clark, Roland W, *The Survival of Charles Darwin: A Biography of a Man and an Idea* (New York: Random House, 1984)

Clark, Stephen RL, *The Moral Status of Animals* (Oxford: Clarendon Press, 1977)

—— 'Ethical Problems in Animal Welfare' in Clark, Stephen RL, *Animals and their Moral Standing* (London: Routledge, 1997)

—— 'Utility, Rights and the Domestic Virtues' in Clark, Stephen RL, *Animals and their Moral Standing* (London: Routledge, 1997)

Clarke, Paul AB and Linzey, Andrew (eds), *Political Theory and Animal Rights* (London: Pluto Press, 1990)

Clarke, Peter, *Hope and Glory. Britain 1900–1990* (Harmondsworth: Allen Lane/The Penguin Press, 1996)

Colley, Linda, *Britons. Forging the Nation 1707–1837* (London: Vintage, 1996)

Commission of the European Communities, 'Background Report: Animal Welfare', 11 October 1993

—— *Report from the Commission to the Council and the European Parliament on the experience acquired by Member States since the implementation of Council Directive 95/29/EC amending Directive 91/628/EC concerning the protection of animals during transport*, COM (2000) 809 Final (Brussels, 2000)

Conservative Political Centre, *Animal Welfare* (London: CPC, 1994)

Cooper, ME, *An Introduction to Animal Law* (London: Academic Press, 1987)

Crown Prosecution Service, *The Code for Crown Prosecutors* (London: CPS, 2000)

Darwin, Charles, *The Origin of Species* (1859) (Beer, Gillian (ed), Oxford: Oxford University Press, 1996)

—— *The Descent of Man* (1871) (London: John Murray, 2nd edn, 1874)

Dawkins, Marian Stamp, *Animal Suffering. The Science of Animal Welfare* (London: Chapman and Hall, 1980)

—— 'From an animal's point of view: Motivation, fitness and animal welfare' (1990) 13 *Behavioural and Brain Sciences* 1

—— *Through Our Eyes Only? The search for animal consciousness* (Oxford: WH Freeman, 1993)

Defoe, Daniel, *A Tour Through the Whole Island of Great Britain* (1724–6) (Harmondsworth: Penguin Books, 1971)

DeGrazia, David, *Taking animals seriously. Mental life and moral status* (Cambridge: Cambridge University Press, 1996) de Montmorency, JEG, 'State Protection of Animals at Home and Abroad' (1902) 18 Law Quarterly Review 31

Dennett, Daniel C, *Darwin's Dangerous Idea. Evolution and the Meanings of Life* (Harmondsworth: Penguin Books, 1996)

Department of the Environment, *Wildlife Crime: A Guide to Wildlife Law Enforcement in the UK* (London: Stationery Office, 1996)

Department of the Environment, Transport and the Regions, *Review of the Operation of the Zoo Licensing Act 1981* (London: DETR, 1997)

—— *Dog Identification Group Report* (London: DETR, 2000)

—— *Secretary of State's Standards of Modern Zoo Practice* (London: DETR, 2000)

Desmond, Adrian and Moore, James, *Darwin* (Harmondsworth: Penguin Books, 1992)

Devlin, Patrick, *The Enforcement of Morals* (Oxford: Oxford University Press, 1965)

Dicey, AV, *An Introduction to the Study of the Law of the Constitution* (Basingstoke: Macmillan, 10th edn, 1959)

Duncan, Ian JH and Fraser, David, 'Understanding Animal Welfare' in Appleby, Michael C and Hughes, Barry O (eds), *Animal Welfare* (Wallingford, UK: CAB International, 1997)

Dunlop, Robert H and Williams, David J, *Veterinary Medicine. An Illustrated History* (St Louis, Missouri: Mosby, 1996)

Eurogroup for Animal Welfare, *Report of the 139th Session of the European Parliamentary Intergroup on the Welfare and Conservation of Animals* (Brussels, 1997)

European Parliament, Report of the Committee on Agriculture, Fisheries and Food on animal welfare policy, Rapporteur: Mr Richard J Simmonds, 19 January 1987, A2-211/86

—— Report of the Committee on the Environment, Public Health and Consumer Protection on animal welfare and the status of animals in the Community, Rapporteur: Mr Gianfranco Amendola, 13 November 1991, A3-0321/91

—— Report of the Committee on the Environment, Public Health and Consumer Protection on the welfare and status of animals in the Community, Rapporteur: Mr Gianfranco Amendola, 3 January 1994, A3-0003/94

Evans, EP, *The Criminal Prosecution and Capital Punishment of Animals* (London: Heinemann, 1906)

Ewbank, R, 'Stress: a General Overview' in Phillips, Clive and Piggins, David (eds), *Farm Animals and the Environment* (Wallingford, Oxon: CAB International, 1992)

—— 'Animal Welfare' in Ewbank, R, Kim-Madslien, and Hart, CB (eds), *Management and Welfare of Farm Animals. The UFAW Farm Handbook* (Wheathampstead, UK: UFAW, 4th edn, 1999)

Fairholme, Edward G and Pain, Wellesley, *A Century of Work for Animals. The History of the RSPCA, 1824–1924* (London: John Murray, 1924)

Farm Animal Welfare Council, *Report on the Animal Welfare Implications of the Harvesting of Deer Antlers in Velvet* (Surbiton: FAWC, 1980)

—— *Advice to the Agriculture Ministers of Great Britain on the Need to Control Certain Mutilations of Farm Animals* (Surbiton: FAWC, 1981)

—— *Report on the Welfare of Poultry at the Time of Slaughter* (Surbiton: FAWC, 1982)

—— *Report on the Welfare of Livestock (Red Meat Animals) at the Time of Slaughter* (Surbiton: FAWC, 1984)

—— *Report on the Welfare of Farmed Deer* (Surbiton: FAWC, 1985)

—— *Report on the Welfare of Livestock when Slaughtered by Religious Methods* (Surbiton: FAWC, 1985)

—— *Report on the Welfare of Turkeys* (Surbiton: FAWC, 1985)

—— *An Assessment of Egg Production Systems* (Surbiton: FAWC, 1986)

—— *Report on the Welfare of Livestock at Markets* (Surbiton: FAWC, 1986)

—— *Advice to Agricultural Ministers on Transportation of Unfit Animals* (Surbiton: FAWC, 1988)

—— *Assessment of Pig Production Systems* (Surbiton: FAWC, 1988)

—— *Advice to Ministers on the Handling and Transport of Poultry* (Surbiton: FAWC, 1990)

—— *Report of the Enforcement Working Group* (Surbiton: FAWC, 1990)

—— *Report on the European Commission Proposals on the Transport of Animals* (Surbiton: FAWC, 1991)

—— *Report on the Welfare of Laying Hens in Colony Systems* (Surbiton: FAWC, 1991)

—— *Guidelines on the Welfare of Farmed Ostriches* (Surbiton: FAWC, 1993)

—— *Report on Priorities for Animal Welfare Research and Development* (Surbiton: MAFF, 1993)

—— *Report on the Welfare of Sheep* (London: FAWC, 1994)

—— *Report on the Welfare of Farmed Fish* (Surbiton: FAWC, 1996)

—— *Report on the Welfare of Pigs Kept Outdoors* (Surbiton: FAWC, 1996)

—— *Report on the Welfare of Dairy Cattle* (Surbiton: FAWC, 1997)

—— *Report on the Welfare of Laying Hens* (Surbiton: FAWC, 1997)

—— *Report on the Implications of Cloning for the Welfare of Farmed Livestock* (Surbiton: FAWC, 1998)

—— *Report on the Welfare of Broiler Breeders* (Surbiton: FAWC, 1998)

—— *Advice to Ministers on the Enforcement of Animal Welfare Legislation* (Surbiton: FAWC, 1999)

—— *Annual Review 1998* (Surbiton: FAWC, 1999)

—— *Annual Review 1999/2000* (London: FAWC, 2000)

Favre, DS, 'Movement toward an international convention for the protection of animals— the further adventures of four rabbits' in Blackman, DE, Humphreys, PN, and Todd, P (eds), *Animal Welfare and the Law* (Cambridge: Cambridge University Press, 1989)

—— 'Equitable Self-Ownership for Animals' (2000) 50 Duke Law Journal 473

Fletcher, Ronald (ed), *John Stuart Mill: A Logical Critique of Sociology* (London: Michael Joseph, 1971)

Foot, Michael and Kramnick, Isaac (eds), *The Thomas Paine Reader* (Harmondsworth: Penguin Books, 1987)

Francione, Gary L, *Animals, Property and the Law* (Philadelphia: Temple University Press, 1995)

—— *Rain Without Thunder. The Ideology of the Animal Rights Movement* (Philadelphia: Temple University Press, 1996)

Fraser, AF and Broom, DM, *Farm Animal Behaviour and Welfare* (London: Baillière Tindall, 3rd edn, 1990)

Fraser, D, 'Science, values and animal welfare: exploring the "inextricable connection"' (1995) 4 *Animal Welfare* 103

—— and Duncan, IJH, '"Pleasures", "Pains" and Animal Welfare: Toward a Natural History of Affect' (1998) 7 *Animal Welfare* 383

Fraser, D, Weary, DM, Pajor, EA, and Milligan, BN, 'A scientific conception of animal welfare that reflects ethical concerns' (1997) 6 *Animal Welfare* 187

Freeman, Edward A, 'The Morality of Field Sports' (1869) 34 (new series) *The Fortnightly Review* 353

French, Richard D, *Antivivisection and Medical Science in Victorian Society* (Princeton: Princeton University Press, 1975)

Frey, RG, *Interests and Rights* (Oxford: Oxford University Press, 1980)

—— *Rights, Killing and Suffering* (Oxford: Blackwell, 1983)

Garner, Robert, *Animals, politics and morality* (Manchester: Manchester University Press, 1993)

—— *Political Animals. Animal Protection Politics in Britain and the United States* (Basingstoke: Macmillan Press, 1998)

Gentle, MJ, 'Pain in Birds' (1992) 1 *Animal Welfare* 235

George, Dorothy M, *London Life in the Eighteenth Century* (1925) (Harmondsworth: Peregrine Books, republished 1966)

Gilmour, Ian, *Riots, Risings and Revolution. Governance and Violence in Eighteenth-Century England* (London: Hutchinson, 1992)

Godlovitch, Stanley, Godlovitch, Roslind, and Harris, John (eds), *Animals Men and Morals* (London: Gollancz, 1971)

Gompertz, Lewis, *Moral Inquiries on the Situation of Man and of Brutes* (London, 1824)

Gregory, NG and Constantine, E, 'Hyperthermia in Dogs Left in Cars' (1996) 139 *Veterinary Record* 349

Griffith, JAG, 'The Political Constitution' (1979) 42 Modern Law Review 1

Habig, Marion A (ed), *St Francis of Assisi. Writings and Early Biographies. English Omnibus of the Sources for the Life of St Francis* (Chicago, Illinois: Franciscan Herald Press, 1983, Fourth Revised Edition)

Haldane, ARB, *The Drove Roads of Scotland* (1952) (Isle of Colonsay, Argyll: House of Lochar, republished 1995)

Hall, Sherwin A, 'The Struggle for the Charter of the Royal College of Veterinary Surgeons, 1844' (1994) 134 *Veterinary Record* 536

Halsbury's Laws of England, Vol 2 (London: Butterworths, 4th edn, reissue, 1991)

Hansard Society for Parliamentary Government, *Making the Law. The Report of The Hansard Society Commission on the Legislative Process* (London: Hansard Society, 1992)

Harrison, Brian, *Peaceable Kingdom. Stability and Change in Modern Britain* (Oxford: Clarendon Press, 1982)

Harrison, Ruth, *Animal Machines* (London: Vincent Stuart Ltd, 1964)

Harrop, Stuart R, 'The Dynamics of Wild Animal Welfare Law' (1997) 9 Journal of Environmental Law 287

—— 'The trapping of wild mammals and attempts to legislate for animal suffering in international standards' (2000) 12 Journal of Environmental Law 333

—— 'Challenges and Dilemmas Faced by Conservation and Animal Welfare Charities Who Both Enforce the Law and Press for Charges' in Dunn, A (ed), *The Voluntary Sector, The State and the Law* (Oxford: Hart Publishing, 2000)

—— and Bowles, D, 'Wildlife Management, the Multilateral Trade Regime, Morals and the Welfare of Animals' (1998) 1 Journal of International Wildlife Law and Policy 64

Hart, HLA, *The Concept of Law* (Oxford: Clarendon Press, 2nd edn, 1994)

Hill, George Birkbeck (ed), *Boswell's Life of Johnson* (Oxford: Clarendon Press, 1934) Vol 1

Hollands, Clive, *Compassion is the Bugler. The Struggle for Animal Rights* (Edinburgh: Macdonald, 1980)

Home Office, *Code of Practice for the Housing and Care of Animals used in Scientific Procedures*, HC 107 (London: HMSO, 1989)

—— *Guidance on the Operation of the Animals (Scientific Procedures) Act 1986*, HC 182 (London: HMSO, 1990)

—— *Code of Practice for the Housing and Care of Animals in Designated Breeding and Supplying Establishments*, HC 125 (London: HMSO, 1995)

—— *The Humane Killing of Animals under Schedule 1 to the Animals (Scientific Procedures) Act 1986. Code of Practice* (London: HMSO, 1997)

—— *The Ethical Review Process* (London: Home Office, 1998)

—— *Guidance on the Operation of the Animals (Scientific Procedures) Act 1986*, HC 321 (London: Stationery Office, 2000)

—— 'Animal Rights Extremism. Government Strategy. A Consultation Document' (London: Home Office, 2001)

—— *Statistics of Scientific Procedures on Living Animals. Great Britain* (London: HMSO/Stationery Office, published annually)

Hood, Christopher, Baldwin, Robert, and Rothstein, Henry, 'Assessing the DDA: when does a regulatory law fail?' [2000] Public Law 282

Houghton, Lord, 'Animals and the Law: Moral and Political Issues' in Paterson, David and Ryder, Richard D, *Animals' Rights—A Symposium* (Fontwell: Centaur Press, 1979)

House of Commons Agriculture Committee, *Animal Welfare in Poultry, Pig and Veal Calf Production*, HC 406 (London: HMSO, 1981)

House of Commons Agriculture Committee, *Animals in Transit*, HC 45 (London: HMSO, 1991)

—— *The UK Poultry Industry*, HC 67 (London: HMSO, 1994)

—— *Health Controls on the Importation of Live Animals*, HC 347 (London: HMSO, 1994)

—— *The UK Pig Industry*, HC 87 (London: Stationery Office, 1999)

—— *Badgers and Bovine Tuberculosis*, HC 233 (London: Stationery Office, 1999)

—— *The Implications for UK Agriculture and EU Agricultural Policy of Trade Liberalization and the WTO Round*, HC 246 (London: Stationery Office, 2000)

—— *The Government's Proposals for Organophosphate Sheep Dips*, HC 425 (London: Stationery Office, 2000)

—— *Badgers and Bovine Tuberculosis*, HC 92 (London: Stationery Office, 2001)

—— *Organic Farming*, HC 149 (London: Stationery Office, 2001)

House of Commons Environment Committee, *London Zoo*, Cm 427 (London: HMSO, 1991)

—— *World Trade and the Environment*, HC 149 (London: HMSO, 1996)

House of Commons Home Affairs Committee, *The Operation of the Dangerous Dogs Act 1991*, HC 146 (London: HMSO, 1996)

House of Lords Select Committee on Science and Technology, *Resistance to Antibiotics and Other Antimicrobial Agents*, HL 81 (London: HMSO, 1998)

—— *Resistance to Antibiotics* (London: Stationery Office, 2001)

Hughes, BO, 'Behaviour as an index of welfare', *Proceedings 5th European Poultry Conference, Malta* II: 1005

Humane Slaughter Association, *Annual Report 1998–99* (Wheathampstead, Hertfordshire: HSA, 1999)

Hume, David, *Commentaries on the Law of Scotland, Respecting Crimes* (Edinburgh: Bell and Bradfute, 1844)

Jenkins, Simon, 'Persuade, don't outlaw', *The Times*, 23 October 1993

Kean, Hilda, *Animal Rights. Political and Social Change in Britain since 1800* (London: Reaktion Books, 1998)

Kelch, Thomas G, 'Toward a Non-Property Status for Animals' (1998) New York University Environmental Law Journal 531

Kennedy, Ian (Chairman), Report of the Advisory Group of Quarantine: *Quarantine and Rabies: A Reappraisal* (London: MAFF, 1998)

Kennedy, JS, *The New Anthropomorphism* (Cambridge: Cambridge University Press, 1992)

Kirkwood, JK, Sainsbury, AW, and Bennett, PM, 'The welfare of free-living wild animals: methods of assessment' (1994) 3 *Animal Welfare* 257

Kitchen, H, Aronson, AL, Bittle, JL, McPherson, CW, Morton, DB, and Pakes, SP, 'Panel report on the colloquium on recognition and alleviation of animal pain and distress' (1987) 191 *Journal of the American Veterinary Medical Association* 1186

Krebs, John (Chairman), *Bovine Tuberculosis in Cattle and Badgers. Report of the Independent Scientific Review Group* (London: MAFF, 1997)

Labour Party, *Who Cares?* (London: Labour Party, 1992)

—— *new life for animals* (*sic*) (London: Labour Party, 1996)

Langford, Paul, *A Polite and Commercial People. England 1727–1783* (Oxford: Oxford University Press, 1989)

Lawrence, John, 'On the Rights of Beasts' in *A Philosophical Treatise on Horses, and on the Moral Duties of Man towards the Brute Creation* (1796, 2nd edn, 1802); extracts from the second edition were reproduced as an Appendix in Nicholson, Edward Byron, *The Rights of an Animal: A New Essay in Ethics* (London: C Kegan Paul & Co, 1879)

Leahy, Michael, *Against Liberation* (London: Routledge, 1991)

Legood, Giles (ed), *Veterinary Ethics. An Introduction* (London: Continuum, 2000)

Liberal Democratic Party, *A Matter of Conscience* (London: Liberal Democrat Publications, 1992)

Linzey, Andrew, *Animal Theology* (London: SCM Press, 1994)

Littlewood, Sydney (Chairman), *Report of the Departmental Committee on Experimentation on Animals*, Cmnd 2641 (London: HMSO, 1965)

Local Government Association, British Veterinary Association, Chartered Institute of Environmental Health, Pet Care Trust, and the Ornamental Aquatic Trade Association Ltd, *The Pet Animals Act 1951. Model Standards for Pet Shop Licence Conditions* (London: LGA Publications, 1998)

Locke, John, *Two Treatises on Government* (1690), A Critical Edition with an Introduction and Apparatus Criticus by Peter Laslett (Cambridge: Cambridge University Press, 1964)

Lynam, Shevawn, *Humanity Dick. A Biography of Richard Martin, M.P. 1754–1834* (London: Hamish Hamilton, 1975)

MacDonald, Melody, *Caught in the Act. The Feldberg Investigation* (Oxford: Jon Carpenter, 1994)

McLynn, Frank, *Crime and Punishment in Eighteenth-Century England* (Oxford: Oxford University Press, 1991)

Main, DCJ and Green, LE, 'Descriptive analysis of the operation of the Farm Assured British Pigs Scheme' (2000) 147 *Veterinary Record* 162

Malcolmson, Robert W, *Popular Recreations in English Society 1700–1850* (Cambridge: CUP, 1973)

Manning, Aubrey and Dawkins, Marian Stamp, *An Introduction to Animal Behaviour* (Cambridge: CUP, 5th edn, 1998)

Marx, K, 'Theses on Feuerbach' in *Karl Marx, Frederick Engels, Collected Works* (Moscow: Progress Publishers, 1975 onwards) Vol 5

Mason, G and Mendl, M, 'Why is there no simple way of measuring animal welfare?' (1993) 2 *Animal Welfare* 301

Midgley, Mary, *Animals and Why They Matter* (Harmondsworth: Penguin, 1983)

Mill, John Stuart, *Principles of Political Economy* (London: John W Parker, 3rd edn, 1852)

—— *On Liberty* (1859) (Harmondsworth: Penguin, 1982)

Ministry of Agriculture, Fisheries and Food, *Animal Health. The Report of the Chief Veterinary Officer* (London: HMSO/Stationery Office, published annually)

—— *Code of recommendations for the welfare of livestock:*
Cattle (London: MAFF, 1983)
Pigs (London: MAFF, 1983)
Domestic Fowls (London: MAFF, 1987)
Ducks (London: MAFF, 1987)
Goats (London: MAFF, 1987)
Rabbits (London: MAFF, 1987)
Turkeys (London: MAFF, 1987)
Farmed Deer (London: MAFF, 1989)
Sheep (London: MAFF, 1989; revised edn 2000)

—— *Code of Practice for the Welfare of Animals in Livestock Markets* (London: MAFF, 1990)

—— *Code of Practice for the Welfare of Horses, Ponies and Donkeys at Markets, Sales and Fairs* (London: MAFF, 1990)

—— *Condition Scoring in Sheep* (London: MAFF, 1994)

—— *State Veterinary Service: service standards for the veterinary field and investigation services, including the code of practice on enforcement* (London: MAFF, 1994)

—— *The Welfare of Dogs and Cats in Quarantine Premises. Voluntary Code of Practice* (London: MAFF, 1995)

—— *An Explanatory Guide to the Welfare of Animals (Slaughter or Killing) Regulations 1995* (London: MAFF, 1996)

—— *Pig Space Requirements. Guidelines on Schedule 3 of the Welfare of Livestock Regulations 1994* (London: MAFF, 1997)

—— *Quarantine for Pets* (London: MAFF, 1997)

—— *Assessment of Practical Experience in the Handling, Transport and Care of Animals* (MAFF, 1998)

—— *Guidance on the Transport of Casualty Farm Animals* (London: MAFF, 1993; amended reprint 1998)

Ministry of Agriculture, Fisheries and Food, *Guidance on the Welfare of Animals (Transport) Order 1997* (1998)

—— 'Proposed revised pre-export procedures for sheep/pigs destined for fattening/production or slaughter in other EC member states' (Surbiton: MAFF, 1998)

—— *Strategy for the Protection of Animal Welfare at Livestock Markets* (London: MAFF, 1998)

—— 'Revised pre-export procedures for sheep/pigs destined for fattening/production or slaughter in other member states' (Surbiton: MAFF, 1999)

—— *The 1998 Strategy for the Protection of Animal Welfare at Livestock Markets: Report on SVS Assessment of Compliance* (London: MAFF, 1999)

Morris, PA and Warwick, H, 'A study of rehabilitated juvenile hedgehogs after release into the wild' (1994) 3 *Animal Welfare* 163

Moss, Arthur M, *Valiant Crusade. The History of the RSPCA* (London: Cassell, 1961)

Murray, KC, Davies, DH, Cullinane, SL, Eddison, JC, and Kirk, JA, 'Taking Lambs to the Slaughter: Marketing Channels, Journey Structures and Possible Consequences for Welfare' (2000) 9 *Animal Welfare* 111

National Farmers' Union, *Caring for Livestock. Report of the Animal Welfare Working Group* (London: NFU, 1995)

Nicholson, Edward Byron, *The Rights of an Animal. A New Essay in Ethics* (London: C Kegan Paul & Co, 1879)

Nollkaemper, André, 'The Legality of Moral Crusades Disguised in Trade Law: An analysis of the EC "ban" on furs from animals taken by leghold traps' (1996) 8 Journal of Environmental Law 237

Paine, Thomas, *The Rights of Man* (1791–2) (London: JM Dent, 1993)

Pattison, Iain, *The British Veterinary Profession 1791–1948* (London: JA Allen, 1983)

Phillips, Lord (Chairman), *The BSE Inquiry: The Report* (15 volumes) (London: Stationery Office, 2000)

Polkinghorne, JC (Chairman), *Report of the Committee on the Ethics of Genetic Modification and Food Use* (London: HMSO, 1993)

Poole, TB, 'The nature and evolution of behavioural needs in mammals' (1992) 1 *Animal Welfare* 203

—— 'Natural behaviour is simply a question of survival' (1996) 5 *Animal Welfare* 218

Porter, Alastair, 'Veterinary Charters and Veterinary Statutes' (1994) 134 *Veterinary Record* 541

Porter, Roy, *English Society in the Eighteenth Century* (Harmondsworth: Penguin Books, 1982)

Primatt, Humphry, *The Duty of Mercy and the Sin of Cruelty to Brute Animals* (1776), republished 1992, edited by Richard D Ryder (Fontwell: Centaur Press)

Puppy Farming Working Group, *The commercial breeding and sale of dogs and puppies* (Puppy Farming Working Group, 1996)

Rachels, James, *Created from Animals* (Oxford: Oxford University Press, 1990)

Regan, Tom, *The Case for Animal Rights* (London: Routledge, 1983)

—— and Singer, Peter (eds), *Animal Rights and Human Obligations* (Englewood Cliffs, New Jersey: Prentice-Hall, 1976)

Ritvo, Harriet, *The Animal Estate. The English and Other Creatures in the Victorian Age* (Cambridge, Massachusetts: Harvard University Press, 1987)

Robertson, CPJ and Harris, S, 'The condition and survival after release of captive-reared fox cubs' (1995) 4 *Animal Welfare* 281

—— and —— 'The behaviour after release of captive-reared fox cubs' (1995) 4 *Animal Welfare* 295

Rodd, Rosemary, *Biology, Ethics and Animals* (Oxford: Clarendon Press, 1990)

Rousseau, Jean-Jacques, *Discourse on the Origins and Foundations of Inequality among Men* (1755) (Harmondsworth: Penguin Books, 1984)

Royal College of Veterinary Surgeons, *Guide to Professional Conduct* (London: RCVS, 2000)

Royal Commission on the Practice of Subjecting Live Animals to Experiments for Scientific Purposes, *Final Report* (London: HMSO, 1876)

Royal Commission on Vivisection (1906–12), *Final Report* (London: HMSO, 1912)

Royal Society for the Prevention of Cruelty to Animals, *Annual Review* (Horsham: RSPCA, published annually)

—— *Vivisection. The Royal Society for the Prevention of Cruelty to Animals and the Royal Commission* (London: Smith, Elder & Co, 2nd edn, 1879)

—— *Farm Animal Welfare* (Horsham: RSPCA, 1995)

—— *Agenda 2000. The future for farm animal welfare in the European Union?* (Horsham: RSPCA, 1998)

—— *Live animal transport in the UK* (Horsham: RSPCA, 1998)

—— *Home to Roost—the future for laying hens* (Horsham: RSPCA, 1999)

—— *Profit with principle. Animal welfare and UK pig farming* (Horsham: RSPCA, 2000)

Royal Society for the Prevention of Cruelty to Animals/Eurogroup for Animal Welfare, *Conflict or concord? Animal welfare and the World Trade Organisation* (Horsham: RSPCA, 1998)

——/—— *Food for Thought. Farm Animal Welfare and the WTO* (Horsham: RSPCA, 1999)

Royal Society for the Prevention of Cruelty to Animals et al, *The commercial breeding and sale of dogs and puppies* (jointly produced and published by the RSPCA, NCDL, BVA, KC, BSAVA) (1996)

—— et al, *Welfare of circus animals* (jointly produced and published by the Chartered Institute of Environmental Health, RSPCA, Association of Circus Proprietors of Great Britain, Wildlife Conservation Research Unit, BVA, and the Born Free Foundation) (Horsham: RSPCA, 1998)

Russell, WMS and Burch, RL, *The Principles of Humane Experimental Technique* (London: Methuen, 1959; reissued by UFAW, South Mimms, 1992)

Ryder, Richard D, *Victims of Science* (London: Davis-Poynter, 1975)

—— 'Putting Animals into Politics' in Garner, Robert (ed), *Animal Rights. The Changing Debate* (Basingstoke: Macmillan Press, 1996)

—— *Animal Revolution. Changing Attitudes towards Speciesism* (Oxford: Berg, 2nd edn, 2000)

Sainsbury, AW, Bennett, PM, and Kirkwood, JK, 'The welfare of free-living wild animals in Europe: harm caused by human activities' (1995) 4 *Animal Welfare* 183

Sainsbury, AW, Cunningham, AA, Morris, PA, Kirkwood, JK, and Macgregor, SK, 'Health and welfare of rehabilitated juvenile hedgehogs (*Erinaceus europaeus*) before and after release into the wild' (1996) 138 *Veterinary Record* 61

Salt, Henry, *Animals' Rights Considered in Relation to Social Progress* (1892; reissued 1980; London: Centaur Press)

Sanderson, Burdon J (ed), *Handbook for the Physiological Laboratory* (London: 1873, 2 vols)

Sandøe, P and Simonsen, HB, 'Assessing animal welfare: where does science end and philosophy begin?' (1992) 1 *Animal Welfare* 257

Sandys-Wynch, G, *Animal Law* (London: Shaw & Sons, 1984)

Sapontzis, Steven, *Morals, Reason and Animals* (Philadelphia: Temple University Press, 1987)

Scientific Committee on Animal Health and Animal Welfare, *Report on the Welfare Aspects of the Production of Foie Gras* (Brussels: Commission of the European Communities, 1998)

Scientific Committee on Animal Health and Animal Welfare, *The Welfare of Chickens Kept for Meat Production (Broilers)* (Brussels: Commission of the European Communities, 2000)

Scientific Veterinary Committee, *Report on the Transport of Farm Animals* (Brussels: Commission of the European Communities, 1992)

—— *Report on the Welfare of Calves* (Brussels: Commission of the European Communities, 1995)

—— *Report on the Welfare of Intensively Kept Pigs* (Brussels: Commission of the European Communities, 1997)

Scott Henderson, J (Chairman), *Report on Cruelty to Wild Animals*, Cmd 8266 (London: HMSO, 1951)

Scottish Office, *Scotland's Parliament*, Cm 3658 (London: Stationery Office, 1997)

Scottish Parliament, Rural Development Committee, *Stage 1 Report on the Protection of Wild Mammals (Scotland) Bill*, SP Paper 376 (Edinburgh: Stationery Office, 2001)

Scottish Society for the Prevention of Cruelty to Animals, *Annual Report* (Edinburgh: SSPCA, published annually)

—— (with Exotic Animal Services, University of Edinburgh, and the Pet Care Trust), 'A Code of Practice for Livestock Trading' (Edinburgh: SSPCA, nd)

Scruton, Roger, *Animal Rights and Wrongs* (London: Demos, 1996)

Select Committee on the Police of the Metropolis, *Parliamentary Papers*, 1822, (440) iv

Serpell, James, *In The Company of Animals. A Study of Human-Animal Relationships* (Cambridge: Canto/Cambridge University Press, 2nd edn, 1996)

Simmonds, Richard, 'The Role of the European Community' in Ryder (ed), *Animal Welfare and the Environment* (London: Duckworth, 1992)

Singer, Peter, *Animal Liberation* (London: Jonathan Cape, 1975; 2nd edn, 1990)

Smellie, William, *The Philosophy of Natural History* (Edinburgh, 1790)

Soros, George, *The Crisis in Global Capitalism. Open Society Endangered* (London: Little, Brown & Co, 1998)

Spinelli, JS and Markowitz, H, 'Clinical recognition and anticipation of situations likely to induce suffering in animals, (1987) 191 *Journal of the American Veterinary Medical Association* 1216

Stafleu, FR, Grommers, FJ, and Vorstenbosch, J, 'Animal welfare: evolution and erosion of a moral concept' (1996) 5 *Animal Welfare* 225

Storer, Tracy I and Usinger, Robert L, *General Zoology* (New York: McGraw-Hill, 4th edn, 1965)

Sweeney, Noël, *Animals and Cruelty and Law* (Bristol: Alibi, 1990)

Tannenbaum, Jerrold, 'Ethics and animal welfare: The inextricable connection' (1991) 198 *Journal of the American Veterinary Medical Association* 1360

—— 'Animals and the Law: Property, Cruelty, Rights' (1995) 62 *Social Research* 539

Taylor, Thomas, *A Vindication of the Rights of Brutes* (1792) (Gainesville, Florida: Scholars' Facsimiles & Reprints, 1966)

Termouw, EM Claudia, Schouten, Willem GP, and Ladewig, Jan, 'Physiology' in Appleby, Michael C and Hughes, Barry O (eds), *Animal Welfare* (Wallingford, UK: CAB International, 1997)

Tester, Keith, *Animals and Society. The Humanity of Animal Rights* (London: Routledge, 1991)

Thomas, Keith, *Man and the Natural World. Changing attitudes in England 1500–1800* (Harmondsworth: Penguin, 1984)

Thompson, EP, *Whigs and Hunters* (Harmondsworth: Penguin, 1990)

Thompson, Flora, *Lark Rise to Candleford* (1945) (Harmondsworth: Penguin Books, 1973)

Thornton, Peter, Morton, David, Main, David, Kirkwood, James, and Wright, Brian, 'Veterinary ethics: filling a gap in undergraduate education' (2001) 148 *Veterinary Record* 214

Todd, Pauline, 'The Protection of Animals Acts 1911–1964' in Blackman, DE, Humphreys, PN, and Todd, P, *Animal Welfare and the Law* (Cambridge: CUP, 1989)

Turner, ES, *All Heaven in a Rage* (1964, republished by the Centaur Press, Fontwell, 1992)

Veasey, JS, Waran, NK, and Young, RJ, 'On comparing the behaviour of zoo housed animals with wild conspecifics as a welfare indicator' (1996) 5 *Animal Welfare* 13

Vines, David, 'The WTO in Relation to the Fund and the Bank: Competencies, Agendas, and Linkages', in Krueger, Anne E (ed), *The WTO as an International Organization* (Chicago: University of Chicago Press, 1998)

Wallace, Alfred Russel, *The Malay Archipelago* (1869) (with an introduction by John Bastin, Oxford: Oxford University Press, 1986)

Webster, AJF, *Calf Husbandry, Health and Welfare* (London: Collins, 1984)

—— *Animal Welfare. A Cool Eye Towards Eden* (Oxford: Blackwell Science, 1995)

—— 'What use is science to animal welfare?' (1998) 85 *Naturwissenschaften* 262

Westacott, E, *A Century of Vivisection and Anti-Vivisection* (Rochford: CW Daniel Ltd, 1949)

Wilkins, David B (ed), *Animal Welfare in Europe. European Legislation and Concerns* (London: Kluwer Law International, 1997)

Williams, Bernard, *Morality. An Introduction to Ethics* (Cambridge: Cambridge University Press, reissued 1976)

Wise, Steven M, 'Animal Thing to Animal Person—Thoughts on Time, Place, and Theories' (1999) 5 Animal Law 61

—— *Rattling the Cage. Toward Legal Rights for Animals* (Cambridge, Massachusetts: Perseus Books, 2000)

Wollstonecraft, Mary, *A Vindication of the Rights of Woman* (1792) (London: JM Dent, 1986)

World Trade Organization, *Trading into the Future* (Geneva: World Trade Organization, 1995)

World Veterinary Association policy statement on animal welfare, well-being and ethology (1991) 7 *World Veterinary Association Bulletin* 38

Wynne-Tyson, Jon (ed), *The Extended Circle. An Anthology of Humane Thought* (Fontwell: Centaur Press, 1990)

Zimmermann, M, 'Behavioural investigations of pain in animals' in Duncan, IJH and Molony, V (eds), *Assessing Pain in Farm Animals* (Luxembourg: Commission of the European Communities, 1986)

Index